CURIOUS TALES FROM THE ANCIENT GRAVEYARD

Celebrating the lives of Settle’s

FOREWORD

'Mighty oaks from little acorns grow'

These words might have been specially written with this publication in mind. What began in May 2018 as a project to decipher and record for posterity the inscriptions on the older graves in Holy Ascension churchyard before they became completely illegible, rapidly turned into something of much bigger and greater significance.

The project, which built on previous work by the late Harold Foxcroft, to identify all the burials in the churchyard as recorded in the church's burial registers, was carried out by a team of dedicated volunteers from the Settle U3A Family History Group, who each brought their individual enthusiasms and energies to the work. None was more highly enthusiastic and energetic than Sarah Lister, who, fresh from her work of uncovering the identities of the 19th century inhabitants of The Folly, concentrated her sleuthing skills on revealing some of the remarkable life stories which lie hidden beneath so many of the grave inscriptions.

The results of Sarah's labours show us quite clearly that there is no such thing as an 'ordinary life'. The amazing range of stories she has brought to light demonstrate the importance of churchyards as a focus for our collective memory. The stories are important not only to the families concerned but also for the better understanding of the close-knit community of Settle, its pivotal place in the social and economic history of our region and its sometimes astonishing links to the wider world.

Sarah's immense enthusiasm and passion for her subject make this book compulsive reading and I predict it will rapidly become a best-seller. It is also an inspiration for further research both now and for generations to come. Make sure of your copy while you can!

Anne Read, MBE

Hon. Curator, Museum of North Craven Life

Settle, June, 2019

CURIOUS TALES FROM THE ANCIENT GRAVEYARD

Celebrating the lives of Settle's ancestors

Every gravestone rests upon a life story waiting to be told. So every grave provides a little slice of history. What better way to discover Settle's heritage than to check out the folks buried in the graveyard? That's what this project is about.

Settle is a quiet, unspoilt market town in North Yorkshire. If its nineteenth century residents came back today, they would still recognise much of the town. Settle was (and still is) a real community, but in those days many more families were related through marriage. The graveyard gives us a colourful mix - aristocracy, professionals, tradesmen, innkeepers, farmers, the working classes and including some incredible women. They tell us how the mills and railways changed Settle and how some clever folk made a real difference - not just to Settle but to the country too. We also discover how a twist of fate can change lives, for better or for worse, and how some resilient and inspirational folk thrived against the odds, despite the incredible events that life threw at them.

IT ALL STARTED A LONG TIME AGO . . . .

Settle's Holy Ascension was the first of several local churches built as part of the Parish of Giggleswick to provide for the expected increase in population, which didn't really happen and for predicted shortages in graveyard space, which did. Holy Ascension was consecrated in 1838, Stainforth in 1842, then Rathmell in 1843, and Langcliffe in 1851. The vicar of Giggleswick raised subscriptions and had Holy Ascension Church built on part of William Bolland's Townhead estate. It was optimistically designed to seat 600, with another 200 in the gallery. Since then, numerous baptisms, marriages and burials have marked the passage of time.

180 years later in June 2018, as part of the church's anniversary celebrations, Sally Waterson asked the Settle District U3A Family History Group to record the inscriptions the gravestones in the churchyard, to preserve them for future generations. But who were these people? What did they do? How did they make Settle the town it is today? Ready for a challenge, I decided to research the burials, and this is how new chapters of Settle's history began to emerge. This book is a celebration of the lives of Settle's ancestors, warts and all. So if you are sitting comfortably, let us begin.

Spare a thought for Luke Ralph, a blacksmith who died in 1849 aged 49, buried in plot *C9* with his wives **Agnes Harrison**, aged 29, and **Elizabeth Capstick,** aged 74, sons James, aged 5, and William, aged 10, and a grandson William Ralph Briscoe, aged 6.

> ***My sledge and hammer both declined,***
> ***My bellows they have lost the wind,***
> ***My fire extinct, my forge decayed,***
> ***and in the dust my vice is laid.***
> ***My coals have spent, My iron gone,***
> ***My nails are drove, my work is done.***

THE ANCIENT GRAVEYARD

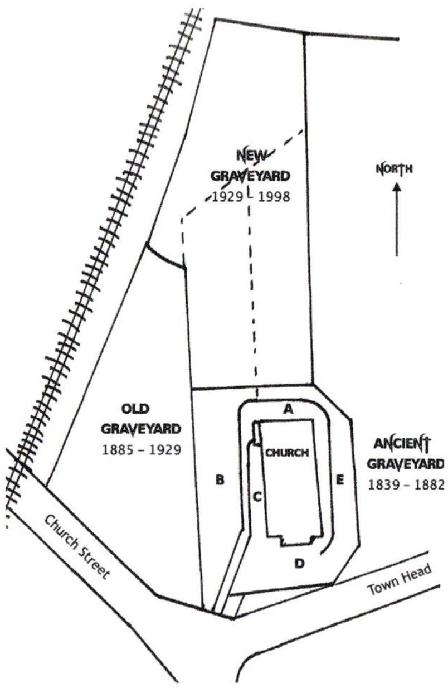

The land next to the church was the first graveyard, now known as the 'Ancient' graveyard, and this is where our stories begin. It has five areas A - E, with numbered plots, for example *D12*. Unmarked graves are shown with X, for example *AX4*. The graveyard plan is inside the back cover of this book. In the Ancient graveyard there are around one thousand burials. The first burial was in January 1839, and the last was in March 1949. The graveyard contains Catholics, Wesleyan Methodists and Primitive Methodists (The Quakers and the Zion Chapel had their own graveyards). The churchyard contained burials from Langcliffe until 1851 when St John's Church was built.

The church sexton had a responsibility of keeping the burial plan up to date, to show where bodies were buried. William Perkin was the sexton from 1843 until the 1880s, but he didn't keep the burial plan up to date, despite being reminded. It was even recorded formally in Vestry records. As a result there are over 400 people in unmarked graves, and we will never know where they are buried. How frustrating! Of course, William was buried in prime plot *DX22* by the church gate with two wives and two of his children.

103 gravestones name 324 people but two stones are too worn to read. Approximately 10% of the people named on gravestones were not actually buried in the grave, but had died elsewhere. *Gravestone D12* names two people, neither of whom are in the grave.

Don't make assumptions from gravestone inscriptions! Many were not inscribed until the man of the house died, or when the last of the family died. By then, memories of dates and ages could be slightly confused. Illiteracy was common, and this included the stonemasons. Take the case of **John Bullock** in *grave E3*, himself a stonemason. He married **Elizabeth Sledding** and they had seven children, three of whom died in childhood. When John died, Elizabeth married **Thomas Bordley**.

In affectionate remembrance of John Bullock of Settle, died March 27th 1854 aged 40 years *- John was only 38, and was not buried in E3 but in plot AX7 with a niece and two nephews*
Elizabeth, widow of the above, died April 10th 1877, aged 60 years *— correct!*
Ellen their daughter, died Jan 13th 1841, aged 5 years. Robert their son, died Jan 12th 1846 aged 5 years. *Ellen and Robert both died just before their 4th birthdays and are buried at St Alkelda's, Giggleswick*
Elizabeth their daughter, died July 29th 1852 aged 5 years. *Elizabeth was nearly 4 and her body is in AX17*
Also of Thomas Bordley, second husband of the above who died Jan 17th 1875 aged 64 years *— correct!*

The only people actually buried in this grave seem to be John's widow Elizabeth with her second husband, Thomas Bordley. Their daughter Mary Ann married Samuel Compston, son of the Minister at the Zion Chapel. Samuel ran a lucrative medical business in Burnley. Impressively, he was a Councillor and Alderman for 25 years and Chief Magistrate. Samuel and Mary Ann may have paid for the gravestone after Elizabeth died and forgotten some of the details. *NB Transcriptions given in this book are exact copies of inscriptions, even if they included mistakes. Brackets include missing details, if known.*

DID YOU KNOW . . .

The average age of death for those burials *with* gravestones in the Ancient graveyard was 44 years. Of those *without* gravestones between 1839 and 1855 the average age was just 21, despite William Beecroft, a labourer who had come to Settle from Ferrybridge. He died in 1852 when he was 98. He is buried in *grave AX1* with his daughter Nancy, aged 75.

Between 1839 and 1855, nearly a third of burials had a gravestone, which is a higher proportion than at most other graveyards. Generally, it was only the wealthy who could afford a gravestone and Settle had plenty of those, although there are a few working class exceptions.

The wealthy folk, including the first two vicars, were buried in areas D and E at the corner of the churchyard behind the altar, or in area C close to the church door so that everyone would have to walk past their gravestone on their way into church. There are two huge family vaults – the Robinsons in *grave C11*, and the Birkbecks in *grave D6*. The wealthy could afford elaborate artwork and inscriptions on their stones.

	Gravestones	Unmarked
Wealthy	11	1
Farmers	13	2
Professional	20	10
Tradesmen	34	34
Innkeepers	9	1
Working class	15	66

Graves were dug across all five areas from the start – families bought a plot to their liking in any part of the Ancient graveyard, with paupers randomly buried where there was a space. Area E contains the 16 infant graves, with three of the infants being illegitimate.

There were numerous people who arrived in Settle to try to find work. Some stayed, but others moved on. Nearly everyone who moved away from Settle went west, often to the Lancashire industrial towns.

There are around 30 gravestones in each of areas B - E, but just two in area A, which was later hard-surfaced. Sometimes churches kept the north side for people who were not christened, which may or may not be the case here. This area contains a large number of burials of people whose families moved away from Settle.

DANGEROUSLY FULL . . .

In January 1882 the graveyard was closed by the Home Secretary as it had become 'dangerously full' – across the country graveyards were the source infectious diseases. No further burials could take place unless there were 'special specified' circumstances to add someone to an existing grave. New burials had to be in Giggleswick. It was not until November 1885 that the land between the church and the (new) railway was bought for the "Old" graveyard [*BNA13*].

ENLARGEMENT OF THE SETTLE CHURCHYARD.— The original burial ground attached to the Church of the Holy Ascension, Settle, having some time ago become exhausted, the then Home Secretary (Sir William V. Harcourt) directed that no further interments should take place within it. Thereupon the Rural Sanitary Authority of the Settle Union raised the question of the provision of a joint cemetery for the parishes of Settle and Giggleswick, but the parishioners at a public meeting, presided over by the vicar (the Rev. Jackson Mason, M.A.), decided by an almost unanimous vote in favour of the enlargement of the Settle Churchyard in preference to a cemetery. New ground was accordingly purchased, and the addition recently made to the old ground virtually settles the cemetery question for all time so far as Settle is concerned. The entire cost of the extension proved to be £1144 1s. 10d. For a parish containing less than four thousand inhabitants this may appear to be a considerable sum to expend on the project, and yet the entire outlay has been provided for solely by voluntary subscriptions and one offertory at the church. It is only fair to add that members of every religious denomination represented in the district have given generously to the fund.

Families were split across graveyards, although the rules were relaxed later as the Old graveyard also filled. **Thomas Ayrton** was a labourer whose wife **Jane Jenkinson** had 12 children. Thomas died in 1881 and is buried in *grave B17*, and his headstone also commemorates Jane. However, Jane died in 1886 and is buried in the *Old graveyard* in the kerbstone grave directly behind Thomas' in *Old A25*. **Elizabeth Chapman** died in 1881 and is buried in *grave D22*. Elizabeth's son Robert died in 1884, before the Old graveyard had opened, so he is buried in St Alkelda's, Giggleswick.

Initially, Holy Ascension Church could conduct baptisms and burials, but weddings weren't permitted until 1849. The first wedding was that of Susannah Hardacre, a farmer's daughter from Long Preston to Joseph Hartley, a manufacturer of cotton from Lancashire. Joseph was the son of the innkeeper of the Golden Lion in Settle. The independent Parish of Settle was established in 1892 and the 'New' graveyard was added in 1928/9.

TO A BETTER PLACE . . .

So far we have discovered eight known cases of suicide who are buried in the churchyard, with five linked to the Ancient graveyard, plus a couple of rather strange accidents which could also have been suicide. Without healthcare and a welfare state, some people became so desperately unhappy that they took their own lives, often recorded as a moment of '*temporary insanity*'. Surprisingly, all of these unfortunate people were from professional, religious or trading backgrounds, and all were men.

Until 1961 suicide was a criminal offence. The Church of England had strict rules about these burials, and subject to the vicar's discretion, prevented funeral services inside the church and burials in consecrated ground or during daylight hours. The General Synod eventually decreed that these burials could have full services inside the church in 2015.

For some reason in 1897 the Craven district suffered '*Suicidal Mania*' with six cases in the district within 12 months. Two of these were in Settle, with another in Langcliffe. Our cases linked to the Ancient graveyard are:

Henry Cowburn, 27 February 1889, the son of a solicitor who shot himself after failing to pass a military exam [*working class heroes*]

James Tomlinson Handby, 19 March 1897, a tailor and Wesleyan minister who shot himself in a moment of temporary insanity [*church folk*]

Henry Hayton, 27 May 1897, a tailor who hanged himself in a moment of temporary insanity [*professionals*]

Charles Alured Swale, 26 November 1913, son of the first vicar of the church who shot himself whilst in a state of depression [*church folk*]

John Himsworth, 27 April 1860, a solicitor's clerk who drowned himself in a moment of temporary insanity [*wenches, wives*]

In the Old graveyard, the men who died of 'temporary insanity' include a member of the clergy, the son of a Wesleyan minister and the son of a French Polisher.

The descendants of all those buried here, with or without gravestones, should be proud of their contribution to making Settle the town it is today. May they Rest in Peace.

1 RAILWAY FOLK

Many of the developments of the Victorian era passed the residents of Settle by. Despite 18th century plans, the canals of the Industrial Revolution didn't reach us, which helped to prevent Settle becoming another sprawling industrial town. But cotton mills and railways did reach us. Some of our folk lived at the forefront of life in the mills and on the railways.

COTTON MILLS IN SETTLE?

Yes! The Settle cotton industry had taken over from local corn mills and handweaving. It was at its peak in the early 1800s with five mills: Bridge End, King's Mill, Runley Mill, Dog Kennel Mill and Watershed Mill as well as the Langcliffe Mills. Cotton manufacture was a true Lancashire trade - Yorkshire specialised in wool. The Luddite riots of 1811 to 1816 protested against mechanisation which improved efficiency but cost workers' jobs. Settle mills were slow to mechanise and so avoided the riots, although this also meant they were less efficient and in the 1850s several had to close. Many Settle workers moved to Lancashire, especially Accrington, leaving many houses empty. Some mills re-opened later, having to bring in workers from other parts of the country.

Charles Ratcliffe, and his tales of the unexpected . . . [A]

Charles Ratcliffe, born in 1786, worked at the peak of cotton manufacture when there were five cotton mills in Settle. Initially he was the agent for George Faulkner and sons who probably ran Bridge End cotton mill, and in the 1840s Charles managed Runley Mill. Charles and his wife **Nancy Hargreaves** came from Colne. By the 1830s they had moved to Settle and Charles was listed on the electoral register - a definite sign of wealth. Only one in 14 men in Settle were wealthy enough to meet the voting criteria at that time. In 1844 Charles owned property on Albert Hill behind Twisleton's Yard - the site of another mill, and also rented property behind the Golden Lion on Duke Street.

In 1841 census Charles and Nancy were living with their only child Ellen and several girls from Colne. At that time Nancy ran a straw bonnet business, employing the girls from Colne. Charles was a witness to the marriage of one of them, Elizabeth Walker, to cotton manufacturer Watson Bracewell, providing us with his signature. Ellen, the widow of a Kirkby Lonsdale surgeon Richard Fell Gregg [BNA1], had run a linen business in Settle before she married.

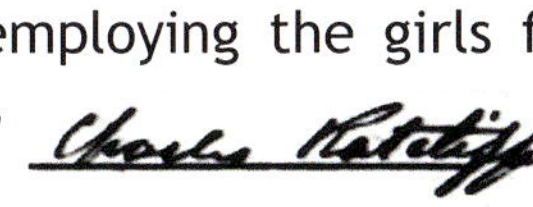

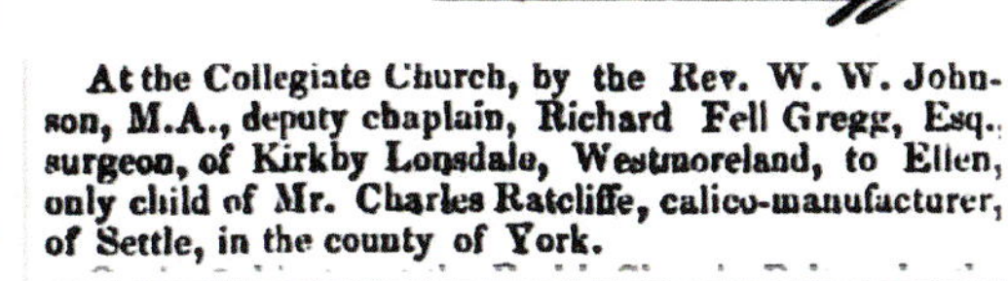
At the Collegiate Church, by the Rev. W. W. Johnson, M.A., deputy chaplain, Richard Fell Gregg, Esq., surgeon, of Kirkby Lonsdale, Westmoreland, to Ellen, only child of Mr. Charles Ratcliffe, calico-manufacturer, of Settle, in the county of York.

D17 Sacred to the memory of Nancy beloved wife of Charles Ratcliffe of Settle, who in sure and certain hope glorious resurrection departed this life February 14th 1848 aged 57 years. Also of the above mentioned Charles Ratcliffe who departed this life on the 10th July 1850, aged 64 years. Blessed are the peaceful.

The gravestone confirms that Nancy died in 1848, followed by Charles in 1850, an elderly (for those days) couple passing away quietly at the end of their lives, which looks like the end of the story. But it isn't.

It seems that as part of Charles' grieving process, he sought the comfort of young **Mary Ann Hartley**. Within six months of Nancy's death, Mary Ann was pregnant with a daughter Mary Ellen. 63 year old Charles 'did the decent thing' and married 21 year old Mary Ann.

Goodness Charles! He was three times Mary Ann's age. Clearly this was all a bit much for Charles as he died just a year later.

Mary Ann was the daughter of a humble coachman from Great Marsden, Lancashire who had died when she was a child. Mary Ann initially tried to continue the cotton business with the help of her brother Henry, but changed to the millinery trade, advertising in 1858 [*SC*].

SPRING GOODS.

M. A. RATCLIFFE

Has now on hand a well selected assortment of

MILLINERY

And Cheap RIBBONS in great variety, also a large quantity of Plain and Fancy

STRAW BONNETS

At extraordinary low prices, to which she respectfully calls the particular attention of her numerous Friends, and the Public generally.

Duke Street, Settle, May 1st, 1858.

N.B.—A good stock of MOURNING BONNETS at all prices, always on hand.

In 1861 Mary Ann had another strategic marriage, this time to widowed inland revenue supervisor **Leonard Ward**. She gave him four daughters and they settled in Ashton-under-Lyme. Leonard already had two daughters and a son from his first wife Mary who had died in Settle in 1860, but it seems Mary Ann didn't want to look after them - they were brought up by other relations. When he died in 1890, Leonard was buried back in Settle with his first wife in an unmarked grave. Mary Ann was buried in Lancashire. Leonard left his (really quite small) estate to Mary Ellen, Charles' daughter who had married headmaster John Hadfield and lived in Derbyshire.

Brother Henry went into partnership with another brother John in cotton manufacture. Runley Mill was destroyed by fire during the 1850s. Henry and John started a business in Kirkby Malham but by the 1870s had established themselves back in Settle, employing over 100 men. Henry lived at King's Mill and John at Marshfield. The cotton industry was in decline, but the brothers cleverly spun cotton waste, which provided a thriving business during the 'Cotton Famine' when cotton imports from America were disrupted by the civil war. In 1886 Henry's wife died, and the partnership with brother John was dissolved. Henry moved to Burnley with his many children, still working in cotton [*ph1*].

Sales by Auction.

KING'S MILL, SETTLE.

PRELIMINARY ADVERTISEMENT.

MR. MATTHEW WATSON has received instructions from Messrs. J. and H. Hartley to catalogue and SELL BY AUCTION (piecemeal), on the above premises on an early date, the whole of the WASTE SPINNING MACHINERY, LOOMS, and Effects in the above Mill, namely, cop bottom, Oldham willow; single breaking-up machine, 4 sets of 3-cylinder breaking machines, soft waste willow, single lap machine for 48in. cards, 15 single carding engines, 48-in. on the wire, with coiler fronts; Derby doubler, 2 roving frames, 120 spindles each; 2 do., 90 spindles each; 2 pairs mules, containing about 3,600 in all; 20 sheeting looms, 20 narrow looms, contents of smithy and mechanics' shop; the whole stock of waste, yarn, and cloth in process of manufacture; strapping, mill stores, and many loose effects.

Fuller particulars in posters, catalogues, and future advertisements.

King's Mill went up for sale in 1887 [*BNA3*], however John continued to work at King's Mill. His wife **Mary Wormwell** had given birth to an illegitimate child called Hartley Wormwell a few years before they married, and this could have been John's child. They had five other children. John left Mary the equivalent of £400,000 today when he died in 1895. They are buried in the *Old grave C18* with their son John who died in the same year as John (Snr). They have a fine gravestone.

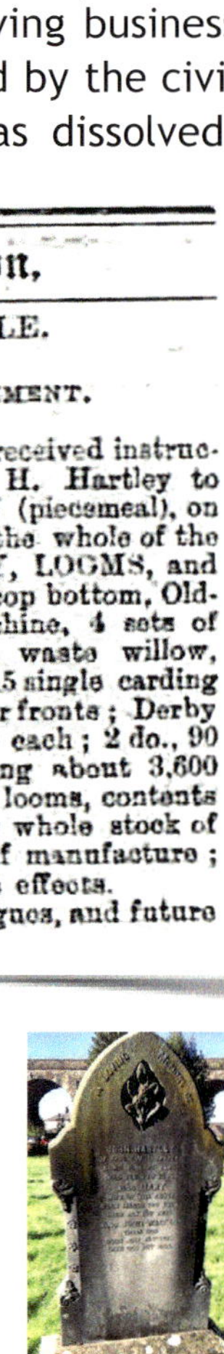

So what happened to Charles and Nancy's widowed daughter Ellen? Well, the surprises keep on coming. She married **Frederick Furlonger**, an aspiring solicitor and son of an innkeeper from Warminster, who had invested in the railways. However, like many others, he was unlucky and lost a considerable amount of money. Unlike many others, he was so desperate that in August 1850 he embezzled one pound and 12 shillings from his employer in Woodbridge, Suffolk [*BNA4*]. During the trial it transpired that he had an alias '*Joseph Symonds*' and had committed bigamy with a previous wife Sophie (and a child Alice) and fraud.

Frederick was found guilty. He was sentenced to 12 months imprisonment, with hard labour, narrowly avoiding transportation. This explains why Ellen was found in the 1851 census as '*Ellen Gregg*' in Staffordshire with their son Charles '*Gregg*'. This whole business may also have something to do with the death of Ellen's dad Charles in July 1850.

Ellen 'officially' married Frederick in 1861 just after the birth of their second son and the death of his first wife. Frederick was then declared bankrupt in 1868 - oh dear!

SINGULAR CASE OF EMBEZZLEMENT.—*Joseph Symonds* alias *Frederick Furlonger*, 31, a respectably dressed man, who took notes during the trial, was charged with having embezzled various sums of money the property of his employer, Mr. John Wood, of Woodbridge.—Mr. Power appeared for the prosecu-

Mr. Coburn then stepped into the witness-box. He said, I am a solicitor, at Settle, in Yorkshire. The prisoner married the daughter of a client of mine during the railway mania he got into difficulties; his real name is Furlonger; he never was a clerk of mine

You have been foolish enough to marry two wives—a very foolish thing to do—at the same time, what was still more foolish, you have been engaged in railway speculations, and lost a good deal of money. Under these circumstances, one ought not to bear too hardly upon a person who has tried to get back into a respectable situation, under such circumstances. Excepting in the matter before me, I do not attribute to you the idea that you came, through the medium of a forged certificate of character, for the purpose of cheating Mr. Wood. But the temptation seems to have come upon you whilst you were there, perhaps from distress owing to railway speculations. As I hope you are not wholly irreclaimable, the sentence is, that you be imprisoned and kept to hard labour for twelve calendar months. If I thought you had done this deliberately, I should certainly sentence you to transportation. But I do not. The prisoner burst into tears, and cried bitterly as he was removed.

Frederick died in 1879, still working as a solicitor's clerk in Wiltshire and Ellen at the Lambeth workhouse three years later. Their son Charles made a living from odd jobs, including painting and selling mineral water. Son Frederick emigrated to New Zealand and had a huge family out there. Frederick leads us nicely onto the railways . . .

CHANGING TRACK: RAILWAY FOLK

Of all Victorian developments, the railways had the greatest impact on the daily life of the residents of Settle. The Skipton to Lancaster line, known as the 'Little North Western', was completed in 1850 and the incredibly expensive Settle to Carlisle line completed in 1875.

The railways benefitted almost everyone, but can you imagine what the locals must have thought while it was being built? [*CH,1923*]. The railways provided thousands of jobs. Farmers could take their livestock to markets by train. Tradesmen could get goods more quickly so new businesses sprang up, including Settle's first 'fish and chip saloon' [*LSA*], the Langcliffe limeworks and the Hoffmann Kiln. The Bank Holidays Act of 1872 meant day trips by train.

The making of the Settle and Carlisle Railway was a very important event in the history of Settle. It brought into the town and neighbourhood an alien population, and soon after operations began the voice of the Cockney was heard in the land. Huts were erected to house the workmen and their families, a "Tommy Shop" was established in an old barn at the bottom of Duke Street to supply food, etc., and there were scenes of bustle and excitement in the somnolent little town.

As a rule the newcomers were well behaved, but occasionally quarrels arose which led to fights in the fields outside the town. Such fistic encounters as these took place were practically unknown in Settle, and I can recall several ghastly exhibitions which we youngsters witnessed with horror. The contestants, stripped to the waist, faced each other in a ring formed by partisans and other spectators, and then began a display of brute force, which increased in violence until one, or, in some instances, both were incapacitated and covered with blood. It was not an edifying spectacle, and I merely mention it to show how an alien element were able to destroy the quietude of our peaceful community.

David Hearsum,
FISH and
CHIP SALOON,
Wholesale Potato Dealer,
The Folly, SETTLE.
Good Accommodation for Tourists.
HOT and COLD BATHS.

Unfortunately, the railways brought a halt to droving trade and the coaching inns. But every cloud has a silver lining - the lack of late trains after theatre productions in Leeds prompted the formation of the Settle Amateur Dramatic Society in 1879, still running today.

THE "RAILWAY MANIA" INVESTORS

After the success of the canals in the 18th century, the railways became the next 'must have' investment for the wealthy. 'Railway Mania' was a speculative frenzy; between 1844 and 1846 investments resulted in 6,220 miles of railway line – more than half of the modern railway network. However, as Frederick Furlonger illustrated, there were winners and losers; around a third of the railways authorised were never built as the companies went bust. The smarter investors bought shares in several companies just in case.

The Burrow family surgeons, multiple railway investors

This talented family played an active part in Settle life. **Thomas Dixon Burrow,** born in 1797, married **Mary Anne Holme** in Bentham. They moved to Settle in time for the birth of son John in 1828 and lived on the corner of Cheapside and Duke Street. The North Craven Heritage Trust articles by Mary Slater state that Thomas *'occupied an old house at the corner of the Market-place, abutting on the main road, and known as Lazy Corner from the fact that there loungers and idlers 'most did congregate' to the annoyance of the peaceful inmates.'* and that he was *'a man of middle stature, always dressed in professional black, had a frilled shirt and neat neckcloth, trousers and short-waisted swallow-tailed coat, had dark brown hair and whiskers, and a capital face for a doctor, a round, pleasant, cheery-looking face, with bright, dark eyes; a face to inspire confidence in a patient ...'*

Thomas was a director of the 'Staffordshire Potteries and the Liverpool and Manchester Direct Railway' (one company), and had shares in other railways including the Cheltenham, Oxford and London Junction Railway.

Eldest son **William Thomas Holme Burrow** qualified in 1848 and so picked up where Thomas left off when he died in 1850. William was the surgeon to the Workhouse and subscribed to the new Settle Mechanic's Institute, which educated men in literacy, numeracy and work skills. Tragically, William died of tuberculosis, aged just 34, in the Isle of Wight which he may have visited for health reasons in 1860 [*BNA5*].

Youngest son **John Holme Burrow** went to Giggleswick School and graduated from Cambridge. He was in the chess club and local theatricals and was a fine marksman with the North Craven Rifle Corps. He was a geologist with a fossil collection and worked closely with Joseph Jackson [*tradesmen*] to promote the Victoria Caves. John was a prolific writer and spent time in London to get his work published. He is perhaps best known as the author of Jabez Oliphant [*SC, LSA*]. It probably wouldn't make the current best sellers

On the 8th inst., at Ventnor, Isle of Wight, aged 34 years, William Thomas Holme, Burrow, Esq., surgeon, of Settle, after a long illness, which he bore with exemplary patience and resignation. He was much beloved for his kindness of disposition and other excellent qualities.

STORIES FOR WEEK-DAYS AND SUNDAYS BY JOHN HOLME BURROW.—We are happy to introduce this little book by a late towns-man to the notice of our readers. The title of the book sufficiently explains its character; and from the hasty glance which we have been able to give to it we think it is likely to become a favourite with the class of readers for which it is intended. The style is agreeable, the incidents are interesting, and, without being too prosy, a decided moral lesson is impressed upon the minds of the youthful readers. A few neat engravings (indispensable in a book to please the young) embellish the volume. From the small size and price (one shilling) of the book it is well suited for a prize book for National and Sunday Schools.

John Holme Burrow, who practised as a surgeon in Settle, wrote a considerable quantity of verse which he published under the non-de-plume of "Bryan Yorke." He is perhaps best known as the author of "Jabez Oliphant," a novel in which local characters are freely introduced.

The following is a parody on "The Charge of the Light Brigade" and refers to a gift of £500 from a London gentleman to Mr. Blakiston, then Head Master of Giggleswick School, as a token of sympathy with him in his controversy with the Governors.

Two hundred and forty miles!
All the way from London!
Now there comes 500 pounds,
That Settle may be undone,
"Fight," is Sir Medlar's eager song,
"No matter whether right or wrong,
Into the gap we'll rush headlong—
We have the 500."

list but was popular in his day and is a gift to historians. Like his brother, John died in London of tuberculosis, aged 43. Thomas' wife Mary Ann died four years later, also in London, and her body was brought back to Settle for burial.

Daughter **Agnes Eliza Burrow** was a talented artist who gave music and drawing lessons in Settle in the 1860s [*SC*]. She exhibited work at London events run by the Society of Lady Artists which had been founded by Settle's **Ann Atherton** [*wenches, wives*].

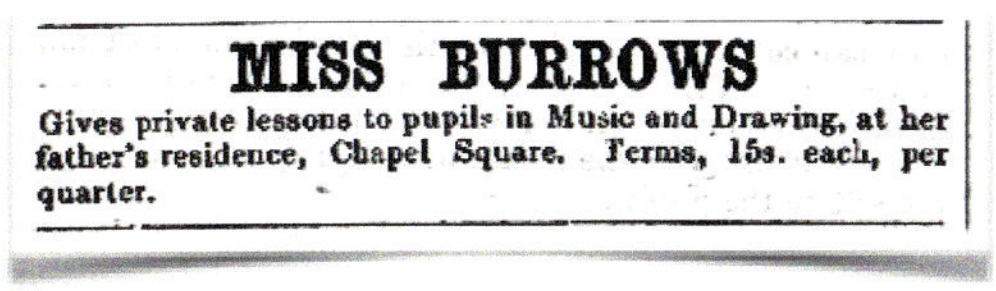

MISS BURROWS

Gives private lessons to pupils in Music and Drawing, at her father's residence, Chapel Square. Terms, 15s. each, per quarter.

The engraving of Warrendale Knotts near Settle [*ph2*] was taken from one of Agnes' oil paintings. Agnes was in London when she died aged 66 and was buried with her brother.

D11 Sacred to the memory of Thomas Dixon Burrow, surgeon of Settle, who died March 14th 1850, age 53. Also of his much lamented son William Thomas Dixon Burrow, surgeon who died at Ventnor, Oct 8th 1860 aged 34 and is interred at the Old Church of Bonchurch, Isle of Wight. Mary Ann, wife of the above who died in London April 18th 1870 aged 65 years. 'Dear mother on thy Saviour's breast, thy gentle spirit now hath rest, but well I know such love as thine will still look down and answer mine. JHB.'

D12 In dear memory of John Holme Burrow who died in London June 20th 1876 aged 43 years and is buried in Brompton cemetery. Also of Agnes Eliza Burrow who died 23rd Feb 1891 aged 66 and was buried beside her brother. 'For whither thou goest I will go and where thy diest there will I be buried.'

Thomas Dixon Burrow went to the expense of purchasing two grave plots but as it transpired, only he and his wife were actually buried here. Plot D12, with its fine stone is empty. Giggleswick School records also list a Henry Burrow, son of Thomas Dixon Burrow but no other records of him can be found.

John Birbeck and George Stansfeld [*wealthy ones*] were also railway investors, signing up for shares in the Manchester, Liverpool and Great North of England Union Railway in 1845.

Isabella Hargraves, who had a lucky escape [B]

Robert Hargraves, born in 1828, was the third son of **Stephen Hargraves** of Stockdale Farm, one of the largest farms in the West Riding of Yorkshire [*farmers*]. Robert married **Isabella Jane Wilson** and took over Stockdale Farm when his dad retired. Unfortunately Robert died of tuberculosis, aged 32, just six months after his dad.

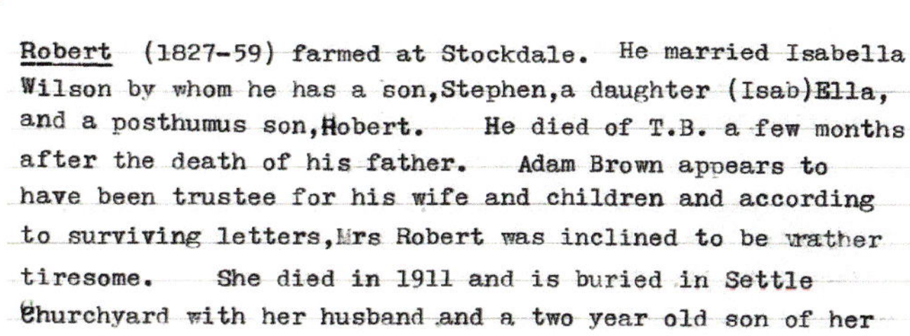

Robert (1827-59) farmed at Stockdale. He married Isabella Wilson by whom he has a son, Stephen, a daughter (Isab)Ella, and a posthumus son, Robert. He died of T.B. a few months after the death of his father. Adam Brown appears to have been trustee for his wife and children and according to surviving letters, Mrs Robert was inclined to be rather tiresome. She died in 1911 and is buried in Settle Churchyard with her husband and a two year old son of her son Robert.

Robert's sister **Jane** married **Adam Brown**, a handsome farmer, and they lived in Dumfriesshire [*ph16*]. Robert's wife Isabella was Adam Brown's cousin. Family notes describe that Isabella was '*inclined to be rather tiresome*'! She outlived her husband by 52 years, and family letters describe how Adam managed Isabella's finances during this time, helping her live off railway investments [ph16]. Family letters written in the 1860s show the precarious nature of the investments.

My Dear Adam
I was indeed glad to read the opening words of your letter this morning and could scarcely realize it would be true. The news was much too good after the past long months of anxiety and I fancy privation to very many poor creatures I cannot grudge the original share-holders their mites. Thanks to your forethought that I have not sufferred. I never for a moment dreaded misfortune coming to a good railway in that manner, but always thought them a perfectly safe investment, experience is at all times a good but dear teacher Will this years income due to me remain in the railway (?)bad stock and how am I to repay the £100,because it must be done I shall be very glad of the extra interest arising from the overdue interest in the railway, as I want to send Ella away to school.

£259.5.9. I saw Mr Geldard the other day he said he should recommend us to invest £250 in the ? North Western 5 per cent Debenture he considered it perfectly safe it is less interest but would it not be better than risking so much in the Railway? .I shall be glad to hear your opinion, There is £230.?.?. accumulation of rents

Isabella lived in Birkenhead with her son Stephen and died there in May 1911. She is buried back in Settle with Robert. Their stone commemorates two year old grandson 'Robbie', the son of their second son Robert, who had emigrated to Melbourne, Australia. Little Robbie died in 1911 in Melbourne and is not in this grave - did Isabella ever meet him?

E24 In memory of Robert Hargraves who died at Stockdale on the 29th Octr 1859 aged 32 years, third son of Stephen and Isabella Hargraves of Rock House, Settle. Also of Isabella Jane Wilson, wife of the above named Robert Hargraves died on the 21st May 1911 aged 78 years. "Robbie" grandson of the above and son Robert and Alice Hargraves of Melbourne Australia died March 1911 aged 2 yrs.

OTHER RAILWAY FOLK

William Knott Stephenson, eccentric accountant

C16 In memory of Annie the wife of WK Stephenson of Settle who died 24th October 1850. Also of Arthur their son who died on the 7th day of November 1850 aged 19 days.

Annie Howe, born in 1815 was the daughter of a Kendal saddler. In 1849 she married the (much younger) **William Knott Stephenson** from Lancaster, born in 1826. Annie died in Settle, aged 35, giving birth to their first child Arthur who soon followed. William's dad Abraham was a Lancaster horsekeeper/innkeeper. His mum was Elizabeth Knott, hence his middle name. After Annie's death William went back to Lancaster. A few years later he married local lass **Ann Birkett** and they had at least seven children, the youngest also named Arthur.

William worked as an accountant and was employed by the railways for most of his life but later worked with his wife in a china and earthenware business. 1866 was a bad year for William as he had a couple of appearances in court in which both judges described his conduct as 'highly improper'. Allegedly, William drunkenly assaulted a coroner [BNA6] and also threatened an employer with *'a heavy oak stick, one of the heaviest I ever saw'* to obtain money whilst drunk. It was reported rather comically in the *Lancaster Gazette*. Both cases were eventually dismissed. In the same year he was also summoned to court for an investigation into electoral fraud, and questioned about bribing voters as a Liberal supporter.

ASSAULT UPON A CORONER.—At the Judges' Lodgings, on Saturday, William Knott Stephenson, accountant was charged with assaulting Mr. Lawrence Holden, coroner. Defendant had been summoned the week previously for an assault and battery on Mr. Holden, on which occasion the information was dismissed, on the ground that no battery had been proved. A summons for assault only was then taken out.—The magistrates on Saturday considered that a most unjustifiable assault had been committed, and fined the defendant 40s. and costs. The assault took place in Mr. Holden's house, to which defendant had gained admittance whilst under the influence of liquor.

time, when he was sober. He said he would not leave the house until Mr Holden paid him £75 he owed him. He used a deal of excited and violent language, and after we had been in the lobby about five minutes, he cried out, "You owe me £75 for keeping the Phœnix Foundry books, and I'll have it." Mr Holden said, "I don't owe you anything of the kind," or words to that effect. Mr Stephenson called out in very loud tones, "You are a liar," at the same time raising a stick, and in my belief was about to strike Mr Holden. Immediately my son took hold of Mr Stephenson's arms, and Mr Holden also took hold of him. He made resistance, but was forced into the road. In the struggle several of us were on the ground. I can't say how many,

In 1891, William was again brought to court for using insulting language. This case was also amicably sorted, with William profusely apologising and paying costs *[BNA8]*.

USING INSULTING LANGUAGE.
William Knott Stephenson, accountant, New-street, was summoned for using provoking and insulting language to Richard Bond, stock and share broker, Lancaster, on the 6th inst.—Mr. Clark appeared for

Obituaries, quite rightly, celebrate success and achievement. In 1896, William's painted quite a different side to this drunken, foul-mouthed accountant and explained why he was in Settle in 1850. He was described as a *'railway pioneer'* and a *'man of some eccentricity, but of great ability'* which sounds as if he could have had a form of Asperger Syndrome. William had surveyed several railway lines and was a promoter of both Settle railways *[BNA9]*. A good man, in some ways.

A RAILWAY PIONEER. — The *Lancaster Times* notices the death last week, of a railway pioneer in the person of Mr. William Knott Stephenson, well known in the six northern counties. He was an uncle of Mr. R. W. Bellis, the present master of the Clewer Green Schools. Mr. Stephenson, who is described as a man of some eccentricity of character, but of great ability, was engaged in the survey of several lines in the early railway days, with Sir Thomas Storey and others. He was one of the promoters of the Settle and Carlisle Railways, and the Little North Western, now known as the Morecombe and Lancaster Branch of the Midland Railway. Singularly enough, only a week previous occurred the death of Mrs. Bellis's uncle, Surgeon General Hendley, C.B.

David and Goliath: David Hall Dale, taking on the railways

Skipton born **David Hall Dale** married **Isabella Green** in 1830, and began their family of ten. David farmed at Paley Green until 1842 and then moved to Cleatop Farm just outside Settle. This was a large farm of 370 acres, all rented from Rev'd Swale of Holy Ascension *[church folk]*. David won many awards in numerous livestock categories at the Agricultural Shows. David was a manager of the Craven Savings Bank in 1871 along with several other men of Settle who are buried nearby *[BNA7]*.

The rate of interest allowed to depositors in this bank is 3 per cent. The following are the Trustees, managers and officers of the bank. Trustees: Josias Atkinson, John Birbeck, Rev. W. T. Pierson, William Robinson, Thomas Stackhouse, and Rev. H. J. Swale. Managers: Joseph Birbeck, John Cowgill, D. H. Dale, William Hartley, James Hartley, Edward Hartley, John Jackson, Joseph Jackson, T. G. Metcalfe, William Procter, John Preston, Mearbeck House, and John Tatham. Actuary: Joseph Tatham, Treasurer: Ellwood Brockbank. Auditor, John Lister.

The Leeds to Lancaster line and, later, the very start of the Settle to Carlisle line ran through David's farm. Rev'd Swale may have invested in these railways and would have probably received compensation for the use of his land. David may not have been quite as enthusiastic - the building of the railway would have been incredibly disruptive.

In 1848, David took action against the North Western Railway who were building the Leeds to Lancaster line. He claimed the fence they used was insufficient to contain his sheep and

Esq., of Lancaster, on behalf of the Railway Company.—David Hall Dale, being sworn, said that the fence was post and wire, the small posts being about three yards from each other, and the main ones about 148 yards. The horizontal wires were about eight inches apart, and are very elastic. Has had sheep gone *through* many times, and cows *over*. The top wire is sufficiently cows. The court agreed with him and made the railway build a new fence within a month! - a very expensive case for the railway [*BNA10*].

hundred landowners in Scotland have this fence. After a lengthy deliberation the magistrates decided that it was not a sufficient fence; and the order of the court was, *that a wood fence of 4 feet 6in. high, and five bars 6in. apart*, be erected by the company, and completed within a month. This decision will be seriously felt by the railway company, as it is understood they have provided material for fencing the whole of their line. It is estimated that their loss in consequence will not be less than eight or ten thousand pounds.—*Lancaster Guardian*.

It's no surprise that David was well respected by colleagues. In 1866, he was the chair of a ratepayers' meeting to tackle Cattle Plague which eventually killed 260 cattle in the area [*BNA11*]. This was a difficult but important job. Just as now, the strategy to eliminate Cattle Plague was to kill all the animals in infected areas, and farmers received some compensation when animals died. There were numerous court cases against farmers flouting the rules.

SETTLE.—At a meeting of ratepayers held at Settle, on Friday, Mr. David Hall Dale in the chair, to select a resident ratepayer to be recommended to the Court of Quarter Sessions for appointment as cattle valuer for the township, Mr. John Parker, of Upper Settle, was unanimously agreed upon.

C22 In loving remembrance of David Hall Dale of Cleatop born at Skipton Sep 9th 1802 died Dec 24th 1871. Isabella Dale widow of the above born March 2nd 1805 died January 11th 1876. Charles Dale MB their son born March 1st 1845 died at Keighley Dec 4th 1869

David's intricately carved gravestone was inscribed by the talented stonemason Kildwick Robert Tillotson, and is positioned in a prime spot in the graveyard, behind the altar. Son Charles had just qualified as a doctor when he was killed by a fever, aged just 24 in 1869 [*BNA7*]. Medical qualifications didn't help in this case.

Keighley.—On the 4th inst., deeply and sincerely regretted, Charles Dale, Esq., M.B.C.M. He had just commenced practice as surgeon, in Keighley when he was seized with a fever prevailing in that town, and at the early of 24 was called to his rest.

Two of David and Isabella's other sons had slightly underwhelming careers as travelling drapers. Others became a lead merchant, a coal merchant, a bookkeeper and son Edward emigrated to Argentina. Just one son, Thomas, remained in farming but died aged 35. Daughter Isabella remained single, and Margaret married a lead merchant.

The Greens, railway surgeons - and a tragic encounter with a horse

Edwin Septimus Green, born in 1843, was one of eight children of **Joseph Septimus Green**, a surgeon in Co Durham. Edwin qualified as a surgeon in Edinburgh. In 1867, he married **Harriet Anderson** from South Shields and they moved straight to Settle, living in Duke Street and had three daughters. Edwin was surgeon to the Settle to Carlisle Railway. His Settle and Horton-in-Ribblesdale district included the Ingleton Fells and Batty Green. Edwin also served the Settle Union Workhouse in Giggleswick. He was only 27 when he died under tragic circumstances, being dragged by his horse for a mile and a half [*BNA12*]. His obituary explains he was the '*surgeon in connection with the Settle to Carlisle Railway*' and '*had never lost a case*'. Even though he was only in Settle for four years before he died, perhaps the manner of his death contributed to the decision to dedicate a church window to him at Holy Ascension?

D2 In loving Remembrance of Edwin Septimus Green, surgeon, born at Houghton-le-spring, Co Durham, Nov 13, 1843, died at Settle Aug 3 1871. Also of Harriet his wife who died June 22nd 1899, and of Harriet Anderson, her mother who died March 22 1904, age 92.

A MELANCHOLY ACCIDENT.—A very sad accident happened a few days ago to Mr. E. S. Green, surgeon, of Settle. Mr. Green had ridden over to his hayfield, and being anxious to assist the men up a steep hill which had to be ascended, he was attaching an impromptu trace to the horse he had ridden, so as to connect it as a leader, and assist the cart horse to pull the load up the hill. Having tied the rope to each end of the trace, he was about to fix it, uncut, to the shafts of the cart, when the horse took fright, and started at a furious pace up the hill, dragging Mr. Green (who was encircled) after him. For a considerable distance, by grasping each side of the rope, he succeeded in keeping his feet. Eventually, however, from exhaustion, he fell, and one foot became entangled. He was in this manner dragged along the road, a distance of a mile and a half, when the runaway horse was stopped. The poor gentleman was immediately conveyed to his residence at Settle. His body was frightfully bruised over the back, hips, and both arms, &c. He lingered from the Tuesday to the Thursday night. He was attended by Dr. Dreghtot, of Clapham, and Mr. Sam. Hey, of Leeds, but all their efforts were of no avail. They were of opinion that rupture of the liver, &c., had taken place. His loss is severely felt, and has cast a universal gloom over the neighbourhood. In his professional capacity, for his years, he had few equals—an expert surgeon and a most successful operator. He was surgeon in connection with the Settle and Carlisle Railway, and of the many operations which he has had for the last two years, he had never lost a case. The great esteem and affection in which he was held was evinced by the large number of sorrowing friends who attended his funeral, and by the tradespeople closing their shops in token of grief for one who was so suddenly removed from amongst them. His mortal remains were on Saturday consigned to their last resting place in the burial-ground of Ascension Church, Settle. A full choral service was given in respect to his memory. He was only 27 years of age, and has left a widow with three daughters to deplore his loss.

Wife Harriet, her mum and their daughters moved to Portsmouth. When they died, the bodies of Harriet and her mum were brought back to Settle for burial. All their daughters married professionals who were also quite wealthy. Daughter Emily married the **Rev'd Thomas Charlesworth**, son of the Settle solicitor. Emily is buried with the Charlesworths, *Old grave E12/13*.

OBITUARY.

We have to announce the death of Mr. Francis Green, M.D., L.R.C.P., which occurred on Monday, at the White Horse Hotel, Settle. After acquiring considerable experience as a practitioner at Newcastle, Dr. Green went to Settle about 20 years ago, and his reputation and skill speedily brought him a large and lucrative practice. His health had been failing for the last two or three years.

This was not the end of the Greens' story in Settle. Edwin's brother, **Francis Green**, took over as railway surgeon until he died in August 1890, at the White Horse Hotel. He is buried in *Old grave B13*. His obituary describes *'His reputation and skill speedily brought him a large and lucrative practice'* [BNA7.]

The building of the railway was a tradesman's dream. Settle blacksmiths, stonemasons, and joiners suddenly found themselves in the right place at the right time and plenty of others moved here.

Abraham Smith, a very wealthy coal merchant

In the industrial revolution, coal was in demand as never before. The arrival of the railways made it easy to obtain supplies [LSA].

Abraham Smith, born in 1840, was a cattle dealer from Bradford. By 1868 he had met **Sarah Ann Tatham**, the daughter of a coal merchant **Elisha Tatham** from whom he learnt the trade. Sarah and a daughter died while they lived in Skipton, so, just in time for the building of the Settle to Carlisle Railway, Abraham moved to Settle. He set up his business in Station Road and married another Bradford coal merchant's daughter, **Ann Wilkinson**. Abraham suddenly died just after the birth of their third daughter Amy [BNA7]. He was described as *'generally respected'* which doesn't sound as good as it could. His gravestone is right next to the church door.

SETTLE.

SUDDEN DEATH.—On Monday morning last Mr. Abraham Smith, coal merchant, New Road, Settle, died suddenly at his residence. Deceased was well known and generally respected

C3 In loving remembrance of Abraham Smith who died May 30th 1881. Also Ann, wife of the above born Jan 21st 1842, died Sep 6th 1931. Also Margaret, eldest daughter of the above died 1st September 1972 in her 96th year.

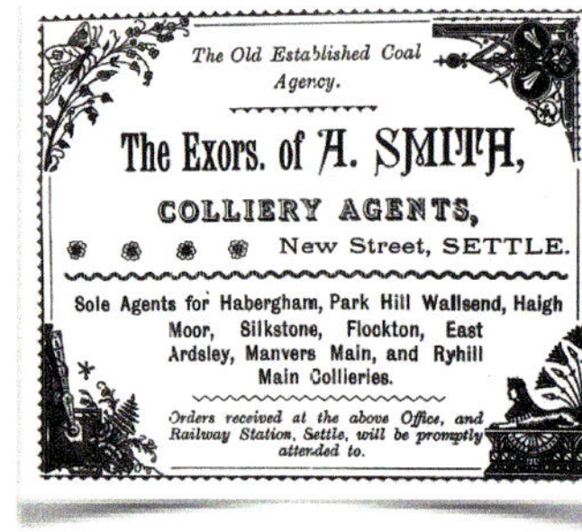

Widow Ann carried on the business with her daughters [*LSA*] and then lived on *'independent means'* which came from Abraham - he left the equivalent of well over £1 million today. A good business, very well run. Ann died aged 89. Daughter Margaret died a spinster, the oldest woman in the Ancient graveyard at 96. Daughter Sarah married an accountant from Bradford, Charles Henry Best and they lived in Mainsfield, Giggleswick.

THE NAVVIES – HEALTH AND SAFETY? ......

Railway navvies had a tough, physical job so most were unmarried men in their twenties. They needed to eat well and so their pay was relatively high - four shillings a week, including 'danger money' which was needed with three deaths for each mile of railway built, and more in tunnelled sections because of the explosives. Plenty of men thought it was worth the risk.

TUNNEL MINERS wanted at Blea Moor Tunnel, Settle and Carlisle Railway, No. 1 Contract. Wages, 6s. per day. Good lodgings immediately adjoining. Station, Ingleton *via* Leeds Parties of ten men will be passed down.—Apply Alfred Terry, Midland Railway Offices, Settle

As this census return shows, most navvies travelled to this area for jobs, following the railway contractors, this one advertising in 1873 [*BNA13*]. Many used false names, such as the boarder in this navvy hut *'Frederick Frattlafarty'*, as there was a stigma about travellers in those days too. It was a rough living and there was plenty of crime in the navvy villages. One of these boarders, James Smith, was fined 5 shillings for being drunk and disorderly in 1872 [*BNA16*]. This doesn't seem the ideal environment in which to bring up children, but some workers, such as **George Gibbs**, did just that. George and his wife Jane had ten children over his career of 40 years as a railway tunneller, and only two died in infancy - quite an impressive achievement.

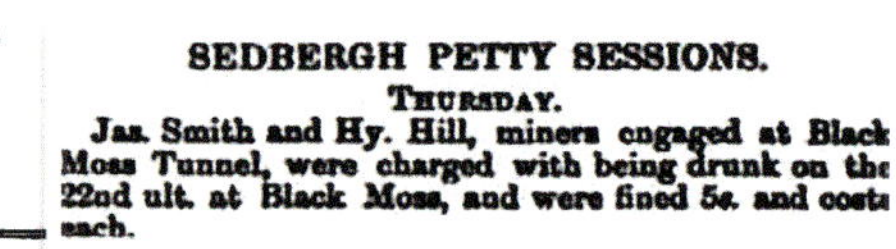

SEDBERGH PETTY SESSIONS.

THURSDAY.

Jas. Smith and Hy. Hill, miners engaged at Black Moss Tunnel, were charged with being drunk on the 22nd ult. at Black Moss, and were fined 5s. and costs each.

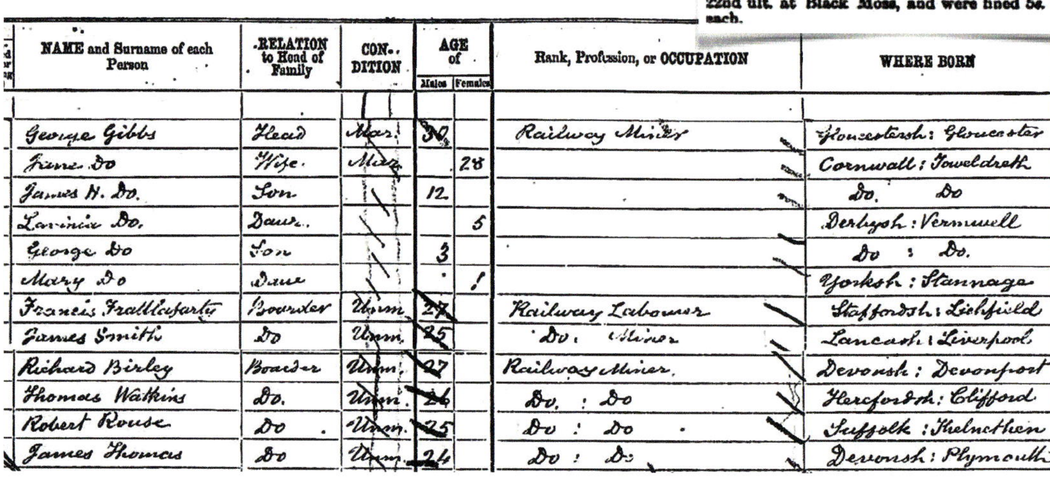

NAME and Surname of each Person	RELATION to Head of Family	CONDITION	AGE of Males	AGE of Females	Rank, Profession, or OCCUPATION	WHERE BORN
George Gibbs	Head	Mar.	30		Railway Miner	Gloucestersh: Gloucester
Jane Do	Wife	Mar.		28		Cornwall: Toweldreth
James H. Do.	Son		12			Do. Do
Lavinia Do.	Daur.			5		Derbysh: Vermuell
George Do	Son		3			Do : Do.
Mary Do	Daur			1		Yorksh: Stannage
Francis Frattlafarty	Boarder	Unm.	27		Railway Labourer	Staffordsh: Lichfield
James Smith	Do	Unm.	25		Do. Miner	Lancash: Liverpool
Richard Birley	Boarder	Unm.	27		Railway Miner.	Devonsh: Devonport
Thomas Watkins	Do.	Unm.	26		Do. : Do	Herefordsh: Clifford
Robert Rouse	Do	Unm.	25		Do : Do	Suffolk : Thelnethen
James Thomas	Do	Unm.	24		Do : Do	Devonsh: Plymouth

At least 20 navvies who died during the building of the Settle to Carlisle Railway are buried in this graveyard, with an average age of just 29. There are just four gravestones and the rest are in unmarked graves. The church porch has a memorial to the navvies who died in this area which reads:

To the memory of those, through accidents lost their lives in constructing the railway works between Settle and Dent Head. This tablet was erected at the joint expense of their fellow workers and the Midland Railway Company 1869 - 1876.

Welsh Navvies John Griffiths Owen and John Jones

B4 Sacred to the memory of John G Owen of Holyhead who died at Settle Feby 18th 1873 aged 19 years. Ai mewn bedd man Ioan back -O I'e. Ioan sy'n llwch bellach. Ond daw'n ol etto'n iach At ail vesi'n hi tlysach. *(Young John is now in his grave, John that is all ashes now, But he'll come back a second time A thousand times better)*

SETTLE.
TEMPERANCE LIFE BOAT CREW.—The members and friends of the above society gave the first of their en-entertainments this season on Saturday evening last. Captain Phillipson in the chair. The Hall was well filled with a very enthusiastic audience. The programme, which comprised songs, readings, recitations, and dialogues, was gone through in a very creditable manner. The reading in the Lancashire dialect by Master R Lambert, entitled "Owd Shunt" kept the audience convulsed with laughter, and was deservedly applauded. The dialogues with the assistance of a few friends were very creditably rendered. Mr. John Owen very efficiently sung a Welsh song.

John Owen from Holyhead on Anglesey, had settled into Settle life by November 1872, performing for the Temperance Lifeboat Crew Society [BNA7]. Incredibly, Settle folk raised enough money to build and launch six lifeboats between 1868 and 1912, saving 148 lives in all. Three boats were stationed in Anglesey so John's contribution was most apt. In February 1873 John was accidentally killed by the leg of a crane falling on him [BNA13].

Tom Twisleton, the local dialect poet, was captivated by John's tragic story and wrote a poem of some 15 verses including: *'But Hark! A strange sound is heard - the crane that o'hangs them is broken, and the heavy jib fall ere a hand call be stirred, or a sentence of warning be spoken.'*

SETTLE—FATAL ACCIDENT.—John Owen, aged nineteen years, whilst working underneath a crane in No. 3 cutting, near Langcliffe, on the new Settle and Carlisle Railway, was killed on Tuesday last by one of the legs or supports of the crane falling upon him, causing his instant death. An inquest was held the same evening, when a verdict of "Accidentally killed" was returned by the jury, who recommended that for the future all the cranes used on the line should undergo an inspection daily by some competent person in the employ of the Midland Railway Company.

A1 In memory of John Jones of Ingleton Fells who died on the 27th of July 1872, Aged 17 years. "Affliction seized my dear son and snatched him from my sight, but Jesus took him to his breast and claimed him as his right"

INQUEST.—An inquest was held on Monday last, at the Commercial Hotel, before Mr. J. P. Brown, Deputy Coroner, respecting the death of John Jones, a young man, aged 17 years, who at the time of the accident was employed as a stoker, at Batty Wife, near Ingleton, on the new Settle and Carlisle Railway. The deceased met with his accident on Saturday last. Whilst in the act of doing something in connection with his engine he fell off, coming in contact with the abutment on the side, causing injuries to his arm and thigh. He was conveyed the same night to the hospital at Settle, but died shortly afterwards. The jury returned a verdict that the deceased was accidentally killed by falling from a railway engine.

John Jones' work on the railways led to his death when he was just 17. He worked as an engine stoker, feeding coal into engines. An inquest was held into his death at the Commercial Hotel in Settle and returned the verdict of being *'accidentally killed by falling from a railway engine'* [BNA7]. The inscription suggests his mum organised his burial.

An Irish family business - Thomas Cooper and Thomas Ferris

Thomas Cooper and **Thomas Ferris** were both born in Newry, Northern Ireland. In the 1870s Thomas Cooper, a stonemason, his wife and three daughters lived in one of the shanty towns on Ingleton Fells. Thomas died in 1875 and two daughters Alice, aged 11 months, and Mary, aged 19 are buried in the graveyard, hopefully with him. Thomas had a sister, **Eliza Jane Cooper**, who married Robert Ferris. Robert's brother **Thomas Ferris**, a railway labourer, is buried with Thomas Cooper.

Yorkshire Batty Wife

Robert Ferris was a grocer serving the shanty towns. Robert and Eliza Jane had eight children - their son William was born at

'Batty Wife' at Ribblehead. It's hard to imagine what it must have been like to give birth under the shadow of a partially built Ribblehead Viaduct. Three of Robert's children are also buried at Holy Ascension. After brother Thomas' death, the family moved to Bootle, Liverpool. They scraped a living together working on the docks and making match boxes.

C13 In affectionate remembrance of Thomas Cooper of Newry who died at Settle Feb 22nd 1875 aged 23 years, also Thomas Ferris of Newry who died at Settle April 30th 1873 aged 28 years. Also Mary Jane Ferris who died at Settle aged 17 months.

Most navvies were not commemorated with a gravestone but had equally tragic deaths, some graphically reported by the papers [*BNA7, BNA13 - Peacock, Burton*].

SETTLE.

FATAL ACCIDENT.—Abraham Colling, a carpenter employed on the new Settle and Carlisle Railway, was accidentally killed on the 21st instant by a piece of timber falling upon his head. An inquest was held on the 23d inst. before Mr. T. Brown, coroner, when a verdict of "Accidental death" was returned.

A MAN KILLED BY A BLAST.—An inquest was held on Saturday last before Mr. T. P. Brown, deputy Coroner, touching the death of James Lashbrook, a miner employed in the tunnel, near Ingleton, on the new Settle and Carlisle Railway. After hearing the evidence, a verdict of "Accidentally killed by a dynamite cartridge," was returned."

An accident, which terminated fatally to a man named William Peacock, employed on the new Settle and Carlisle Railway, happened on Tuesday. The deceased, along with others, was on the bridge at Sherwood Brow, near Stainforth, engaged in lowering some timber. Whilst the chain was being loosed from the timber the crane overturned and fell into the river below, taking with it the man Peacock and another. The rest of the men succeeded in getting clear of the crane before it fell. Peacock was found much crushed, and was at once conveyed to the hospital, where he died the same night. The other man was not much injured. Deceased was 25 years of age, and a native of St. Albans.

SETTLE.

MAN DROWNED.—On Sunday last the body of a man was seen in the river Ribble near to King's Mill, Settle, and on its being got out of the water, it was identified as the body of Thomas Smith *alias* Bill Farrer, who had been employed on the new line of railway here. The body was conveyed to the Royal Oak Inn, where an inquest was held on Tuesday last, before Thomas P. Brown, Esq, deputy coroner, when evidence was given that deceased was seen the worse for liquor late on Saturday night, going in the direction of Giggleswick, and it is supposed he had mistaken the road, and wandered down to the river side, and accidentally fallen in. There were no marks of violence found on his body, and the jury returned a verdict of "Found dead." The deceased was 43 years of age, and resided at Stainforth.

FATAL ACCIDENT.—An accident happened on Saturday last, to a man named Thomas Burton, an employee on the new Settle and Carlisle Cailway. The accident occurred at number seven cutting at Elworth Bridge, near to Settle. It appeared Burton had got behind some earth wagons to protect himself whilst a blast was being let off, and about the same time an engine with wagons attached came up, and before the poor fellow was aware of his dangerous position, he was jammed between the wagons and sadly crushed. He was immediately conveyed to the Hospital, but with very little hope that he would survive, he lingered, however, until Tuesday last, when he died. An inquest was held on Wednesday at the Commercial Hotel, Settle, before Mr Brown, coroner, when a verdict to the effect that the deceased accidentally met with his death under the above circumstances was returned. The jury, sitting in the above inquest resolved to send the following recommendation to the directors of the Midland Railway Company:—"The body of Thomas Burton, 26 hours after death being in an advanced state of decomposition, the effluvia offensive and sickening to the jury, cannot but be detrimental to the health of the patients confined in the Hospital, and to the Master and matron of the establishment, and during the hot weather is likely to be a prolific source of disease in the locality; and the jury therefore urgently recommend the erection of a dead house detached from the Hospital as a means of remedying the present unsatisfactory state of things.

Navvy **Thomas Burton**, also Irish, was married with children. At the inquest, the Midland railway was recommended to set up a 'dead house' so that dead bodies couldn't infect others in hot weather. The result of this could be the 'hearse house' built on Church Street in Giggleswick today.

Some residents of Settle joined the railway workforce and died at work. **James Todd**, aged 21, was a railway plate worker. He was the son of Henry Todd, Townhead gardener [*wealthy folk*].

Workers travelling across the country carried diseases with them. Disease accounts for many of the deaths, for example stonemason Robert Ralph and his wife who both died within a week leaving several children.

Grim stuff, but what a wonderful legacy they left.

2 CHURCH FOLK

From its consecration, Holy Ascension was fortunate to appoint clergy and musicians with fine credentials.

Rev'd Hogarth John Swale, the first vicar, a good and wealthy man

Hogarth Swale was born in Kendal in 1810 and his dad John, an attorney at law, died when he was only two. He went to Giggleswick School when he was eight, and his mum Ann (Hogarth) came to live in Langcliffe Hall. One of Hogarth's school chums was the son of Rev'd Ingram at St Alkelda's church in Giggleswick, who initiated the building of Holy Ascension Church. Ann contributed £1000 towards the building of the church, a third of the total cost, and has a window dedicated to her *'placed by her affectionate children'*. Hogarth inherited and invested in huge amounts of land – in 1844 he owned over 500 acres, most rented out to farmer David Hall Dale [*railway folk*]. Some land was shared with sister-in-law Ellen Eliza Lambert. Hogarth was also a Trustee of the Craven Savings Bank.

Hogarth graduated at Oxford University. After his ordination, he became a curate at Clitheroe. From there, it was only a short hop back to Settle when the church opened to become the first incumbent for ten years until 1848. He undertook the building of Ingfield Hall for his retirement, now the Falcon Manor. In 1841 he married **Mary Lambert**, the daughter of a solicitor, descended from the Peart family of Settle lawyers. Mary died at the birth of their second child **John Lambert Swale** in 1844.

Hogarth then took up a post in Kensington and married **Emily Charlotte Goter**, the daughter of a London fish merchant, who was to bear him another six children. Hogarth was soon appointed chaplain to the British Embassy in Paris for nine years [*SC*], after which he retired as planned to Ingfield Hall, back in Settle.

NORTH RIBBLESDALE ADVERTISER

FOREIGN CHAPLAINCY.—The Rev. H. J. Swale, of Ingfield, near Settle, has just received the appointment of Chaplain to the Right Honourable Lord Cowley, British Ambassador to the Court of the Emperor of the French at Paris.

Soon after Hogarth's departure, the 1851 religious census criticised Holy Ascension for the fees charged for pews and services, as it deterred attendance by the poor. Interestingly, Hogarth's first wife Mary donated £5000 in her will of 1844 *'to build a church in the colonies, on the condition that pews are rent free and the altar visible from all seats'*. The Church of the Holy Trinity was built in Toronto by 1847. She left a similar sum for a church for convicts in South Australia. In Settle, it wasn't until 1867 that an endowment fund was set up for free pews. Free pews eventually became available in 1908.

Mary's son, **John Lambert Swale**, had a wonderful 21st birthday celebration at Ingfield in 1865 [*SC*] before embarking on his military career. Soon after, in India, he married **Blanche Voyle** from a military family and they had a son, **Charles Alured Lambert Swale.** John worked his way up through the ranks to become Captain of the 7th Hussars Cavalry. But in February 1876 he was reported missing from Tenby, Wales, and adverts were placed in a number of regional

BIRTHDAY REJOICINGS.—The 21st birthday of John Lambert Swale, Esq., eldest son of the Rev. H. I. Swale, and cornet in the 4th Hussars, was kept up by the retainers and tradesmen of the family, on Monday the 17th May, with suitable rejoicings. Early in the morning the union jack was seen floating from the highest pinnacle of Ingfield. In the evening a salute of three guns boomed accross the valley from the battery on the summit of Castlebergh, and was replied to from Ingfield. A supper was provided at the latter place, where upwards of thirty of the tradesmen and servants of the family sat down to the excellent fare, after which the health of Mr. J. L. Swale was duly honoured and toasted, and suitable speeches were made by several of the company. The arrangments were made under the zealous direction of Mr. James Hudson, gardener and ground bailiff to the Rev H. I. Swale.

newspapers for over 15 months, asking for help to find him [*BNA7*]. He was not a tall man, we are told.

GENTLEMAN MISSING.—£200 is offered to any person who will supply authentic information of the present abode of Captain John Lambert Swale, of Ingfield, near Settle, Yorkshire, if living, or proof of his death if he be dead. He was a Captain in one of her Majesty's Hussar Regiments, and on the 1st of February, 1876, left Tenby, South Wales, where he was temporarily residing, and has not since been heard of. He is about 5ft. 6in. in height, has brown hair, pale brown complexion, short heavy moustache, small whiskers.

John's substantial estate was finally agreed in April 1881, but his body was never found. Son Charles was just six when John went missing. Understandably, John's wife Blanche found this difficult to cope with and in 1880 was admitted to a lunatic asylum where she remained for over 40 years until her death.

Meanwhile, Charles studied at a private school in Godalming, Surrey and then went to Cambridge to qualify as a barrister. He came back to Settle to live with grandfather Hogarth, who died when Charles was 23. Charles took over Ingfield Hall. He was a Trustee of Settle Church and President of the Conservative Club (and a member of its billiards team). He was Vice President and Captain of the First XI cricket team, was on the committee of several other sporting clubs, and a regular in the Settle Amateur Operatic Society [*ph6,15*].

The end of Charles' life, aged just 43, was tragic. Charles had become depressed over local criticism that he had a pecuniary interest in the sale of some land [*BNA11,13*]. Dr Hyslop had warned '*those living with him to watch him*'. The Giggleswick vicar suggested that he was 'morally murdered – hounded to his untimely end'.

If this tragic occurrence does not impress this neighbourhood with the wickedness of traducing an honourable man for some petty personal or other unworthy end, nothing ever will. There are some people whose role in life seems to be that of mischief-makers, and who are not in the least perturbed by any untoward circumstances they may bring about. There is no getting out of the fact that Charles Alured Lambert Swale has been morally murdered—hounded to his untimely end. He felt that his high personal honour had been foully and unjustly aspersed; this to a man of his peculiar sensitiveness, known to all, was not only iniquitous, but cruelly mean.

YORKSHIRE BARRISTER'S DEATH

A strange story was told at an inquest at Settle, yesterday, on the body of Charles Alured Lambert Swale, a barrister, of Inglefield.

Mr. Swale was found drowned in a pond, and it was stated that he had been depressed over trouble in connection with the purchase of a farm. Dr. B. S. Hyslop said that at the end of March Mr. Swale threatened to shoot himself, and he warned those living with him to watch him.

A gamekeeper said Mr. Swale went out with him on Wednesday morning to look at same snares. He complained of cold, and said he thought he would have a run. The gamekeeper said: "I hope you will run straight home," and Mr. Swale walked away in the direction of the house.

Half an hour later the man found Mr. Swale had not returned to the house, and a search revealed his body standing upright in a pond.

A verdict of "Suicide during temporary insanity" was returned.

Maybe Charles had inherited his mum's tendency towards fragile mental health? At Ingfield Hall, Thomas and Margaret Bulcock [*working class heroes*] worked as his gamekeeper and housekeeper. When he died, unmarried, Charles left an annuity to them both and provision for his mum's asylum fees – she died in 1923.

D3 In memory of Mary Swale of Ingfield who died May 26 1844 aged 25 years. Blessed are the poor in spirit for theirs is the Kingdom of Heaven Matt VIII. Rev. Hogarth John Swale, first incumbent of this parish, born Sept 26 1810, died Aug 10 1893. Charles Alured Lambert Swale, grandson of the above who entered into rest 26 Nov 1913 age 43 years. This is my rest forever. Here I will dwell for I have desired it. In memory of Ann Swale of Langcliffe Hall who died Feby 9 1859 age 86 years. To thee Lord I resign my spirit.

Rev'd William Frederick Pierson, the second vicar

Despite his wealthy background, Rev'd Swale ran the church along simple lines and procedures. In contrast, his successor Rev'd Pierson donated the very ornate font: '*William Frederick Pierson and Margaret Pierson dedicate this font to the glory of God*'. A plaque at the back of the church explains William was responsible for setting up the endowment fund to eliminate pew rents.

William was born in 1821 in Hitchin, Hertfordshire. By 1848 he had moved to Holy Ascension in Settle. In 1850 he married **Margaret Birkbeck** [*wealthy ones*] and lived with her family at Anley. They had two daughters and three sons. In 1856, the new Vicarage on Station Road was completed for them to live in - William had contributed a quarter of the cost [*SC*]. Along with his brother-in-law John Birkbeck and predecessor Rev'd Swale, William was a Trustee of the Craven Savings Bank. William died in 1883, after 35 years' service and a brass lectern was dedicated in his memory.

SETTLE PARSONAGE.

THE following Subscriptions have been already received towards the purchase of a site, and building of a Parsonage House for this town. The amount subscribed is still below the estimated cost, and further subscriptions will be thankfully received by the Churchwardens, Mr. Richard Greenwood, and Mr. Thomas Stackhouse, or at the Craven Bank.

	£		£
The Craven Bank	100	Miss Robinson........	10
Wm. Robinson, Esq. ..	100	Rev. J. Robinson......	10
John Birkbeck, Esq. ..	100	Miss Bolland	10
Rev. W. F. Pierson ..	200	S. Hargraves, Esq.	10
Miss Lambert	50	Mrs. Henlock, Ousburn	10
John Preston, Esq.....	40	F. Dawson, Esq..... .	10
Thomas Birkbeck, Esq.	30	Rev. H. Dawson......	10
Thomas Clapham, Esq.	25	A. Stackhouse, Esq., (Stainforth)	10
Miss Dawson	20	Anonymous	5
George Hartley, Esq...	20	Mr. Geo. Wilkinson ..	1
Wm. Robinson, Junior, Esq.	20	Rev. R. Procter	1

E26 William Frederick Pierson priest, interred into rest August 18 1883. Vicar of Settle 1848 - 1883. Faithful until death

E27 Margaret Pierson died Feb 27 1871. Rest in the Lord. And her son John Ernest Pierson Late major of the Royal Sussex Regiment, died at Worthing May 18 1912. Then are they glad because they are at rest

E28 Mary Emily Pierson, July 2nd 1853 X

His wife Margaret was buried with their son John who had a distinguished military career [*BNA7*]. Their daughter Mary Emily had her own gravestone. She was just two and a half days old.

Major John Ernest Pierson died at Worthing on Saturday, aged 54. He saw service in Egypt in 1882, and was with the Nile Expedition in 1884-5. He was Adjutant of the 1st Royal Sussex Brigade and Major in the 3rd Brigade at Aldershot. He was also a J.P. for the Worthing Division.

Daughter Lucy Margaret married a vicar and had six children. Son William Birkbeck Pierson also became a vicar, but met a sudden death aged 52 [*BNA1*].

CLERGYMAN'S SUDDEN DEATH.

A FORMER CREWE VICAR.

The Rev. William Birkbeck Pierson, Vicar of Rothwell, died suddenly yesterday while attending a meeting of the Leeds Day School Association. The business had just about concluded when the rev. gentleman was noticed to be breathing rather heavily. He at once collapsed, and lost consciousness, expiring within five minutes. Mr. Pierson, who was fifty-one years of age, was from about 1882 for eight years curate at the Leeds Parish Church, after which he was appointed to the living of St. Barnabas's, Crewe, where he remained for nearly five years. In 1894 he was appointed to Rothwell, and for the past two years had acted as Rural Dean of Whitkirk. He was an excellent preacher, was possessed of remarkable powers of organisation, and had taken great interest in education. At the inquest held at night a verdict of "death from apoplexy" was returned.

So far, all very respectable. However, not all children follow their father's footsteps and youngest son Alfred Graeme Pierson certainly didn't, as we shall see. It's quite possible that Alfred's misdemeanours could have contributed to his father's demise [*wives, wenches*].

CHURCHWARDENS

Churchwardens were the vicar's right hand men (yes, they were always men!) who managed the day to day life of the church. One churchwarden was appointed by the vicar and often remained in post for many years. The other was appointed annually by 'the pew-renters'. Churchwardens had to be 'fit and proper persons' and tended to be well respected tradesmen.

Vestry records list their responsibilities: '*to perform and execute all lawful acts, matters and things necessary and requisite for and concerning the repairs, management, good order and decency of behaviour to be kept and observed in the church by the congregation. In the case of non-payment of Pew Rent, to enter upon and sell the same or else to sue for and recover the same by Action in the names of the Churchwardens of the church*'. There was plenty of controversy over pew rents in Anglican churches throughout the nineteenth century, especially as nonconformist churches were free to all.

Thomas Hardacre, draper and first churchwarden (and bankrupt)

Thomas Hardacre, born in 1803, was the eldest son of Turner Hardacre and Elizabeth Dodgson. Turner was a successful Settle businessman, and a 'tax assessor' in the town. Turner died, aged just 40, in 1815. In 1834 Thomas married **Sarah Littlewood** from Birmingham and they had two daughters and two sons. The daughters survived but the sons died in infancy - George in 1844, and Charlie in 1853. Sarah died at the birth of Charlie when she was 44 and they are all buried together.

C23 In memorial of Sarah Hardacre Obit 22nd February AD 1853, AET 44

In April 1839 Thomas became the first 'vicar's churchwarden' of Holy Ascension Church and remained in post until February 1844. His retirement may have been linked to son George's death. Like his dad, Thomas was a successful business man. In 1844 he owned several properties on Castle Hill and in the Market Place backing onto Castle Hill where his drapery business was located.

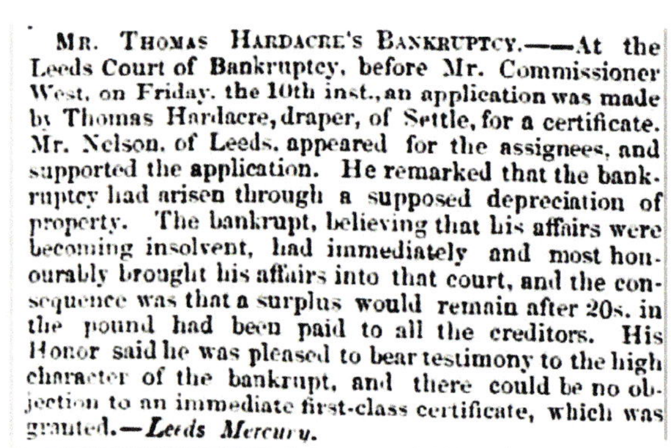

MR. THOMAS HARDACRE'S BANKRUPTCY.——At the Leeds Court of Bankruptcy, before Mr. Commissioner West, on Friday, the 10th inst., an application was made by Thomas Hardacre, draper, of Settle, for a certificate. Mr. Nelson, of Leeds, appeared for the assignees, and supported the application. He remarked that the bankruptcy had arisen through a supposed depreciation of property. The bankrupt, believing that his affairs were becoming insolvent, had immediately and most honourably brought his affairs into that court, and the consequence was that a surplus would remain after 20s. in the pound had been paid to all the creditors. His Honor said he was pleased to bear testimony to the high character of the bankrupt, and there could be no objection to an immediate first-class certificate, which was granted.—*Leeds Mercury.*

Unfortunately the death of Sarah and the children seems to have affected business. In 1857 Thomas applied for bankruptcy due to the depreciation of his property. The Commissioner made a point of Thomas' good character [*BNA11*].

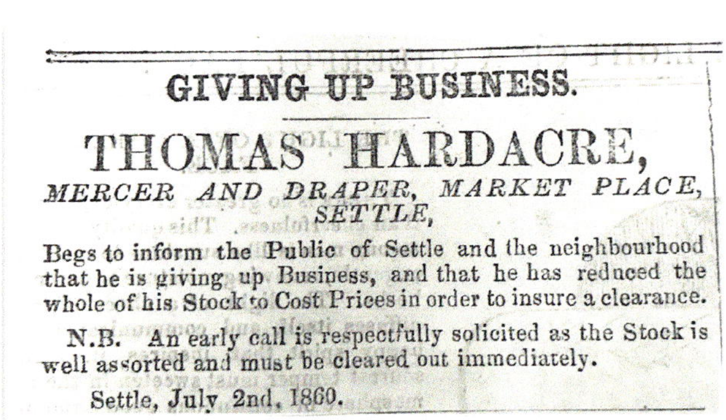

GIVING UP BUSINESS.

THOMAS HARDACRE,

MERCER AND DRAPER, MARKET PLACE, SETTLE,

Begs to inform the Public of Settle and the neighbourhood that he is giving up Business, and that he has reduced the whole of his Stock to Cost Prices in order to insure a clearance.

N.B. An early call is respectfully solicited as the Stock is well assorted and must be cleared out immediately.

Settle, July 2nd, 1860.

Two years later, aged 56, Thomas married 36 year old **Eliza Josine Robinson** who was the daughter of the Settle surgeon Thomas Robinson and cousin to the church verger William Perkin [*below*]. In July 1860, Thomas Hardacre advertised that he was giving up business [*SC*], however he was still working as a linen draper in Settle at the time of the 1861 census. Thomas' two remaining (adult) daughters were boarding with aunts in Leeds. Thomas and Eliza moved to Liverpool to try their luck but Thomas died there in 1867, leaving an estate of under £100.

In 1871 Eliza was 'housekeeper' to her elderly uncle and retired surgeon John Marshall in the incredibly imposing Wray House in Wray. When Eliza died in 1876, she left an amazing £30,000 which would be worth several million today. How is this possible? Well, Eliza was from a wealthy family. Her widowed mum and aged uncle John died earlier in the 1870s and may well have left her a legacy.

What happened to the daughters? Emily died a wealthy spinster in Derbyshire in 1906. Poor Lucy married an insurance agent but died at the birth of her first child in 1873.

John Handby, plumber and churchwarden for over 40 years

A CARD.
JAMES HANDBY,
GARDENER,
Rock Cottage, Back Lane, Settle.
Country orders punctually attended to.

The Handbys were pillars of the community. **James**, born in 1815 in Clapham, married **Ann Tomlinson** in 1840. They had three sons and moved to live in Rock House Cottage, behind Rock House on Castle Hill. James was a gardener [*SC*].

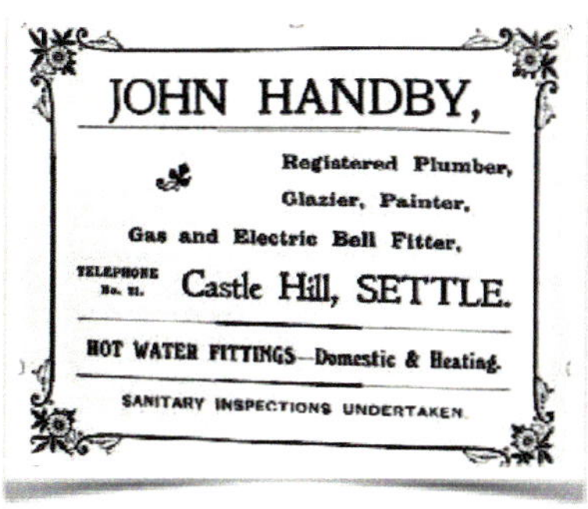

JOHN HANDBY,
Registered Plumber,
Glazier, Painter,
Gas and Electric Bell Fitter,
TELEPHONE No. 11. Castle Hill, SETTLE.
HOT WATER FITTINGS—Domestic & Heating.
SANITARY INSPECTIONS UNDERTAKEN.

Eldest son, **John Handby**, born in 1841, became a plumber having been apprenticed to plumber and cave explorer Joseph Jackson [*tradesmen*]. John married **Hannah Lord,** son of John Lord [*wenches, wives*] who died giving birth to her second daughter. So he married **Mary Slinger** who also died soon after the birth of her second son Joseph. Her first son William had died aged just ten days. John then married **Mary Barns** who gave him another two children and survived, thank goodness.

As well as plumbing, glazing and fitting 'gas and electric bells' [*LSA*], John invested in the Settle Market Buildings Co. Ltd. This was set up to build an additional storey on to the Shambles buildings in Market Place and John probably generated some more trade for himself as part of the project. John was a foundation governor of the National School in Settle and the manager of Settle Gas Company from 1875, taking over from Joseph Jackson, his previous boss and later business partner [*ph2*].

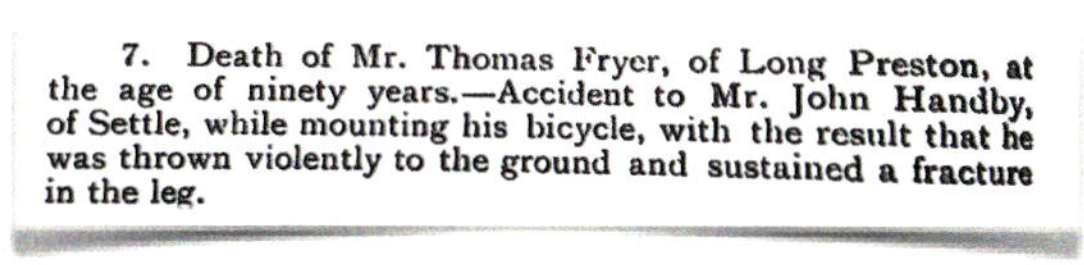

7. Death of Mr. Thomas Fryer, of Long Preston, at the age of ninety years.—Accident to Mr. John Handby, of Settle, while mounting his bicycle, with the result that he was thrown violently to the ground and sustained a fracture in the leg.

Local press reported that 59 year old John fractured his leg whilst mounting his bicycle [*LSA*]. John became the vicar's churchwarden and served for over 40 years. He regularly organised day trips for the choristers and bell ringers. When John died, in 1918, he was described as a '*stalwart worker for the church,*' and a memorial fund raised sufficient to purchase two silver mounted churchwardens' wands, inscribed with his name. His widow Mary was presented with a gold wristlet watch. A popular man indeed.

John is the only person named on this gravestone, but several of his family are probably with him: his parents, first two wives Hannah and Mary and infant William.

D5 In loving memory of John Handby died August 27th 1918 age 77 years. Until the day break and the shadows flee away.

Son Joseph continued the plumbing business; note the named taps [*ph7*], and is buried with wife Edith in *New grave H12*. Several of John's other children emigrated to Australia.

James' second son **James Tomlinson Handby**, born in 1846, was not a happy chap. He ran a tailoring business on Castle Hill [*SC*]. He married **Margaret Walling** in 1871 and their son James Walling Handby followed. The family spent eight years in Blenheim, New Zealand with John still working as a tailor, but returned to Settle in 1895 for some reason.

James had been a vocal teetotaller and a Wesleyan local preacher who had suggested: *'the sale of intoxicating liquors on a Sunday is a special service of intemperance, immorality and crime'* [*BNA7*].

SUNDAY CLOSING OF PUBLIC HOUSES.—On Monday evening last a public meeting was held in the Mechanics' Hall, the object being to consider the desirability of presenting a petition to Parliament in favour of the closing of public houses during the whole of Sunday. The chair was occupied by Mr. T. A. Harvey, who after opening the meeting by explaining the purpose for which it had been called, requested Mr. I. T. Handby to propose the following resolution :—" That your petitioners believe that the sale of intoxicating liquors on Sunday is a special service of Intemperance, immorality and crime." On the motion of Mr.

James Tomlinson Handby died in March 1897, aged 51, in the midst of what was reported as a 'spate of suicides' in the area [*CH*].

SAD SUICIDE.—An inquest was held at the Court House, Settle, on Saturday last, by Mr T. P. Brown, coroner, on the body of James Tomlinson Handby, master tailor, of Castle Hill, Settle, who committed suicide on Friday morning by shooting.—James Walling Handby, tailor, of Settle, said deceased was his father, who had returned to England in August, 1895, from New Zealand, and had of late seemed to be low in spirits, and in bad health. He last saw him alive on Thursday evening between nine and ten p.m., when his father had scarcely anything to say, which was very unusual. The deceased was found between seven and eight a.m. on Friday morning.—Emma Bryning, domestic servant and housekeeper to the deceased, said that he rose about the usual time and lit his workroom fire, and then went into the vinery. She came down at 7 a.m. and made the breakfast, and then called the deceased to his breakfast, but there was no answer. She went upstairs and could not find him. On looking in the boiler house attached to the greenhouse she found him there in a sitting position. She then went for help.—Dr Elgar said he saw the body on Friday morning and deceased appeared to have been dead about half an hour. He found a wound in the head caused by a revolver, which he found in the right hand of the deceased, and the wound was probably self-inflicted.—The jury returned a verdict of "Suicide whilst temporarily insane," and expressed their sympathy with the family of the deceased.—The deceased was formerly a Wesleyan local preacher and throughout life a consistent teetotaller. This sad close of an exemplary career has cast quite a gloom over the town and district. The interment took place at the Holy Ascension Church on Monday. This is the fourth suicide in this locality within a few months.

The coroner's inquest at Settle Court heard that James killed himself with a pistol shot *'suicide whilst temporarily insane'*. Margaret and son James, now a commercial clerk, lived in Austwick until Margaret died in 1907. She is buried with husband James in the unmarked *Old grave CX28*. Son James immediately left for New Zealand where he married and worked in the armed services until he died aged 55. You can't blame him really. James Handby (Snr)'s third son Edmund is with the musicians [*below*].

Churchwardens also include William Bilton in 1840, John Johnson Hartley in 1841, Peter Skirrow in 1844, Joseph Jackson in 1846, John Armistead in 1850, [*all tradesmen*] and John Winskill in 1862, *page 92*. Charles Ratcliffe in 1848 [*railway folk*], Arthur Brewin in 1867, William Shepherd in 1870 [*both professionals*], Capt Robert Stansfeld Birkbeck in 1874 [*wealthy ones*], Elias Davis in 1902 [*farmers*].

SEXTONS AND VERGERS

The men who held these overlapping roles were responsible for the order and upkeep of the church and the care of sacred relics and preparations for liturgy. They had to maintain the church buildings and grounds and dig graves. These were paid roles, earning a salary of £5 per half year. The early vestry records tell us that the man appointed *'is to have the yearly salary of five pounds for attendance on Sundays, Good Friday and Christmas Day. He will be in attendance during Divine Service to see that all be kept orderly and quiet and persons properly seated in their pews. He is to attend to the warming apparatus and lighting of the church and keep it clean and in good order".* The heating and lighting apparatus was fraught with problems. This report of 1866 explains how the steam from the heating apparatus and the soot from the camphine lamps (using distilled turpentine) had damaged the organ machinery [SC].

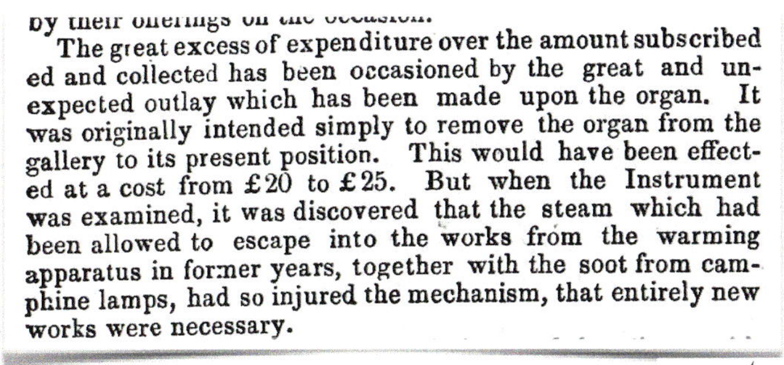
by their offerings on the occasion.
The great excess of expenditure over the amount subscribed and collected has been occasioned by the great and unexpected outlay which has been made upon the organ. It was originally intended simply to remove the organ from the gallery to its present position. This would have been effected at a cost from £20 to £25. But when the Instrument was examined, it was discovered that the steam which had been allowed to escape into the works from the warming apparatus in former years, together with the soot from camphine lamps, had so injured the mechanism, that entirely new works were necessary.

Poor William Butterfield, gardener and first verger

William Butterfield, born in 1784, was a gardener from Shipley. He found his way to Settle where he married **Ann Dibb**. They had at least four children but only son James survived. William was the first sexton at the church from 1838, but resigned in November 1843. There were two very good reasons for his resignation. Firstly, wife Ann died in July 1843, which may be linked to the second reason, son James' accidental transgression.

William Lodge Paley's diaries tell us that on June 2nd 1843, son James accidentally shot 46 year old William Hargreaves in the shoulder while they were shooting sparrows and he died. Amazingly there are no records of a coroner's inquest – did James just run away? He wouldn't be the first.

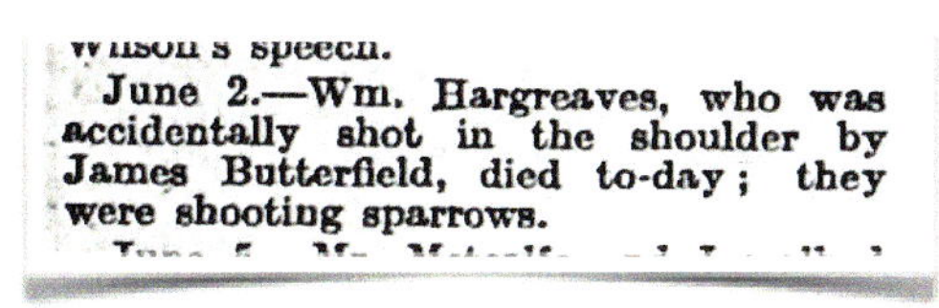
Wilson's speech.
June 2.—Wm. Hargreaves, who was accidentally shot in the shoulder by James Butterfield, died to-day; they were shooting sparrows.

Four years later in Lancaster, on 22 April 1847, James married **Isabella Jackson** who was the illegitimate daughter of Elizabeth Jackson, a domestic servant from Caton. Did Isabella know anything about the shooting? In a twist of fate and just 15 weeks after their marriage, in Liverpool, James died, perhaps due to the rampant cholera in the city at the time. William went to the expense of bringing James' body back to Settle for burial and also paid for a notable inscription, perhaps feeling the need to reinforce his good character?

B9 Sacred to the memory of Ann wife of William Butterfield died July 26th 1843 aged 65 years. Also of James Butterfield, son of the above died at Liverpool August 8th 1847 aged 29 years.

If upright worth and virtue claims the tears, reader tis due to him who sleepeth here. Grateful, affectionate, sincere and kind. His memory's dear to those he left behind.

Also of the above named William Butterfield who died April 12th 1860 aged 76.

What happened to James' widow Isabella? Isabella and her mum moved to Settle and worked as servants at Stackhouse. Nine years later, in 1856, Isabella married **John Laytham**, who worked as a 'druggist'. John was the son of **Christopher Laytham**, a 'cow leech doctor' – an early vet, based in Upper Settle. Christopher got himself into a spot of trouble with this assault in 1852 [*BNA7*].

ASSAULT.——**Mr. Christopher Laytham, of Settle, horse breaker, was summoned before the magistrates on Tuesday, for assaulting and beating Richard Coates. The assault was admitted, but it was contended that the defendant was provoked to it. Mr. Cowburn appeared for the complainant, and Mr. H. Robinson for defendant. Fined 10s. and costs.**

PIPES! PIPES!! PIPES!!!

Mrs. LAYTHAM,

CHAPEL STREET,

Has in stock the following assortment of **PIPES**, viz ,—

Meerschaums from 5s. to 20s., Briarwood from 6d. to 2s. 6d. Swanbone (in cases) 3s. Plain and Ornamental Clay, 4d. to 1s. 6d. Churchwardens 4d. and 6d. per dozen. Southorn's Patent Broseley's, 2s. per doz.

Cigar Holders in Meerschaum and Briarwood 4d. to 1s. 6d. Cigar Cases. 1s. to 4s. 6d. Indian Rubber Tobacco Pouches, 1s. to 2s. Tobacco and Snuff Boxes, 3d. to 1s.

TOBACCO,

Kendal Shag, 4s. and 4s. 2d. per lb. Kendal Returns, 5s. per lb. Dawson's Rough cut, 4s. 8d. per lb. DUNCAN'S celebrated SMOKING MIXTURE, composed of Cavendish, Latakia, &c., in ¼ lb. Canisters, 2s. 6d. each.

CIGARS,

Havannah and Vevey Fins, 12s. to 30s. per lb.

SNUFFS,

Kendal Brown, and S. P., 5s. per lb., Best Princes' Mixture, 5s. 6d. per lb.

Chapel St., Settle, April 2nd, 1866.

Isabella's husband John died just four years after their marriage and six months after the death of both his parents. These deaths bear the signs of an infection such as tuberculosis. Isabella really didn't have much luck with husbands.

Isabella continued to run the tobacconist part of John's business [*SC*]. Ten years later Isabella and her mum died within a week of each other and they are both buried with the Laythams.

B3 In memory of John Laytham of Settle who died December 11th 1860 aged 36 years. Also of Christopher Laytham, father of the above who died June 1st 1861 aged 61 years. Also of Ann wife of the above who died June 18th 1861 aged 75 years. Also of Elizabeth Jackson of Settle who died Decr 6th 1870 aged 78 years. Also Isabella wife of th(e above n)amed John Laytham and (daughter) of the above named Elizabeth (Jackson) who died Decr 13th 1870 (aged) 56 years.

William Perkin, stonemason and naughty sexton for 46 years

William Perkin, born in 1808, was the son of Christopher Parkin, a farmer. His mum Ellen was the sister of Thomas Robinson, a respected surgeon in Settle. Somehow the family name of Parkin had changed to Perkin by the 1840s. William made quite an income from his work at the Church, which conveniently supplemented his stonemasonry business based in the Market Place and Constitution Hill. In 1843 he became sexton/verger, replacing William Butterfield, a post which he held for an amazing 46 years.

William had the responsibility of maintain the churchyard grave plan showing where bodies were buried. As we have found out, he did this until 1855, but then just stopped. In 1866, the Vestry records describe that churchwarden *'Mr Winskill do require Messrs Perkin to supply the necessary sketch for completing the map of the graves in the church yard without delay.'* There was a further request in May 1867 as the churchwardens were required to send copies of records to the Diocese. William never completed these records, so we will never know where over 400 bodies are buried. That's really not helpful William! Was he just lazy or was there another reason he was unable to do it? He was remembered as having quite a relaxed attitude to the job [*CH*].

The old sexton, William Perkin by name, who had been grave digger since the church was built till he retired through old age and infirmity, had generally to be consulted before a grave was started. On one occasion he was asked about a certain space as to whether it would hold another body or not, he replied it would not "because old Tommy so-and-so is buried there and he made me promise before he died to bury him as near the top as possible so that at the resurrection he would find no trouble in getting out when his body had to rise again, so I put him in a very shallow one; he lies very near the top."

William had married **Mary Wildman** from Tatham in 1830 and they had five children, two of whom died in 1841 aged just one and 11. Mary died in June 1852. In October the same year William married **Nancy Cornthwaite** of Milnthorpe and they had another daughter, Fanny. Poor Nancy died suddenly in 1868, aged 48 [*BNA7*]. Just a year after Nancy's death William married again, this time to **Martha Satterthwaite.**

> SUDDEN DEATH.—A very sudden death happened here on Tuesday last. The wife of Mr William Perkin, sexton, whilst preparing her husband's tea, was seized with a fit of apoplexy, and died in less than two hours afterwards. Up to the moment of the attack which so suddenly proved fatal deceased, who was aged 45, was in her usual health and spirits. Mr. Altham, surgeon, was called in immediately she was seized with the fit, but there appeared little hope of her rallying, and, as the result shows, his services were unavailing.

As William was the verger, it was custom and practice that his wife should be the church cleaner. Nancy had done a good job. After Nancy died, the church agreed that daughter Fanny could do the cleaning in the absence of a wife. However, William's third wife Martha obviously didn't enjoy cleaning – the church 'redefined' her job description and arranged payment to her '*only when the tiling and stone steps have been washed.*' A few years later, they decided that '*in the future the cleaning and dusting of the church be committed to the charge of a few ladies to be selected and authorised by the vicar and churchwardens.*' Martha was probably very relieved!

William saw out his days with Martha on Constitution Hill. William, his two children and first two wives are buried in prime position, *grave DX22* right by the church gate. As a stonemason and having such a prestigious role at the church for so many years it's surprising William and his family didn't have a gravestone.

THE MUSICIANS

William Henry Barnett, church organist for 50 years

William Henry Barnett, born in Leeds in 1808 was an organist with fine credentials. After the death of his dad in the Napoleonic wars, William became a pupil of Edward Booth, a celebrated violin maker. He joined the orchestra of the Royal Italian Opera Company, specialising in flute and cello. He was a 'Professor of Music' at the age of 23. In 1840 William's reputation brought about his recruitment to Holy Ascension Church through a friend of Thomas Hardacre, the churchwarden. Classical music played a much greater part in nineteenth century society than today, and so an organist of such high standing was well paid. William was the leader and conductor of Settle's new Choral Society and led numerous concerts at the new Music Hall (Victoria Hall) which had been built in 1853 by the Rev'd John Robinson, a music enthusiast. William was a true classical musician composing numerous pieces for the organ and piano.

William had married **Rebecca Reynolds** when he was 23 but she died at the birth of son George Frederick. So William married Irish **Margaret Dunn** and she quickly gave William another four children within five years. Unfortunately two of them died in infancy. The family lived on the Market Place close to what is now Boots' Chemist and in each census return William described himself as a '*professional organist, musician, music teacher.*' In the 1860s William and George Stansfeld [*wealthy ones*] visited the Conservatoire in Leipzig, which had been founded by the composer Felix Mendelssohn [*CH*]. Margaret died aged 53 leaving William to bring up the children, living in the same house until he retired to Prospect Terrace on Station Road. William outlived Margaret by almost 30 years.

> Mr. Barnett and Mr. George Stansfeld (just returned from the Conservatoire of Music, Leipsic) organised an Orchestra and gave the Settle folk their first taste of theatrical venture on a grand scale, which provided a handsome sum for the benefit of the Lancashire sufferers during the great cotton famine.

D14 In loving memory of William Henry Barnett Died June 26 1895 aged 87. I know that my redeemer liveth. Margaret his wife died Jany 6 1867 aged 52. Rebecca Core Barnett died Nov 1845, aged 5 years. William Percy died Feb 27 1848 aged 2 years. Julia Barnett entered into rest August 10th 1922 aged 79. Faithful unto death. Clara F Barnett died at Stuttgart in Germany December 29th 1835. George Frederick Barnett died July 21 1872 Aged 39. George Joseph, son of the above died at Kurrachee Jan 1884 Aged 20

D10 RG and WP Barnett *(gravestone with a tiny cross pictured to right behind their parents' grave)*

Upon William's death at the very respectable age of 87, the Parish Magazine reported '*the church on earth has lost a faithful servant. For nearly 50 years he was Organist of our Parish Church. He was an organist and composer of hymn tunes of no little merit. One of the last acts of his life was to make a very handsome contribution to the fund which has been raised for the heating of our National Schools.*' Lambert's Settle Almanac printed a generous obituary.

Mr. Barnett was a most capable performer upon the organ, pianoforte violin, flute and 'cello, but his predilection lay in the direction of the organ, and it was indeed a treat to hear him extemporise upon that instrument when he happened to be in the vein to do so.

He led a singularly beautiful and quiet life, gaining the respect of all with whom he came in contact, and at the time of his decease it may safely be affirmed that he had not an enemy in the neighbourhood. Interred in the peaceful churchyard at Settle, a handsome rustic cross has been erected to his memory by his two daughters Miss Julia and Miss Fanny Barnett.

William left an estate worth the equivalent of £280,000 to his two surviving spinster daughters Julia and Fanny Ann. It seems they took the money to run a school together in Devon. Son George Frederick married and had four children before he died, aged just 39. Clara and George Joseph commemorated on the stone are George's children. Rebecca and William Percy died in childhood and are remembered on William's stone and also have a stone of their own.

Also: William Moorby was the Church cleaner, clerk and choirmaster [*wenches,wives*].

Edmund (Ted) Handby, artiste and chorister for over 60 years

Edmund Handby, born in 1850, was the brother of churchwarden John Handby [*above*]. When he was 16, Edmund was seriously injured about the head on an excursion [*BNA8*], but there was no lasting damage. Edmund married **Jane Holmes**, daughter of Thomas Holmes [*tradesmen*] and they had five children. They lived on Castle Hill and Duke Street. Edmund was a talented artist - portraits, landscapes stage decor and paper hangings. [BNA13, *WSA*].

THE WINDERMERE EXCURSION ACCIDENT. — Our usually quiet little town was thrown into a state of great excitement on Wednesday, when the news came that an accident had happened to the excursion train which had that morning taken a great many passengers from Settle to Windermere. Those who had friends or relatives amongst the passengers were concerned to know whether they had escaped injury, and several persons met the train at the station on its return to learn the truth. Then, and not till then, it was ascertained with certainty that no Settle persons had been seriously injured, except a young man of the name of Edmund Handby, who got badly hurt about the head, and was brought home by an earlier train and placed under medical care Very

ARCHERY BALL AT SETTLE.

The North Ribblesdale Archers gave a ball at the Lion Hotel, Settle, on Monday evening, the event proving an unqualified success. The ball-room had been decorated in Mr. Edmund Handby's best style. The walls of the room were made gay with trophies of banners, the Royal Arms, targets and arrows, whilst plants and ferns of splendid foliage appeared on every hand. Across the room was suspended the appropriate motto, "Stout arm, strong bow, and steady eye; Union, true hearts, and courtesie." Some very pretty dresses were worn by the ladies. Mr. Law, of Leeds, supplied the excellent dance music. The supper, provided by Mr. Alfred Simpson,

Edmund Handby,
Painter, Paper-Hanger,
SIGN WRITER,
Gilder & General Decorator,
Calls attention to his Stock of
PAPERHANGINGS
Which have been carefully selected to suit the requirements of all classes.
OIL PAINTINGS CLEANED AND RESTORED.

Edmund could thank Mrs McClelland (Epsey Robinson) [*wives, wenches*] for organising the fine art exhibition in 1886 [*BNA7*]. Edmund was a very active member of the Dramatic and Operatic Societies and starred in numerous productions. Edmund was sometimes described as '*the portly Mr Handby*' especially in photos of his dramatic personae [*ph13*]. He is credited with painting the fire screen at Victoria Hall which is still in use today.

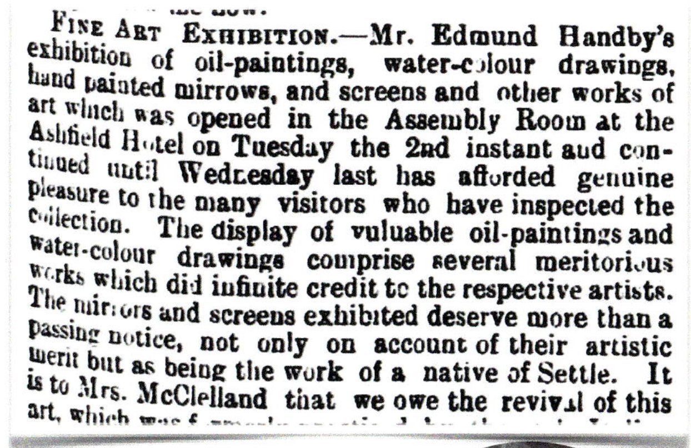

FINE ART EXHIBITION.—Mr. Edmund Handby's exhibition of oil-paintings, water-colour drawings, hand painted mirrors, and screens and other works of art which was opened in the Assembly Room at the Ashfield Hotel on Tuesday the 2nd instant aud continued until Wednesday last has afforded genuine pleasure to the many visitors who have inspected the collection. The display of vuluable oil-paintings and water-colour drawings comprise several meritorious works which did infinite credit to the respective artists. The mirrors and screens exhibited deserve more than a passing notice, not only on account of their artistic merit but as being the work of a native of Settle. It is to Mrs. McClelland that we owe the revival of this art, which

Edmund was an excellent singer and a chorister for 60 years at Holy Ascension. He was also a churchwarden. He died six months before his brother John in 1918, aged 67, being described by the vicar as *"the oldest member of the choir, and a most highly respected parishioner"*.

Edmund and Jane are buried in *Old graveyard G28* with son Edmund, another painter, and his wife Elizabeth, who ran the refreshment rooms on the site of the old Crown Inn, next to the Old Naked Man [*LSA*].

In loving memory of Jane wife of Edmund Handby died Feb 17 1909 aged 62. Also Edmund Handby died (?) Feb 1918, aged 67. Also Edmund ...their son died Sept 10 1935 aged 57 years. Also of John their son died at Germiston South Africa March (?) 1904 aged 28 years.

...JT...

John Cook, choirboy

John Cook (Snr) was the only child of Irish tailor James Cook and his second wife **Ann Winnera**, who died at John's birth. James already had eight children with his first wife Dorothy and then married a third wife Eleanor. John became a joiner and worked from Constitution Hill and then Duke Street with his wife **Elizabeth Grime** from Clapham. Elizabeth's brother was William Grime [*working class heroes*]. Elizabeth was 10 years older than John, so lied about her age on the wedding certificate (and for the rest of her life), to suggest she was only five years older. Did John know? They had five children. The fourth, John, died aged two so they also named their next child John. This John, born in 1873, was a choirboy at the church. Tragically, aged just 13, John drowned in the Ribble at Birkbeck Weir near Anley [*BNA11*]. Both sons called John, and mum Elizabeth are buried in the Ancient churchyard in unmarked graves, hopefully together. Later, dad John lived with son William, a joiner, on Belle Hill in Giggleswick.

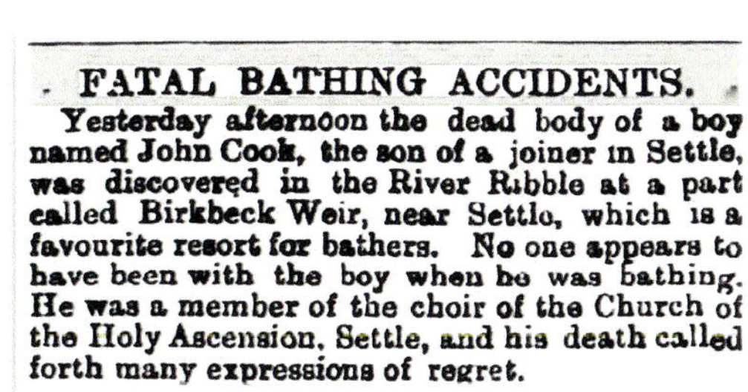

FATAL BATHING ACCIDENTS.

Yesterday afternoon the dead body of a boy named John Cook, the son of a joiner in Settle, was discovered in the River Ribble at a part called Birkbeck Weir, near Settle, which is a favourite resort for bathers. No one appears to have been with the boy when he was bathing. He was a member of the choir of the Church of the Holy Ascension, Settle, and his death called forth many expressions of regret.

...JT...

WESLEYAN CHURCH FOLK

The churchyard was the burial place for other denominations including Catholics and Methodists. There are several ministers in the churchyard but none had lives quite like those of William Towler's family.

Rev'd William Towler, Wesleyan missionary in the West Indies

William Towler was born in 1811 in Lincolnshire, the son of Edward Towler, a Wesleyan Minister. In 1837 William, working as a draper, married **Sophia Wainwright** whose family were originally from Kent but came to work in the woollen trade in Leeds. Straight after the wedding a Weslayan mission called them to Haiti. William died in 1853, aged 41, in Haiti. His Wesleyan Ministry obituary tells us:

At the (Wesleyan) conference of 1837, William received an appointment to Haiti, and for nearly sixteen years faithfully and zealously laboured in Haiti and St Domingo. For the greater part of that time he was resident in the town of Puerto Plata, and, in consequence of the hostilities subsisting between the empire and the republic, was cut off from all personal intercourse with his brethren, and subjected to many and grievous privations, both personal and domestic. But, notwithstanding all, he fulfilled his course with diligence; his work was his delight. His death was a fitting sequel to a holy and devoted life. For him death had no terrors. He died on the 25th August 1853, in the forty-second year of his age, and the sixteenth of his ministry.

Copies of letters tell of natural and man-made destruction, with earthquakes perforating the fighting. Meanwhile, in the midst of those horrendous conditions, William and Sophia brought up at least four children: **Eliza**, **Sophia**, **Emily** and **Mary Ann**. After William's death Sophia and the girls returned to England.

By 1871 Sophia and the girls were running a *'school for ladies'* in Station Road in Settle. Two of the daughters married good Methodist men; in 1874 Eliza married **Thomas Dixon** and in 1877 Emily married **William Walker**. Mum Sophia died just a month after Eliza's wedding. This left Mary Ann and Sophia running the school, now in the Market Place, and with enough money to have a servant.

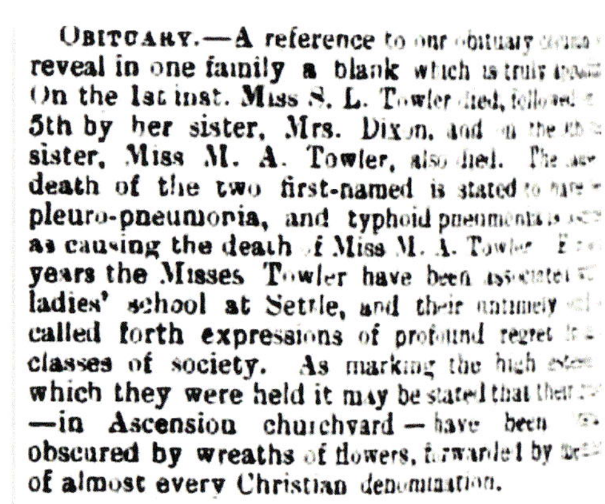

OBITUARY.—A reference to our obituary ... reveal in one family a blank which is truly ... On the 1st inst. Miss S. L. Towler died, followed ... 5th by her sister, Mrs. Dixon, and on the ... sister, Miss M. A. Towler, also died. The ... death of the two first-named is stated to have ... pleuro-pneumonia, and typhoid pneumonia is ... as causing the death of Miss M. A. Towler. ... years the Misses Towler have been associated ... ladies' school at Settle, and their untimely ... called forth expressions of profound regret ... classes of society. As marking the high ... which they were held it may be stated that their ... —in Ascension churchyard — have been ... obscured by wreaths of flowers, forwarded by ... of almost every Christian denomination.

The first week of October 1885 turned out to be unbelievably tragic as three of the four sisters died [*BNA7*]. Sophia died on the 1st October, followed by Eliza (Dixon) on the 5th, both dying of pneumonia. Sister Mary Ann followed on the 9th October, dying of typhoid.

D26 In memory of Sophia, widow of the Revd William Towler, Wesleyan Missionary who died 23rd February 1874 aged 60 years. Also of Sophia Louisa daughter of the above who died 1 Oct 1885 aged 43. Also of Mary Ann daughter of the above who died 9th Oct 1885 Aged 37.

The only surviving sister Emily and her husband William Walker lived in Ribble Terrace in Settle. William had served an apprenticeship with chemist William Shepherd [*professionals*], and later went into business with the Shepherd family. Their son William Towler Walker continued the chemist business and his descendants ensured that 'Shepherd and Walker' was a successful business, trading until 1978. Emily was the President of the Women's Temperance Association in 1901 [*LSA*]. William was an active Methodist and was honoured, together with brother-in-law Thomas Dixon, for their services to the Sunday School in 1915 [*LSA*]. Their daughter **Alice Emily Walker** remained a spinster and spent a while working as a nurse back in the West Indies before retiring to Ribble Terrace in Settle. Son **John Fraser Walker** also remained in the chemists' business with brother William, working as a travelling salesman, selling chemists' products. Emily lived until she was 89 and is buried in the *Old grave L36*, with husband William and daughter Alice Emily.

BRITISH WOMEN'S TEMPERANCE ASSOCIATION.

President	Mrs. Walker.
Secretary	Mrs. Marlor.
Assistant Secretary	Mrs. Best.
Treasurer	Mrs. Whiteley.
Literary Secretary	Miss G. Harger.

MAY.

2. A memorable Tea and Meeting, at Settle, for the purpose of chronicling 105 years of history, and unveiling the enlarged photographs of the two honoured superintendents of the Wesleyan Methodist Sunday School, Mr. William Walker and Mr. Thomas Dixon.

Sister Eliza had married **Thomas Dixon**, a banker's clerk from Halifax, who would later be the manager of Craven Bank in Settle. Eliza died of pneumonia just a year after their third child was born. Thomas brought up the children and a niece Emma Louise Dixon who had also been born in the West Indies. They lived in Duke Street and could afford a servant to help.

MR. T. DIXON, OF GIGGLESWICK.

Mr. Thomas Dixon, of The Mains, Giggleswick, near Settle, died yesterday, in a Leeds nursing home, in his 69th year, after an operation for appendicitis. Mr. Dixon went to Settle 54 years ago, from Halifax, and entered the Settle branch of the present Bank of Liverpool (Limited), which was then known as Alcocks, Birkbeck, and Co., afterwards as Birkbeck, Robinson, and Co., and later as the Craven Bank (Limited). He became manager on the retirement of Mr. Francis Ellis, in 1892, and himself retired in March, 1913, after an unbroken period of 51 years' service. The staff of the Settle branch of the bank, having been greatly depleted by enlistment, Mr. Dixon offered his services again, and they were gladly accepted, so that it may be said that he died in harness.

When the war broke out, and the Settle and District War Relief Committee was formed, Mr. Dixon was appointed treasurer, and he did much good work. He was a man who was ever wishful to do good, and was greatly respected by rich and poor alike. In his quiet way, he took a great interest in local affairs, and for a long time he had been one of the most prominent supporters of the Wesleyan community in the district. In temperance and other work, as well as in musical circles, he was most enthusiastic. In sport he took the greatest interest in bowling, being the treasurer of the local club, and he also was a keen follower of the local cricket club.

movement was great in those days. I remember attending the singing lessons in the Wesleyan Chapel (now Mr. Yeadon's warehouse) under the leadership of that very sincere enthusiastic gentleman, Mr. Thos. Dixon, who, with his violin, used to teach us temperance songs such as "Dare to be a Daniel," and many others similar, which we enjoyed quite as much as the present day kiddies enjoy singing such flimsy songs as "Yes, we have no bananas," etc. I suppose we didn't know any better in those far-off days.

Thomas was an active member of the Methodist church [*CH*] and the Settle Gospel Temperance Union. He retired in 1914 but died two years later after an appendicitis operation. A glowing obituary was written about him— a good man [*BNA13*]. Thomas and Eliza are buried next to the Towlers.

D27 In memory of Eliza the beloved wife of Thomas Dixon born 26th Sept 1840 died 5th Oct 1885. Also Thomas Dixon who died May 15th 1916 aged 68 years. Also their niece Emma Louise Dixon who died March 17th 1975 in her 90th year.

Daughter **Annie Fraser Dixon** married the rather dashing **Sidney Reginald Daniels**. Sidney was a graduate of Oxford and worked for the Indian Civil Service, later becoming a high ranking judicial commissioner. After retiring in 1928, he stood for parliament four times between 1929 and 1935, but was unsuccessful each time. Sidney was a Liberal Party candidate and later became the deputy president of the executive committee for proportional representation.

3 WENCHES, WIVES, SPINSTERS AND SUFFRAGETTES

Would you want to be a woman in the nineteenth century? History has a habit of treating women harshly with the law, attitudes and customs stacked against the 'fairer sex'. This was certainly the case throughout the Victorian era.

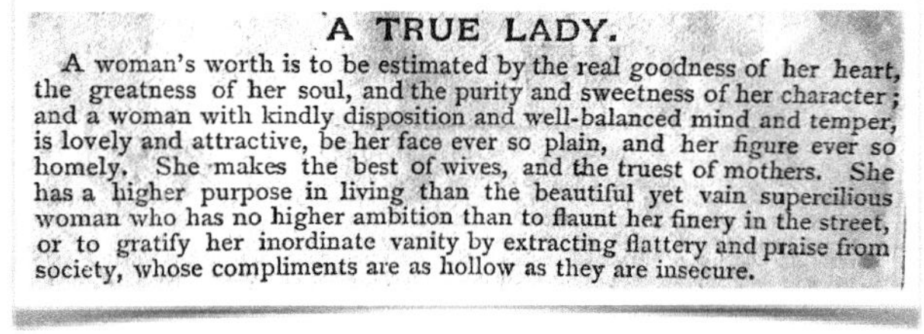

A TRUE LADY.

A woman's worth is to be estimated by the real goodness of her heart, the greatness of her soul, and the purity and sweetness of her character; and a woman with kindly disposition and well-balanced mind and temper, is lovely and attractive, be her face ever so plain, and her figure ever so homely. She makes the best of wives, and the truest of mothers. She has a higher purpose in living than the beautiful yet vain supercilious woman who has no higher ambition than to flaunt her finery in the street, or to gratify her inordinate vanity by extracting flattery and praise from society, whose compliments are as hollow as they are insecure.

Marriage and motherhood was seen by many as 'God's purpose for women' [*CH*]. 80% of women married. Journalist WR Greg commented on '*the unnatural number of redundant women* (spinsters), *which is indicative of an unwholesome social state, and is both productive and prognostic of much wretchedness and wrong.*'

The husband had legal ownership of his wife's body, possessions, children and any earnings. This could be a disincentive for wealthy women, such as spinsters Margaret Bolland, Susanna Robinson and the Jarry sisters [*wealthy folk*]. For the wealthy, marriage was a way of declaring status and enhancing business or political prospects.

The average age of marriage was 25 for women and 26 for men, which is similar now. A quarter of women were pregnant when they married. In some parts of the country women had to 'prove fertility' by getting pregnant before the marriage. Attitudes to sex varied – some women entered marriage without the slightest idea of male anatomy or function.

In theory, marriage for working class women provided protection and income, in return for a relentless round of housekeeping and childcare without any mod-cons. Childbirth was a risky business; 1 in 200 mothers died giving birth (now it is around 1 in 10,000). Working class women had stronger bodies and a simpler diet than the wealthy, so were actually better prepared for childbirth, although poverty meant more of their babies died once born. In 1891 a law was passed to prevent women going back to work until four weeks after childbirth but women couldn't afford to do this and so it was unenforceable.

Fans of Victorian literature will know that 'wench' was not an insulting term, but the usual name for a single young woman. The term became associated with serving girls, particularly if she was shapely (buxom). There weren't many options for single women to earn money apart from spinning, hence the term 'spinster'. It was socially unacceptable for a woman to 'do a man's job', but you could work in the mills or be a governess (if you were educated). However, a widow could continue her deceased husband's occupation.

It was incredibly difficult to find information about our women as they were seen as 'just the wife' of the men. But behind every good man there is often a very good woman.

Typically nineteenth century marriages lasted 14 years before the death of one partner, but many didn't last that long . . . .

Jane Barker, opportunist business woman

Jane Barker, born in 1816, was an unlucky but determined woman. A shoemaker's daughter from Grindleton near Clitheroe, Jane had two illegitimate daughters. In 1859, aged 42, Jane moved to Settle and became the second wife of **Phineas Butler**, *grave E13*, a beer seller from Tosside who had also moved to Settle to be the innkeeper at the New Inn. Poor Phineas died just a year after their wedding, leaving Jane a good £450. Undaunted, Jane took the money and became the landlady of the New Inn with help from her sister Susannah.

In 1869, Jane caught the eye of widower and stonemason **Lawrence Hodgson**. Lawrence, born in 1817 in Kirkby Lonsdale, ran his business in Chapel Street and the Market Place. Amongst many others, he carved the gravestone for Thomas Dixon Burrow [*railway folk*]. Lawrence's proudest achievement could well have been the building of the 'New Savings Bank' completed in 1865 [*SC*].

Lawrence had moved to Settle for his marriage in 1838 to his first wife, **Mary Hurtley,** a shoemaker's daughter. Mary died in 1842 and is buried in Giggleswick churchyard with their first born James who died in infancy. Their second child Edward would be brought up by Lawrence's second wife who was **Catherine Harger** son of Robert Harger [*tradesmen*]. They married in 1844. Catherine's sister Maria had married the cave explorer Joseph Jackson [*tradesmen*]. Lawrence worked closely with Joseph in the 1850s and 1860s collecting items from the Settle cave complex.

Wife Catherine died in 1867 without any further children and Lawrence found solace in landlady Jane. He clearly liked his alcohol; in 1871 he found it impossible to leave the White Horse Inn [*BNA7*]. His fine of 40 shillings plus costs is very harsh compared to similar offences and perhaps reflects his status/wealth. Lawrence died in 1876, just seven years after their wedding. Again Jane used her husband's deaths an opportunity. She continued his stonemasonry and building business and seemed to be better at it – when Lawrence died he left Jane £100, but when she died in 1900 she left £600 to her sister, worth over £80,000 today. Well done Jane.

THE NEW SAVINGS BANK.

The new building, which has been erected on the site of the house and shop formerly occupied by Mr. Waugh, saddler, has just received the roof and is so far advanced as to give the inhabitants of the town a tolerably complete idea of what will be its outward appearance. It has of course been pretty freely commented upon by onlooking critics as it gradually rose from the foundation; the general complaint being that the building is too low for one of some pretension to architectural display. It is, however, a handsome edifice of one lofty story, combining elegance of appearance with substantial masonry. The walls are finished with a bold cornice and battlement which gives additional elevation. The principal front, facing west towards the market place, contains a lofty doorway in the centre with handsome mullioned windows on each side. The doorway and windows are surmounted by ornamental arches with massive mouldings. Over the whole is an elegant entablature with a centre block bearing the inscription "Savings Bank, established 1818," The south side contains five windows and side entrance, also arched and ornamented, in a rather plainer style than the principal front. The interior contains Bank and Committee rooms with safe &c. The rooms are 15 feet 10 inches in height. The designs are by E. G. Paley, Esq., Lancaster, and the masonry has been executed by Mr. Lawrence Hodgson, builder, Settle.

LAWRENCE HODGSON
BUILDER, STONE MASON, & GRAVE STONE DRESSER,
SETTLE,

BEGS to announce that he keeps in Stock TERRA COTTA CHIMNEY POTS and SANITARY TUBES,
YORKSHIRE GREY SLATE, FLAGS, AND RIDGE STONE,
Of the best quality.
The Grey Slate and Flags may be seen at the Railway Station, Settle, or in his yard, and will be delivered at any Station on the North Western Railway at moderate charges.
Sold by THOMAS HALL at the Station.

PETTY SESSIONS, Tuesday last.—Before J. Birbeck, Esq., (chairman), Rev. H. Swale, and H. Christie, Esqrs., Lawrence Hodgson, of Settle, stonemason, was fined 40s. and costs, 8s. 6d, in default one month's imprisonment, for being drunk, and refusing to quit the White Horse Inn on Saturday last.—Mr. H. D.

Jane is buried with a fine stone in *Old grave D33* with her sister Susannah Foster and her husband William Foster, a butcher. As a stonemason, it's surprising that Lawrence is buried in the Ancient graveyard without a gravestone – perhaps Jane had better things to do with his money? Lawrence was probably buried with wife Catherine and son Edward who died aged just 22.

Old D33** **In Loving Memory of Jane widow of the late Lawrence Hodgson who died Jan 10th 1900 aged 83 years also of William Foster died Oct 28th 1904 aged 67 years also Susannah widow of William Foster died April 26th 1917 aged 78 years

Ann Hardacre, a stonemason's widow and supermum

Ann Hardacre's husband **John Lord,** a stonemason, died after 17 years of marriage and just after their eighth child was born, leaving Ann to bring up the children alone in Upper Settle. John and their infant daughter Sarah are buried together in *grave BX19.*

Ann lived for another 30 years and, to make ends meet, she worked as a baker – a really physical job, usually for men. (There were no male bakers in Settle as so many men were needed for farming.) Most of Ann's children found work at the cotton mills which helped to bring in some money. To Ann's credit the whole family thrived, despite the poverty of a widow in Upper Settle. Son **Thomas**, a grocer and carrier, married his first cousin **Jane Hardacre** and they had 12 children. Three year old daughter Mary and infant son Robert are buried in *grave B12*, and Thomas and Jane are in *Old F32*. Daughter **Jane** married **Luke Ralph**, a weaver, who was the grandson of blacksmith Luke Ralph. Daughter **Hannah** became the first wife of plumber **John Handby** [*church folk*]. Ann died in 1884 aged 84, and is buried in an unmarked grave. It would be nice to think she was with John.

Eldest son John was one of Settle's well known characters. He was a grocer/fruiterer living in Cob Castle in Upper Settle [*SC*]. His wife, **Rose Martha Preston**, the daughter of a Long Preston clogger, gave him seven children and three are buried with her – she died aged 46.

PARAFFIN OIL LAMPS.

The cheapest and most pleasant light for shops or domestic use. A large stock containing great variety in pattern and size from 1s. 6d. upwards, may be selected from at the shop of

JOHN LORD,
GROCER AND TEA DEALER, &c,
THE SQUARE, UPPER SETTLE.

Paraffin Oil at 2s. 11d., per gallon; double refined at 3s. 2d. Moderator or Oil Lamps fitted with the New Burner.

B19 In affectionate remembrance of Rose Martha, the beloved wife of John Lord of Settle who died March 1st 1876 aged 46 years. Also Charles son of the above who died Jany 11th 1855 aged 8 months. Also Alice Hall daughter of the above who died Novr 25th 1863 aged 1 year and 7 months. Also John Edward son of the above who died April 1st 1865 aged 7 months. Blessed are they that die in the Lord.

John remarried, this time to Rose Martha's sister, **Ellen Preston**, who helped to bring up the remaining children. If being a dad and grocer were not enough, John celebrated 50 years as a Methodist Local Preacher in 1899 [*LSA*], and was on Settle's first Parish Council [*ph4*].

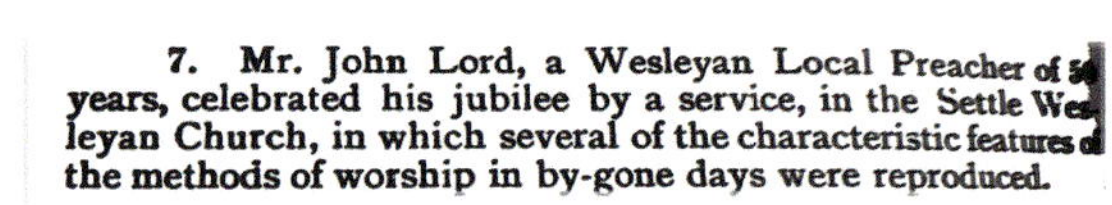
7. Mr. John Lord, a Wesleyan Local Preacher of 5[0] years, celebrated his jubilee by a service, in the Settle Wesleyan Church, in which several of the characteristic features of the methods of worship in by-gone days were reproduced.

John died in 1904, with an estate of £315. When Ellen died just seven years later, she left an incredible £1262 worth nearly £150,000 in today's value. Where did she get that from? John and Ellen are buried in *Old grave F18* with his son Thomas Preston Lord, a successful Lancashire shipping merchant.

Ellen Redmayne, another great businesswoman

E8 In memory of John Greenwood of Settle who died January 30th 1868 aged 34 years. Blessed are the dead which die in the Lord. Also of Ellen widow of the above, died at Croylands, Spring Grove, Middlesex, June 5th 1900 Aged 71 years. Peace perfect peace.

This gravestone is made of a particularly fine slate, positioned amidst other wealthy folk in the graveyard, so there was money here.

Ellen Redmayne came from humble roots, born in Thornton in Lonsdale in 1829 and worked as a house servant. In 1854 Ellen married **John Greenwood**, the son of a farmer from Horton-in-Ribblesdale. By age 18 he was an apprentice to a carpenter in Ingleton. They married in Cheshire for some reason – perhaps they didn't want people to know? They had a son William (named after both their dads) and daughter Mary Elizabeth (with a name from each of their mums) and John worked as a grocer and provision dealer in Upper Settle. Perhaps the expense of a family curtailed his apprenticeship? John died in 1868, at the young age of 36, (the inscription is wrong) leaving Ellen a widow to look after children aged 12 and 10. She continued their grocery business.

Ellen's next step was a good one – in 1870 she became the second wife of **Edward Hartley**, a Methodist whose wife had died four years previously leaving five children. Edward was from the farming family at the Capon Hall estate on Malham Moor.

SETTLE PETTY SESSIONS, TUESDAY LAST.—G. Towler and Ambrose Preston, both of Settle, and J. Gill, of Giggleswick, were each charged with trespassing in search of conies on land occupied by Mr Edward Hartley, of Barrel Sykes. The charges were clearly established (being proved by Mr Cockshutt, superintendant constable) and the defendants, all of whom were represented by Mr Pearson's clerk, of Kirkby Lonsdale, were fined £2 each and costs.

WESLEYAN MISSIONS.—On Sunday last, afternoon and evening, the Rev. Thos. M. Rodham, of Kendal, preached in the Wesleyan Chapel, Settle, in behalf of these missions. The anniversary meeting was held in the same Chapel on the following evening, Edward Hartley, Esq., in the chair.

In 1853 Edward become the tenant farmer at Barrel Sykes just opposite the Watershed Mill. He had all the usual poaching issues, this one in 1854 [*BNA18*]. The advert for its sale in 1863 gives an indication of its size and quality [*BNA14*]. This was before the railway was built so Barrel Sykes had plenty of land. The estate included the land which later became the Holy Ascension '*Old*' graveyard.

VALUABLE FREEHOLD ESTATE AT SETTLE, in the County of York.

TO BE SOLD BY AUCTION, by Mr. JOHN CRAGG, at the Golden Lion Inn, in Settle, on TUESDAY *the Eighteenth day of August*, 1863, at six o'clock in the evening, the BARREL SYKE ESTATE, in the several Townships of Langcliffe and Settle, in the Parish of Giggleswick, in the County of York, in the occupation of Mr. Edward Hartley, as tenant thereof.

The Estate consists of the following particulars:—

	A.	R.	P.
Homestead and Garden	0	1	12
Lady Well Close	0	2	22
North Field or North Close, Holy Acre, Great Barrel Syke Close } now in Two Closes	15	3	10
Home Close	3	0	16
Stable Close	1	2	36
Back Garth	2	0	10
South Kirk Bank, West Kirk Bank, North Kirk Bank } now in one	10	3	30
Banks Close (otherwise Carlow)	9	0	15
High Barn Close	3	1	28
North High Close	2	1	0
First High Carlow, including the road on the West Side thereof	9	1	4
Second High Carlow	32	0	30
Third High Carlow	29	1	24
Blewhawe, or Carlow Inclosure	18	2	16
The Copy	10	1	8
Total	A149	0	30

The land tax has been redeemed.

The tithes on the Estate were in 1844 commuted under the Tithe Commutation Acts, at £6. 17s. per annum.

The buildings and fences are in excellent condition.

The whole of the land is in grass, and the Estate is well timbered.

The property adjoins the town of Settle, and is within 1½ miles of the Settle Station on the Leeds and Lancaster Railway.

Printed particulars, with a plan of the Estate, may be had three weeks before the sale from the Auctioneer, at his offices at Skipton; or at the Golden Lion Inn, Settle; or on application to

Messrs. W. & B. WAKE, Solicitors, Sheffield.

Sheffield, 8th July, 1863.

In 1854, the Settle Cricket Club for working classes and apprentices used Edward's 'North Field' for free. There was another, more expensive club for the wealthy folk. In 1880, after the railway was built, cricket moved to Marsh Field [*BNA7*].

CRICKET.—A great many of the old members of the Settle cricket club, which, from some cause or other, was broken up a long time ago, have, by themselves and a number of new members, lately established another; and as they practice almost daily, we hope they will be soon ready to give challenge for a friendly game to one of our neighbouring clubs. Their subscriptions being somewhat higher we understand than some persons can afford, a similar club is also being formed, composed of apprentices and working classes, who will have the use of a field (kindly offered by Mr. Edward Hartley) for nothing. The other club have to pay £12 a-year for their field. As a further encouragement to apprentices and working classes, funds are being raised, from the subscriptions of other parties, for the purchase of bats, &c.; and almost sufficient has already been collected for that purpose.

Edward was a manager of the Craven Savings Bank along with several other high status men of Settle.

Edward and Ellen's marriage may have caused some issues. Second spouses often lived with their step-children but not in this case. Edward left Barrel Sykes, leaving his quite grown up

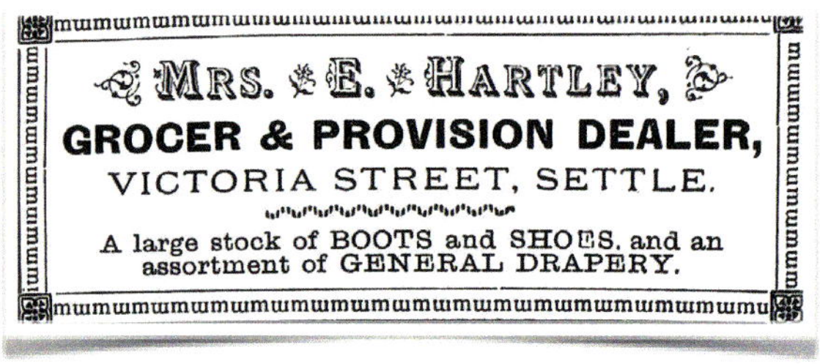

children and moved in with Ellen and her two children in Upper Settle. Edward continued to farm and Ellen continued to run her grocery business. They had enough money for a servant. Perhaps Edward's children felt he was marrying beneath himself?

Ellen was widowed again eight years later - Edward was buried with his first wife in Langcliffe. Ellen continued to run her business with enough money to employ a servant for another 20 years [*LSA*]. She did well.

John Greenwood can rest in peace. His daughter Mary Elizabeth married **John Scaife**, a barrister and lived in Dublin with their four children. Son William became a barrister and worked in Middlesex, living with his wife, daughter and servants. John's children could definitely afford that fine gravestone. Ellen moved to live with William in Middlesex and died there, aged 71.

John Greenwood is alone in the grave with that fine stone.

Also: **Betsy Wilman** outlived husband **John Turner** by 49 years [*tradesmen*], **Isabella Jane Wilson** outlived husband Robert Hargave by 52 years [*railway folk*], **Isabella Jackson** had two particularly brief experiences of marriage [*church folk*].

...JF...

Settle's Suffragette Sisters, by Royal Appointment . . . yes really

23. A Paper on "Woman's Suffrage" was read before the Settle Wesleyan Mutual Improvement Society, by Miss Anderson.

CHRONOLOGY OF EVENTS (continued.)

15. A Public Debate on "Woman's Suffrage," at Settle Conservative Club, when a paper in favour of the cause was read by Mrs. Mott, of Giggleswick, and Mr. W. Simpson, of Catteral Hall, opposed. A warm discussion followed, and, on a vote being taken at the close, there was a large majority against granting the Franchise to Women.

Settle has always been a little behind the times. Mechanisation in cotton mills, gas lighting and credit card swipe technology all took ages to arrive. So did Settle really produce women who were suffragettes and were appointed to the queen? Well, yes it did.

In 1897 Miss Anderson read a paper on women's suffrage to the Settle Wesleyan Improvement Society - a relatively liberal group [*LSA*]. In 1909 the Conservative Club ran a debate on woman's suffrage. After a 'warm discussion' there was a large majority against giving women the vote [*LSA*].

The Robinson family tomb [*K*] [*E*]

C11 In memory of Epsey, wife of Henry Robinson, who died 14th October 1861 aged 44 years. Henry Robinson, solicitor of this town died 27th February 1870, aged 54 years. Eleanor, who died 30th September 1854, aged 4 months. Fanny who died on the 17th April 1856 aged 7 months. Charlotte who died 13th October 1901 aged 42 years. Epsey, widow of John McClelland who died 6th February 1912 aged 65. George Marshall who died 21st April 1925 aged 74 years. William Augustus, who died 27th May 1896 aged 51 years. Henry Duncan, who died 5th July1875, aged 31 years.

The people commemorated on this impressive family tomb were academically and artistically gifted, but also passionate about social and political reform. (We must remember that there were many working class residents who were just as talented but did not have time or money to demonstrate their talents.)

Henry Robinson, born in 1815, was a cooper's son from Lincolnshire. Somehow he managed to get an education which set him up for a very successful life. In 1842, he married **Epsey Dale**, the daughter of a successful London piano manufacturer who carried an important artistic gene. Henry found work in Kirkby Lonsdale, articled to solicitor Francis Pearson and by 1847 had moved to Settle where he would live for the rest of his life, working as a solicitor. They lived on or near Cheapside and then in the large 'Terrace' on Duke Street, bringing up nine children. Settle residents of 1924 remembered a serene picture of innocent family life in the Craven Herald.

In those days kite-flying in Settle reached a high standard of excellence, largely due to the lead given by the Robinsons, who then lived in The Terrace. There were "G. M." "W. A." and Harry, all keen flyers, whilst the sisters Epsy, Annie and Charlotte seconded their efforts. The kites were home-made, some of them of large size—one, indeed, I remember was over six feet in height, and bore the name of "Porter," in honour of a local curate of that name, a very giant in stature. The kites required careful construction, and the long tails were so adjusted that the kite could be flown without wobbling in the air. A wobbling kite was anathema in those days. The Robinsons occasionally put up half a-dozen kites, one behind the other, on one string; at other times long distance flights were made, and it was no uncommon thing for a kite to sail away until it was invisible to the eye. The pull on the larger kites was so great that it required two or three boys to hold them, and even they were in danger of being lifted into the air. Then there was the excitement of a broken string, and the subsequent hunt to retrieve the kite. I recall one escaped kite, flown from the fields above The Terrace, was found entangled in the tops of trees at Scaleber.

Henry's business included local petty sessions and company law, representing business and mills across the north of England. As soon as his sons were old enough, Henry included three of them in the family business, with branches in Skipton and Keighley as well as Settle. The fourth son worked as a land agent and accountant. Henry was a passionate Liberal and often represented Liberal interests in Settle.

Epsey died in 1861 just after the death of their ninth child, Charlotte. Two other daughters, Eleanor and Fanny had died in infancy. Henry owned a property in Widcombe Crescent, one of the massive Georgian Crescents in Bath - very Jane Austen. He was living in that house, perhaps for health reasons, when he died aged just 54. He left an estate worth the equivalent of millions of pounds today. With a legacy like that Henry's children could easily have spent the rest of their lives mixing with high society and enjoying the finer things in life. However, Henry and Epsey's parenting and Liberal politics led most of them into lives as equality activists.

THE LATE MR. ROBINSON, OF KEIGHLEY.

Mr. William Augustus Robinson, solicitor, Keighley, who died in Leeds last night, is the second son of the late Mr. Henry Robinson, solicitor, Settle. He was a member of the defunct Keighley Local Board for a short time, sat several years on its successor, the Town Council, and last November, after being defeated in the Central Ward, was subsequently returned unopposed for the West Ward for three years. He was admitted a solicitor in 1867. He carried on business with his elder brother, Duncan Robinson, until the latter's death in 1875, and subsequently with his younger brother, Mr. George Marshall Robinson. He had been Registrar of the Settle County Court since 1875. He played cricket with the Settle Club for several years, and appeared in the Keighley first eleven from 1871 to 1875. He was unmarried, and was aged about 50 years.

Sons **William Augustus**, **Henry Duncan** and **George Marshall** Robinson continued Henry's business. William's obituary of 1896 told how he worked hard for Keighley Town Council and was a Registrar at Settle County Court, (as was brother George). William played cricket for Settle and Keighley [*BNA26*]. Another obituary for William explained his *'indefatigable exertions in the Radical cause'*. The Radical cause was the Liberal Party campaigning for democratic reform.

Son Henry Duncan [*ph14*] could also have had a successful life but died of cirrhosis of the liver just four years after marrying. He enjoyed his alcohol, according to his family. However, generations of his descendants were highly successful cotton mill managers in the Barley (Pendle) area.

Now, what about Henry and Epsey's three daughters?

Ann Elizabeth married **Francis Henry Atherton** in 1870. Two years later Francis was on board a ship bound for Australia where he spent the rest of his life working in gold mines.

Daughter **Epsey** married **John McClelland**, a Scottish accountant who became a salesman. After fathering daughter Elspeth, John spent the rest of his life travelling, so Epsey and sister Ann had time on their hands in London. They worked together as interior designers, exceptionally unusual for women in those days. In 1886 Epsey organised a 'Fine Art Exhibition' back in Settle showcasing Mr Edmund Handby's work [*church folk, BNA7*].

> ...nection. The display of vuluable oil-paintings and water-colour drawings comprise several meritorious works which did infinite credit to the respective artists. The mirrors and screens exhibited deserve more than a passing notice, not only on account of their artistic merit but as being the work of a native of Settle. It is to Mrs. McClelland that we owe the revival of this art, which was formerly practised by the early Italian masters and used simply as a wall decoration. Now however Mrs. McClelland has applied it to a variety of objects which have taken prominent places in artistic English homes.

Very soon Ann became friends with artist **Kate Thornbury**, the daughter of a Lieutenant Colonel in the Indian Army. They lived together in Hertfordshire for the rest of their lives. When Ann died, in 1913, she left her whole estate to Kate. When Kate died in 1920, a publication of the *National Union of Societies for Equal Citizenship* called *Common Cause* printed her obituary, explaining Kate and Ann's part in the Suffragette movement. They promoted female artists and founded the Society of Artists. Agnes Burrow used this to showcase her work [*railway folk*].

> **PERSONAL.**
>
> The late Miss Louisa Kate Thornbury, of Shire Lane, Chorley Wood, who died on October 27th, 1920, left a legacy of £100 to the National Union. Miss Thornbury was connected with the Suffrage movement from its earliest beginning, and was at one time Hon. Secretary of one of the branch societies in London. She gave up this work to enter into business partnership with Mrs. Atherton, and they founded the Society of Artists in Bond Street, and for many years carried on business as house decorators and experts in furniture. They retired from business shortly before the war, and the death of Mrs. Atherton, a life-long friend, was a blow from which Miss Thornbury never recovered. She continued her interest in the woman's movement to the last, and though no longer engaged in active work for the Cause, shared in the rejoicing when the vote was won. For those of us who are still at work building on the foundations laid by others, there is something at once moving and inspiring in these gifts that reach us from time to time—the last visible mark of the devotion of a lifetime.

Youngest daughter **Charlotte**, another incredible artist, was appointed 'Home Art Decorator' to Queen Victoria. The Princess of Wales was particularly fond of her work [*BNA1*].

> The Princess of Wales has purchased the original *billet doux* table, designed and registered by Miss Charlotte Robinson, of King-street (home art decorator to her Majesty). Her Royal Highness expressed great admiration for the ingenuity Miss Robinson has displayed. Her stand at the Glasgow Exhibition may safely be pronounced the gem of the woman's industry section.

An article in 1887 [*BNA28*] explained her career and provided a sketch portrait, provided by **Miss Emily Faithfull.**

> **THE QUEEN'S HOME ART DECORATOR.**
>
> Miss Charlotte Robinson, who has been appointed Home Art Decorator to her Majesty the Queen, has been for some time engaged in art decorative work of various kinds. Her exhibits at the famous Manchester Exhibition, and also at Saltaire, have attracted great attention this year, and she has quite established herself in Manchester as adviser in general on matters relating to house decoration and furnishing. Her father was a well-known Yorkshire lawyer. After leaving Queen's College, Harley-street, she expended a great deal of energy on the usual engagements which fall to the lot of an ordinary young lady in society. She was also associated with the entertainments organised by Mr. Titus Salt at Saltaire, and finally determined on a career of honourable work rather than a life of dull inactivity or intermittent charitable enterprises. Regardless of the bugbear which terrifies weaker women—the loss of social status—she opened a shop in King-street, Manchester; and the result has been eminently satisfactory. She has now won the recognition of her Majesty, who has always been ready to show a kindly interest in ladies who are trying to open out new paths for the remunerative employment of women in appropriate directions. Miss Robinson had at first some difficulty in making people understand that her work was commercial, not charitable; but she feels that until a healthy public sentiment is created, the false pride which keeps ladies afraid of entering on industrial pursuits will never be overcome. Her clever sister, Mrs. M'Clelland, is the presiding genius of the London studio, in which a number of lady artists are busily at work in various directions.
>
> The Portrait is from a photograph taken while Miss Robinson was travelling in America, and forwarded to us by Miss Emily Faithfull.

Charlotte had met Miss Emily Faithfull whilst at Queen's College, London, an independent girls' school '*promoting a non-competitive spirit to produce confident, open-minded young women*'. It certainly did that. Charlotte and Emily travelled together and set up businesses in London and Manchester. Emily was a vicar's daughter from

MISS CHARLOTTE ROBINSON,
HOME ART DECORATOR TO HER MAJESTY.

Bloomsbury, with family links to India, and was well known as a *'petticoat philanthropist'*. Emily said of Charlotte, *'Her furniture designs are simple and unique; she has dainty and quaint arrangements for cosy nooks and odd corners, and has good reason to be proud of the work of the artists employed in the studio over which her clever sister, Mrs McClelland is the presiding genius.'*

Emily, known as Fido, was a women's rights activist promoting education for girls, women's employment and suffrage. She published material to support her cause through her 'Victoria Press' publishing company and was appointed publisher to Queen Victoria. In 1888 she received an inscribed portrait from the Queen in recognition of 30 years' work on behalf of women.

In 1863, soon after the divorce laws of 1857, Emily was involved in a high profile divorce case, in which she was suspected of being *'the other woman'* to the wife of Royal Naval officer Henry Codrington, after being initially employed as her companion. Emily was known to dress in *'manly clothes'*. Outrageous! This case was recently listed number 2 in *'Marriage Scandals that Shocked the 19th Century'* and is the basis of the book *'The Sealed Letter'* by Emma Donoghue, which is a great read.

In one of her talks, Emily Faithfull said *"....True marriage is the crown and glory of a woman's life; but it must be founded on love...nothing can be more deplorable, debasing, and corrupting than the loveless marriages brought about in our upper society by a craving ambition and a longing for a good settlement."* Emily's experience in the divorce case and those of Charlotte's siblings may have inspired these thoughts - Epsey, Ann Elizabeth and Edward all found themselves spending their lives estranged from their spouses – a result of arranged marriages?

When Emily died in 1895, she left her whole estate to Charlotte, *"my final love, as some little indication of my gratitude...for the affectionate tenderness and care which made the last five years of my life the happiest I ever spent."* When Charlotte died in 1901, *Lambert's Settle Almanac* highlighted the fact that she was one of the first educated woman to have a business career as an art decorator. It's good to know this was appreciated back home.

13. Death of Miss Charlotte Robinson (youngest daughter of the late Mr. Henry Robinson, Solicitor, Settle), at her home, in Plymouth Grove, Manchester. Miss Robinson was one of the first women of education, in this country, to enter upon a business career as art decorator.

Charlotte left her estate to her niece **Elspeth McClelland**, a talented and rare female architect who worked in the style of the 'Arts and Crafts Movement' inspired by John Ruskin and William Morris *[BNA28,29]* promoting simple, romantic and traditional craftsmanship.

WOMEN IN INDUSTRY.

The Woman Architect: Where She Excels.

We take the following facts from a very interesting interview with Miss Elspeth McClelland, the woman architect, by Mary Mortimer Maxwell, which appeared in *The Daily Chronicle* of February 28, and should be stimulating to other women to follow the excellent example courageously set by Miss McClelland. She was found on a roof, examining certain building materials, to make sure that they were according to her orders for the particular work, for Miss McClelland is not satisfied to be simply a designer; she understands the practical requirements of building. Indeed, a few years ago, when she was "the only woman student amongst 600 men at the Polytechnic who were qualifying for the business of house-erection, she even learnt the proper way to make bricks, and how to lay them," writes Mary Mortimer Maxwell.

Miss Elspeth McClelland, the girl architect, who sprang into fame among women workers last year, has been rising steadily in her profession. Her latest achievement is a design for a house at Grange-over-Sands, overlooking Morecambe Bay.

Unsurprisingly, Elspeth was swept into the Edwardian suffragette movement, regularly contributing to 'Votes for Women' publication.

Elspeth achieved a certain notoriety on 23rd February 1909 when she was a *'Human Letter'* along with Christabel Pankhurst. They sent themselves as a letter to 10 Downing Street as a publicity stunt [*BNA28*], costing 3 pence. Downing Street would not sign the postman's forms so they had to be returned as a *'dead letter'*.

SUFFRAGETTES' LATEST SCHEME.

"HUMAN LETTERS" TO PREMIER

RETURNED AS "DEAD LETTERS."

Two members of the Women's Social and Political Union ingeniously attempted on Tuesday afternoon, to convey a message personally to the Prime Minister. There is a clause in the Post Office regulations which allows of any individual being "posted" by express messenger, and Mrs. Drummond—accompanied by Miss Christabel Pankhurst, Miss Solomon, and Miss McLellan—presented herself at the counter of the West Strand Post Office, and astonished a lady clerk with the remark: "I want to send a human letter." She duly received an official form, and promptly addressed Miss Solomon and Miss McLellan to "H. H. Asquith, 10, Downing-street, S.W." The threepenny fee having

MARYLEBONE.—The meetings in Marylebone get more and more enthusiastic as time goes on, and the women especially understand our tactics. We have sold the paper very well, and each week the sale has increased. On Friday, Saturday, and Sunday of last week we had already sold 438, so we hope to double our previous total. We have been very fortunate in getting speakers who have ungrudgingly given their time for the furtherance of this campaign. We have also brought out several new speakers, all of whom are very promising.

Committee Rooms: 64, Blandford Street.

Elspeth McClelland.

The extremes of high society life were also prevalent in the lives of the siblings of Henry's wife, Epsey Dale. Her brother **John Duncan Dale** was a Catholic priest working in Manchester and London. Meanwhile her brother **Augustus Dale**, a property valuer in London married **Jane McCulloch,** but spent most of his life living with a 'housekeeper', **Emma Howell** who was a singer. Emma bore him at least nine children, many of whom continued to work in the arts.

A WIFE'S DUTY . . .

"The man, with his reasoning faculties, muscular power and courage is best qualified as the protector of the feeble timid woman. Under these circumstances, the man naturally governs, the woman as naturally obeys."
Physiologist Alexander Walker 1840

The 'purpose' of a Victorian woman was to procreate. Child mortality was high, so giving birth to many children ensured the family line, in theory. Childbirth was dangerous for women but despite this some of our women took it to extremes.

Elizabeth Boothman, first prize for procreation

Elizabeth Boothman, born in 1818, was a weaver's daughter from Long Preston. In 1838 she married **William Moorby**, a weaver and the son of a Tatham labourer. Six months after the wedding, Elizabeth gave birth to the first of an amazing nine sons and five daughters over 23 years – yes, 14 children. Just three died in infancy, and sons Cleopas and James Boothman Moorby were buried in *grave CX2*. Eldest daughter Margaret died aged one, but there are no burial records for her....

With all these mouths to feed, William needed money. He found a job at the Church; Vestry records for 1843 say he was asked to '*to keep the whole of the church well swept and the pews and choir washed out once a month or so as often as occasion shall require at the yearly salary of five pounds.'* Later he became the Church clerk and choirmaster earning £7 per year.

Somehow, William managed to become an infant schoolteacher and, by all accounts, was quite a good one, especially in music. He lived in Upper Settle, a cheaper part of town, and later Castle Hill. William was the secretary of Settle Co-op in its early days, with James Twisleton taking over from him 1864.

William and Elizabeth retired back to her roots in Long Preston. After Elizabeth died William moved to Hull where, for some reason, all his surviving children had moved. Most families who left Settle moved west for work in the industrial towns and cities.

William died in Hull, but was brought back to Settle for burial in *Old A28*, to be with Elizabeth and (adult) children John and Fanny. William's death merited a mention in *Lambert's Settle Almanac* so he was a respected man, even though they got his name wrong. His children remained in Hull and had successful careers, remaining in education, and one son worked in the shipping business [*BNA30*].

[redacted]16. Mr. Thomas Moorby, an old native of Settle, died [redacted]ull, in the 81st year of his age. He was for many years [redacted]ol-master at Settle, and choir-master of Ascension Church.

The death has occurred at Newland, near Hull, at the residence of one of his sons of Mr William Moorby, formerly of Settle. Mr Moorby thoroughly mastered the details of the tonic-sol-fa method of teaching music, and he may fairly be said to have been the father of this method so far as the Craven district was concerned.

Mr Edwin Corris, late H.M. Inspector, spoke to the great work the late Mr William Moorby had done during his 40 years of office.
Mr Thomas Moorby, who was headmaster of the school previously to his late brother accepting that position, also spoke a few words.
The portrait is framed in oak, and bears the inscription:—"In affectionate remembrance of William Moorby, 40 years headmaster. Presented to the Newland School by his old scholars, 1910."

Mr. Christopher Charles Allen Moorby, head master of the Newland School, Sculcoates, Hull, died on Saturday at Cottingham, in his 52nd year. His first appointment was in Manchester, and after being Principal of St. Mary's School, Sculcoates, he succeeded his brother as head master at Newland. For 51 years Newland has had a Moorby as head master, three members of the family having filled the position. Mr. Moorby's father was the late Mr. William Moorby who was a schoolmaster at Settle, and was one of the first teachers to introduce the tonic sol-fa in Yorkshire.

Alice Bowskill, beyond the call of duty

Alice Bowskill, born in 1817, was the youngest of eight children and the sister of William Bowskill, the blacksmith who built Bowskill's Yard on Castle Hill. In 1840, Alice married **John Himsworth**, a solicitor's clerk and the son of a Wakefield farmer who had come to Settle to work for the Hartley firm of solicitors. Alice promptly set about a production line of nine children, one every two years while they lived on Belle Hill in Giggleswick. In the early 1850s, John was one of several solicitor's clerks appealing to their employers to be given time off on a Saturday [*ph13*]. Other clerks included with James Twisleton [*below*], John Armitstead [*professionals*] and John Lister [*wealthy ones*]. John's is the second signature on the left hand side.

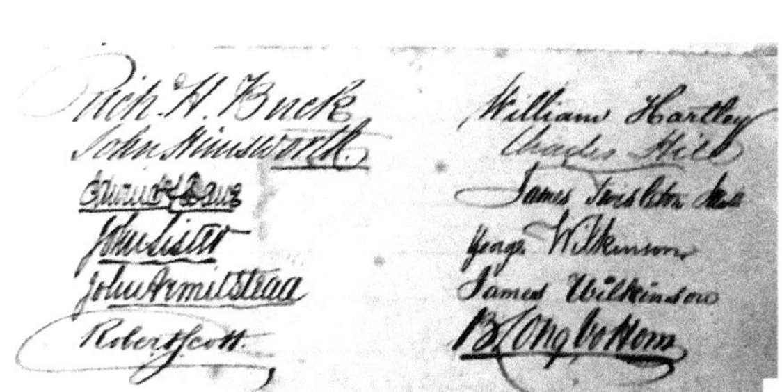

In 1860 John drowned himself in a moment of 'temporary insanity', leaving poor Alice with the nine children. The youngest, William was just two [*SC*]. Imagine that.

SUICIDE.—Mr. John Himsworth, who for a period of 21 years has creditably held an important situation as clerk in the office of Messrs G. and W. Hartley of this town, solicitors, was found drowned in the river Ribble on Saturday morning, April 21st. The deceased had left his home as it was thought to take a walk on the preceding afternoon. For a few days before the deceased appeared to be in a rather low state of mind. The coroner's jury returned a verdict of "Temporary insanity." Deceased, who was 43 years of age, and from his position was well known and respected, has left a widow and nine children.

John left Alice £200, not a bad sum. Saving money, Alice moved to Howson's Yard behind the church side of the Settle Market Place and then Victoria Road in Upper Settle which was probably even cheaper. Little William died aged four. Daughter Eliza was described as an 'imbecile' – a term which described many mental health and learning difficulties at that time. Eliza spent her last 20 years in Giggleswick workhouse which was the only medical provision available, especially for the poor. She died aged 50. William and Eliza are buried in unmarked graves in the Ancient graveyard. The other children had successful lives, several moving to the coast of West Cumbria to work in the new iron industry. They were often found living together. Well done Alice.

And what about poor Alice? Mental health issues may have featured in both sides of this family as Alice died in an asylum in York in 1879, having been a widow for nearly 30 years.

WERE THERE REALLY MORE CHILD DEATHS IN THOSE DAYS?

Sadly, yes there were. The records show that between 1839 and 1855, 42% of all burials were for children aged five or under and the average age at death of all burials was just 30. Chances of survival increased considerably after the age of five. Cholera, typhus, scarlet fever and tuberculosis were an ongoing hazards in the nineteenth century although epidemic directories don't suggest any particular outbreaks in this region.

The recorded mortality of illegitimate babies in the first year of life was twice that of legitimate babies, and was probably even higher as some would not have been buried or recorded. The south east corner of the graveyard is the infants' section containing 16 infants and three of these were illegitimate.

13 of our infant children are remembered with their very own stones, including two sets of twins. Most child deaths went unmarked of course. Some were buried with their families, others wherever there was a space. We spare a thought for all those families, especially John Waller, innkeeper of the Black Horse in Giggleswick [*innkeepers*] who lost six of his 12 children in infancy and John Slinger, a pauper weaver [*working class heroes*], who lost six of his ten children in infancy.

UNTIL DEATH US DO PART

Marriage was for life, so mistresses, desertion and bigamy were not uncommon. The divorce laws of 1857 allowed divorce but only in person in a London court. It cost 18 months of solicitors' fees, so it really was a privilege for the wealthy rather than for working class Yorkshire folk. Men just had to prove a 'criminal conversation' (adultery) but before equal rights, women had to prove a 'criminal conversation' and also physical cruelty, bigamy or incest.

The wives of Alfred Graeme Pierson, unfortunate twists of fate . . .

Born in 1862, **Alfred Pierson** was the youngest child of the second vicar, William Frederick Pierson, and his wife Margaret Birkbeck. One of Alfred's sisters died in infancy, another married a vicar. Brother John Ernest Pierson served in the military and brother William Birkbeck Pierson became a vicar. Both brothers died in their 50s and received glowing obituaries [*church folk*].

Alfred had a good education at Giggleswick School and went to Cambridge, but the school register says that an accident to one of his eyes prevented him from finishing his degree.

This cruel twist of fate must have been frustrating for Alfred and may have shaped the rest of his life.

Alfred lived in London, describing himself as a '*gentleman of no occupation*'. When he was 25, Alfred married **Beatrice Lonsdale Bing.** She was a stage singer with the stage name of **Minnie Palmerstone** who specialised in acting and burlesque dancing, singing and comedy and performed all over the country to rave reviews [*BNA31*].

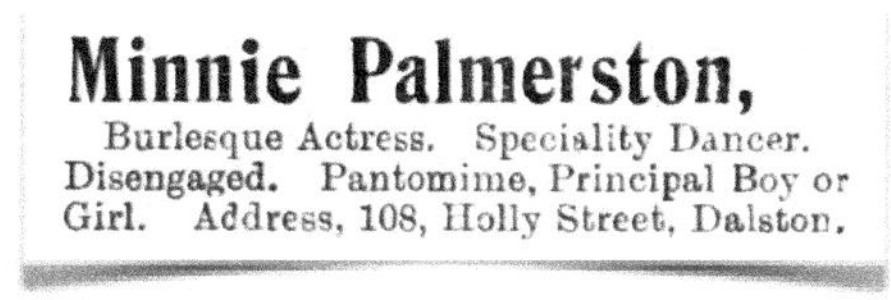

Minnie Palmerston,

Burlesque Actress. Speciality Dancer. Disengaged. Pantomime, Principal Boy or Girl. Address, 108, Holly Street, Dalston.

Five years later, after finding letters delivered to her in several names, Alfred discovered she was already married at least twice before. She had married **James Bardsley** in 1878 and then **Charles Couzens** in 1882, much to the amusement of the journalists [*BNA30*]. Alfred's dad Rev'd William Frederick Pierson, who had died in 1883, would be quite justified in turning in his grave.

, SATURDAY, NOVEMBER

A WOMAN WITH THREE HUSBANDS.

In the Divorce Division, yesterday—before Justice Butt—two suits for nullity of marriage were heard in

heard. Mr. Deane appeared for the petitioner, Mr. Alfred Green Pierson, who, he said, was married to the respondent on September 9, 1885, she being the same respondent as in the previous case. The petitioner asked for a decree of nullity of his marriage with Beatrice Lonsdale Bing, otherwise Couzens, otherwise Bardsley, on the ground that at the time of the marriage she had husbands living of the name of Bardsley and Couzens. Mr. Pierson made the acquaintance of the respondent at Boulogne in 1884. She was then engaged as a public singer at a public entertainment, under the name of Minnie Palmerston. His Lordship: She had a good many names one way or the other. (Laughter.) Mr. Deane said she informed his client that she was well connected, and that she had run away from home and adopted the musical profession as a means of livelihood. So far as he could tell she was a person of perfect propriety, and her behaviour all that could be desired. Eventually he married her at St. Andrew's Church, Holborn. Since the

The marriage was annulled.

Beatrice, or Minnie, provided completely different details on the three wedding certificates so we have no idea who she really was, but she carried on performing until her death of typhoid in 1904 [*BNA31*].

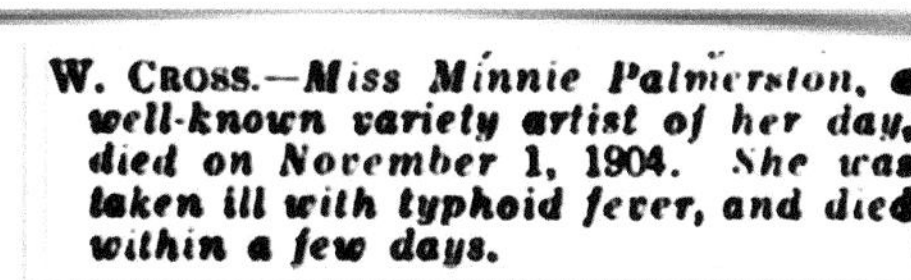

W. CROSS.—*Miss Minnie Palmerston, a well-known variety artist of her day, died on November 1, 1904. She was taken ill with typhoid fever, and died within a few days.*

Two years after the divorce, Alfred married **Lucia Kathleen D'Esterre.** Lucia was the daughter of Henry Vassall D'Esterre and Mary Elisabeth Sandes from Sixmilebridge, Limerick in Ireland. The D'Esterres were a Huguenot family who had arrived in Ireland in the late 17th century. They were granted 3000 acres of land, and made their fortune as French Protestants renting out land to the Catholic working classes during a tumultuous period of Irish history. Henry had a shocking reputation as a landlord. There are numerous newspaper reports of unrealistically high rents, evictions and local protests.

One report said, *"As seen throughout this study the D'Esterre family was never far from controversy within Sixmilebridge. Far from investing in the local economy and supporting their tenants, they chose to do the opposite. From when the family first arrived and built Rossmanagher Bridge and basically cut all nautical traffic to Sixmilebridge and killed trading just so the family could benefit themselves with extra traffic through their lands despite the consequences for the village. The D'Esterre family further blackened their name in Sixmilebridge when making headlines over the eviction of the Frost family in 1887 which was heard across the county for all the wrong reasons and to this day when the D'Esterre name is mentioned it is still remembered for all the wrong reasons without many positives if any at all."*

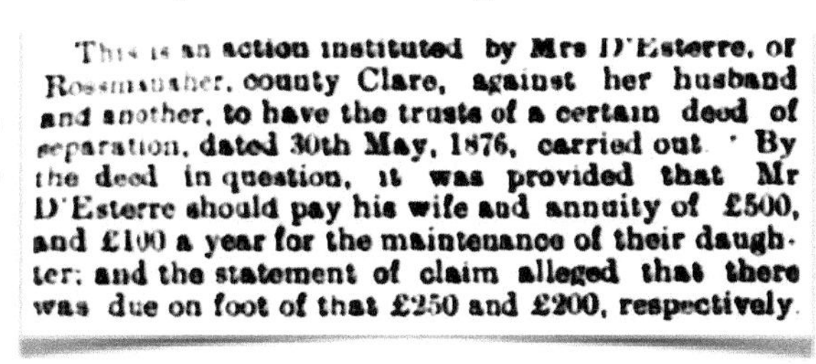

This is an action instituted by Mrs D'Esterre, of Rossmanagher, county Clare, against her husband and another, to have the trusts of a certain deed of separation, dated 30th May, 1876, carried out. By the deed in question, it was provided that Mr D'Esterre should pay his wife an annuity of £500, and £100 a year for the maintenance of their daughter; and the statement of claim alleged that there was due on foot of that £250 and £200, respectively

The private life of Lucia's parents was also fraught. In 1884 Mary took Henry to court to force him to pay maintenance as part of a deed of separation. Ironically, to avoid social embarrassment, Mary had requested this as an alternative to divorce. Her social standing must have been very important to her but it all came out in the end. The divorce claim would have been on the basis of Henry's *'criminal misconduct'* and also because of bringing their 13 year old son into *'evil associations'* [*BNA32*]. Mary spent the rest of her life living in a selection of fine English hotels.

> writing or otherwise, to do so. She explained that in 1870 she instituted a suit in the Divorce Court against her husband on account of his criminal misconduct, and, through the influence of friends, litigation was stopped, and the deed of May 30th, 1876, was executed. In April, 1877, she was obliged to file a bill in the Court of Chancery for an account of the moneys due under the deed, and in 1882, having discovered that her husband was bringing their son, then in his thirteenth year, into evil associations, she took steps to have him made a ward of court.

So this was the background of Alfred's second wife Lucia. They had plenty to share with each other. What would Rev'd Pierson have thought? Did they live happily ever after? Sadly not. Lucia managed to have two children before Alfred died aged just 34 in Sussex. Lucia spent the rest of her life in Dublin with her children and servants, of course.

Annie Amy Sanderson, a passionate woman

Annie Amy Sanderson was born in 1834 in Bolton-by-Bowland to grocer, labourer and innkeeper **John Sanderson**. In 1853 she married an aged salesman **Robert Hamilton** who died just after the birth of their son, another Robert. Annie came to Settle where her dad John had bought her the licence for **The Old Naked Man** and she became the landlady. It was here that she caught the eye of **James Twisleton** (Jnr) who married her in 1859 [*BNA18*].

> On the 31st ultimo, at the Ascension Church, Settle, by the Rev. W. F. Pearson, vicar, Mr. James Twistleton, head clerk in the office of C. J. Geldard, Esq., to Mrs. Ambleton, landlady of the Naked Man Inn, Settle.

James Twisleton's dad, another **James Twisleton**, born in 1787, came from Stainforth. He married **Mary Lofthouse** from Cold Cotes near Ingleton and they settled in Settle, having three children - James (Jnr), Alice and little Mary Isabella who died in infancy. Initially James described himself as a butcher but by 1861 was a 'proprietor of houses' having been responsible for the development of Twisleton's Yard on Albert Hill.

Daughter Alice, born in 1829, found herself pregnant at the age of 16 and gave birth to son Gregory, a good Twisleton family name. Alice died aged 21, and Gregory died nine years later, aged 13, and they are buried in *grave CX7*. Alice's parents are probably buried with them.

In the meantime Alice's brother James, born in 1825, had inherited his dad's business sense – he was described as an 'accountant' in the census at the age of 15. He was actually a clerk at Geldard's solicitors and he worked there for over 50 years. Incredible. James made a fair contribution to life in Settle, as a secretary for the newly formed Co-op in 1864 [*BNA7*], taking over from William Moorby [*above*]. He was also secretary to the North Ribblesdale Agricultural Association for over 20 years.

> non-members. Mr. James Twisleton was appointed secretary in the place of Mr. Moorby, who resigned a short time ago. After the usual business of the society had been concluded it was resolved to give, on an early day, an open air tea party on the Green in Upper Settle, with the view of giving an impetus to the society's operations and promoting conviviality amongst the members and their families. The proposal was very favorably received, and a committee was duly appointed for the purpose of carrying out the necessary arrangements.

A couple of reminiscences in the *Craven Herald* suggest that James was a gentle and caring man, if a little gullible, which seemed to cause a few problems for the seemingly vivacious Annie.

> ... pints enlivened his captivity.
> Many people will remember Mr. James Twisleton, commonly known as "Spinney," and how one Sunday he went along the beck in the Ings with a friend.
> Seeing a trout hide in the wall he prostrated himself and put his hand in saying "I can just touch his tail but if you'll sit on my feet I may reach further and get it." This was done when suddenly the poacher sang out "By Jove, he's gone." "Eh! where?" says the watcher jumping up, but before a reply could be obtained Spinney had rolled into the beck in his Sunday best, as his friend had forgotten the law of leverage.

After their wedding, the license for the Old Naked Man was transferred to James. Strangely though, in the next census, there is no mention of it being run as an inn. However, they put on a good spread for Hector Christie's employees in 1861 *[BNA18]*. James still worked as a solicitor's clerk.

SETTLE.—The workpeople in the employ of Messrs. Christy, at the Langcliffe Mills, enjoyed a treat at the house of Mr James Twisleton, the Naked Man Inn, on Saturday evening last. The treat consisted of a tea party and dance afterwards; all passed off pleasantly.

Old Mary Wilson, too, was one of the best known of Settle characters of that period. She lived by begging, and a good living she made. If she visited any of the houses of those who were in the habit of helping her and she found them out she would often sit down on their door steps awaiting their return. She lived in a small house the property of a well-known lawyer's clerk named James Twisleton, himself quite one of the characters of the town. Now old Mary could not be prevailed upon to pay her rent and was so far in arrears that her landlord decided to apply for an ejectment order and so get rid of her as notices to quit were of no use at all. On Monday he attended the Magistrates' Court to apply for the order; old Mary put in her appearance to oppose it. After the landlord had stated his

case the Chairman of the Bench, the Rev. Mr. Swale, asked old Mary why if she couldn't pay her rent she didn't go out of the house when she had received her notice to quit. Her reply was, "Go out of t' 'ouse! Why should I go out of t' 'ouse? I'm sure it's a very comfortable 'ouse, and I've the kindest little owd landlord anybody could wa[illegible]. Go out indeed! Why should I go o[illegible]?" The Court was convulsed. Her landlord told me afterwards he could have wished the ground to open and swallow him up. He would have given his right hand never to have applied for the order of ejectment. He said "I never felt such an old fool in my life." He, however, obtained an order but old Mary withstood it for a long time, keeping her door always locked except when she slipped out on her begging expeditions. In the end, however, she was obliged to settle down in the Workhouse on account of old age and other infirmities. I think her old landlord felt he would only bring further ridicule upon himself if he took steps to carry out the order.

James and Annie had four children in the next five years which takes some doing. So far so good.

Unfortunately, James and Annie were not living together in the next two census returns - James was with his mum and a son or two in Settle, Annie was nowhere to be found. A report from 1872 indicates that all was not well with James and Annie *[BNA7]*.

amount from his assignees.—*Harrison v. Twisleton.*—This was an action brought by the plaintiff, a tailor and draper, at Settle, against Mr. James Twisleton, of the same place, Attorney's Clerk, for £3 16s. for goods supplied to defendant's wife and children. At the time a portion of the goods were supplied it appeared the defendant's wife and children were living apart from him, who allowed her £1 per week for maintenance but he was in the habit of meeting her at her house and cohabited with her. His Honour gave a verdict for £1 16s. 6d., being the value of the goods supplied during this cohabitation, disallowing the remainder of the plaintiff's claim. Mr. Robinson appeared for the plaintiff, and Mr. Vant for the defendant.

James was paying Annie 'maintenance' as they were officially separated but occasionally 'cohabiting'. Annie was still charging expenses to James - a woman scorned? In 1884, from a Surrey address, Annie took James to the divorce courts on the grounds that he *'hath refused and still refuses to render her conjugal rights'* - clearly he wasn't doing his fair share of washing up. The divorce courts could be used as an extreme measure to force a spouse to accept conjugal demands, although it was almost always led by the man.

That the said James Twisleton without any just cause whatsoever hath refused and still refuses to render to your Petitioner her conjugal rights.

Mr. James Twisleton, of Settle, died on Wednesday last. He was for upwards of fifty years in the service of Messrs. Geldard and Charlesworth, solicitors, of Settle, and for more than twenty years he held the position of secretary of the North Ribblesdale Agricultural Society. Aged 78.

James and Annie couldn't live together, yet couldn't live apart — in the next census in 1891, they were back together in Settle, but apart again by 1901. Annie died in 1905 in Essex, James died in 1907 in Settle *[BNA18]* and is buried in *Old E66*. Despite all this, James and Annie's children all had successful lives in military and professional careers based in London so they managed to get child rearing right.

In affectionate memory of James Twisleton who died on the 18th day of June1902 aged 79 years and of Amy his wife who died on the 6th day of May 1905 aged 72 years, and is interred in Plumstead Cemetery, Kent.

James (Jnr) was a first cousin once removed to Tom Twisleton, the famous Yorkshire dialect poet.

4 THE WEALTHY ONES, and some of their servants

The 'gentlemen', businessmen and clergy ran Victorian Settle, making a good living from their inheritance, investments, foreign trade and property. They employed workers, were the workers' landlords and held all the positions of responsibility. Without local authorities, the wealthy were responsible for the collection of taxes to spend on drainage, lighting, education, a justice system of sorts and some provision for the poor. The wealthy were also generous benefactors to the town.

Upper class women filled their time with leisure and a variety of philanthropic societies often linked to the church, fulfilling their self-appointed duty to teach the less fortunate about Christian morality. Whilst it is easy to criticise their actions, these women had a real impact supporting the poor and reducing cruelty to women, children and animals.

Many of the wealthy were Settle born and bred, often with several additional residences around the country. Many had family tombs at St Alkelda's Church in Giggleswick. In our Ancient graveyard, many of the wealthy were buried behind the south east corner of the church behind the altar, believed to be the best place for a good resurrection.

...JT...

Bollands and Perfects, perfectly aristocratic

The Bollands were originally from Kettlewell, but had bought the old Townhead farmhouse in Settle by 1763. This was a fantastic residence [ph2], now the site of Town Head medical centre and housing.

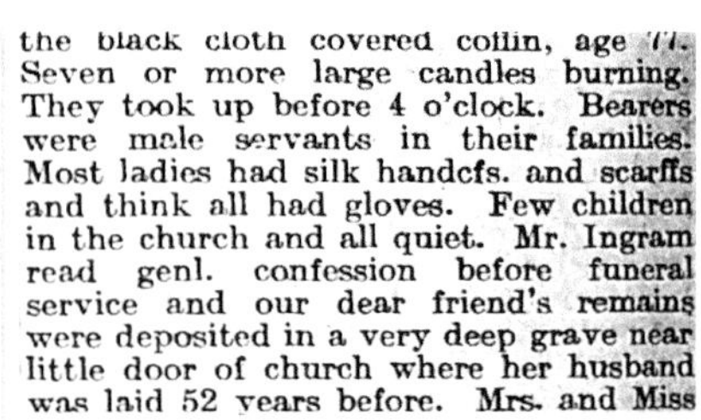
the black cloth covered coffin, age 77. Seven or more large candles burning. They took up before 4 o'clock. Bearers were male servants in their families. Most ladies had silk handcfs. and scarfs and think all had gloves. Few children in the church and all quiet. Mr. Ingram read genl. confession before funeral service and our dear friend's remains were deposited in a very deep grave near little door of church where her husband was laid 52 years before. Mrs. and Miss

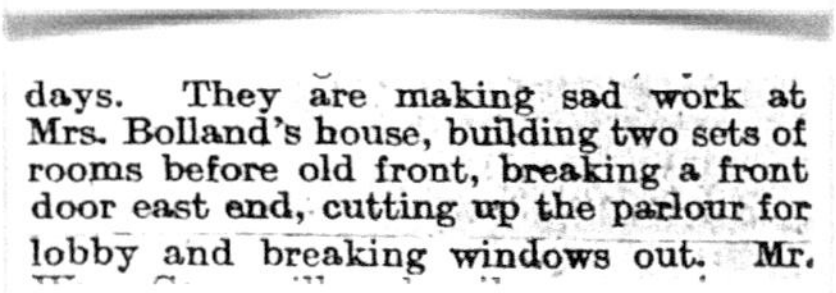
days. They are making sad work at Mrs. Bolland's house, building two sets of rooms before old front, breaking a front door east end, cutting up the parlour for lobby and breaking windows out. Mr.

Anthony Bolland married **Elizabeth Dawson** in 1771 but died in 1777. When widow Elizabeth died in 1826, diarist William Lodge Paley described the funeral at St Alkelda's in Giggleswick. After her death, the first of many structural changes took place, with more in the 1870s. Anthony's son, **William Bolland**, had five daughters: **Margaret**, **Elizabeth**, **Mary**, (who died, unmarried, aged 27) **Jane** and **Susanna**.

...JT...

Margaret Bolland *and her gardener Henry Todd*

In 1837 Townhead was inherited by **Margaret Bolland**, born in 1805. There are numerous articles describing Margaret's generosity. She contributed to events for the workhouse and smallpox vaccinations. She provided the grounds of Townhead for the annual celebrations of the Band of Hope (Junior Temperance Society) [BNA7].

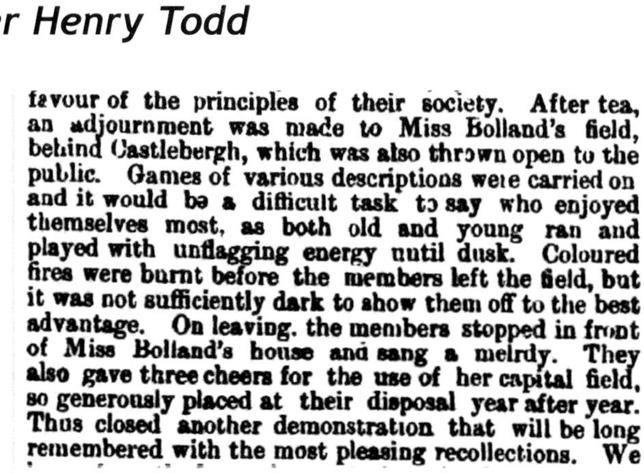
favour of the principles of their society. After tea, an adjournment was made to Miss Bolland's field, behind Castlebergh, which was also thrown open to the public. Games of various descriptions were carried on and it would be a difficult task to say who enjoyed themselves most, as both old and young ran and played with unflagging energy until dusk. Coloured fires were burnt before the members left the field, but it was not sufficiently dark to show them off to the best advantage. On leaving, the members stopped in front of Miss Bolland's house and sang a melody. They also gave three cheers for the use of her capital field, so generously placed at their disposal year after year. Thus closed another demonstration that will be long remembered with the most pleasing recollections. We

Margaret was perhaps a little eccentric, once described as '*a wealthy old woman who lived in a nice house on Constitution*

Hill, who collected peacock feathers diligently. She stitched them in rows on a long cloak she wore down to her heels and as she trotted around in the summer sunshine she was quite a gorgeous spectacle' [Mabel Horner, Dalesman 1951].

When Margaret died aged 73, her estate was worth the equivalent of £2 million today. She is buried with her sister [*below*]. Margaret didn't marry, but with a nod to Queen Victoria, had a lifetime gardener at Townhead, Henry Todd, of whom she was very fond.

Henry Todd, Townhead gardener and companion [*C*] [*D*]

Henry was born in 1806 just south of Kendal. In 1839 he married **Sarah Harrison** and they had six children. Henry's descendants explain that he left home to help with haymaking and never went back. After that, he spent his whole life working as the gardener at Townhead. When he wasn't 'living in', he resided at Townhead Cottage at the far end of Bowskills Yard, owned by Townhead. Sarah died, aged 44, giving birth to their last child, Robert, so Henry brought up the children with the help of his eldest daughter **Ann**.

E18 In affectionate remembrance of Henry Todd, for 53 years the faithful servant and friend of the family at Townhead, Settle, died 25th March 1892 aged 85 years. Also of Sarah his wife died 1st May 1854, aged 44 years. And of James their son died 25th November 1871 aged 21 years.

Henry must have been quite a special gardener and person to remain at Townhead for 53 years. He was often awarded prizes in numerous produce categories at the local Agricultural Show [*SC*].

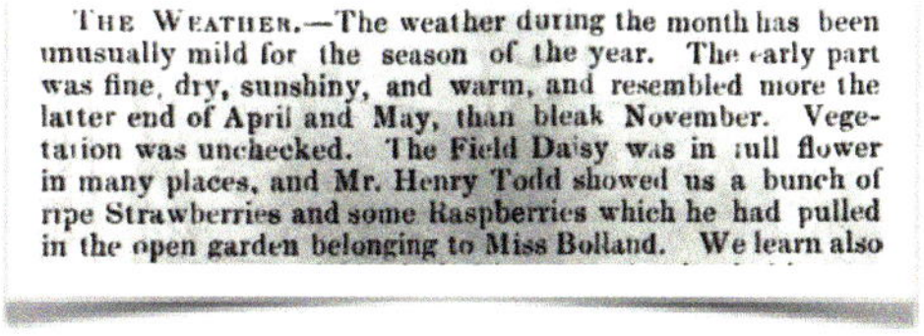

THE WEATHER.—The weather during the month has been unusually mild for the season of the year. The early part was fine, dry, sunshiny, and warm, and resembled more the latter end of April and May, than bleak November. Vegetation was unchecked. The Field Daisy was in full flower in many places, and Mr. Henry Todd showed us a bunch of ripe Strawberries and some Raspberries which he had pulled in the open garden belonging to Miss Bolland. We learn also

Henry [*ph3*], is buried with his wife and 19 year old son James, a railway platelayer who died working on the Settle to Carlisle Railway. Townhead's owner, then **Susannah Edgar**, Margaret Bolland's niece probably contributed to the cost of his gravestone – it's in the midst of their family *graves E16, 17, 21.*

Despite Henry's longevity, there may have been a weak gene in this family. Henry outlived three of his children. Daughter Ann spent most of her life bringing up children, initially her siblings, then an illegitimate daughter **Sarah Ann**, two children from her marriage to **Thomas Waterhouse,** a butler (to banker William Robinson, sister of Susanna Constantine Robinson [*below*]), and then five from her second marriage to **John Dickinson.**

Widowed John Dickinson was the ideal son-in-law for Henry, being the son of estate gardener **Elias Dickinson** of Stackhouse [*farmers*] and perfectly experienced to take over at Townhead when Henry died. John was a good man – when wife Ann died, John continued to bring up his extended family including Sarah's children and grandchildren from previous relationships. Amongst other things, John was the groundsman for Settle Tennis Club, but resigned in 1900, aged 75, because of 'poor health'. He died in 1902 and is buried in the same grave as both his wives on the back (east) wall of the churchyard.

E2 In loving memory of Margaret, wife of John Dickenson who died Oct 5th 1856 aged 32 years. Also of Ann, his second wife who died Sept 19th 1887, aged 48 years. Also of the above John Dickenson who died June 4th 1902 aged 77 years

Ann's illegitimate daughter Sarah Ann died giving birth to her own illegitimate son **James Cleave Todd**, who was brought up by a half-aunt. James was killed in the WW1, and his body was never found. Sarah Ann and half siblings Mary Annie Dickenson and John Henry Dickenson, a solicitor's clerk, are in an unmarked *Old grave CX45*.

Back to the Bolland sisters . . . meet the Perfect brothers

Brothers **John Crowder Perfect** and **William Mosley Perfect** were sons of John Perfect, the principal of the 'Perfect John and William Banking Co' in Pontefract. Their mum Elizabeth Crowder descended from a Mayor of Pontefract. Very eligible! They made a fortune from banking and land investments and took quite a fancy to the Bolland girls. In 1834 John Crowder Perfect married **Maria Bolland** from Leeds, a third cousin to Margaret Bolland, but Maria died in 1836. John sold up, even selling paintings and his *'fifty dozen of choice old port'* collection, [*BNA14*] and then married Settle's **Elizabeth Bolland** in 1838. They had two sons, both of whom died in infancy, and a daughter. John died when he was just 34 and is buried at Giggleswick. Elizabeth spent the rest of her life living with sister Margaret at Townhead. Margaret, Elizabeth and daughter Elizabeth, aged just 17, are buried together.

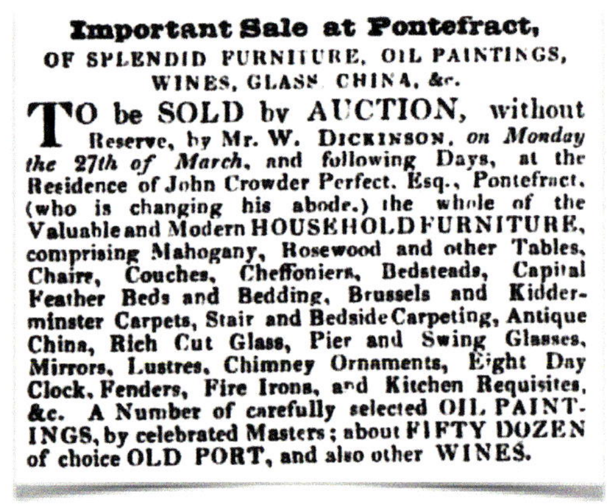

Important Sale at Pontefract,
OF SPLENDID FURNITURE, OIL PAINTINGS, WINES, GLASS CHINA, &c.

TO be SOLD by AUCTION, without Reserve, by Mr. W. DICKINSON, *on Monday the 27th of March*, and following Days, at the Residence of John Crowder Perfect, Esq., Pontefract, (who is changing his abode,) the whole of the Valuable and Modern HOUSEHOLD FURNITURE, comprising Mahogany, Rosewood and other Tables, Chairs, Couches, Cheffoniers, Bedsteads, Capital Feather Beds and Bedding, Brussels and Kidderminster Carpets, Stair and Bedside Carpeting, Antique China, Rich Cut Glass, Pier and Swing Glasses, Mirrors, Lustres, Chimney Ornaments, Eight Day Clock, Fenders, Fire Irons, and Kitchen Requisites, &c. A Number of carefully selected OIL PAINTINGS, by celebrated Masters; about FIFTY DOZEN of choice OLD PORT, and also other WINES.

E16 Elizabeth Margaret Perfect, daughter of John Crowder Perfect Born 10 November 1841, died 17 August 1858. Elizabeth Perfect, widow of John Crowder Perfect, born 10 July 1807, died 12 January 1878. Margaret Bolland of Townhead, Settle born 28 August 1805, died 29 September 1878

In 1845 John's brother **William Mosley Perfect**, a solicitor, received an irresistible offer from Dixon Robinson of Clitheroe Castle (the brother of Susanna Constantine Robinson [*below*]) to move to Blackburn. He worked *'obtaining the acts of Parliament for the construction of the railways from Blackburn to Bolton and Clitheroe'* [BNA1], and was a partner of Dixon Robinson in the firm of Robinson, Perfect and Robinson Solicitors.

William's first wife had died after the birth of a son, and then he married **Jane Bolland**, one of the Settle Bolland sisters. The vicar presiding over the wedding was Rev'd William Clayton who was the husband of youngest sister **Susannah Bolland**. William Mosley Perfect and Jane had a further four daughters and a son. Their daughter Mary married George Robinson, the son of Dixon Robinson, so family links remained strong. William suddenly dropped down dead in 1865 aged just 42 and Jane spent the rest of her life living either in Langcliffe

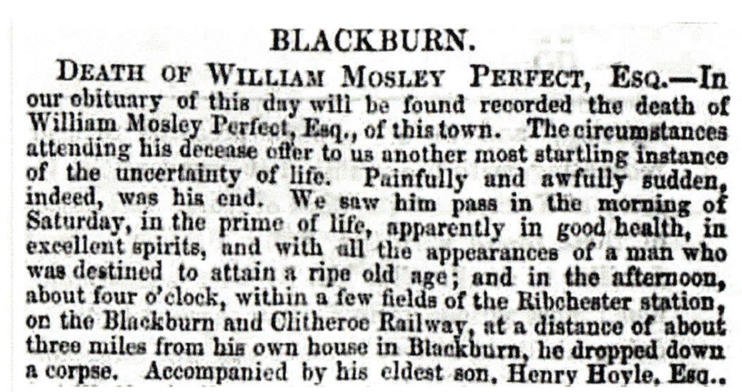

BLACKBURN.

DEATH OF WILLIAM MOSLEY PERFECT, ESQ.—In our obituary of this day will be found recorded the death of William Mosley Perfect, Esq., of this town. The circumstances attending his decease offer to us another most startling instance of the uncertainty of life. Painfully and awfully sudden, indeed, was his end. We saw him pass in the morning of Saturday, in the prime of life, apparently in good health, in excellent spirits, and with all the appearances of a man who was destined to attain a ripe old age; and in the afternoon, about four o'clock, within a few fields of the Ribchester station, on the Blackburn and Clitheroe Railway, at a distance of about three miles from his own house in Blackburn, he dropped down a corpse. Accompanied by his eldest son, Henry Hoyle, Esq.,

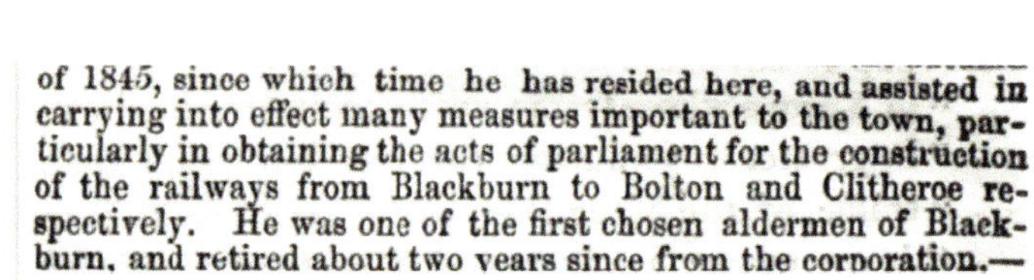

of 1845, since which time he has resided here, and assisted in carrying into effect many measures important to the town, particularly in obtaining the acts of parliament for the construction of the railways from Blackburn to Bolton and Clitheroe respectively. He was one of the first chosen aldermen of Blackburn, and retired about two years since from the corporation.—

Hall or Devon. Daughters Margaret and Katherine are buried in the same grave as their parents. Daughter Susanna Frances was just 19 when she died on Christmas Day at Langcliffe Hall, and has her own grave.

E17 William Mosley Perfect died 26 January 1856, aged 42 years. Jane his wife died 13 November 1885 aged 74 years. Margaret Jane Dawson of Langcliffe Hall died 5 January 1917 and Katherine Elizabeth Perfect of Langcliffe Hall died 2 May 1934.

E21 Susanna Frances Perfect died Christmas Day 1870 aged 19 years.

On the gravestone, Margaret Jane's name has become 'Dawson' instead of 'Perfect', even though she was unmarried. Why is this? In 1879 Queen Victoria decided that the Perfect name could change to Dawson to uphold the ancestry of Langcliffe Hall, [*BNA15*]. Perfect!

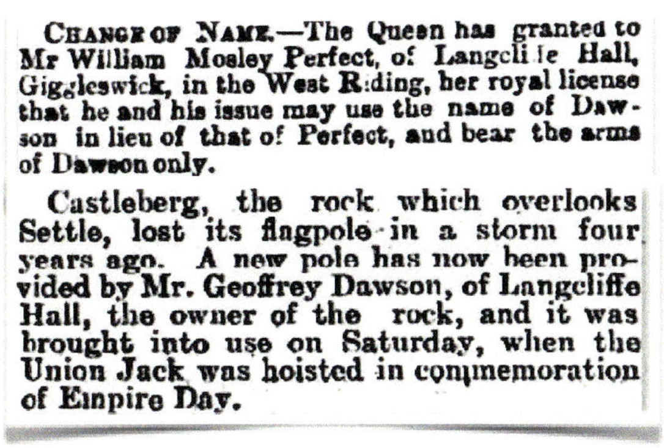

CHANGE OF NAME.—The Queen has granted to Mr William Mosley Perfect, of Langcliffe Hall, Giggleswick, in the West Riding, her royal license that he and his issue may use the name of Dawson in lieu of that of Perfect, and bear the arms of Dawson only.

Castleberg, the rock which overlooks Settle, lost its flagpole in a storm four years ago. A new pole has now been provided by Mr. Geoffrey Dawson, of Langcliffe Hall, the owner of the rock, and it was brought into use on Saturday, when the Union Jack was hoisted in commemoration of Empire Day.

The Dawsons had been at Langcliffe Hall almost continuously since 1645 and Elizabeth Dawson had married Anthony Bolland in 1771. The William Mosley Perfect (Junior) mentioned in this article tragically died at sea.

William and Jane's grandson Geoffrey Robinson (now Dawson of course) also lived at Langcliffe Hall - this article [*BNA7*] was written in 1930. Geoffrey was the editor of The Times from 1910 to 1942, and was a West Riding Magistrate.

Widowed Bolland sister Susanna Clayton lived at Townhead after Margaret Bolland died, followed by Susanna's widowed daughter Susanna Isabella Edgar who is buried in *Old grave E54*. After the death of the last of this line in 1947, Townhead was taken over by Tot Lord.

Susanna Constantine Robinson *and her servant Mary Maria Blundell*

Susanna was born in 1791 in Chatburn, near Clitheroe, the daughter of Josias Robinson and Susanna Dixon. Susanna was a spinster who made a comfortable living from the proceeds of invested inheritance in the large house just below Fern Hill at the top of Constitution Hill.

MR. WILLIAM ROBINSON.

The Robinsons were a well known and successful Settle family. Most of the sons went to Oxbridge. Susanna's brother **William Robinson** was a JP for North Yorkshire and a banker in Settle. William had married **Jane Peart**, whose father Robert built Cragdale, which later became the police station on Duke Street. (Rev Hogarth John Swale married Mary Lambert who also descended from the Pearts.) William and Jane had a son, John, who became the **Reverend John Robinson.** John and William Robinson were responsible for building both the Music Hall (Victoria Hall) and the National School in Upper Settle in 1853. Brother Dixon Robinson was the solicitor based at Clitheroe Castle. The siblings each have a memorial window dedicated to them in Chatburn Church. Susanna's grave has a foot stone.

E20 Here lie the remains of Susanna Constantine Robinson only daughter of Josias and Susanna Robinson of Chatburn who died 19th Decr 1862 aged (71) years

Susanna's servants were widow **Mary Maria Blundell** and her daughter Harriet who was born in Spain. Spain was in turmoil in the early 1800s, occupied by Napoleon until 1814, and then afflicted by numerous civil wars eventually bringing about the end of the monarchy. Harriet's dad Thomas died in those wars. No wonder Settle seemed an attractive place.

B28 M (Mary Maria) Blundell. Ob Nov 29, AD 1849, Age 66

The design of Mary's gravestone is similar to that of Susanna's - it's likely that Susanna paid for Mary's gravestone. Harriet continued to work for Susanna Constantine Robinson after her mum died. After Susanna died in 1862, Harriet, perhaps with a legacy from her generous employer, moved to Darwen, Blackburn. When Harriet died in 1878 she left her estate to the local hospital [*BNA3*].

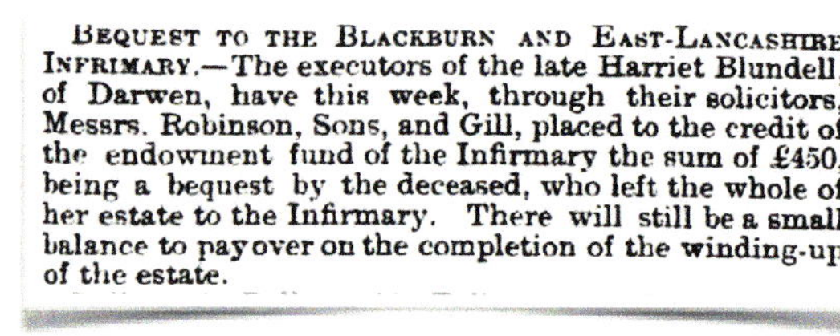

BEQUEST TO THE BLACKBURN AND EAST-LANCASHIRE INFIRMARY.—The executors of the late Harriet Blundell, of Darwen, have this week, through their solicitors, Messrs. Robinson, Sons, and Gill, placed to the credit of the endowment fund of the Infirmary the sum of £450, being a bequest by the deceased, who left the whole of her estate to the Infirmary. There will still be a small balance to pay over on the completion of the winding-up of the estate.

The Jarry sisters, les aristocrates, des chiffons aux richesses [*E*]

Maria Louisa, born in 1818, and **Alphonsine Sarah Jarry**, born in 1822, were the daughters of Frenchman **Etienne** (otherwise known as Stephen) **Jarry** and his wife **Sophia Milbourn**. In 1851 the family lived in Halifax. Stephen ran a French school and provided an excellent French library for his students. However, this settled image of middle class contentment gave no inkling of Etienne's incredible past.

According to *Malcolm Bull's Calderdale Companion*, Etienne was born at Versailles in 1775, his dad being a steward for King Louis XV1 - yes, incredibly so. Little Etienne performed as a chorister in the Chapel Royal from the age of five. But this lifestyle was to come to an abrupt end with the French Revolution in 1789 and the beheading of the King in 1793. People associated with the King were hunted down and often slaughtered. Etienne found himself begging for bread for several years – and there was no cake! Amazingly he survived and being an able man of good character became a secretary to a general, travelling through Europe. He signed up to the French army and saw plenty of action. Eventually wounded by a British sabre in Spain in 1809, Etienne was brought to England as a prisoner of war and was released at Northampton at the end of hostilities. In 1812, aged 36, he married 20 year old Sophia within the Church of England, having converted from Catholicism. Etienne's occupation was given as a *'French Prisoner of War'*. Sophia had been orphaned at the age of six and her siblings were agricultural labourers. Etienne and Sophia settled in Halifax. In 1818, Etienne was listed in a Trade Directory working in 'British Lace manufacture, wool shops', before teaching French. Despite all his adventures, Etienne lived until an incredible 82 years of age.

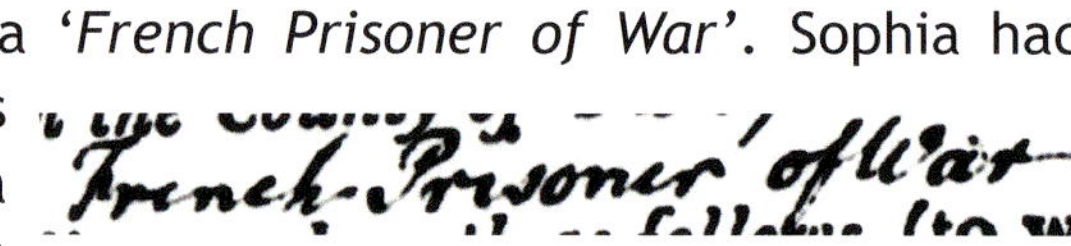

In the 1840s, the sisters were governesses. **Maria** worked for John Birkbeck at Anley [*below*] and **Alphonsine** worked in Halifax where she taught John Lister, the last inhabitant of Shibden Hall who first deciphered the code to Anne Lister's famous diaries. After the death of both of their parents in the 1850s and equipped with their sizeable inheritance, the sisters moved to Fern Hill on Constitution Hill in Settle with their aged aunt Sarah who died in 1863.

Alphonsine helped with the work of the Church and Sunday school for over 40 years. When she retired, she was presented with a purse containing more than 50 guineas with letters from over 80 people.

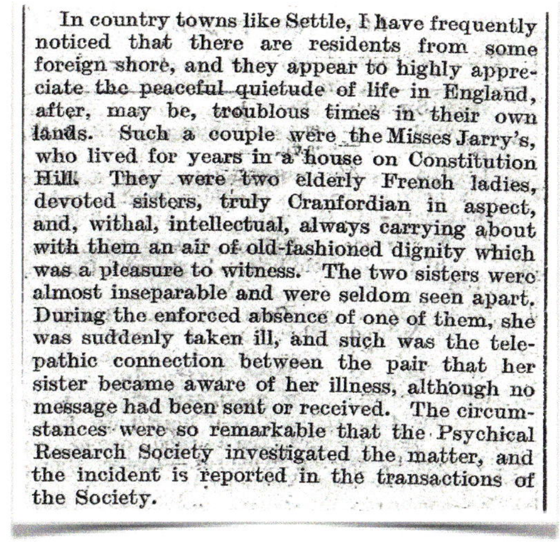
In country towns like Settle, I have frequently noticed that there are residents from some foreign shore, and they appear to highly appreciate the peaceful quietude of life in England, after, may be, troublous times in their own lands. Such a couple were the Misses Jarry's, who lived for years in a house on Constitution Hill. They were two elderly French ladies, devoted sisters, truly Cranfordian in aspect, and, withal, intellectual, always carrying about with them an air of old-fashioned dignity which was a pleasure to witness. The two sisters were almost inseparable and were seldom seen apart. During the enforced absence of one of them, she was suddenly taken ill, and such was the telepathic connection between the pair that her sister became aware of her illness, although no message had been sent or received. The circumstances were so remarkable that the Psychical Research Society investigated the matter, and the incident is reported in the transactions of the Society.

The sisters were remembered in the *Craven Herald 1923* series *'A Veteran's Reminiscences of Settle'*. The sisters were born in Halifax rather than 'some foreign shore', but after their dad's early years it's no wonder the sisters appreciated the 'peaceful quietude of life in England'.

Maria died in 1893 and left her estate to Alphonsine who died in 1912, aged 89, leaving the equivalent to over £1.1 million today. Three-quarters of that went to charity. That's not bad for the daughters of a Versailles escapee! Alphonsine generously donated to the Settle church endowment scheme for pew rents, and to a charity set up by Rev'd John Robinson - *'the object of the charity is the benefit of the aged and infirm of the Parish of Giggleswick'*. She left a legacy to the Halifax infirmary where her dad had died, together with a portrait of him which subsequently went missing.

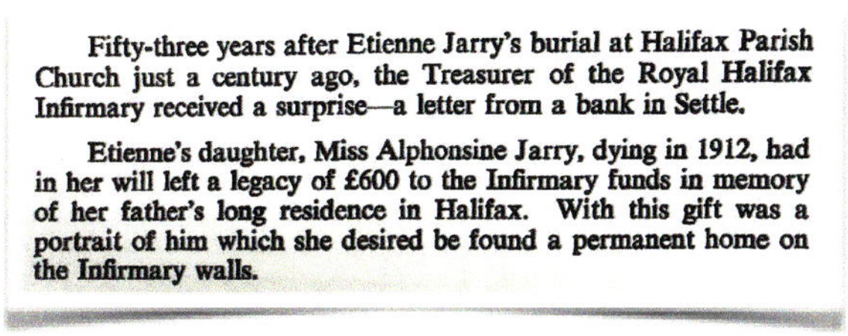
Fifty-three years after Etienne Jarry's burial at Halifax Parish Church just a century ago, the Treasurer of the Royal Halifax Infirmary received a surprise—a letter from a bank in Settle.

Etienne's daughter, Miss Alphonsine Jarry, dying in 1912, had in her will left a legacy of £600 to the Infirmary funds in memory of her father's long residence in Halifax. With this gift was a portrait of him which she desired be found a permanent home on the Infirmary walls.

It's not clear where the family money came from, although Etienne clearly moved in high circles. One of the executors of his will was Sir James Stansfeld from Halifax, a neighbour and 'Radical' Liberal MP who was the first cousin of George Stansfeld [*below*]. This could explain why the girls moved to Settle from Halifax.

A William Morris stained glass window and plaque in the Church reads: *'To the memory of two sisters devoted to kind and good works.... Erected AD 1913 by parishioners and friends.'* Their grave is in a prime position, right by the door of the church.

C2 Maria Louisa Jarry died April 17th 1893 aged 75 years. Until the day break. Alphonsine Sarah Jarry died 6th Nov 1912 aged 90 years, Sarah Chapman died Jan 30th 1863 aged 75.

John Moffat, a Scottish banker and gentleman [*F*]

C20 Sacred to the memory of John Moffat OB June 19th 1841 AET 64. Also Mary his widow OB Dec 16th 1846 AET61. She was the daughter of Joseph Hall who practised many years as a surgeon in Settle.

John Moffat was born in 1877, an only child from Canonbie, Dumfriesshire. By 1803 he was in Settle working as a banker's clerk. At this stage in the Napoleonic wars, he was also a lieutenant in the 'Settle Militia'. He quickly worked his way up at the Craven Bank, becoming a partner with some of the well known Birkbecks, Pearts and Redmaynes. In 1830, aged 53, John withdrew from the partnership and lived as a 'gentleman'. John was one of the Founder Trustees of the Holy Ascension Church.

John married **Mary Hall** in Carlisle in 1817. Mary's dad, Joseph, had been a surgeon in Settle. From 1826, they lived in a large house at the lower end of Constitution Hill. John died of liver disease in 1841 and left a detailed will *[BNA14]*. He left provision for his widow who died of heart disease five years later. He asked William Robinson and John Birkbeck to manage his estates in Langcliffe and in Coniston in the Lake District. John had shares in the Leeds to Liverpool Canal (opened in 1820, and making a healthy profit transporting coal across the Pennines) and the Lancaster Canal which opened in 1826. The main beneficiary of his will was **Jane Creighton**, a daughter of his widowed cousin, another Jane Creighton who herself died when young Jane was six. Jane continued to live in the same house and make a living from John's property until she died in 1877. Jane is buried at Giggleswick church, alongside relations including her uncle **Rev'd John Armstrong** who had become Classical Assistant at Giggleswick School in 1803. Jane's headstone at St Alkelda's in Giggleswick was erected by the Rev'd Henry Arthur Starkie 'as a token of his esteem' – she left a considerable sum to Henry and several other young men of the cloth.

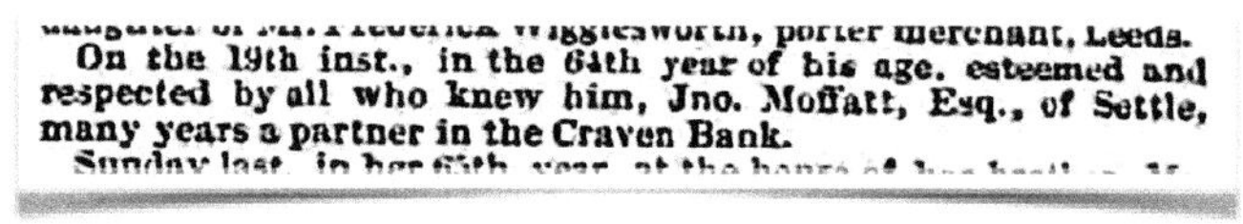
On the 19th inst., in the 64th year of his age, esteemed and respected by all who knew him, Jno. Moffatt, Esq., of Settle, many years a partner in the Craven Bank.

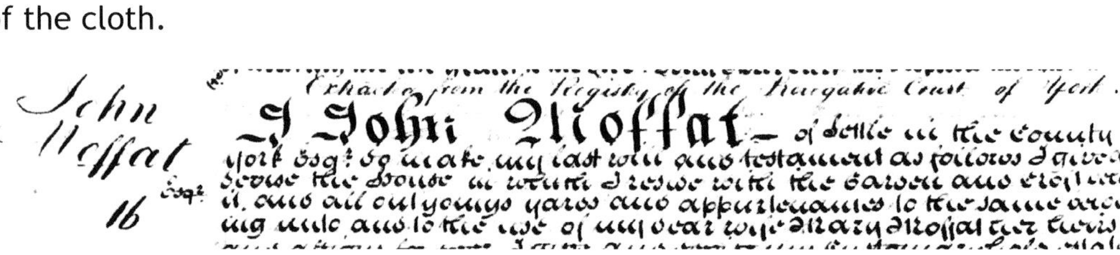
John Moffat Esq. 16

Extract from the Registry of the Prerogative Court of York.

I John Moffat of Settle in the County of York Esq. do make my last will and testament as follows I give and devise the house in which I reside with the garden and ... and all outbuildings yards and appurtenances to the same belonging unto and to the use of my dear wife Mary Moffat ...

The Birkbecks and Stansfelds dynasty of bankers, barristers, JPs *[E]*

The Birkbecks and Stansfelds were two of the wealthiest and most influential families in Settle. Their lives have been well documented by The North Craven Heritage Trust. The Birkbecks were Quakers who came to Settle in the early 1700s. They were held in high repute as trustworthy businessmen and magistrates. They made the equivalent of millions today from textiles, cotton and the Craven Bank, which they had set up. The Birkbecks were founder shareholders in the Leeds to Liverpool Canal in the 1770s, and may have been disappointed that the planned branch to Settle was never completed. George Birkbeck pioneered the national 'Mechanics Institute' movement, which addressed the need for adult education for working men. They built and/or lived in several of Settle's most extravagant houses including Anley, Ashfield, Marshfield, Ingfield Hall and Bankwell in Giggleswick.

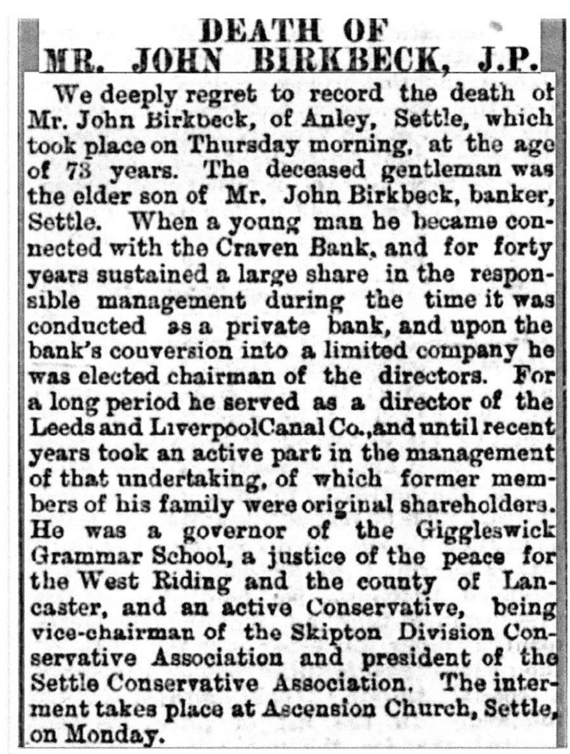
DEATH OF
MR. JOHN BIRKBECK, J.P.

We deeply regret to record the death of Mr. John Birkbeck, of Anley, Settle, which took place on Thursday morning, at the age of 73 years. The deceased gentleman was the elder son of Mr. John Birkbeck, banker, Settle. When a young man he became connected with the Craven Bank, and for forty years sustained a large share in the responsible management during the time it was conducted as a private bank, and upon the bank's conversion into a limited company he was elected chairman of the directors. For a long period he served as a director of the Leeds and Liverpool Canal Co., and until recent years took an active part in the management of that undertaking, of which former members of his family were original shareholders. He was a governor of the Giggleswick Grammar School, a justice of the peace for the West Riding and the county of Lancaster, and an active Conservative, being vice-chairman of the Skipton Division Conservative Association and president of the Settle Conservative Association. The interment takes place at Ascension Church, Settle, on Monday.

Business links in Halifax introduced **John Birkbeck**, born in 1817, to **Lydia Stansfeld**. The Stansfelds were Anglicans, which may have led this branch of the Birkbecks to defect from the Quakers and so find themselves here in this graveyard. John had been educated at Giggleswick School and

Cambridge. They married in 1841 and had four children including twins George and Robert who are buried with them. The reports of John's death and funeral in 1890 [*BNA3*] give an indication of the influence and respect the family commanded. The Craven Herald had a slightly different perspective! John and his son, also John, had the means to explore British caves and mountains and were pioneers of mountaineering in the Swiss Alps in the Golden Age of the 1850s. A fall of over 1500 feet in the Alps may have contributed to son John's death at the age of 49 in 1892.

FUNERAL OF THE LATE MR. JOHN BIRKBECK.

On Monday afternoon the remains of the late Mr. John Birkbeck, of Anley, were interred in the family vault at Ascension Church, Settle. In accordance with the wishes of the deceased gentleman the ceremony was devoid of all pomp and display. At two o'clock the funeral procession left Anley. A detachment, composed of twenty-

...number of local tradesmen. A large number of wreaths and crosses were forwarded, one being furnished by the staff of the Craven Bank at Keighley. At Settle the shops were closed, and the blinds of private houses were drawn during the funeral service, and at least 1,000 persons gathered at the churchyard, most of them taking a last look at the coffin at the close of the service at the graveside.

It is indeed remarkable what changes take place in half a century, types of characters entirely disappear, and the manner of living and environment is altogether different. In many respects the Settle of the past had an affinity with Mrs. Gaskell's "Cranford," and many of its inhabitants were of the type drawn by that talented novelist in her charming idyll. I can see in my mind's eye many of the quaint characters which formerly walked about the streets of Settle. An old maiden-lady from Skipton, taking a walk over Racy Hill, saw a gaunt figure approaching, dressed in a thread-bare suit, and taking him for a dangerous-looking tramp, she rushed back to The Terrace in a fright, but she was re-assured when she was told that it was only "old Mr. John Birkbeck, the Banker."

B6 *This huge family tomb commemorates the lives of John and Lydia Birkbeck of Anley, children Lydia Margaret, Robert Stansfeld, George, John, John's wife Rachel Wilhelmina (Stansfeld), grandchildren Victor John, Hylbert John, Mary Inez*

John Birkbeck's groom was **William Grime** [*working class heroes*]

The Stansfelds

Lydia Stansfeld's brother **George Stansfeld** had recently married **Sarah Birkbeck**, a third cousin to John, who was also in Settle. The Stansfelds' money came from the Calderdale mills. They lived in the impressive Field Hall House, Sowerby Bridge near Halifax, the family home since 1630.

George, a barrister, banker and JP lived with Sarah at Ashfield (now the social club) in Settle and had seven children, three of whom are buried with them. They had another residence, also called 'Ashfield' in Burnley. George's sons followed him into the profession. Daughter Rachel Wilhelmina Stansfeld married her cousin John Birkbeck and is buried in the Birkbeck family tomb.

Their son George was an excellent violinist and the conductor of Settle Choral Society. There are frequent reports of him providing

PRESENTATION.—Our readers will all have heard with regret of the coming departure of Mr. Geo. Stansfeld, jun., who for several years has been the life and soul of our musical entertainments. The working members of the Settle Choral Society have seized this opportunity of presenting to one who has contributed so largely to their musical pleasures, some acknowledgment of his unwearying and cheerful services, and accordingly on Friday the 13th, Mr. Stansfeld was invited to attend a meeting of the members in the Music Hall, when after some delay consequent on the arrangement of the Programme, Mr Barnett took the chair, and called upon Mr Brewin to state the object of the meeting. This he did in a humourous speech. He commenced by saying that on a report of Mr. Stansfeld being about to leave the town getting abroad, the idea seemed to arise simultaneously in the minds of several members of the Society that some acknowledgment of his services on its behalf should be made. Accordingly a committee and treasurer was appointed. Mr. Brewin humorously related how on one occasion, when they were holding a preliminary meeting under the orchestra Mr Stansfeld came suddenly upon them and but for the presence of mind of one of the ladies the secret might have been prematurely exposed. He said that the subscription had been confined to the working members of the Society, or it would have been much larger; he hoped Mr Stansfeld would not look upon this small present as an adequate acknowledgement of his deserts, but would receive it in the spirit in which it is given—as a slight token of their good will. After paying a warm tribute to Mr Stansfeld on personal as well as public grounds, he called on Mrs. Ellis to present the piece of plate which is an embossed Silver Tankard (quart) with cover, with this inscription, "Presented to George Stansfeld jun, by the members of the Settle Choral Society, in grateful acknowledgment of his zealous services for the welfare of the Society. April, 1866." Mr. Stansfeld in replying said that some lady had told him he must speak twenty minutes which he did *not* intend to do.

hilarious entertainment together with friend **Arthur Brewin** [*professionals*], a schoolmaster at Giggleswick School. Arthur Brewin's twin sons are buried very close to the Stansfeld grave, in *grave E25*. George was paid a fine tribute before heading off to work as a JP and Banker in Keighley in the 1860s [*SC*]. Even though he moved away, George remained Chair of the Craven Bank for many years.

E30 In memory of George Stansfeld of Ashfield, Settle who died March 3rd 1869 aged 65 years. Also of Sarah his wife who died July 18th 1869 aged 63 years. In memory of Elizabeth Stansfeld who died October 13th 1931 aged 93 years. In memory of Kenneth Adrian Stansfeld who died March 24th 1881, aged 35 years. Also Harold Eugene Stansfeld, Barrister in law who died August 10th 1894, aged 50 years.

Daughter **Sarah Stansfeld** married **Charles Henry Charlesworth** in 1863, [*SC*],of the wealthy firm of solicitors 'Geldard and Charlesworth'. The Charlesworths are buried in *Old grave E67/8*.

One of George Stansfeld's servants was Annie Grime, daughter of **William Grime**, John Birkbeck's groom [*working class heroes*]. George's gardener was **Robert Weymes** [*farmers and gardeners*].

WEALTHY FOLK LOOKING AFTER THE POOR

In the nineteenth century there was no welfare state. The Poor Law of 1834 decreed that workhouses should be established and run as a deterrent to the poor. So the Giggleswick workhouse was built to provide for the poor of the 'Settle Union' of seven local districts, housing 150 inmates. As part of their keep, the poor were expected to work in the community. William Lodge Paley wrote that they were used to clear roads, and to help out in cotton mills when water levels fell and water-driven machinery failed.

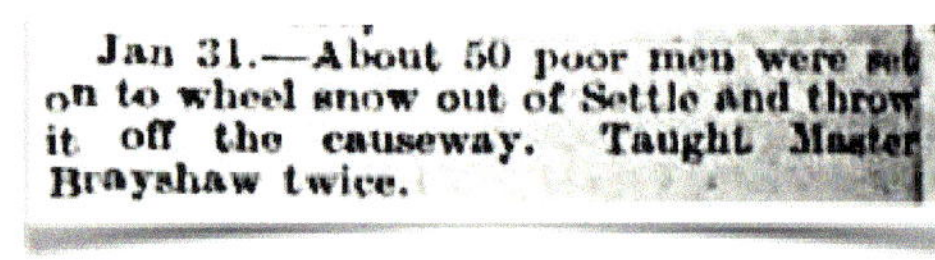

Jan 31.—About 50 poor men were set on to wheel snow out of Settle and throw it off the causeway. Taught Master Brayshaw twice.

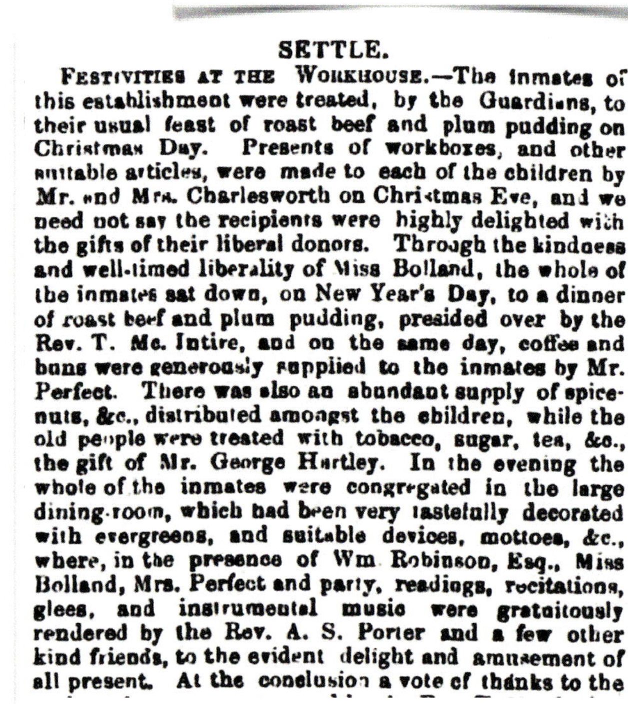

SETTLE.

FESTIVITIES AT THE WORKHOUSE.—The inmates of this establishment were treated, by the Guardians, to their usual feast of roast beef and plum pudding on Christmas Day. Presents of workboxes, and other suitable articles, were made to each of the children by Mr. and Mrs. Charlesworth on Christmas Eve, and we need not say the recipients were highly delighted with the gifts of their liberal donors. Through the kindness and well-timed liberality of Miss Bolland, the whole of the inmates sat down, on New Year's Day, to a dinner of roast beef and plum pudding, presided over by the Rev. T. Mc. Intire, and on the same day, coffee and buns were generously supplied to the inmates by Mr. Perfect. There was also an abundant supply of spice-nuts, &c., distributed amongst the children, while the old people were treated with tobacco, sugar, tea, &c., the gift of Mr. George Hartley. In the evening the whole of the inmates were congregated in the large dining-room, which had been very tastefully decorated with evergreens, and suitable devices, mottoes, &c., where, in the presence of Wm Robinson, Esq., Miss Bolland, Mrs. Perfect and party, readings, recitations, glees, and instrumental music were gratuitously rendered by the Rev. A. S. Porter and a few other kind friends, to the evident delight and amusement of all present. At the conclusion a vote of thanks to the

It was left to the wealthy benefactors to provide funding and run the workhouse. They gave treats to the poor, for example at Christmas in 1867 [*BNA7*] and for special events such as the Queen's jubilee. Trustees of the Settle Union appointed a 'Clerk to the Union' to manage the workhouse. John Lister was appointed in 1855.

John Lister, Clerk to the Settle Union for 35 years

D7 In loving memory of Emily Liztrr (Lister) died Oct 15th 1880, age 17 years. Isabella, beloved wife of John Lister died Nov 15th 1893 age 64 years. John Lister, for 35 years clerk to the Settle Union. Died June 27th 1894, aged 64 years. Rest in the Lord.

John, born in 1830, came from humble roots, his dad **William Lister** being an ostler ('Hostler', who looked after visitors' horses at hostelries) [*ph4*].

John was educated, probably at Giggleswick School, and found work as a solicitor's clerk. In 1855, John married **Isabella Robinson**, a farmer's daughter from Langcliffe and they had four daughters, the youngest being Emily who was buried with them. In the same year John was appointed 'Assistant Clerk to the Settle Union' and in 1859 was given the full responsibility, taking over from William Foster. The adverts he placed, such as this one in 1877, give a fascinating picture of workhouse life [*BNA8*]. John needed a lot of coffins.

SETTLE UNION.

CONTRACTS FOR PROVISIONS, &c.

THE Guardians of the above Union are desirous of contracting with one or more person or persons for the supply of the undermentioned articles for the use and consumption of the inmates of the Workhouse at Giggleswick, for the next Six Months, commencing on the 2nd day of October next:—

Good Beef, sound and sweet, in equal proportion of Brisket, Thick Flanks, and Veiny pieces, the whole not to contain more than 10lbs. of bone for every 112lbs. supplied .... per lb.
Meat for the Master's and Matron's Table:—
Beef .... per lb.
Mutton .... per lb.
Australian Beef and Mutton, in Tins of 4 and 6lb. each.
Flour .... per pack of 240lbs.
Good House Coal, well riddled, and Slack ...... per ton.

Separate Tenders will be required for the delivery of the Coal and Slack at the Workhouse, or at the Station.

Coffins, including Shrouds, and dues for Paupers dying in all or any of the Townships comprised in the Union, (including the Workhouse),
For persons under 4 years old.
For persons under 10 do.
For persons under 16 do.
For persons 16 years old and upwards.

The coffins must be three-quarters of an inch thick and the material perfectly dry.

The Guardians also invite tenders for the undermentioned articles in the quantities hereinafter specified, and to be delivered at the Workhouse within a reasonable time after the Tenders are accepted:—

Cheese 20lbs.; Coffee 15lbs.; Moist Sugar 3cwts.; Loaf Sugar 60lbs.; Split Peas 2cwt.; Black Pepper 4lbs; Rice 2cwt.; Salt 3cwts.; Black Tea 65lbs.; Yellow Soap 2cwt.; Dipped Candles per lb.; Soda 1cwt.; Gin, Rum, Brandy, and Wine, each per gallon.

Cash will be paid for these articles on the Board day next following the delivery thereof.

Sealed tenders (free of expense) must be delivered at the Clerk's Office, in Settle, on MONDAY, the 1st day of October next, before Twelve o'clock at Noon, with the samples of such articles as will admit thereof, after which time no Tenders will be received.

The persons whose Tenders may be accepted will be required to enter into bonds (with a surety or sureties if deemed necessary) for the due performance of their respective contracts, and the articles contracted for will be required to be of good qualities, and must be delivered at the Workhouse free of carriage.

By Order of the Board,
JOHN LISTER, Union Clerk.
Settle, September 18th, 1877. [1641

John was the manager of Settle National School for nearly 20 years, the Treasurer of the Church of England Temperance Society and a churchwarden at St Alkelda's Church. He was the auditor of the Craven Savings Bank and a fine cricketer in the 1850s and 60s. His obituary confirms that he was 'well known and highly respected' [*BNA8*].

DEATH OF MR. JOHN LISTER.—We regret to announce that on Wednesday afternoon last Mr. John Lister, Clerk to the Settle Board of Guardians, died at his residence, Duke-street, Settle. The deceased gentleman has held the appointment of Clerk to the Settle Board of Guardians for the long period of 35 years, having been elected to the office on the 3rd of April, 1859. Although his health had been failing for upwards of a year Mr. Lister continued to discharge the duties of Clerk up to the time of his demise. He was a Manager of the Settle National School, and for nearly 20 years was a Churchwarden at the Parish Church, Giggleswick. He was widely known and highly respected. In politics Mr. Lister was an ardent Conservative. He had reached the age of 64 years.

Daughter Mary Annie married surgeon **Oliver Scattergood**, the son of consultant surgeon Thomas Scattergood from Leeds. Thomas was an obstetrician and pioneer of forensic medicine, especially related to poisons and particularly strychnine. He was consulted on cases all over the country. He was the first Dean of Leeds Medical School. Oliver didn't achieve the eminence of his dad. After working as a surgeon in Settle and in Leeds, he spent his last 20 years working as a clerk at a woollen mill in Leeds. What happened there then?

Daughter Isabella married **Charles Glover Ratcliffe**, a Colne cotton manufacturer, in 1881 with a glorious celebration [*BNA7*]. Charles could be related to our other Charles Ratcliffe [*railway folk*].

SETTLE.

Marriage of Miss Lister.—The marriage of Miss Isabella Lister, of Settle, to Mr. Charles Glover Ratcliffe, manufacturer, of Colne, was celebrated on Wednesday last, at the Church of the Holy Ascension, the ceremony which was performed by the Vicar (Rev. W. F. Pierson), being witnessed by a considerable number of interested personages. The bride, who is the daughter of our well-known and highly respected townsman, Mr. John Lister, was attired in a dress of Ruby velvet trimmed with satin. Her two sisters (Miss Amy and Miss Annie Lister) were the bridesmaids, and wore cream coloured cashmere dresses trimmed with lace and bonnets to match. The bride's father gave her away. For many years Miss Lister has been a teacher at the Church Sunday School, and it is not too much to say that her loss will be keenly felt.

John's younger brother William was a bank manager for the Kendal Bank, based in Ambleside, but died after an attack of flu in Settle in 1898 *[BNA16]*. William, his wife Ann and two children William and Agnes are also buried in the unmarked *Old grave EX73*.

Death of Mr. William Lister.—Many were the expressions of regret when the news reached Ambleside on Tuesday morning that Mr. W. Lister, manager for the Bank of Liverpool, at Ambleside, had died the previous night at the residence of his brother at Settle, whither he had gone but little over a week before in the hope of recruiting his health. Mr. Lister had partially recovered from a somewhat severe attack of influenza, but after reaching Settle he was taken seriously ill. On Monday he became unconscious and died about 11 o'clock at night. His life has been one of usefulness and activity, and he will be greatly missed. He was a native of Settle and was educated at Giggleswick Grammar School. He entered the Kendal Bank in 1859 and in 1871 was appointed to the management of the Ambleside branch. During his 12 years residence in Kendal Mr. Lister made many intimate friends, identifying himself with the work carried on at the Mechanics' Institute. He was a very prominent member of the debating society held there. He was also a keen cricketer, belonging to the Kendal team for whom he rendered useful service. At Ambleside he was closely connected with the church and schools, filling the office of churchwarden for many years. He was a staunch Conservative in politics.

. . . . . .

Sometimes the workhouse was just too little, too late. . . .

The Armitstead family

At the time of the May 1841 census, **Christopher Armitstead**, born in 1794, was in Langcliffe working as a labourer with four children and his mum Ann Armitstead. After the death of two infant daughters, Christopher had moved the family to Langcliffe from Horton-in-Ribblesdale, presumably to find work. Christopher's dad had died the previous year in Giggleswick workhouse, and was buried at Giggleswick.

Christopher's wife **Martha Hesleden** had died a few weeks before and was buried in Ancient *grave DX8*. (Holy Ascension buried those from Langcliffe until St John's church was built.) Son William died on 28th July the same year, 1841, in *grave BX11*.

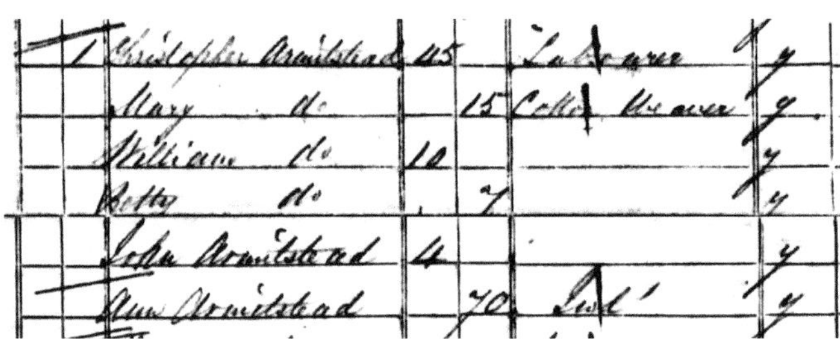

Christopher Armitstead	45		Labourer	y
Mary do		15	Cotton Weaver	y
William do	10			y
Betty do		7		y
John Armitstead	4			y
Ann Armitstead		70	Ind.	y

Christopher himself died on 2nd September the same year, buried in *grave BX11* with son William leaving John, Mary and Betty orphaned. Perhaps mum Ann in her 70s was able to look after the children?

Daughter Mary died in January 1842. Mum Ann died in January 1845. Daughter Betty died in Giggleswick workhouse in April 1949 aged 14, and is buried at Giggleswick.

There are no further records for son John. There are no burial records for daughter Mary, or mum Ann, so what happened to their bodies? There are no gravestones, newspaper cuttings or obituaries for families like these, but they are just as an important part of Settle's heritage.

Infections were the cause of more than 50% of deaths in those years, and tuberculosis killed most. It's possible that disease, linked to poverty, wiped out this whole family.

5 FARMERS AND ESTATE GARDENERS – WORKING THE LAND

In the 1850s, over a third of Craven workers were involved in farming. After land owners, tenant farmers were some of our wealthiest residents. They rented farms from the land owners and made money primarily from mainly cattle and some sheep. Several farmers were also gardeners. Houses didn't have domestic gardens as such; families kept pigs and wildfowl in back yards for a bit of extra food. 'Gardeners' worked in the grounds of the large estates – think Capability Brown in Settle. As gravestones show, despite being in service to someone else, this was a lucrative occupation.

THE FARMERS

The Hargraves, farmers of the largest farm in the County *[B]*

Stephen Hargraves, born in 1792 was *'a landed proprietor and farmer of 2250 acres'*, yes 2250 acres, at Stockdale Farm (behind Upper Settle). In 1851 there were only three other farms of this size in the whole of West Yorkshire. Stephen rented most of the land from the Dawsons (who also owned Langcliffe Hall, the Folly and Marshfield amongst others) and from Thomas Clapham of Stackhouse. Stephen was one of the few farmers involved in the droving trade, providing grazing for herds of sheep and cattle as they were marched across the country to market.

Stephen and his son Robert were regular prizewinners at the North Ribblesdale Agricultural Show, this in 1853 *[BNA14]*.

BLACK-FACED AND OTHER SHEEP.—Best black-faced tup, Stephen Hargraves, Settle, £1 ; 2, James B. Chapman, Wharfe, 10s. Best four black faced shearling gimmers, Stephen Hargraves, Settle, 10s. ; 2, Robert Hargraves, Stockdale, 5s. Best four black-faced stock ewes that have suckled lambs this season, John Proctor, Long Preston, 15s. ; 2, Stephen Hargraves, Settle, 10s. Best four

In 1818, Stephen married **Isabella Holgate** who allegedly descended from Archbishop Robert Holgate of York. Robert just about managed to survive the turmoil of Henry VIII's rule, although was defrocked by Queen Mary. Stephen retired in 1853 after the death of son William and lived at Rock House on Castle Hill, which his wife had inherited. Stephen and Isabella had 11 children, including twins but only three survived him. Stephen died in 1859, aged 67, after a failed gall bladder operation, according to family records.

Stephen Hargraves died in Leeds on 19 Feb.1859 aged 67, subsequent to an operation for gall stones. He survived the operation,but his death was probably due to inefficient and perhaps unhygenic nursing afterwards.

E19 Sacred to the memory of Stephen Hargraves formerly of Stockdale and late of Settle who died February 19th 1859 aged 67 years and Isabella his wife who died September 7th 1861 aged 68 years. Also of William their second son who died June 19th 1853 aged 28 years. Two daughters survive by whom this stone is erected.

Stephen has the honour of two gravestones in his name. In addition to this grave at Holy Ascension, Stephen also has a family tomb right next to the front door of St Alkelda's Church in Giggleswick inscribed *'The family grave of Stephen Hargrave'*. It probably contains his dad John and children John, aged 28, twins Alice and Elizabeth who died in their teens, infant Isabella and toddler Thomas. Next to it is the grave of Stephen's daughter **Annie Batten** and her husband John, who was the principal clerk in Her Majesty's Customs and Excise. Annie died in 1900, leaving the equivalent of nearly £1 million to her son. In 1910, John died leaving the equivalent of just £40,000. Interesting.... The grave inscription bears the Batten coat of arms and John and Annie have a memorial window dedicated to them in the choir vestry at St Alkelda's. Stories of son Robert and daughter Jane Hargrave are in *[railway folk]*.

The Parkers, an incredibly resilient family *[A] [E]*

Stephen Parker was born in 1801 in 'Parkers Yard', Giggleswick. Stephen started life as a carpenter – the whole family were carpenters and undertakers, so will have said a last farewell to many of our folks in the graveyard. They were a family who just kept going in the face of several tragic twists of fate.

March 28.—Sorry to hear that Stephen Parker has broken his thigh, loading wood up. Twenty-seven or eight children said Catechism at church, chiefly from Meth. Chapel Sunday School.
March 29.—Did sit ½ hour with Stephen Parker, who seems much resigned and left him my largest volume of tracts to read.

In 1823, diarist William Lodge Paley noted that Stephen broke his thigh. A year later, Stephen married **Elizabeth Blackwell** from Gisburn in 1824 and in the 1830s set up his farming business whilst bringing up at least nine children – sons **John**, **Richard**, **Stephen** and **Joseph** and daughters **Rebecca**, **Ann**, **Eliza**. Daughters **Sarah** and **Elizabeth** died in infancy, and **Rebecca** died of scarlet fever aged 13.

In the 1830s Stephen took over the tenancy of the wonderful Lodge Farm *[ph10]*. He farmed and burnt lime on 200 acres of land, renting most of it from Quaker families: the Birkbecks *[wealthy folk]* and John Moore of Eldroth.

It wasn't all a bunch of roses though. In 1846 (not 1848 as on the gravestone), sons Richard and John went to play with the sons of David Hall Dale *[railway folk]* from Cleatop Farm. Neither brother could swim and tragedy struck. They were just 15 and 17. Appropriately, a record number of people attended the funeral *[BNA 18]*.

SETTLE.—ACCIDENT.—We have this week to record a most melancholy and fatal accident, which occurred to two sons of Mr Stephen Parker, of the Lodge, near Settle, on Sunday last. The two boys went to Cleatop, to Mr Dale's, and, in company with his (Mr Dale's) two sons, went down the river Ribble for the purpose of bathing. The youngest boy, about fifteen years of age, undressed himself, and went into a very deep part of the river called "Wall-end Dub," and not being aware of its depth, which then was about six yards in the middle, waded up to his neck, and having been asked if he dared go no farther, he replied "Yes," when his foot slipped off the stone and he went to the bottom, but came to the top twice, and called for help to his brother John, a fine young man about 19 years of age, who was with him. His brother John then threw off nothing but his hat and leapt into the river, and as neither of them could swim, they both immediately sank; and, the distance to Settle being about a mile and a half, before any assistance could be rendered, the unfortunate youths were both drowned. Their bodies were got out of the river about four hours after the accident occurred.

It appeared they went down the river Ribble for the purpose of bathing, and having got out of their depth, were drowned, as neither of them could swim. A verdict of "Accidental death" was returned.—The bodies were interred on Wednesday evening, and were followed to the grave by the largest concourse of people ever seen at a funeral in settle.

SETTLE.
INQUEST.—An inquest was held on Tuesday last, before Thos. Brown, Esq., coroner, on the body of Elizabeth Parker, aged 58, the wife of Stephen Parker, of Settle, farmer, who was found dead on Monday morning, in a small rivulet. On Sunday evening, deceased before going to bed, complained to her husband of pain in her head, and the husband on awaking about one o'clock found his wife missing, he procured assistance, but could find no trace of her, till it was light, when her footsteps were traced to a small stream, called Lodge Gill where they found her. The water was so shallow as not to cover deceased, who was found laid on her back, with only her night dress on. Wm. Altham, surgeon, was immediately sent for, but life was found extinct. Though no marks of violence, or any external injury were found on the body, still the depth of the water (only 6 inches), rendered drowning almost impossible; but exposure to the cold for several hours without clothing, would have caused death. The Jury, returned a verdict, in accordance with the above facts, being unable to determine the precise cause of death. It is a singular coincidence that the deceased is the fourth member of her family whose deaths have been the subjects of a coroner's inquest, and the other three were her children, two of whom were drowned at the same time.

As if that wasn't enough trauma, Stephen's wife Elizabeth also met a tragic end in 1860, at the age of 58 *[BNA7]*. One of the reports suggests there was a coroner's inquest for a further child, although we can't prove that. Perhaps Elizabeth never got over the deaths of her children.

Poor Stephen. However, he had great resilience and a fine business brain. He

had built Pendle View, next to the Hart's Head in Giggleswick and the five dwellings in Sutcliffe Buildings in Settle [*ph1*] completed in 1841 with a date stone 'SEP' - Stephen and Elizabeth Parker. In 1859 Stephen had bought New Butts farm in Bentham to set up a business making drainage tiles for farmers. After Elizabeth's death he lived in Bentham with some of his children, but just a year later he married a butcher and farmer's widow, **Margaret Dugdale**, and spent the rest of his life with her in Sutcliffe Buildings. In 1872, Stephen was appointed the valuer for stock affected by contagious diseases (after recent attacks of cattle plague). He was obviously a well regarded man.

Stephen died aged 85, an incredible age considering the events in his life. He is buried with his first wife and sons. Second wife Margaret died in 1889 and is buried with her first husband at Kirkby Malham.

E15 Sacred to the memory of Stephen Parker, of Sutcliffe House, Settle, who died January 23rd 1886 aged 85 years, also of Elizabeth wife of the above who died at Lodge, near Settle, February 20th 1860 aged 58 years.

Also of John, and Richard their sons both of whom were drowned whilst bathing in the River Ribble, on Sunday evening June 26th 1848 aged respectively 18 and 16 years. Also of John their nephew who died at Morecambe, December 30th 1885 aged 53 years.

Unmarried son Stephen and daughters Ann and Eliza lived together at Butts Farm in Bentham. They are buried together in the *Old grave A65*

Son Joseph Parker took over Lodge Farm

Understandably, after the tragic death of his wife, Stephen moved out of Lodge Farm. However, by the 1881 census, youngest son **Joseph Parker** was back there, again renting from the Birkbecks. Joseph, born in 1845, was the only child of Stephen to marry and have a family of his own, justifying the Victorian principle of having many children in order to ensure surviving family heirs.

Joseph married **Mary Clarke** in 1872. During their very short marriage, Mary gave birth to twins who survived just 16 and 17 days. They were named **John** and **Richard**, the same as Joseph's brothers who had drowned. Mary survived that birth, however, two years later the effort of giving birth to **Joseph Clarke Parker** killed her.

A couple of years later, Joseph married **Alice Ayrton**, daughter of Thomas Batty in *grave B24* and the widow of John Ayrton [*innkeepers*]. Alice gave Joseph a further three sons before she also died. One of the sons, toddler Stephen, is in the grave with her.

E14 In loving memory of Mary the wife of Joseph Parker, The Lodge, Settle who died Dec 30th 1874, aged 32 years. And two children, twin sons of the above, also in remembrance of Alice the beloved wife of the above Joseph Parker who died Oct 7th 1883 aged 40 years. Stephen son of the above who died Dec 21st 1883 aged 4 years. The Lord's will be done.

Not one to give up, in 1886 Joseph married **Elizabeth Marsden Ayrton**, who was already pregnant with their son **James.** Elizabeth was the sister of John Ayrton, the first husband of Joseph's second wife Alice. We find several of these complex family links in the small town of Settle.

Elizabeth had experienced her own share of tragedy and perhaps this understanding brought them close [*working class heroes*].

Joseph (pictured right) and his first cousin once removed, John Parker (left) were both on the first Settle Parish Council in 1894 [*ph4*]. Joseph died in 1908 and is buried in the *Old grave E65* with his third wife Elizabeth and son of his first wife, Joseph Clarke Parker who died aged 24. The style of the gravestone matches that of Joseph's parents and siblings.

Old E65 In Loving Remembrance of Joseph Parker of the Lodge, Settle who entered into rest May 2nd 1903 aged 58 years. Also of Joseph Clarke Parker, son of the above Joseph and the late Mary Parker who died Sept 3rd 1899. Also of Elizabeth M Parker, widow of the above Joseph Parker who died July 1914 aged 69 years.

Joseph was survived by two farming sons, Thomas and James, and a daughter, Elizabeth Ann who lived with her husband John Carr Chapman at Cleatop Farm near the scene of the death of her uncles John and Richard. The tragedy is not quite over. After farming near Slaidburn, son James later lived in Sutcliffe House. In 1909, he married **Hannah Elizabeth Haining** who gave him two children. Hannah was a descendant of the Hainings [*below*] and the Hartleys [*railway folk*]. Like so many others, James died of dysentery in July 1918 in Salonica, Greece aged just 32. Total respect to this family.

...JT...

THE ESTATE GARDENERS

Elias Dickinson, who knew a thing or two about ferns [*D*]

Elias Dickinson, born in 1799, was the son of farmer **John Dickinson** and his wife **Ann Hardacre** of Long Preston. In 1822 he married **Mary Woodworth** in Bolton-by-Bowland and they had at least three children, **Elizabeth**, **John** and **Thomas**. Elias was a labourer who found work in Wigglesworth, Mearbeck and then at Langcliffe, probably attracted by the opportunities at the Claytons' cotton mill at Langcliffe Place.

Work began to decline at the mill, but somehow Elias managed to secure a job as a gardener working for **Thomas Clapham** at the Old Hall in Stackhouse. This wonderful house had been built in 1695 by a previous Thomas Clapham and had been in the family ever since.

In 1857, Elias won particular praise and several prizes for his ferns at the North Ribblesdale Horticultural Show [*BNA7*]. In 1888, Thomas Clapham's son's obituary included: '*Abraham Clapham was a keen naturalist and horticulturalist specialising in the rearing of ferns.*' So who did Abraham get his expertise from?

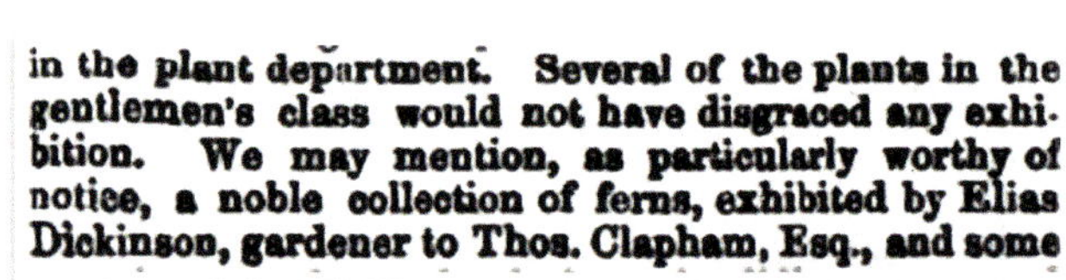

in the plant department. Several of the plants in the gentlemen's class would not have disgraced any exhibition. We may mention, as particularly worthy of notice, a noble collection of ferns, exhibited by Elias Dickinson, gardener to Thos. Clapham, Esq., and some

Elias stayed at Stackhouse until Mary died in 1872 so had been there for nearly 30 years. Mary is buried somewhere in the Ancient graveyard. Elias was 74 by then and moved to Settle to live with daughter Elizabeth and her family. Elias' eldest son **John** married **Ann Todd**, the daughter of Henry Todd, the gardener at Townhead [*wealthy ones*].

In 1887 Elias was seen as part of 'a remarkable group of four persons, whose united ages reached 340' [BNA25]. In November 1888, Elias aged 90!, had an unfortunate accident and broke his thigh [LSA]. He eventually died in 1891, aged 93.

Longevity in the Settle District.—A remarkable group of men was formed by chance on the Town Hall steps, Settle, yesterday. It was composed of four persons, whose united ages reached 340 years, or an average of 85 years. The names and ages are as follows:—Elias Dickinson, 88; Joseph Garner, 88; Thomas Hardacre, 82; Thomas Hardacre, Long Preston, 82.

6—Accident to Elias Dickinson, of Settle, who was knocked down by a butcher's cart and had his thigh broken.—Entertainment for the benefit of the Mechanics' Institute at Long Preston.

Elias was buried with daughter Elizabeth and her husband **John Davis**, who worked as a labourer, light porter and warehouseman, in *Old B47* [ph6]. The fantastic *photograph 6* was given to the family following the erection of the stone. It shows the really quite empty Old graveyard soon after the building of the railway.

In Loving Memory of Elias Dickinson Born Feb 25th 1799 died April 24th 1891. Also of Elizabeth (his daughter) wife of John Davis Born March 24th 1823 died June 9th 1897. Also of John Davis Born July 26th 1829. Died Feb 7th 1904. Their Children Rise Up and Call them Blessed

John and Elizabeth's son **Elias Davis**, born in 1859, was a fine looking man [ph6] who bought his tailoring business at the corner of High Street and Chapel Street from John Snell in the early 1900s [LSA]. In 'Memoirs of a Settle Boy', James F Riley recalls '*keeping an eye on the slim silhouette and side whiskers of his neighbour, Elias Davis the tailor, still the model of the well-dressed Edwardian'*. Elias Davis and his wife Ellen are buried in *Old C49* with their five year old daughter Mildred. Their daughter Ellen Davis married Richard Mason Tomlinson, son of William Tomlinson. William worked as coachman to the Edgar family at Townhead for 45 years, continuing this family's links with Townhead.

"It is Policy to Dress well."

Elias Davis,

MILITARY, CIVIL, AND CLERICAL TAILOR : : : : : AND COSTUMIER

Newest Materials.

Cut and Fit Guaranteed.

HIGH STREET, SETTLE.

Elias Dickinson's son Thomas, born in 1827, retired to Settle after a life working as a policeman and insurance salesman in Liverpool and Cheshire [ph6]. His son Elias Thomas Dickinson became a Wesleyan Minister who was known for promoting the Temperance cause. Elias Thomas died in 1895 of an infection which he appears to have caught whilst taking a ferry to the Isle of Man for a holiday. He was just 39 [BNA3].

DEATH OF THE REV. E. T. DICKINSON, OF PADIHAM.

We regret to announce the death, from peritonitis, of the Rev. E. T. Dickinson, which took place at Dalton-in-Furness, on Friday last. About three weeks ago Mr. and Mrs. Dickinson left Padiham for their holidays, and it appears that in the passage to the Isle of Man the rev. gentleman caught a chill which induced an attack of peritonitis.

Robert Weymes, the gardener to the Stansfeld family

Elusive **Robert Weymes**, born in 1812, named a variety of birth places throughout his life including Northamptonshire, Westmorland and London! In 1845 he married **Ann Saville** from Heworth, York, and their first child, Louisa was born at Kilnwick Percy, a small village in the grounds of the Kilnwick Percy Hall (now a Buddhist meditation centre). The current building was completed in 1845 and Robert was employed as a gardener, probably to help establish the gardens.

Robert moved to the impressive Cowling Hall near Colne, working as Head Gardener. By 1853, son George Robert was born in Settle. Robert ran his own business as a gardener and seedsman, living at Green Head in Upper Settle [*SC*]. By 1857 they had moved to Chapel Street and could afford a servant, probably linked to his appointment as gardener to George Stansfeld [*wealthy ones*] at Ashfield on Duke Street.

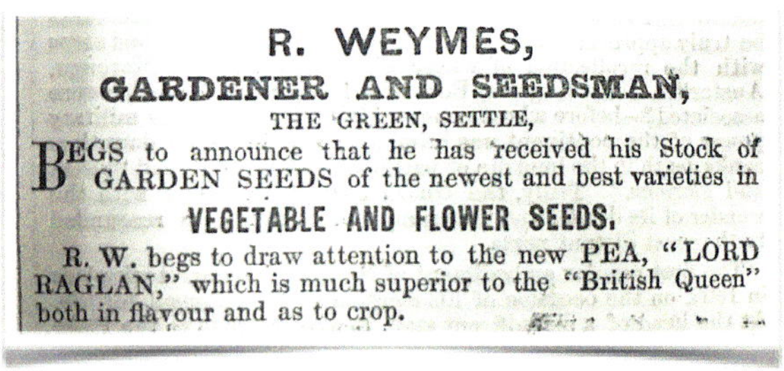
R. WEYMES,
GARDENER AND SEEDSMAN,
THE GREEN, SETTLE,
BEGS to announce that he has received his Stock of GARDEN SEEDS of the newest and best varieties in
VEGETABLE AND FLOWER SEEDS.
R. W. begs to draw attention to the new PEA, "LORD RAGLAN," which is much superior to the "British Queen" both in flavour and as to crop.

B2 In affectionate remembrance of Robert Weymes of Settle who died Feb 2, 1868 aged 54 years. The Lord is my shepherd I shall not want. Also Mary Louisa Agar niece of R & A Weymes who died June 17 1872 aged 22. years. Her end was at peace. Also of Ann, widow of the above who died June 8 1885, aged 74 years. Rest in the Lord.

Robert and Ann's daughter, Louisa, had the honour of working as nursemaid to the family of Rev'd Swale, the first vicar of the church at Ingfield Hall [*church folk*] before she married a carpenter James Aitkins. James later became the 'estate carpenter' at Bolton Abbey.

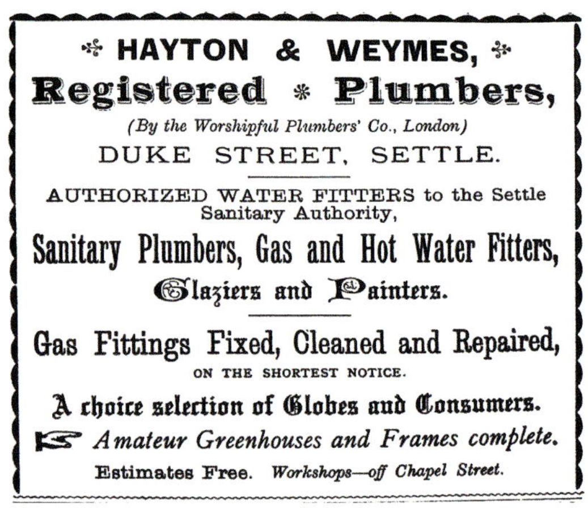
HAYTON & WEYMES,
Registered Plumbers,
(By the Worshipful Plumbers' Co., London)
DUKE STREET, SETTLE.
AUTHORIZED WATER FITTERS to the Settle Sanitary Authority,
Sanitary Plumbers, Gas and Hot Water Fitters,
Glaziers and Painters.
Gas Fittings Fixed, Cleaned and Repaired,
ON THE SHORTEST NOTICE.
A choice selection of Globes and Consumers.
Amateur Greenhouses and Frames complete.
Estimates Free. Workshops—off Chapel Street.

Robert and Ann's son, **George Robert**, became a plumber and married **Alice Ann Overing**, a tailor's daughter. Alice died, aged 37, and is buried in the *Old grave E39* all by herself. After Alice died, George went into business with William Hayton who was the son of John Hayton the bookbinder [*professionals, LSA*]. George married again and his new wife brought up the children with him in Clitheroe.

Robert and Ann also brought up their niece, **Mary Ann Louisa Agar**. She has her own grave and gravestone. Mary Ann was born in Sheriff Hutton, York, the youngest of five children of Ann Saville and James Agar, an agricultural labourer. Mary Ann was less than a year old when her mum died in 1851 and still only four when her dad died in 1854.

Mary Ann Louisa was brought up by her aunt Ann Weymes in Settle. Her brothers all went on to have successful careers as skilled tradesmen. In 1871, Mary Ann Louisa worked in the grand Hanover Square in Leeds with her cousin Elizabeth Ann Saville. They were 'waiting maids' to Mrs Sarah Charlesworth, the mother of Charles Henry Charlesworth who had established himself as a solicitor in Settle. Mary Ann Louisa died a year later, aged just 22.

James Haining, a farmer and gardener with two desperate sons [*A*]

James Ralph Haining, born in 1807, and his wife **Mary Dixon** came to Settle by 1837 with a son William from Northumberland. James worked at the gardens of Langcliffe Place, where mill owner William Clayton and his family lived. An infant son, Dixon, died while they were in Langcliffe and is buried in *grave DX4*, close to his parents. The decline of the mill probably affected James' post, as they had moved to the Upper Settle by the next census. James made a living as farmer/seedsman and they had another two children, James and Mary Jane. When he died in 1868, aged 61, James' quite substantial inheritance will have helped to pay for the gravestone of such excellent quality, just behind the south (altar) church wall.

E29 In memory of James Haining who died December 14th 1868 aged 60 years. Also of Mary, wife of the above who died March 18th 1883 aged 80 years.

Eldest son **William Haining** was an interesting character. In August 1855, aged 19, he married **Elizabeth Marsden**, an illegitimate daughter of Grace Marsden who later married John Lord. Elizabeth already had two illegitimate children. When they married, Elizabeth was already six months pregnant with son **Joseph**, but this must have been too much for William. In November 1855, he was on a ship bound for New York, describing himself as a farmer, and then records stop – perhaps he changed his name, or died? In 1871, 'widow' Elizabeth married a stonemason **John Hounds** who was working at Ribblehead, probably on the viaduct. There are no further records – navvies often gave false names. Son Joseph married Jane, daughter of the cotton manufacturer Henry Hartley [*railway folk*] and worked as a grocer in Upper Settle. Joseph died, aged just 51 and poor Jane was killed by a car on Penny Bridge, Giggleswick on Christmas Eve 1940 when she was walking home during a black out. One of their daughters married James Parker [*above*].

Three years before James' death, and perhaps contributing to it, son James was caught poaching rabbits. Times were tough and many working class folk supplemented their diets with nature's gifts. James was let off subject to paying costs [*BNA7*]. However, just a year later, James was caught red-handed again, by Sergeant Whincup [*SC*]. Rather than face up to the consequences, James fled to Indiana, America to farm with an American wife and son Ira.

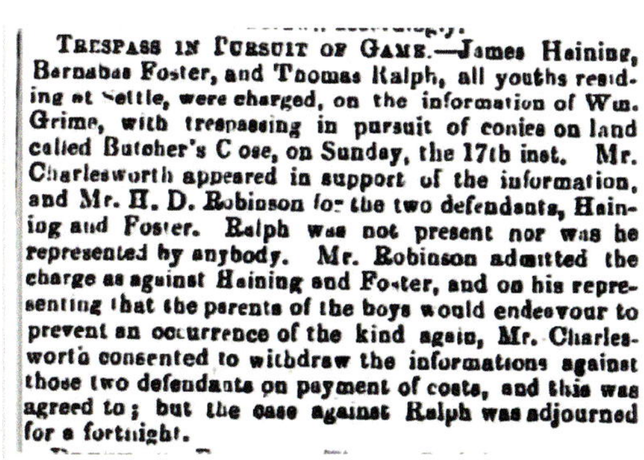

TRESPASS IN PURSUIT OF GAME.—James Haining, Barnabas Foster, and Thomas Ralph, all youths residing at Settle, were charged, on the information of Wm. Grime, with trespassing in pursuit of conies on land called Butcher's Close, on Sunday, the 17th inst. Mr. Charlesworth appeared in support of the information, and Mr. H. D. Robinson for the two defendants, Haining and Foster. Ralph was not present nor was he represented by anybody. Mr. Robinson admitted the charge as against Haining and Foster, and on his representing that the parents of the boys would endeavour to prevent an occurrence of the kind again, Mr. Charlesworth consented to withdraw the informations against those two defendants on payment of costs, and this was agreed to; but the case against Ralph was adjourned for a fortnight.

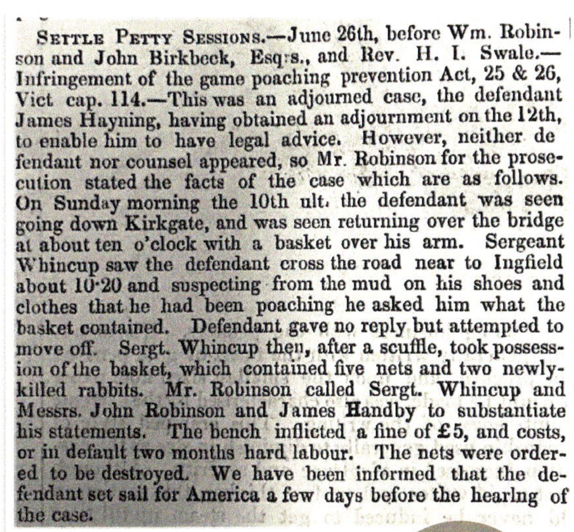

SETTLE PETTY SESSIONS.—June 26th, before Wm. Robinson and John Birkbeck, Esqrs., and Rev. H. I. Swale.—Infringement of the game poaching prevention Act, 25 & 26, Vict cap. 114.—This was an adjourned case, the defendant James Hayning, having obtained an adjournment on the 12th, to enable him to have legal advice. However, neither defendant nor counsel appeared, so Mr. Robinson for the prosecution stated the facts of the case which are as follows. On Sunday morning the 10th ult. the defendant was seen going down Kirkgate, and was seen returning over the bridge at about ten o'clock with a basket over his arm. Sergeant Whincup saw the defendant cross the road near to Ingfield about 10·20 and suspecting from the mud on his shoes and clothes that he had been poaching he asked him what the basket contained. Defendant gave no reply but attempted to move off. Sergt. Whincup then, after a scuffle, took possession of the basket, which contained five nets and two newly-killed rabbits. Mr. Robinson called Sergt. Whincup and Messrs. John Robinson and James Handby to substantiate his statements. The bench inflicted a fine of £5, and costs, or in default two months hard labour. The nets were ordered to be destroyed. We have been informed that the defendant set sail for America a few days before the hearlng of the case.

Meanwhile, back in Settle, daughter Mary Jane lived with her parents. In the late 1860s, a young labourer **John Lund** arrived in Settle from Sheffield, possibly looking for work on the Settle to Carlisle Railway. He worked as a servant to a farmer at the Folly and married Mary Jane in 1874. Soon after Mary died, Mary Jane and John (who was a distinguished looking man [*ph11*]), and their five children also left for America, to live in Ohio, the state adjacent to brother James in Indiana.

6 THE PROFESSIONALS

Most professionals could afford a decent gravestone. Most professionals in our graveyard were born elsewhere and moved to Settle for work, some marrying a local girl (of suitable class of course).

Christopher Edmundson, solicitor, the first burial in the graveyard

D9 Sacred to the memory of Christopher Edmundson, solicitor, Settle who died January 21st 1839, Aged 36 years. In the midst of life we are in death.

Christopher was born in 1802 into a wealthy farming family in the Forest of Bowland. In 1829 he married 'well' to **Sarah Watson**, a solicitor's daughter. Her family home had been the impressive fourteenth century Borwick Hall near Carnforth, Lancashire. Christopher was a solicitor in Settle and clerk to the magistrates in Sedbergh.

SUDDEN DEATH.—On Monday afternoon last, Mr. Christopher Edmondson, of Settle, solicitor, with another gentleman, was laying out a portion of ground near to his residence, for the purpose of having it converted into a garden, and when in the act of placing a peg in the ground, he fell and instantly expired. The deceased, who was clerk to the magistrates at Sedbergh, was in excellent health the moment previous to his death, and was a gentleman of the most temperate habits.

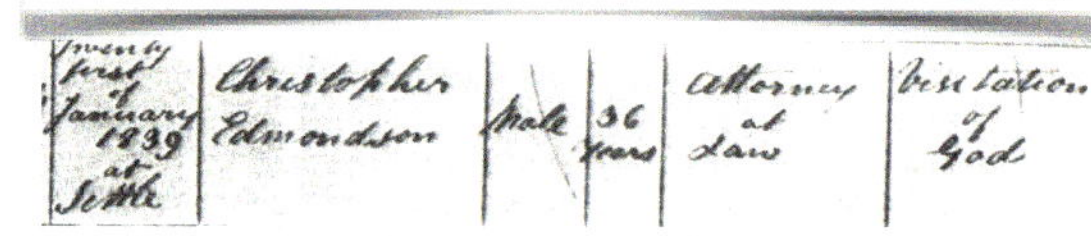
Twenty first of January 1839 at Settle | Christopher Edmondson | Male | 36 Years | Attorney at Law | Visitation of God

Christopher and Sarah had six children and lived on Church Street. In November 1838, daughter Sarah was the second baptism at the 'new' Church. Christopher suddenly died in 1839, recorded as a *'visitation of God'* [BNA16], becoming the first burial in the graveyard. Sarah stayed in Settle bringing up the children who were all successful in professional careers.

only second in elegance to that of the fair bride herself. The bride wore a tulle dress over white glacè silk, bands of silver in the hair, and an elegant lace veil covering the whole. The bridesmaids wore white embroidered grenadine, small white bonnets and blue ornaments. All the ladies carried beautiful bouquets of hot-house flowers. The *dejeuner* provided by Mrs. Wetherell, in her best style, was partaken of in a tent erected for the occasion on the lawn in front of Ivy Cottage. After breakfast, we understand the happy couple left for Venice. The numerous company after spending the day in visiting some of the romantic scenes for which our neighbourhood is famous, dined together at the Lion in the evening at the invitation of Mr. Heseltine. Amongst the company we ... and Mr

In 1858 daughter **Jane** married her first cousin **John Dawson Watson** in Giggleswick, a lavish affair [SC]. John, an unusually talented artist, specialised in watercolours and pioneered black and white line drawings for use in early newspapers before photography. John also illustrated books including The Pilgrim's Progress and Arabian Nights. He died in 1892 [BNA7].

The London correspondent of a daily contemporary says:—"The papers this morning record the death of J. D. Watson, the artist. He was a member of the Society of Painters in Water Colours, the Royal Cambrian Academy, and a frequent exhibitor in many of the principal galleries in London. But it is not for his pictures shown in recent exhibitions that he is best known, or will be longest remembered. His chief work was done years ago (he was in his sixtieth year when he died) for the *Graphic*. He was one of the group of brilliant artists who gave that paper its present importance and artistic reputation by contributing to it at the start the best black-and-white drawings that have ever been produced in England. Since he

Jane and John's children were also talented dancers and artists, the most well known being **Dawson Dawson Watson**, who was one of the first members of the Impressionist colony in Giverny, France before emigrating to the States.

Christopher's daughter **Sarah** married **John Postle Heseltine** who made his millions on the stock exchange. Three of their children were awarded Honours, with daughter Sylvia awarded an OBE for work during WW1. Others married into the aristocracy – daughter Dorothea famously helped the young Princess Elizabeth change tyres [*ph5*].

Christopher was an impressive first burial. In contrast, the second was **James Clemmy**, an illegitimate baby buried in *grave EX30*, in the infants' section.

John Hayton, a bookbinder of skill and taste

In the nineteenth century newspapers and books were still just for the rich, although Settle had a 'subscription library' if you could afford it. John was on the crest of a booming trade.

John Hayton was born in 1810 in Kendal. He served his apprenticeship in bookbinding with **John Wildman** in Settle. In 1845 he married the young **Ann Armistead Duckett** born in 1821. Ann was the daughter of Charles Duckett, who ran the beer house at the King William IV Hotel on High Street. They lived in Chapel Square, just opposite Ann's parents' beerhouse. Ann had six children in quite rapid succession and died at the birth of her seventh, little Isabella who also died shortly after.

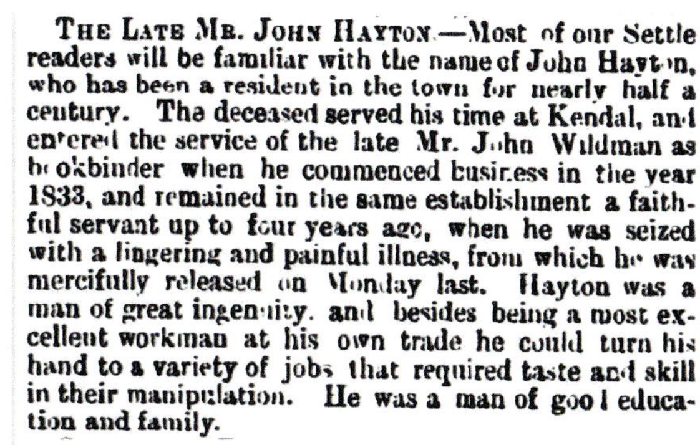

THE LATE MR. JOHN HAYTON.—Most of our Settle readers will be familiar with the name of John Hayton, who has been a resident in the town for nearly half a century. The deceased served his time at Kendal, and entered the service of the late Mr. John Wildman as bookbinder when he commenced business in the year 1833, and remained in the same establishment a faithful servant up to four years ago, when he was seized with a lingering and painful illness, from which he was mercifully released on Monday last. Hayton was a man of great ingenuity, and besides being a most excellent workman at his own trade he could turn his hand to a variety of jobs that required taste and skill in their manipulation. He was a man of good education and family.

John and the children stayed in the same house until his death after a long illness, aged 68. His obituary describes a good man [*BNA7*].

B8 In memory of Ann Armistead Hayton wife of John Hayton, died March 4th 1859, aged 37 years. Also to the above John Hayton died May 27th 1878 aged 68 years. Jane Hayton, daughter of the above, died July 17th 1852 aged 2 years and 4 months. Isabella Hayton daughter of the above died June 5th 1859 aged 14 weeks. Thomas Hayton, son of the above, died Feby 13th 1872 aged 26 years. Henry Hayton son of the above died May 27th 1897 aged 40 years.

Son Henry had been apprenticed to tailor John Snell, on the corner opposite the Folly and then worked as a tailor in Barrow-in-Furness. Henry's eyesight failed so that he couldn't work and he returned to Settle where his brother William, a plumber, and sister Annie were still living. Tragically, Henry ended his own life in 1897 by hanging in an outhouse of the Royal Oak. This was the fifth suicide in the area over the past year. The newspaper report (of poor quality) read:

'The deceased was found hanging from a beam in an outhouse adjoining the Royal Oak Hotel on the previous evening. William Hayton, plumber said the deceased was his brother. He said prior to coming to Settle he had been staying at Liverpool and had been out of work for 15 weeks . His eyesight had failed, so that he could not follow his trade, and he had come to the place where he was bred and hoped to end his days here. He seemed very depressed. . . The jury returned a verdict of 'suicide by hanging whilst in an unsound state of mind'. This is the fifth suicide which has been committed in this district within a comparatively short period of time.'

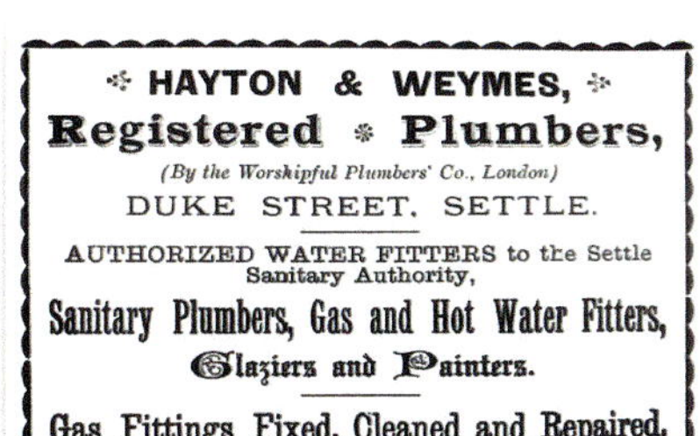

Henry is buried alone in unmarked *Old grave CX48*. Son William became a plumber, advertising in the *Settle almanac,* and later going into business with George Robert Weymes [*farmers, LSA, ph7*]. William took an apprentice, Edward Percy, who later took over his business. William's wife was Louisa Clarke, the daughter of Thomas and Thirza, the successful grocers, buried in *Old grave 003.*

John's daughter Ann was a housekeeper and boarding house keeper in Settle for several medic lodgers such as Oliver Scattergood, the son-in-law of John Lister [*wealthy ones*], James Edgar and Balfour Hyslop.

John Armitstead, rags to riches

D4 In memory of Mary, daughter of William and Isabella Armitstead of Settle who died June 16th 1839 aged 12 years. Also of Elizabeth their daughter who died June 26th 1847 aged 21 years.

William Armitstead and his wife **Isabella Robinson** married in 1824. They lived at Halton Gill and had four children, **Jane**, **John**, **Mary** and **Elizabeth**. William and Isabella both died in the 1830s leaving the four young children orphaned. Isabella's dad, **John Robinson** worked in Settle as an agricultural labourer, living on Constitution Hill, and he brought up the children.

Son **John Armitstead**, born in 1831, was educated at Giggleswick School, probably taking advantage of the endowment scheme. Sisters Mary and Elizabeth died in their early years and are buried in this grave. John Robinson died in the 1840s leaving sister Jane housekeeping for John who worked as a solicitor's clerk. Jane married **William Bell**, a Scottish linen draper who worked in Skipton. 18 months after the wedding, upon the birth of her second child, (yes, do the maths!) Jane died. William remarried and moved to Darlington.

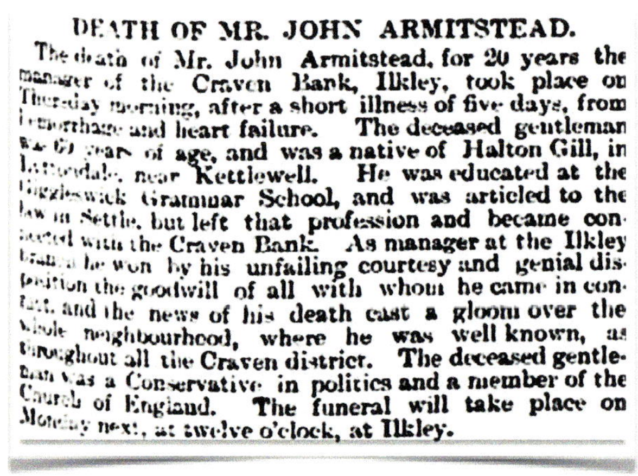

DEATH OF MR. JOHN ARMITSTEAD.

The death of Mr. John Armitstead, for 20 years the manager of the Craven Bank, Ilkley, took place on Thursday morning, after a short illness of five days, from [illegible] and heart failure. The deceased gentleman was 60 years of age, and was a native of Halton Gill, in Littondale, near Kettlewell. He was educated at the Giggleswick Grammar School, and was articled to the law in Settle, but left that profession and became connected with the Craven Bank. As manager at the Ilkley branch he won by his unfailing courtesy and genial disposition the goodwill of all with whom he came in contact, and the news of his death cast a gloom over the whole neighbourhood, where he was well known, as throughout all the Craven district. The deceased gentleman was a Conservative in politics and a member of the Church of England. The funeral will take place on Monday next, at twelve o'clock, at Ilkley.

In the meantime brother John found work in the Craven Bank, also in Skipton. John became a director of the Ben Rhydding Hydropathic Establishment which provided leisure facilities for 160 residential visitors wishing to use spa waters. John was promoted to Bank Manager of the Craven Bank in Ilkley where he served for another 20 years before he died in 1891 [*BNA13*]. Well done John.

The Shepherd family of chemists

William Shepherd, born in 1825 in Horton-in-Ribblesdale, was the son of **Richard Shepherd**, a farmer. By 1841 William had moved to Giggleswick and was apprenticed to druggist and grocer **John Hayhurst** in Settle Town Hall. William may have encouraged his dad to move this way; in the 1851 census he was found as the innkeeper at the Hart's Head in Giggleswick.

Meanwhile William [*ph2*] married **Mary Slinger**, also from Horton and they had eight daughters and two sons. They lived on Church Street and then in the larger houses at The Terrace on Duke Street. William established his chemist and druggist business in Settle on the site of Boots' Chemist [*LSA*]. After William died in 1871 aged just 46, his apprentice **William Walker** continued the business until son **John William** qualified as a pharmacist in 1880. William Walker married **Emily Towler** [*church folk*], and had a son William Towler Walker, also a chemist. His descendants ensured that Shepherd and Walker was a successful business, trading until 1978.

MESMERISM.—On Friday Evening, March 30th, Mr. Wm. Shepherd delivered a very interesting Lecture on this subject, to the Members of the Settle Mechanics' Institute. He had a good subject for his practical illustrations He put him in the somnolent condition in 2 minutes, and catalepsed his arm and leg. He was not quite successful in some experiments. A Public Room is not a favourable place for a first appearance. We witnessed a private exhibition before the Lecture, in which the experiments were decidedly successful. However in the Room he put his subject into the mesmeric state, the Lecturer being out-side the door. There were upwards of 40 Members present who were all highly gratified by the evenings instruction and amusement. We hope Mr. Shepherd may be induced to bring the subject before the people, as well as the Members of the Institute.

In the 1850s William Shepherd was a Director of Settle Gas Company. He gave a lecture 'Mesmerism' (hypnotism) [*SC*] in 1855. William became a churchwarden in 1870, but died a year later. William's gravestone is amidst those of the most wealthy. Out of the ten children, three died in childhood and are buried with William and Mary. Daughter Edith died just a week after her dad, aged 4.

Sons Ernest and John William went to Giggleswick School. Ernest, a doctor, died in Bloemfontein unmarried aged 27, after being advised to go there on account of his health [*LSA*].

24. Death of Mr. Ernest Shepherd (youngest son of the late William Shepherd, The Terrace, Settle), at Bloemfontein, Orange Free State. He had been advised, on account of his health, to go to the Cape.

E22 In memory of William Shepherd of Settle, who died February 5th 1871 aged 46 years. Also Mary Shepherd, who died 27th April 1915 aged 87 years. Also children of the above, Elizabeth Eleanor Shepherd who died January 24th 1863, aged 5 years. Francis Slinger Shepherd who died February 4th 1863 aged 11 days. Edith Alice Slinger Shepherd who died February 13th 1871 aged 4 years. Ernest Shepherd who died at Bloemfontein January 24th 1897 aged 26 years.

Remaining son John William was the only one of the ten children to marry and he married twice with just one son, William who went into banking. John William was a JP, and a fellow of the meteorological society. He became a churchwarden at Holy Ascension in 1918, replacing John Handby [*tradesmen*] and was also a bellringer. John was the Chair of Settle Gas Works in 1906 [*ph6*] and vice president of the cricket club in 1912.

William Shepherd left money to daughters Clara Jane and Helena Frances who used it to set up a school in Devon and then retired together to Gloucestershire. John William and the remaining sisters lived extraordinarily long lives, all surviving to their 80s or 90s, seeing out their last years together in Helwith Bridge. John William and both his wives are buried in *Old grave C76*.

...JT...

William Lodge Paley, a schoolmaster and top diarist

Education was a privilege for the wealthy until the Church of England started National Schools to provide a basic education and promote good morals, and William was a schoolmaster at Giggleswick National School. Settle's National School was built on the site of Victoria Hall before moving to Upper Settle in 1853. Giggleswick Grammar School provided for those who could afford it but also for a proportion of the poor, funded by endowments.

E5 Here lie the remains of W L Paley who was Master of the National School Giggleswick for 27 years. He was born at Walden, Wensleydale on 13th Jany 1785, died at Settle Novr 16th 1847, aged 62 years 11 months

William's gravestone inscription gives little hint of the life of this rather eccentric man. William's diaries were found and transcribed by Dr Charles William Buck in the early 20th century and paint a fascinating picture of Settle life in the early 1800s [*ph4*]. It seems that

A VILLAGE "PEPYS" AT GIGGLESWICK OVER 100 YEARS AGO.

(BY C. W. BUCK, SETTLE.)

[Copyright Reserved.]

William Lodge Paley was born at Walden, Wensleydale, Jan 13th, 1785, and commenced teaching at Lodge, 1803, afterwards at Long Preston, and ultimately at Giggleswick National School 1812. He resigned in 1839 and set up at Settle as a bookseller in his private house, but returned to Giggleswick 1844 and died at Settle, 1847.

His tombstone is behind Settle Church (belfry end). He was not a very efficient teacher, and ludicrous stories were told of him. He left a voluminous Diary extending over many years and which is still in existence.

The boys nick-named him "Old Putty Legs," as he wore drab kerseymere small clothes, stockings, shoes with buckles, and a swallow-tailed blue coat with brass buttons.

He smoked a long clay pipe which he sucked long and loudly; wore a wig made by Sylvester Cork, of Settle, and was always very particular how he took off his hat in Church. He went to Skipton to study Dr. Bell's improved system of education (with sand trays), which he introduced at Giggleswick in 1814.

As our diarist died in 1847, very few people now alive will remember him but I have heard him described as a shy, serious simple-minded man. He acted as the local bookseller and accountant, preserving a copy of all his letters and business transactions.

William, born in 1785, was not a good teacher, *'the boys nick-named him Old Putty Legs'*, and later he turned to selling books, travelling all around the region on foot; Halton Gill and back in a day was quite common. He didn't marry and lived as a lodger, mostly at the Black Horse in Giggleswick. His diaries have frequent complaints about fellow guests, especially when he was forced to share a room with them. In no particular order:

Aug 19 - Took supper with 10 tanners and shoemakers from near Ulverstone who had come for the Settle leather fair. Mr Waller had only 6 of them staying so that I got to sleep in my own bed.

Jul 15 - Drank sea water which acted well *(for constipation)* - Coronation of George IV. Joined procession in Dalton Square where "God Save the King" was sung by children and the Corporation Band. Proceeded to the Market Place but the crowd was so immense could never see 1/2 of it, nor can I describe it. Bid all farewell and walked to Hornby Castle Inn but was much annoyed with the noise of drunken people and was awoke before daylight by awful storm and lightning. Was not so much afraid as I sometimes am.

Feb 26 - the remains of Rev W Peart were interred with great pomp - Pall and supporters. The body in 3 coffins *(?)* upon a bier from Gisburn made for the late Lord Ribblesdale. No ladies in the procession.

June 1 - Took down a list of about 90 scholars who have not had the small or cow pox; think they will be inoculated by subscription *(donations from the wealthy)*. Mrs Bolland desired me to call on Dr Rogers to remunerate him.

June 9 - Went to Settle Fair after 3, was chiefly with Mr Broader who is nervous with smell of Small Pox as he is not certain he ever had *(it)* so intends being inoculated tomorrow. Hope he will be preserved from having them naturally as he is very fat and it might be dangerous.

Aug. 17—Mob stopped weaving at Gargrave but were not allowed to enter Skipton. Mr. Garforth much hurt about head with stones. The magistrates met and swore in 250 special constables. Saw John and Stephen Green who had been turned out of Gargrave Mill.

Aug. 20—J. Charnley told me the mob stopt coach in Burnley, till soldiers beat them off.

Aug 17 - Mob stopped weaving at Gargrave but were not allowed to enter Skipton. Mr Garforth much hurt about head with stones. The magistrates met and swore in 250 special constables. Saw John and Stephen Green who had been turned out of Gargrave Mill. *(The Luddite riots were protests against mechanisation in mills.)*

Aug 20 - J Charnley told me the mob stopt coach in Burnley, till soldiers beat them off.

Sept 7 - Was surprised we had 91 scholars at Sunday school.

July 18 - Attended church twice and had an unpleasant altercation with *(scholar)* H Ingham after and thought myself obliged to whip him which his rebellion increased manyfold.

March 13 - A fox hunt and much intoxication in the neighbourhood – sad proof of depravity.

Sept 22 - Heard *(Rev'd)* Ingram and Thompson at G'k Church and Henley in Meth Ch at night. I liked him better than the first time.

March 12 - Taught all day to prevent the scholars attending the cock fight, on the sinfulness of the practice and our weak natures. Was sorry some of them did from perversity. Was disturbed in bed by a rat and the noise 11 soldiers and 2 women made.

Sep 27 - Pain very bad and met Dr Robinson on the road about having a tooth drawn. I had an instinctive fear of the operation. He could clearly see the farthest tooth was bad and it was painful as he had to go in my mouth so often. There was a hole down the middle and it bled till I went to bed, but I enjoyed a good night's repose.

Arthur Brewin, assistant master at Giggleswick School

E25 Frank and Guy twin sons of Arthur and (Mary) Brewin, . . buried 10 August 1874 IHS. *[IHS - the first three letters in the Greek name for Jesus.]*

Frank and Guy Brewin were the twin sons of **Arthur Brewin**, a Middlesex gardener's son and his wife **Mary Mossop**, the daughter of Moses Mossop, a landed proprietor from St Bees, Cumbria. They came to Giggleswick straight after marrying in 1861 and lived at Bankwell. Arthur worked as an assistant master at Giggleswick School for 35 years. This was a privileged position and he was able to give his four other sons a good education.

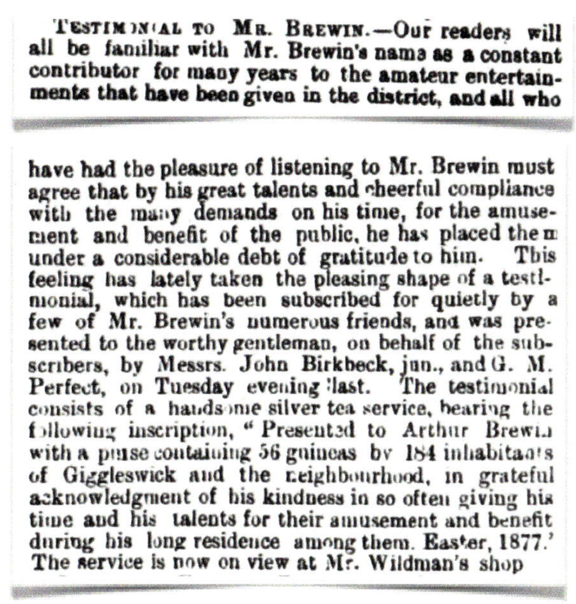

TESTIMONIAL TO MR. BREWIN.—Our readers will all be familiar with Mr. Brewin's name as a constant contributor for many years to the amateur entertainments that have been given in the district, and all who have had the pleasure of listening to Mr. Brewin must agree that by his great talents and cheerful compliance with the many demands on his time, for the amusement and benefit of the public, he has placed them under a considerable debt of gratitude to him. This feeling has lately taken the pleasing shape of a testimonial, which has been subscribed for quietly by a few of Mr. Brewin's numerous friends, and was presented to the worthy gentleman, on behalf of the subscribers, by Messrs. John Birkbeck, jun., and G. M. Perfect, on Tuesday evening last. The testimonial consists of a handsome silver tea service, bearing the following inscription, "Presented to Arthur Brewin with a purse containing 56 guineas by 184 inhabitants of Giggleswick and the neighbourhood, in grateful acknowledgment of his kindness in so often giving his time and his talents for their amusement and benefit during his long residence among them. Easter, 1877.' The service is now on view at Mr. Wildman's shop

In 1877, Arthur was presented with a tea service and a purse containing 56 guineas as a thank you for his generosity and amusing entertainment over the years, often in a double act with George Stansfeld (Jnr) [*wealthy ones, BNA7, CH*].

Arthur was a choirmaster at Holy Ascension Church. Vestry records of 1893 tell us *'the Church choir, assisted by a number of ladies attended the Northern Diocese Choral Festival in York Minster. The bellringers had gone to Scarborough for their outing. In particular thanks to Mr Brewin without whose careful training such excellent results could not be attained.'*

Arthur retired to the southern Lake District. Arthur's surviving sons were well educated at Oxford and moved in high circles, as did his daughter. Son Clement became a vicar, with a stint at Long Preston. The other sons became military officers and lived all around the world. Daughter Helena Margaret became a military nurse and settled in South Africa. Not bad for a gardener's son.

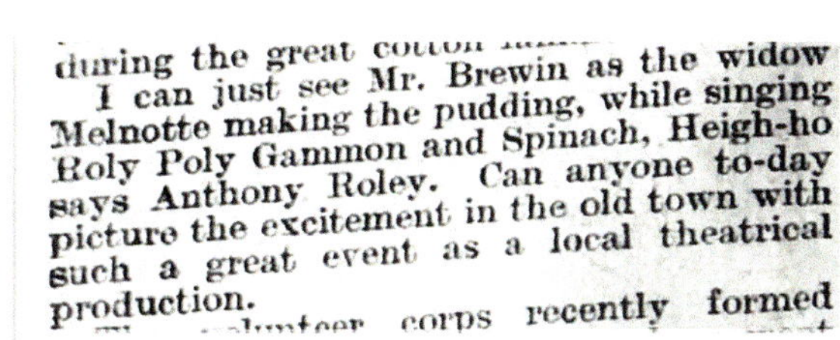

during the great cotton
I can just see Mr. Brewin as the widow
Melnotte making the pudding, while singing
Roly Poly Gammon and Spinach, Heigh-ho
says Anthony Roley. Can anyone to-day
picture the excitement in the old town with
such a great event as a local theatrical
production.
corps recently formed

7 THE INNKEEPERS

The decision to build the church was made in a meeting at the Golden Lion on Duke Street in 1835. Since then, numerous innkeepers have found their final resting place in the graveyard, usually affording a gravestone.

Everything happened at the inns – news and gossip, auctions and inquests and even a place to hold prisoners or store dead bodies. They were usually run by and for men, although this was an acceptable and popular job for a married couple or a widow. Several innkeepers worked at the inns for decades, occasionally transferring from one to another. In nineteenth century Settle there were at least nine inns, plus beer houses and spirit merchants – which would you have frequented?

NI - New Inn on what was then New Road, now Station Road

JA - Joiner's Arms, later Commercial (Temperance) Inn

GL - Golden Lion, as now, previously on Cheapside

SE - Spread Eagle Inn on Kirkgate

CV - Crown Inn/Vaults

ONM, RO -(Old) Naked Man and Royal Oak, as now

WH - White Horse

OBB - Obadiah Bayne's Beerhouse - the tiny house in the row

TA - Talbot Arms, as now

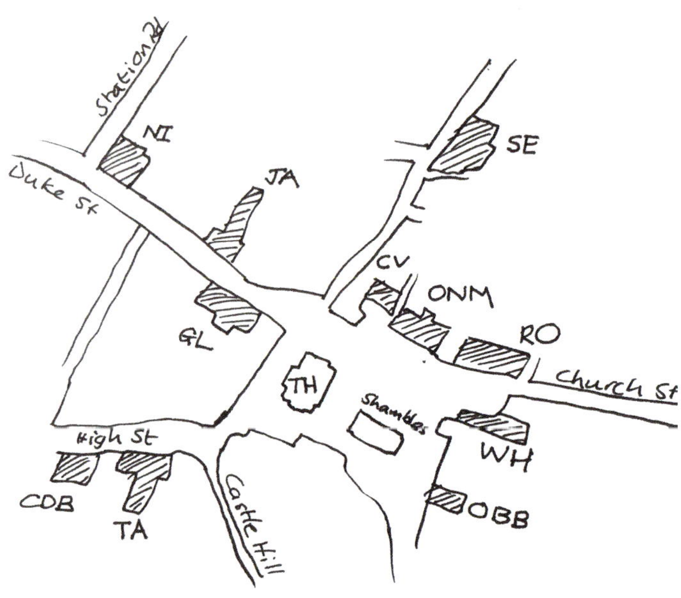

CDB - Charles Duckett's beerhouse, now the King William guesthouse.

Obadiah Baynes and his beerhouse

The wonderfully named **Obadiah Baynes** rented his beerhouse from Elizabeth Banks, the widow of another wonderfully named man, Columbus Banks. Before 1818, Columbus had used the building as a tallow chandler's shop [*BNA7*].

> TO LET,
> *And enter upon immediately,*
> A TALLOW-CHANDLER'S SHOP, situated in Settle, Yorkshire, and late in the possession of Columbus Banks, deceased.
> The Stock-in-Trade and all the Utensils of the above business may be taken at a fair valuation.
> *§* Particulars may be had by applying to ELIZABETH BANKS, widow and administratrix of the deceased, on the premises.

Obadiah, baptised in 1803 in Giggleswick, married the much younger **Mary Gifford** and they ran the beerhouse for the rest of their lives. Their infant son Robert died in 1844, but daughter Alice survived.

> FALSE ALARM.—On Thursday Evening, Feb. 22nd, Mr. and Mrs. O. Baines were dreadfully alarmed about half-past eleven o'clock, by a supposed attempt to break into their house. They called up both Mr. Cockshott, and Mr. Wilkinson, saying people were breaking into the house and had taken the window out. William of Austwick notoriety was not however, to be disturbed by attempts, he quietly continued his rest. On an investigation being made, it turned out that Obadiah's dog being locked out, had made forcible entry through the window.

Obadiah had a couple of meetings with local PC Cockshott who had a reputation of being quite officious. In the 'opening during the hours of divine service' case in 1853, Obadiah's customers were very loyal and he was let off [*BNA7, SC*]. His defence lawyer was Henry Robinson [*wenches, wives*].

BEERHOUSE CASE.—Mr. Obadiah Baynes, beer-seller, Settle, appeared to answer a charge of keeping his house open during the hours of divine service on Sunday the 9th inst., for the reception of persons not travellers, and another charge of refusing to admit the constable at the same time. The former charge was taken first. Mr. Cockshott, the superintending constable stated on oath, that on the evening of the above named Sunday he went to the defendant's house and found the door fast; that he knocked and kicked at the door for the space of 8 minutes before gaining admittance, and then found 4 persons in the house. Mr. H. Robinson, the as to whether there was any case which required an answer. The Bench intimated a wish that the defendant's witnesses should be examined and Mr. Robinson accordingly called 3 of the 4 persons above alluded to, all of whom positively stated that defendant's wife went to open the door immediately they heard the knocking, and that the defendant kept a very orderly house, no drink having been drawn after the bell ringing for church. This like the previous charge was dismissed.

Obadiah and Mary's only daughter **Alice** married **Thomas Taylor**, an agricultural labourer from Litton. Perhaps inspired by an advert like this [SC], Thomas became one of the fleet of Dales farmers to move to Liverpool as Cowmen, to supply the expanding city with milk. Alice had 12 children.

A CAPITAL LIVING FOR A FAMILY FOR £350, NEAR LIVERPOOL.

TO BE SOLD

A

MILK HOUSE,

With 9 Cows, Pony, Shandry, Cans, and all complete, with a connection established 12 years, in the best part of the north end of Liverpool.

Apply, without delay, for full particulars to Mr JOHN BATTERSBY, Duke Street, Settle; or to Mr BROWNE-CAVE, Farm Stock Auctioneer and Valuer, Bootle Village, near Liverpool.

B10 In remembrance of Obadiah Baynes of Settle who died Jany 5th 1870 aged 66 years. Also Mary wife of the above who died Feby 21st 1873 (aged) 53 years... their son Robert who died in infancy.

The Calverts, "Terror of Settle Tradesmen", (Old) Naked Man [D]

Henry Calvert was one of five sons of Settle butcher, **William Calvert**, who worked in the Shambles with his wife **Margaret Hornby**. There are several reports of the Calverts' fine butchery [SC,CH]. They owned land by Watery Lane and several properties on Kirkgate, and also the **Old Naked Man**. They lived in the cottage on the Market Place corner next to the **Crown Inn**, (now part of Boots) and Henry's brothers, John and Robert [ph15], both butchers stayed in this cottage until they died. Next door were **Joseph** and **Susannah Forrester** and their daughter Susannah, who Henry married in 1865.

FAT COW.—On Monday, February 9th, the celebrated Cow RUTH, the property of Wm. Carr, Esq. of Stackhouse, was killed by Mr. Calvert, in the Shambles. She weighed the enormous weight of 58 Score, her Hide weighed 75 lbs., and she yielded 11 Stones of Fat.

Above, beneath the arches, were the butcher's shops, kept by Robert and John Calvert, John Wilman, George Beardall, etc., where, at that period, the animals were slaughtered, and the meat sold in the same room. In those days, regulations for the safeguarding of the public well-being were conspicuous by their absence, but we got along very well without them, and

HENRY CALVERT,
AUCTIONEER & APPRAISER,
NAKED MAN INN, SETTLE.
A large room adjoining the Inn, for the convenience of parties wishing to remove Furniture &c. for sale.

They had three children, **Margery**, **William** and **Margery Susannah** whilst running the Old Naked Man, with daughter Margery dying when she was just three - allegedly from meningitis after a fall from Castleberg Rock. Henry died of cirrhosis of the liver aged 53...not uncommon for innkeepers.

C19 In loving memory of Henry Calvert of Settle born Feb 14th 1827, died July 14th 1880 and of Susannah Harwood born March 10th 1839 died April 25th 1915

Widow Susannah took over Henry's business in style, investing in lands, businesses and properties in Ingleton and Settle. She sold land to the railway companies. She was a shrewd business woman, leaving the equivalent of £1 million to son William when she

died. Susannah would turn in her grave if she knew that William managed to fritter most of it away during his lifetime. Susannah reacted to Henry's death by running the Old Naked Man [*LSA*] with a 'rod of iron', not allowing any drunkenness, earning her reputation as the '*Terror of Settle Tradesmen'*. She sent son William to Giggleswick School and he went on to study pharmacy in Edinburgh and London. She also insisted that he become teetotal and sign the Temperance pledge.

In 1887 Susannah met and married a man brave enough to take her on – railway inspector **John Harwood**, a widower from Nottingham. John was in Settle organising work for the Settle to Carlisle Railway. Because of his work they moved frequently, but spent several years in Carlisle.

Susannah's daughter Margery Susannah died of scarlet fever, aged 20, in Carlisle. Descendants say that husband John didn't tell Susannah about Margery's illness until it was too late and she was so angry that she left him. This is borne out by John's obituary in the paper in 1898; he had moved to Sheffield to live with his two spinster daughters and left his whole estate to them, with no reference to Susannah [*BNA17*]. Margery Susannah's body was brought back to Settle for burial, *Old grave C15*. Henry Calvert's brothers Robert and John are buried next to Margery Susannah in *Old grave CX16*.

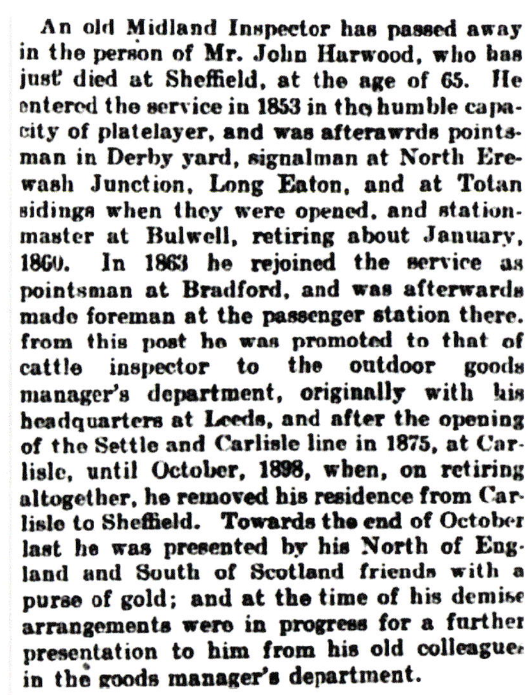
An old Midland Inspector has passed away in the person of Mr. John Harwood, who has just died at Sheffield, at the age of 65. He entered the service in 1853 in the humble capacity of platelayer, and was afterawrds pointsman in Derby yard, signalman at North Erewash Junction, Long Eaton, and at Totan sidings when they were opened, and stationmaster at Bulwell, retiring about January, 1860. In 1863 he rejoined the service as pointsman at Bradford, and was afterwards made foreman at the passenger station there. from this post he was promoted to that of cattle inspector to the outdoor goods manager's department, originally with his headquarters at Leeds, and after the opening of the Settle and Carlisle line in 1875, at Carlisle, until October, 1898, when, on retiring altogether, he removed his residence from Carlisle to Sheffield. Towards the end of October last he was presented by his North of England and South of Scotland friends with a purse of gold; and at the time of his demise arrangements were in progress for a further presentation to him from his old colleagues in the goods manager's department.

Susannah retired in Settle, back in the original cottage, helping to bring up her grandchildren. Son William and wife Mary Matilda settled at number 3, The Terrace with their six daughters and one son. William worked as a druggist and pharmacist in a small shop at the top of Kirkgate, backing onto their cottage [*LSA*]. In 1908, Mary Matilda donated funds for the building of the Methodist church on Duke Street, now a free church. She is remembered with a foundation stone.

Susannah is buried with Henry, almost next to her parents **Joseph and Susannah Forrester** in *grave C24*. Joseph was a 'stationer' who sold paper goods in and around the Craven district. The detail of the inscription is now lost but the grave contains Joseph and Susannah, Henry's eldest daughter Margery, aged three, and a granddaughter Mary Ann Forrester, who was aged 10. Two other grandchildren named Forrester are in *grave BX13*.

William Towler, his rather attractive governess and the White Horse

William Towler was born in 1829, a Rathmell farmer's son. His elder brother John was a self-proclaimed Professor of Languages who travelled Europe and the States, had three marriages (including two at the same time in different continents) and numerous children.

In 1854 William was a coin dealer at Hollin Hall, near Rathmell and married **Alice Holden,** the daughter of a farmer and land owner. Alice gave him six children, but little Mary died at one day old. In 1856, William took over the licence of the **White Horse** from William Cork. By 1864 William had moved into Rock House on Castle Hill and worked as a corn merchant storing grain in the barn next door. He must have done well - William could afford to educate his sons at Giggleswick School. Alice died in 1864, at the birth of their daughter Emily Alice, who also died, so in the 1871 census William was a widower with three sons and a daughter, helped by a young Scottish governess **Elizabeth Manson**.

Now you know how these things sometimes work – by the next census, William was still a corn merchant at Rock House, but had a further three sons with his new wife Elizabeth, the governess. William died in 1887 after fathering yet another son. He is buried in Settle churchyard with his first wife Alice and the two daughters who died in infancy.

E23 In remembrance of Alice, wife of William Towler, Rock House, Settle who died Decr 23rd 1864, aged 32 years. Also 2 of their children Mary Towler died June 30th 1857 aged 1 day. Emily Alice Towler died August 5th 1864 aged 6 months. Also of the above William Towler who died... April 1887 aged 59 years

William left a sizeable estate which may explain how the family could afford the grand gravestone amidst the other wealthy folk. The estate is likely to have gone to William's children, leaving widow Elizabeth with relatively little. Elizabeth took her remaining sons to Lancashire where she made a living as a music teacher. A daughter **Jessie Elizabeth Manson** lived with them – she was born in Stockport 18 months before Elizabeth married William and was brought up by a couple in Stockport (probably to avoid gossip in Settle).

In 1880 William and Alice's eldest son, **Joseph Towler** had a bit of a lucky escape [*BNA7*]. He used his expensive education to be landlord of the **Hart's Head** in Giggleswick. He was described as an 'Innkeeper and coindealer' and advertised in *The Ribble-land*. Later he became a hotel manager in Leeds.

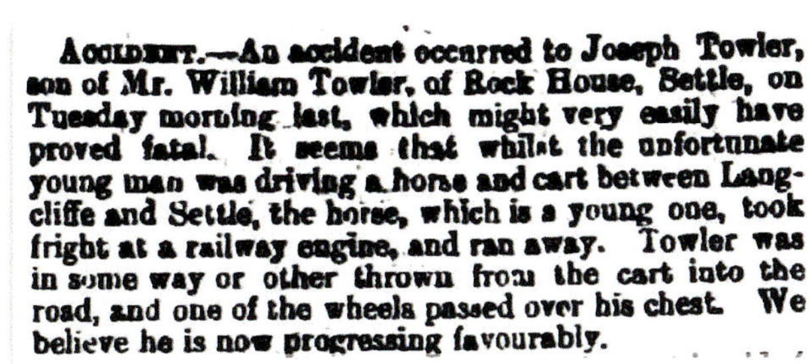

ACCIDENT.—An accident occurred to Joseph Towler, son of Mr. William Towler, of Rock House, Settle, on Tuesday morning last, which might very easily have proved fatal. It seems that whilst the unfortunate young man was driving a horse and cart between Langcliffe and Settle, the horse, which is a young one, took fright at a railway engine, and ran away. Towler was in some way or other thrown from the cart into the road, and one of the wheels passed over his chest. We believe he is now progressing favourably.

William's second son, **Charles Edward Towler** tried his hand at several jobs including a draper and an auctioneer/innkeeper at the Craven Inn [*LSA*]. He lived at **The Talbot** before marrying **Mary Hodgson**, the landlord's daughter. In 1896 he went bankrupt, so left for Morecambe which appears to have been a destination for several of Settle's bankrupts.

William's third son was **Edwin Holden Towler,** who took over the corn business for a short while. Edwin married **Annie Huthersall,** whose

CHAS. E. TOWLER,
Hosier and Draper,
DUKE STREET, SETTLE.
ORDERS PROMPTLY ATTENDED TO.

parents had also previously run **The Talbot**. They had a son William Edwin who died in infancy, two daughters who became governesses and a further son, **Edwin Holden Towler** (Jnr). Unfortunately, both Edwin (Snr) and Annie died in their mid 30s and are buried with infant William Edwin in the *Old grave A74*, next to Annie's parents. Young Edwin married and worked as a clerk in Doncaster.

The Ayrtons, innkeepers for over 30 years, New Inn, Royal Oak

Henry Ayrton was born in 1808 near Kirkby Lonsdale. Henry, a widower, married **Mary Marsden** from Long Preston in 1840 and they started their family of seven children. Henry had a partnership with **John King**, renting the **New Inn**, grounds and outbuildings and 15 acres of land from the Birkbecks. Henry ran the carrier service while John ran the inn. In 1848, Henry took over the **Royal Oak** from **Joseph Harger** [*tradesmen*] and was the innkeeper until he died after a long illness aged 59 [*BNA18*]. Henry generously supported the Cricket Club in 1846 [*BNA7*].

SETTLE—CRICKET MATCH.—On Thursday, the 3d inst., a grand cricket match was played between the members of the Settle Cricket Club, and those of Gargrave. The wickets were laid at 10 o'clock in the morning, and after a severe struggle on both sides, till seven in the evening, for the honors of victory, the knights of Gargrave were proclaimed conquerors. After the fatigue of the day, the members of each club spent the evening joyously at Mr. Henry Ayrton's, New Inn, Settle, where an excellent supper was prepared and served up in the first order. Every guest seemed to manifest the greatest satisfaction with the evening's entertainment. The members of the Settle Club (much to their credit) by the good feeling shewn towards their opponents, almost convinced them that—
" The pleasure is as great
In being beaten as to beat."

On the 7th inst., after a long illness, aged 59 years, Mr Henry Ayrton, innkeeper, Settle.

B26 In memory of Henry Ayrton of Settle who died October 7th 1857 aged 49 years. Also Henry Ayrton, son of the above who died September 27th 1852 aged 4 years, 8 months and 27 days. Also and an infant. Also of Mary Ayrton, wife of the above who died Jany 20th 1882 aged 76 years. (gravestone now well hidden behind the tree)

After Henry's death, widow Mary continued to run the **Royal Oak** for a further 25 years. She did a good job according to this report from 1860 [*BNA7*]. Mary's daughter Elizabeth, who was born before Mary's marriage to Henry, moved in with the family. Henry and Mary are buried with their five year old son Henry, and infant daughter Ann who died in April 1844. Daughter Margaret, aged 14, may also be with them. Henry's daughter **Elizabeth** became the third wife of Joseph Parker [*farmers*] of Lodge Farm.

THE U. O. OF MECHANICS.—On Whit-Wednesday, the United Order of Mechanics held their 9th anniversary. The members, to the number of 76, headed by the Rathmell brass band, walked in procession from the Royal Oak to church, where a most impressive sermon was preached to them by the Rev. W. F. Pierson. At the conclusion of divine service the whole of the members, including some few friends, adjourned to the Royal Oak, where a very sumptuous dinner was provided by the worthy hostess, Mrs. Ayrton, in her usual style, and to which, we need scarcely say, ample justice was done. After the removal of the cloth, the

Henry Ayrton's son **John Ayrton** is buried next to him in *grave B25*. John married **Alice Batty**, daughter of Thomas and Alice Batty who are buried in the next *grave B24*. (The **Royal Oak** and **Crown Hotel** were run by other members of the Batty family during the 1880s.) John and Alice ran the **Craven Arms** (on the A65 at Giggleswick) for three years, until he died in 1872, aged just 31. John is buried with their infant son, Henry, also with a gravestone hidden behind a tree. After John died, **Alice** became the second wife of **Joseph Parker,** until she died in childbirth. Yes that's right – two Ayrton women that married the same Joseph Parker. Settle is a small place.

B25 In memory of John Ayrton of Settle who died December 25th 1872 aged 31 years. Also Henry son of John and Alice Ayrton who died February 2nd 1873 aged 6 months.

John Johnson Waller at The Black Horse in Giggleswick

June 17.—J. Waller, junr., was thrown by a horse and split a shoulder bone—he had cans in his hand—Wm. behind him was unhurt.

back. Wm. Waller died of a ruptured blood vessel in his head, wh: the doctors had wanted to operate on.

April 18.—John Waller jr. set off early with his wife and yng'st son Fran's to Leeds; she is going to the Eye Infirmary in London, by recommendation of Dr. R. Paley to get the child's eyes cut, in hopes to get it sight. She seemed down, but having an uncle in Town she will not be so lonely.—Was shocked to

the Coronation.
July 26.—Jane Waller and child returned from London and the latter has got to see surprizingly. They have benn 14 weeks away.
[illegible] of turf for school

John Johnson Waller was born at The **Black Horse** and baptised in June 1816, the first of at least 12 children of **John Waller** and his two wives, both called Jane. The survival rate in this family was appalling – at least six died in infancy or childhood.

Resident diarist William Lodge Paley [*professionals*] recorded that John split a shoulder bone after being thrown from a horse in June 1828. John's brother William died of a ruptured blood vessel in his head six months later. The diaries suggest that young William was quite a naughty boy. John's brother Francis spent 14 weeks at the Eye Infirmary in London to have his 'eyes cut' and it worked, 'surprizingly'! Sadly Francis died aged 15.

John's dad (and granddad, both called John) were the landlords of the Black Horse Inn in Giggleswick. It was a thriving inn and William Lodge Paley frequently commented on Mr Waller and the way he dealt with boarders: *'Sep 24 - had 17 soldiers and 3 women at Mr Waller's last night, being part of the detachment of the North Lincoln Militia on their march to that city to be discharged'*, and *'Apr 21 - Got my half year's salary and paid Waller for board, who grumbled about my using candles in the parlour so often'*. William was only paid his salary twice a year, and so paid rent twice a year. That would have caused a few problems for the more impulsive residents of Settle.

With all those younger siblings and visitors to the inn, it's not surprising that John Johnson Waller quickly moved to Kendal, beginning his life as a curate. However, that didn't last long as he married Kendal girl **Hannah Compston** and they moved back to Settle. John Johnson worked as a draper, opening a shop just after their wedding.

B11 In memory of Samuel Waller, son of John J Waller who died July 19th 1847 age 6 weeks. Francis who died Feby 5th 1849 aged 14 weeks.

Their sons Samuel and Francis both died in infancy and this may have prompted a move back to Kendal with their remaining daughter. They had another two children. John was a partner in the 'Garnett and Waller' drapery business with several assistants and apprentices. When Hannah died, John married a much younger **Agnes Bownas**. John was 78 when he died in 1894. Agnes outlived him by 25 years.

PETTY SESSIONS.—Tuesday Last.
Before J. Birkbeck, Esq. (chairman), Rev. H. J. Swale, C. Ingleby, and H. Christie, Esqrs.
Extension of Hours.—Thomas Waller, of the Black Horse Inn, Giggleswick, applied for an extension of hours until 12 p.m. on the occasion of the workpeople at the Hostel having a "rearing supper" on Wednesday evening next. The Bench granted until 11 p.m.

Back in Giggleswick, John's brother Thomas ran the Black Horse for over 20 years after their dad died, providing celebrations for guests in 1874 [*BNA7*].

John's other siblings became farmers and brother Edward Green Waller emigrated to Honolulu and worked as a farmer with his wife and seven children.

Entrepreneur William Cork with meat, wigs and three inns

William Cork, born in 1790, was the son of a Skipton draper. He moved to Settle by 1810 to marry his first wife **Elizabeth Charnley** who gave him four children before she died. He worked as a butcher. By 1821 William had become a hairdresser and wig maker in the days when gentlemen could not be seen without their (very itchy) wig, as described by William Lodge Paley's diaries. William's son Sylvester also became a hairdresser and wig maker, living in the Market Place with his unmarried sister Elizabeth.

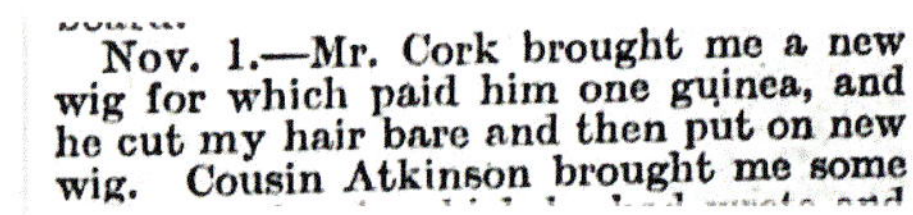
Nov. 1.—Mr. Cork brought me a new wig for which paid him one guinea, and he cut my hair bare and then put on new wig. Cousin Atkinson brought me some

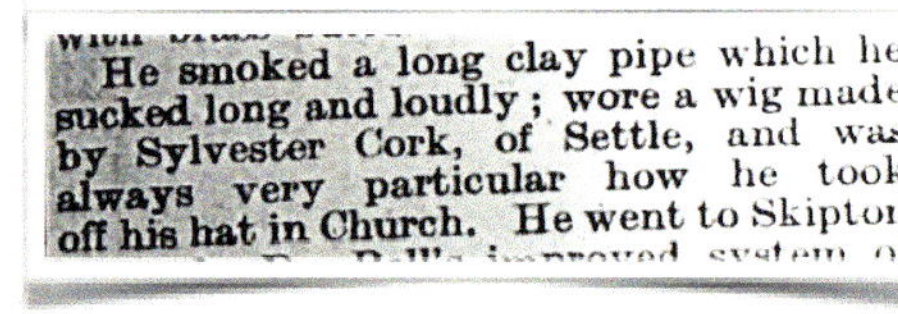
He smoked a long clay pipe which he sucked long and loudly; wore a wig made by Sylvester Cork, of Settle, and was always very particular how he took off his hat in Church. He went to Skipton

William married again, this time to **Jennett Moorhouse**. In the 1837 trade directory William was listed as a hat manufacturer. By the 1840s, entrepreneur William had another new business, taking on the tenancy for the **New Inn** and then for the **Old Naked Man**.

In 1856, William swapped his license at the **New Inn** for **The Talbot** for some reason [*BNA7*]. Two years later, William died aged 67. Jennett spent the rest of her life as a visitor to wealthy people, describing herself as being 'formerly innkeeper'.

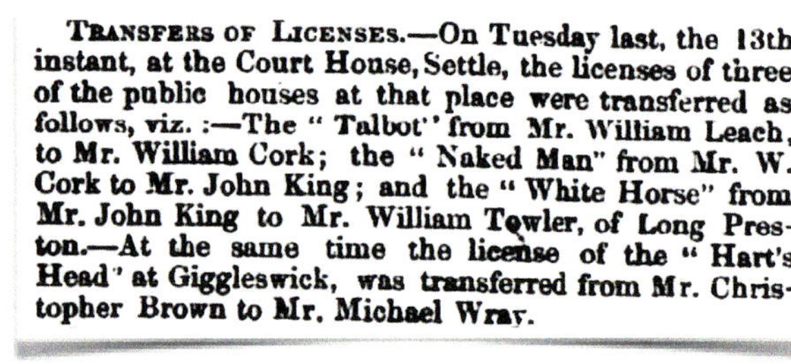
Transfers of Licenses.—On Tuesday last, the 13th instant, at the Court House, Settle, the licenses of three of the public houses at that place were transferred as follows, viz. :—The " Talbot" from Mr. William Leach, to Mr. William Cork; the " Naked Man" from Mr. W. Cork to Mr. John King; and the " White Horse" from Mr. John King to Mr. William Towler, of Long Preston.—At the same time the license of the " Hart's Head" at Giggleswick, was transferred from Mr. Christopher Brown to Mr. Michael Wray.

William made a good living through his enterprise. William is buried with his first wife in Long Preston and Jennett is buried in an unmarked grave somewhere in our Ancient Graveyard.

...JT...

Robert Atkinson, innkeeper for over 30 years, Spread Eagle Inn

Robert Atkinson and **Margaret Dent** were from Preston, Lancashire, but moved to Settle to become innkeepers at the Spread Eagle Inn. Several auctions and coroner's hearings took place there, including the sale of Armitstead Hall, Lawkland in 1819. In Tithe survey of 1844, Robert was recorded as owner of the inn, neighbouring stables, garden, cottages, 18 acres of land and he rented a further 10 acres. A busy man. Robert and Margaret died within a couple of months of each other.

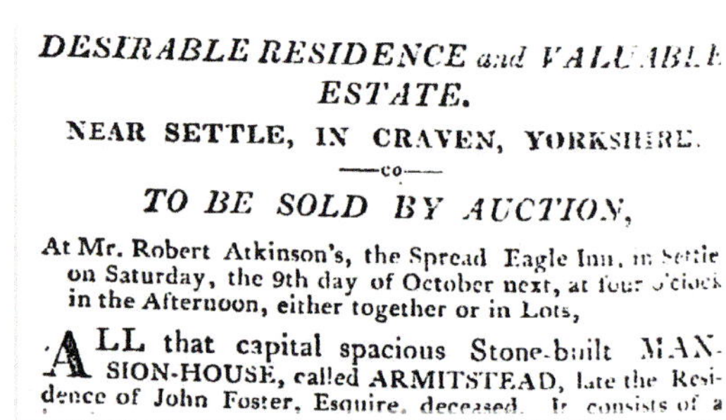
DESIRABLE RESIDENCE and VALUABLE ESTATE.

NEAR SETTLE, IN CRAVEN, YORKSHIRE.

—co—

TO BE SOLD BY AUCTION,

At Mr. Robert Atkinson's, the Spread Eagle Inn, in Settle on Saturday, the 9th day of October next, at four o'clock in the Afternoon, either together or in Lots,

ALL that capital spacious Stone-built MANSION-HOUSE, called ARMITSTEAD, late the Residence of John Foster, Esquire, deceased. It consists of a

C15 In memory of Robert Atkinson of Settle, innkeeper died 11th April 1850 aged 75 years. Also of Margaret his wife died 18th June 1850 aged 73 years.

After they died, the Spread Eagle was bought by Thomas Brigg, governor of Giggleswick workhouse, and was run by for a short while by William Duckett of Ingleton. In the census of May 1851 one of William Duckett's lodgers was Robert's son, Robert Atkinson (Jnr), a painter from Preston who was lodging with several other painters, perhaps testing the water for trade in Settle; unsuccessfully – he returned to Preston.

In 1852, the license of the Spread Eagle was surrendered. It became a Temperance Hotel run by John Bordley, a teetotal Primitive Methodist and talented artist/photographer [*working class heroes*]. In 1853, land from the Spread Eagle was used to build the new Music Hall, later renamed Victoria Hall.

...JT...

8 TRADESMEN, the backbone of settle

Settle tradesmen make up 35% of all the burials. Some were local and others were 'offcumdens'. We had a wonderful variety of businesses in our bustling town.

The explorers who discovered Victoria Cave

Michael Horner and **Joseph Jackson** discovered Victoria Cave on the hills behind Settle in 1837. Michael Horner was walking nearby the cave with friends and saw some foxhounds disappearing into some foxholes. He later went back and dug out the rocks and entered the cave, the first time it had been entered for 1200 years. Michael told his boss Joseph Jackson about it and Joseph took the very first early photographs of the cave and its findings. With these as evidence, he obtained permission to explore the caves. Joseph was the first man to enter the back chamber and, more importantly, to realise its archaeological significance. This became a life's work for Joseph, according to George Brown [*LSA*].

MR. JACKSON'S WORK IN THE CAVE.

The Cave was discovered by Mr. Michael Horner, then of Langcliffe. After he had made a few visits to it he spoke of his discovery to Mr. Joseph Jackson, whose servant he then was. Mr. Jackson who had already interested himself in questions of local geology soon saw that the Cave was one of exceptional importance. Mr. M. Horner's interest in the Cave soon ceased; Mr. Jackson's lasted to the end of life.

gloom of their native-place. During those same years Mr. Joseph Jackson was making frequent visits to the Cave and was finding not a few things of exceptional interest and value. These were found a little below the level of the floor, and included ornaments, coins, and fragments of pottery,—all testifying to a British occupation of the Cave; and must have been left there undisturbed for not less than 1200 years. Mr. Jackson's "finds" were numerous. Eventually part of his collection was sold to the British Museum, and the rest of it, which is of much and varied interest, is in the hands of his son-in-law, Mr. Knowles.

Michael Horner, a tinsmith, gunner, musical instrument maker

Michael was born in 1813 in Feizor, one of 13 children [*ph2*]. In 1844 he married **Ellen Coulton** and they lived on Castle Hill in Settle. He ran his busy shop in the north west corner of the Town Hall. They had five daughters, although Catherine died in infancy.

Michael and Ellen died in the 1870s. Michael left a legacy for widow Ellen '*as long as she remained a widow*' but she died within a year.

B27 In loving memoriam of Michael Horner of Settle who died Feby 11th 1878 aged 65 years. And also Ellen the beloved wife of the above who died March 8th 1879 aged 53 years. Also Catherine Ann their daughter who died in infancy March 21st 1855

Daughter **Mary Horner** continued living in Castle Hill, making a living as a dressmaker for some 46 years. Daughter **Elizabeth Horner** married a German, **Hermann Paul Jerome**, who was a wig maker with a shop in Ripon. Their son Tanny Jerome ran a photographic shop on the far left of the Shambles. In his spare time Tanny, '*a little man with dark brown eyes*' was busy. Cinema came to Settle in 1912 at 'The Picture House' in the Assembly Rooms on Kirkgate. Tanny was the manager and licensee. He ran silent films with projectionist Harold Smith. In 1927 the venue switched to the Victoria Hall as '*The Picturedrome*' and '*Kirkgate Kinema*', later to become known as the '*Vic*'. In 1939 Arthur Graham opened the '*NuVic*' on the other side of the Market Place, where the Coop is now, taking over from Tanny. Tanny also ran a draper's shop behind the Shambles and was known to be an unofficial bookie. He retired to the Isle of Man.

Michael's parents are also in this grave. His daughters Mary, Elizabeth (Jerome) and Jane (Grimshaw) are buried together in *Old grave G13* whilst daughter Margaret (Taylor) moved to Blackburn with their ten children.

Michael's nephew Michael Horner, talented photographer

Michael had a brother **Thomas Horner**, a house painter, who was the father of Michael and Anthony Horner, the Settle photographers. They had a shop opposite the end of the Shambles, now Field to Home, before moving to Station Road.

Young **Michael Horner** was fascinated with the new scientific process of photography, probably inspired by family friend Joseph Jackson. Michael spent four months at the leading photographic studios in Manchester and was working commercially as a photographer from 1864 [*SC*]. In 1866 he married a recently widowed Lincoln girl **Betsy Brown**. They had two daughters, one of whom died an infant. Michael's brother James married Betsy's sister Ellen Selina a few years later.

Our clever townsman Mr. M Horner has just completed a beautiful series of photographs of that famous "*lusus naturæ*" Gordale—and we are sure that we are not exaggerating when we say that three of the stereoscopic views—the 'upper' and 'lower falls,' and 'a peep through the natural arch' will for grandeur of scene and excellence of reproduction bear favourable comparison with the Alpine and Swiss views of similar scenes which have hitherto been supposed to reign without rivals. The new series consists of eight views which can be had either as cartes or stereoscopic slides. The list will be found in our advertizing columns.

PHOTOGRAPHY.

M. HORNER, JUN.,

Desires to announce that he has commenced the above business at his father's address, Market Place, Settle.
Cartes de Visite. Portraits on Glass or Paper.
Pictures &c., copied.
M. H. having spent four months in one of the leading Photographic Studios in Manchester, confidently hopes to give satisfaction to those who may favour him with their patronage.
Carte de Visite Portraits of the Rev. H. Bunn, 1s each or by Post thirteen Stamps

Michael died aged just 26. His younger brother Anthony quickly learnt the ropes and continued the business along with Michael's widow, Betsy. To say it was a successful business is an incredible understatement. Michael is also commemorated on his wife's gravestone with infant daughter Selina in *Old grave D15*. Their other daughter, Mabel, married a gardener, Edward Thompson. Mabel worked as a music teacher and later as a journalist in London - nicely progressive.

B29 ***MH died Dec 2(9 1869) Aged 26 years*** *(a very small stone under the trees)*

Joseph Jackson, a plumber and explorer

Joseph was born in 1815 in Melling, near Hornby, the son of Christopher Jackson, a maltster and his second wife Elizabeth Thompson. Joseph was an apprentice to his future uncle-in-law **Richard Harger** whose successful plumbing business was on Castle Hill. Richard died before the end of the apprenticeship, but Joseph's mum Elizabeth, now a widow, bought the business for him. It was ideally located - Castle Hill was the hub of skilled tradesmen.

Joseph [*Ph2*] married **Maria Harger** the daughter of Richard's brother Robert Harger [*below*]. Joseph and Maria had three children. Joseph gave an apprenticeship to a young **John Handby** [*church folk*] and later went into business with him. Joseph was the manager of Settle Gas Company for nearly 20 years and partner John Handby took over from him.

Mr Jackson, of Settle, in the most courteous manner submitted his fine collection of cave relics, collected in the neighbourhood, to the inspection of the visitors. They are chiefly of the Romano-British period, and are in fine preservation. Mr J H Burrow, B.A., also rendered most valuable services to the excursionists, not only by the facilities which he afforded for the inspection of his collection of limestone fossils, but by the indefatigable and cordial manner in which he ministered to every intellectual want and personal comfort of his fellow students in geological science and their literary and other friends.—*Preston Guardian.*

Joseph supplemented his income by letting people view his caving discoveries and being a '*site superintendent*'. In 1864, Joseph hosted '*a most delightful and instructive*' meeting of geologists from Yorkshire and Lancashire [*SC*]. Brother-in-law Lawrence Hodgson [*wenches, wives*] and surgeon John Holme Burrow [*railway folk*] shared Joseph's interest in the caves and worked with him.

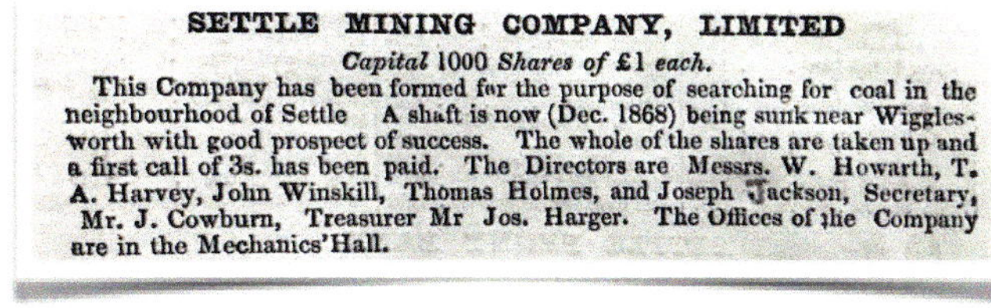

SETTLE MINING COMPANY, LIMITED

Capital 1000 *Shares of £1 each.*

This Company has been formed for the purpose of searching for coal in the neighbourhood of Settle A shaft is now (Dec. 1868) being sunk near Wigglesworth with good prospect of success. The whole of the shares are taken up and a first call of 3s. has been paid. The Directors are Messrs. W. Howarth, T. A. Harvey, John Winskill, Thomas Holmes, and Joseph Jackson, Secretary, Mr. J. Cowburn, Treasurer Mr Jos. Harger. The Offices of the Company are in the Mechanics' Hall.

Joseph and Thomas Holmes [*below*] were directors of the Settle Mining Company which was set up in 1856 to try and find local coal, unsuccessfully [*SC*]. However, Joseph was also a Trustee of the Craven Savings Bank, a far more productive enterprise.

Maria died in 1867 and is buried with son George who died aged just 28. George had been to Giggleswick School and then worked as a plumber and glazier. He died in 1871 so his death could perhaps have been linked to the building of the Settle to Carlisle railway?

E11 In memory of Maria, the beloved wife of Joseph Jackson, of Settle, who died on 25th of April, 1867, aged 51 years. Also George Jackson who died Sep 3rd 1874 aged 29 years.

Joseph died suddenly in 1886, aged 69. Joseph would not have been allowed to be buried with his wife as the Ancient graveyard had been closed in 1882, so he is one of the first people buried in *Old graveyard A13*. This gravestone commemorates their daughters Eleanor and Agnes Annie (Knowles) and Maria and George, again.

Thomas Holmes, the father of a plumbing dynasty

Thomas Holmes was born in 1811 in Glasson Dock, Lancashire. He married **Betty Richmond** in Giggleswick and they had 8 children. Thomas set up a plumbing business in Castle Hill which was to last over 100 years and also had land and property back in Glasson Dock. Thomas worked until he died aged 71, one year after Betty's death. They are buried together in a top spot, right by the door of the church, close to their children Ann, Betty and William who, for some reason, all died when they were 17 years old.

C1 In memory of Thomas Holmes of Settle who died Feb 15th 1882 aged 72 years. Betty the beloved wife of Thomas Holmes of Settle who died Octr 9th 1881 aged 71 years.

C4 In memory of Ann, daughter of Thomas and Betty Holmes, who died January 10th 1850 aged 17 years. Also of William their son who died Novr 1852 aged 17 years. Also of Betty their daughter who died April 14th 1866 aged 17 years.

Thomas's eldest son **John Richmond Holmes**, born just before his parents' marriage, was also a plumber. His wife **Elizabeth Burniston** gave him four children. Their son, another Thomas, made a living as a painter. His name and that of his partner George Armistead, was found on a wall of a house in Giggleswick where they had been working [*ph8*]. John Richmond Holmes, his wife, and four children are commemorated in *Old grave C37*.

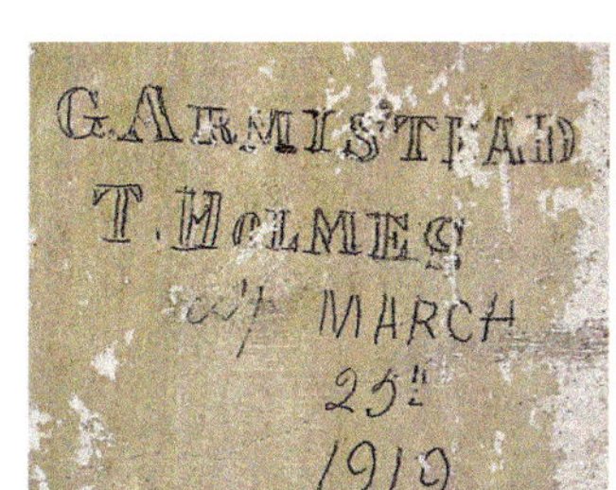

Son **Thomas Holmes** (Jnr), born in 1838, also became a plumber [*WSA*] and lived on Castle Hill. He married **Isabella Johnson** and they had at least 11 children! In 1880 Thomas had a bit of an accident stepping on a plank [*BNA7*].

ACCIDENT.—On Tuesday afternoon last, whilst Mr. Thomas Holmes, plumber, Settle, was engaged upon some work in connection with the building of a new house at Craven Terrace, he stepped upon a wrong plank, which caused him to fall to the ground, a distance of several yards. He sustained injury to both wrists, and was also bruised in several places.

THOMAS HOLMES,
PLUMBER, GLAZIER,
GAS FITTER AND PAINTER,
SETTLE,
Respectfully thanks his numerous friends and supporters for their past patronage, and hopes by strict attention to business to merit a continuance for the future.
PUMPS, BATHS & W. CLOSETS
Fitted up and repaired.
Iron Eaves Troughs & Pipes
Always on hand.

Thomas (Jnr) was a member of the first Settle Parish Council in 1894, which is when his photo [*ph4*] was taken. In the 1901 census the Castle Hill house was occupied by five of Thomas's children, but not Thomas. Why? 58 year old Thomas had married 39 year old **Mary Ann Lamb**. They lived in Goldielands, Settle with their two daughters and Mary Ann's mum who was just seven years older than Thomas. Thomas died in 1908, and Mary Ann took over the house and business in Castle Hill which she described as 'Plumba's business', now with three daughters. Thomas is buried in unmarked *Old grave FX66* with his second wife and some children.

Thomas (Snr)'s youngest son **Robert** was a cabinet maker, upholsterer and bell hanger [*SC*]. In the 1881 census, he was lodging in London describing himself as a widower and an American farmer. He will have had some interesting stories! Thomas (Snr)'s daughter **Jane** married **Edmund Handby** [*church folk*].

ROBERT HOLMES
Respectfully announces that he has commenced Business as
CABINET MAKER,
UPHOLSTERER, AND BELL HANGER,
On CASTLE HILL, SETTLE, and trusts to be favoured with the orders of his friends and the public which he will endeavour to execute with the utmost punctuality.
June 1st 1866

William Ralph, a blue flag merchant and a true Settle man

William Ralph and his wife **Mary Lord** were first cousins. They were members of some of Settle's largest families and so are related to many others in the graveyard. Their grandparents were **John Lord** from Long Preston and **Mary Bordley** who was the sister of Francis Bordley, corn dealer [*working class heroes*]. William's mum was **Margaret Lord** and his dad **Samuel Ralph**, an agricultural labourer who was a first cousin to **Luke Ralph** the blacksmith. Mary's mum was **Mary Lord** who gave birth to Mary before her marriage to **James Ellel.**

William, born in 1822, started working as a rag dealer but then took up quarrying before becoming a slate flag dealer employing five men (which included his son and step-sons). They lived at 18 Victoria Street in Upper Settle, which is built with some beautiful blue flagstones, of course. Son Christopher, known as Kit, took over the business [*LSA*].

WM. RALPH & SON,
BLUE FLAG MERCHANTS,
SWARTH MOOR, nr. SETTLE.
Makers of Brewers' and Dyers' Vats,
WATER CISTERNS, LIQUID MANURE TANKS,
Headstones, Founts, and Tablets.
ESTIMATES ON APPLICATION.
All Letters addressed—Victoria Street, Settle.

Young Mary followed her mum's example and had three children before marrying William. Their names **Lot Bordley Lord**, **Johnson Lord** and **Christopher Charles Lord** may give a clue to their paternity. Once married to William in 1860, Mary had another four children. Two sons, infant Samuel and William aged 16 are in their grave.

Christopher Ralph,
BLUE FLAG MERCHANT and QUARRY OWNER,
Helwith Bridge, near SETTLE.

Maker of Brewers' and Dyers' Vats, Water Cisterns, Liquid Manure Tanks, Headstones, Tombs & Tablets, and every description of FLAG WORK.

DIVISION FLAGS FOR CATTLE a speciality.

HEADSTONES in Marble, Granite, or Stone.

THEFTS BY A RAILWAY WATCHMAN.—At the Todmorden Police Office, on Wednesday, Lot Bordley Lord, a watchman in the employ of the Lancashire and Yorkshire Railway at Todmorden, was charged with stealing two quarts of whisky from a cask under his care for a night on the siding at Todmorden; and also with stealing four pairs of boots from a case also under his charge. A cask containing 23¾ gallons of Scotch whisky was sent from the Wishaw Distillery, on the 21st April, by the Caledonian Railway; at Carlisle and Preston the weight was about the same, but on arriving at Holmfirth, to which town it was consigned, it was found considerably lighter, and on measuring the contents they were nearly a gallon short of the invoiced quantity. Two spile holes were found in the side of the cask. The train in which the cask was conveyed from Preston was under the prisoner's care for the night on a siding at Todmorden, and on his cupboard being searched a bottle containing about a quart of whisky was found, and there were also found two gimlets, which were of the same size as that by which the cask had been bored.

Son **Lot Bordley Lord** found work on the railways in Todmorden as a nightwatchman. In May 1870 Lot was found guilty of larceny, stealing two quarts of whisky from barrels and four pairs of boots [*BNA19*]. For this he was imprisoned for 15 months. It didn't cramp Lot's style as he married Eliza Guyer, a shoemaker's daughter, in Settle soon after his release. They moved to Halifax and Lot worked in quarrying. William's other sons and step sons continued working in the trade. Son Edwin is buried in *Old grave H46*.

A2 In loving memory of Samuel the beloved son of William and Mary Ralph of Settle who died December 18th 1862 aged 10 months. Also of the above Mary Ralph who died Nov 1st 1890 aged 62 years. Also of the above William Ralph who died April 14th 1895 aged 74 years.

Peter Skirrow, a tallow chandler

Tallow chandlers worked closely with butchers to obtain the fat to make the candles. It was a really unpleasant, caustic and smelly job, but someone had to do it [*CH*].

There have been many changes in the business life of Settle during the past sixty years. Some of the industries have died out entirely. I can remember the old chandlery business run by Mr. Skirrow on Castle Hill, where he manufactured the old-fashioned tallow candles. These have since been supplanted by the wax candle, but there was a considerable local demand for the "dips" in those days. As I write these lines I can almost catch a whiff of the rancid odour that rose from the vats in which the wicks were dipped, and re-dipped until they reached the proper consistency.

Peter Skirrow was born in 1797 in Carnforth and came to live in Settle with his new wife **Ellen Harrison**. Peter was a tallow chandler based in Castle Hill and then Kirkgate, renting from the Calvert family [*innkeepers*]. William Lodge Paley's diaries suggest Peter struggled with money. In the 1844 Tithe Survey Peter rented 9 houses, cottages, stables, meadows and barns in Kirkgate, Castle Hill, in the Back Stables behind Cheapside and in Upper Settle - quite ambitious.

April 10.—Peter Skirrow walked with me to Austwick for the sale of late Mr. Scott's books and bo't 2 pieces of his penmanship in frames. Fear Mrs. S. will have little left as they say there is a deal of debt. Saw Mrs. Baxter, who

Peter and Ellen had five children in 13 years. Peter had a lingering illness before his death 'advanced in years' aged just 57! [*BNA7*] There is a mistake on the gravestone inscription.

On Wednesday, the 23rd inst., after a lingering illness Mr Peter Skirrow, tallow chandler, Settle, advanced in years.

Wife Ellen and son Henry kept the business going [SC]. Son **Robert** enjoyed life on the railways, being a stationmaster and then coal merchant in Matlock, Derbyshire. He also dabbled rather sloppily in the building trade in 1868 [BNA21].

ELLEN SKIRROW & SON,
TALLOW CHANDLERS, SETTLE.

E. Skirrow begs to return thanks for past favours during the long period of thirty years in which the business was conducted by her late husband, and to solicit a continuation of those favours, the business being now carried on by herself and Son, who hope by strict attention and a good article to merit a share of the public patronage and support.

Moulds and Rushlights always kept in Stock.

his horse to stray on the highway at Chelmorton, on the 27th ult.....Robert Skirrow, coal dealer, of Matlock, was summoned by Mr. Edward Jones, clerk to the Darley Local Board of Health, for erecting a house at Darley without sufficient accommodation.—John Wildgoose, surveyor and inspector to the Board, said the defendant had recently erected six cottages at Darley, five of which are now occupied by thirty-eight persons, and there is not a water-closet, petty, or ash-pit on the premises for their accommodation. All the ashes, rubbish, and refuse are thrown into the street. A quantity of mortar, stones, and other rubbish had been left in the street since the houses were built some six months ago. Notices had been served on the defendant to remove the nuisance, and provide the requisite accommodation, but he had not attended to them.—Fined £10 and costs.—Witness asked the Bench if

Peter's son **Henry** had the honour of being apprenticed to saddler James Waugh, father of Benjamin Waugh, the founder of the NSPCC. Henry took over his dad's tallow chandler business. He married shoemaker's daughter **Hannah Bowerbank**, and they are buried in *Old grave D29*.

B14 In memory of Peter Skirrow of Settle who died November 23rd 1853 aged 55 years. Also William son of the above who died January 15th 1855 aged 23. Also Ellen Skirrow wife of the above Peter Skirrow who died Augst 28th 1872 aged 71 years. Also of Ann Skirrow daughter of the above who died May 25th 1873 aged 33 years.

William Capstick, a blacksmith and fisherman

Blacksmiths and saddlers were at the heart of Victorian England as horses were used for all transport – people, goods and materials for building railways. So William Capstick struck lucky when the railways were built.

William Capstick was born in 1824 into a Clapham family of blacksmiths. His brother Charles was a blacksmith and sister Elizabeth married blacksmith Luke Ralph who had the wonderful inscription on his stone. In 1848 William married **Agnes Garnett** and they lived in Chapel Street in Settle, bringing up four daughters and a son.

Agnes died in 1882 and is buried with infant daughter Annie. William married **Ann Carter** in 1884.

AN UNSATISFACTORY VISITOR.—At the Settle Police Court yesterday, Josiah Taylor, of Bolton, who described himself as an ironfounder, was charged in custody with having stolen £30 and two gold rings from the dwelling-house of Mr. William Capstick, blacksmith, Settle, on the 21st November, 1891. The prisoner has admitted to the police that he took a smaller sum than that stated whilst on a visit, Mrs. Capstick, the wife of the prosecutor, being his aunt. Formal evidence having been tendered, the prisoner was remanded in custody until to-day.

In November of 1891, William had an 'unsatisfactory visitor' who stole from him. The burglar was his wife's nephew Josiah Taylor. Josiah was remanded in custody until the court session 11 months later in October 1892, and was then given a further two months imprisonment. This was Victorian justice! [BNA20]

In the early 1890s, William and two fishing friends were the butt of some banter in the form of a 15-verse poem called 'The Three Fishers'. Fisher William is in the centre [ph4]. It was written by 'WC and TA' – probably William Clark, an innkeeper and Thomas Altham, a grocer. It included a verse:

'Now a bottle they's got, full of whisky they'd thought, As Nowell remarked, "good as ever was bought". When Capstick sings out, and Jim says' "What's matter", "I'm denged if they haven't put up mineral water".

THE THREE FISHERS.

2nd Canto.

NOW Capstick and Hartley, and bold little Tti
Went up to the Tarn in the month of July;
They went up in style in a nice waggonette,
On a fishing excursion, no doubt, you may bet.

18. Mr. J. B. Wookey visited Settle with a number of boys from Dr. Barnardo's Homes, and gave an Entertainment in the Victoria Hall.—Mr. Wm. Capstick died at his residence, in Chapel Street, Settle, after a long and painful illness.—First Annual Meeting of the members of the Settle Golf Club.

Not everyone appreciated the joke. Friends of the fishermen issued a leaflet attacking the authors: *'There's two men in Settle who sit at their ease, to scandalise people just as they please, They walk up and down and call themselves mashers, they can't leave alone Three Poor Little Fishers.'*

William died after 'a long and painful illness' aged 72 [*LSA*].

C8 In memory of Annie, infant daughter of William and Agnes Capstick of Settle who died October 15th 1854 aged (5) months. A few ....feld, and she....dead. Also of William Capstick, died Nov 18th 1896. Also of Agnes his wife, died Jan 12th 1882.

Widow Ann died in Austwick in 1905. Both of William's wives worked in service before marriage. Agnes worked at the impressive Casterton Hall in Kirkby Lonsdale and Ann worked for Lorenzo Christie, owner of the Langcliffe Mills when he had retired to Stackhouse Hall. Daughter Margaret also worked as a housemaid for the Birkbecks [*wealthy folk*] before she married farmer Richard Metcalfe.

William Bilton, a master saddler at the Town Hall [*H*]

C21 In memory of Mary Bilton who died July 11th 1820, aged 7 years, Sarah Bilton who died March 17th 1822 aged 3 years, William Bilton who died January 29 1847 aged (36) years, Betty wife of William Bilton of Settle and mother of the above who died July 24th 1851 aged 71 years. William Bilton husband of the above named Betty Bilton who died March 28th 1871 aged 91 years. Margaret Bilton who died July 12th 1878 aged 70 years.

William Bilton was born in 1780 in Ripon, but had moved to Settle by 1806 when he married **Betty Rigg.** They had six children. Daughters Mary and Sarah died in childhood and are buried in Giggleswick but are commemorated on William's stone. He worked as a saddler in the Town Hall all his life [*SC*]. William became a churchwarden in 1840 and spent some time working as treasurer and librarian at the 'Subscription Library' in the Town Hall, recorded in a very early 1840 edition of the Settle Almanac [*ph4*].

WILLIAM BILTON,
SADDLER and HARNESS MAKER,
MARKET PLACE,
SETTLE,

In returning thanks to the inhabitants of Settle and neighbourhood for the very liberal support he has received for the last 58 years, begs leave to inform them, that in addition to the Saddle and Harness business he is combining that of

CARRIAGE PAINTING,
VARNISHING & TRIMMING,

And for that purpose has engaged clever and experienced Workmen from first class London Houses whom he can with confidence recommend.

Manufacturer and dealer in every description of Saddlery and Harness, Horse Clothing, Blankets, Kerseys, Roller, Girth and Brace Webs, Linen and Woollen Checks, Bandage Serges, Saddle Cloths, Goodman's Patent Saddle Cloths, Felt Saddle Cloths, ...

SETTLE LITERARY SOCIETY AND NEWS ROOM.

Mr. Bilton, Librarian.

This Society, which is merely a Book Club, established 1770, has a very good collection of Books—it has about 86 Members. Annual subscription £1.—entrance £3. 3s. The News Room adjoining it has four Daily Papers—Subscription £1. 1s. per annum.

Betty was aged 71 when she died. William was an incredible 91, still working as a saddler and outliving four of his children. He is the oldest man commemorated on a stone in the Ancient graveyard.

Son **William** is buried with them. He had married Dent born **Nancy King**, daughter of William King who had been the innkeeper at the Joiner's Arms in Settle. William followed his dad to become another saddler, but died aged just 36. They had three children but youngest daughter Elizabeth died in infancy and is buried in *EX25*, the infants section of the graveyard. Widow Nancy [*ph9*] miraculously had a further daughter Emily four years after William's death, which may have had something to do with her lodger Thomas Holden, and/or could be the child of her 17 year old daughter Mary. Soon afterwards, Nancy and the girls went with son William to Holbeck, Leeds where William found work as a cashier at a railway goods department. Later, they moved to Bradford.

William (Snr)'s son **John** is buried nearby:

D8 In remembrance of Betty Bilton who died 2nd Feb 1840 aged 25 years. Also of John Bilton who died 18th Feb 1869 aged 53 years. Also of Elizabeth Bilton daughter of the above who died 11th August 1877, aged 37 years. Margaret Elizabeth Bilton granddaughter of the above who died 21st Nov 1865 aged 7 months, Joseph Edward Bilton, grandson of the above who died August 24th aged 11 weeks.

John's wife **Betty Carr** died just a few weeks after the birth of their second child Elizabeth. John brought up his children in the Town Hall helped by his dad and sister, also working as a saddler. He predeceased his dad William by two years.

John Turner, a hatter and property investor [*G*]

Believe it or not, Settle markets were well known for hats in the middle of the nineteenth century, so John Turner was in the right place at the right time. The expression 'mad as a hatter' is based on fact - the vapours produced in hat manufacture caused mercury poisoning. This may or may not have affected John Turner, who died aged just 47.

John Turner, born in 1805, was the only child of **William Turner** and his wife **Elizabeth Blackburn**. Elizabeth died when John was just three, and dad brought him up alone. William and son John were both hatters and ran their business from a shop in the Market Place just at the bottom of Constitution Hill. They also owned and rented out the cottages in **Turner's Yard** behind the shop fronts of the Market Place.

In 1835, John married **Betsy Wilman**, the illegitimate daughter of **Margaret Wilman** who ran a lodging house next door at Jessamine Cottage with her spinster sister Mary. They provided comfortable lodgings for several well-to-do residents including surgeon Edward Harrison and solicitor George Dudgeon-Hartley. John and Betsy had five children over the next ten years. Their daughter **Elizabeth Turner** was the first child to be baptised in the new Holy Ascension Church on 4th November 1838.

C14 In memory of John Turner who died Decr 22nd 1852 aged 47 years. For here have we no continuing city. Betsy beloved wife of the above who died Jany 11th 1901 aged 87 years. He giveth his beloved sleep.

Betsy sold off the hatting business in 1854 [*SC*] but continued to live off the rental income and helped her mum run the lodging house business. They must have run it well as they had the luxury of a servant in each census return. Betsy outlived her husband by 49 years and died with an estate worth £50,000 today. Well done Betsy! Their properties were eventually sold off to the Graham grocery business, based further along the row.

HATS, CAPS, &c.
MRS. TURNER, MARKET PLACE, SETTLE,
Begs to announce that she has commenced
SELLING OFF
THE WHOLE OF HER
STOCK-IN-TRADE,
Comprising Silk and Stuff HATS, CAPS, and Umbrellas.
ALSO, TO BE LET,
THE DWELLING HOUSE AND SHOP,
With or without the Workshops.
The House contains front Parlour, Kitchen, Scullery with hard and soft water, 2 good Cellars, and 5 Lodging Rooms; there is also a good Garden behind.
To be entered upon at Martinmas.
For particulars apply to MRS. TURNER.

Their youngest son **Joseph Turner** went to Giggleswick School and then worked as a druggist. He married **Hannah Wetherell**, the daughter of Thomas Wetherell, *grave B15*, the innkeeper of the Golden Lion - the paper got it wrong! [*BNA7*] Joseph learnt Thomas' trade. They moved to Keighley with their five children and Joseph worked as an innkeeper before emigrating to the States. Daughter Elizabeth took the plunge and went to find work in Manchester. There she met and married Joseph Taylor, a hotel proprietor. Now, a few generations later, one of Elizabeth's descendants lives back in Settle. Daughter Margaret married a grocer, James Bentham and they brought up their family in Lancashire. It seems son William may have died at Port Talbot, South Wales, aged 29.

Giggleswick.—Recently, at the Parish Church, by the Rev. T. Mc.Intyre, Mr. Joseph Turner, chemist and druggist, Settle, to Miss Hannah Wetherell, third daughter of the late Mr. Thomas Wetherell, of the Red Lion Hotel, Settle.

George Wilkinson Newsholme, a cabinet maker defying illegitimacy

George Wilkinson Newsholme, born in 1791, was the illegitimate son of **Bridget Newsholme**, and had been fathered by the much older and very wealthy **George Wilkinson** in Slaidburn. By 1817 George (Jnr) had moved to Settle and married **Sarah Ingham.** They had at least five children all given the surname 'Wilkinson Newsholme', but confusingly they referred to themselves as both Newsholme and/or Wilkinson over the years. George was a cabinet maker in the Market Place, owning and renting property in Kirkgate and Bishopdale Court.

D20 In affectionate remembrance of George Wilkinson Newholme died December 18th 1866 aged 75 years. Also of Sarah wife of the above who died March 26th 1867 aged 77 years. The memory of....Catherine eldest daughter died May 13th 1889 aged (71) years.

Son **John Wilkinson Newsholme** married **Agnes Bateson,** one of the nine children orphaned when her parents **Thomas Bateson** and **Nancy Harger** died in 1849, *grave CX3* [*below*]. Son George married three times in the space of four years – the first two wives died. He is buried with his third wife **Jane Hardacre** and only child, **Sarah Ellen**, in *Old grave C13.* When she was 22, daughter **Mary Wilkinson Newsholme** became the second wife of her 67 year old second cousin **William Wilkinson**, a very wealthy 'gentleman' in Hellifield. William was a founder of the delightful Dale Head Church at Stocks Reservoir in 1852. Daughter Ellen married **Robert Grime**, who died aged just 24 and is buried in *grave D24.* They had three sons. two of whom died in childhood. Ellen spent the rest of her life helping out in the family business. Ellen is buried in unmarked *Old grave BX8* with her unmarried sister Catherine, but commemorated with her husband and sons:

D24 In memory of Robert Grime of Settle who died April 10th 1847 aged 24 years. Also of John Grime, son of the above who died September... 1846 aged 9 months. Also of George Grime son of the above who died Jany 1866 aged 22 years. Ellen Grime died Nov 19th 1890 aged 70 years.

The Hargers, a successful Settle family business [J]

Brothers William, Robert, and Joseph Harger account for at least eight of the graves in the Ancient graveyard and numerous others in the Old and New graveyards.

1. William Harger, a farmer

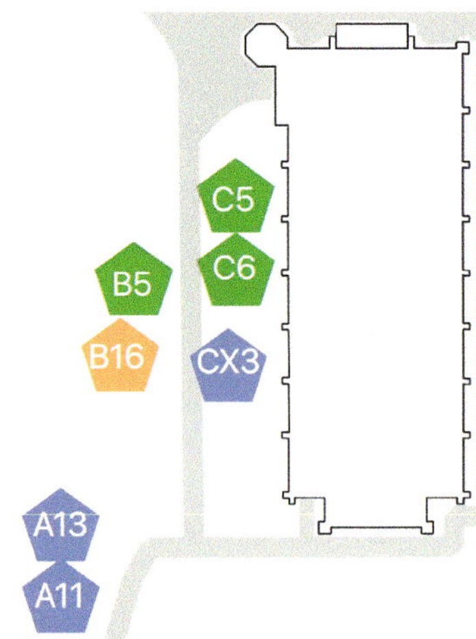

William Harger, born in 1771, was a successful farmer who married **Mary Holden**. They had seven daughters.

B16 In memory of William Harger who departed this life Jany 27th 1854 aged 82 years. Also of Agnes his daughter who died April 2nd 1829 aged 19 and who was interred at Giggleswick. Also of Mary widow of the above who died July 19th 1878 aged 91 years.

William and Mary's third daughter **Ellen** and fifth daughter **Maria** married brothers **John** and **William Armistead**, sons of Hugh Armistead, a wealthy landed proprietor in Tatham, just beyond Ingleton. **John Armistead** [*ph2*] was a draper with his business in the Market Place [*SC*]. John was a Director of the Settle Gas Company. Two daughters married Cambridge graduates: Mary Jane married William Simpson Bamber, a headmaster of Appleby Grammar School, while Annie Elizabeth married Horace Orford, a cleric who worked as an assistant master to William Bamber at Appleby Grammar School before serving in Bloemfontein, South Africa. Annie gave birth to eight children, but was killed by disease, one of thousands of typhoid victims in South Africa at that time.

SPRING &S UMMER FASHIONS.

JOHN ARMISTEAD,

Wholesale and Retail Draper,

SILK MERCER, &c.,

Begs to announce that his Stock is now replete with every novelty for the Season in

SHAWLS, MANTLES, DRESS MATERIALS,

and every description of Fancy Goods. His extensive Stock of

WOOLLEN CLOTHS,

has been replenished with the newest and cheapest Goods the Market can offer.

The remainder of last Summer's Stock of SHAWLS, FANCY DRESSES, MUSLINS, DE LAINES, PRINTS, LIGHT TROUSERINGS, and VESTINGS, &c., is now being sold off at about ONE HALF their original price.

MARKET PLACE, SETTLE.

E10 In memory of John Armistead of Settle born January 28th 1819, died March 7th 1864. Also Ellen, wife of the above born Aug 7th, 1816, died Dec 28th 1885 laid to rest at Shelford. Also Annie Elizabeth Orford their daughter died at Bloemfontein, South Africa, July 5th 1897, aged 45 years. RIP

Daughter **Maria** married John Armistead's brother **William Armistead**, a chemist who died aged just 38. Maria spent the rest of her life alone in 'Castle Villa' in Kendal. Their sons John and Hugh were also chemists. They were both confirmed bachelors, although 62 year old Hugh eventually married his housekeeper Eleanora Mounsey, a 37 year old mason's daughter. Eleanor was the beneficiary of this branch of the Armistead estate, lucky girl!

2. Robert Harger, a joiner

Robert Harger, born in 1775, married **Agnes Hallpike** in 1801 and they had at least ten children with just two sons, one of whom died in infancy. Robert was the instigator of the Harger Brothers North Craven Saw Mill and Furnishers – the business allegedly started 'at the time of the Battle of Trafalgar' in 1805 [*LSA*]. Agnes' dad, Vincent Hallpike, ran a successful furniture business in Settle Market Place, next to the White Horse Hotel and Robert had been apprenticed to him.

ESTABLISHED AT THE TIME OF THE BATTLE OF TRAFALGAR

STATION RD.,
SETTLE
Phone: 2533

Harger Bros.
FURNISHERS

H. BROS. EXECUTE ALL KINDS OF JOBBING WORK AT REASONABLE CHARGES.

HARGER BROS.,
Cabinet Makers & Furnishing & Bedding
WAREHOUSE.

DEPARTMENTS.

Cabinet Furniture	Fancy Cabinet Goods
Brass and Iron Bedsteads	Carpets, Oilcloths, & Linoleums
Venetian and Roller Blinds	Mats and Mattings and other
Chimney and Toilet Glasses	Floor Coverings
Spring, Hair & Wool Mattresses	Washing & Wringing Machines

H. Bros. would draw special attention to their new PERFORATED WOOD CHAIR SEAT, for re-seating chairs.
Special advantages—They are cheap, durable, easily fixed, and have a good appearance.

N.B.—They are made square in different sizes, and if required to be cut to shape a paper pattern should be taken large enough to cover the old cane.
Prices, with Brass Pins for fixing—

Size........	12 in.	14 in.	16 in.	18 in.	20 in.
Price........	8d.	9d.	11d.	1/2	1/4 per seat

BE FORWARDED FOR INSPECTION, OR PARTIES CAN BE WAITE

Robert and Agnes' first daughter **Nancy** married the stonemason **Thomas Bateson** and had ten children. Tragically they both died in 1849, probably from an infectious disease. Youngest son Joseph Harger Bateson died with them, and they are buried in unmarked *grave CX2*. The other children all survived, miraculously, looked after by a variety of relatives.

Son **Joseph**, born in 1809, continued the family business. The Harger building empire succeeded in Settle for generations, well known for their quality fretwork and carving [*SC,LSA*]. Their business was at Goldielands with premises reaching down to the river and headquarters on Station Road.

JOSEPH HARGER,
JOINER AND CABINET MAKER,

Thanks his numerous friends for the liberal support himself and late father have received for upwards of 60 years and assures them it will always be his study to merit a share of their patronage.

J. H. invites attention to his stock of Kidderminster, Dutch and other Carpets and Hearth Rugs, Door Matts, Cocoa and Manilla Mattings, Wood and Iron Bedsteads, Flock Beds, Mattrasses, Cabriole and other Chairs, Sofas, Washstands, Looking Glasses and other articles belonging to the trade.

An Apprentice wanted.

Chapel Street, Settle, Nov. 28th, 1866.

WESLEYAN SUNDAY SCHOOL.—The scholars belonging to the Sunday School in connection with the Wesleyan Methodist Chapel, Settle, met at their annual Christmas Breakfast on Monday morning, the 26th, at eight o'clock. The teachers and friends of the school then partook of breakfast together, after which suitable addresses were delivered by Mr. Joseph Harger, the superintendent, Mr. James Redmayne, and several other friends. A few Christmas Hymns were also sung by the children, and the meeting was kept up with great interest until 12 o'clock.

The Hargers were active Methodists [*SC*] and were, appropriately, the building contractors for both the Methodist Chapel built on Chapel Street in 1810 and the second Chapel built on Church Street in 1893, recently demolished. Joseph was associated with the Wesleyan Sunday School for over 70 years, becoming the school superintendent [*ph4*]. The Hargers also built Prospect Terrace (Goldielands) and Halsteads at the top of Duke Street.

Joseph is buried in *Old grave A11*, the earliest dated gravestone in the Old graveyard. Robert's daughter Catherine became the second wife of Lawrence Hodgson [*wenches, wives*]. Daughter Maria married Joseph Jackson [*above*], and is buried next to him in *Old grave A13*

In loving memory of Joseph Harger who died April 14th 1886 aged 76 years. Also Margaret his wife died Sep 12th 1891 aged 74 years. Robert, eldest son of the above died at Skipton Nov 25th 1885 aged 41 years. Also Annie his wife died Dec 27th 189(3) aged 4(9) years.

...JF...

3. Joseph Harger, the innkeeper of the Royal Oak

Joseph Harger, born in 1781, married **Ellen Holden**, the sister of Mary who married Joseph's brother William. They had at least nine children, four of whom are buried with them. Joseph was the innkeeper of the **Royal Oak**, renting from George Dudgeon Hartley who lived at Whitefriars next door. Four of their unmarried children, Joseph, a Cheshire wine merchant, John, a farmer, Nancy and Sarah are buried next to them, with the stone now doing battle with a tree.

C6 In memory of Joseph Harger of Settle, who died 10th June 1848 aged 68 and of Ellen his wife who died 23 Jany 1863 aged 78 years. Also their children viz, Eli who died 26th May 1834 aged 5 years. William who died 4th Octr 1851 aged 40 years. Mary who died 24th Octr 1864 aged 50 years, Richard who died 19 Decr 1866 aged 48 years.

C5 In memory of Joseph Harger of Oxton, Cheshire, eldest son of Joseph and Ellen Harger of Settle, who died 30 Nov 1869 aged 61 years. Also John who died 5th Dec 1872 aged 48 years. Nancy their daughter who died 19th May 188(3) aged 67 years. Sarah who died 29th Feb 1896 aged 74 years.

TO SPORTSMEN AND OTHERS.

ON SALE,

A newly invented

PATENT THREE BARREL GUN,

Containing Fowling piece and Rifle; admirably adapted for Rook and Sea Fowl shooting, in addition to the usual appliances of a Double Barrel Gun; on view.—Apply to

J. J. HARTLEY,

Ironmonger, Settle.

Joseph and Ellen's daughter **Mary Harger** married **John Johnson Hartley** in 1839. John was the eldest son of Isabella and Robert Hartley who ran the **Golden Lion** for decades. John worked in the Market Place as an ironmonger and tinsmith, but had fingers in many pies [*SC*].

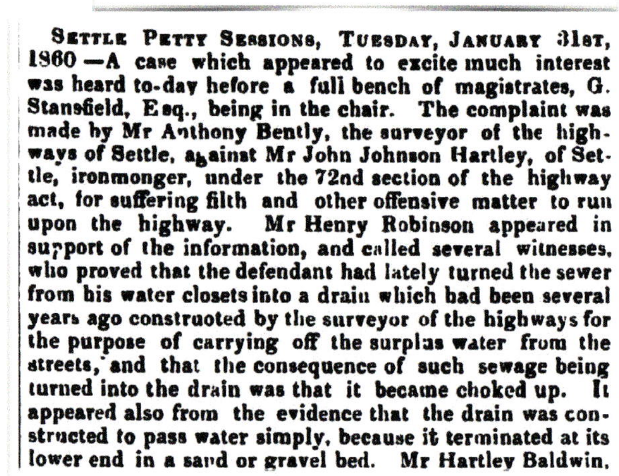
SETTLE PETTY SESSIONS, TUESDAY, JANUARY 31ST, 1860 —A case which appeared to excite much interest was heard to-day before a full bench of magistrates, G. Stansfield, Esq., being in the chair. The complaint was made by Mr Anthony Bently, the surveyor of the highways of Settle, against Mr John Johnson Hartley, of Settle, ironmonger, under the 72nd section of the highway act, for suffering filth and other offensive matter to run upon the highway. Mr Henry Robinson appeared in support of the information, and called several witnesses, who proved that the defendant had lately turned the sewer from his water closets into a drain which had been several years ago construoted by the surveyor of the highways for the purpose of carrying off the surplus water from the streets, and that the consequence of such sewage being turned into the drain was that it became choked up. It appeared also from the evidence that the drain was constructed to pass water simply, because it terminated at its lower end in a sand or gravel bed. Mr Hartley Baldwin,

In 1860 John used his entrepreneurial spirit to divert the waste from his water closet down a street water drain which emptied out onto gravel. Unsurprisingly the drain blocked up [*BNA18*]. Not John's smartest move! Incredibly, he got away with a one shilling fine, which may reflect his good reputation in the town. The magistrate was George Stansfeld [*wealthy ones*], and the prosecution solicitor was Henry Robinson [*wenches, wives*].

B5 Sacred to the memory of John Johnson Hartley who died May 27th 1864 aged 53, and Mary, wife of the above who died October 27th 1864 aged 50 years. Also William Hartley brother of the above who died February 24th 1858 aged 38 years. Also Robert Hartley nephew of the above who died August 17th 1852 aged 4 years.

William, Robert and Joseph's brother **Eli** was the innkeeper at the **Old Naked Man**. He was predeceased by all of his five children. This may help to understand why William Lodge Paley's diaries say Eli was *'addicted to liquor'*. Brother **Richard** owned several properties and the plumbing business on Castle Hill. William Lodge Paley described him as *'very flighty'* and *'very fat'* after another spell in an asylum. Eli and Richard are buried in Giggleswick churchyard.

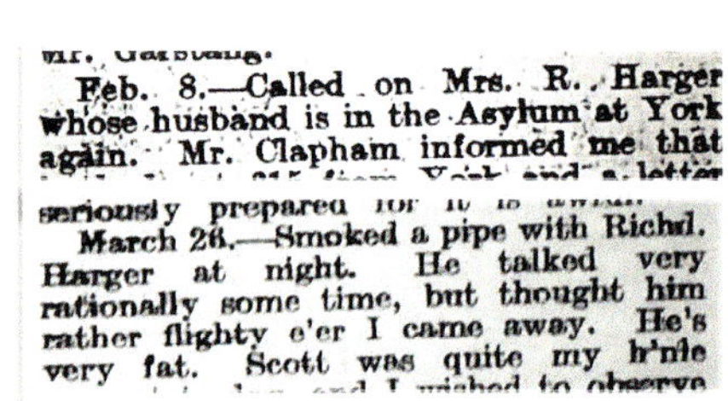
Feb. 8.—Called on Mrs. R. Harger whose husband is in the Asylum at York again. Mr. Clapham informed me that

seriously prepared

March 26.—Smoked a pipe with Richd. Harger at night. He talked very rationally some time, but thought him rather flighty e'er I came away. He's very fat. Scott was quite my h'nle

9 WORKING CLASS HEROES

The working classes made up 80% of the Victorian population but only 15% of our gravestones. Burials were expensive and gravestones cost even more. The working classes often subscribed to insurance schemes to afford a burial. Women often shared the expensive black mourning clothes that they were expected to wear for up to two years. Of course, these were the lucky ones – several poor people, especially infants, had deaths certified in Settle but didn't appear in any local burial records....

Thomas Bordley, a popular Settle postie

D19 In loving memory of Thomas Bordley died October 2nd 1878 in his 71st year. Sarah his wife died November 14th 1870 in her 64th year.

Dad **Francis Bordley** was born in 1781 in Tosside into a Quaker family. He was a corn dealer and lived in Castle Hill/Bowskills Yard. He died in 1854, aged a respectable 74 and is buried in this grave.

Son **Thomas Bordley**, born in 1807, began his working life as a house painter. He married **Sarah Thompson** in 1828 and they had six children. The new 'Penny Post' in 1840 meant that anyone could send a letter to anywhere in Britain for a penny so there was suddenly a need for more postmen and post boxes. Thomas became a letter carrier with his daily round going through the villages all the way to Horton. In 1860, his retirement was celebrated by the good folks on his round with a new suit! [BNA7]

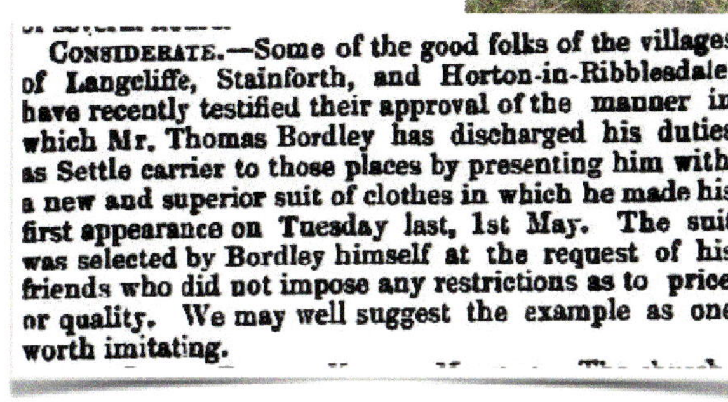

CONSIDERATE.—Some of the good folks of the villages of Langcliffe, Stainforth, and Horton-in-Ribblesdale, have recently testified their approval of the manner in which Mr. Thomas Bordley has discharged his duties as Settle carrier to those places by presenting him with a new and superior suit of clothes in which he made his first appearance on Tuesday last, 1st May. The suit was selected by Bordley himself at the request of his friends who did not impose any restrictions as to price or quality. We may well suggest the example as one worth imitating.

Thomas took up the slightly less energetic occupation of house-painting again. He had been a teetotaller for 40 years but met a sudden death in 1878 [BNA7]. Sarah had died in 1870. Sons Francis, aged 12, and James, aged 25, are probably buried with them.

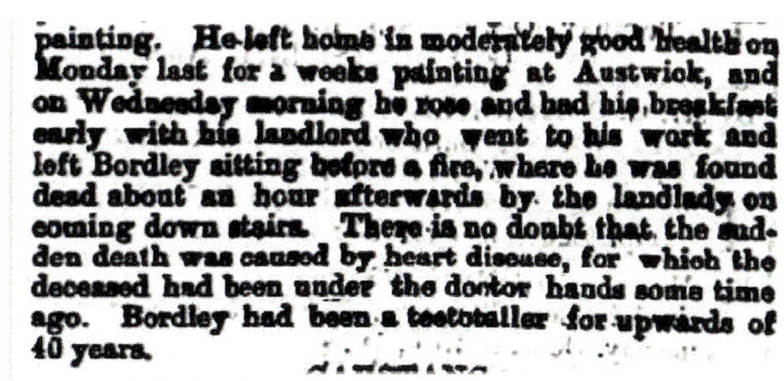

painting. He left home in moderately good health on Monday last for a weeks painting at Austwick, and on Wednesday morning he rose and had his breakfast early with his landlord who went to his work and left Bordley sitting before a fire, where he was found dead about an hour afterwards by the landlady on coming down stairs. There is no doubt that the sudden death was caused by heart disease, for which the deceased had been under the doctor hands some time ago. Bordley had been a teetotaller for upwards of 40 years.

Thomas's daughter **Ann** married Charles Gibbins, the son of Thomas' boss, the postmaster John Gibbins who was also a wealthy bank manager. Thomas' half brother, **John Bordley,** was a well known painter, decorator and photographer [LSA]. John and his wife, **Esther Wellock**, were Primitive Methodists and active members of the Temperance movement. They ran the Temperance Hotel, formerly the Spread Eagle Inn in Kirkgate until Esther died in 1862 and she is buried in an unmarked grave. John is buried with his second wife Alice in the Quaker graveyard in Kirkgate.

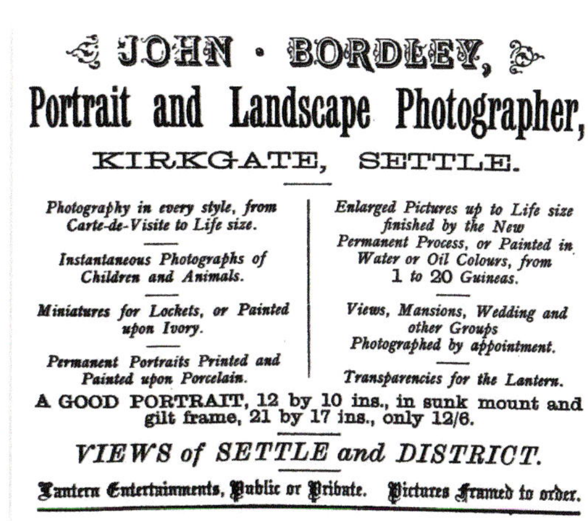

Thomas' cousins Margaret, Ann (Hargreaves) and John are buried in *grave AX2*, cousin Thomas in *grave E3*, grandchildren Francis James Bordley and Mary Pratt in *grave AX12*.

John Slinger, a pauper with a gravestone?

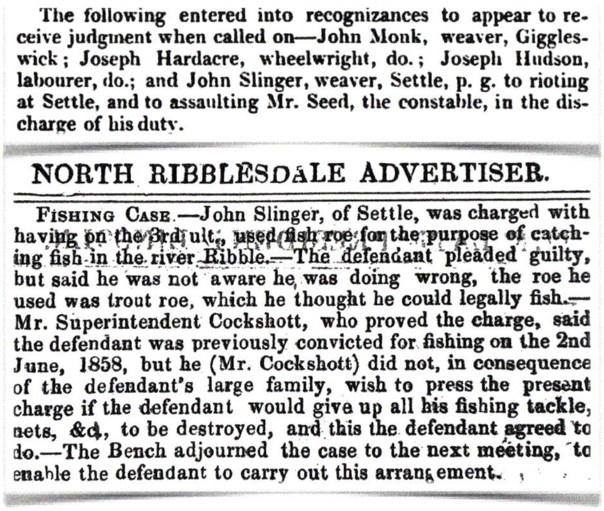

The following entered into recognizances to appear to receive judgment when called on—John Monk, weaver, Giggleswick; Joseph Hardacre, wheelwright, do.; Joseph Hudson, labourer, do.; and John Slinger, weaver, Settle, p. g. to rioting at Settle, and to assaulting Mr. Seed, the constable, in the discharge of his duty.

NORTH RIBBLESDALE ADVERTISER.

FISHING CASE.—John Slinger, of Settle, was charged with having on the 3rd ult., used fish roe for the purpose of catching fish in the river Ribble.—The defendant pleaded guilty, but said he was not aware he was doing wrong, the roe he used was trout roe, which he thought he could legally fish.—Mr. Superintendent Cockshott, who proved the charge, said the defendant was previously convicted for fishing on the 2nd June, 1858, but he (Mr. Cockshott) did not, in consequence of the defendant's large family, wish to press the present charge if the defendant would give up all his fishing tackle, nets, &c., to be destroyed, and this the defendant agreed to do.—The Bench adjourned the case to the next meeting, to enable the defendant to carry out this arrangement.

John Slinger, born in 1816, started life as a cotton weaver at Runley Bridge Mill. In December 1842 he got into a spot of trouble, OK a riot with assault, at the Spread Eagle Inn [*BNA22*]. The landlord was the elderly Robert Atkinson [*innkeepers*]. John was let off and bound over to keep the peace. In 1845 he married a local lass **Mary Hargreaves** who gave him ten children. By the 1851 census John was described as a pauper weaver living in Upper Settle. They would have lived hand to mouth.

John liked fishing, a cheap hobby which helped to supplement a meagre diet for the poor. However, he drew the attention of the officious Superintendent Cockshott on more than one occasion, this one in 1865 [*SC*]. John died four years later, when his youngest son was just five.

D16 In memory of John Slinger who died August 3rd 1869, aged 53 years. Also Mary wife of the above who died Nov 2nd 1878 aged 59 years. Also of Thomas their son who died Dec 2nd 1902. (Interred at Warton) Aged 53.

Six of John's children died in infancy/childhood and three could be buried in this grave. The other three are in Giggleswick graveyard. Of those that survived, all but one moved away. Two sons worked on the railways at Carnforth and nearby Warton.

Daughter **Harriet** married **David Plank** and they moved to Lancaster. David found work on the railways while Harriet brought up ten children. In 1913, most of the family emigrated to Canada. In May 1915, Harriet booked a trip back to Lancaster (New York to Liverpool) to see her other children, travelling second class. The ship was called the Lusitania. The Lusitania Resource website tells us: *'Her son, Hargreaves Plank, residing in England was a disabled naval seaman, and was the first violinist at Loew's Winter Garden. He strongly advised his mother not to travel until the war was over.'* The Lusitania sank on 5th May 1915. Amazingly Harriet was one of the survivors, but the shock killed her and she died on 31st July 1915. Son Hargreaves was killed in November 1918 in France.

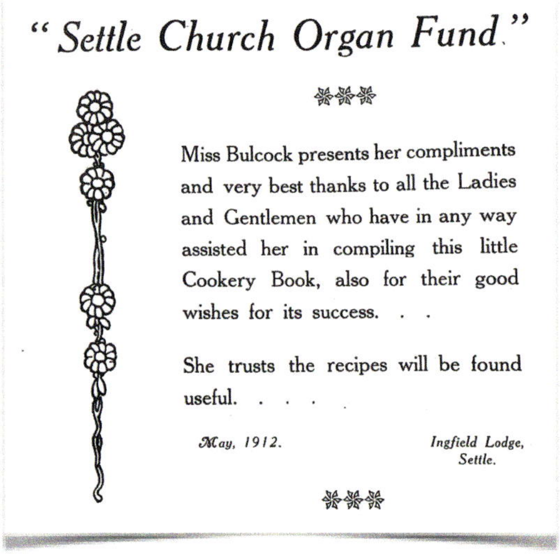

"Settle Church Organ Fund."

Miss Bulcock presents her compliments and very best thanks to all the Ladies and Gentlemen who have in any way assisted her in compiling this little Cookery Book, also for their good wishes for its success. . .

She trusts the recipes will be found useful. . . .

May, 1912. Ingfield Lodge, Settle.

Daughter **Margaret** stayed in Settle and married **Thomas Bulcock**, who became gamekeeper to Charles Swale, the grandson of the first vicar of Holy Ascension who lived at Ingfield Lodge [*church folk*]. Charles was a Trustee at Holy Ascension and their daughter Mary Jane showed her support by compiling a recipe book to raise money for the Church Organ Fund. Mary Jane was obviously an excellent cook – in 1909 she won a silver medal at the Food and Cookery Exhibition in London [*LSA*].

When he died, Charles Swale left an annuity to Margaret and Thomas which may have paid for John's gravestone. Thomas and Margaret are buried in *Old grave G14.*

4. Miss Bulcock, of Ingfield Lodge, Settle, obtained a silver medal for chocolate bon-bons and other sweets, at the Food and Cookery Exhibition held at London.

William Grime, John Birkbeck's groom

William Grime, born in 1828, was related to the many Grime families of Clapham, some of whom changed their name to 'Graham' in the 1840s which you can understand. William went straight into domestic service as a groom for Thomas Ingleby Esq. of Lawkland Hall, which was an impressive post. By the 1860s he had started working as groom to John Birkbeck where he spent the rest of his working life.

IN AFFECTIONATE REMEMBRANCE OF

William Grime,

Who entered into rest December 28th, 1877,

AGED 49 YEARS,

And was interred at Ascension Church, Settle, on New Year's Day 1878.

"Whosoever shall call on the name of the Lord shall be saved."

William married **Lydia Athey**, a servant from Doncaster, who had been brought up by her aunt and uncle and they had four daughters. William died in 1877, aged 49, five years after the birth of the youngest daughter Isabel who was promptly dispatched to be brought up by her aunt and uncle (Athey), a family tradition. William is in an unmarked grave.

Widow Lydia worked as a nurse in the 'Giggleswick sanitorium' (the workhouse) and then lived at the newly built 1 Ribble Terrace [*ph15*]. Lydia and her daughters ran an apartment rental business from here until the 1950s – over 70 years. Daughter Annie worked in domestic service, at one time working for George Stansfeld (Jnr) [*wealthy ones*]. Daughter Mary married **Frank Cowburn**, the youngest son of **John Cowburn**, the successful solicitor, who had died aged just 39. Frank's grandfather, another **John Cowburn**, had died in 1855, aged 44, after a particularly nasty skating accident on 'Birkbeck Wear' at Anley. Those were proper winters! *[SC]*

MELANCHOLY ACCIDENT. On Monday, February 12th, an accident, attended with fatal consequences, occurred to John Cowburn, Esq., of Settle. He had been skating on Birkbeck Wear, and was about to finish, when he unfortunately went against a piece of rough ice, and fell heavily. His cheek was cut through under the eye. He was out on the Tuesday and Wednesday, but on the following Tuesday he was no more. It is supposed that Erysipelatous inflamation had spread fataly to the brain. He held the offices of Clerk of the County Court and Chief Constable for the Division of Staincliffe West, for which offices his Son is a candidate.

Frank's mum was **Elizabeth Ayrton**, who was a daughter of Henry Ayrton of the Royal Oak [*innkeepers*]. She later became the third wife of Joseph Parker [*farmers*]. Frank's sister Maggie married William Lambert who was the nephew of the Settle printer John Wilcock Lambert.

SHOCKING DEATH OF A SETTLE YOUTH.—On Thursday the inhabitants of Settle and neighbouring villages were greatly shocked upon receiving intelligence to the effect that on the previous evening Henry Cowburn (20), sailor, a native of Settle, had committed suicide at Hellifield. It seems that about 4·45 p.m. on Wednesday Mr John Winder, of Gallaber Farm, Hellifield, noticed a flash of fire and heard the report of fire-arms in one of his fields, and after proceeding about 200 yards he found the young fellow lying on the ground. A bullet wound was visible in the right temple and a pistol was lying by his side. The sufferer was conveyed to Long Preston where he was attended by Doctors Lazenby and Williamson, but death ensued about five hours after the fatal shot was fired. Deceased was the eldest son of the late Mr John Cowburn, of Settle, and his untimely end, which is said to be attributable to failure to pass an examination for second mate's position on his vessel, is universally deplored in the district. An inquest is to be held on the body at the Boar's Head Hotel, Long Preston to-day (Friday).

Frank was a troubled young man. Two of his brothers died in childhood in 1873 when

Frank was just one. His brother Henry took his own life in 1889 as he had failed to pass an examination [*CH*]. Poor Frank was just 17. Frank got a job in the London and Midland Bank. He married Mary in 1895 and they moved to Pontefract. Frank and Mary had a son **Henry**, named after Frank's brother. Then, in 1904, Frank was arrested for embezzlement having caused his employer considerable trouble. After profuse apologies from Frank and his mother he was given a lenient sentence of two months imprisonment [*BNA24*].

Mr. Moxon, in opening the case, said it was one of the most painful he had ever known. Accused had been cashier in this bank, and for some time had given the management considerable trouble. The bank, however, in an excess of kindness and leniency had given him every chance of reformation. He had abused these opportunities by embezzling money to the extent of close upon £200. The bank were in which they had treated the matter. Mr. Cowburn had been in this bank since he was 16, for he left school to go there. Since he had been in this position of trust and responsibility, his character had been absolutely without blemish. When the question of bail arose, hundreds were willing and anxious to stand for him. Accused, who was a married man, with a child, attributed his fall to drink, and the difficulty of making both ends meet. There had been no betting or anything of that kind, and accused during the whole of his 16 years in the bank had never got into debt, and did not owe a penny to any tradesman. His mother had offered to recoup every penny to the bank, but they had very properly refused that offer. He urged the Bench to deal with accused as leniently as possible.

After about a quarter of an hour's retirement, the Chairman said it was a most serious charge, and they very much regretted that Cowburn had had to appear before them. Seeing that he and his family had offered to repay the money, and seeing the bank did not press the case, the Bench had taken a very lenient view of the case. But they had decided in the interests of justice, and of the public, to commit him to Wakefield for two months, in the second division.

By the next census, Mary was back in Settle with her sisters describing herself 'a widow'. However, Frank was alive and well in a lodging house in London. Oh dear. Mum Lydia died in 1906 and is buried with daughters Emma and Mary (Cowburn) in the unmarked *Old EX17*. Daughters Annie and Isabel are in *New EX9*.

Young Henry Cowburn was the only heir of this line of Cowburns and Grimes, and benefitted from all of his aunts' wills, lucky lad. He made a living selling coal in Settle and married Rose Martha Lord, granddaughter of Wesleyan Preacher John Lord [*wenches, wives*]. Henry is buried in the *New grave K50*.

Henry Puttenham, a travelling paper maker

Henry Puttenham was one of numerous working class men who travelled around the country to try and find work. Henry, born in 1768, came from Aylesford, Kent. In 1794 he married **Mary Bailey** and they had four children: Richard, Louisa, the wonderfully named Theopolis and Napoleon (an interesting choice at that stage in history). In the early 1800s the family moved to the thriving metropolis of Liverpool where Henry and his sons made a living as paper makers. In the late 1830s, with Henry approaching his 70s, he moved to Langcliffe to work in the paper mill with wife Mary and daughter Louisa. They lived at the 'Paper Mill Houses' in Langcliffe.

In 1838, daughter Louisa became the second wife of **Alexander Gliddon**. Alexander had moved up to Langcliffe from Somerset, probably looking for a fresh start after a six month spell in Ilchester Gaol for '*assault and want of sureties to keep the peace'* with a fine of one shilling. Alexander's first wife had died giving birth to their son John who was brought up by maternal grandparents in Langcliffe.

Assault and for
Want of Sureties to keep the Peace

Louisa gave birth to daughter Mary Ann. In March 1840, dad Henry died, aged 72. A year later, little Mary Ann died and was buried at Holy Ascension on 28th May next to her grandfather in the unmarked grave *DX16*. Incredibly, within the space of a week, by the date of the 1841 census on 6th June, Alexander, Louisa and mum Mary Puttenham were living in Liverpool. Mary was working as a schoolmistress, and Alexander was a papermaker. Louisa died in 1846 and Alexander then moved to London with son John. Mary continued to work as a matron in Liverpool until she died in 1858, aged 77.

The elusive Elizabeth Chapman, a war hero's mum

D22 In remembrance of Elizabeth, relict of the late Thomas Chapman of Kirkby-in-Ashfield born April 11th 1806, died February 4th 1881. RIP

This is an exquisitely carved gravestone, so this family had money somewhere. Frustratingly, Elizabeth was not once found on a census return. She was born **Elizabeth Beighton/Britain** in 1806 to an agricultural labourer near Mansfield, Nottinghamshire. At the age of 16 and seven months pregnant she married **Thomas Chapman**, an equally elusive young chap who worked as a framework knitter, using machinery to make stockings – a real Nottinghamshire trade. Thomas died in 1843. They lived near Sutton-in-Ashfield and had four children. Both daughters were called Rebecca as the first one died aged 4, and second died when just 12. Sons **John** and **Robert** survived.

John and Robert lived with aunts and uncles, even when they were young children so obviously things weren't quite right at home. By the late 1870s Robert, his wife **Louisa Smith** and his mum Elizabeth had moved to 'Crag View' at the top of Commercial Street in Upper Settle. Here Robert worked as a baker but had previously worked as a salesman and a servant. Louisa came from Barnoldswick so this may be why they moved in this direction. Elizabeth died in 1881.

Robert died in 1884, aged just 51. This was during the years when Holy Ascension graveyard was closed. The Ancient graveyard was 'dangerously full' but the church had not yet purchased land for the Old graveyard. This may explain why Robert is buried at Giggleswick rather than with his mum.

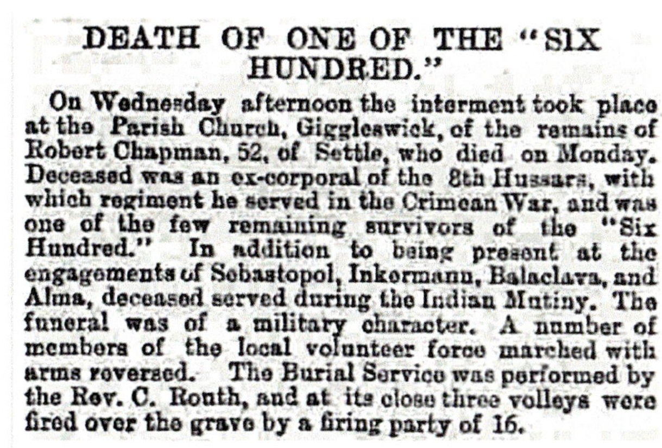

DEATH OF ONE OF THE "SIX HUNDRED."

On Wednesday afternoon the interment took place at the Parish Church, Giggleswick, of the remains of Robert Chapman, 52, of Settle, who died on Monday. Deceased was an ex-corporal of the 8th Hussars, with which regiment he served in the Crimean War, and was one of the few remaining survivors of the "Six Hundred." In addition to being present at the engagements of Sebastopol, Inkermann, Balaclava, and Alma, deceased served during the Indian Mutiny. The funeral was of a military character. A number of members of the local volunteer force marched with arms reversed. The Burial Service was performed by the Rev. C. Routh, and at its close three volleys were fired over the grave by a firing party of 16.

The news reports of his death and detailed gravestone inscription explain his life and how he could afford such a beautiful gravestone for his mum and also for himself and Louisa at Giggleswick Church [*BNA1*]. Robert had was one of the Gallant 600 in the Balaclava Charge of 1854, otherwise known as the Charge of the Light Brigade. The Light Brigade included the 8th Hussars Cavalry, armed only with lances and sabres so they could move quickly in a reconnaissance charge. However, a series of blunders meant they were completely outmanoeuvred by heavy artillery. There were nearly 300 human British casualties and 335 horses slain. With this service, Robert will have had a good pension.

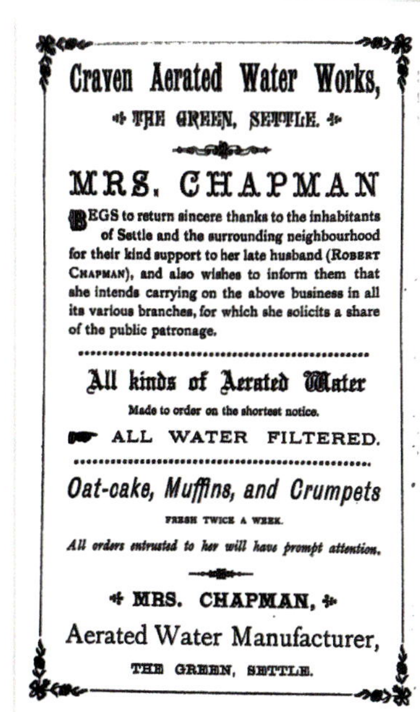

Robert's wife Louisa outlived him by 14 years and continued his aerated water business [*LSA*]. When Louisa died, she left her quite substantial estate to her 30 year old boarder, Mary Agnes Proctor, a music teacher. Just a year later, Mary Agnes married a respectable bookkeeper George Clark. Perhaps Louisa's inheritance somehow made Mary seem more attractive?

A SNEAKY PEAK INTO THE OLD GRAVEYARD . . . . John Winskill

John Winskill, born in 1817 in Kirkby Lonsdale, was a stonemason, advertising his business in 1854 [*SC*]. He married **Margaret Parkinson** in Settle and they had three daughters and then three sons living in the Back Stables area, behind the Golden Lion. John was a churchwarden at Holy Ascension for five years, and had the difficult job of trying to persuade William Perkin to update the burial plans, unsuccessfully. John had responsibility in the town as 'Vice Chair of the Sanitary Authority', the equivalent of Health and Safety with an 'Inspector of Nuisances'. We could do with one of those now! John and Margaret lived long lives, and died within a year of each other in 1889 and 1890. They are buried in an unmarked *Old grave BX31*. Their children had varying fortunes. The daughters married farmers and a blacksmith.

> JOHN WINSKILL,
> Builder, Stone Mason, and Grave Stone Cutter,
> SETTLE,
> BEGS to announce that he keeps in Stock TERRA COTTA CHIMNEY POTS,
> YORKSHIRE GREY SLATE and FLAGS
> Of the best quality.
> The Grey Slate and Flags may be seen at the Railway Station, Settle, or in his yard, and will be delivered at any Station on the North Western Line, at moderate charges.

Eldest son James, born in 1847, worked a large farm of 360 acres in Airton and then in Cumbria with his wife **Elizabeth Coates** (whose step-mother was also James' aunt!). Strangely, at the time of the 1891 census they lived in Nottingham. James described himself as a '*retired farmer*'. Later that year several newspaper articles suggested that James was having problems, writing insulting letters to both the Queen and the Archbishop of Canterbury [*BNA30*]. The full details of the hearing explained that he had been a successful Yorkshire farmer. He had been assessed, but doctors said they were '*too afraid to say he was insane*'. In 1896, James appeared in Calais dressed in red and carrying a wooden cross [*BNA33*]. Oh dear, poor James. He died in Calais the following year. His wife Elizabeth returned to Settle and lived by herself on Mains View.

> James Winskill, a clerk, was remanded in custody at Nottingham on Tuesday on the charge of writing insulting letters to the Queen and the Archbishop of Canterbury.

> A PECULIAR ARREST.
> CALAIS, May 24.—A man named James Winskill, said to be a British subject, was arrested here to-day under singular circumstances. It appears that a decree of expulsion had been issued against Winskill for being concerned in a publication directed against Queen Victoria. This afternoon he appeared in the streets of Calais attired in red, and carrying a wooden cross on his shoulders. A considerable crowd collected, and Winskill was taken into custody.

Son John was the land agent for Walter Morrison at Malham Tarn Estate for over 30 years, and was left £1000 in Mr Morrison's will [*BNA13*]. John and his two wives are buried in the graveyard in unmarked *Old grave BX32* next to his parents.

> MALHAM TARN ESTATE AGENT.
> The death has occurred at Settle of Mr. John Winskill, aged 79, for over thirty years estate agent for the Malham Tarn Estates, being employed in turn by the late Mr. Walter Morrison, his nephew, Major J. A. Morrison, the late Mr. E. W. Fisher, of Oakfield Lodge, Huddersfield, and the present owner, Capt. Hutton-Croft.
> There were few better known men in North Ribblesdale than Mr. Winskill, who for over forty years had had an unbroken connection with the local government of the district, being a member of the Settle Board of Guardians from 1890 until 1930. At his death he was a member of the Settle Rural District Council. He was also a prominent Freemason.

Son Edward began life as a butcher [*LSA*] and then moved into farming, with wife Judith. They emigrated to Saskatchewan, Canada, in 1905 but came back again.

CURIOUS TALES FROM THE ANCIENT GRAVEYARD

Celebrating the lives of Settle's Ancestors

This book has been generously funded by Stories in Stone, a scheme of conservation and community projects in the Ingleborough area. The scheme was developed by the Ingleborough Dales Landscape Partnership led by Yorkshire Dales Millennium Trust, and supported by the National Lottery Heritage Fund. Contact www.storiesinstone.org.uk.

AUTHOR'S NOTE:

I am not a historian, nor an academic, but I do have a passionate interest in local and family history. I have had the pleasure of researching Settle's ancestors for many years and they have never ceased to amaze and inspire me. I hope this collection of real life stories helps you, the reader, appreciate the wonder and importance of these people and that it will be an inspiration to others to research their local ancestors.

There isn't space for all of the stories in this book, but many others have been written. Research into more recent graves in the 'Old' and 'New' graveyard continues. Holy Ascension Church currently has a rolling display of the latest research. Eventually, we hope all the findings will be available at the church and online. Inscriptions and stories will be added to the 'Old Settle' family tree in ancestry.co.uk.

This is not a history book, however, the stories have been based on historical fact, using publicly available documentation and resources. They are written in good faith, with no offence intended. If I have inadvertently included errors or breached any copyright I apologise and would welcome corrected and additional information.

Do you have ancestors in Holy Ascension graveyard? If so, I would love to hear from you, please get in touch.

Contact: settleresearch@gmail.com

This book is dedicated to Settle's ancestors, without whom there would be no stories, no history and no book. It's also dedicated to my own ancestors, without whom I wouldn't be here to write it. In particular to my dad, Fred Youell, an eccentric preserved railway pioneer, for those nerdy genes and to my dear mum Susan Youell, one of life's unforgettable enthusiasts, despite my dad. She would have been so proud, and would have loved to have read this book.

Sarah Lister, July 2019

ACKNOWLEDGEMENTS

This book could not have been written without the friendship and support of wonderful people. I give my sincere thanks to every one, and owe you a coffee at one of Settle's finest coffee shops.

To **Stories in Stone**, particularly Don Gamble whose generous support has enabled the publication of this book, and the **Yorkshire Dales Community Archives**, **Capturing the Past** website team for their support, and Nigel Robinson at **iprint.**

To **Settle District U3A Committee**, for supporting the book publication, the **Family History Group**, and the **Graveyard Team** for inscriptions, typing, proof reading, ideas, meetings, publicity, listening, encouragement and support. They include Sally Waterson (of course), Eileen Bamford, Jackie Allot, Anne Webster, Dot Lambert, Lynda Boyce, Rosemary Padgett-Roberts, Alan and Dorothy Hemsworth, Chris Taylor, Jennifer Scholey, Phil Robinson, Liz Brown, Sue Simpson, Vicky Cooper, Hilary Brown, Marion McNichol, Pauline Elliot, Mike and Sue Howarth. To **Holy Ascension Church**, in particular John and Edith Diggles, Paul Cochrane and Beryl James for their generous support. To Giggleswick School and Giggleswick Horticultural Show for display boards.

To **North Craven Buildings Preservation Trust** at the Folly, Settle for their support over the past five years with particular thanks to Anne Read, Mel Cookson-Carter and Pamela Jordan. Thanks for having the faith in me to compile the material for the Momento Mori Exhibition in Spring 2019. To the **Folly**, **Settle District U3A** and **Holy Ascension Church** for selling the book and to the **Folly**, **North Craven Heritage Trust**, **Settle District Rotary Club**, **Giggleswick Women's Institute**, **Long Preston Heritage Group** and **Clapham Age UK** for inviting me to talk about the stories of Settle's ancestors. To **St Mary's Embsay Churchyard Survey Project** for sharing expertise on RTI imaging of gravestones, and Long Preston Heritage Group for sharing experiences. To members of the excellent **'Back in Settle'** facebook site for sharing photos and numerous Settle folk for their interest. Of course, there are many other stars who remain unnamed.

Most of all I thank my husband, soul mate and best friend, **Ken Lister.** This project has taken his patience, love and support to new levels. I'm so very lucky to have him by my side.

RESOURCES

Stories have been compiled using documents from Ancestry and FindMyPast genealogy websites. Parish records at Holy Ascension by TH Foxcroft, and at St Alkelda's Giggleswick by Nigel Mussett. Other records from the Church, the Folly, NCHT website and Settle Community Library.

Descendants and local researchers have helped to bring stories to life: **[*A*]** Robert Currie, **[*B*]** descendants of the Hargraves, **[*C*]** Algy Metcalfe, **[*D*]** Mike Howarth, **[*E*]** Pamela Jordan, **[*F*]** Catherine Vaughan-Williams, **[*G*]** Rodney Hooper, **[*H*]** Jane Milner, **[*J*]** Allan Gould, **[*K*]** Bridget Sunter, and also Norma Lowery. It has been such a pleasure to share the stories of these families.

Great photographs: [*ph1*] Robert Currie, [*ph2*] Tom Lord, [*ph3*] Algy Metcalfe, [*ph4*] NCBPT, [*ph5*] descendants of Edmundsons, [*ph6*] Mike Howarth, [*ph7*] Sandra Cowin, [*ph8*] Chris Chandler, [*ph9*] Jane Milner, [*ph10*] Ann Gee, [*ph11*] Descendants of John Lund, [*ph12*] Liz Metcalfe, [*ph13*] Pamela Jordan, [*ph14*] Bridget Sunter, [*ph15*] Paul Cochrane, [*ph16*] descendants of Hargraves. Group photos by Ken Lister, Gravestones by Eileen Bamford. Other photos in the public domain from Wikipedia.

Newspaper cuttings with kind permission from the **British Newspaper Archive**, supplied by the British Library: [*BNA1*] Manchester Courier and Lancashire General Advertiser, [*BNA2*] Huddersfield Chronicle, [*BNA3*] Burnley Express, [*BNA4*] Essex Herald, [*BNA5*] Yorkshire Gazette, [*BNA6*] Preston Chronicle, [*BNA7*] Lancaster Gazette, [*BNA8*] Lancaster Guardian, [*BNA9*] Windsor and Eton Express, [*BNA10*] Blackburn Standard, [*BNA11*] Leeds Mercury, [*BNA12*] Cambridge Independent Express, [*BNA13*] Yorkshire Post and Intelligencer, [*BNA14*] Leeds Intelligencer, [*BNA15*] Edinburgh Evening News, [*BNA16*] Westmorland Gazette, [*BNA17*] Peterborough Advertiser, [*BNA18*] Kendal Mercury, [*BNA19*] Leeds Times, [*BNA20*] Lancashire Evening Post, [*BNA21*] Derbyshire Advertiser and Journal, [*BNA22*] Bradford Observer, [*BNA23*] Aberdeen Press and Journal, [BNA24] Sheffield Daily Telegraph, [*BNA25*] Bradford Daily Telegraph, [*BNA26*] Yorkshire Evening Post, [*BNA27*] Illustrated London News, [*BNA28*] Vote, [*BNA29*] Mid Sussex Times, [*BNA30*] Hull Daily Mail, [*BNA31*] The Era, [*BNA32*] Dublin Daily Express, [*BNA33*] Cheltenham Chronicle.

Other cuttings

[*SC*] Settle Chronicle, [*WSA*] Wildman's Settle Almanac, [*LSA*] Lamberts Settle Almanac, and the diaries of William Lodge Paley, with kind permission of the Folly, NCBPT. Thanks also to Lamberts Printer and Design, Settle.

[*CH*] with kind permission of the Craven Herald and Pioneer, generously provided by Mike Howarth. Thanks to the Craven Herald for their supportive features.

INDEX OF GRAVESTONE (OR FAMILY) NAMES

Eileen Bamford, Sarah Lister, Sally Waterson

PLAN OF THE ANCIENT GRAVEYARD

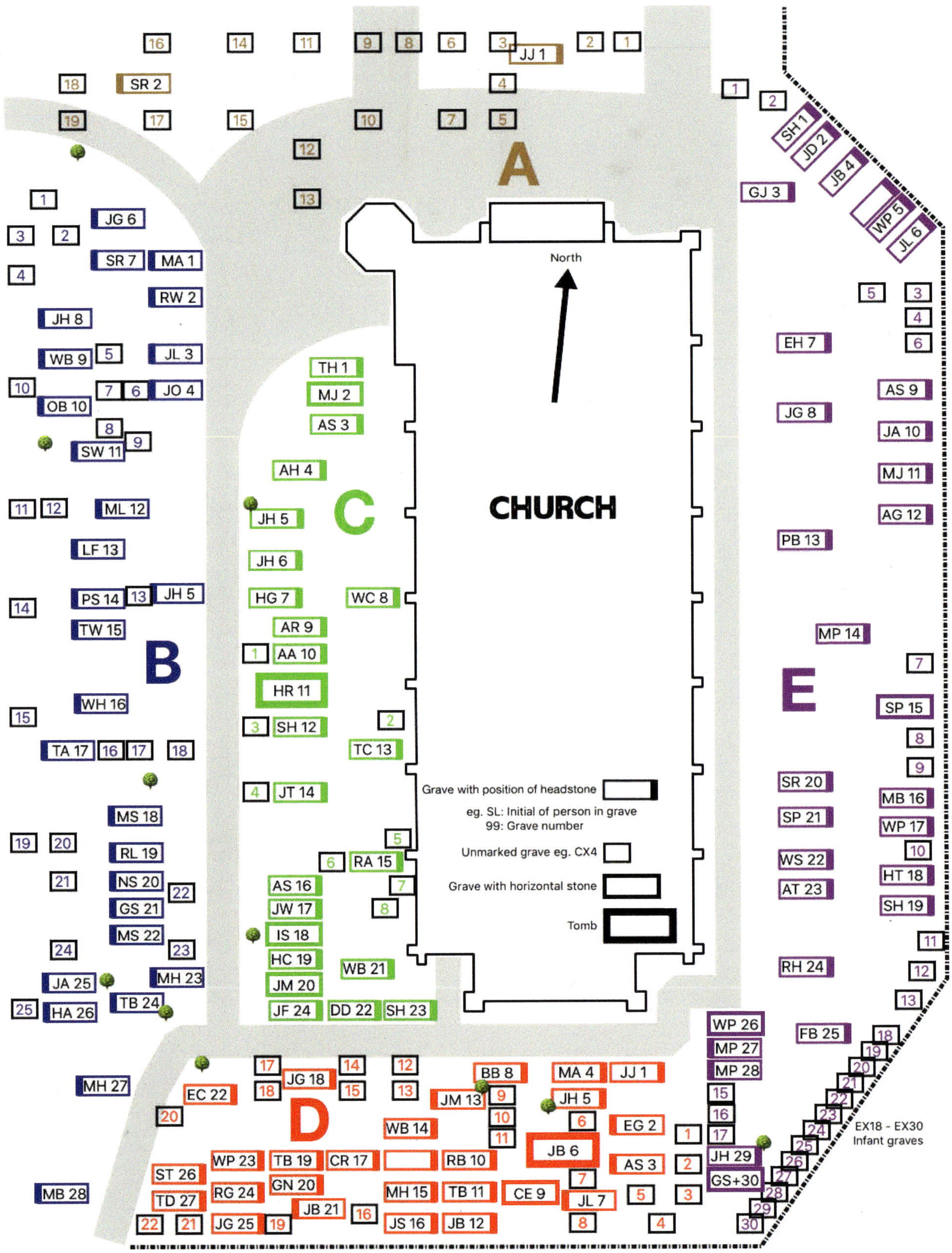

QSE

QUICK SMART ENGL

Intermediate

TEACHER'S GUIDE with Photocopiable Resources

Ken Wilson

and

Mary Tomalin

BROOKEMEAD ENGLISH LANGUAGE TEACHING

QSE
QUICK SMART ENGLISH

Intermediate
TEACHER'S GUIDE

Series editor: Duncan Prowse
Contributor: Deborah Friedland
Consultant: Rosemary Harris
Editors: Deborah Friedland, Anna Whitcher Kutz
Designers: John Anastasio, Wendi Watson, e-Bookservices

QSE Intermediate Common European Framework Level B1-B2

QSE Series *Title*	*Common European Framework*	*Cambridge ESOL*	*Michigan*	*TOEFL (New TOEFL)*	*Trinity College, London, ESOL*	*Edexcel London Test of English*
Quick Smart English Pre-Intermediate	A2-B1	PET	BCCE		ISE I, GESE Grade 4,5,6	Level 1- 2
Quick Smart English Intermediate	B1-B2	FCE	ECCE	450-525 Target 485 (NT 163)	ISE II, GESE Grade 7,8,9	Level 2-3
Quick Smart English Advanced	B2-C1	CAE	ALCE	Target 525 (NT 197)	ISE III, GESE Grade 10,11	Level 3-4

QSE Intermediate B1-B2 Teacher's Guide
ISBN:978-1-905248-19-3
1-905248-19-9
Also available:
QSE Intermediate Student's Book, ISBN 1-905248-04-0
QSE Intermediate Workbook, ISBN 1-905248-05-9
QSE Intermediate CD 1 Listening + Unit 0, ISBN 1-905248-24-7
QSE Intermediate CD 2 Reading, ISBN 1-905248-07-5

Other books in the QSE Series:
QSE Pre-Intermediate (CEF A2-B1)
Student's Book, Workbook, Audio CDs, Teacher's Guide
QSE Advanced (CEF B2-C1)
Student's Book and Workbook, Audio and video DVD, Teacher's Guide

Published by:
Brookemead English Language Teaching, PO Box 58230, London N1 1RP
www.brookemead-elt.co.uk

QSE
QUICK SMART ENGLISH

Intermediate TEACHER'S GUIDE

CONTENTS

Unit	Title	Subject *The BIG question*	Functions, Language Banks (See SB cover flaps)	Grammar / Supplementary Grammar	Reading CD 2	Listening CD 1
0	Think global, act local	National and local produce and products *Are you a 'good' shopper?* SB4	0 Advantages and Disadvantages SB4, WB46	*should*; present simple passive; *because of*, *due to* SB4, WB2	19 CD 1 Shopping in supermarkets or local shops? SB5	20 kNOwtrash Exhibition at Eden Project SB6, WB67
1	Mr and Ms Right	Youth culture *Is the internet a good place to meet people?* SB8	1 Asking for and giving advice and suggestions SB9, WB46 2 Asking for and giving opinions SB10, WB46 3 Filling pauses SB11, WB46	*should, ought to, could, you'd better* SB8, WB4 *so, such, too, enough* PR190	1 CD 2 Relationships, online dating: advantages and dangers SB9	1 Late night radio phone-in show for lonely hearts SB10, WB67
2	Bright lights, big city	Country and city life *Is life better in the city?* SB12	4 Comparing and contrasting SB13, WB47 5 Asking for clarification SB15, WB47	Comparatives with modifiers SB12, WB6 Prefixes, suffixes PR191	2 Living in San Francisco and New York compared SB13	2 Three contrasting views of immigration SB14, WB68
3	Fame and fortune	Public figures and celebrity *What is the price of fame?* SB16	6 Expressing possibility and uncertainty SB17, WB47 7 Expressions used to gain time for thought SB19, WB48	*may, might* SB16, WB8	3 Plusses and minuses of being as famous as Nicole Kidman, Einstein or Madonna SB17	3 Interview with pop musicians about their tours and gigs SB18, WB68
4	Animal passions	Environmental concerns *Do animals have feelings?* SB20	8 Expressing feelings and emotions SB21, WB48 9 Ways of agreeing and disagreeing SB23, WB48	Relative clauses; definite article SB20, WB10 *where, whose, what, which, whom* PR192	4 Animal behaviour: the emotions of whales, dolphins and elephants SB21	4 Anti-vivisection campaigner and scientist discuss experiments on primates SB22, WB69
5	Did it really happen?	Early memories *How well do we remember things?* SB24	10 Talking about past habits SB25, WB49 11 Hesitation fillers SB27, WB49	*Would, used to*, past perfect SB24, WB12 Defining / non-defining relative clauses PR193	5 *Recollections of a happy life*, by Annie L. Burton, ex-slave, USA SB25	5 Life of servants and masters in a great house in England in the early 20th century SB26, WB70
6	You are being watched	Technology *Is security more important than privacy?* SB28	12 Asking about and describing pictures SB31, WB49	Present and past simple passives SB28, WB14 Countable, uncountable nouns, plurals PR194	6 Underwater surveillance device saves lives in swimming pools SB29	6 Being monitored everywhere you go: RFID tags and CCTV cameras SB30, WB70
7	Oil crisis	Environmental issues *What will we do when the oil runs out?* SB32	13 Speculating SB33, WB50 14 Future time expressions SB35, WB50	*when, unless, in case*, zero and first conditionals SB32, WB16 Future tense, future perfect PR195	7 When will we reach Peak Oil? When will oil run out? Alternative energy sources SB33	7 Interview about solar-hydrogen powered house with Malaysian professor-inventor SB34, WB71
	Extended reading 1	Love and romance SB36			8 *Captain Corelli's Mandolin*, by Louis de Bernieres SB37	
8	Exam pressure	Education *Why are students so stressed?* SB38	15 Persuading and encouraging SB39, WB50 16 Giving examples SB41, WB51	Second conditional SB38, WB20 *Prefer, I'd rather...* PR196	9 Exam pressure on Korean students causes some to commit suicide SB39	8 Students discuss studying at an American university SB40, WB71
9	Give peace a chance	Personal values and ideals *Can we stop wars?* SB42	17 Cohesive words SB43, WB51	Cohesive devices SB42, WB22	10 Interview with inventor of AK-47 rifle, Mikhail Kalashnikov SB43	9 Three different personal campaigns for peace SB44, WB72

Key:
SB = Student's Book TG = Teacher's Guide
WB = Workbook PR = Photocopiable Resources in TG

Speaking (see also Role Cards for each Unit WB57-66)	Writing	CLIL (Content and Language Integrated Learning)	Teacher's Guide Photocopiable Resources	Pages
What do you do about recycling? CONTROVERSY: Discussion about growing your own food SB6, WB57 YOUR TOPIC: Products you use SB7	Review of exhibition SB6 Product report WB3	ECONOMICS: BRIC economies (Brazil, Russia, India, China) SB7	Teacher's notes and answer key TG256 Quick Smart Test 0 PR267	Unit 0 SB4-7 WB2-3 TG256-266
Advice and suggestions about dating CONTROVERSY: Best ways of meeting Mr or Ms Right SB10, WB55 CONVERSATION: How do people meet their ideal partners? SB11	Survey on dating habits; writing up results of dating survey SB10 WB5	PSYCHOLOGY: Professor Solomon Asch's Conformity Experiment SB11	Teacher's notes and answer key TG33 Supplementary grammar PR190 FCE Exam 1 PR205 Quick Smart Test 1 PR226	Unit 1 SB8-11 WB4-5 TG33-40
Comparing where you would most like to live CONTROVERSY: Argument between a refugee and someone who is against immigration SB14, WB55 YOUR TOPIC: Why move to another country? SB15	Send a postcard home, describing where you live now SB14 WB7	HUMAN GEOGRAPHY: World's largest cities; Push and pull factors in migration SB15	Teacher's notes and answer key TG41 Supplementary grammar PR191 FCE Exam 2 PR206 Quick Smart Test 2 PR227	Unit 2 SB12-15 WB6-7 TG41-47
Advantages and disadvantages of fame and fortune CONTROVERSY: Can a famous pop star hide from publicity? SB18, WB55 INTERACTIVE TASK: How does the media manage the news? SB19	Devise and answer a questionnaire about how fame changes people SB18 WB9	MEDIA STUDIES: How the media select and manage the news that we see and read SB19	Teacher's notes and answer key TG48 FCE Exam 3 PR220 Quick Smart Test 3 PR228	Unit 3 SB16-19 WB8-9 TG48-56
Your ideas about whether animals have emotions CONTROVERSY: Do animal rights come before scientific research? SB22, WB56 CONVERSATION: Are people more important than animals? SB23	Formal letter to editor of a newspaper SB22 WB11	ECOLOGY: How habitat loss and bush meat affect threatened species in Africa SB23	Teacher's notes and answer key TG57 Supplementary grammar PR192 FCE Exam 4 PR207 Quick Smart Test 4 PR229	Unit 4 SB20-23 WB10-11 TG57-63
Could a life of slavery really be happy? CONTROVERSY: Tell a story in a whisper and pass it on SB26, WB57 INTERACTIVE TASK: Talking about being a servant or a slave SB27	Essay about things you remember from your childhood SB26 WB13	HISTORY: The Slave Trade across the Atlantic Ocean SB27	Teacher's notes and answer key TG64 Supplementary grammar PR193 FCE Exam 5 PR208 Quick Smart Test 5 PR230	Unit 5 SB24-27 WB12-13 TG64-70
The benefits of electronic security systems CONTROVERSY: Police, politicians and ordinary people debate privacy SB30, WB57 CONVERSATION: Discussion about surveillance SB31	Creative writing: a world where everyone is watched SB30 WB15	PHYSICS: Communication waves; wavelengths; digital and analogue signals SB31	Teacher's notes and answer key TG71 Supplementary grammar PR194 FCE Exam 6 PR209 Quick Smart Test 6 PR231	Unit 6 SB28-31 WB14-15 TG71-78
Your opinion about the future of oil CONTROVERSY: Will technology find a solution to the energy crisis? SB34, WB58 YOUR TOPIC: Presenting your ideas for alternative energy SB35	Article for environmental magazine SB34 WB17	CHEMISTRY: Hydrocarbons, pollution, greenhouse gases SB35	Teacher's notes and answer key TG79 Supplementary grammar PR195 FCE Exam 7 PR210 Quick Smart Test 7 PR232	Unit 7 SB32-35 WB16-17 TG79-87
Describing people's characters Continuing the story SB36	Writing informal letter to a friend SB36		Progress check 1 WB18-19	SB36-37 WB18-19 TG88-90
Helping each other through exams CONTROVERSY: Parents and students debate the need for and kinds of further education SB40, WB58 YOUR TOPIC: Studying abroad: why and where? SB41	Formal letter of application to a college abroad SB40 WB21	ENGLISH FOR ACADEMIC PURPOSES: Why study EAP? Where to study SB41	Teacher's notes and answer key TG91 Supplementary grammar PR196 FCE Exam 8 PR211 Quick Smart Test 8 PR233	Unit 8 SB38-41 WB20-21 TG91-98
Would stopping arms manufacturing stop wars? CONTROVERSY: Can you refuse to fight in a war? SB44, WB59 INTERACTIVE TASK: Do you have the right to kill in self-defence? SB45	Article for magazine about peace and war SB44 WB23	PEACE STUDIES: Role of the United Nations SB45	Teacher's notes and answer key TG99 FCE Exam 9 PR222 Quick Smart Test 9 PR234	Unit 9 SB42-45 WB22-23 TG99-107

Unit	Title	Subject *The BIG question*	Functions, Language Banks (See cover flaps)	Grammar / Supplementary Grammar	Reading CD 2	Listening CD 1
10	I must have one of those	Society and living standards *How much is enough?* SB46	18 Expressing wishes and hopes SB47,WB51 19 Checking that you understood what someone said SB49,WB52	Verb patterns after *wish* and *hope* SB46, WB24 *to, so as to, in order to, so that* PR197	11 Rich family from London downshifts to the simple life in Wales SB47	10 Poverty – making a living from garbage in Brazil and South Africa SB48, WB72
11	Globesity	Habits and obsessions *Are people fatter?* SB50	20 Evaluating options SB51, WB51	*although, (even) though, in spite of, despite* SB50, WB26 *can, could, to be able* PR198	12 Houston, fat capital of America SB51	11 Diary of a diet and a date SB52, WB73
12	Cities of the future	Design *Where will we all live?* SB54	21 Asking for extra information and eliciting further ideas SB57, WB52	Simple passive – present perfect, future SB54, WB28 Participle clauses PR199	13 New types of cities: 1.6 km high Sky City; Pyramid City SB55	12 Maglev trains and trans-atlantic tunnel SB56, WB73
13	Call of the wild	National customs *Is hunting a sport, tradition, or cruelty?* SB58	22 Paraphrasing SB61, WB53	Reported speech SB58, WB30 Reporting verbs PR200	14 Bear hunting for sport in Russia SB59	13 Expedition to Kamchatka Peninsula in the Russian Far East SB60, WB74
	Extended reading 2	Pollution and recycling SB62			15 *Dumped computers sold illegally* SB63	
14	Fantasy worlds	Dreams and nightmares *Why is fantasy so popular?* SB64	23 Expressing abstract ideas SB67, WB53	Passives with modals (*can be seen, should be read*) SB64, WB34 Gerund and the infinitive PR201	16 Book extract: Ursula K Le Guin's, *A Wizard of Earthsea* SB65	14 Friends discuss which video to watch: horror or fantasy SB66, WB74
15	Think big!	The world of work *Would you like to make 81m?* SB68	24 Expressing likes and dislikes SB69, WB53	Verbs + *ing* or an infinitive SB68, WB36 Verbs followed by gerund or infinitive PR202	17 How student Geoff Cook made a million SB69	15 Two applicants interviewed for a job building a hospital in India SB70, WB75
16	Throw away the key	Crime and punishment *Is prison best to stop crime?* SB72	25 Expressing regret SB73, WB53 26 Showing respect SB75, WB54	Third conditional, past use of *wish* SB72, WB38	18 Drugs: therapy in Holland or the death penalty in China? SB73	16 Three Strikes Law sends people to jail for life SB74, WB76
17	Surviving disaster	Risk and adventure *Are you a survivor?* SB76	27 Evaluating past actions / course of events SB77, WB54	*should / could* + present perfect SB76, WB40 *It is said that; he is said to...* PR203	19 Did climber Aron Ralston have to cut off his arm to save his life? SB77	17 Lost in a snow storm on a mountain in Scotland SB78, WB76
18	Alone in space	The supernatural *Are we alone in space?* SB80	28 Hypothesising SB81, WB54	*must / might / could / can't* + present perfect SB80, WB42 *To have / get done; it's time we...* PR204	20 The Roswell incident: have aliens visited the Earth? SB81	18 Search for Extra Terrestrial Intelligence and Life. SB82, WB77
	Extended reading 3	Adventure and achievement SB84			21 *West with the Night*, by Beryl Markham SB85	

Language banks and exercises WB46-56 **Language bank answer keys** TG268 **Audio text** WB67-77

Key:
SB = Student's Book TG = Teacher's Guide
WB = Workbook PR = Photocopiable Resources in TG

Speaking (see also Role Cards for each Unit WB57-66)	Writing	CLIL (Content and Language Integrated Learning)	Teacher's Guide Photocopiable Resources	Pages
Is the simple life boring? CONTROVERSY: Is poverty the most important problem in the world? SB48, WB59 CONVERSATION: What makes people poor, or think they are poor? SB49	Email a friend about the cost of living SB48 WB25	SOCIAL STUDIES: Child poverty in Britain SB49	Teacher's notes and answer key TG108 Supplementary grammar PR197 FCE Exam 10 PR212 Quick Smart Test 10 PR235	Unit 10 SB46-49 WB24-25 TG108-116
What do people do to keep fit? CONTROVERSY: Putting pressure on people to eat more or diet more SB52, WB60 YOUR TOPIC: Survey and report on people's eating habits SB53	Write an advertisement for a fitness club SB52 WB27	HEALTH EDUCATION: Worldwide evidence of increasing obesity SB53	Teacher's notes and answer key TG117 Supplementary grammar PR198 FCE Exam 11 PR213 Quick Smart Test 11 PR236	Unit 11 SB50-53 WB26-27 TG117-124
Would you live in a building that is 1.6 km high? CONTROVERSY: Is it a good idea to build projects like transatlantic tunnel? SB56, WB60 INTERACTIVE TASK: For and against modern architecture SB57	Report on your plans for your ideal city of the future SB56 WB29	DESIGN: The Bauhaus and the beginning of modern design in Germany and America SB57	Teacher's notes and answer key TG125 Supplementary grammar PR199 FCE Exam 12 PR214 Quick Smart Test 12 PR237	Unit 12 SB54-57 WB28-29 TG125-131
Reporters interview hunters CONTROVERSY: For and against hunting wild animals SB60, WB61 CONVERSATION: Right to bear arms in USA and tragedy at Colombine High School SB61	Write an article describing an old national custom SB60 WB31	CONSTITUTIONAL LAW: US Bill of Rights, Second Amendment, the right to bear arms SB61	Teacher's notes and answer key TG132 Supplementary grammar PR200 FCE Exam 13 PR215 Quick Smart Test 13 PR238	Unit 13 SB58-61 WB28-29 TG132-140
Presenting your ideas on recycling SB62	Making a summary SB62		Progress check 2 WB32-33	SB62-63 WB32-33 TG141-144
Your own ideas about fantasy writing CONTROVERSY: Do you prefer fantasy movies or horror movies? SB66, WB61 CONVERSATION: Which stories would make good films? SB67	Write a film review SB66 WB35	LITERATURE: Mary Shelley had a dream which became the first horror story - *Frankenstein* SB67	Teacher's notes and answer key TG145 Supplementary grammar PR201 FCE Exam 14 PR216 Quick Smart Test 14 PR239	Unit 14 SB64-67 WB34-35 TG145-151
What kind of job do you want? Is it right to have help with college essays? CONTROVERSY: Interview for jobs SB70, WB62 YOUR TOPIC: Present your ideas on a subject connected with work SB71	Writing a formal job application letter SB70 WB37	BUSINESS: Changing types of employment, manufacturing and service industries SB71	Teacher's notes and answer key TG152 Supplementary grammar PR202 FCE Exam 15 PR217 Quick Smart Test 15 PR240	Unit 15 SB68-71 WB36-37 TG152-160
Attitudes to drug problems CONTROVERSY: Debating the Three Strikes Law SB74, WB62 INTERACTIVE TASK: Human rights SB75	Diary of a prisoner in jail for life SB74 WB39	HUMAN RIGHTS: The Universal Declaration of Human Rights SB75	Teacher's notes and answer key TG161 FCE Exam 16 PR224 Quick Smart Test 16 PR241	Unit 16 SB72-75 WB38-39 TG161-168
What should people do in emergencies? CONTROVERSY: Emergency at sea-to the rescue! SB78, WB63 INTERACTIVE TASK: Discussion about dangerous adventures SB79	Creative writing: a story of survival in the wilderness SB78 WB41	PHYSICAL GEOGRAPHY: Supermen of the Andes and effects of altitude on people SB79	Teacher's notes and answer key TG169 Supplementary grammar PR203 FCE Exam 17 PR218 Quick Smart Test 17 PR242	Unit 17 SB76-79 WB40-41 TG169-175
Do you think that UFOs are real? CONTROVERSY: Have we been visited by aliens, or is there a scientific explanation? SB82, WB63 YOUR TOPIC: Do ghosts exist? SB83	Article for a UFO magazine SB82 WB43	ASTRONOMY: The Solar System and the speed of light SB83	Teacher's notes and answer key TG176 Supplementary grammar PR204 FCE Exam 18 PR219 Quick Smart Test 18 PR243	Unit 18 SB80-83 WB42-43 TG176-183
Success and failure; optimism and pessimism SB84	News report SB84		Progress check 3 WB44-45	SB84-85 WB44-45 TG184-187

Role cards WB57-66 **Unit-by-Unit Glossary** (with monolingual definitions) SB86-96

- ***Quick Smart English*** is a topic-based English language course at various levels in line with the **CEF (Common European Framework)**.
- ***QSE*** uses affective, topical and sometimes controversial reading and listening material to present and revise structures and vocabulary and to develop communication skills.
- The language structures are those found in widely-accepted international curricula.
- The topic-based vocabulary is wide-ranging and based on real-life ideas and issues.
- The learning tasks include integrated skills activities, with a particular focus on speaking.
- Integrated **CLIL** (Content and Language Integrated Learning) activities are in each Unit.
- Although ***QSE Intermediate*** is not a dedicated exam preparation course, the structure and vocabulary practice, skills work, question types and supplementary test materials are all designed to help students prepare for international ESOL examinations.
- ***QSE Intermediate*** is designed to cover a 70-90 hour course, although it can also be used in modules for skills development, in particular speaking practice.

QSE and the CEF

The structure and approach of the course are based on the Council of Europe's Common European Framework of Reference (**CEF**). Like the **CEF**, ***QSE Intermediate*** takes a very broad view of what language students need to learn in order to use a foreign language and what knowledge and skills they need to develop in order to communicate effectively. ***QSE*** aims to provide the widest possible cultural context, using examples from the great cultural diversity of global English (British, American, Australian, South African and others).

QSE helps to provide learners with strategies to activate general and communicative competences in order to carry out the activities and processes involved in the production and reception of texts and the construction of discourse dealing with particular themes.

The objectives, content and methods of ***QSE*** follow the guidelines of the **CEF**, aiming to equip students to deal with communicating in English, not only in English-speaking countries, but also in using the language as a *lingua franca* in other countries. ***QSE*** helps students to exchange information and ideas and to communicate their thoughts and feelings. Its wide range of topics, many of which are unusual in EFL courses, help students to achieve a wider and deeper understanding of the way other people live and think and of their cultural heritage. The methods of language teaching and learning with ***QSE*** are based on the needs, motivations, characteristics and resources of the learners themselves. The course is above all student-centred. The language learning activities are based on action-orientated tasks and relevant authentic texts (oral and written).

The topics (including the **CLIL** materials) help students to face the modern challenges of international mobility and closer co-operation, not only in education, culture and science but also in trade and industry. ***QSE*** aims to promote mutual understanding and tolerance, respect for identities and cultural diversity through more effective international communication.

The course visits all four **Domains** identified by the **CEF**. The Public Domain, for example, is represented in many Units including Environmental issues in Unit 7, Society and Living Standards in Unit 10 and Crime and Punishment in Unit 16. The Personal Domain is visited in Unit 1 (Youth Culture) and Unit 14 (Dreams and Nightmares) among others. The Educational Domain features in Unit 8 (Exam Pressure) and the Occupational Domain appears in Unit 15 (Think Big!).

The **CEF** is a framework not only for language learning, but also for **assessment**, which is central to the methodology of ***QSE***. Trinity College London recognises that ***QSE*** makes a valuable contribution to preparation for the **Graded Examinations in Spoken English** (**GESE**) and **Integrated Skills Examination** (**ISE**). ***QSE Intermediate*** is also compatible with preparation for the **Cambridge ESOL** suite of examinations, featuring a special set of exam preparation materials at **FCE** (**First Certificate in English**) level. Other levels of ***QSE*** are coordinated with other Cambridge exams – ***QSE Pre-Intermediate*** with **PET** level and ***QSE Advanced*** with **CAE** and **IELTS**. The chart below shows how the various levels of the ***QSE*** course have been planned to match the levels of the **CEF** and the requirements of international examinations.

QSE levels, the CEF and international examinations

QSE	*Common European Framework (CEF)*	*UCLES (University of Cambridge ESOL)*	*Trinity College, London ESOL*	*Michigan /* HAU	TOEFL *(New TOEFL)*	*IELTS*	*Edexcel London Test of English*
Quick START English	A1-**A2**	**KET** (Key English Test)	**GESE Grade 1, 2, 3**				Level (A1) **1**
QSE Pre-Intermediate	A2-**B1**	**PET** (Preliminary English Test)	**ISE 0, ISE I, GESE Grade 4, 5, 6**	BCCE		3.0 to 4.0	Level 1-**2**
QSE Intermediate	B1-**B2**	**FCE** (First Certificate in English)	**ISE II, GESE Grade 7, 8, 9**	ECCE	450-525 Target 485 *(NT 163)*	4.0 to 5.5	Level 2-**3**
QSE Advanced	B2-**C1**	**CAE** (Certificate in Advanced English)	**ISE III, GESE Grade 10, 11**	ALCE	Target 525 *(NT 197)*	5.5 to 6.5/7.0	Level 3-**4**

QSE Intermediate takes students from Level **B1** to **B2**. These are the **CEF Reference Levels Global Descriptors** for the two levels. There are more detailed examples of the **CEF Can-do Statements** in the four skill areas in the self-assessment charts on pages 251-255 of this book.

	B1 ———————————	——————————→ **B2**
Listening	• I can understand the main points of clear standard speech on familiar matters regularly encountered in work, school, leisure etc. I can understand the main point of many radio or TV programmes on current affairs or topics of personal or professional interest when the delivery is relatively slow and clear.	• I can understand extended speech and lectures and follow even complex lines of argument provided the topic is reasonably familiar. I can understand most TV news current affairs programmes. I can understand the majority of films in standard dialect.
Reading	• I can understand texts that consist mainly of high frequency everyday or job-related language. I can understand the description of events, feelings and wishes in personal letters.	• I can read articles and reports concerned with contemporary problems in which the writers adopt particular attitudes or viewpoints. I can understand contemporary literary prose.
Spoken interaction	• I can deal with most situations likely to arise whilst travelling in an area where the language is spoken. I can enter unprepared into conversation on topics that are familiar, of personal interest or pertinent to everyday life (eg family, hobbies, work, travel and current events).	• I can interact with a degree of fluency and spontaneity that makes regular interaction with native speakers quite possible. I can take an active part in discussion in familiar contexts, accounting for and sustaining my views.
Spoken production	• I can connect phrases in a simple way in order to describe experiences and events, my dreams, hopes and ambitions. I can briefly give reasons and explanations for opinions and plans. I can narrate a story or relate the plot of a book or film and describe my reactions.	• I can present clear, detailed descriptions on a wide range of subjects related to my field of interest. I can explain a viewpoint on a topical issue giving the advantages and disadvantages of various options.
Writing	• I can write a short, simple connected text on topics which are familiar or of personal interest. I can write personal letters describing experiences and impressions.	• I can write clear, detailed text on a wide range of subjects related to my interests. I can write an essay or report, passing on information or giving reasons in support of or against a particular point of view. I can write letters highlighting the personal significance of events and experiences.

QSE for exams

QSE is not designed to be a specific exam-preparation course. But no teacher or class these days can ignore the fact that exams are a very important and almost unavoidable presence in the language classroom. All international exams today have been written or have been calibrated to fit into the levels and requirements of the **CEF**. Styles of examination differ, however. As ***QSE*** is a course with a very strong emphasis on **spoken English** and the development of **oral skills**, the authors decided to use the syllabus of the **Trinity College, London, GESE** (**Graded Examinations in Spoken English**) and **ISE** (**Integrated Skills in English**) examinations (revised 2010). However, we are aware that many students will take other exams, so there are many question types, tasks and exercises in the **Student's Book** and **Workbook** that provide exam practice in all four skills for several exam types. In addition, there are special photocopiable pages in this **Teacher's Guide** that practice the **University of Cambridge ESOL First Certificate in English** – see details below. This makes ***QSE*** an ideal course for general study at the end of which students may go on to take a variety of exams, including those of Trinity and Cambridge. Many, but not all the requirements (not for example, the poetry or phonics) of the Cambridge International GCSE (**IGCSE**) are also covered; however the speaking activates are highly suitable for this exam.

QSE and Cambridge FCE exam practice

QSE is not an exam-practice book, and students taking any examinations, including the **Cambridge FCE**, should prepare by using actual sample papers before they sit any exams. However, ***QSE*** does provide a great deal of practice in every skill necessary for the **FCE** exam (revised 2008+).

FCE Paper 1 Reading:
Throughout ***QSE*** there are many reading comprehension tasks. Some are in the exam format, and some practice the same skills in similar formats. For example, the Paper 1 Part 2 format (text with sentences removed) is used in the reading texts of Units 4, 5, 7, 8 and 15. In the Workbook, Progress check 1 uses the format for Paper 1 Part 2; Progress check 2, for Paper 1 Part 3; and Progress check 3 for Paper 1 Part 1.

FCE Paper 2 Writing:
The Portfolio Writing section provides practice in **FCE**-style writing tasks, as does the Portfolio Writing section in the **Workbook**. In particular, the **Photocopiable resource** pages for Units 3, 9 and 16 in this Teacher's Guide provide guidance and tasks in the format of the **FCE** exam.

FCE Paper 3 Use of English:
In every Unit of the **Workbook** there is practice in **FCE**-style Use of English tasks. These are in abbreviated form, as it is not necessary to practice a complete exam paper for every activity. Each of the **FCE** exam practice pages provides tasks in the format of the Use of English paper, and covers all question types in the revised exam 2008+.

FCE Paper 4 Listening:
Many of the listening activities in the Units are based on **FCE**-style tasks. With 140 minutes of Audio material, ***QSE*** provides ample listening material.

FCE Paper 5 Speaking:
All the speaking activities in the main Student Book Units practise the skills and functions necessary for the **FCE** exam. The **FCE** exam practice pages for Units 3, 9 and 16 offer both guidance and tasks in the precise format of the **FCE** exam.

FCE Exam Practice Pages:
Teacher's Guide has 36 photocopiable pages of exam material, divided into **Grammar Supplement** and **FCE exam practice**. The Grammar Supplement consists of explanations and exercises which round out the **FCE** syllabus. The photocopiable **FCE** exam practice material is in the format of the Use of English Paper. In addition, Units 3, 9 and 16 focus on the **FCE** Speaking Paper 5 and Writing Paper 2. You can use these pages at the same time as the main Units, or separately for homework. Each set of materials can be marked by the teacher (or students). There is a score box on each Activity.

QSE and the Trinity College, London GESE and ISE exams

Because they are based on the structures, functions and subject areas of Trinity's Intermediate (Grades 7, 8, 9) Graded Examinations in Spoken English (**GESE**) and Integrated Skills in English (**ISEII**) Examination (covering CEF levels **B2** to **B2+**), the Units in the ***QSE Intermediate*** coursebook provide a thorough preparation for students wishing to take either oral or integrated skills examinations at these levels.

The **READING** (Activity 3 of each Unit) and **LISTEN IN** (Activity 5 of each Unit) sections in the book offer the opportunity to become familiar with the vocabulary specific to the subject areas in the **Trinity** examinations. Students then learn how to present and discuss their knowledge and ideas with the examiner in **CONTROVERSY** (Activity 6) and **YOUR TOPIC** (Activity 9) in each Unit, using the structures and functions of the appropriate grade. This preparation applies to the topic and Conversation phases of the interview component of both **GESE** and **ISE** examinations.

In the **GESE** and **ISE** interviews, Trinity examiners will be looking for candidates to show their ability to use a good range of the communicative skills, grammar, lexis and functions in the syllabus for the appropriate grade, while having a sufficient grasp of English pronunciation to be intelligible to the examiner and a more confident, fluent use of the language than at the previous level.

Students will need guidance in selecting a topic, which may be any theme that they are interested in, knowledgeable about and able to talk readily about. In preparing the topic, candidates should be actively discouraged from producing and memorising a written text, as this will have an adverse effect on the candidate's pronunciation and ability to use spontaneous spoken English. Candidates are also advised to think carefully about the amount of material necessary for their topic, bearing in mind the time available. They should prepare enough material to sustain a discussion of the topic for up to five minutes, but not more. The discussion should provide opportunities for the candidate to use the language of the specific grade, *eg* at Grade 8 or ISE II, exponents of reported speech and the present perfect continuous tense.

In the Topic phase of the **Trinity Intermediate** exams the candidate needs to be prepared to:

- communicate facts, ideas, opinions and viewpoints linked across a series of extended turns
- maintain coherence and cohesion throughout the phase by organising the discourse
- engage the examiner in discussion of the topic
- ask and answer questions about the content of and views about the topic

Candidates may like to take with them into the exam one or more pictures, photos, models or other suitable objects to illustrate their prepared topics.

The **INTERACTIVE TASK** in the coursebook (Activity 9 in some of the Units - see the Speaking column of the Contents list on pages 4-7 of the **Student's Book**) gives students the opportunity to prepare for the Interactive Task phase of the **GESE** and **ISE** exams at this level. Here candidates are expected to be able to:

- initiate the discourse (after a preliminary prompt by the examiner)
- maintain the discourse by asking for information and commenting on the responses
- take, give up and offer turns as appropriate
- take the opportunity to use exponents of the functions of the grade

This task in particular marks the **transition from the Pre-Intermediate stage** by putting more responsibility on the candidate for initiating and maintaining the discourse.

QSE Intermediate also provides ongoing guidance in the **writing** skills needed to tackle the Portfolio tasks and Controlled Written examination of the **ISE**. On page 6 of this Introduction, under the heading **PORTFOLIO WRITING** (Activity 7) you will find details of what this element of the **ISE** consists of. There is also a requirement for candidates to talk to the examiner about one or more of their pieces of Portfolio Writing, giving more details about what they have written. In the **ISE Controlled Written** examination, which takes place at the candidates' place of learning, before the examiner comes to mark the Portfolio and interview the candidates, they are expected to complete a Reading into Writing task which requires them to read a text of about 300 words and use their understanding to complete the accompanying Writing task, as well as an additional writing task of one of the types covered in the Portfolio.

Rosemary Harris, Trinity Examiner

QSE and CLIL

One of the most significant aims of recent educational thinking in many countries has been to make learning a relevant preparation for the students' real lives in the widest sense. This can mean relevance not just to vocational training but also to personal development, citizenship, further education and the use of information technology. In addition, education reforms in many countries now encourage a greater emphasis on political, economic, historical and cultural world awareness, as globalisation affects everyone's lives.

QSE features a cross-curricular **CLIL** (Content and Language Integrated Learning) topic as part of every Unit. Some of these are traditional school subjects like Chemistry, Physics, Geography and History. Others reflect the nature of the modern syllabus with subjects like economics, literature, design and media studies. The course approach to **CLIL** also reaches out more widely to embrace a range of topics that interest and are useful to students even if they are not being formally studied. These include ideas such as Psychology, Ecology, Human Rights, Astronomy and English for Academic Purposes. In ***QSE*, CLIL** is truly integrated so that it becomes a natural part of what we use language for – talking about the things that interest us.

The objective of the cross-curricular sections in this book is not to add to the students' own knowledge of science, history or geography. Instead it is to equip students with an English language strategy (and the relevant conceptual and linguistic tools) so that they can extend their understanding of the world through the use of a foreign language. It is not aiming to teach geography to the students – they are probably already learning that separately. It is intending to give them the equipment to combine their language studies with their other subject areas.

"**CLIL** is an approach to bilingual education in which both curriculum content – such as Science or Geography – and English are taught together….. Hence it is a means of teaching curriculum subjects through the medium of the language still being learned….. **CLIL** can also be regarded the other way round – as a means of teaching English through study of a specialist content. … **CLIL** is compatible with the idea of **JIT** education ('just in time learning') and is regarded by some of its practitioners as the ultimate communicative methodology" (David Graddol, *English next*, British Council, 2006).

QSE and Multiple Intelligences

The theory of Multiple Intelligences, first posited by Dr Howard Gardner in 1983 and modified many times since then, has divided teachers and educators as much as it has brought them together. But this is really a matter of the details. Most educational theorists now agree that the long-established methods of teaching and testing, which only appealed to a learner's linguistic or logical-mathematical intelligences, work well for some students but exclude others whose intelligences are of a different type.

What we have tried to do in this book is address certain other aspects of the theory, particularly the distinction between interpersonal and intrapersonal intelligences. Students do not always want to interact with each other and provision needs to be made for 'lone' activities as well as pair and group work. However, we also feel that the notion of bodily-kinaesthetic intelligence is a key factor in language learning and enjoyment of the process. But as these are choices and decisions which are best made by the teacher, activities that involve sharing, moving around to find the answers with other students, participating and mingling have been included here in the **Teacher's Guide** rather than on the pages of the **Student's Book**.

Auditory learners will find plenty of stimulation in the 140 minutes of varied audio material on the two CDs. Visual learners will find that ***QSE*** is lavishly illustrated with photos that make the texts come alive. Most of the photographs are authentic news pictures and there are **Picture notes** that describe the back story to many illustrations in the Unit-by-Unit part of the guide.

We have also tried to balance giving teachers and learners what they like, expect and are used to and giving them something new and different, without making them alarmed or uncomfortable.

The principles of Accelerated Learning also inform what we write, particularly ideas of multi-sensory teaching and learning and, in particular, how teachers can pay more attention to their students' physical and emotional well-being. Many of these ideas are here in the **Teacher's Guide** rather than on the **Student's Book** pages.

English as a meme

Content and Language Integrated Learning (**CLIL**) represents an evolution in second language acquisition. It is an idea that is changing the way people learn English. One of the key concepts of **CLIL** is that, by changing the context in which a foreign language is learned, teachers can make it more relevant to the students' needs and thus more readily acquired.

In 1976, Professor Richard Dawkins of Oxford University suggested that there are units of cultural inheritance and transfer which he called 'memes'. He suggested that they work in a way that is similar to the way that genes pass on biological information. Memes are ideas (such as the 'Earth is flat') or fashions (like short skirts) or skills (such as skiing), which can be rapidly transmitted from one person to another.

The skill of speaking English as a foreign or second language is now a globally successful idea, or a meme. Over a billion people worldwide are learning English as a Foreign Language. Dawkins and others think that memes reproduce by both mutation and recombination, rather like genes in process of biological evolution itself. A mutation in thought may take centuries to take root. For example, Leonardo da Vinci's ideas on mechanical flight never caught on in the fifteenth century because the technical environment of the time could not support them. Five hundred years later, the meme of flight is so commonplace we hardly question it.

Memes are also propagated by recombination, such as when existing ideas and skills come up against a new environment and adapt rapidly to suit it. Thus, mobile phones and the internet have dramatically changed the ways in which people communicate. We still talk and write, but now we do this instantly with people anywhere in the world. The result is an explosion of global communication - an extremely successful meme, evolved to fit the 21st century environment.

CLIL may be another example of memetic recombination. The learning environment is filled with subjects like Geography, History and Physics. If language learning moves into these new environments, it becomes an improved meme – one that combines old ways of teaching with new situations and thus provokes students to acquire improved skills and new ideas.

Students not only learn *about* the subject of Geography or Maths with **CLIL**, they also turn the process upside down and learn the language *from* the subject. If they are already learning geography, discussing it in English enables them to recombine the subject with the second language, producing a form of learning that is better adapted to their environment. It's more fun, more relevant and more motivating, and like a gene or a meme, more successful.

QSE Intermediate – the course at-a-glance

QSE Intermediate consists of 19 separate Units of six-pages each, plus various additional materials, such as **Extended Reading**, **Exam Practice** and **Language Banks**. Every Unit of the course works in the same way. The same ingredients appear in the same order in each Unit. The activities are explained with an intentionally limited repertoire of rubrics, which are repeated throughout. The activities are varied, but the instructions are kept as simple and similar as possible. This means that students only have to learn how to use the course once in the first Unit, and can then expect the same structure in the rest of the Units. This makes it exceptionally clear and user-friendly, further defining the student-centred approach of the whole course.

Scope and sequence of the course:

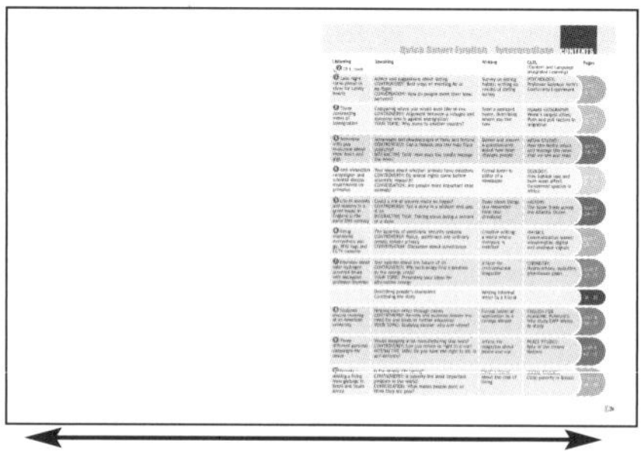

Student's Book Contents p4-7

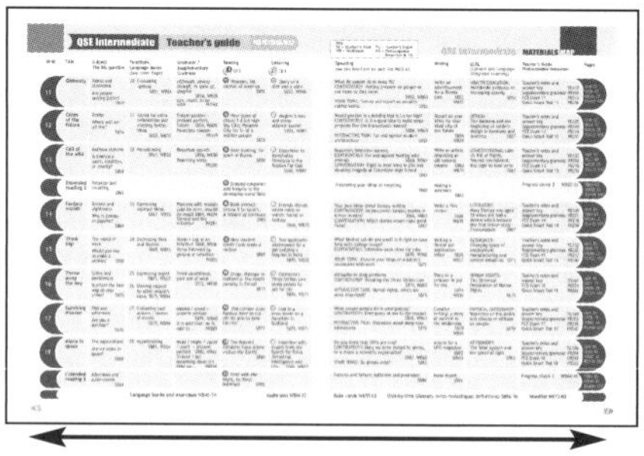

Teacher's Guide Materials Map p4-7

Workbook p3

Every Unit consists of:

***4 Student's Book** pages in colour*

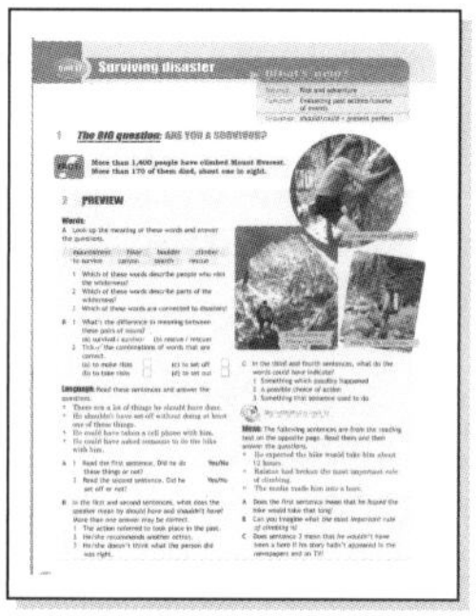

Page 1:
Preview: Words, Grammar, Ideas

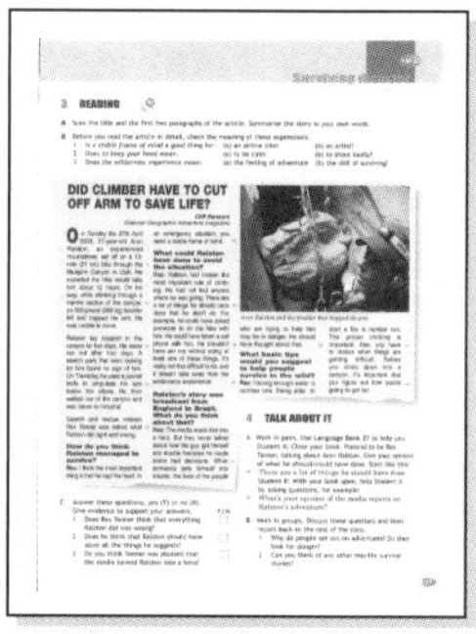

Page 2:
Reading Speaking

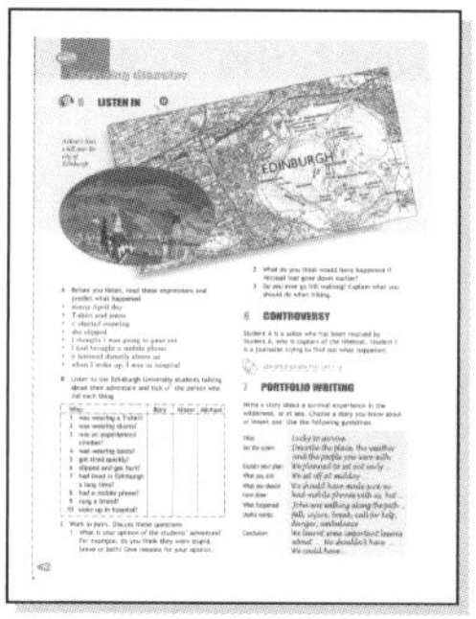

Page 3:
Listening, Speaking, Writing

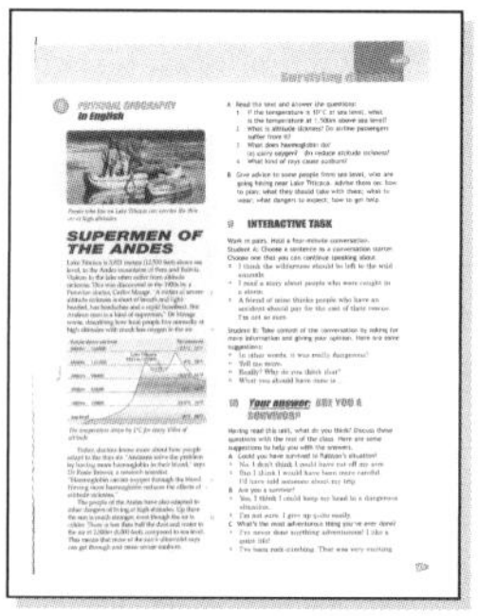

Page 4:
CLIL, Speaking

***2 Workbook** pages and*

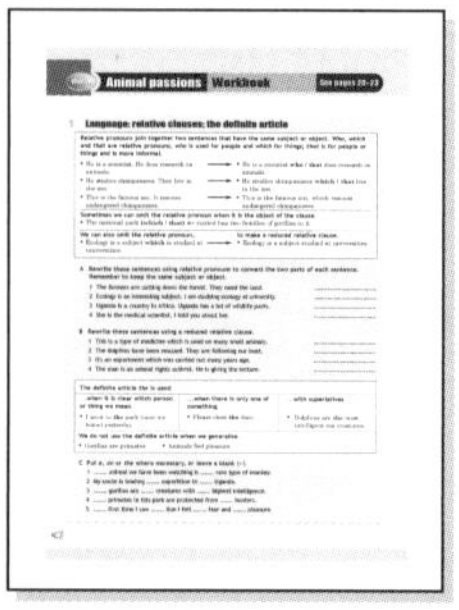

Page 1:
Grammar explanations and exercises

Page 2:
Use of English exercises Connections, Writing

***Role cards** for every Unit*

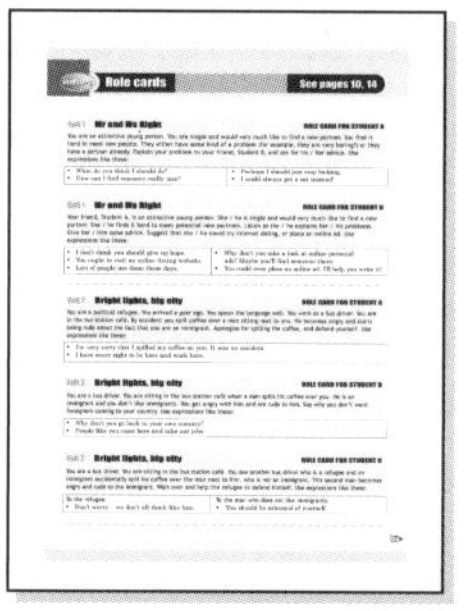

Role cards
For every Unit in the Workbook

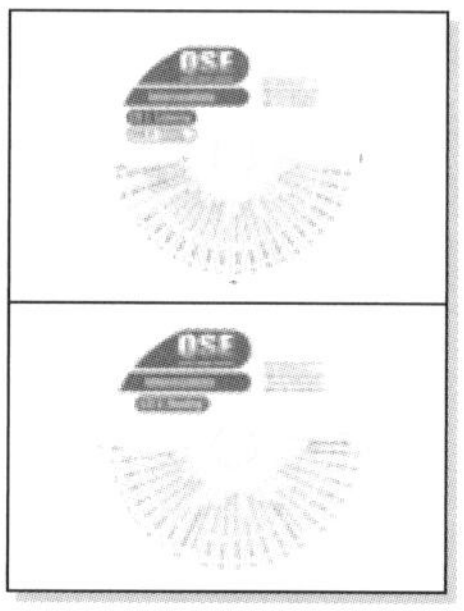

2 Audio CDs
CD1 (Blue) Listening + Unit 0
CD2 (Red) Reading

Photocopiable Resources (in this Teacher's Guide) for each Unit:

Supplementary Grammar (pages 190-204)

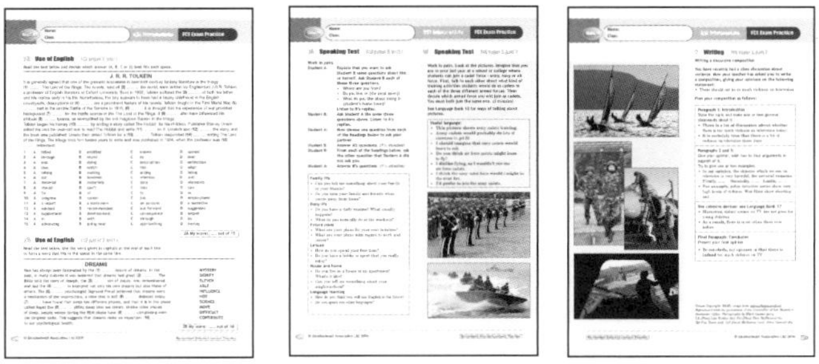

Cambridge FCE Exam practice materials (pages 205-225)

Quick Smart Tests 1-18 (pages 226-243)

Plus various other resources:

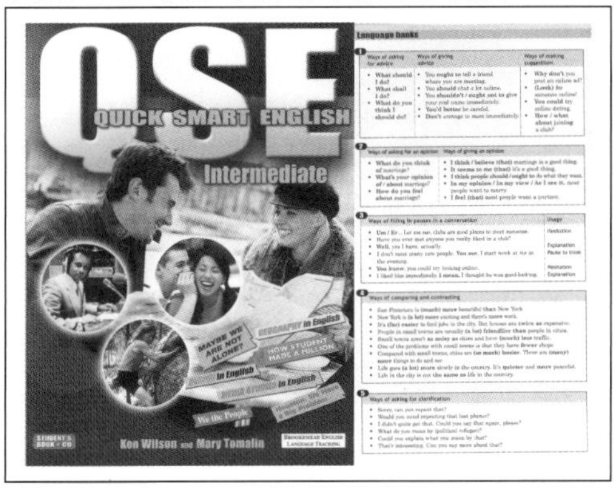

***Language Banks**, on the Student's Book cover flaps*

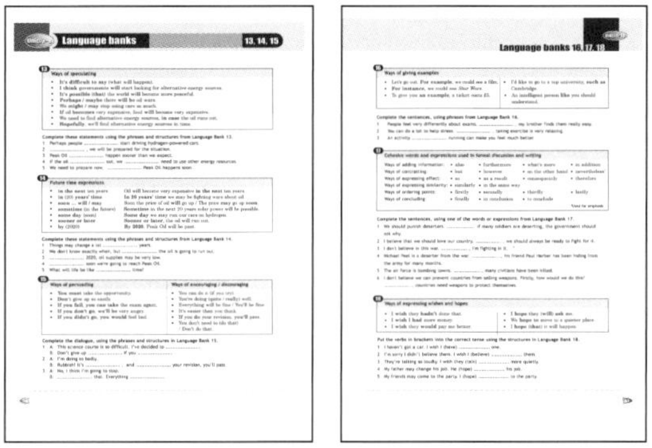

The Language Banks are also in the Workbook with exercises

3 Extended Reading sections

3 Progress Checks

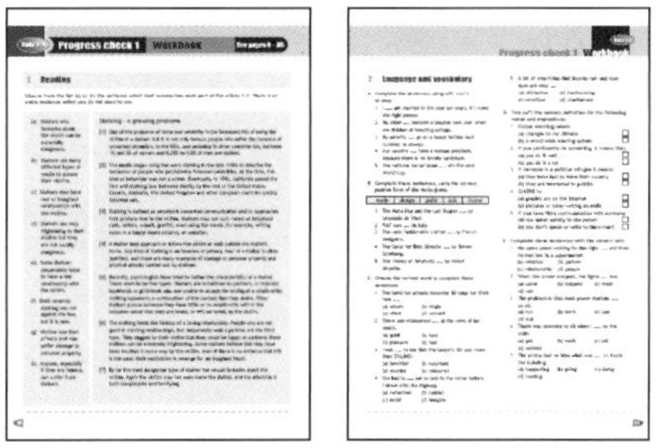

Audio texts (CD 1 Listening)

CD1 (Blue) Listening also contains both the Reading and Listening passages for Unit 0 (Zero)

Unit-by-Unit Glossary in the Student's Book

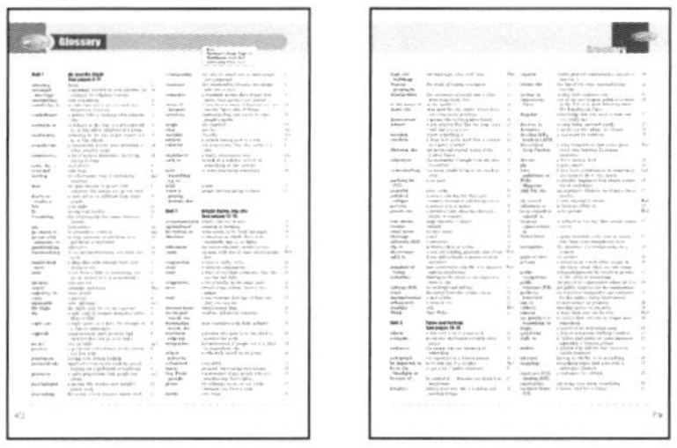

QSE Intermediate – guide to the Unit structure

The 4 pages of each Unit in the Student's Book consist of:

Student's Book Page 1:

What's new?
Subjects, functions and language introduced in the Unit.

1 *The BIG question*
Grabs the attention of the students.

FACT
An amazing or amusing fact to engage immediate attention on the topic.

2 PREVIEW
Words
Pre-teaching of new vocabulary using word fields and collocations. Developing new and wider lexis for the students is an important element of the course.

Language
Inductive grammar activities, cross-referenced to grammar explanations and exercises in the Workbook.

Cross-reference to Workbook grammar Explanation and exercises.

Ideas
Personalised and intercultural speaking activities based on the new vocabulary. Introduction to thinking about the reading text on the next page.

Unit 3 **Fame and fortune**

What's new?
Subject: Public figures and celebrity
Function: Expressing possibility and uncertainty
Grammar: *may, might*

1 *The BIG question:* WHAT IS THE PRICE OF FAME?

FACT: **A series of robberies at the houses of rich and famous people became known as the *Hello!* Burglaries, because celebrities were robbed after appearing in *Hello!* Magazine.**

2 PREVIEW

Words:

A Why are the people in the photographs famous?
1 Nelson Mandela
2 Albert Einstein
3 Bill Gates
4 Nicole Kidman
5 Queen Elizabeth II
6 Tiger Woods

B Discuss these questions with other students.
1 What is a *celebrity*? How do people become celebrities?
2 What are the *media*? How do the media treat celebrities?
3 What is a *stalker*? Why do you think people become stalkers?
4 Are famous people always *talented*?

Language: Read these sentences and then answer the questions.
- Photographers **may** hide because they want a photo of you.
- You **may** not be famous ten years from now.
- The public **may** lose interest in you.
- They **might** even forget all about you.

A Do the words *may* and *might* refer to:
a) a possible situation?
b) a situation that will definitely happen?
B Which sentences refer to the future?
C Which sentence talks about something that can happen in a certain situation?
D Write two sentences saying what you may or may not do tomorrow.
E Write two sentences saying what you might do next year.

SEE WORKBOOK UNIT 3

Ideas: The following sentences are from the reading text on the opposite page. Read them and then answer the questions.
- Fans may decide that they have a 'special relationship' with you. They may stalk you, and climb into your bedroom.
- When you're famous, people say things like, "I think you're wonderful, can I have your autograph?"
- If you're famous, you may have to say goodbye to your privacy.

A Which sentences refer to the disadvantages of fame?
B What are the advantages and disadvantages of fame, in your opinion?
C Why do you think people are so interested in famous people? Why do people want their autographs?
D Have you ever met anyone famous? If so, describe how you met them and what happened?

16

Texts are from authentic sources. Some have been adopted to reflect the structures, functions and vocubulary of the Unit.

The photographs and illustrations are an important aid to learning. They provide talking points, aid understanding and motivate students to read the text.

Student's Book Page 2:

3 READING ⑩
Text(s) with track number (⑩) for audio CD 2 Reading. Students can either just read or follow the CD. High degree of authenticity in all the texts.

Pre-reading questions (reading for gist; prediction, personal reaction).

Comprehension questions on the reading texts(s).

Reading for gist, specific information and reading for detail.

Unit 3

Fame and fortune

3 READING ③

A Scan the article. Which paragraphs are about the plus (+) and which are about the minus (-) factors of being famous?

SO YOU WANT TO BE FAMOUS?

(a) .... **All the trappings:** Fame can make you very rich. And money can bring you the high life -- a private plane, a villa in the South of France. Bill Gates' house near Seattle has only seven bedrooms, but it has 24 bathrooms and six kitchens, and is worth $97 million.

(b) .... **If it doesn't work out:** Fame gives you the opportunity to fall in love with famous and attractive partners. Nicole Kidman met Tom Cruise co-starring in the film *Days of Thunder*. Within a year, she and Cruise were married. They divorced ten years later. Fame might not make you happy in the long run!

(c) .... **In the limelight:** We all want to be admired. When you're famous, people say things like, "I think you're wonderful; can I have your autograph, please?" Famous people may pretend not to like the attention, but in fact, they're secretly pleased.

(d) .... **Power and influence:** Fame may bring you power. If you're famous, you may have a better chance of getting your opinion heard. If, like Bono from U2, you have Nelson Mandela's number on your speed-dial (and he has yours), you definitely have influence!

(e) ...... **Public recognition:** Many brilliant people want their achievements to be recognised by the public. It makes them feel their work is worthwhile. Few great achievers are like Albert Einstein, who said: "My scientific work is motivated by a desire to understand the secrets of nature -- by nothing else." But he did become world famous and won the Nobel Prize.

(f) .... **Adopt a disguise:** If you're famous, you may have to say goodbye to your privacy. Photographers may hide near your vacation home, waiting to get a picture of you in your swim suit. You may have to wear a disguise. When the Rolling Stones appeared on television in the 1970s, they went into the studio via the back door -- in trash cans!

(g) .... **Beware of stalkers:** Fans may decide that they have a 'special relationship' with you. They may stalk you, and climb over your backyard five-metre garden wall and into your bedroom. The Queen of England and Madonna have both had problems with stalkers.

(h) .... **Keeping up appearances:** Once you're famous, you may want to stay famous. But you have to accept that you may not be a celebrity ten years from now. The public may lose interest in you. Don't worry! Just enjoy your fame while you have it.

B Match the phrases above in **bold** (a – h) with these definitions:
1 Something that you wear so that people will not recognise you.
2 Pretend everything in your life is wonderful.
3 Luxuries that you can buy if you are rich.
4 Getting a lot of attention from the public and the media.
5 Having the chance to put your ideas into practice.
6 Watching out for people who take too much interest in you.
7 Having people know who you are and what you do.
8 When something does not last as long you might like.

C What does the text say about these things or people?

1 bathrooms	2 autographs	3 Bono
4 Nobel Prize	5 dustbins	6 marriage

D Read the text carefully.
1 What might a photographer do to get celebrity photos?
2 What might a stalker do, according to the writer?
3 What advice does the writer give to famous people?

4 TALK ABOUT IT

Use **Language Bank 6** to help you.
A Is there anything in the article you disagree with? If so, say why.
B Can you think of other advantages or disadvantages of fame?
C Do you know anyone who may become famous?
D Do you want to become famous?
E Do you think that the price of fame might be too high for you?

17

4 TALK ABOUT IT
Discussion and chance to activate new language functions with the help of Language Banks.

Student's Book Page 3:

5 LISTEN IN ⑩

Listening material with track (⑩) number for audio CD 1 Listening.

Illustrations aid understanding and improve motivation to listen and also form the basis of activities.

Pre-listening activities (pre-discussion of the general topic, prediction, pre-teaching of vocabulary).

Listening comprehension questions (listening for gist and listening for detail; personal reactions and opinions).

Unit 3

Fame and fortune

5 LISTEN IN ③

A Before you listen to an interview with two members of a new band, put these words and expressions into the correct sentences.

(a) album	(b) single	(c) drummer
(d) gig	(e) on tour	(f) come out
(g) in the charts	(h) appear on TV	

1 Can you name the band's ....?
2 Are they going to ....?
3 Is their chart single also on their ....?
4 When did the album ....?
5 Are they doing a .... next Saturday?
6 Does the band have a song .... at the moment?
7 What is the title of their latest ....?
8 Does the band ever go ....?

B Listen to the interview and answer the questions.
1 Why does the audience laugh when Dave speaks?
2 What doesn't Dave know about Sharon?

C Listen again and decide if these sentences are true (T) or false (F). T / F
1 The band's first single went into the charts at number six. ☐
2 They're writing material for a new single. ☐
3 They are going to Scandinavia and Germany. ☐
4 The new album will come out in the autumn. ☐
5 Sharon has been asked to appear on TV in *The Girl Next Door*. ☐

D Work in pairs. Take turns to talk about your favourite band.
- My favourite band is ...
- Their latest single is ...
- I may see them on tour ...
- I might buy their next album ...

6 CONTROVERSY

Student A is a pop star who does not want to do publicity interviews for a new album because he wants a holiday. Student B is the PR manager who wants the star to appear on TV chat shows.

SEE ROLE CARDS FOR UNIT 3

7 PORTFOLIO WRITING

Work in pairs and write a questionnaire to find out people's ideas about fame and celebrity. Write seven questions then give it to another pair to complete.

Example questions:	Example answers:
• Do you think fame changes people?	• Yes, I think fame almost always changes people.
• In what way does it change them?	• It is very difficult for them not to become arrogant.

18

6 CONTROVERSY

Role play and discussion using the language and functions introduced in the Unit, based on the ***Role cards*** *in the Workbook.*

7 PORTFOLIO WRITING

Writing activities in the style of the Trinity examinations, with guidance to help students get the most out of the questions.

Student's Book Page 4:

8 *CLIL TOPIC in English*

A cross-curricular topic connected with the Unit. Comprehension, specialist vocabulary questions and other CLIL activities using the cross-curricular material presented. Charts, diagrams, maps and illustrations in the style used in the cross-curricular subject area.

Unit 3

Fame and fortune

8 MEDIA STUDIES in English

MAKING NEWS

Are the media simply reporting world events? Do they give us images of famous people and events as they really are? Or do media editors **manage the news** in order to present a **particular point of view**?

In reality editors **select the images** that we see. For example, during the 2003 war in Iraq, American TV news did not show pictures of dead American soldiers, although hundreds of Americans were killed. Was this because the media wanted people to support the war?

The media, which include **Public Relations (PR) managers**, select images and stories that show the type of news that they want to present. For example, the photos on this page show that both Democratic Party candidate John Kerry and President George W Bush are strong military leaders. Photographers may use techniques **such as choosing the camera angle** and the location. All these things **influence the message** that the picture has for the viewer.

US President George W Bush

US Senator John Kerry

A Look at these photos, taken when the US occupation of Iraq was an important issue for American voters. What images are the photographers trying to present and how is this done?

B Think of two captions for each photo, one that presents the person in a positive way, and one that presents him in a negative way.

C Read the text quickly and check the meanings of the phrases in **bold**.

D Read the text again and answer these questions.
1 How do the media influence the news?
2 Give examples of their methods.

9 INTERACTIVE TASK

Work in groups of four, two pairs in each group. Both pairs prepare a 3–4 minute talk on the same topic, for example, *How The Media Works*. Make a list of four or five main points.

Pair A: Start talking about the topic. Be prepared for Pair B to take control of the conversation. Answer their questions and reply to their comments, for example:	**Pair B:** Listen while Pair A starts the discussion. Let Pair A do most of the talking, but take control of the discussion by asking questions and making comments, for example:
• The media don't show us real news. They show us what they want us to see. • Yes. For example, they set up exactly the images they want to show us.	• Really? That's an interesting idea. Can you explain how they do that? • I think I understand. You mean, they select which images they show?
Use **Language Bank 7** for expressions used to gain time for thought.	

10 *Your answer:* WHAT IS THE PRICE OF FAME?

Having read this unit what do you think? Discuss these questions with the rest of the class. Here are some suggestions to help you:

A Do you want to be famous?
- No. If you are famous, you have no private life.

B Is the price of fame too high for you?
- No it's worth it for all the trappings.
- I'm not sure I would like to be recognised in public.

C Can you be a public figure and remain real?
- Yes, I think it's possible to be rich and real.

19

9 CONVERSATION, YOUR TOPIC, INTERACTIVE TASK

Speaking activities based on three different parts of the Trinity GESE exam. Each Unit has one of the three possible types of activity. The Language Banks help with functions.

10 *Your answer:*

Questions with suggested models to help answer <u>The BIG question</u> that opened the Unit.

Workbook Page 1:

Unit number
Page cross-reference to Student's Book

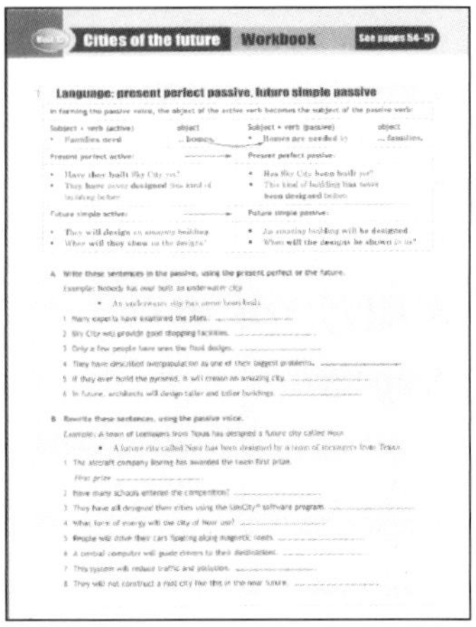
Cities of the future Workbook See pages 54–57
1 Language: present perfect passive, future simple passive

1 Language

Grammar explanations and examples with exercises based on language presented in the Unit. Presentation in the Student's Book Unit is inductive. Students can then refer to these pages for explanations and exercises. In some cases there is more than one grammar point explained and practiced. There are Supplementary Grammar points (explanation and exercises) available as photocopiable pages in this Teacher's Guide.

Workbook Page 2:

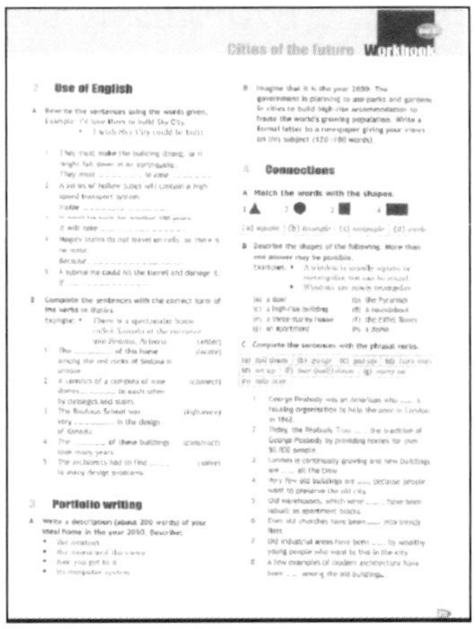
Cities of the future Workbook
2 Use of English
4 Connections
3 Portfolio writing

2 Use of English

This section uses the various formats of the Cambridge FCE Paper 3 Use of English. There are shortened versions of exercises from all five parts of the Paper. Sentences and structures are based on material in the Unit.

3 Portfolio Writing

Exam-style writing activities.

4 Connections

Prepositions and opposites, language awareness, idioms, collocations and

Photocopiable Resources for each Unit:

Role cards

6 CONTROVERSY

In every Unit of the Student's Book, in Activity 6 there is a brief description of a Role play. This description is set out in full in the Workbook, where each student in the pair or the group is given a part to play.

Role Cards
Surviving disaster
Alone in space?

Supplementary grammar and exercises

Grammar supplement
1 Language: ability and possibility – can / could / to be able to

Exam practice including Use of English exercises

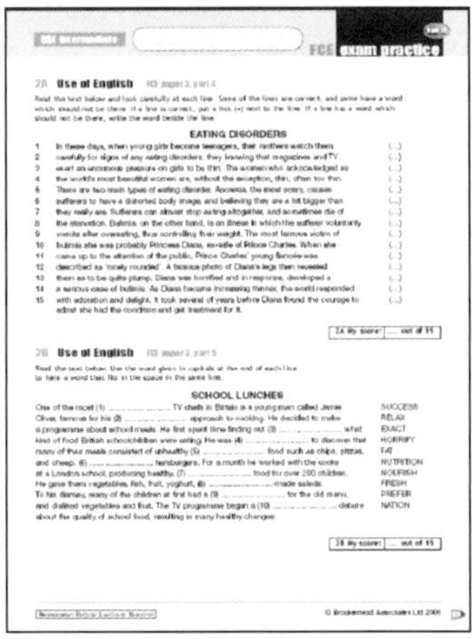
FCE exam practice
Use of English
EATING DISORDERS
SCHOOL LUNCHES

QSE Intermediate – how the sections of each Unit work

Map of the course

Student's Book, Contents pages 4-7. See also **Teacher's Guide**, Materials Map pages 4-7.
The syllabus of ***QSE Intermediate*** is based on an extensive survey of current international standards in EFL teaching. Increasingly these are based on the **CEF**, or, if non-European, they are now being aligned with it (for example the **University of Michigan** examinations). The functional, structural and topical basis of the course is the syllabus of **Trinity College, London**, but it also takes into account the requirements of the **University of Cambridge ESOL** syllabus.

Given that **communicative competence** is one of the main aims of the ***QSE*** course, care has been taken not to overload the students with grammar. However, extra language work is available in the **Teacher's Guide**, with a photocopiable page of Supplementary Grammar for each Unit. The **Student's Book** takes care to concentrate on skills work, particularly **speaking**.

The Contents pages show the scope and sequence of the whole book as well as each Unit, with headings for **Topic** (or Subject), *The BIG question*, **Functions (Language Banks)**, **Grammar**, **Reading**, **Listening**, **Speaking**, **Writing** and **CLIL**. These pages can be used as a quick reference for both students and teachers, including a list of **CD tracks** for both CDs.

Student's Book Units

The colour pages of the **Student's Book Units** contain all the main language input material of the course. The authors have chosen to have many short Units, rather than a few long ones, so there is lots of variety and interest for students of widely different tastes. There are 18 Units, plus three **Extended Reading** sections. There is also a series of **Language Banks**, examples of functional language presented in meaningful and useful written or spoken examples. The **Language Banks** are on fold-out cover flaps for easy reference in class when students are working on any Unit. The functions chosen for these **Language Banks** are taken from the **Trinity College GESE** syllabus, Grades 7, and 9. The format of each Unit is as follows:

Unit title and What's new?

Student's Book Page 1
The title gives a clue to the Unit topic, and the **What's new?** box tells you what the Unit covers. All three areas – Subject, Function and Grammar – are in the **Trinity College GESE** syllabus, and they are also to be found in many other curricula and the **CEF**.

Before you open the book ...

At the beginning of the notes to every Unit in this **Teacher's Guide**, there is a suggested activity for something you can do before you open the book. We appreciate that teachers all have their own ways of approaching new material, and that they have an unrivalled awareness of how their students cope best when confronted with new lexis and grammar. However, we have added a suggestion here which we feel will enhance the students' interest in and appreciation of the material they find in the opening spread of the Unit.

1 *The BIG question* and FACT box

Every Unit begins and ends with an important question related to the topic. The question is intended to immediately grab the attention of the students. They are not asked to give an opinion at this stage. It is simply there to make them think. At the end of the Unit, after consideration of the evidence in the Unit and consultation with other students about their opinions, the class will be much more prepared and confident to answer the question.
Using *The BIG question*:

- Read the question out. Check students understand it by asking questions.
- Elicit answers.
- Ask students to write a 1-2 sentence answer in their notebooks.
- Tell them that at the end of the Unit you will ask them to reread their answers and see if they have changed their minds.

There is also a boxed **FACT** at the beginning of the Unit. Wherever possible, the **FACT** is informative and / or surprising, There are occasionally amusing facts, such as in Unit 3 *Fame and fortune*, which reads as follows:
A series of robberies at the houses of rich and famous people became known as the Hello! *Burglaries, because celebrities were robbed after appearing in* Hello! *Magazine.*
Using the FACT box:
- Read the **FACT** out or ask students to read it silently.
- Teach new vocabulary items and ask questions to check comprehension.
- If you do not want to exploit the **FACT**, you can simply tell students it is something for them to think about.
- Alternatively, you can use the question to stimulate interest in the topic by asking questions, for example: *What's your reaction to this? Does this surprise you? Why / why not?* If you do this, spend only one or two minutes eliciting answers and don't worry about correcting mistakes.

2 PREVIEW

The **PREVIEW** section prepares students for the reading and speaking tasks on the next page. It consists of three parts, **Words**, **Language** and **Ideas**.

Words

This section presents and highlights words that appear in the **READING** text on page 2, and also adds other related vocabulary. This is vocabulary that the students need to help them deal with the Reading text and it appears with words from the same context, providing students with a wider lexical set. Students are often encouraged to provide words they already know at this stage, as well. The words section is accompanied by two to four interesting photographs, providing stimulus for activation of the new words.
Using PREVIEW Words:
- Put students into pairs and ask them to work through the activities, looking up new vocabulary where necessary.
- Elicit answers and teach new vocabulary, writing new language on the board.
- Alternatively, go through the activities with the whole class. Either read out the activities yourself or ask different students to read them out. As you go through the activity, ask questions to check comprehension and teach new vocabulary. Give students time to think about their answers before eliciting them.

Language

In this section, sentences from the Reading text on page 2 are highlighted because of the grammatical structure(s) they contain. Wherever possible, new grammar items are dealt with inductively. This means that we offer clues about how the structure works, and students embark on a voyage of discovery. Not all grammar can be taught in this way, but when it can be, students can only benefit from discovery learning. By working it out for themselves they are much more likely to put the ideas into their long-term memories.

It may be that the structure material is new to the students, or it may be revision. It is possible that the structure items in the first few Units (*should / ought to*, comparatives, *may / might*) are revision items for your students, and structure items later in the book are new. Only you know the realities for your class. Therefore, we will make a suggestion for the aspects of the structure item that you need to revise or present so that students can deal with the material they encounter later in the Unit.

This section is cross-referenced to the **Workbook**, where there is an explanation with exercises. If you wish, you can at this point spend some time working on the structure practice material you will find there.
Using PREVIEW Language:
- If the language is new to the students, it's probably best to read out the sentences and questions that follow. Ask questions to check comprehension and teach any new vocabulary. Ask students to think about their answers to the inductive questions. You may want to put them in pairs to discuss their answers. Then read out the questions again and elicit answers. If necessary, give the answer yourself. Use the answers to highlight both the concepts behind the structures and the way the structure is formed.

- If the language is revision, you can simply ask students to read the section and think about their answers. Again, you may prefer for students to do this activity in pairs. Then continue as outlined above.

Ideas

Other phrases and sentences from the Reading text are highlighted here, for their ideas content rather than for any grammatical structure they may contain. In other words, students are given a preview of some of the facts and opinions that may appear in the Reading text. In this way, we balance the preparation of the structure content and ideas content of the Reading text.

The Reading texts are often about controversial subjects, so students should be aware that the ideas expressed here are not necessarily mainstream, and are certainly not intended as standard opinion in the English-speaking world. For example, in Unit 3 *Fame and fortune*, the following sentence appears in the **Ideas** section: *Fans may decide that they have a 'special' relationship with you. They may stalk you and climb into your bedroom.* This may read like an endorsement of stalking and similar behaviour! This of course is not the intention. Students may express surprise at the ideas expressed in this section. The important thing is, as with the **Language** section before it, this activity will allow them to read the Reading text with more confidence.

In many places throughout the book, students are invited to speculate on the possible meaning of an idea, why the writer said it. The language of speculation can become complicated: *The writer might be describing* or *The writer might have been unhappy about…* Students of this level may have problems with this kind of utterance. We recommend that you encourage them simply to start their replies with, *Maybe*….. In the example just quoted, the student could say: *Maybe the writer is describing…* or *Maybe the writer was unhappy about* …. It helps if you the teacher do the same thing when you are offering your ideas.

Using PREVIEW Ideas:

- Read out the sentences and questions, or ask students to read them out. Ask questions to check comprehension and teach new vocabulary.
- Put students in pairs to discuss their answers. Alternatively, give them time to think about their answers.
- Elicit answers. Encourage brief discussion and correct major errors.

3 READING ⑩

Student's Book Page 2

Each of the next three pages of each Unit has a main feature, plus one or two other activities. The main feature of this page is the Reading text. There is a red CD symbol (⑩) next to the title of this section. It shows the CD track number for the audio recording of the text on **CD 2 Reading**. At the beginning of the Unit-by-Unit teaching notes on this section, there is a box of **Key words and expressions**. These are words your students need to know, or will have to work out the meanings of, in order to get the most out of the activity. There are occasional notes with this box, suggesting words and expressions that you may want to focus on before the students read the text. There are similar boxes for the listening and **CLIL** activities later in the Unit (Activity 8). It is possible that teachers may skip one or more of the activities in a Unit and, for this reason, the same words may appear in more than one box. Words may appear in key words boxes in more than one Unit.

- The text is designed to give students practice in the skill of reading. It also aims to present the target structure and vocabulary in context, and provide students with material to help them deal with later activities in the Unit, including **YOUR ANSWER** (Activity 10) to ***The BIG question*** at the end.

The reading topics have been chosen in line with the specifications of the **Trinity College** spoken exams and other curricula. The text is sometimes divided into sections to make reading more manageable. Thanks to the **PREVIEW** preparatory work, students should be in a position to deal with the passage confidently, so first reading can be done quite quickly. Students should try to grasp the overall gist of the text and not worry at this stage if they don't understand everything. There is usually a reading for gist exercise to help students with the overall meaning. The exercises which follow are designed to get students to re-read the passage for more detailed understanding.

The material in the Reading texts is mainly from authentic sources – print and online (newspapers, magazines, websites, advertising). In some cases, the material has been modified so that it contains the target structure items. These modifications never change the original flavour and feel of the text, and we avoid forcing multiple examples of a structure into a Reading text, to avoid what is sometimes called TEFLese.

We have chosen Reading texts which may occasionally shock or surprise, but which will always draw the attention of the reader. Students want to find out more after seeing the visuals and reading the headline and the first few lines of text. The notion of grabbing the attention of the reader through the triple attraction of image, headline and affective first paragraph is a fundamental principle behind all kinds of journalism and creative writing. It also provides a strong motivation to read ELT materials as well.

Some of the texts offer a variety of different political, moral and philosophical standpoints. For example, one part of the reading material in Unit 13 is an advertisement for bear-hunting in the Kamchatka Peninsula in Eastern Russia. It contains the line: *Kamchatka gives you a unique opportunity to shoot a huge brown bear, the dream of every real sportsman.* Lines like this in ***QSE*** are always authentic!

The Reading text is accompanied by standard examination-style activities and exercises.

Using the comprehension activities:

- Read out the questions or ask students to read them silently. Ask questions to check comprehension.
- Put students into pairs or small groups to discuss their answers. Alternatively, give students time to think about their answers individually. Elicit answers, giving the answer yourself if necessary. Where appropriate, ask students to justify their answers by quoting the relevant sentence(s) from the text.

Reading in class:

Most students like reading in class. It's more predictable and less challenging than listening, speaking and writing. Often it's a chance for them to work by themselves, which is a welcome break for the ones who find the whole English-only classroom process a bit overwhelming. Plus, they can always do some pre-reading work of their own, which usually means going through a reading text with a bilingual dictionary. You can often see students doing this at the start of the class. There's absolutely nothing wrong with this. It shows a commendable desire to be ready for the activity.

From our experience of watching classes in many different countries, there are some techniques for reading activities which we really admire and some we aren't sure about.

All the activities listed below are things we've seen. Just because we aren't sure about something doesn't mean you shouldn't do it!

We like these reading ideas:

- When students are asked to read a text at home and do some preparatory work of their own, and then come to class with questions about the content.
- When the teacher pre-teaches certain words and expressions in a dialogue of discovery with the class, and then the students read the text in silence.
- When students work in pairs or groups with a new text, using prior knowledge, dictionaries, and questions to the teacher.
- When the teacher cuts the text into small pieces, a paragraph for example, and gives each piece to a different group. The different group work on their fragment of text and then tell the rest of the class about it. One of them can read it aloud, as long as the others can't see the text themselves (see below for more thoughts about reading aloud in class).

The aim of all the above activities should be to bring the class to a point where they can deal with the reading tasks in the book. Several of our pre-reading tasks in the book aim to help the above processes.

We are not sure about these ideas:

- Asking students to read aloud in class – particularly when they are sitting in rows so that all most of the students can see are the backs of the heads of the students in front of them. It's impossible to understand what people are saying, even if they are speaking clearly, which most students don't. It is a very dispiriting experience to sit in a class where this is happening if you haven't got a book. Does this mean students shouldn't read in class? No. But it's better if they read to each other in small groups, and when one student is reading, the others should close their books.
- Sometimes teachers read a passage, or ask students to read, and stop after a sentence containing a new or unknown word. The teacher asks, '*What does X mean?*'. Again, there is nothing wrong with the principle behind identifying problem vocabulary. But sometimes the words defy simple definition – even by a native speaker.

How to solve this problem? Read the ideas that we like (above)!

4 TALK ABOUT IT

This section is an innovative way of combining the chance to discuss the topic and also activate some key functional language. **TALK ABOUT IT** offers various ways of giving your opinion, and is cross-referenced to the numbered **Language Banks** (**LBs**) which appear on the covers of the book and in the **Workbook** with exercises.

Before you ask students to try to carry out this task, go through the relevant **LB** with them. But bear in mind that the **LB** function will probably only be appropriate for one of the questions in this section.

It is also important to bear in mind that with any productive task, speaking or writing, successful completion of the task is more important than actually using the target functional language. In other words, if students carry out the task successfully, but don't use any of the target expressions, this is not a reason to criticise them!

Using TALK ABOUT IT:

- Go through the relevant **LB**. Either read out the sentences yourself or ask students to read it out. Teach new language.
- You may want students to complete the short exercise that follows the **LB** in the **Workbook**, as a check on comprehension. Check their answers.
- Read out the questions or ask students to read them out. Check comprehension by asking questions.
- Put students in pairs or small groups to discuss their answers. As students talk, walk round and listen to students, noting major errors. Alternatively, give students time to think about their answers individually.
- Elicit answers and encourage discussion. Make notes of students' major errors, particularly errors involving the target structure and vocabulary items. It's probably best to point out major errors after the discussion and write the correct versions on the board.
- It can prove to be very helpful, in a follow-up session, to briefly go through the activity again as a way of revising the language.

5 LISTEN IN ⑩

Student's Book Page 3

The main features of this page are the activities which relate to the listening text. There is a blue CD symbol (⑩), next to the title which shows the track number on **CD 1 Listening**. The **Audio script** for each of the recordings is in the **Workbook**. In the Unit-by-Unit notes of this **Teacher's Guide**, there is a box of **Key words and expressions**, the words your students need to know or will have to work out the meanings of in order to get the most out of the activity. There are notes suggesting words and expressions that you may want to focus on before the students listen.

Listening is a vitally important language skill and it is important that listening material should sound authentic as well as interesting. However, we appreciate that listening can be quite arduous for the students. To begin with, listening to a CD player on the teacher's desk is not the same as listening to a real native speaker. Also, the quality of the sound may be affected by the machine it is played on and the room it is played in. Often the speed of the delivery is daunting for students, and sometimes they lose the thread of the meaning and find it hard to pick it up again. Students may be helped by downloading the audio recordings from the CD to their own personal stereos.

Slowing down the texts to an artificially degree is not the answer – this does not prepare students for real listening experiences. What we try to do in ***QSE*** is present focused pre-listening activities, which make the listening experience a successful one. Often there is more than one pre-listening task.

In our view, it is pointless to make the listening tasks so challenging that students lose both confidence and motivation. As with the presentation of the reading material, the listening preparation tasks are designed to motivate students to listen with a purpose.

Whilst the listening texts are all studio-recorded, the text types are authentic and varied – from street *vox pop*, where members of the public give their opinions, to interviews with experts, radio reportage and discussions. Whilst all factual information in the listening is to the best of our knowledge accurate, the texts may contain some non-standard opinions. For example in Unit 2 *Bright lights, big city*, people in the street give their views on immigration, some of which are quite extreme.

There are usually four to five activities in the **LISTEN IN** section. The first activity prepares students for the listening passage, often by focusing on key vocabulary items that will appear in the passage. The second and third activities are comprehension activities based on the listening passage. The first of these activities focuses on the gist of the passage, while the second deals with more detailed comprehension. The final activity / activities are speaking activities based on topics arising from the passage.

Using LISTEN IN:

- **Pre-listening activity / activities:** Ask students to go through the activity, either singly or in pairs. If you want, ask them to look up new vocabulary in their dictionaries. Then check answers, teaching new vocabulary where necessary.
- **Listening for gist activities:** Read out the questions and check students understand them. Play the tape – you will probably need to play it twice. Elicit answers. If necessary, play relevant sections of the tape to elicit the correct answers.
- **Detailed comprehension activities:** Go through the procedure described above.
- **Speaking activities:** Put students in pairs or small groups to discuss the questions. Walk round and listen to students. Alternatively, give students time to think about their answers. Then elicit answers and encourage discussion. Make notes of major errors and offer corrections after the discussion.

6 CONTROVERSY

This is one of the most innovative sections of the ***QSE*** **Student's Book**. It is essentially an opinionated **Role play**, on a subject related to the listening passage or topic of the Unit. The roles are explained in abbreviated form on the page of the **Student's Book**, and in more detail but in simple language on **Role cards**, which are in the **Workbook**. The cards also suggest useful phrases that students can use in their roles. Students need to have the Role cards in front of them to be able to familiarise themselves fully with their role. There is a cross-reference from the Student's Book to the **Workbook**. If you do not want the students to know the roles of others, it is a good idea to photocopy the Role cards and cut them up, so that each student only receives his or her actual role.

There are two general points to make about this activity. The first is, how do you end an open-ended discussion, argument or Role play situation? In Unit 4 for example, the roles are of an animal rights activist and a medical research scientist. In this case, the roles mirror the characters that the class heard having an argument in the listening activity. It is clear that these people will never agree about anything. The answer to this question is in the timing. Give students a very small amount of time to do the activity. You can tell them that they only have say five minutes (in fact you may give them more, especially if they are doing well), but it concentrates the mind to know that time is limited.

The second point can be more problematic. In almost every case, students are being asked to take on the role of someone who may be outside their experience and, more important, who may have opinions and beliefs which are not be the same as their own. There are two ways to deal with this: (a) tell students that they don't have to play the role if they feel uncomfortable with it; (b) tell them to try the role anyway, as it will be good communication skills practice and may come in useful in an examination.

The problem with the first of these solutions is that a lazy class can end up doing nothing at all! The problem with the second is that students may feel upset about having to express certain opinions, especially if there are cultural reasons why they object to taking a certain role. The teacher will know where there are sensitivities, and could opt to omit this activity, if it is too controversial. But controversy is the name of the activity!

Even so, we feel that the second option is the better one, and students can be mollified by knowing that the tasks are designed in a very systematic way to help them with their fluency.

Using CONTROVERSY:

- Make sure each of the students has his or her Role card, either in the **Workbook**, or as a photocopy.
- Read out the rubric, which summarises the Role play.
- Divide students into pairs or groups, according to the numbers needed in the Role play. Assign students roles as A, B or C, as suggested on the Role card.
- Teach new vocabulary necessary for the Role play.
- Ask students to read the Role cards. Ask questions to check comprehension.
- Point out the suggested phrases on the Role cards and ask students to read them carefully. But tell them they don't have to use them! They can use their own words if they like.
- Students perform the Role play. Encourage them to enjoy themselves! Walk round and listen.
- Ask one or two groups to perform their Role play for the class. While they do this, ask students to note down two things that they really liked about the Role play and two mistakes that they noticed.
- Ask the class for their comments, both positive and negative.
- Ask students for their real opinions!

7 PORTFOLIO WRITING

This section provides guidance for the students to carry out writing tasks. The tasks include emails, postcards, letters, articles, reports and creative writing. The key word here is guidance. There are clear examples of the kind of writing required on the page itself, especially at the beginning of the book. It is our belief that there is no value in asking people to write if you don't offer them a model to work from. **PORTFOLIO WRITING** is a student-centred activity that many teachers and learners will find motivating and creative.

Using PORTFOLIO WRITING:

- Explain the task.
- Go through the guidance section, asking questions to check comprehension.
- You may want students to do the writing task in class. It can be very helpful for them to do the task in pairs. Alternatively, you can give it to them for homework. If students do the writing in class, walk round and offer help where necessary. Encourage students to use their dictionaries. Set a certain time limit, for example 10 minutes.

With regard to correction, try these approaches:

- Put students into pairs and ask each one to correct their partner's work.
- When you go through students' answers, make notes of sentences containing major errors.
- In a follow-up session, write these sentences on the board or hand them out as a photocopy (without the name of the person who made the error). Ask the class to correct the sentences.
- When correcting written work, devise symbols for different types of errors, for example *G* for

grammar, and *Sp* for spelling. Give students a photocopied handout of these symbols. Make sure that students write out incorrect sentences correctly.
- These tasks make ideal homework activities.

8 *CLIL in English*

Student's Book Page 4

In this section, the cross-curricular aspects of the central theme of the Unit are explored. The title of each **CLIL** (Content and Language Integrated Learning) section makes this connection clear. Titles include ***PSYCHOLOGY in English***, ***ECOLOGY in English*** and ***PEACE STUDIES in English***, as well as traditional curriculum subjects such as ***PHYSICS in English*** and ***HUMAN GEOGRAPHY in English***.

At the beginning of the notes in the **Teacher's Guide** on this **CLIL** section, there is a box of **Key words and expressions**. These are words your students need to know, or will have to work out the meanings of, in order to get the most out of the activity. There are occasional notes within this box, suggesting words and expressions that you may want to focus on before the students read the text.

The input material is presented in a variety of forms – statistics, charts, graphs or lists, for example – as well as more conventional reading texts. Often the reading is more dense and challenging (although it is always short), and we recommend that the class should deal with it in a different way from the **READING** texts on page 2. Group work, with students supporting each other and adding their own prior knowledge, is important here. These sections are not expected to add seriously to the students' store of knowledge on geography or history. It is more a question of them realising what they already know and putting it into the new context of learning English. As with the more conventional reading texts on the second page of each Unit, the texts are accompanied by vocabulary and comprehension activities.

Cross-curricular material is more and more in demand by teachers and syllabi. We think there is great value in cross-curricular study, with students using English to accomplish tasks which refer directly to other aspects of their studies or work.

Students who excel in the particular subjects under discussion in this section may of course find them easier to deal with. They will even be able to help the rest of the class who may not be as expert at chemistry, for example, as they are. In fact the ***CHEMISTRY in English*** information in Unit 7 may be quite easy for students who are scientists and they should be encouraged to show the rest of the class (and the teacher) what they know – as long as it is in English. The advantage of this is that these students can then help other students, for whom chemistry is more complex.

Using the CLIL section:
- **Pre-reading activity:** The first activity often prepares the student to read the text, by teaching relevant vocabulary items or asking questions that will focus students' minds on the topic in question. Explain the task and check comprehension. Students work individually or in pairs or small groups to complete the task. You may want them to look new vocabulary up in their dictionaries. Elicit answers, teaching new vocabulary where necessary.
- **Comprehension activities:** Make sure students understand the questions before reading the text. Tell them not to worry about understanding every word. They should just try and answer the questions. Elicit answers, correcting where necessary.

9 CONVERSATION / YOUR TOPIC / INTERACTIVE TASK

This section is based on the speaking tasks in the **Trinity College GESE** exams. In each Unit there is one of three tasks: **CONVERSATION**, **YOUR TOPIC** or **INTERACTIVE TASK**. Students are often referred to a **Language Bank** in this section, since it will practise a function that is relevant to the task. Go through the **Language Bank** with students, reading the language out and asking students to repeat it. Ideally, students should then do the exercise that follows.

Using CONVERSATION:

As its title suggests, this requires students to discuss certain aspects of a topic in pairs for up to five minutes.

- Make sure that the students understand the questions they are going to discuss.
- Pre-teach any new vocabulary and expressions necessary for the discussion.
- In order to integrate the **Language Bank** function into the conversation task, it can be helpful to choose two students to discuss the questions. Encourage them to use phrases from the **Language Bank** as a model for other students.
- Put students into pairs to discuss the questions. Walk round and listen and note major errors.
- Ask one or two pairs to re-enact their conversation in front of the class. Ask students to listen and note two things they liked about the conversation or agreed with, and two mistakes that they heard.
- Go through major errors and write the correct versions on the board.
- In a follow-up session, ask students to go through the conversation again with a different partner. This is a good way to revise the language.

Using YOUR TOPIC:
Students are progressively prepared to talk on a given subject for up to two minutes. They are taught to make notes and then give their talk, and also to listen attentively to others in their group as they do the same.

- Go through the relevant **Language Bank** as outlined in **CONVERSATION** above. Elicit from students ways of incorporating the functional language into their talk.
- Pre-teach any new vocabulary and expressions necessary for the talk.
- Put students into pairs or groups to make notes in preparation for their talk.
- Students give their talks in pairs or groups. Walk round and note major errors.
- Ask two or three confident students to stand up and give their talk. Ask students to listen and note two things they liked about the conversation or agreed with, and two mistakes that they heard.
- Go through major errors and write the correct versions on the blackboard.
- For homework, ask students to write up their talk.

Using INTERACTIVE TASK:
A student is required to take the responsibility for maintaining interaction in a discussion for up to five minutes.

- Go through the relevant **Language Bank** as outlined in **CONVERSATION** above. Elicit from students ways of incorporating the functional language into their talk.
- Put students into pairs or groups to make notes in preparation for the task. It can be helpful to ask one of the more confident groups to go through the task. As they do so, make notes of helpful new vocabulary and phrases. Afterwards, elicit / teach these items.
- Students then go through the task.
- Proceed as outlined above at the same stage in the **CONVERSATION** notes.

10 *Your answer:*

And finally, we come back to *The BIG question* which started the Unit. Students will now be in a much better position to answer it. To prove this, we recommend that, before you start using the book with your class, you experiment by reading *The BIG question* of a particular Unit and making a note of what your answer would be on first reading. Then read and listen to the Unit content, and read the question again. Is there anything you would change or add? We think so, and we are sure that students will benefit from this approach.

As usual with *QSE* activities, this section offers guidance, and even lists opinions that the students might feel happy to express themselves. Some students will of course prefer to express themselves in their own words, but the 'example opinions' are valuable for equally opinionated but less articulate students.

Using YOUR ANSWER:

- Ask students to look back to *The BIG question* and the answers that they noted down. Ask them to think about their answers for a few minutes and whether their opinions have changed.

- Read out the questions and the answers or ask students to read them out. Explain that the answers are just examples – they don't have to agree with them.
- Put students into groups to discuss the questions. Walk round and listen, noting major errors.
- Afterwards, or alternatively, have a whole class discussion, encouraging students to reply to each other.
- Point out major errors and write the corrected versions on the board.
- Ask students if their opinions have changed since they first answered *The BIG question*, and if so, why?
- For homework, ask students to write one or two paragraph answers to the questions.

Extended reading

The three **Extended Reading** Units are situated after Units 7, 13 and 18. The reading texts here are longer and more substantial than the texts on page 2 of the other Units. In ***QSE***, the texts are an extract from a novel, a newspaper article and a biography. All three are authentic texts without adaptation. Apart from the text itself, these two-page Units provide activities and strategies for coping with longer texts and encourage learners to read for pleasure. They are paired with Progress Check pages in the **Workbook**.

Glossary

At the back of the **Student's Book** there is a monolingual **Glossary** section. This contains approximately 800 head words, with English-language explanations in the style of popular learner's dictionaries. This does not replace a dictionary, which students will need and should use frequently, but it does provide a quick reference to the most difficult vocabulary in a lexically rich book. There is a fuller Unit-by-Unit **Wordlist** without explanations at the back of the **Workbook**.

Language Banks

There are **Language Banks** (**LBs**) on the **cover flaps** of the **Student's Book**. In this way they can be kept open in front of the students for constant reference. These **Language Banks** (**LBs**) also appear in the **Workbook**, with accompanying exercises. There is one **LB** for each of the **Functions** listed in the scope and sequence of the course (see Contents pages 4-7 of the **Student's Book**). The functions chosen for the ***QSE Intermediate*** **Language Banks** equate to CEF levels B1-B2.

Students should be encouraged to use the **LBs** for ready reference in speaking activities particularly. Each **LB** can be used in conjunction with many different Units of the book. However, each one is introduced and practised for the first time in the order of Units shown in the Contents list. Reference to the new **LB** for each Unit is usually made for the first time in Activity 4 **TALK ABOUT IT** and followed up in Activity 6 **YOUR TURN TO SPEAK**. Thereafter students are expected to be able to use the **LBs** on their own initiative, and when prompted in the text.

Workbook Units

The ***QSE Intermediate*** **Workbook** is designed to be used in class or for self-study, making it ideal for **homework**. The contents follow those of the **Student's Book** Units, the aim being to reinforce knowledge of the main themes as well as provide further practice with vocabulary, language structures and writing skills. There are also three Progress Check activities, located at the same position in the **Workbook** as the Extended Reading Units are in the **Student's Book**, namely after Units 7, 13 and 18. There are four sections to each workbook Unit. The Progress Checks use **Cambridge FCE**-style exercises.

1 Language

The main grammar item is presented in diagrammatical form, with information about rules and explanations. This is in contrast to the **Student's Book** grammar presentation, which is inductive. Following this, there are practice exercises. In addition, there is usually information and exercise material relating to a secondary grammar item, which featured in the **Student's Book** reading text but was not focused on in the page 1 grammar presentation.

2 Use of English

This section has exercise material in the format of the **Cambridge FCE Examination** Use of English paper, mainly based on sentences from the core texts (reading, listening or cross-curricular themes text) of the **Student's Book** Unit.

3 Writing

The writing activity is also in **Cambridge FCE** format, with of course no writing model to help the students. The choice of tasks is of the length and type specified in various exams. The writing tasks are diverse and include conversations, interviews, letters, emails and for / against opinion pieces. We hope to encourage students to appreciate the differences in register and style that are needed when writing for different purposes. The tasks here are useful ideas for homework, as they follow-up work already undertaken in the **Student's Book** Unit.

4 Connections

This is another innovative and useful vocabulary activity, which follows on from the lexis-building activities on page 1 of the **Student's Book** Units. There is not only more practice with the lexis of the main topic but also an opportunity for students to widen their awareness of related words – how words connect. Synonyms, collocations and chunks are highlighted here.

Role cards

This section contains the Role cards which are required to carry out the speaking task in Activity 6 **CONTROVERSY** on the third page of each **Student's Book** Unit. There is more about using the Role cards in the section on Activity 6 **CONTROVERSY** above.

Audio scripts

Transcripts of the listening material are provided with track numbers of **CD 1 Listening**.

Wordlists

Finally, there is a list of words and collocations. The words are listed Unit-by-Unit, alphabetically and with a page reference.

QSE methodology

The Units are topic-based. The **topics** we have chosen are genuinely affective – stimulating, controversial and designed to make students want to express their own views in speaking and writing and to help them do it. Activities promote the sharing of ideas and opinions, the aim being to present both sides – or sometimes many sides – of a highly debatable issue. The issues chosen are those that affect everyone in our **globalised society** – from the highly personal (exams, ambition, education, finding a partner), to the most public of debates (environment, oil, peace, fame).

Vocabulary enrichment

Because all the topics are real life issues, and the input materials for them are from authentic sources, the vocabulary range is challenging. ***QSE*** is intentionally a rich source of new vocabulary for students' use. The benefit for students is that they have to deal with language they would actually meet in genuine written or spoken exchanges with native English speakers.

In addition, we provide activities to help students understand and activate new terms or concepts, both before they read or listen and afterwards. Then, after they have worked through the **Student's Book** activities, the **Workbook** recycles and practises vocabulary items. This too helps learners to consolidate their knowledge and to become more confident in using the structures and expressions they have learnt.

Using vocabulary sections:

Students may encounter new vocabulary items in all sections of a Unit. For example, the sentences in the **PREVIEW Language** section on the first page of every Unit may have words and phrases that are new to students. Here are two approaches to dealing with new vocabulary:

- Pick new words and phrases out beforehand and pre-teach them. Writing these items on the board in sentences is a good way to contextualise them.
- Ask students to use their dictionaries to look up any words they do not know as they work through the activity.

- For each lesson it can be helpful to decide on your target vocabulary items. Then towards the end of the lesson you can briefly revise them, making sure that students have noted the items in their notebooks, preferably in sentences.

Unit development

There is a systematic and structured development in each Unit which follows a logical cognitive pattern – words, ideas, grammar awareness, reading, discussion, listening, writing, followed by the cross-curricular (**CLIL**) information which relates the topic to other subjects the students may be studying. Finally, the wheel comes full circle and students, older and wiser, answer the question that started the whole thing off.

QSE illustrations

The illustrations in this book have been carefully chosen to be an affective resource in their own right. They are almost entirely news-style photographs, not included simply to decorate the page, but to be used as a resource. As in the best of printed and online competitive media, the pictures are designed to draw students' eyes when they open the book at a particular spread.

We suggest that, especially when you look at the opening double-page spread of the Unit, you should start with an activity about the photos. Students can describe them but they may also want to comment on them. There are suggestions for exploiting these photos in the Unit notes.

However, there may be some photos that you may not want students to comment on, so we have drawn your attention to the more controversial ones. For example, the photo on page 12 of the Student's Book , which is a scene-setter for the reading text about San Francisco, actually shows a gay and lesbian parade (although the relevant banners are not shown in the picture). This could be a talking point in its own right. Alternatively, you may want to avoid drawing attention to it. Similarly, in Unit 4 there is a photograph of a dog used in a laboratory experiment. In some cultural contexts it may not be suitable to emphasise these pictures. In the **CLIL** sections there are often graphics, diagrams and charts. Students going on to business English qualifications, such as the **Cambridge BEC** and **IELTS** for academic qualifications, have to be familiar with describing and using graphics in English.

Where it is useful and appropriate, there are separate notes with some extra information about the photographic material in the Unit-by-Unit section of this **Teacher's Guide**, under the heading **Picture notes**.

Many forms of testing today require students to discuss and comment on images, and the pages of ***QSE*** provide ample opportunities for students to develop this form of **visual awareness** which is such an important part of modern literacy and communication.

Internet sources

There are lists of **Internet references** for further research in each of the Unit-by-Unit sections of this **Teacher's Guide**. We also recommend that teachers and students take advantage of the fantastic research and study opportunities offered by search engines such as Google. Online sources are correct at time of print. The publishers cannot guarantee that websites will not change. This is the reason why the internet links have not been printed in the **Student's Book**. Both teachers and students should be aware that all websites and online resources are constantly changing. They should be checked before they are used for educational purposes. **The contents of any online references cited in this book do not represent the opinions of or any manner of endorsement from the publishers, who cannot be responsible for any online content beyond their control.**

Using the Photocopiable resources

There is a full list and user notes on pages 188-189 of this **Teacher's Guide**.

We hope you enjoy using ***Quick Smart English Intermediate*** and find the ideas in this **Teacher's Guide** useful.

Ken Wilson and **Mary Tomalin**, London 2009

What's new?

Subject:	Youth culture
Function:	Giving advice, making suggestions, giving opinions
Grammar:	*should, ought to, could, you'd better*

For Unit 0 Teacher's notes and answer key, see pages 256-266 of this Guide.

Before you open the book ...

Tell students that one of the main topics of the Unit is internet dating. Ask: *Have you ever visited an online dating website*? Write the question on the board and elicit the meanings of the words *online / dating / website.* Students write *Yes* or *No* on a slip of paper. A student then collects up the pieces of paper and divides them into a Yes pile and a No pile. Count up the answers and announce them to the class. Are the students surprised by the answer?

1 *The BIG question:* IS THE INTERNET A GOOD PLACE TO MEET PEOPLE?

FACT: Nearly a quarter of Japanese high school students regularly visit online dating websites.

Picture notes / Background information

If students use a search engine such as Google to look for internet dating agencies they will find about 61 million references (at the time of publishing). Great care needs to be taken with such sites. For information about the dangers of online dating websites, go to this website:

www.kno.org.uk/internetdating.php

The pictures on this page show:

(a) an art gallery
(b) a pop music festival
(c) an internet café

For information on Glastonbury Festival:
http://www.glastonburyfestivals.co.uk

For information on the Tate Modern (an art gallery in London) go to this site:
http://www.tate.org.uk

This page is mostly preparation for the reading passage on the opposite page, so do not feel that you need to spend a lot of time in discussion. There will be plenty of discussion on the following pages! Check students understand the word *internet.* Ask them if they use the internet and why they use it. Check students understand the word *online* by asking: *How often do you go online?*

2 PREVIEW

Words

A To check comprehension, ask students which of these places they have been to, *eg Have you been to an art gallery / an internet café / a pop music festival? What did you do there? When did you go? Did you meet new people there?*

B Students may disagree amongst themselves here. For example, some students may think that an art gallery is a great place to meet people. Encourage students to justify their opinions.

C Students will probably enjoy learning these words! Teach collocations, such as *to have a relationship / to make friends / to be involved in a romance / to go on a date.*

D This could develop into quite a lengthy discussion. Decide how long you want to spend on the questions. You may only want to spend a short time as there will be plenty of time for discussion later in the Unit. Use the questions to teach the vocabulary. Encourage students to answer the questions, without overcorrecting them. However, make sure that students use the language in the activity correctly.

2 PREVIEW Words A / B / C / D **Answers**

A Picture **(a)** 4 Picture **(b)** 5 Picture **(c)** 1
B **1**, **2** and **3** are probably the best. But you could meet people at the other places.
C **1** the way in which people are connected to each other (although it usually means a romantic connection between two people)
2 a relationship between two people who are friends
3 an exciting relationship between two people who are in love with each other
4 an arrangement to meet someone who you are having a romantic relationship with
D Example answers
1 These are websites where people place personal ads in which they describe themselves in the hope of meeting new friends. Other people read the ads and can reply to them online. Personal advertisements of this kind are sometimes called *lonely hearts ads* and websites or newspaper pages are called *lonely hearts websites*, or *lonely hearts columns*.
2 In online personal ads, people describe themselves and their interests. Often they post a photo of themselves as well.
3 It's a very easy way to meet people. You don't have to pay a lot of money. You can meet a lot of different people online in a very short time. It's easy to end the relationship (at least if you are only meeting online).
4 People can lie about themselves, for example, their age, and their job. They can even use a photo that isn't really them at all! You don't know anything about them except what they tell you – and it may not be true.

Language

If this is mostly revision work for students, they will go through the activity very quickly. Elicit more sentences from students using *should / ought to*. As an example, ask them:

What should you do if you have a bad cold? Point out that *should* is used with all persons (*I / he / they etc*). The question form is *Should I / should you?* The negative form is *should not / shouldn't*. Similarly, *ought to* is used with all persons. The question form is *ought (you) to…?* The negative form is *ought not to / oughtn't to.*

Students may not know the use of *you could* in suggestions. To give them more practice, say: *The old lady next to me lives alone and is very lonely. What could she do, or what could I do to help her?*

Elicit suggestions, for example:
1 She could get a pet.
2 She could join a club.
3 She could ask volunteers to visit her.
4 You could visit her more often.
You'd better is used to give advice only in particular situations, not in general ones. For example, we might say:
• It's late, **I'd better** go to bed.
However, we can't say as a general comment:
• **You'd better** go to bed earlier.
Instead we must say:
• You **should / ought to** go to bed earlier.
Refer students to the **Workbook Unit 1** (page 4 WB), where they will find clear explanations as to the difference between *should / ought to* and *you'd better.*

2 PREVIEW Language A / B / C / D **Answers**

A Sentences 1, 2 and 4.
B Sentence 3.
C *ought to*
D Yes. *Should* is more common than *ought to.*
E 1

Ideas

Encourage students to express their opinions in answer to question **B**. Elicit the fact that the word *hard* (in question **C**) means *difficult*. At this stage, don't expect students to express their opinions in completely correct English. However, in answering question **B**, encourage students to use the words *should* and *ought to.*

2 PREVIEW Ideas A / B / C **Answers**

A In an online personal ad (or its printed equivalent in a newspaper or magazine).
B Because you will find out what they are like. You must decide if you are happy to meet this person and if you will feel safe with him / her.
C **Example answer:** Yes, it can be very hard, especially if you work with only a few people or work on your own.

3 READING CD 2 (Red) track 1, Page 9 SB

Key words / expressions
- partner • search • mate • independent
- passionate • adventure • identity
- secret • honest
- internet services = businesses offering services on the internet
- (the US) market = a particular place (in this case the USA) or group of people that a product is sold to
- there's a lot under the surface = things that a person doesn't immediately show about themselves

Point out that there are three texts, all relating to different aspects of online dating. Pre-teach key vocabulary items. Alternatively, during the detailed reading that accompanies questions **C** and **D**, students can look up new words in their dictionaries (see comments on **3A** and **3B** below).

Background information / Internet references

As the internet has become more and more popular, so have online dating websites. The basic procedure for all dating websites is the same: The user signs on and chooses a user name and password. He / she then answers a questionnaire and this information (profile) is entered into the website database. A photo is often posted. The user then has access to other users' profiles and can email them, or talk in an online chat room. More and more, specialist websites cater for people with different interests: there are websites for gym-users, university graduates and people over 50. Recent research shows that websites with chat rooms where users can talk to each other online in real time provide the best way of getting to know someone before meeting them. Research also shows that online dating is a successful way of finding a potential partner for many people. For general information on online dating websites go to this website:
http://en.wikipedia.org/wiki/Online_dating
For information on recent research into online dating websites and also descriptions of people's experiences of online dating, go to this website:
news.bbc.co.uk/2/hi/uk_news/education/4250281.stm

3A Ask students to read the questions and check they understand them. They should then read all three texts without looking up words they don't understand. Say that their job is simply to answer the questions, which will show that they understand the main idea of each text.

3B1 Explain that the next question helps students deal with unfamiliar vocabulary without using their dictionaries. Make sure that students understand that in bold means 'in heavy black print'. Tell students to try and guess the meaning from the context.

3B2 Suggest that students write the questions down. Make sure that they all find the answers in the passage and understand why the questions are correct. Write the correct answers on the board.

3C Ask students to point out the words that show the answers are correct. They can use dictionaries.

3D Elicit answers. Allow students to disagree! You might want to teach some new vocabulary here, *eg safety / safe / danger / dangerous.*

3 READING A / B / C / D **Answers**

A 1 3 **2** 1 **3** 2a, 2b, 2c
B 1 (a) is likely to (b) posted (c) surfed
(d) the word is getting around
(e) according to research
2 (a) How many men did Leeane have a date with before she met Mr Right?
(b) What per cent of US internet users have surfed a personal website?

(c) How much are single people willing to pay in order to find a mate?
(d) What do people think the US market for online personal ads will rise to by 2007?

C **1** 2c **2** 2a **3** 2b

D **Example answer:** I think the fourth piece of advice is the most important. Safety is the most important thing of all!

4 TALK ABOUT IT

Using the Language Banks

There are **Language Banks** (**LBs**) on the cover flaps of the Student's Book. These **LBs** also appear in the **Workbook** (pages 46-54), with accompanying exercises. There is one **LB** for each of the Functions listed in the scope and sequence of the course (see **Contents** pages 4-7 of the Student's Book).

Students should be encouraged to use the **LBs** for ready reference in speaking activities. Each **LB** can be used in conjunction with many different Units of the book. However, each one is introduced in the order of Units shown in the Contents list. They can fold out the flaps of the book in class, so they can see the LBs, no matter which page they using in the SB.

4A This exercise practises the function of giving advice. Direct students to **Language Bank 1** (**LB1**) on the fold-out cover flaps, and in the **Workbook**, where the **LBs** are repeated with exercises. Either read out the questions (in the left hand column of **LB1**) and the answers (in either the centre or right hand column of **LB1**) or ask students to read them out. Note that the answers are general examples and not meant to be exact replies to each of the questions.

Point out that the natural answer to *What shall I do?* is an imperative, for example:

- Phone him / Don't phone him.

Explain and practise.

The imperative is often used when giving advice.	Then elicit advice, for example:
• I have difficulty sleeping. What shall I do?	• Have a hot drink. • Don't watch TV before you go to bed.

Students should not find question **A** difficult as the answers are all clear in Text **3**. If you think students need help, choose one or two pairs to demonstrate the conversation before the rest of the class do the activity, and ask the class to offer corrections and suggestions afterwards.

4B Explain that the point of not talking about your own experiences, or about anyone else in the class is in order not to embarrass anyone. However, students may be happy to talk about their own experiences – or they may choose to talk about their own experiences using another name. If students can't think of any stories to tell, then they can make up a story. Students can then vote for the best story.

5 LISTEN IN

CD 1 (Blue) track 1, Page 10 SB

<u>Picture notes</u>

The picture on this page shows the presenter of a radio programme at a mixing desk. He is hosting a phone-in chat show and wearing headphones so that he can talk to members of the public live on air. Use the photo to teach vocabulary items, *phone-in programme / to phone in / host.*

<u>Key words / expressions</u>

- attractive • slim • considerate
- sense of humour • superhero
- sociable • guy • single • nasty
- sensitive • make conversation
- stare • miserable • darling
- phone-in = radio programme in which people call the host to discuss a topic or talk about themselves
- caller = the person telephoning
- fit = healthy and physically strong (in BE slang it means attractive)
- go on (about something) = to talk in a boringly way for too long
- go out with (someone) = have a date with someone

The **Audio text** is in the **Workbook** (page 64). In the listening passage, a woman called Michelle telephones a midnight phone-in programme to ask for advice about how to find the right man. The host is called Jason Lynch. Michelle talks about the different kinds of men she meets and her problems with them. The presenter seems to understand completely. His words at the end suggest that he might possibly be gay: '*Some of us know just what you're talking about, darling.*' However, if you or the class are sensitive about this kind of issue, there is no need to point this out (and it is only noticeable on the audio to native speakers or the most experienced listeners).

5A This is preparation for the listening passage, as all these words and phrases appear in the listening. Elicit / teach the word *partner*, and explain that it is a useful general word for someone you live with and have a sexual relationship with – you may or may not be married. Here are some useful phrases when describing an ideal partner:

- He / she needs to be (sensitive).
- I'd like him / her to be (sensitive).
- My ideal partner has (a sense of humour).

5B This activity asks students to understand the main ideas of the passage. In fact, Michelle points out more than three problems and the class may be able to describe most of them.

5C To help students with this exercise, pause the audio CD after each of the listed sentences, and ask them to repeat the sentence as they heard it. You may need to play the sentence two or three times. Write the corrected sentences on the board. Students can then explain whether the new words change the meaning, and if so, how they do this.

5D This activity practises the function of suggestions. Direct the class to **LB1**. Point out that *How / what about .....?* can be followed by either a noun, or verb+*ing*.

To practise, say:	Elicit suggestions:
• I want to go out on the weekend. Where shall I go?	• Go to (the cinema)! • How about going to (the cinema)?

Before students do the activity in pairs, elicit advice and suggestions on how to meet people, for example:

- Get a dog and take it for walks. That's a good way to meet people.
- Why don't you go on an educational course, for example, a painting course?

If the class are not very confident, choose one or two more confident pairs to perform the role play first. You and the class can offer corrections and suggestions, making sure they include some of the advice / suggestion structures (see **LB1**). You can then put students into pairs to perform the role play.

5E Again, if students are not confident in voicing opinions, elicit opinions from the whole class before putting them into groups. Point out that we often use *I (don't) think...* when giving an opinion. If you choose to do group work, afterward have a whole class discussion. Some possible opinions:

- I don't think she's being fair at all.
- There are a lot of nice men out there!
- Women can be awful too!
- She obviously doesn't like men.

5F This practises the function of asking for and giving opinions. Direct students to **Language Bank 2**. Point out that the phrases *in my opinion / in my view / as I see it* are quite formal. Make sure students understand these phrases:

- to live together = to live in the same house and have a sexual relationship with someone.
- arranged marriage = when parents choose their daughter / son's marriage partner.

Teach the following phrases:

- it's a good thing / idea.
- to marry someone / to get married (to someone).

Useful structures for the questions:

- I think it's a good thing, because if you live with someone before you marry them you find out if you really like them.
- **It's not necessary to** get married **these days**.
- **It's better to** marry later, in my opinion.
- I think they can work (= be successful).

5 LISTEN IN A / B **Answers**

B 1 She'd like to get married and have children but she can't find the right man.
2 Some men talk too loudly or don't wash enough. Others go on about sport too much. Some are gay, or if they are attractive, they're probably going out with three women. Some can't make conversation.

C 1 Do you have a picture *in your head* of Mr Right? (The extra words don't change the meaning.)
2 In fact, I think he sounds rather *like me.* (The word *nice* is wrong and completely changes the meaning.)
3 But the really nice guys are all *taken.* (*Taken* in this context means more or less the same as *married*).
4 They get *this kind of* light in their eyes. (The extra words completely change the meaning, suggesting that the men become interested and excited, whereas, to get light in your eyes suggests that there is an outside light shining on your eyes.)
5 Or if they are really attractive, you can be sure they're going out with three women at once. (The words *three women at once* change the meaning to some extent.)

6 CONTROVERSY

See Role cards, Page 57 WB

Read the notes about this section in the Introduction. For each of the Units there are Role cards in the **Workbook** (pages 56-63). These can be photocopied and given to students separately so that they cannot see each others' cards if you wish to use them as information gap activities. The Role cards offer a variety of tasks, some for just two students, some for three or more students and some for larger groups. For this particular role play, start by checking that students understand these vocabulary items:

- potential = possible
- give up = stop doing something

Remind students that this role play practises the functions of asking for and giving advice and asking for and making suggestions. They should use **Language Bank 1**. You may want to go over these functions again before students perform the role play.

7 PORTFOLIO WRITING

You may want to do this writing task over two sessions. In the first session students write their questionnaire. After the class, appropriate numbers of students' questionnaires are photocopied, either by you or the students. In the second session, they are handed out and students answer them. The questionnaires are then collected and collated. Group reports can then be written.

First session: Put the class into groups to prepare their questions. If you think ten questions are too many, lower the number. It will help students if you then elicit their questions and write them on the board, using the opportunity to teach relevant vocabulary: *boyfriend / girlfriend / to go out with someone* = to have a sexual or romantic relationship with someone / *steady (boyfriend)* = someone who you go out with for a long period of time.

Groups then decide on their questions and write their questionnaire. Below is a list of possible questions:

1. Have you got a steady boyfriend / girlfriend? If not, would you like to have one?
2. How did you meet your (previous) boyfriends / girlfriends? *eg* Were they at your school / a friend of a friend / a neighbour?
3. What's the longest time you've ever been out with someone?
4. Do you think it's alright to go out with more than one person at the same time?
5. Have you ever visited an online dating website?
6. If so, how many times?
7. Have you ever had a date with someone you met online?
8. Do you think online dating websites are a good way to meet people? Briefly explain why / why not.
9. What's the best way to meet someone, in your opinion?
10. How do you feel if you don't have a boyfriend / girlfriend? For example, do you feel unhappy or do you feel fine?

Second session: Each group hands their questionnaire out to students in the class, who write their answers. They then gather in the questionnaires. Elicit answers from the class for each question and offer corrections where necessary. Then in their groups, students can read out the different responses and make notes.

Read out the examples of language in the example of a Survey Report shown on the page. Point out that the report should have four clear sections: introduction, questions asked, results and comments on results, and the general conclusion. Give students some more useful phrases:

- We found that (most students) …
- Almost no one …
- Only one person says (that) …
- Ten per cent of students said (that) …

Students write their report, either in class or for homework. If they write it in class, allow them 15-20 minutes. See the Introduction for ways to correct. The **Writing model** below can be used either before or after students have written their report. See the Introduction for ways of using the **Writing model**.

Writing model

> This is a report on a survey of students' dating habits. A group of us gave a questionnaire to five students. These were the questions that we asked:
> (See questions above)
> The results were very interesting. We found that most students met their boyfriends or girlfriends through friends. Almost no one has been out with someone they met online and only one person says they would like to meet someone online. Six people say that they don't want to try online dating websites because they are afraid people will not tell the truth about themselves.
> It is clear from the survey that in our class most people prefer to meet people through other friends.

8 *PSYCHOLOGY in English* Page 11 SB

This is the cross-curricular section of the Unit. Check students understand the meaning of *Psychology* (the study of the mind and how it affects behaviour). Find out who in the class is interested in studying Psychology or is already studying it. If some are interested, ask them to explain why. You may want to teach the title words conformity (behaving in a way that most people think is correct or suitable) and experiment (a scientific test to find out what happens in particular conditions) before students read the text.

Background information

The experiment described in the passage is well-known to all Psychology students. It demonstrates that many people have a strong desire to conform, and that they will change what they think is true and right in order to gain the approval of others. A similar but even more frightening experiment was carried out in 1961 by Stanley Milgram. Psychologists asked volunteers to give electric shocks to subjects if they did not perform a task correctly. Volunteers were encouraged by the psychologists to give bigger and bigger shocks each time subjects got the task wrong. Subjects often cried out when they received the shocks and asked the volunteers to stop. When the shocks got really bad some even seemed to pass out. What the volunteers were not told was that the 'subjects' were actors and the shocks were not real. The volunteers were the true 'subjects' of the experiment, whose aim was to discover how people reacted when asked by an authority figure to punish someone. The study revealed that many of the volunteers (but not all of them) were happy to punish someone if ordered to do so by someone in authority. Note: This experiment is described in the Unit 1, First Certificate Exam practice page, Use of English, activity A. These activities are photcopiable pages in this Teacher's Guide (see pages 205-225).

8A Explain that this activity will help students with the meaning of some key words used in Psychology. When students read the text, tell them not to try and understand every word, but simply to try and match the words in bold with the definitions.

8B Question **1** is a more detailed comprehension activity – students will need to read the text more closely to answer the questions. Check students understand the word *task* (something that you have to do). Elicit answers and point out the words in the text that give the answers. questions **2** / **3** are opinion questions. Elicit answers (see suggested answers in **Answers** box below). For question **3**, students may point out that many people are very frightened of being 'different' in some way – it takes courage to be different. Most people try to be the same as other people – if their friend buys a new gadget, they buy one too.

8 *PSYCHOLOGY in English* A / B Answers

A **1** to conform **2** confederates
3 experiment **4** majority
5 results **6** trial
7 psychologist **8** subject

B 1 a) The idea was to test people's desire to conform.
b) To say which of three lines on a card matched the line on another card.
c) Other people in the experiment gave a different (and obviously wrong) answer.
d) 76% of the subjects agreed with the incorrect opinion of the majority in at least one trial. The subjects conformed to the incorrect majority in 35% of the trials.
e) To choose the wrong line.

2 Example answer: Yes, they do. I think it's astonishing that people can choose the wrong answer when they're certain that it's wrong.

3 Yes, if you look around, it's very clear that people need to conform. For example, teenagers all wear the same kind of trainers and clothes.

9 CONVERSATION

Read the notes about this section in the Introduction to this **Teacher's Guide**. **Language Bank 3** practises phrases that we use to fill in pauses in a conversation, for example when we hesitate or pause to think. Before the class looks at **LB3**, elicit from them words and phrases that they use when they hesitate or pause to think.

9A Some interesting stories may come out of this. Students can tell the best ones to the class. Suggest that they write their parents' stories for homework.

10 *Your answer:*

These questions focus on the big issues dealt with in the Unit. Either read out the questions and answers or ask students to read them out. Ask students to be really honest in their answers. They can look back to their original answer to *The BIG question*, and write a second answer. Ask some students to read out both their first and second answers.

WORKBOOK answers Pages 4-5 WB

1 Language: *should, ought to, could, you'd better*

1A **1** ought to **2** think you should **3** shouldn't **4** you think I should **5** should

1B **1** 'd better **2** shouldn't **3** should **4** 'd better **5** should

1C **1** You could work abroad for a while.
2 How about taking up a new sport?
3 What about learning a new language?
4 You could study an interesting subject.
5 Why don't you join a gym?

1D *Example answers*
- You could get a part-time job.
- You could work in the evenings.
- You could ask your boss for a rise.
- You could work as a taxi driver.

2 Use of English

2A **1** The internet dating market will probably grow a lot.
2 She hasn't had a boyfriend since February.
3 My boyfriend and I broke up last month.
4 You don't have to give your name.
5 Is card 1 the same as card 2?

2B **1** (j) behave **2** (d) if **3** (e) also **4** (f) that **5** (g) because **6** (h) to **7** (i) especially **8** (c) important **9** (b) like **10** (a) while

3 Portfolio writing

Students' own answers

4 Connections

4A **1** (d) had **2** (a) asked **3** (b) went **4** (c) lived **5** (e) lasted

4B **1** (a) **2** (a) **3** (b) **4** (a) **5** (b)

4C adolescent / teenager
baby / infant
man / guy
young person / youth
adult / grown up

What's new?

Subject:	Country and city life
Function:	Comparing and contrasting
Grammar:	Comparatives with modifiers

Before you open the book ...

If your students live in a city, ask them to write down a single word that describes what living in the country would be like. If they live in the suburbs, a smaller town or the countryside, they can write a word to describe what living in the city centre would be like. They can then either read their word out and explain why they used it, or you can put all the words in a box, asking different students to pick a word out of the box and say if they agree or disagree with it.

1 *The BIG question:* IS LIFE BETTER IN THE CITY?

FACT: More people live in the cities of China, Brazil and India (such as Shanghai, Sao Paulo and Mumbai), than in all the cities in the rest of the world.

As explained in the Introduction, *The BIG question* is intended to immediately grab the attention of the students. However, when it first appears, they are not asked to give their opinion or respond in any way. It may be that very few students have actual experience of living in both the country and the city, but if there are any who have done both over an extended period of time (ie not just on holiday), encourage them to give their personal experience at this point.

As always, the **FACT** box contains something informative and, we hope, surprising. Everyone knows that there are a lot of people in China, Brazil and India, but to think that the urban populations of these three countries exceed the urban population of the rest of the world is astonishing. Students only need to read and think about this fact, but if they wish to comment on it further, encourage them.

Internet reference

For up-to-date information about world population, Google "World population" or go to this United Nations website:
http://esa.un.org/unpp/

Picture notes

The pictures on this page show:

Top – a rural scene from Montana, one of the least densely-populated states in the US. **Below** – a street parade through San Francisco.

Background information

San Francisco is the gay capital of the US, and one of the few cities in the world where gay people set the agenda for the cultural life of the city. You may or may not want to discuss this fact. The city's gay community was portrayed in literature by Armistead Maupin in his series of best-selling novels called *Tales of the City*.
For more information on Armistead Maupin go to: http://www.talesofthecity.com/.
If you do wish to discuss this, there are lots of websites about gay life in San Francisco. Information about events and the changing cultural face of the city is available at www.sfpride.org.

2 PREVIEW

This section prepares students for the reading and speaking tasks on the next page.

Words

As with all Units in this book, the link between lexis, topic and structure has been carefully worked out. The words that we present here are the words we think students need, to compare life in the city and the countryside. We realise that students may wish to use other words, but we always provide some base lexical material to get them started.

A The opening activity asks students to use words from a list to describe the images in two photos. One photograph is of the remote countryside, the other is of a street parade in the city centre of San Francisco. Most or all of the words should be known to students at this level. We don't wish to force opinions on them, so there are no right or wrong answers for this exercise.

B Another feature of the book is our regular attempts, in the main Unit pages and also in the workbook, to encourage students to think about and learn the possible variations on root words. In this case, students have to modify a list of adjectives to complete sentences.

2 PREVIEW Words B — **Answers**

1 bored **2** noisily **3** excited **4** colour

Language

Another five adjectives are introduced, and this time they are used to complete a series of comparative statements. Comparisons are the featured structure item of the Unit. Do your students know comparatives? To complete this exercise, they need to know how to make comparatives using *as … as / less / more*. This means that they must understand that when you make a comparison with *less*, the form is the same with short or long adjectives – *less hot / less expensive*. Students should also be reminded that certain collocations with *less* are unlikely – *this street is shorter than that street*, rather than less long.

If you want students to do more structure practice work before they proceed, they can do the structure exercises in the **Workbook** (page 6).

2 PREVIEW Language A — **Possible answers**

Note: the answers are all sentences from the **Reading** text **(Exercise 3)**, but alternatives are possible.
1 less expensive **2** hotter **3** angrier / more angry **4** less exotic **5** as hectic

Ideas

This section also contains extracts from the reading text. In this case, students are invited to consider the ideas that they contain, not the structure content. There are three questions to consider. Here are some notes about the questions:

- The quote about San Francisco – *Freedom sips a cappuccino in a sidewalk café in San Francisco* – is a wonderful image about life in a city which takes its freedom for granted. The quote is by a writer named Joe Flower, who has written a lot about future change. He is the author or co-author of several books, including *China's Futures* (2000) and *The Encyclopaedia of the Future* (1996). For more information on Joe Flower go to www.imaginewhatif.com
- The second quote creates an image that can be seen as paradise or hell, depending on your point of view. This should be clear from the reactions of the students.
- This extract is different. It describes both what happened to someone and how they reacted. Encourage students to think about ways the clothes could have been ruined. *Maybe the writer took them to a dry-cleaners.* As students will find out, it actually describes what happened to someone who was involved in the New York power cut in 2003.

3 READING — CD 2 (Red) track 2, Page 13 SB

Picture notes

The pictures on this page show:

1 Old and new San Francisco architecture. The city is built on a series of small but steep hills and the older houses are made of wood.
2 People emerging from the New York subway on the day of the power cut (blackout) in August 2003.

Key words / expressions
- advertising agency • afford • cappuccino
- exhausted • groan • hectic • parking lot
- sidewalk café • manhole = opening in the road big enough for a man
- bohemian = enjoying an alternative lifestyle
- sip = to drink slowly
- clams, crabs and lobsters = types of seafood

The reading texts are about living in San Francisco and New York. The texts are different in style. Text **1** consists of four quotations about San Francisco from (mainly) famous people.

Background information / Internet references

John Lennon (1940-1980) and Yoko Ono (1933-) John Lennon was a member of The Beatles. Yoko Ono, a Japanese musician and artist, was his second wife. Many people thought that Lennon's relationship with Ono led to the break up of the group. Lennon was shot dead aged 40 by a deranged fan outside his apartment in New York on 8th December 1980.
http://en.wikipedia.org/wiki/The_Beatles

Oscar Wilde (1854-1900) was an Irish dramatist and poet, who angered polite society in 19th century London with his flamboyant lifestyle. He is famous for a large number of memorable quotations, such as "*The only thing to do with good advice is pass it on; it is of no use to oneself.*"
http://www.cmgww.com/historic/wilde/index.php

Dylan Thomas (1914-1953) was a Welsh poet who wrote many great poems. Encourage your students to read *Do not go gentle into that good night*, or listen to the Richard Burton recording of the play *Under Milk Wood.*
http://www.bbc.co.uk/wales/dylanthomas/bibliography/pages/under_milk_wood.shtml
http://www.dylanthomas.com/

Note: There is information about **Joe Flower in 2 Preview Ideas A** above.

Text 2 is the true story of a woman who was caught in the New York power cut in August 2003. Ask students to think about what it would be like to be stuck underground for several hours on a hot summer afternoon.

The power cut of August 2003 didn't just affect New York. It extended from the north east of the United States to parts of eastern Canada, including the city of Toronto. It was the largest blackout in North American history, affecting 40 million people in the US and more than a third of the population of Canada. The financial loss was estimated at 6 billion US dollars.

3A As with many first reading activities in this book, this one is quite easy. Students scan both texts to decide whether the people love or hate San Francisco. The quotes indicate that the people love San Francisco. The woman who has the nightmare journey home on the subway hates New York.

3B This is a scanning activity for Text **1**. There is a choice of possible meanings for key words, which should be clear from the context.

3 READING B **Answers**

1 (a) sea creatures **2** (b) an artist or writer
3 (a) a place to leave cars

3C Students now read the quotes about San Francisco and decide which they think is the key word in each one.

3D Text **2** contains a lot of phrases in CAPITAL LETTERS. The text is written like this to indicate the extremes of emotion felt by the writer, both positive and negative. Each capitalised phrase refers to a different topic.

3 READING D **Answers**

1 THE CENTER (*US spelling*) OF THE WORLD – **New York**
2 THERE WAS A BLACKOUT – **the result of a power cut**
3 THERE WAS NO WAY I COULD AFFORD – **cost of city accommodation**
4 IT WAS REALLY HECTIC – **city life**

4 TALK ABOUT IT

As we explained in the Introduction, this section is an innovative way of combining discussion on the topic and also some key functional language. This section is always cross-referenced with the **Language Banks**, in this case, **Language Bank 4 (LB4)** – Ways of Comparing and Contrasting.

Ask students to look at **LB4** and then encourage them, in groups or as a class, to discuss the three questions which are listed here.

The first question concerns their response to the two texts. The second asks them to say how the information about New York and San Francisco has affected them. However, the texts about San Francisco are all positive, and the experience of the New Yorker is negative. Encourage the class to add any more they know about the two places to balance the discussion.

The third question takes the conversation into the more general area of city v country. Students should not only be able to use the comparative forms they find in **LB4**, but also the vocabulary they learnt or revised in **2 Preview Words**.

The conversation can be judged successful even if students fail to use the functional language and/or the target vocabulary. Don't criticise them if they have a good conversation without using a comparative form!

Key words / expressions
• economic migrants • immigrant • ethnic minorities • immigration • multi-cultural society • political refugees • unemployed

5 LISTEN IN   CD 1 (Blue) track 2, Page 14 SB

Picture notes / Internet references

The picture on this page shows a street in New York where there is a great deal of ethnic diversity. It happens to be a picture of the same blackout event as shown on the previous page. As there was no power, people had to walk instead of taking the subway.

For more information on immigration in America go to:
http://en.wikipedia.org/wiki/Immigration_to_the_United_States

The **Audio text** is in the **Workbook** (page 64). As we pointed out in the Introduction, listening activities can be quite arduous for the students. We have devised a series of pre-listening activities, which we hope will make the listening experience a successful one. As mentioned earlier, we think it is pointless to make the listening tasks so challenging that students lose both confidence and motivation.

This listening text is what is known as a vox pop, a series of three short interviews with members of the public, who are asked for their views on immigration.

5A The first pre-listening exercise requires students to familiarise themselves with four expressions:

- Economic migrants = people who move to a new country or society for economic reasons.
- An ethnic minority = an ethnic group who are in the minority in the society in which they live – Asian British people for example, or the Chinese community in San Francisco.
- A multi-cultural society = a place where several different ethnic groups live in harmony in the same place.
- A political refugee = someone who has to leave his or her own country because he / she is in danger of persecution by the authorities.

5B The second pre-listening task requires students to look at a photo, a street scene from a clearly multi-ethnic society and consider two questions. The first question is about whether there are ethnic minorities in your country. Obviously, the students will have similar answers to this. The advantage of this kind of question is that students who are more confident about speaking can answer for the whole class. The second question, on the other hand, requires students to give an opinion about immigration and freedom of movement between countries.

5C The first listening task is to find general information about the three people who are interviewed.

5 LISTEN IN C — **Answers**

Sarah: for immigration **Craig:** mixed opinions
Mike: against immigration

5D In their own words, students now try to give more specific details about the opinions of the three interviewees.

5 LISTEN IN D — **Answers**

1 Sarah (a) it's right that we should share what we have **(b)** we should help them **(c)** immigrants do the jobs no one else wants to do
2 Craig (a) we should help political refugees **(b)** some people want a better life in a richer country **(c)** ethnic minorities sometimes don't mix
3 Mike (a) foreign people take our jobs **(b)** they also take our houses **(c)** they send their children to our schools and they can't speak the language

5E There are three sentences here which have been changed slightly from the original. Students should identify what is different and how it changes the meaning. If at any time, students seem to have difficulty remembering the details, offer to play the tape again.

5 LISTEN IN E **Answers**

The corrections are as follows:

1 We should help people who are IN DANGER IN their own countries (the changed version suggests these people are the ones who are posing the danger).
2 Ethnic minorities often live in their own COMMUNITIES, not countries. (The danger here is in thinking that ethnic communities have another country which is their own. Often they were born in the country where they now live).
3 I can see you feel quite STRONGLY about the subject. (Not wrongly! Whatever the interviewer's own feelings, it would be wrong to say that the Mike's views are wrong).

6 CONTROVERSY See Role cards, Page 58 WB

Read the notes about this section in the Introduction. In this section, students work in groups and act out a scenario, which is explained to them in the instructions. In this case there are three students. Student A is a refugee and spills some coffee over Student B, who responds in a racially unacceptable way. Student C tries to mediate.

There are three role cards for the students to read in the **Workbook**. However, if possible, it's better to photocopy the role cards so that students don't read each other's. This role play is simple to stage. A spilt cup of coffee leads to an aggressive, potentially racist response. Teachers who have different ethnic groups in their classes will know that they have to be careful with this activity.

7 PORTFOLIO WRITING

The writing task is a postcard home from someone who has moved to live in a new country. An extra detail is that the immigrant lived in a big house in the old country and now lives in a small city apartment, giving another chance to practice the main structure item of the Unit, comparatives.

As always, with the first example of a particular type of writing, there is plenty of help in an accompanying box. In fact, there are enough ideas to complete half of the required 120 words quite easily.

If the students have any problems with this activity, you can show the following, more complete model. Remember to tell the students that this is just one of many possible ways to write this.

Writing model

Informal postcard

Dear Mum and Dad,
I'm writing to you from my new apartment in Leeds. It's much colder here in the north of England than it is at home. And this little apartment is much smaller than our house! People here aren't as friendly as they are back home.

But I mustn't complain. I have a job and the people I work with are OK. I also have somewhere to live and there is a lot to see and do here. There are some wonderful shops, and lots of cinemas, although all the films are American, and I find American English harder to understand than British English.

So, please don't worry about me because I'm doing fine.

Take care. I miss you all so much!
Edwin

8 *HUMAN GEOGRAPHY in English* Page 15 SB

This is the Content and Language Integrated Learning (CLIL) section of the Unit, where the aim is for students to deal with tasks which connect them to other areas of their study or work. As with many CLIL sections, this one does not consist of a conventional reading text, but begins with a list of the world's largest cities and urban areas. Many countries have super cities that are so large that they dominate the rest of the country. In Europe, Athens, Paris and London, for example, all dominate their home nations. By contrast, some countries such as Italy and Germany, have many smaller cities, which do not individually have such a large effect on the nation as a whole. The growth of mega-cities is a feature of rapidly developing nations, such as China, India, Brazil and Egypt. If any members of the class have studied this aspect of human geography in their other classes, they may be able to use their specialist knowledge for the benefit of the whole class (and the English language teacher). Becoming the teacher is often an excellent way for the student to learn the language.

Key words / expressions

• congestion	• entertainment	• health care
• lack (noun)	• poverty	• pull factors
• push factors	• rural areas	• shortage

Push factors and *pull factors* mean things that encourage people to move in (attract them into) or out of (repel them from) a particular area. After looking at the list, students discuss three questions.

8A1 This question asks them if they know the difference between a city and an urban area. The official definition, which appears on the World Resources website (http://pubs.wri.org) states that all cities are urban areas, but not all urban areas are cities. Urban is a statistical concept defined by a country's government. A city, on the other hand, is more than just large numbers of people living in close proximity to one another; it is a complex political, economic, and social entity. Cities around the world symbolise their nation's identity and political strength. Cities are also centres of economic production, religion, learning, and culture. It should be enough for students to realise that an urban area includes cities where there is no real distinguishing line between the city and its suburbs.

8A2 This question asks them to say which of the cities are in the developed or developing world. This is a tricky question with a constantly changing answer but should start an interesting exchange of views. Are all cities in Asia developing? What about Sao Paulo, Brazil?

8A3 This question allows the students to discuss the relative sizes of the different cities, considering why some are so much larger than others.

8B The second text illustrates and describes 'push' and 'pull' factors, the factors that encourage some people to leave cities and others to move to them. The task is to find specific words and expressions that describe certain things.

8 *HUMAN GEOGRAPHY in English* B
Possible answers

1 Poverty in rural areas.
2 Rich people want space and a clean environment, so they move.
3 Shops and entertainment are better in the city.

8C Now students read the text more carefully and answer questions.

8 *HUMAN GEOGRAPHY in English* C
Possible answers

1a) push factor **b)** pull factor **c)** pull **d)** pull
2a) city **b)** country **c)** city or country

9 YOUR TOPIC

Read the notes about how to develop a **YOUR TOPIC** activity in the Introduction. Students work in groups of four, comprising two pairs. One pair prepares a short talk on something they have read about in this Unit. Here are some possible topics which have been dealt with or alluded to:

1 The gay community in San Francisco
2 The dangers of being dependent on a city transport system
3 Racism
4 Cities that get bigger and bigger

The pair who have prepared the talk take it in turns to make their points. The listeners are encouraged to ask for clarifications, and to this end are directed to **LB4**, which provides them with this information.

10 *Your answer:*

Finally, we return to the question that set things off in the Unit. Students have more information to form their opinions now. They have read about San Francisco and New York, they have heard a variety of opinions and attitudes about immigration, and have seen the vast size of the world's largest cities.

As stated in the Introduction, we feel that students still need guidance in this section, so we include a set of subsidiary questions, with possible answers, which constitute opinions. We don't expect students to repeat these opinions as if they were their own, but we feel that they may gain confidence by seeing sentence structures which they can use to articulate what they want to say.

WORKBOOK answers Pages 6-7 WB

1 Language: comparatives with modifiers

1A *Suggested answers*

1 much more dangerous
2 even noisier
3 much cheaper
4 a bit more modern
5 much hotter
6 far more quickly

1B *Students' own answers*

Example: New York is **much more** crowded than Boston. Kyoto is **far more** beautiful than Tokyo.

1C **1** I don't think London is as beautiful **as** Paris.
2 OK
3 OK
4 I travel **farther** than you to work.
5 People say that New York is **the** most exciting city in the world.
6 Which is the **oldest** building?
7 This is the **worst** part of my journey
8 Is there as **much** noise in the suburbs as there is in the city centre?

2 Use of English

2A1 It was tiny, it was noisy, but it belonged to me.
2 I couldn't find anywhere to sit down.
3 When I came out on Houston Street, I was covered in oil.
4 I tried hard to look good today.

2B Choose a word from the box to fill the gaps.
1 (h) **2** (f) **3** (d) **4** (e) **5** (c) **6** (j) **7** (i) **8** (b) **9** (a) **10** (g)

3 Portfolio writing

Students' own answers

4 Connections

4A Words

1 a) same **b)** different – urban = city; rural = countryside
c) same **d)** different – suburbs are outside the city
e) different – an emigrant leaves a country; an immigrant comes into a country

4B Useful phrases

1 a) peace and quiet **b)** bustle **c)** get away from it all

What's new?

Subject:	Public figures and celebrity
Function:	Expressing possibility and uncertainty
Grammar:	*may, might*

Before you open the book ...

Tell students that the title of this Unit is *Fame and fortune*. Elicit the fact that *fame* is the noun of *famous* and explain that *fortune* means *a large amount of money*. Ask: *Do you want fame and fortune?* Elicit answers (*eg I want fortune but not fame*).

Ask students to name their favourite celebrity. Teach the word *celebrity* if necessary. As you elicit celebrity names, write them on the board. You'll almost certainly find that the same names come up and it will be interesting to see who the class' favourite celebrity is.

If possible, bring in a copy of *Hello!* Magazine (or any similar publication featuring the lives of celebrities). Hold up the magazine and / or pass it round. Ask if anyone reads it. If students do, ask them to explain why (*eg I enjoy reading about celebrities / I enjoy reading gossip about celebrities*). If no one reads it, ask students what they know about the magazine (*eg It's a celebrity gossip magazine).*

1 *The BIG question:* WHAT IS THE PRICE OF FAME?

FACT: A series of robberies at the houses of rich and famous people became known as the *Hello!* Burglaries, because celebrities were robbed after appearing in *Hello!* Magazine.

The phrases, *What is the price of fame / a successful career / having children?* etc mean, *What are the bad things you have to accept when you have fame / a successful career / children*? To check students understand *The BIG question*, elicit answers such as *The price of fame is no privacy.*

Ask students what their reaction is to the FACT. They may reply that it's rather amusing! Ask why they think the burglaries took place. Perhaps criminals read *Hello!* in order to find wealthy people to rob!

2 PREVIEW

Words

Picture notes / Background information

Nelson Mandela (1918-): Black South African statesman and president (1994-99). Trained as a lawyer, for 20 years he campaigned against the racist policies of the South African government (Apartheid). In 1964 he was sentenced to life imprisonment for political offences. Released from prison in 1990, he is famous for presiding over a peaceful change of regime from white minority government to a multi-racial society with equal rights.

Nicole Kidman (1967-): Australian film actress, who has become a top Hollywood star. Her films include *Dead Calm*, *To Die For*, *Moulin Rouge* and *The Hours*, for which she won an Oscar. She was married to film star Tom Cruise; they divorced in 2001.

Queen Elizabeth II (1926-): Queen of the United Kingdom, head of the Commonwealth, and daughter of George VI. Elizabeth was crowned Queen in June 1953. Married to Prince Philip, the Duke of Edinburgh, she has three sons, Charles, Andrew and Edward, and a daughter, Anne.

Albert Einstein (1879-1955): Mathematical physicist, born in Germany, he took Swiss nationality in 1901. Einstein developed the theory of relativity, which caused physicists to rethink the laws of physics. He became a

US citizen in 1940. After the war, he urged international control of atomic weapons.

Tiger Woods (1976-): Real name Eldrick Woods, in 1997 he won the US Masters (the top US golfing championship) at the age of 21, the first Afro-American to do so as well as the youngest. Since then he has consistently remained at the top of his profession.

Bill Gates (1955-): American computer engineer and entrepreneur. At the age of 22 he co-founded Microsoft, a company that produces basic operating systems for computers. By the 1990s Microsoft had become the world's leading computer company, and by the late 1990s, Bill Gates had become the wealthiest man in America. Gates and his wife Melinda give enormous sums of money to charity, particularly in the area of world health, and have set up their own charitable institutions.

To find *Hello!* Magazine online, go to: www.hellomagazine.com

A First, ask students to match names with pictures. They may not be able to name all the people in the pictures. Then ask students to say why each person is famous. Fill in the gaps in students' knowledge.

B The words in italics are key words connected with fame. Questions **1** and **4** focus on the fact that more and more, people are becoming celebrities who have no real talent – for example, perhaps they have been on a TV reality programme. What is strange is that people seem to become celebrities so easily. You may want to quote American Pop Art artist Andy Warhol (1927-87), who said, 'Everyone will be famous for 15 minutes.'

Someone might point out that the media has a habit of 'building up' celebrities (writing a lot about them and saying how wonderful they are), and then 'knocking them down' (taking advantage of their vulnerable aspects). For example they might expose their love life and be very cruel about them.

2 PREVIEW Words A / B **Answers**

A Page 16, left to right:

Nelson Mandela, Nicole Kidman, Queen Elizabeth II of Great Britain

Page 17, top down:

Albert Einstein, Tiger Woods, Bill Gates

B 1 A celebrity is a famous entertainer or sports personality. Traditionally, people become famous because of a talent that they have. But recently, people have become famous for appearing in reality TV programmes or for modelling in newspapers and magazines.

2 The media are radio, television, newspapers, the internet and magazines, considered as a group. The media are very interested in celebrities because celebrities 'sell' newspapers etc. Paparazzi (media photographers) pursue celebrities so that it can be difficult for them to find privacy.

3 A stalker is someone who follows and watches someone in a way that can be dangerous and obsessive. People probably become stalkers because they are lonely.

4 If you are talented, you have a natural ability to do something well. More and more these days, it seems that famous people are not necessarily talented.

Language

Point out that we use *may / might* to express possibility, either in the present or the future. *I may see him = Perhaps I will see him.* Elicit the fact that we use *may* and *might* interchangeably. To present or revise, elicit from students what their possible plans are for the weekend (*eg I may go away for the weekend. I'm not sure*).

2 PREVIEW Language A / B / C / D / E **Answers**

A a)
B The last three sentences
C The first sentence
D Example answers:
I may go to the cinema tomorrow. I may stay in tomorrow evening.
E I might go to California for a holiday. I might leave my job.

Ideas

Check students understand the words *autograph* and *privacy*. There is a lot to discuss in these questions, and you need to decide how much time you want to devote to discussion. You could usefully use the discussion to teach new vocabulary connected with fame.

Question **C** is explored in detail in the reading text on page 17, so you may not want to spend too long on it here. However, you could teach the phrase *An advantage / disadvantage of fame is that...* Students should also find question **D** very interesting. If they haven't met anyone famous, perhaps their parents or family friends have – almost certainly one or two students will have an interesting story to tell. If they have, then the class can write the story up for homework.

2 PREVIEW Ideas A / B / C **Answers**

A The first and third sentences

B **Example answers:** The advantage of fame is that if you like attention, you get a lot of it. A big disadvantage of fame can be that you have no privacy.

C **Example answers:** Perhaps because they seem in some way special, and most of us want to be special.

Extension activity

Ask students to go online and print out an article from *Hello!* Magazine - give them the magazine website (above). Students then bring the article to class, describe it and give their opinion of it. Alternatively, print out an article yourself and use it as a basis for comprehension activities and discussion.

3 READING **CD 2 (Red) track 3, Page 17 SB**

Key words / expressions

- the high life • in the long run
- to admire • to pretend
- attention • power • influence
- Bono (U2) • achievement
- public • worthwhile
- the Nobel Prize • disguise
- the Rolling Stones

- trash cans (AmE) • to beware
- the high life = a life lived in a very expensive and exciting way
- in the long run = in the end
- speed dial = a way of dialling fast / automatically on a phone
- backyard = a garden behind a house (AmE)
- to lose interest = not to be interested any more

Background information

Bono is the lead singer of the famous Irish rock group, U2. Bono uses his celebrity to try and diminish world poverty, and is in constant talks with leading politicians.

Nobel Prizes: important Swedish prizes awarded each year to those who have contributed most in the fields of physics, chemistry, physiology, medicine, literature and peace. The prizes were founded by Alfred Nobel, Swedish scientist and businessman who invented dynamite explosive in 1866.

The Rolling Stones are an English rock and roll group that became world-famous in the 1960s and have remained one of the world's biggest rock bands. The band's lead singer is Mick Jagger.

This passage takes a light-hearted look at the advantages and disadvantages of fame.

3A This activity helps students to practise their ability to scan a passage for the main ideas. Tell them not to try and understand every word. In particular, tell students to ignore the headings at the start of each paragraph – explain that they are not necessary to understand the paragraph.

3B Explain that the definitions give very simple explanations of the headings in bold. This activity encourages students to guess the meaning of unfamiliar phrases by looking at the context. Guessing the meaning of unfamiliar words and phrases is a useful reading skill that needs practice.

Here are some more notes on the phrases, some of which are very idiomatic:

(a) all the trappings = all the possessions that show someone is rich, powerful or important
(b) if it doesn't work out = if it doesn't end well or successfully
(c) in the limelight = in a situation in which you are getting a lot of public attention
(d) power and influence = when someone has the ability to change things
(e) public recognition = when people in general know who you are and admire you
(f) adopt a disguise = if you adopt a disguise, you wear things that change your appearance.
(g) beware of stalkers = be careful of people who may watch and follow you
(h) keeping up appearances = to make things appear as they have always been, even if the situation has changed for the worse

3C / D These activities focus on more detailed comprehension.

3 READING A / B / C / D **Answers**

A plus factors / advantages: (a) (c) (d) (e)
minus factors / disadvantages: (b) (f) (g) (h)

B **1** (f) **2** (h) **3** (a) **4** (c) **5** (d) **6** (g) **7** (e) **8** (b)

C **1** Bill Gates house near Seattle has 24 bathrooms.
2 When you're famous, people ask for your autograph.
3 Bono has Nelson Mandela's phone number and Mandela has his. This means Bono has power and influence.
4 Albert Einstein won the Nobel Prize for science.
5 In order to get away from photographers, in the 1970s the Rolling Stones got into a television studio by hiding in trash cans (rubbish bins).
6 Nicole Kidman married Tom Cruise. Ten years later they divorced.

D **1** He or she might hide near your vacation home.
2 They might climb over your five-metre garden wall and into your bedroom.
3 You should accept that you may not be a celebrity ten years from now. Just enjoy your fame while you have it.

4 TALK ABOUT IT

Language Bank 6 gives ways of expressing possibility and uncertainty. Elicit sentences from students that begin with: *It's possible that … / You can't be certain that …* Encourage students to focus on the questions that they find most interesting.

To give more practice with *may / might*, ask: *Which celebrities do you think will still be famous in ten years' time?* Possible answers: *I think (Brad Pitt) will still be famous. But Orlando Bloom, for example, may not be famous in ten years' time. People may forget him.*

4B Other advantages of fame: You get the best table in a restaurant, the best seats in the theatre, it's good for your self-esteem and successful people have better health than other people. Other disadvantages: You may feel that you're not as good as people say you are. You may be afraid that your next book / film will not be as good as your last one.

4C / D Encourage students to give reasons for their opinions.

4E Check students understand that if the price of fame is too high, then there are too many disadvantages, so that you may not want to be famous.

Extension activities

Most students will know the story of Diana, wife of Prince Charles (heir to the British throne), and her tragic death in 1997 as a result of a chase by paparazzi (celebrity photographers) through Paris. Ask students to research this story online and write an article reporting it as if it had just happened.

This could then lead to a discussion on the paparazzi and their relationship with celebrities. Celebrities love them because they give them publicity and hate them because they destroy their privacy.

For a fun talking exercise write the names of famous celebrities on pieces of sticky paper and stick them to the foreheads of your students so that they cannot see the name that is written there. Then tell students to walk around the room asking each other questions in order to guess what celebrities they are. Questions might include: *Am I a singer? Am I an actor in Hollywood movies? Am I very handsome / pretty?*

Internet reference
For articles on the tragic death of Diana, Princess of Wales, go to these websites:
http://news.bbc.co.uk/onthisday/hi/dates/stories/august/31/newsid_2510000/2510615.stm
http://www.cnn.com/SPECIALS/1998/08/diana/
http://www.cnn.com/WORLD/9708/30/diana.dead/
www.lospettro.it/ pagina751.htm

5 LISTEN IN

CD 1 (Blue) track 3, Page 18 SB

Key words / expressions
- newcomer • studio • drummer • fan
- album • serious • pub
- in the charts = the charts are the official list of the most popular songs, produced each week.
- single = a musical record with only one song or piece of music on each side.
- gig = a public performance of pop music or jazz.
- (on) tour = a journey in which a person or group visits several different places in order to perform.
- to come out = to become available to buy or see, eg *The album is coming out in February.*

The **Audio text** is in the **Workbook** (page 65). The listening passage is a radio interview with two members of a pop group called *Dark Star*. Sharon, the singer / songwriter, is clearly very competent, but the drummer Dave seems to have no idea about what is going on.

5D The bulleted sentences are examples of things students might say about their favourite band. You may want to expand on this activity and take the opportunity to teach / revise vocabulary connected with pop music. If this is the case then ask a student who his / her favourite band is. Write the name of the band on the board – teach the word *band* (pop group) if necessary. Ask students to tell you as much as they can about the band, who the *lead singer / lead guitarist / drummer* is etc. Teach these words if necessary. Ask questions, like *What was their first / latest album / single? When did it come out? What's the highest they've been in the charts? Have they ever been on tour? Have you been to any of their gigs?* Then elicit the name of another favourite band and put students into pairs to ask and answer similar questions.

5 LISTEN IN A / B / C **Answers**

A **1** (c) drummer **2** (h) appear on TV **3** (a) album **4** (f) come out **5** (d) gig **6** (g) in the charts **7** (b) single **8** (e) on tour

B **1** Because he doesn't seem to know much about the band or about Sharon.
2 He doesn't know that she wants to be an actress, and that she's been asked to appear in *The People Next Door.*

C **1** False. The band's first single went into the charts at number 26.
2 False. They're writing material for a new album.
3 False. They may go to Scandinavia and Germany.
4 False. It may come out in the autumn.
5 False. She has been asked to appear in *The People Next Door.*

6 CONTROVERSY

See Role cards, Page 58 WB

Key words / expressions
- to release (an album) • to publicise
- publicity • manager • chat show
- PR (public relations) = the job of giving people information about something and making it popular.
- (to need) a break = a period of time when you are not working and can rest and enjoy yourself.

Read the notes about this section in the Introduction. Begin by eliciting / teaching the phrase *PR manager.* Ask students to say what kind of thing a PR manager does for a pop star (arrange interviews with the media, give information to the media about the pop star, and create publicity). Allow students to choose whether to be the pop star or the PR manager. Suggest that the students playing the pop star should behave like a typical pop star, ie demanding and selfish!

Optional activity

When students have performed the role play, choose one or two of the most confident pairs and ask them if they would be willing to be recorded performing their role play for the class. If they are willing, go ahead and record them. Explain that you will use the recording as a basis for a future language session.
When preparing the session, transcribe the recording, and make photocopies for the class. During the session, hand out the photocopies, and put students into pairs to correct and improve on the dialogue. Elicit corrections and suggested improvements and write the improved dialogue on the board. Finally, students can perform the role play again, acting different roles.

7 PORTFOLIO WRITING

When students have written their questions, elicit them and write them on the board, with corrections. After they have written their answers, ask certain students to read them out. Some answers could be the basis for an interesting discussion. For homework, students could write one or two paragraphs in answer to the most interesting questions.

For a variation on this, put students into groups of four and get each student in the group to choose one of four categories: music, film, politics and fashion. Every student must choose a different category. Students then think of a famous person from that category and tell the rest of the group. If a student's category is music, for example, she might choose Madonna as a celebrity. If a student's category is politics, he might choose Nelson Mandela.

Now ask students to split into pairs and write questions together for the two celebrities that the other pair chose. Each student must then take it in turns to imagine they are their chosen celebrity, while answering questions from the other pair as if they were in an interview. Ask students to write down answers as if it were a real interview. If a pair has chosen Madonna, the questions and answers should be very different to questions asked of, for example, Nelson Mandela.

Writing model

Example questions
- Why do so many people want to be famous?
- Can fame be a burden?
- Do you think fame makes people happy?
- What is the price of fame?
- Do you think it is true that the media likes to destroy famous people? If so, why?
- Why are people so fascinated by celebrities?
- Are you interested in reading about celebrities? Say why / why not. Be honest!

8 *MEDIA STUDIES in English* Page 19 SB

Key words / expressions
- editor • image • select
- Democratic Party • candidate
- military • technique
- camera angle • location
- to influence
- particular = a particular thing or person is the one you are talking about and not any other
- point of view = one way of thinking about a situation
- to manage the news = to select the information that is given out so that a particular point of view is presented
- message = the main idea that is contained in something such as a speech or advertisement

Picture notes / Background information

Media studies: A communication social science which studies the nature and effects of mass media upon individuals and society. Media Studies uses techniques from cultural studies, psychology, art theory, sociology, information theory and economics.

Democratic Party: one of the two main political parties in the US. The other party is the Republican Party.

George W Bush (1946-): Known as George Bush Junior, he is a member of the Republican Party and the 43rd US president (2001-2008). He is the son of George Bush Senior, the 41st US president. His election as president in 2000 was marked by five weeks of complex legal argument over the voting procedures. He was eventually judged to have won the election over Al Gore, the Democratic Party candidate, by a US Supreme Court decision in his favour.

John Kerry: US politician who opposed George W Bush in the 2004 presidential elections as the Democratic candidate. He narrowly lost the election.

Both these photographs were taken during the 2004 presidential election campaign, as both candidates attempted to show that they were fit to be President, and hold his title of Commander-in-Chief.

2003 war in Iraq: a coalition headed by the US and Great Britain invaded Iraq (without United Nations support) with the intention of removing Iraqi president Saddam Hussein from power and finding and removing the weapons of mass destruction (WMD) believed to be possessed by Iraq. Saddam was removed and eventually captured. No WMD were found. The coalition troops have remained in occupation in Iraq due to widespread unrest and violence in which many civilians and soldiers have died.

Begin by asking if any students are doing Media Studies. Elicit from students what is studied in Media Studies (see **Background information** above.) You may want to use the photos to briefly ask students' opinion of George Bush (students may be vociferous in their opinions!), and what they know about John Kerry (see **Background information** above).

8A This activity focuses on the photos in preparation for the text. Briefly ask students what they know about the US occupation of Iraq. (See **Background information** above). Elicit answers to the questions and teach any new vocabulary that arises.

8B Students should have fun writing the captions. Write the best ones on the board.

8C It is good practice for students to use their dictionaries to look up words from time to time in class. If dictionaries are not available, teach the phrases instead.

8 *MEDIA STUDIES in English* **Answers**

A / B / C / D

A The photographers are trying to present both Bush and Kerry as strong military leaders. This is done by showing them performing a military-style salute.

B Example answers

Photo of George W Bush

Positive caption: Yessir, I will lead our country to victory!

Negative caption: Why am I pretending to be a soldier when I've never been one?

Photo of John Kerry

Positive caption: I have medals, I'm a war hero!

Negative caption: I'm saluting like a soldier but inside I'm not so sure!

C manage the news = select the information that is given out so that a particular point of view is presented

point of view = one way of thinking about a situation

Public Relations (PR) manager = someone whose job it is to give people information about something and make it popular

camera angle = the position from which the camera shoots

influence the message = to change the main idea contained in an advertisement or speech, for example.

D 1 The media manage the news by presenting a particular point of view.

2 During the 2003 war in Iraq, American TV news did not show pictures of dead American soldiers, even though hundreds of soldiers were killed. Photographers use techniques such as choosing the camera angle and location.

<u>Optional extension activity</u>

In preparation for a future session, ask students to choose a current news story they are interested in. Pick two newspapers that demonstrate different attitudes to the same story. You can find British newspapers online – *The Daily Mail*, *The Guardian* and *The Daily Telegraph* all have very different points of view. Make copies of two articles that express different points of view on the same story and appear to 'manage the news' very differently. Do comprehension activities based on the articles and then go on to ask how the articles differ in their attitudes and how the news is 'managed'.

Alternatively, having chosen an interesting news story, ask students to bring in an article (in their native language) about the story. Put students into pairs to talk about their articles and compare the different points of view.

9 INTERACTIVE TASK

Read the notes about this section in the Introduction. Go through **Language Bank 7**. Briefly revise **Language Bank 3** and elicit the fact that the phrases in **Language Bank 7** are longer and more sophisticated. Explain that *How can I put it? / What's the best way of putting it?* both mean *How can I explain it? / What's the best way of explaining it?*

Write the title of the topic on the board – *How the media works.* To teach the meaning of *to work* in this context, point to a machine or a gadget like a mobile phone or a computer, and ask: *How does this work?* You could also point to your mobile phone and say: *It's no good, it's broken – it doesn't work.*

If you feel that students need help in preparing their talk, hold a discussion on the topic first. In this case, elicit points from the class and write notes on the board. Ask: *Do you think the media manages the news? If so, how do they do this? Why do you have that opinion?* Elicit answers from students. They will probably talk about newspapers they read in their own country and how they notice the lack of objectivity.

Students may go on to explain that the point of view of a newspaper depends on the politics of its owner and which political party he / she supports. If possible, elicit specific examples of bias in various newspapers or TV channels. Teach new vocabulary where necessary. If the students simply want to repeat the content of the text *Making News* rather than come up with their own ideas, tell them that is fine.

When explaining the **Interactive Task**, make sure students understand that Pair B are acting as interviewers, and that they should really feel that they are controlling the situation. Once students have performed the role play, they should then swap roles. However, you may want to do this in a following session as revision.

10 *Your answer:*

Check students understand the phrase *public figure* (well-known person). Something that may come out of this final discussion (if it hasn't emerged before) is the fact that the less responsible newspapers and magazine sometimes (often?) print stories about celebrities that simply aren't true. This is an extreme example of 'managing the news'!

Workbook answers

Pages 8-9 WB

1 Language: *may, might*

1A 1 In ten years' time, people may not remember her.
2 You may meet someone famous at the party.
3 I might go to the concert tomorrow.
4 Michael Jackson might sell his home.
5 Madonna's next book may be a big success.
6 He may not ever be famous.
7 We might go to New York or L.A.

1B 1 Might this photo not be genuine?
2 Do you think he might not be telling the truth?
3 Might this house belong to someone famous?
4 Might he get a job in TV?
5 Do you think it might only be a rumour?

1C *Example answers*
1 I might start work immediately after university, or I might travel for a year.
2 I may not go for a swim this evening, instead, I might see my friend Maria.

2 Use of English

2A 1 Almost no one recognised him.
2 It is more likely that people will listen to the opinions of famous people.
3 He has been famous for five years.
4 What are the requirements of fame?
5 If you are famous, you can become very rich.

2B 1 won 2 made 3 famous 4 of 5 Sadly

6 more **7** fears **8** problems **9** In
10 fame

3 Portfolio writing

Students' own answers

4 Connections

4A **1** celebration (n) celebratory (adj)
2 influence (n) influence (v)
3 publicise (v)
4 talented (adj)
5 famous (adj)
6 privacy (n)
7 reality (n)
8 fortunate (adj)

4B **2** (j) **3** (i) **4** (h) **5** (a) **6** (b) **7** (e)
8 (g) **9** (c) **10** (f)

4C **1** in the public eye **2** fortune **3** fans
4 in disguise **5** keeps herself to herself
6 autograph

What's new?

Subject:	Environmental concerns
Function:	Expressing feelings and emotions
Grammar:	Relative clauses

Before you open the book ...

Ask students to make a list of five animals that they would expect were in the top ten for intelligence. You can, if you wish, allow students to say what they know about these animals, and if they have ever seen them, in zoos or in the wild.

1 *The BIG question:* DO ANIMALS HAVE FEELINGS?

FACT: Apart from humans, the ten most intelligent animals are: chimpanzees, gorillas, orang-utans, baboons, gibbons, monkeys, whales, dolphins, elephants, pigs.

It is likely that initial answers to *The BIG question* will vary according to where the students are from. People who live in the city tend to anthropomorphise animals (think of them as having similar feelings to humans) a lot more than people who live in the country. In other words, city people give animals some 'human' characteristics and emotions. And, of course, they give affectionate names to their pets! People in the country, especially if their livelihood has something to do with the raising and killing of animals for food or sport, may have different ideas. However, everyone should be in the same position when it comes to the facts about the intelligence of animals.

Picture notes

There are seven photos on the opening spread; they are of the following creatures:

On the left-hand page: a group of chimpanzees, a dolphin, a flock of sheep, a tree frog. If you wish to discuss the idea of ascribing human emotions to animals, you could ask students what they think each of the animals in these four pictures is thinking!

On the right-hand page: whales, elephants and a very distressing photo of some dolphins being killed by hunters. Many of these creatures are mentioned in the **FACT** box.

2 PREVIEW

Words

The lexical set for this Unit is words which express emotions, like *joy* and *grief.* There are grammatical factors involved with abstract nouns like these, particularly for students who speak Latin languages – we only use the definite article with them in certain restricted uses: *joy is a wonderful thing; I can't express* ***the joy I felt*** *when I saw her again.*

Note that abstract nouns which are preceded by the definite article are usually followed by some kind of relative clause, often a contact clause involving a person – *the joy I felt, the disappointment they suffered, the anger he displayed* etc.

2 PREVIEW Words A / B / C **Answers**

A The animals which are in both the **FACT** box and the photos are: chimpanzee and dolphin (on this page); dolphins and whales on the next page.

B Students give their own answers about unintelligent animals.

C **Example answers**

Opposites: *joy – sorrow / grief – joy; love – hatred; pleasure – pain; fear – courage*

D This activity personalises the new language for the students. They may prefer to talk about great joy, grief and fear in small groups, or they may not want to talk about it at all, especially grief. Don't push any students who don't want to talk about sad times in their lives.

Language

The target structure is relative clauses with *which, who* and *that*. As usual, the examples are taken from the reading text on the next page. The relative pronouns in each sentence are highlighted and the first activity requires the students to turn them into two sentences again. When they read the two sentences, it becomes clear why the idea is better expressed in its combined form! Relative clauses may be a nuisance to learn, but they help to make a student's speaking and writing more sophisticated.

The difference in the use of *who* and *that* when referring to people, and *which* and *that* when referring to things is partly a matter of personal style, although some people say that *that* is more informal in both cases. This is true for defining clauses. For non-defining clauses, which this phrase is an example of, you have to use *who* for people and *which* for things, of course.

The Language section on this page is an inductive activity. In other words, the activity is designed to help students discover the rules of usage for themselves, or hopefully to remind themselves of the rules they already know. For students at this level, relative clauses like this should be revision. But, as all teachers know, there are some structures which you simply can't revise too much! If you want students to do more structure practice work before they proceed, at this point, they can do the structure exercises in the **Workbook** section.

2 PREVIEW Language A / B / C / D / E
Suggested answers

A The sentences, written as two sentences, are as follows:
She found a young chimpanzee. It had starved to death after its mother died.
There are so many kinds of food. We can eat them.
He's an environmentalist. He regularly observes whales.
The scientists had studied chimpanzees for many years. I interviewed them.

B In these sentences *that* refers to things (chimpanzee) and people (the scientists; *which* refers to things (food) and *who* refers to people.

C In every sentence except the last one (about the scientists), the words in bold are the subject of the verbs which follow.

D In the last sentence (about the scientists), the word in bold is the object of the sentence.

E You can omit *that* in this phrase and say simply: *the scientists I interviewed;* this is called a contact clause.

Ideas

There are three sentence-extracts from the reading text on page 21, each one describing actions by animals that suggest very 'human' emotions. Students read about the emotional responses of whales, female sea lions and elephants, and then there are three questions to guide their discussion, and activate the words such as *love*, *fear* and *grief* which were presented in the earlier **Words** section.

3 READING CD 2 (Red) track 4, Page 21 SB

Key words / expressions
- biologist • dolphin • embrace
- flipper • inlet • amorous • right whale
- mating strategy • (sea lion) pup
- to purr • revive • killer whales
- sea lions • to stroke • to surface
- to trap • (elephant's) trunk
- to wag (your tail)

The three texts are about the behaviour of certain animals and the similarity to human behaviour. Activity **A**: As per Cambridge ESOL 2008+ exam, sentences have been removed from the text (A, C, D) and placed in a jumbled order (plus an additional, unused sentence, B). Students have to show that they understand specific information in each text by choosing which sentence fits where. Actvities **B / C / D** work on the individual texts. Try dividing the class into groups of three; each member of each group reads one text and then describes it to the others.

3 READING A / B / C / D **Answers**

A The missing sentences are **(1) D** (Are they in love?) **(2) A** (The hunt is an important part of local culture, which dates back 400 years.) **(3) C** (She says that he died of grief.) **B** is the sentence not used.

B 1 the female **2** yes **3** scientists disagree about this

C 1 F **2** T **3** T

D 1 grief **2** starve **3** trunk

Internet references

Right whales are one of many different kinds of whales. For more information about all the different kinds of whales, go to these sites:
42explore.com/whale.htm
http://www.enchantedlearning.com/subjects/whales/

You can find out more about the work of Izumi Ishii and his campaign to stop the killing of dolphins on his personal website:
http://www.gjallarhorn.com/dolphin/

Other websites about the Taiji dolphins:
http://news.bbc.co.uk/1/hi/programmes/this_world/3956355.stm
http://www.seashepherd.org/taiji/taiji.html

This website is in Japanese but it has some interesting pictures:
http://homepage2.nifty.com/KOHKAIMARU/

4 TALK ABOUT IT

The content of the three reading texts offers very different evidence that animals feel emotions. From the calmness of the right whales to the slaughter of the dolphins, there is a lot of information, some of which is quite depressing. However, the texts provide the class with material they can refer to in this discussion phase. As usual, there is a **Language Bank** reference, where students will find useful language for expressing their own feelings after reading the information about the animals.

5 LISTEN IN CD 1 (Blue) track 4, Page 22 SB

Picture notes / Background information

The pictures on this page deal with the things that humans do to animals. On the left-hand page is a dog which is being used to test for skin diseases in a laboratory; on the right-hand page are some gorillas in Uganda. The gorillas are endangered because they are hunted for meat and souvenirs and because their habitat is disappearing. For more information on the bush meat trade, see photographs on the website of campaigner Karl Amman, whose work is mentioned in the **Internet references** box in section ***8 ECOLOGY In English*** below. Activity **9B** invites students to discuss the priorities of hunting primates that are so like humans.

Key words / expressions

- Alzheimer's disease
- animal rights (activist) • ape • come on!
- cosmetics • cruel • drug company
- embarrassment • endangered species
- experiment (verb and noun) • extinction
- mammal • medical scientist • mosquito
- non-essential • primate • properly
- research • resemble
- sophisticated behaviour • vivisection

The **Audio text** is in the **Workbook** (page 65). The listening text is a radio debate about the rights and wrongs of vivisection. Apart from the interviewer, the two people taking part in the debate are Tony Cavell, an animal rights activist, and Carla Robinson, a medical scientist who uses animals in her research.

As we said in the Introduction, in this book, we aim to give students as much help as possible with the listening texts. We would rather have a lot of pre-listening activities than slow the exchanges on the tape down so much that they no longer sound like real English.

Before the class listens to the debate, make sure that everyone understands clearly what *vivisection* means. *Vivisection* is the process of operating on living animals for scientific research. In case *animal rights* and *animal rights activists* are rare or unheard of in the students' countries, you may want to bring some information about animal pressure groups. There is plenty of information on the internet about these groups, in the UK, the US and worldwide.

Background information / Internet reference
For information about a US organisation called PETA (People for the Ethical Treatment of Animals), go to www.peta.org. For a more general overview of the animal rights movement worldwide, go to www.animal-rights.com. In fact, there are more than six million websites that concern themselves with animal rights. For the other side of the argument visit this website: www.pro-test.org.uk

It is interesting to note that this group in favour of animal testing grew out of concern about the tactics of the animal welfare groups campaigning against and delaying the building of a new animal testing laboratory at Oxford University. Most protests against this new lab have been peaceful. However, elsewhere people have been subjected to intimidation and even threats of violence by animal rights campaigners, especially those campaigning against certain companies that carry out laboratory tests on animals. There is no support for animal testing for cosmetic purposes (banned in the UK since 1998), but the Pro-Test group does represent many people who feel that without tests on animals, medicines cannot be developed to benefit humans who suffer from terrible diseases.

This is a highly emotive subject and, not surprisingly, the two participants in the discussion have deeply contrasting views. It is also clear from the moment that they start speaking that the two guests on the programme are not going to agree or find any common ground.

5A This is a pre-listening task where students can make their views clear before they hear the views of the experts. There will be more opportunities to discuss this issue later, but it is helpful to have a discussion at this point, to make sure that everyone knows what the subject-matter really deals with.

5B The second pre-listening task requires students to make sure they understand some of the key words and expressions from the text. Ask the students to read the list and check that they know the meanings. Ask them to give examples of *sophisticated behaviour* – in humans and in animals. And ask them if they know of any campaigns to *save* certain creatures *from extinction.*

5C This prediction activity allows the students to read the main arguments that they will hear before they listen. It seems likely that Tony Cavell, the animal rights activist, will have opinions 1 and 4, and that Dr Carla Robinson, the medical research scientist, will have opinions 2 and 3.

5D When students listen to the tape, they will hear the opinions expressed in activity **C**, and they will hear the opposite view expressed as well. For example, when Tony Cavell says *'Animals have many of the same feelings (or emotions) that we do',* Carla Robinson replies by saying that only mammals have these emotions, and uses the classic line: *Mosquitoes don't feel pleasure or grief and they certainly don't feel embarrassment.* Students are not expected to remember the opposite view word for word, and they should try to express what they heard in their own words.

5E Students now have to recall the arguments that they heard for and against three specific things.

5 LISTEN IN E **Answers**

E 1 For – animals feel pain like we do. Against – human lives are more important.
2 For – they are our closest relations. Against – nothing is said against the rights of primates.
3 For – they save endangered species. Against – they resemble prisons.

6 CONTROVERSY See Role cards, Page 59 WB

Read the notes about this section in the Introduction. As usual, the instructions direct students to the section of the book where the role cards are located. In this case, the role cards are for two characters that mirror the roles and attitudes of the two people we heard in the discussion on the tape. If possible, give the students a photocopy of just their role, so they can concentrate on what they have to say, and not be distracted by the other student's role.

As we mentioned in the Introduction to this

book, some students may not be happy with certain roles. Decide whether you should accept their concerns, or suggest to them that it will help their fluency if they try to act the part out.

7 PORTFOLIO WRITING

The writing task is a formal letter, the first one in the book, so a writing model is given below. The positioning of the addressee's address, the date and the sender's address are standard usage. If the writer is using headed notepaper, the positions are the same for the addressee's address and the date.

A useful guideline for students writing a formal letter is that they should avoid contractions (*I'm, he's* etc) and try to use formal expressions (*In my opinion* is more formal than *I think*). As with all letter-writing (especially for exam purposes) the key is NOT to repeat any of the useful phrases and expressions that we give you. If you are going to use *In my opinion*, only use it once! If you are required to write a formal letter of 120-180 words, this does not include the address and your name at the end.

Writing model

35 Queen's Road
York YK1 8BH

The Guardian
119 Farringdon Road
London EC1R 3ER

25th September 200X

Dear Editor,

I am writing in connection with the article that appeared in your newspaper last week about building more zoos in this country. I believe that zoos are not a good thing, and the animals which have to live in them are not kept in suitable conditions.

In my opinion, the argument that zoos are important for helping endangered species is not a good one. Why are the species endangered? I think the reason is almost always because of what humans have done to their environment and habitat.

I agree with your correspondent who says that zoos in some countries are improving, but I don't think this is true in every country in the world. And I certainly don't agree with the idea of capturing animals in the wild and bringing them to zoos in countries where they do not normally live.

I hope that the government will not continue with its idea of building more and bigger zoos.

Yours faithfully,
Tom Donovan

8 *ECOLOGY in English* Page 23 SB

Internet references

For more information on the anti-bush meat campaign, see the website of Karl Ammann, the Swiss photographer and conservation activist. Karl Ammann has devoted his life to trying to protect endangered species from being killed for meat. For more information on the Bushmeat Campaign, go to this website:
http://www.bushmeat-campaign.net/engsite/
For more information about the Ruwenzori mountains of East Africa go to this website:
http://www.worldwildlife.org/wildworld/profiles/terrestrial/at/at1013_full.html

Key words / expressions

- competition
- deforestation
- DNA
- ecosystem
- habitat
- rainforest
- resources
- survival
- to threaten

The text in this cross-cultural activity is a standard reading text. The subject matter is deforestation and destruction of habitat. Most of the words in this key word box are activated in activity **A**.

8A To help students with problem words, the pre-reading task is a gap exercise which highlights the new vocabulary.

8B Students read the text again and then, in their own words, talk about the effect that a number of people and organisations have on gorillas.

8 *ECOLOGY in English* A / B Answers

A **1** ecosystem **2** threatened
3 competition **4** resources
5 survival **6** habitat
7 deforestation **8** DNA

B Suggested answers

1 farmers – threaten survival by cutting down trees
2 timber companies – threaten survival by cutting down trees
3 hunters – threaten survival by killing the gorilla for meat
4 tourists – help survival by providing funds; threaten survival by introducing diseases
5 national parks – help survival by protecting gorillas
6 diseases – threaten the gorillas with extinction

9 CONVERSATION

Read the notes about this section in the Introduction.

9A There are three discussion starters and a reference to **Language Bank 9** (**LB9**), where students will find words and expressions they can use for agreeing and disagreeing. This is the first reference to **LB9**, but students will be able to refer to it many more times in this book, when there are activities where they need to give their opinion.

9B This activity gives students a chance to react to the idea of hunting gorillas for meat. Having started the Unit by thinking about animals having 'human' emotions and behaviour, they can use **Language Bank 9** to say how they feel now about eating primates which share 98% of human DNA.

10 *Your answer:*

Finally, the question that started the Unit. Now you can find out what the students have learnt from the reading, listening and cross-curricular material and also the discussions and role-plays that they have generated. *The BIG question* is here sub-divided into three different aspects, and suggested responses are given to answer each one.

Workbook answers — Pages 10-11 WB

1 Language: relative clauses; the definite article

1A **1** She is a biologist who / that works with elephants.
2 The farmers who / that need land are cutting down the forest.
3 People who / that keep pets have better health.
4 Uganda is an African country which / that has many wildlife parks.

1B **1** He's the animal researcher I met last week.
2 The book I'm reading now has some useful information.
3 She is the medical scientist I told you about.
4 The gorillas we saw didn't notice us.

1C **1** The animal we have been watching is a rare type of monkey.
2 My uncle is leading an / the expedition to Uganda.
3 Gorillas are the creatures with the highest intelligence.
4 The primates in this park are protected from hunters.
5 The first time I saw a lion, I felt fear and pleasure.

2 Use of English

2A *Example answers*
1 The animals spent a long time swimming together.
2 It is important that animals have rights in the same way that people do.
3 It is wrong to experiment on animals and put them in zoos.
4 We must stop using live animals for experiments and (even) cutting them up.

2B **1** c **2** a **3** g **4** f **5** e **6** i **7** d **8** j **9** h **10** b

3 Portfolio writing

Students' own answers

4 Connections

A Words:

1 trunk

2 *Students' own answers*

B Idioms:

1(a) *the lion's share* (= most of it)

(b) *a whale of a time* (= a good time)

(c) *a wolf in sheep's clothing* (= he's more dangerous than he looks)

2(a) *A white elephant* is something that you can't sell or get rid of; it's useless and takes up too much space.

(b) *A dog's life* means not a very nice life.

(c) *The cat's whiskers* is something that's nice and smart. *This suit is the cat's whiskers.*

(d) *A red herring* is something which is a deliberate distraction and not relevant to an argument or investigation. It may be derived from the habit of hunt saboteurs, who drag a herring (a fish) across the path of hunting dogs so that they lose the scent of the animals they are following (a fox, for example). The expression dates back to the late 1600s.

What's new?

Subject: Early memories
Function: Describing past habits
Grammar: *used to;* past perfect

Before you open the book ...
Ask students to write a short note describing their earliest memory. Invite them to exchange their notes with a partner and ask questions about their partner's memory. At the end of the activity, ask them to say how confident they are that the memory is correct.

1 *The BIG question:* HOW WELL DO WE REMEMBER THINGS?

FACT: Memories are not stored in our brains like books on shelves. When we remember something, we re-make the memory from many words, images and experiences kept in different parts of our brains.

How well do we remember things? The question seems like a simple one, but in fact memory is a very uncertain thing. You can prove this to the class by asking them to remember details of something that they all remember, an event which took place in your town, or what you did on the first day of the course, for example. Very quickly, they will realise how imprecise their memory of quite recent events can be.

Picture notes
There are three photos on page 24. They depict infancy (top left), childhood (below) and adolescence (top right), and the dominant relationships of those eras, with parents, school friends and adolescent friends. Everyone in the class will have memories or experiences of these periods in their lives. Ask them to comment on the difference in their memories of each of the ages. Activity **1C** is directly related to these photos.

2 PREVIEW

Words

2A This section starts by focusing on words that will be very important in any discussion of memory. There are two lists of words, one of verbs, the other of nouns. Start the lesson by using all the words in context. Elicit examples, if possible. Draw the class's attention to the future use of *remember* – *I must remember to do my homework* – as well as the past use – *I remember doing my homework last week.*

2 PREVIEW Words A / B **Answers**
A1 (a) *Remember* and *recall* mean more or less the same thing, when referring to the past. But you can also remember to do things in the future; you can't recall things in the future. You *remind* someone else to do something, or someone / something *reminds* you *of* something; *this picture reminds me of my holiday in France. Imagine* is the odd one out; you imagine things that haven't happened.
(b) A *memory* of something and a *recollection* of something are similar; but *memory* is also the word we use to refer to the part of your brain that remembers things. A *reminder* is something that helps you remember to do something, or reminds you of things in the past; again, *imagination* is the odd one out.
B **1** reminds **2** recollection **3** imagine **4** remember

2C This activity is directly related to the three photos on the page. If there are any students in the class who knew each other as children, it will be interesting to hear their separate memories of the events in their lives and places that they remember.

Language

There are two structure items focused on in this Unit, *used to / would* and the past perfect. As usual, we have some inductive concept questions for the students to answer. It's quite easy to explain or demonstrate the concept of *used to – We used to live in Canada.* Conceptually, it is clear: we lived in Canada for a long time. We don't live there any more. *Used to* can't refer to a single event, and is rarely used with a definite time period: *we used to go to Canada for our holidays* is OK, and *we used to go to Canada for our holidays during the 1990s* is OK, although the past tense would work just as well. But *we used to go to Canada for our holidays for the last five years* is not OK and *we used to go to Canada for our holidays last year* is definitely not OK.

The use of *would* in this context is a little more complicated. But the simple rule you can tell the class is that you can use *used to* or *would* for repeated events or actions in the past, but not for states. Therefore, the following two sentences are possible:

- We used to go to the beach every day.
- We would go to the beach every day.

However, in the following sentences, you can't use *would:*

- We used to live in Canada.
- We used to have a dog.

In addition to this, and this is not so easy to convey to students, *would* is often used to give a flavour of nostalgia or colour to a sentence. For example, *When we were on holiday in Canada, we would go for a walk in the forest every day.* This sounds as if you enjoyed it! If you replace *would* with *used to* in that sentence, the meaning is the same, but it sounds more matter-of-fact. However, *would* can also evoke memories that are not necessarily pleasant ones. Here is an extract from the reading text: *When the workers returned home, they would complain and we would be whipped.* Students will find this sentence when they read the text on page 25.

2 PREVIEW Language A **Answers**

A 1 The sentences refer to things that happened many times.

2 They don't refer to things that still happen.

3 *used to* and *would* mean the same thing (use the explanation above to indicate how and when they are different)

The secondary structure item in this Unit is the past perfect tense, and specifically its use to indicate that one action happened before another one in the past. If the structure is new to the students, give a few examples that make the concept clear. *By the time* is a very useful expression to use in a marker sentence. Use an example from their own experience to present it for the first time.

Teacher: Tell me three things you did before you left home this morning,

Student: I ate some breakfast, I listened to my MP3 player and I played a video game

Teacher: So … by the time you left home, you had (already) eaten breakfast, listened to some music and played a video game.

2 PREVIEW Language B **Answers**

B 1 The second event in the sentence happened first.

2 The use of *had* + past participle indicates an action that happened before another action in the past.

If you want students to do more structure practice work before they proceed, they can at this point do the structure exercises in the **Workbook**.

Ideas

There are three sentences from the text and students are invited to imagine what the context is. Knowing that the lines are taken from the reading text on the next page, they will of course combine their understanding of the words with the message given by the images on the next page. This conceptualising from images and words is to be encouraged.

2 PREVIEW Ideas A / B / C

Suggested answers

A The children appear to have lived in crowded and poor conditions. The students may want to make suggestions about where they might have lived and in what country.

B The idea of selling a human being is usually connected with slavery.

C The father is definitely someone that the child doesn't live with. We don't know yet if he was a stranger.

3 READING

CD 2 (Red) track 5, page 25 SB

The reading text is in three parts: information about Annie Burton and two extracts from her autobiography, *Memories of Childhood's Slavery Days*. The relevant section of the book is entitled *Recollections of a Happy Life*. Four sentences (A, B, D, E) have been removed (FCE 2008+) and there is one extra, unused sentence (C). Students choose which sentences go in which gaps.

Picture notes

On page 25 are two very evocative images, one of a slave market, and the other of Annie Burton, a former slave who wrote an autobiography during the second half of the nineteenth century. When they read the text, the class will find out more about her, including the fact that she is very positive, despite the terrible things that happened to her. But before reading, students might want to take a minute to discuss what it must have been like to be a slave.

Key words / expressions

- bones • carefree • (American) Civil War
- debt • exclaim (=shout)
- marriage ceremony • oyster shell
- plantation • wander • to whip
- mistress = female boss / owner

Background information / Internet reference

The American Civil War (1861-1865) was fought between the Union of States which called itself the United States, and the Confederate States of America, a coalition of southern States that declared itself independent. There were many complicated reasons why the two sides went to war, but slavery was a key cause, because cotton plantations worked by slaves were essential to the economy of the South. The South wanted to protect their right to own slaves, and the North wanted to end it. There is information about slavery and the slave trade in the cross-curricular activity on page 27.

For more information about Annie Burton go to this site:
http://www.spartacus.schoolnet.co.uk/USASburton.htm

You can find the entire text of the book on this site:
http://digilib.nypl.org/dynaweb/digs-b/wwm97252/@Generic__BookView

For more information on the history of slavery in America go to these sites:
http://www.innercity.org/holt/slavechron.html
http://en.wikipedia.org/wiki/History_of_slavery_in_the_United_States

3A Ask students to read the text carefully. This FCE 2008+ type exercise is designed to focus on "text structure, cohesion and coherence". Students have to work out which sentence fits where and which is not needed.

3B Students now read the text more carefully to find the answers to the comprehension questions.

3 READING A / B — **Answers**

A 1B 2A 3E 4D (C ×)

B **Suggested answers: 1** *Mistress* means the woman of the house; probably the wife of the owner of the house, and therefore the wife of the person who owns the slaves.
2 They ate the food on the way, and were punished for it later.
3 Definitely not! They only ate a little in the morning.
4 Slaves were sold to pay off debts; women slaves who didn't have children were also sold.
5 No. He obviously didn't want to have anything to do with her.

4 TALK ABOUT IT

The discussion task is designed to do three things. (1) to describe the life of Annie and the other slaves; (2) to imagine for yourself what slavery must have been like; (3) to add any prior knowledge the students might have about slavery in America. Students are also directed to **Language Bank 10**, where there are words and expressions they can use to talk about life in the past.

4A Students really have to use their imagination to understand how Annie can possibly have thought that her life was happy. She was a slave, she was whipped for misbehaving, she had hardly anything to eat, and she was always in danger of being sold. Plus her real father disowned her and wanted to have nothing to do with her. So what made her happy? Presumably the friendship of other children, the places they could play, the kindness shown to her by her mistress. Encourage students to imagine, but also to go back to the text for evidence to support their opinions.

4B / C For this section, students must really try to envisage themselves living a life where whipping, starvation and family separation were always possible.

4D Students can offer their prior knowledge of the slave trade to help this discussion. Those who have read the following pages may have picked up some information from there. There is nothing wrong with students reading later parts of the Unit and finding information for themselves. We feel that this attitude to the book should be encouraged.

5 LISTEN IN CD 1 (Blue) track 5, Page 26 SB

Picture notes / Internet references

The two photographs on this page relate to Listening activity **A**. They show Manderston House, a large country mansion near Edinburgh in Scotland.
http://www.manderston.co.uk/default.asp

Houses like this in Britain are usually referred to as stately homes. You can find all you need to know about other houses like this at this website: www.stately-homes.com

The second picture is of a group of servants in a Victorian house. The lady in the centre was the House Keeper, the boss of the servants.

Key words / expressions
- chauffeur • domestic service
- housemaid • inherit • servant
- tiny • passage

The **Audio text** is in the **Workbook** (page 66). The listening text is an interview with a woman who used to work as a housemaid in a stately home when she was a girl. The listening text does not contain too many new words, but it is about a kind of lifestyle which has more or less disappeared in British life, the time when many large houses had servants. It is important to note two things –

1 the difference between servants and slaves.
2 that domestic staff are today no longer called servants – even if they work for the Queen! They are known by their job title (a nanny, who looks after children; a cleaner, a cook, a gardener, a chauffeur (driver), even a butler – a few still exist). Domestic staff who work for the British Royal family today are notoriously badly paid, in some cases little more than the national minimum wage.

5A This is a pre-listening pair work activity, to help students engage with the period. There is a list of occupations and students have to decide if the people would work or live in a house like the one in the picture. Housemaids, chauffeurs and cooks work in the house, lords and film stars live in them. In order to imagine the kind of work the servants did, students have to think about what these big houses were like. In Victorian times, there was no running water (maybe one cold tap in the kitchen), no electricity, so no electric light and no central heating. How did they see anything? How did they heat the house? How did they do any washing? This is a very useful activity for the iPod generation to imagine what life was like in the past!

5B Students now listen to the tape and answer the questions.

5C The second listening activity requires students to listen for specific information.

5 LISTEN IN B / C **Suggested answers**

B **1** She went into domestic service because there weren't many jobs for young girls.
2 She had to clean the stairs and passages, light the fires and put clean sheets on the beds.
3 She liked having her own room; there was a special bathroom for the girls who worked in the house. It was interesting because there were lots of visitors.
4 Students express their opinion about her answers.

C 1b 2b 3a 4b 5b 6a

5D In this activity, there is a transcript of a section of the listening, showing all the hesitations and lubrication expressions which are typical of spoken English, but can be deleted without affecting the meaning of the utterance. These are the words and phrases which can be deleted.

Julie: Was it very hard?
Mary: ~~Er …~~ well, it depended on the job. I worked in… ~~oh I can't remember~~… in five different houses, ~~I think.~~ They were all, ~~how shall I say? …~~ great houses – stately homes – that I worked in, with lots of servants.
Julie: ~~U-huh …~~ How much were you paid?
Mary: For my first job, I was paid ~~… um, let me see,~~ I THINK it was eighteen pounds a year.
Julie: A YEAR?

6 CONTROVERSY See Role cards, Page 59 WB

Read the notes about this section in the Introduction. This is an activity known colloquially as 'Chinese whispers', although this is not an expression that we recommend you teach to your students! There are many expressions like this in English that give a nationality to something (French windows), but many of them are not now politically correct. This is essentially a simple activity, where the students work in groups. One student whispers a story to the next student, who whispers it to the next student. The last student re-tells the story, which has often changed beyond recognition, as it is passed from one student to the next. There are two stories in the Role cards, so two different groups can do different stories. The activity helps students with their narrative and listening skills.

7 PORTFOLIO WRITING

The writing style we want to practise here is essay-writing, a major feature of most examination formats, rather than an example of authentic writing. There are extensive instructions on the **Student's Book** page of this Unit about the process of writing an essay. A feature of some examinations is that they want to see evidence of the notes you make before you write, so we also recommend that here.

Writing model

Title: Memories of my childhood

Notes

- *I'm the youngest of three children; older brother and sister.*
- *Age 0-5 – lived in Oxford; dad teaching at university; mum also academic, but didn't work full-time; my first memories are of my kindergarten.*
- *5-12 – lived in Paris – dad doing PhD at university; mum taught English; I went to international school.*

Essay

I have strong memories of my childhood, because we lived in two very different cities, Oxford and Paris. My father worked at the university in Oxford. He was an English lecturer. My mother didn't work very much. She had decided that she wanted to be a full-time mother and not work too much.

I'm the youngest of three children. My sister Martha is four years older than me and my brother Duncan is a year older than Martha. My first memories are of them going to primary school. I remember wanting to go with them.

Then one day, my mother took me to a kindergarten, where there were hundreds of children. Well, there were probably only 10 or 12, but I remember it was very noisy! I cried all day, but eventually I began to like it.

Then suddenly, when it was time for me to go to primary school, we moved. I remember that it was very hard for all of us. Duncan was about to move to secondary school and Martha was unhappy to leave her friends. We went to an international school in Paris. At first, it was really difficult, because it was a very organised place, and we weren't used to that. But eventually, we liked it.

It was an unusual childhood, and I think it gave me the desire to travel and experience new things.

Picture notes / Internet references

The images on page 27 are a map of the Atlantic, showing the routes taken by slave ships and the different nationalities who were mostly responsible for the trade, and an illustration of the classic image of white men rounding up Africans to transport them to America as slaves. Slavery, of course, had existed long before the events shown on this map. Arab slaver traders had been making raids across the Sahara to West Africa and down the east coast of Africa to Zanzibar for centuries. The scale of the Atlantic slave trade was enormous and whole European cities prospered because of it. Bristol in England was a port which profited greatly from the slave trade. See http://www.discoveringbristol.org.uk/

If you Google the words *slave trade* you find around 18 million references.

The information on this site is very useful: www.spartacus.schoolnet.co.uk/slavery.htm

8 *HISTORY in English* Page 27 SB

The text is a short history of slavery. Some students may have studied this in their history classes. If so, they may have done projects on the topic. They may have useful material from other parts of the curriculum to bring to the English class, which may help them discuss the subject in English. One of the benefits of this cross-curricular study is that students can bring their pre-existing knowledge to the language class and teach their peers, using the target language.

Key words / expressions

- abolish • to chain • (tribal) chief
- cotton plantations • deck (of a ship)
- election • slave traders • slavery
- textiles • to transport

8A Students have already had an opportunity to say a little about what they know about slavery, but here their prior knowledge of specific information is requested. Once again, this prior knowledge will be enhanced by the visual information available. The map will help students answer the second and third questions in the pre-reading task, and a quick glance at the reading text will tell them when slavery started.

8B Now they read the text and check their answers.

8C This is a true or false activity based on the reading text.

8 *HISTORY in English* A / C

Suggested answers

A
1 The slave trade started in 1490.
2 Most of the slaves came from West Africa.
3 They ended up in the Caribbean, Brazil, Spanish America and the United States.
4 Slavery in the US ended after the American Civil War.

C 1F 2T 3T 4T 5T

9 INTERACTIVE TASK

Read the notes about this section in the Introduction. This is a group work activity, and offers students the chance to practise discourse skills which will also come in useful in certain oral examination situations. Students work in groups of four, divided into two pairs, Pair A and Pair B. Pair A prepare a topic, and Pair B listen to what Pair A have to say, but also try to take control of the situation. As we pointed out in the Introduction to this **Teacher's Guide**, the key to an interactive task is the interaction between the two pairs, one wishing to make points about the topic, the other wishing to take control. The important thing for both pairs to realise is that the interaction must take place in an atmosphere of polite mutual respect. In other words, Pair B must take control without being rude.

10 *Your answer:*

As always, the Unit ends with a re-consideration of *The BIG question* and, as we often do, we divide the original question into two or three subsidiary questions. We ask students to recall their earliest memories. We have chosen three questions which your students may have common memories of, especially if they have known each other since they were children.

If they HAVE known each other for a long time, the lesson may end with them disagreeing about, for example, what their first teacher was like, when and where a memorable event took place and who was responsible for certain things happening. As the FACT at the beginning of the Unit points out, memories are not as simple as we think they are!

Workbook answers

Pages 12-13 WB

1 Language: *would, used to,* past perfect

1A 1 ✓ **2** × **3** ✓

1B 1 didn't use to love **2** used to live
3 used to have **4** would / used to play
5 would / used to climb **6** used to live
7 would / used to go **8** would / used to walk
9 would / used to

1C 1 When we got to the station, the train left.
(= It waited until we got there before leaving.)
When we got to the station, the train had left.
(= It left before we got there.)
2 After we had eaten, we went for a walk.
After we ate, we went for a walk. (The meaning is the same.)
3 When I turned around, the dog disappeared.
(= It waited until I turned before disappearing.)
When I turned around, the dog had disappeared. (= It disappeared as I was turning round.)
4 I asked him what he thought of the film, but he hadn't seen it. (*didn't see it* not possible.)
5 Before he bought the car, he checked it carefully.
Before he bought the car, he had checked it carefully. (The meaning is the same.)
6 I woke up at eight. I had slept very badly.
(= refers specifically to that one night)
I woke up at eight. I slept very badly. (= This could be a common problem for me.)
7 Maria opened the fridge and saw that Brian and James had eaten all the food. (*ate* is not possible.

2 Use of English

2A *Variations are possible*

1 Fifteen children had to share one bowl of food.
2 We used to eat all the food that was meant for the workers.
3 We children didn't use to have any supper.
4 'You should speak to your darling child,' my mistress would say.
5 Do you remember swimming in the river?

2B (1) nothing **(2)** to **(3)** least **(4)** with / remembering **(5)** because **(6)** carefully / well **(7)** same **(8)** memory **(9)** turn **(10)** ability

3 Portfolio writing

Students' own answers

4 Connections

4A 1 (a) *memorise* – to commit something to memory because you need it (a telephone number or the answers for an examination, for example, *remember* – to recall an event).
(b) *souvenir* – something you buy to remember a place; *memory* – a purely mental image.
(c) *recollection* – a memory; *collection* – when something is collected, for example the post from a post box.
(d) *to have a good memory* – you are good at remembering things; *remember something well* – an event left a strong impression on you.
(e) *imagine* – to form a picture of something or someone in your mind, possibly in circumstances that haven't arisen yet; *fantasise* – to imagine something pleasant or exciting happening to you.

4 A 2 *Example answers*

(a) I memorised all the dates of the kings for the examination.
I remember falling asleep during his speech.
(b) I have a souvenir from the holiday – an ashtray from the hotel!
I have the most wonderful memory of a little beach in Spain.
(c) I have absolutely no recollection of what happened.
There is a post collection at 5pm.
(d) I imagine they're living in a nice place now.
He's always fantasising about being a professional soccer player.

4B 1c **2**d **3**e **4**a **5**b

What's new?

Subject: Technology
Function: Describing pictures
Grammar: Present and past simple passives

Before you open the book ...
Write the title of the Unit on the board and ask students: *What does this mean to you?* Elicit reactions and teach new vocabulary as it arises. Students may answer, for example, *There are cameras everywhere.* Ask: *What are these cameras called?* Elicit / teach the phrase *CCTV cameras* (closed circuit television cameras). Then ask: *How do you feel when you are walking along a street or train platform, and you see a CCTV camera?* Elicit reactions and teach new vocabulary as it arises. Typical answers might be, *I feel safe / I feel angry because it means I have no privacy.*

1 *The BIG question:* IS SECURITY MORE IMPORTANT THAN PRIVACY?

FACT: Surveillance cameras can find the face of one person in a crowd of 50,000.

Write *The BIG question* on the board. If you want to explore the question a little, ask: *What does security mean to you?* Give a model answer such as, *Security means that I have a job with regular money.* Elicit answers. Similarly, ask: *What does privacy mean to you?* Elicit answers such as, *Privacy means that people don't know too much about me.* Students will have an opportunity to respond to the **FACT** in activity **B** below.

Picture notes

(a) This picture shows people on a train platform (it happens to be on the London Underground). They are obviously being monitored by a surveillance camera.
(b) This picture shows a security officer monitoring images from CCTV cameras.
(c) In this picture, a road sign tells motorists that there are speed cameras on the road. This photograph was taken in Australia, where speed limits on roads are strongly enforced – even in the remote outback. Australia and Canada use kilometres per hour. Britain and the USA use miles per hour. The general speed limit in Australia is 100 kph, even slower than the usual speed limit in the USA of 65 mph (about 105 kph). In Britain the general speed limit is 70 mph (112 kph).

2 PREVIEW

Background information / Internet references

CCTV stands for *Closed Circuit Television.* CCTV is the use of television cameras for surveillance. It was first used as a way of increasing security in banks. Airports and casinos, that had a similar need for high security, then started using them. Surveillance cameras are now increasingly used in public places, for example, on the high street, in shopping malls, in underground stations. They can also be used as part of a home security system.

There is a lot of argument about whether CCTV deters criminals. However, it is clear that CCTV use reduces crime in certain places such as car parks. It is also agreed that surveillance cameras can be effective in detecting crime. CCTV is now routinely used to track missing children. In London, the 2005 July 7 suicide bombers were identified through the use of CCTV. However, the use of CCTV in shopping streets, housing estates and on roads is regarded by many as a worrying form of social control. Britain now has more CCTV cameras than any other country in the world. In some places, people can connect their own domestic TV sets to the CCTV network and watch everything going on their own community area.

Some people think this an important way of improving local security, and others think it is giving neighbours power over each other which might lead to blackmail. To find out about the advantages and disadvantages of surveillance, see:

http://news.bbc.co.uk/1/hi/uk/2071496.stm

http://www.findarticles.com/p/articles/mi_m0EPF/is_2_103/ai_107896318

http://www.telegraph.co.uk/news/main.jhtml?xml=/news/2004/10/25/nscho25.xml

http://www.newscientist.com/article.ns?id=dn3725

http://63.135.115.158/article.asp?ID=569

http://www.secureeng.co.uk/cctvfacts.htm

http://www.liberty-human-rights.org.uk/privacy/cctv.shtml

http://www.privacyinternational.org/article.shtml?cmd[347]=x-347-73837

http://www.iee.org/oncomms/circuit/members/Paper_J%20Doonan.doc

Words

A After students have matched the photos with the sentences, check they understand these words: *to track* (to follow someone by using special equipment), *to monitor* (to regularly check or watch something or someone). Instead of using the sentences to teach new language, you could instead ask students to describe the pictures. Example answers:

(a) This picture shows people on a train platform. There are circles round their heads. This probably means that there are cameras on the platform.
(b) In this photo, a man is watching CCTV screens.
(c) In this picture, cars are going along a road. There is a sign that says there are speed cameras on the road.
Use the photos to teach these words and phrases: *speed camera, security officer.*

2 PREVIEW Words A — **Answers**
A 1 c **2** a **3** b

B These adjectives may need explaining: *horrified* (very shocked), *reassured* (made to feel less worried about something). Ask students to explain their reactions, *eg I feel reassured because it means the police can find criminals.*

C One way to do this activity is, for each question, to ask those who agree to put up their hands. Count the numbers and write the result on the board. Then ask those who disagree to put up their hands. Again, count the numbers and write the result on the board.

Language

This section introduces the present and past simple passive. If the structure is new to the class, you may want to present it before doing the activities in the book. Here is a suggestion for how to present it. Ask the students: *Where do they grow rice?* Elicit and write on the board: *They grow rice in (India).* Follow on by asking and eliciting answers to similar questions, writing the answers on the board:

- Where do we find diamonds? We find diamonds in Africa, Russia…
- Where do they make the best cars? They make the best cars in …
- Where do they produce the best leather? They produce the best leather in …
- Where do they catch the biggest fish? They catch the biggest fish in …

Now ask the students who we are referring to when we say *they / we* in these sentences. Do we know? Is it important? Elicit the fact that this information is not important. Now write the first two sentences as passives:

- Rice is grown in India.
- Diamonds are found in South Africa.

Ask students if these sentences mean the same as the first two sentences on the board. Point out that they do, but that now, the objects of the first two sentences have become the subjects, and the most important words in the sentences are *rice* and *diamonds.*

Point out that *is / are* are the present simple of *to be* and that *grown / found* are the past participles of the verbs in the first two sentences. Explain that this structure is called the passive voice and that we use it when we are not interested in the subject of the sentence. Ask students to put the other three sentences into the passive:

- The best cars are made in......
- The best leather is produced in ......
- The biggest fish are caught in ......

Now ask students to put the present simple sentences into the past simple passive. If they have understood the principle they should not find this difficult: *Rice was grown in India. / Diamonds were found in South Africa etc.*

A At this point, elicit from students that the first sentence uses the active voice, while the second sentence uses the passive voice.

B Elicit the fact that we don't know who performed the actions in the sentences and we aren't interested. It's not important information. That is why the passive is used in these sentences. Point out the use of *by* in the second sentence: *by speed cameras.* Elicit the fact that this is where you put the subject of the active sentence, if you want to use it.

C Explain that in the active sentence, the subject (*speed camera)* is the most important part of the sentence. However, in the passive sentence, the object of the active sentence (*thousands of drivers*) becomes the focus of the sentence. Suggest to the class that they use the useful word 'they' as the subject of these sentences.

2 PREVIEW Language A / B / C **Answers**

A **1** Yes
2 Sentence 1: speed cameras
Sentence 2: thousands of drivers
3 Sentence 1: speed cameras
Sentence 2: thousands of drivers

B **1** is programmed
2 was invented, were introduced
3 We don't really know the answers. Computer programmers, inventors, scientists.
4 No, it isn't.

C **Sentence 1:** They program the computer to recognise swimmers.
Sentence 2: Think of your life before they invented the answering machine.
Sentence 3: Think of your grandparents' lives before they introduced the television and aeroplane.

Ideas

Check students understand the vocabulary in the sentences. Encourage them to speculate in answer to the questions, but don't give any answers. They will have their answers as soon as they read the passage on the opposite page.

Optional activity: Have a discussion about whether CCTV cameras are a good thing. As the basis for the discussion, use the article recommended in the Web reference above.

2 Preview Ideas A / B / C.
Suggested answers

A The Reading text is about the use of surveillance cameras to save people from drowning.
B *they* refers to surveillance cameras; the cameras might also watch out for terrorists carrying bombs.
C *they* (the cameras) are watching out for people who show signs of drowning.

3 READING CD 2 (Red) track 6, Page 29 SB

Key words / expressions

- drown • splash • sink • unconscious
- electronic surveillance system
- lifeguard • to connect • to program
- device • to beep • to detect
- save (life) • to invent • fingerprint
- terrorist • bomb • signal

This article describes how an electronic surveillance system called Poseidon saved a young Frenchman from drowning in his local swimming pool. The story is true and was reported all over France. Since then, there have been other instances in other countries including Britain, of this system saving lives in swimming pools. See the whole story (in French) from the company which developed the system:
http://www.poseidon-tech.com/fr/pressRelease001128.html

Before students read the passage, ask them to look at the diagram and pictures and then try to deduce what the article is about. Use the diagram and pictures to teach relevant vocabulary items, *eg lifeguard, save, drown, signal, electronic surveillance system* (shown in the diagram – *computer, underwater cameras, monitor).* Elicit students' deductions and then ask them to read the passage and answer the questions in activity **A.**

3C 2 Elicit only brief answers to the question *Do you agree?* as the question will be explored more fully in **TALK ABOUT IT**.

3C 3 Students may give answers such as, *I think a device that monitors a baby's breathing is very useful.*

3 READING A / B / C **Answers**

A 1 He was testing how far he could swim underwater on one breath. While he was doing this he became unconscious and sank to the bottom of the pool.

2 An electronic surveillance system called Poseidon saved him. There were underwater cameras that recognised that a swimmer was not moving normally.

3 They will recognise our faces and fingerprints. They will watch for drowning people, terrorists carrying bombs, speeding drivers and heart patients. They will monitor a baby's breathing and track children as they go to school. They will send information to your doctor, your lawyer, your car mechanic, and the local police.

B 1 unconscious **2** beeped **3** sinking **4** drowning

C 1 (a) check that a baby is breathing properly **(b)** patients who have heart problems **(c)** watch children as they go to school to check that they are safe **(d)** regularly checked by machines

2 He says that machines are already monitoring us.

3 Students' own answer

4 TALK ABOUT IT

Break the discussion into two halves. In other words, elicit answers to the first question before going on to the second. With regard to the first question, ask students to quote any sentences that show how the writer really feels. The final sentence, *'They'll know all about us,'* does in fact suggest that the writer is worried that there may be too much surveillance at some time in the future.

With regard to the question, *How do you feel about it?* students may give answers such as *I think surveillance systems are a good idea, they keep us safe.* Before you start the discussion, you may want to tell students a bit about a famous novel called *1984,* which describes the abuse of surveillance in a police state (see **Background information** below.)

If students are not very confident about performing this role play, choose two of the most confident students to act it out. Afterwards, the class can offer corrections and improvements and you can write these on the board. The class will then go into the role play feeling more confident.

<u>Background information / Internet reference</u>

The world-famous novel ***1984*** by George Orwell was first published in 1949. It describes a future social system that allows no privacy – people are even watched in their own homes. There are police known as the *Thought Police* and their job is to monitor what you think. The book is a warning of how systems of surveillance could be misused in a police state. The novel had and still has an enormous effect on people's attitudes towards surveillance. In the book, the government authorities are known as Big Brother, and there are placards everywhere that warn, *Big Brother is watching you.* To find a summary of the plot of *1984,* go to this website: <u>www.online-literature.com/orwell/1984</u>

5 LISTEN IN **CD 1 (Blue) track 6, Page 30 SB**

<u>Key words / expressions</u>

• consumer • issue • consultant
• to take place • store • CD • constant
• radio signal • to link • unique • to identify
• shoplifting • shoplifter • item
• shop assistant • to trigger • security system
• manufacturer • business • baggage
• efficient • service • constant
• tag = a small piece of paper or plastic that is fastened to something and gives information about it.
• microchip = a very small piece of silicon (a chemical element) that contains the electrical connections for making a computer work.
• smart tag = RFID tag (that communicates with a computer).

The **Audio text** is in the **Workbook** (page 66).

5A Begin by using the picture on the left to explain what an RFID (radio frequency identification) tag is. Explain that it is a very small object that can be placed in objects, animals or even people. It sends out a signal to a computer, so that the computer can follow it wherever it goes – each signal is unique and is easily identified.
Now ask the class to describe the pictures. In the middle picture a boy is shoplifting.
The picture on the right shows baggage at an airport. Use the pictures to teach the vocabulary items *to shoplift, shoplifter, baggage.* Ask students how they think RFID tags can end shoplifting and find lost airline baggage. Elicit answers but don't tell students if they are right or wrong. Tell them they will listen to a passage about RFID tags and this will give them the answer.

5B Tell students to use their dictionaries in order to match the words with their definitions. Alternatively, teach the meaning of these words and other key words and expressions from the box above. It will probably be helpful to students if they are taught some of the more difficult words that appear in the listening passage.

Picture notes / Background information

The full name for RFID tags is radio frequency identification tags. An RFID tag is a small object that can be attached to or incorporated into a product, animal or person. Each RFID tag contains a computer chip and antenna which can be read by a scanner – each item contains a unique identification number. The picture on the left is of an RFID tag. The picture in the middle shows a boy shoplifting. The right hand picture shows airline baggage piling up in the baggage hall of an airport. When the baggage arrives from the plane it is put onto a *carousel* (named after the fairground entertainment), from which passengers collect their own suitcases.

RFID tags have many uses. In libraries, security gates can check that a book with an RFID tag in it has been properly checked out. The tags can be used to sort goods into different categories. Wherever a piece of airline luggage is in the world, if it has an RFID tag, it can be found by a scanner which sends a signal back to the computer. Tags are commonly used for animal identification, buried under a dog's skin for example. Similarly, the tags can be used to monitor prisoners on parole.

Although RFID tags are undeniably of great potential benefit, those who oppose their use fear their potential for misuse. For example, companies or governments could make everyone carry a card (or even insert the tags under people's skins) as a means of discovering what they are doing at any time of day or night. The potential for using the tags as a way of controlling people is very great and needs to be thought about.

On the other hand, tags can be very useful, enabling companies to keep track of deliveries and stocks over entire distribution networks.
For articles and information on RFID tags, go to these websites:
http://news.bbc.co.uk/1/hi/technology/4247275.stm
http://www.theregister.co.uk/2003/06/27/rfid_chips_are_here/
http://www.rfidjournal.com/
http://www.channel4.com/news/2003/07/week_4/28_chips.html

5 LISTEN IN B / C / D / E **Answers**

B **1** (h) microchip **2** (c) unique **3** (e) to shoplift **4** (d) manufacturer **5** (f) consumer **6** (a) to trigger **7** (g) constant

C **1** (f) **2** (a) **3** (b) **4** (d) **5** (e) **6** (c)

D RFID tags can end shoplifting in the following way: If a shopper pays for an item, the shop assistant 'kills' the tag so that it no longer sends out a signal. However, if you don't pay, the signal from the smart tag will trigger the security system as you walk out of the store. RFID tags can find lost airline baggage because each RFID tag signal sends out a constant radio signal to computers. Each signal is unique and is easily identified. If a piece of luggage has an RFID tag, it is very easy to identify it, wherever it is.

E **1** RFID tags will make it very easy to catch

shoplifters. Also, when an item with an RFID tag is bought from a shop, a computer can recognise this and quickly order another from the manufacturer. This will keep prices down.
2 RFID tags can follow your airline baggage round the world so that it doesn't get lost.
3 If the tag signal is not killed at checkout, every time you wear the item with the tag, manufacturers will know exactly where you are. Many see this is an invasion of privacy. They ask who will use this information? The police? Other interested people?

6 CONTROVERSY See Role cards, Page 60 WB

Read the notes about this section in the Introduction. This is a general debate about the use of both RFID tags and CCTV cameras. Divide the class into small groups – group A and group B. Group A and B should sit next to each other so that they can work together. Ask them to write down their arguments. Elicit the arguments and write them on the board as notes. Students can then have their debate. Below are suggestions of arguments for and against.

Arguments in favour of RFID tags and CCTV cameras:

1 CCTV cameras help to catch criminals and terrorists. (Give examples). They are caught on camera and the police are able to identify them.

2 RFID help to catch shoplifters. This is really helpful to shop owners.

3 RFID tags help to track luggage and any product being delivered anywhere in the world.

4 They tell manufacturers how many of their products they have sold so they can order more in time.

Arguments against RFID tags and CCTV cameras:

1 RFID tags and CCTV cameras provide a huge amount of information about us. Criminals (and possibly the government) can find this information and misuse it.

2 If the use of RFID tags and CCTV cameras grows, we will find that we are watched everywhere we go. Do we want to lose our privacy?

3 Technology is not always reliable. Mistakes can be made with disastrous results.

4 These methods provide a way to control people. Governments and the police may misuse these methods.

7 PORTFOLIO WRITING

Tell students to write the story in the present simple tense. Explain that the present simple tense can sometimes be used to tell a story – it is a way of making it more dramatic.

If you think they will have difficulty inventing a story, put them into pairs or small groups, to come up with an idea. Elicit the ideas, and write the best ones on the board in note form. You may want to use the writing model below as a way of providing a stimulus for the class.

Writing model

Sophia unlocks her front door and walks inside her small flat. She puts her hands to her face and starts to cry. Then she remembers that a camera is watching her. She doesn't want them to see her crying. Where can she go? The only place is the bathroom - but at least she has privacy there.

She has a warm bath and lies in the water and cries. Her boyfriend has left her. They have been together for five years and only two months ago they were talking about marriage. Her life seemed perfect. Then this morning he rang her at work. 'I'm leaving you,' he said. 'Our relationship isn't working.' She couldn't protest because there were people all around her, listening. Also, there were others listening – she knew that. It was routine for her bosses to listen to their employees' telephone calls.

Sophia dries herself and dresses. The phone rings and she answers it. It's her boyfriend, Matt. 'I meant it,' he says. 'I'm leaving you. I'm coming round this evening to pick up my things.' The idea is unbearable. Sophia goes and stays with her parents for the night so that she won't see Matt – he has a key to the flat.

The next evening, after work, she returns

to her flat. The phone rings and she picks it up, hoping that it is Matt. 'I hear your boyfriend's left you,' says a voice. 'Well, there are lots of other men available. Me, for example.'

8 *PHYSICS in English* Page 31 SB

Key words / expressions

- image • to record • cable • signal
- analogue / digital • reflect
- video cassette • to store • to transmit
- to link • curve
- wave = the way in which sound, light, a radio signal etc travels
- radio waves • short / medium / long wavelengths • ground / sky / space waves
- ionosphere = the region of the earth's upper atmosphere
- satellite = an object that is sent into space to travel round the Earth in order to receive and send information

Elicit the fact / explain that Physics is the science that deals with heat, light and other forms of energy and how they affect objects. Find out from the class who enjoys / enjoyed Physics and is / was good at it.

The class will probably feel that this text looks very difficult at first sight. Reassure students and tell them that they will find the diagram very helpful in explaining the text. Explain that the numbered words in bold in the text refer to the diagram numbers, and that the illustrations help to explain the meaning of the words.

To make the text as easy as possible for students, it will be helpful to pre-teach / check students understand these words: *image, to record, cable, to store, to transmit, wave(length), curve, ionosphere, reflect, medium, space, satellite.* Students can then read the text, using the diagram to help them. They should then find activity **A** quite easy to do.

If there are students in the class who have taken physics at school, they will have covered topics such as waves in their own language. This could be an opportunity to allow the scientists in the class to explain their speciality to everyone, including the teacher. As scientists they will already know that a great deal of scientific literature is in English and they may need the skill to explain scientific concepts in English later in their careers. English for Special Purposes (ESP) was once regarded as merely a bank of specialist vocabulary, but recently teaching ESP has developed into discourse competence – marshalling arguments, describing diagrams and processes, for example. Parts of the IELTS exam for entry into English-speaking universities concentrate on these skills.

8 *PHYSICS in English* A / B Answers

A **1** produce **2** Computers **3** signal **4** two **5** digital **6** ground waves, sky waves and space waves **7** Space **8** transmitted

B **1** A camera produces an image.
2 Computers store digital signals.
3 A video cassette records the image.
4 The ionosphere reflects sky waves.

9 CONVERSATION

Read the notes about this section in the Introduction. The **Language Bank** connected to this activity, (**Language Bank 12**, Ways of asking about and describing pictures) may be important for students who are taking exams. To practise the language, bring in a good assortment of pictures. Put students into pairs and ask them to describe the pictures to another pair, who do not see the pictures. The pictures can then be displayed and the second pair can say if the picture was as they imagined it.

Explain that the task is not only to describe the picture. It is also to use the subject matter of the picture as a basis for discussion. If you feel that you would like students to discuss something other than surveillance and privacy, use the pictures you have brought in or other pictures in the book.

10 *Your answer:*

Students should now have a very good idea of their own opinion on the matter.

Optional activity: Obtain a copy of *1984* by George Orwell, and choose three or four short passages, through which the storyline becomes clear. Put the passages in the wrong order. Ask students to decide what the correct order for the passages is.

Background information

Benjamin Franklin (1706-90): US statesman, writer and scientist. He proved that lightning and electricity were identical. In 1776 he was actively involved in writing the American Declaration of independence (from the British).

London terrorists of July 2005: On the morning of July 7, four suicide bombers attacked three different trains on the London Underground, and a London bus. Their bombs all went off, killing all the bombers. Fifty-two commuters were killed and 700 people were badly injured. All the bombers were later identified, thanks to CCTV cameras that filmed them outside a station preparing for a trial run some days before the attack. The bombers were not foreign terrorists – they were British.

Workbook answers — Pages 14-15 WB

1 Language: present and past tense passives

1A **1** Camera phones are used for many different things.
2 For example, a new car is taken by a customer for a test drive.
3 But first, a photo is taken of the customer by the car salesperson.
4 Sometimes the car isn't returned by the customer.
5 The thief is found easily, thanks to the photo on the camera phone.

1B **1** A man was bitten by a poisonous spider.
2 A photograph of the spider was taken by the man.
3 He started feeling ill and was taken to hospital by a friend.
4 The spider was identified by experts from the photo on the man's phone.
5 He was then treated by the doctor with the correct medicine, and his life was saved.

1C **1** Were CCTV cameras installed in schools?
2 Where are students observed from?
3 Students are not filmed in the classroom.
4 Is the film shown to students and their parents?
5 Letters of complaint were not written to the head teachers.
6 How was smoking in schools reduced?

2 Use of English

2A **1** There are other jobs that RFID tags can do.
2 While he was doing this, he became unconscious.
3 When an item is bought from a shop, the RFID tag is recognisable by the computer.
4 Are RFID tags something that we really want?
5 The doctors didn't send him home until he was completely well.

2B **1** (c) try **2** (f) ruining **3** (a) chip
4 (h) stadium **5** (g) scanner **6** (d) identify
7 (i) technology **8** (j) problem **9** (b) however
10 (e) privacy

3 Portfolio writing

Students' own answers

4 Connections

A **1** (b) notice **2** (c) recognise **3** (e) identify
4 (f) study **5** (a) glimpse **6** (d) watch

B **1** watch **2** glimpse **3** study **4** recognise
5 notice **6** identify

What's new?

Subject:	Environmental issues
Function:	Speculating, future time expressions
Grammar:	*When, unless, in case,* zero and first conditionals

Before you open the book ...

Write the words *Oil crisis* on the board and ask students what the phrase means to them (*crisis* = an urgent and difficult or dangerous situation). Elicit answers, for example:

1 Only certain countries have oil and that means they have a lot of power over other countries that need oil. They can put up the price of oil and make it very expensive.

2 Oil is becoming more and more expensive because it's difficult to find new supplies and we are using more and more of it.

Tell the class that this Unit is about the oil crisis and about different kinds of energy. Ask students to name as many sources of energy as possible. Some examples are: *oil, petrol, gas, electricity, coal, hydrogen, wind energy, solar energy, wave energy.* Write these words on the board. Tell the class that in this Unit they will learn more about alternatives to oil. Finally, write the following chart like this on the board:

Over the last	1 150 years	we have used	(a) 15%	of the world's total oil supplies.
	2 100 years		(b) 23%	
	3 50 years		(c) 35%	

Ask students to choose what they think are the correct answers. Then tell them to open their books and check the answer by reading the FACT.

1 *The BIG question:* WHAT WILL WE DO WHEN THE OIL RUNS OUT?

FACT: Over the last 150 years we have used over 23% of the world's total oil supplies.

Check students understand the phrasal verb *to run out (We've run out of coffee / milk).*

Briefly elicit answers to *The BIG question* and tell the class that they are going read more on the subject. Take the opportunity to teach the words *optimistic* (think things will be OK) and *pessimistic* (think things will end badly). Ask who feels *optimistic / pessimistic* about the oil crisis and count the show of hands.

Picture notes

The pictures on this page show:

Left – an oil well in Siberia. Russia has some of the world's greatest reserves of oil and natural gas, which gives it a great deal of political influence in the world. It has also brought enormous wealth to some Russians, especially since the oil price rises of 2005-2006.

Top right – a wind farm in which turbines are producing electricity from wind energy. Many countries, such as Germany and Denmark are developing wind power.

Bottom right – a house with solar panels on its roof. The solar panels produce electricity which is used to power the house.

2 PREVIEW

Words

Teach the meaning of these phrases: *fossil fuels, alternative energy sources, renewable energy sources.* Elicit the fact that *alternative energy / renewable energy* mean more or less the same thing. Use the pictures to elicit students' knowledge about oil, wind energy and solar energy (see **Background information** notes below.) You may want to elicit the fact that solar panels placed on the roofs of a house can generate electricity, and that hydrogen can be used to power cars.

Ask if any forms of energy have been left out. Students will probably point out that nuclear energy and hydropower have not been included. Explain that these are not viewed as alternative energy sources, but that many governments are in favour of their use (France has 56 nuclear plants producing 76% of its electricity). The fact that hydropower is *renewable* but not *alternative* may be elicited during the discussion and show up the difference between the two expressions.

Background information / Internet references

Fossil fuels: A fossil is the remains of a once-living organism. Fossil fuels are fuels made from the fossilised remains of plants that lived millions of years ago. Oil, natural gas and coal are examples of fossil fuels. Fossil fuels are a non-renewable source and burning them contributes significantly to pollution and global warming.

Alternative energy sources: Alternative energy sources do not rely on burning fossil fuels or nuclear power to provide energy. Pollution is rarely a problem with alternative energy sources. Alternative energy sources include solar power, tidal power, hydroelectric power and wind power. As yet most alternative energy sources are not fully economic.

Renewable energy sources: Renewable energy sources, as their name suggests, can be used without danger of exhaustion. They include solar power, wind power, tidal power and hydroelectric power. They are not without problems. For example hydroelectric dams mean flooding very large areas of land, for example the Three Gorges Dam in China, which is creating a lake 600 km (375 miles) long and displacing between 1 and 2 million people from their homes.

Wind energy: The energy of the wind is harnessed by means of tall towers supporting turbines. Many of them are needed to provide power and collectively they are known as wind farms. Many people object to wind farms on the grounds that they look terrible on the landscape. Another disadvantage is that the weather is not always windy.

Solar energy: The sun can provide energy to make electricity and heat. Solar panels are placed on the roofs of houses. The panels extract energy from the light of the sun, using photovoltaic cells that produce electricity, or from the radiant heat of the sun which heats water or air in the panels. Like wind energy, solar energy is limited by its dependence on sufficient amounts of sunshine.

Hydrogen: Hydrogen can be used as a source of clean power for transport and houses. In the most favoured method, hydrogen is turned into electricity through fuel cells which then power electric motors. However, at the moment producing hydrogen uses large amounts of electricity.

For more information on alternative energy sources:
www.greenenergy.org.uk
http://www.carbonfootprint.com/
http://www.eere.energy.gov/afdc/altfuel/altfuels.html
http://www.foe.co.uk/

2 PREVIEW Words A / B **Answers**

A **1** All of them
2 Petrol, oil, and hydrogen are fuels used in cars. The most commonly used fuels in houses are oil, gas, electricity, coal, and solar energy.
3 Coal, oil, petrol, natural gas
4 sun / wind / wave energy, hydrogen
5 sun / wind / wave energy, hydrogen
B **1** America, Russia, countries in the Middle East, such as Saudi Arabia, Kuwait, Iraq, Libya
2 America, China

Language

A These sentences introduce two types of *when* clauses:
when + present simple + present simple, used to refer to general truths, for example:

- **When** cars **burn** petrol, they **give out** carbon dioxide.

when + present simple + future simple, used to refer to a future event, for example:

- **When** oil production **starts** to go down, prices **will go** up dramatically.

Point out that with this structure, both parts of the sentence refer to the future.

To provide more practice, ask students to complete these sentences:

1 When I feel lonely, I ....
2 When I feel angry, I ....
3 When I feel sad, I ....
4 When I feel hungry, I ....
5 When I feel stressed, I ....
6 When I get home this evening, I ....

B These sentences practise two types of conditional clause:

The zero conditional, *if* + present simple + present simple, referring to general truths:

• **If** things **seem** alright at the moment,	most people **don't** worry about the future.
The first event may happen.	The second event is the result of the first.
Its meaning is almost identical to the similar structure above with *when*.	

The first conditional, *if* + present simple + future simple, referring to two future events:

• **If** the price of oil **goes** up,	renewable energy **will** become economic.
The first event may happen.	The second event is the result of the first.

To provide more practice, ask students to complete these sentences:

1 If you heat water, it...........
2 If you throw a piece of wood into water, it ....
3 If you have flu, you ....
4 If you drink too much alcohol, the next day, you ....
5 If the weather is very cold, it usually ....
6 If I have a free weekend sometime soon, I ....

Unless means *except if* or *if not,* for example:

- **Unless** we do this, the world will face major energy problems.

To provide more practice, ask students to complete this sentence in several different ways:

- Unless we find alternative energy sources, ...

We use *in case* to refer to the things we do, so that if a certain situation happens, we are ready for it, for example:

- We need to find alternative energy sources **in case** the oil runs out.

We can use *in case* to refer to the past, present or future, for example:

- I took an umbrella **in case** it rained.

To provide more practice, ask students to complete these sentences:

1 Bring some warm clothes in case ....
2 I took some money in case ....
3 Let's take a small tent in case ....
4 Buy some more milk in case ....

2 PREVIEW Language A / B **Answers**

A **1** The second sentence (When cars burn petrol…)
2 The first sentence (When oil production starts…)
3 The first sentence (… prices will go up dramatically)
B **1** No
2 The first sentence. The present simple is used in both parts of the sentence.
3 The last three sentences **4** *unless* **5** (a)

Ideas

A The first quotation refers to the oil-rich states in the Middle East, such as Saudi Arabia.

- My father rode a camel.

People in these places lived a nomadic life (moving from place to place) in the desert, living on very little and riding camels.

- My son flies a jet plane.

With the discovery of oil, these countries have become very rich.

- His son will ride a camel.

However, one day the oil will run out and the

country will be poor again.

- A drop of petrol in war…

This second quotation refers to the First World War, when petrol first became very important as a fuel for military vehicles and aeroplanes.

- The Oil Age will end…

In the third quotation, the suggestion is that countries will find alternatives to oil long before oil supplies run out.

B Ask students to talk about their emotional reactions to these statements. How would it affect them if the Middle-Eastern states ran out of oil? How do they feel about the second statement?

C Plastics are made from petroleum and consequently many everyday goods are ultimately made from oil such as plastic bags, combs, plastic components of computers, plastic bottles.

3 READING CD 2 (Red) track 7, Page 33 SB

Key words / expressions

- barrel • to consume • dramatic
- drop(n) • major • minister • crop
- to add • petrol • to pollute/pollution(n)
- carbon dioxide • limitless
- quantity • vapour
- to run on = to use something as a fuel, *eg* most cars run on petrol / computers run on electricity.
- peak (n) = the time when something is at its highest level, *eg* The artist was at the peak of his career.
- economic = providing a satisfactory profit, *eg* It's not economic to sell the product at this price.
- The Stone Age = a period of pre-history when man's existence was characterised by the use of polished stone tools.
- biofuel = fuel made from plant material, *eg* wood, straw and ethanol from plant matter.

Background information / Internet references

Bio-fuel is any fuel that is made from recently living organisms. Agricultural products grown for use as bio-fuels include sugar, corn (maize) and soybeans. Waste from industry, agriculture, forestry and households can also be used to produce bio-energy. Bio-fuels can be used for the production of electricity. Sweden and Finland supply around 20% of their energy needs with bio-energy. Over half of new cars sold in Brazil can run on bio-fuels, mainly alcohol made from sugar cane. The picture on this page shows a hydrogen-powered car designed and built by students at the University of California, Los Angeles (UCLA) in 1972. Several car companies are now building hydrogen-powered cars and buses. In 2005 California passed a law to start a Hydrogen Highway project. For information on the UCLA Project and California's Project:
http://www.engineer.ucla.edu/history/hydrocar.html
http://hydrogenhighway.ca.gov/

For information on bio-fuels:
http://www.biofueloasis.com/
http://www.biodiesel.co.uk/
http://news.bbc.co.uk/2/hi/business/4581955.stm

This reading text discusses the idea of 'Peak Oil' and possible solutions using various alternative energy sources.

3A Students should show that they understand specific ideas in the text by choosing one of the sentences (A to F) for each of the spaces (1 to 5). There is one extra sentence that is not used (D). This is an activity type used in the Cambridge ESOL FCE 2008+.

3B Encourage students not to use their dictionaries but to try and guess meanings from the context.

3C The answers are all in the text with the exception of question **3**, where students need to think about the answer.

3 READING A / B / C **Answers**

A **1** A **2** E **3** B **4** F **5** C (D ×)
B **1** barrel **2** crisis **3** crops **4** carbon dioxide **5** economic **6** bio-fuel **7** drop **8** use up **9** run on **10** The Stone Age
C **1** The USA uses a quarter of the world's oil.
2 Experts fear that it will be sometime between 2010 and 2020.
3 Because oil-rich countries will become poor again, either because the oil is all used up or

because the world no longer needs oil (the latter seems unlikely!).
4 In case the oil runs out sooner than we expect.
5 Wind farms, bio fuels, hydrogen
6 It is made from electricity and water and can be produced in limitless quantities. Also, it produces no pollution.

4 TALK ABOUT IT

4A / B An obvious answer to these questions is that it depends on what a country's government has done to set up alternative energy sources. In Britain, for example, there is debate about whether a new generation of nuclear power stations should be built, or whether wind farms can provide sufficient energy. Those against the use of nuclear power cite Chernobyl, a city in the Ukraine which was the scene of the world's largest nuclear disaster in 1986. They also point out that nuclear power plants could become targets for terrorist attacks, and there is also the problem of where and how to dispose of the nuclear waste.

4C During the discussion, students may well point out that although America is the world's largest consumer of oil at present, China's fast-growing economy means that it too is using greater and greater amounts. India's economy, also growing fast, is not far behind. America has recently begun a drive to consume less oil. One of the ways in which it aims to do this is by producing hydrogen-powered cars.

4D One option is to use the car less and take public transport, walk or bicycle.

5 LISTEN IN CD 1 (Blue) track 7, Page 34 SB

The **Audio text** is in the **Workbook**. The listening passage involves a discussion between a journalist, Tony Forbes, and Professor Sopian of the Advanced Engineering Centre in Malaysia. The Professor has built an Eco-house that uses energy from the environment to create electricity and power. Solar panels create electricity, and rainwater is collected in a water tank. The electricity from the solar panels is then used to convert the rainwater into hydrogen and oxygen. A gas pipe takes the hydrogen into the house, where it powers the central heating, cooking and hot water.

Picture notes / Background information

The picture on this page shows the actual Eco-house built for Professor Kamaruzzaman Sopian's project at the Advanced Engineering Centre of the Universiti Kebangsaan in Malaysia. There are quite a few references on the internet to this project (Google *Universiti Kebangsaan Eco-house*).

Ecology is the study of the interaction of living organisms with the environment. The 1960s saw the beginning of the ecological movement, which argued that the Earth only has a finite supply of resources, and that people must learn to live within these limitations. The argument also is that humanity is dependent on its environment and must respect it. So far, governments have paid little attention to these arguments, but as the oil and global warming debates continue, the arguments of the ecological movement grow stronger.

Key words / expressions
• engineer • traditional • technology
• solar panel • to convert • pipe • tank
• oxygen • to power • stove
• air conditioning • to turn down • design
• to flow • heating

5A Begin by getting students to look at the picture and asking what an *eco-house* is (see **Background information** notes above.) How is the name made up? (=a combination of the words *ecology* and *house*). Elicit or provide a simple, easily comprehensible answer:
• a house that uses the energy in the environment to provide electricity and power.
Emphasise to the class that the house (and professor) actually exist. By this point in the Unit, students may have learnt enough to give a very general answer to **5A1**:
• the house has solar panels in order to create electricity and a hydrogen tank in order to power the heating etc…
Even if students' answers aren't correct, it

doesn't matter. Encourage them to speculate. They may suggest, for example, that rainwater is collected in order to drink or water the garden – both very reasonable answers!

5B / C Since the description of how the house's energy system works is fairly complex, the comprehension activities are at a fairly simple level.

5D In order to help students with this activity, it could be helpful to play the listening passage one more time in order for students to understand how power is created:

- the solar panels create electricity
- the electricity converts the rainwater into hydrogen and oxygen
- the hydrogen powers the house's central heating, hot water, air conditioning, etc.

The pair should argue that the environment has limited energy resources, and that is why eco-houses, which use energy from the environment, are a good idea. The opposing pair can argue that eco-houses sound very complicated and are a lot of hard work. They can question whether eco-houses actually work. What would happen if the system broke down in the middle of winter? Supposing there isn't enough rainwater or heat from the sun. They can point out that eco-houses are too dependent on the environment.

5 LISTEN IN A / B / C **Answers**

A **1 (a)** To make electricity from the sun
(b) To store hydrogen gas for powering the house
(c) Water is needed to make hydrogen
2 It is a mixture of modern technology and traditional design

B **1** (f) **2** (a) **3** (c) **4** (d) **5** (e) **6** (b)

C **1** True **2** False. It's the first house in the world to run on hydrogen. **3** True **4** True **5** False. It's cold. **6** False. The air-conditioning works too well.

6 CONTROVERSY See Role cards Page 60-61 WB

Read the notes about this section in the Introduction. Students may find it hard to play the part of oil executives who are not worried by or do not believe there is an oil crisis. If so, they may be more enthusiastic about a debate between those in favour of nuclear power stations as a primary source of electricity and those in favour of renewable energy sources such as wind power. If you decide to go this route, it will help students to elicit the arguments beforehand. Some of the main arguments are outlined below:

Arguments in favour of nuclear energy	**Arguments against nuclear energy**
• It's very efficient and can provide electricity for large numbers of people. In France, 76% of the energy comes from nuclear power stations. • It does not cause short-term pollution.	• Nuclear energy's radioactive waste takes thousands of years to become safe. Deciding where to safely bury nuclear waste is a huge problem. • Nuclear power stations are very expensive to build and maintain. • Nuclear power stations are potentially very dangerous. If they blow up, it is a disaster for the environment. They are also a target for terrorists.
Arguments in favour of wind power	**Arguments against wind power**
• It's cheap. • It's a renewable energy source. • It doesn't pollute the environment.	• Wind farms destroy the beauty of the landscape. Many see this as a very powerful argument. • The wind doesn't blow all the time. Many experts believe that wind farms are able to provide only limited amounts of electricity.

If students choose to debate the advantages and disadvantages of nuclear energy over wind power, take a vote on the matter at the end of the discussion – it will be interesting to see the result!

7 PORTFOLIO WRITING

Explain to the class that their task is to write an article for an environmental magazine on the oil crisis and environmental solutions to it. In preparation for writing the article, take the class through the Journalist's Notes, eliciting suggestions and writing them up on the board in note form.

Writing model

Many countries are realising that they have a big problem. They depend on oil for their energy, but there is an oil crisis. If you live in a country that produces huge amounts of oil such as Saudi Arabia, then there is no real problem yet, although the oil will run out one day. However, if you live in a country that does not produce oil, then you are dependent on oil-rich countries for your oil supplies, and sooner or later the oil will become more and more expensive.

The solution is to start using alternative energy sources, because they are renewable and do not pollute the environment. There are many different kinds of alternative energy. Wind energy is cheap and we can certainly use it to supply some of our energy needs. Scientists are developing hydrogen-powered cars and people will probably start using them in the next ten years. We will also see the use of cars that run on biofuel, which is cheap and does not pollute the air. The problem at present is that alternative technologies are not yet good enough. This is not a reason to ignore alternative technologies. It simply means that we must invest a lot of money in these technologies now so that we can develop them quickly.

In conclusion, I believe that if we invest the necessary money in alternative energy sources, in ten years' time we will no longer find that we have an 'oil crisis'.

8 *CHEMISTRY in English* Page 35 SB

Begin by asking who has studied chemistry and to what level. Tell the class that although the text may look scary, it's not as difficult as it looks and the diagram will help. Also say that during this session classes will learn the words for some basic concepts in chemistry.

Write the words *hydrogen* and *oxygen* on the board and elicit the fact that they are *gases.* Explain that they are *elements* and cannot be divided further (except, in the case of hydrogen, by nuclear fission!). Elicit examples of substances that are not elements such as water (H_20), or carbon dioxide ($C0_2$). Teach the word *atom*, and the fact that elements, like oxygen, only have one kind of atom.

Ask students what they know about greenhouse gases, acid rain, air pollution and global warming. You will probably find that they know quite a lot. Teach key vocabulary items. Ask students to look at the diagram. Teach the phrase *oil refinery.* Ask students to try and explain the diagram. They should be able to explain that when crude oil is heated, different substances are produced at different temperatures. Explain that these different substances are called *fractions.* You may now decide to teach certain key words in the text, for example, *microscopic creatures / plastics.* However, students should now be ready to approach the text with confidence.

Background information / Internet reference

Greenhouse effect: a term used to describe the heating of the atmosphere due to the presence of *greenhouse gases* such as *carbon dioxide*. The presence of these gases means that the sun's heat is unable to escape back into space. Instead, the gases absorb some of heat and this heat warms the Earth. This effect is similar to what happens in a greenhouse, where the glass traps heat and warms the air.

Global warming: the gradual increase in temperature of the Earth's lower atmosphere as a result of the increase in greenhouse gases.

Air pollution: Pollution of the air caused by waste gases from vehicles, factories *etc*.

Acid rain: Polluted rainfall caused by the burning of fossil fuels. Acid rain damages forests, soils and lakes.

For more information on the greenhouse effect: http://www.newscientist.com/channel/earth/climate-change

Key words / expressions, first text
- to form • million • creature
- combination • carbon • to divide
- gas • liquid • atom
- crude oil = oil in its raw form, as it comes out of the ground
- hydrocarbon = chemical compound made of hydrogen and carbon, *eg* gas, oil
- element = a substance that consists of only one type of atom, *eg* hydrogen, oxygen
- microscopic = very small
- oil refinery = a factory where oil is treated to produce different substances
- diesel oil = fuel used in diesel engines

Key words / expressions, second text
- product • fossil fuels (oil, coal, gas)
- formula • plastic • polymer • increase
- poisonous • greenhouse gases
- air pollution • acid rain • global warming
- oil rig = a large structure used to dig for oil and gas
- gasoline (AmE) = petrol (BrE)
- molecular = a very small group of atoms that form a particular substance

8 *CHEMISTRY in English* A / B / C

Answers

A Answers in **Key words / expressions** and **Background information** above.

B Gases: hydrogen, methane, carbon monoxide, sulphur dioxide, carbon dioxide, nitrogen dioxide, dioxin, methane (natural gas)

Elements: carbon, hydrogen

Pollution: greenhouse gases – carbon monoxide, sulphur dioxide, carbon dioxide, nitrogen dioxide, pollution from oil rigs, ships at sea, dioxin

C **1** Microscopic creatures that were under the sea millions of years ago
2 The different gases and liquids that are created when crude oil is heated.
3 Methane
4 Burning fossil fuels produces gases.
5 They cause air pollution and acid rain and increase global warming.
6 A very poisonous gas called dioxin is produced.

9 YOUR TOPIC

Read the notes about how to develop a **YOUR TOPIC** activity in the Introduction.
This task gives students the opportunity to give a three-minute talk in pairs. The example given as the topic for the talk does not have to be used. By this point in the Unit, students may want to talk about something different! Encourage them to choose their own topic, but say that it should be on the issue of energy and / or pollution. They may, for example, decide to discuss global warming.

Explain to students that while Pair A is preparing their talk, Pair B should be preparing their own talk, as when Pair A's talk is finished, you will expect Pair B to give a three-minute talk too. Rather than prepare their notes for their talk in class, students may prefer to do the preparation for homework. If this is the case, and they have access to the internet, encourage them to go online to get information.

10 *Your answer:*

By now, students will be a lot more able to answer this question than they were at the beginning of the Unit and should enjoy a class discussion on the subject. One approach to the discussion is to ask the class to put themselves into one of the following categories:

1 Very worried about the oil crisis
2 Worried about the oil crisis
3 Not very concerned about the oil crisis
4 Completely unconcerned about the oil crisis

Students then have to explain the reasons for their position and the consequences of their position, for example, if they are very worried about the oil crisis, and what ideas do they have to help the situation? If they are not very concerned, what ideas do they have for transport when oil is too expensive to use?

Workbook answers — Pages 16-17 WB

1 Language: *when, unless, in case,* zero and first conditionals

1A **1** it creates **2** will explain **3** will **4** turns
1B **1** build / will supply **2** continues / will

increase **3** drop / sinks **4** do not water / dies

1C **1** it gets cold **2** it will be too late **3** you won't understand **4** there's a lot of traffic **5** I had to wait

2 Use of English

2A **1** Have we got enough petrol?
2 You'd better fill up the petrol tank as it is very low.
3 There's a tank in the garden that collects rainwater.
4 Crude oil is heated in a refinery.
5 By 2014, China may consume 14 million barrels a day.

2B **1** why **2** life **3** which **4** depends **5** and **6** gone **7** If **8** also **9** needed **10** cost

3 Portfolio writing

Students' own answers

4 Connections

4A **1** alternative **2** used up **3** run on **4** economic **5** give out **6** resources

4B

to convert / to change	to face / to confront	to give out / to emit
to carry / to transport	to rise / to go up	to create / to make

4C **1** (d) the environment **2** (a) economy **3** (f) affect **4** (c) industrialised **5** (e) work **6** (b) developing

The Extended Reading Units contain longer and more substantial texts than in the rest of the Units. Perhaps the best use of them is to set the texts for homework for students to read in their own time. Alternatively, they can be studied in class.

The text in this Unit is an extract from the bestselling novel, *Captain Corelli's Mandolin*, by Louis de Bernières, first published in 1994. In spite of his French-sounding name, the author is English. He was born in 1954 and worked as a teacher, mechanic and gardener before finding success as a novelist. This is an example of a book that became well-known through readers advising each other to try it. Initially, it was not heavily promoted by publishers. But many Reading Circles (groups of friends who meet regularly to discuss a book they have been reading) took up the book and its fame spread by word-of-mouth.

The story takes place on the Greek island of Cephallonia during the Second World War. The Italians have invaded the island and stationed their troops with the islanders. An Italian captain called Corelli is sent to stay at the house of a Greek doctor and his lovely daughter Pelagia. Although they do their best to resist their feelings, the captain and Pelagia start to fall in love. Food is scarce, and the extract describes how the doctor, Pelagia and the captain go hunting for snails to eat among the undergrowth nearby. Pelagia's hair gets caught on briars and Corelli untangles her. They kiss for the first time …

Below are the key words and expressions that appear in the text. Ten key words are focused on in the **2 PREVIEW** section for students to check their meaning. They are in **bold** in the text.

Key words / expressions

- **crawl** • **tangle** • **briars** • snail • **tunnel**
- contented • to strike (p.p. *struck*)
- **to paralyse** • **thorn** • **to murder**
- to press • chest • uniform
- to squash • to sniff • **strand** (n.)
- to wind (p.p.*wound*) • **vulnerable**
- grateful • to tug • **to kiss**
- to reproach • to gaze • tear (n.)
- to drown • **lousy** • filthy
- enclosed • unpatriotic

- for God's sake = this is an expression used to emphasise what you are saying, especially when you are annoyed
- legions (of snails) = a very large number (of snails). The actual meaning of *legion* = a large group of soldiers, especially in the Roman army
- shrapnel = small pieces of metal from a bomb or bullet that has exploded
- posture = position (especially how a person stands)
- irritation = a feeling of annoyance
- consternation = a feeling of shock or worry
- to yield to temptation = to allow/surrender to a strong feeling that you want to have or do something that you know you should not

1 *The BIG read:* CAPTAIN CORELLI'S MANDOLIN by Louis de Bernières

The opening box of text on page 36 contains brief background information to the novel and provides a context for the extract. Ask the class if they recognise the actors in the photo (Nicholas Cage and Penélope Cruz, stars of the film *Captain Corelli's Mandolin*, released in *2001*). Ask if anyone has read the book or seen the film and what they thought of them. Even if no one has actually done so, they may well know something about the story.

Background information

Cephallonia: This Greek island (also spelt *Kefalonia*) is the largest of the Ionian Islands in western Greece and is popular with tourists. It is in the middle of an earthquake zone, and in 1953 suffered a massive earthquake that almost destroyed the island. This earthquake is described in *Captain Corelli's Mandolin.* In World War II, the island was occupied by the Axis powers – first the Italian army (until late 1943) and then the German army. The islanders suffered terribly under the Germans. A battle on the island between the German forces and the Italians resulted in the Germans taking full control of the island. The remaining Italian prisoners were brutally executed. These events are a main part of the novel.

2 PREVIEW

2A The answers to these questions provide the background to the extract.

2 PREVIEW A **Answers**
1 Because the Italian army has invaded the island and the Italian soldiers have been sent to live in the islanders' homes.
2 Because the captain is part of the invading army.
3 Because there is very little food and they intend to eat the snails for supper.

2B This activity focuses on ten key words in the text. Either teach the words or ask students to use their dictionaries to check the meanings.

2 PREVIEW B **Answers**
crawl = to move on your hands and knees
tangle = a mass of hair, wires etc that are twisted together untidily
briar = a bush with thorns on its branches
tunnel = a passage that has been dug under the ground
paralyse = to make someone lose the ability to move their body or part of their body
thorn = a sharp pointed part on a plant, *eg* a rose
murder = to kill someone deliberately
strand = a single thin piece of thread, hair etc
vulnerable = easily hurt
kiss = to touch someone with your lips as a greeting or to show them love
lousy = very bad

3 READING CD2 (Red) track 8, Page 36 SB

Explain that this text provides practice in reading a longer and more difficult passage. Tell students that they should not try and understand every word, since it takes far too long and kills enjoyment of the text. Instead, they should first try and understand the main points of the text and then try and understand it in more detail – but without looking up every word they do not know! They should also try and guess meaning from context.

If the text is being studied in class, you may decide to teach key words and expressions before students read the text. Alternatively they can use dictionaries. Set a certain time to complete the activities, eg 15-20 minutes. Depending on the class's level, consider asking them to do activity **3A** without any vocabulary pre-teaching, as this provides excellent practice in reading for gist. In this case, you would teach key vocabulary items after activity **3A**.

3A This activity provides practice in reading a challenging text in order to understand the main points. Explain its purpose to students and encourage them to read the extract without using a dictionary.

To help students understand the main points, ask those who chose the correct answer to read out the sentences that helped them make the right choice.

3B This activity focuses on key phrases in the section. Key words to teach include: *legions / shrapnel / posture irritation / cheek.* Point out the following to show how meaning can be deduced from context:

Question 1: The word *impossible* suggests the briars were difficult to crawl through.

Question 4: The use of the words *neck / backwards / on her hands and knees* suggest she was not comfortable.

3 READING A / B **Answers**
A paragraph 3 is the best summary
B **1** No **2** Yes
3 Shrapnel had fallen on her and hurt her.
4 No **5** Because she couldn't move.
6 Her cheek

3C These questions focus on the main points of the section. Key words include: *chest / uniform / squash/ tug / kiss / tears / gaze*

3 READING C **Answers**
1 Because the captain is reaching over Pelagia's shoulders so that her face is pressing into his chest.
2 Because he has untangled Pelagia's hair from the briars without hurting her.
3 He shouldn't have kissed her cheek.

3D This activity returns the reader to the whole text, focusing on Captain Corelli's feelings. If you wish, you can add some questions focusing on Pelagia's feelings:

1 *How do Pelagias' feelings and actions change during the extract?* (First, she seems cross and upset. When Corelli kisses her cheek, she is reproachful. Then she cries, showing her real feelings for him – and finally they kiss.)

2 *What does Pelagia mean by the words, 'I can't stand it any more, not any of it. I'm sorry.'?* (She has to hide her feelings for Corelli because he is an invader, and she hates doing this.)

3 READING D **Answers**

1 He feels very contented.
2 He is frightened that she has been hurt by falling shrapnel.
3 He is amused and laughs.
4 He thinks he might cry too.

4 TALK ABOUT IT

If the class have done the Extended Reading as homework, this section will provide a useful revision of the extract as well as providing stimulating discussion.

4A Ask students what the word *romantic* means to them. (*romantic* = related to love and with treating the person you love in a special way) Ask what kind of things they find romantic, *eg a candlelit meal.*

Possible answer to question **A**: Yes, the text is very romantic. The lovers try to fight their feelings but are unable to. Finally they admit their true feelings and kiss – this is real romance!

4B Possible answer: Corelli clearly has a sense of humour. He laughs when he sees Pelagia's problem and makes some amusing comments. He seems to really care for Pelagia and is very gentle with her.

4C You may find there is a boy / girl split here since women are far more interested in reading romance than men. If this is the case, point it out and make it a point for discussion.

4D Encourage students to speculate. If some have read the book / seen the film, ask them to briefly describe how the novel ends.

5 PORTFOLIO WRITING

Prepare the class for the task of writing the letter by establishing that Pelagia and Captain Corelli are in love with each other.

Elicit / teach useful phrases: *to be in love / to fall in love / to have srong feelings for someone.*

Discuss with the class the problems that their falling in love creates: Corelli is part of the invading army and the islanders would never forgive Pelagia for falling in love with / marrying an invader. They will have to be very careful to keep their love a secret and it seems doubtful that there is any real future for them.

Writing model – an informal letter

Dearest Maria,

I'm writing to you because I have a problem I need to discuss. It's a very serious problem and I must ask you not to discuss it with anyone else. This is very important and you will understand when I tell you about it.

You know that we have an Italian soldier livng with us called Captain Corelli – you have met him on your visits to me. Maria, my problem is that he is an invader but I have fallen in love with him! And he feels the same about me! For the last month or two I have tried so hard to hide how I felt. But yesterday we kissed for the first time, I have never been so happy – and at the same time so frightened – in all my life.

What would people say if they knew? They would kill us, or send me from my home. I cannot see that there is any future for our love. But I have such strong feelings for him.

At the moment it is enough for me to know that he loves me. But we have to hide our feelings from other people (though it is clear my father knows.)

What will happen to us? I do not know. Please write.

Love
Pelagia

What's new?

Subject: Education
Function: Persuading and discouraging
Grammar: Second conditional

Before you open the book …

Write the following on the board: *When I know I have to take an exam, I ....*

Ask students to complete the sentence in their notebooks. Students then read out their completed sentences. Write the best sentences on the board, *eg When I know I have to take an exam, I get nervous.* Teach any vocabulary that arises.

Write the title of the Unit on the board – you will probably have to teach the word *pressure* (= a worried feeling that you get when you have to deal with a difficult situation). Explain that the theme of the Unit is education.

1 *The BIG question:* WHY ARE STUDENTS SO STRESSED?

FACT: A 24-hour telephone helpline in Britain receives over 900 calls a year about exam stress. Most are from students aged 12 to 15. Thousands more ask for a leaflet about exam stress.

Read out *The BIG question*. Check students understand the word *stressed* (worried and unable to relax). Say (with a smile!), *'You are all students. Are you stressed?'* Elicit answers and ask why. Teach new vocabulary where necessary.

Ask students to write down a number, on a scale of 1-5, to describe how stressed they are about their studies. They should write this figure down on a large piece of paper. Students then hold up their pieces of paper and read out their figure.

2 PREVIEW

Words

A Check students understand the vocabulary. They should then find it fairly easy to describe the pictures.

B Like activity **A**, this activity teaches some basic vocabulary connected with education. If students have dictionaries, they can do this activity in pairs. If not, go through the words, eliciting answers and teaching new vocabulary where necessary. Students will probably be able to explain why they have paired certain words, but their grammar won't be too good. Don't worry about this. You only want to check that they understand the meanings.

C Again, this activity introduces more vocabulary connected with education. Check students understand the phrases *full / part-time student.* Put students into pairs to answer the questions, then elicit full answers to the questions, *eg I'm studying at college / I'm studying Journalism / I intend to go to university.* Teach any new vocabulary that arises, and correct prepositions.

2 PREVIEW Words: A / B **Answers**

A Picture 1: Students are probably taking an exam.

Picture 2: A student has probably received the result of an exam. She looks delighted, so the exam result must be good.

Picture 3: A young man is looking upset. Perhaps he has failed an exam.

B 1 (e) Both graduates and undergraduates study at college or university. A graduate has already completed an academic degree. An undergraduate is someone who is still studying for their first degree.

2 (d) To revise, and to do revision mean the same thing. They both mean to study your notes and information again in order to prepare for an exam.

3 (b) Both exams and tests ask questions to find out how much someone knows about a subject. An exam is longer and more important than a test.
4 (c) A grade gives a letter or number that shows the quality of a student's work. A score gives the number of points.
5 (a) Both degrees and diplomas are qualifications that you get after completing a course of study at a college or university.

Language

If students have not met the second conditional before, give them an example of an obviously imaginary situation, *eg If I were president / prime minister, I would (try to reduce global warming).* It is clichéd to use the example, *If I had a million pounds, I would (buy a yacht),* but it is nonetheless an excellent example of a situation that is obviously imaginary!

Make sure that students understand that although the first part of the sentence is in the past, the first conditional does not refer to the past but to something imaginary or unlikely. Invite students to complete the second half of the examples above.

Ask students to give complete answers to these questions, beginning with *if.* Students may need you to write the questions on the board – the second conditional is difficult to learn first time around.

1 What would you do if you found a wallet with £1000 in it?
2 If you could meet a famous person, who would it be?
3 What would you do if you saw a bank robbery?
4 What would you do if you woke up and saw a burglar?
5 Where would you go on holiday in America?

After students have given complete answers, explain that we often answer with the second part of the sentence only, *eg I'd (I would) go to California / I'd go to the police.*

Finally, write the phrase, *If I were you* on the board and explain that we use it to give advice. Ask students to give you advice about buying a car that is rather more than you can afford but that you like very much. Elicit sentences such as *If I were you, I'd buy it / If I were you I'd find something cheaper.*

2 PREVIEW Language A / B / C Answers
A The second sentence. Present simple and future simple.
B The first and third sentences. After *if,* the past simple is used, followed by *would* plus verb. These sentences do not refer to the past. They refer to an imaginary situation.
C The third sentence.

Ideas

Explain that the third sentence refers to the S.A.T. test, the very important college entrance exam in Korea. Students may have very different reactions to these sentences, depending on their nationality. For students in Japan and Korea for example, exam results are extremely important and may more or less decide the limits of a person's future career – hence the extreme stress that some students may feel.

Encourage students to speculate in answer to question **A**, *eg Perhaps she really believed that the exam result showed she was no good / Perhaps she was frightened of her parents' reaction.* Ask students to briefly describe the exam system in their countries. Encourage students to be honest about their feelings about exams. If they hate exams, get them to try and explain why.

3 READING

CD 2 (Red) track 9, Page 39 SB

<u>Key words / expressions</u>
- high school • distressed • commit suicide
- level • anxious • failure • to achieve
- realistic • professor • psychiatry • cause
- serious • to judge • intense • competition
- spokesman • to reform • tragedy
- high school = In American English: a school for students between the ages of 14 and 18; In British English: a school for students between the ages of 11 and 18.
- Union (Trades Union) = an organisation that is formed by workers in order to protect their rights.
- private education = when parents pay for a child's education at a school that is not supported by government money. In Britain, private, fee-paying schools are often known confusingly as 'public schools'.

This article describes how Korean students are committing suicide due to the pressure on them to do well in the college entrance exam which more or less determines their future career.

3A Students should show that they understand specific ideas in the text by choosing one of the sentences (A to E) for each of the gaps in the text (1 to 4). There is one extra sentence that is not used (A). It is a good idea to check students' reaction to the passage. Some may be quite upset by the idea that a student could kill themselves because of exam pressure – they may even be feeling very stressed themselves about an exam. If any students seem upset, it may be a good idea to talk to them briefly and find out how they are feeling and why. You could give them advice on how to handle exam stress – see **Internet reference** notes below.

3B Students should be able to identify these words from the context without using a dictionary.

3C / D These activities test more detailed comprehension.

Background information / Internet reference

Tips for coping with exam stress

It is not just in Korea that exams cause stress for students. As a result there have been cases of student suicide in many countries. See http://news.bbc.co.uk/1/hi/health/3758359.stm

- Have confidence in yourself. Your teachers are there to help you make it.
- Don't try to be perfect. Aim to do your best but you don't have to get the top grade.
- If there is a problem, think about how to solve it. For example, if you don't understand something, see your course tutor or get help from your classmates.
- Talk about your feelings. Talk to someone you trust. It will really help.
- Take the long view. Exams might seem the most important thing in the world right now, but they are only a small part of your life.

Tips for the revision period

- Leave plenty of time to revise. This will really reduce exam stress.
- Develop a revision timetable. Make sure you allow time for fun and relaxation.
- As soon as you notice that you can't concentrate, take a short break. You will then come back to your revision able to work again.
- Experiment with different exam revision techniques. Make your revision more interesting.
- Don't drink too much tea, coffee or fizzy drinks, as caffeine makes you think less clearly.
- Eat healthily and regularly.
- Take regular exercise. This will give you greater energy and reduce stress.
- Try some yoga or relaxation techniques. This can be very calming.

Tips for the exam itself

- Try and avoid panic. When you panic it is difficult to think clearly.
- To stop feelings of stress and panic during the exam or while studying, close your eyes and take several long, slow, deep breaths. It is important that the breaths are very slow. At the same time, say to yourself, 'I am calm and relaxed,' or 'I know I will do fine.'
- If you still can't think of the information, move on to another question, and go back later.

After the exam, don't keep thinking about what you did wrong. Instead, think about the things you did right and learn from the bits where you could have done better. The above tips and more are on this website: www.isma.org.uk/exams.htm

3 READING A / B / C / D **Answers**

A **1** C **2** D **3** E **4** B (A ×)

B **1** (a) unfortunately (b) commit suicide (c) fear
2 (a) cause (b) unhealthy (c) reform

C **1** False. Five students have killed themselves in recent months.
2 True.
3 False. She felt she had done badly. We don't know if she did badly.

D **1** Because the exam more or less decides the type of college a student can go to. The type of college then decides the type of job a person will have.

2 They seem to feel they have failed. They feel they have not achieved what their parents wanted them to achieve.
3 They feel that the college entrance system is a serious problem and must change.

4 TALK ABOUT IT

4A Student A may find it difficult to think of things to say, so elicit suggestions from the class. Here are some examples:

- I can take the exam next year.
- I'm going to pretend to be ill.
- I'm just going to tell my parents I'm not taking the exam.
- I know I'm going to fail so it's stupid to take it.
- I haven't done enough revision / work.

4B Elicit suggestions from the class in answer to this question and encourage discussion.

Since the situation is imaginary, encourage students to use *would / I'd* …Here are some example answers:

- I'd feel very stressed.
- I'd stop caring.
- I'd study just a few of the most important subjects.
- I'd ask friends to give me advice.
- I'd ask friends to give me photocopies of their notes.
- I'd work very hard for the next few days.

4C Put students into pairs and ask them to imagine that they are offering advice to other students. (See **Background information** and the **Internet reference** above) Elicit advice from students and teach new vocabulary where necessary. Write the best tips on the board.

Optional activity: Use the **Background information** above on coping with exam stress as a reading comprehension. Write a set of questions based on the tips. You could, if you wished, give the text to the class for homework. Then in the next session you could ask students which tips they found the most useful.

5 LISTEN IN

CD 1 (Blue) track 8, Page 40 SB

Key words / expressions
- to calm down • to make a decision
- to miss (home) • sensible
- to change (your) mind • opportunity
- bilingual • advantage • fluent
- homesick • to make friends
- job market = the number of jobs that are available at any time.
- facilities = places, services or pieces of equipment that are provided for people such as libraries and swimming pools.
- counsellor = person who advises or supports someone who has problems.

The **Audio text** is in the **Workbook** (page 67). In the listening passage, three foreign students, who are studying at an American university, begin a conversation about the end-of-year exams they have just taken. One of them, Lufti, (a boy) is very unhappy and stressed. He does not feel he has done well in the exam and is very homesick. He has decided not to return to university for the next semester. The other two girls (Yana and Emiko) try to persuade him to change his mind, pointing out the advantages of studying at the university, but Lufti is not to be persuaded.

5A This activity introduces key words in the listening passage. Check students understand the words and teach them if necessary. Elicit answers to the questions but do not spend too long on them – they are simply preparation for the listening passage.

5B Explain the basic situation of the passage as outlined above. Students then listen and answer the questions. They may need to hear the passage more than once. Don't worry if students are unable to give all the reasons for why Lufti wants to leave, so long as they understand that he is homesick and stressed and feels he has done badly in the exam.

5C This activity tests for more detailed comprehension. In question **5**, you could take the opportunity to teach the words *determined* (*Lufti is determined to leave*) and *frustrated* (*Yana and Emiko probably feel frustrated because they cannot persuade Lufti to stay*).

5D The listening passage has pointed out the main advantages and disadvantages of studying abroad. If you feel students need the help, go through these before they begin the discussion:

Advantages

- Speaking a second language well
- Better qualifications
- Better job opportunities
- Job opportunities in the country where the student has studied
- Opportunity to discover another country
- Opportunity to make international friends

Disadvantages

- Feeling homesick
- Difficulties with the new language and, as a result, with the course
- Loneliness because unable to make many friends due to language problems

5E Make sure that Student C (who plays the part of Lufti) understands that he / she can allow him / herself to be persuaded to stay, if he / she finds the arguments of the other two students very persuasive. Take a show of hands at the end of the role play to see how many of the 'Lufti's' were 'persuaded' to stay.

5 LISTEN IN B / C **Answers**

B **1** Lufti thinks she has probably failed an important exam. He is studying at an American university but is very stressed and homesick, and complains that he has not made any American friends. He says that his English is not fluent and that because of this he has difficulties with his studies. He has decided to go home and not return to university after the vacation.
2 Yana and Emiko try to persuade Lufti to remain at university. Because Lufti will soon have a degree from a top American university, the job opportunities will be excellent.
C **1** They say that the university facilities are excellent and that they have had a wonderful time because the university is so international.
2 Yes, she has a few.
3 She agrees with Yana that she's had a great time.
4 She suggests that Lufti sees a counsellor.
5 Lufti is still determined that he will not return after the exam in September. Yana and Emiko probably feel a little upset that they have not been able to persuade Lufti to stay.

6 CONTROVERSY See Role cards Page 61 WB

Read the notes about this section in the Introduction. Check students understand the words *temporary / disappointed / academic*. If you feel that students need preparation for the role play, ask these questions:
1 How important is it to have a degree, in your opinion?
2 Can you get a good job without going to college / university?
3 Why do so many young people want to travel and see the world?

7 PORTFOLIO WRITING

Remind the class that, in a formal letter, when you do not know the name of the person you are writing to, you begin *Dear Sir / Madam*, and end, *Yours faithfully.*

When you know the name of the person you are writing to, you begin *Dear Mr (Brown),* and end *Yours sincerely.* Here are some more useful phrases:

- I understand that you (offer ESOL courses)
- I am interested in studying .....
- I would like details of these courses.
- Could you also give / send me details ..... ?
- I would be grateful if you would (send me details) ...

Writing model - formal letter

Dear Sir
I am an Italian student from Rome in my last year at secondary school. I understand that you offer ESOL courses and I would like details of these courses. I am interested in studying English and Business Studies and feel that an ESOL course abroad could be very helpful for me. In a recent TOEFL test, my score was ...... If there is a course that is suitable or me, I would like to start in September of this year. I will also need details of fees for two semesters and I would like to know about the

accommodation that is available.

Do you also offer courses in Business Studies? It is possible that after completing my ESOL course, I will want to do a Business Studies Course. I would be grateful if you would send me details of these courses and their fees.

Yours faithfully,
(Your name)

8 *EDUCATION in English* — Page 41 SB

Picture notes

The picture on the left is of Harvard University, one of the most famous universities in America. It is near Boston. The picture on the left is of Trinity College, Cambridge University, England. Both universities are in towns called Cambridge. Harvard is in Cambridge, Massachusetts and Trinity College is part of Cambridge University, England.

Key words / expressions

- academic • purpose • scientific
- communication • research • publish
- journal • enrol • talent • engineering
- provide • instruction
- peer = your peers are people who are the same age as you or who have the same job or social position
- overseas students = students from abroad
- study skills = training in the skills needed for academic study
- critical thinking = the ability to think critically, needed on university courses, and sometimes a course itself (training in how to think critically)

The text on this page concerns a topic that may be of great interest to some of your students. It focuses on the growing importance of English as the international language of academic and scientific communication and the fact that, as a result, over half a million overseas students go to American universities to study their subjects in English.

The text refers to courses offered at American universities called English for Academic Purposes (EAP). (These courses are of course offered in other countries too.) As the titles suggest, these courses train students in the academic skills required for study at university, for example, Academic Reading and Writing and Critical Thinking. A course in Academic Writing would train students how to write an academic paper according to the correct conventions, and a course in Critical Thinking would help students to ask the right kind of questions when studying a novel or an academic paper. An important point to make is that different countries give different kinds of academic training to students. For example, in some countries it is more important to be able to memorise information than to think critically, and this is where a course in Critical Thinking could be helpful.

Begin the session by asking the class to look at the pictures at the top of the page and the caption. Ask students if they know what the buildings are. Harvard is a top American university and Cambridge is a top English university. Once these facts have been established, ask students if they can work out which college is which. The picture on the left shows Harvard. The picture on the right shows Trinity College, Cambridge. If the students know that Cambridge University is much older than Harvard University, they may be able to work out that the picture on the right, which shows a much older building, is Trinity College.

Continue the session by asking if anyone in the class intends to study for any length of time abroad. If the class is taking place in an English-speaking country, ask students why they came to this country to study. Also ask if any students intend to continue their English studies to a high level because they intend to be scientists, for example.

8A Either check students understand the vocabulary items or ask students to look the items up in their dictionaries. In the latter case, ask questions to check that students have understood the meanings.

8B Write the title *English for Academic Purposes (EAP)* on the board, and ask students what they think it means. Elicit answers but don't say whether they are correct. Tell students they will find the answer in the text.

8C When students have read the text and answered the question, ask the class what they think they would learn from courses entitled Academic Writing, Critical Thinking or Study Skills (See notes above and also **Answers** below.)

8D The answer to question **3** is implied in the text but not actually stated. (See **Answers** below).

You could conclude this section by asking students, *If you could study abroad in an English-speaking country, which country would you choose and why?* This question provides excellent opportunities to practise the second conditional, the target structure for this Unit.

8 *EDUCATION in English* B / D Answers

B You would study subjects such as academic reading and writing, critical thinking, study skills and research.

D 1 Because English has become the language of scientific and academic communication all over the world. English is particularly important for scientific research. Scientists publish in English because they want their work to be read by their peers all over the world.

2 Because they realise that they need to speak and write English well, if they want to do work in scientific or academic subjects.

3 If students are taking a university course designed for native speakers, then they may need help with some of the language used. Also, perhaps the academic training at American universities is different to the way their country trains its students.

9 YOUR TOPIC

Read the notes about this section in the Introduction. Encourage students to think broadly when choosing a topic to discuss. Here are some suggestions:

1 Why learning English is hard
2 How to relieve stress
3 The importance of a gap* year
4 My favourite three courses
5 Why I am (not) going to university
6 Why I hate / enjoy exams

*A 'gap year' is the year that many students take time off (often going travelling, or working) between school and university. They often use the year to travel and to do voluntary work. It is generally agreed that a 'gap year' is very useful in helping students to mature enough to cope with the freedom and pressures of university life.

10 *Your answer:*

By now students will have acquired a lot more of the vocabulary needed to discuss the questions raised here. Explain that question **A** *Why do students get so stressed?* is to some extent a question aimed at helping students to revise the language of the first two sessions in the Unit. Questions **B** and **C** are new questions for the class and should create genuine interest. Both questions provide opportunities to practise the second conditional answer *I'd (I would).*

Workbook answers — Pages 20-21 WB

1 Language: second conditional

1A 1 If I found a subject really difficult, I would talk to my teachers about dropping it.
2 If I didn't want to go to university, I wouldn't have to work so hard.
3 If I went back home, my parents wouldn't be pleased with me.
4 You could finish the project in time if you started work on it right now.
5 What would you do if you won a scholarship to university in the States?

1B 1 If my exams were finished, I would feel less stressed.
2 If the book were less expensive, I would buy it.
3 If you went to bed earlier, you wouldn't be so tired in the morning.
4 If you did some exercise while you were revising, you would have more energy.
5 If the exam weren't so difficult, students wouldn't get so stressed.

1C 1 What would you say if someone offered you the answers to your next exam paper?
2 What would your parents do if you didn't do well this year?
3 What would you do if you thought that

someone copied your answers in an exam?
4 What would you do if you overslept and were late on the morning of an exam?

1D *Example answers*
1 I would refuse to look at them.
2 They would ask me to explain why I hadn't done well.
3 I would talk to them and say that it wasn't fair.
4 I would explain the situation to the exam supervisor.

2 Use of English

2A **1** The student had discussed her fears with a friend.
2 The university or college a student eventually attends depends on exam results.
3 Young people often feel they have failed.
4 They don't have enough help.
5 Too much is expected of us by our parents and teachers.

2B **(1)** ways **(2)** Plan **(3)** subjects **(4)** time
(5) approach / method **(6)** when / as
(7) try / find **(8)** difficult / hard
(9) draw **(10)** marks

3 Portfolio writing

Students' own answers

4 Connections

4A **1** (c) **2** (b) **3** (e) **4** (f) **5** (a) **6** (d)
4B **1** taking / dropped out of **2** picked up
3 enrolling for **4** take up **5** passed / got

What's new?

Subject: Personal values and ideals
Function: Adding and contrasting information
Grammar: Cohesive devices

Before you open the book ...

Have any of the students in your class attended a course called Peace Studies, or something similar? If they have, ask them to describe what goes on in these classes. If they have not, ask them to tell you why they think wars start, and what happens when two nations or rival groups go to war.

Secondly, do they know anything about the history of wars? Are they familiar with the causes and results of the most important worldwide conflicts of the twentieth century – the First World War (1914-1918), the Second World War (1939-1945), Korea, Vietnam, the Palestinian-Israeli conflict, or the Gulf or Iraq wars? If not, you may want them to do some internet research. Are wars different in the 21st century? Can they explain what US President George W. Bush's 'War on Terror' means?

1 *The BIG question:* CAN WE STOP WARS?

FACT: There is one gun for every 12 people in the world. 90% of people killed by small arms are civilians. 800 people are killed by land mines every month.

Picture notes / Internet references

The images on the opening spread are all about war. On the first page, there's a gun, a land mine and an aircraft carrier.

http://www.landmines.org/crisis/ Land mines are a threat to the people of about one third of the countries in the world and kill over 15,000 people every year and maim many more.

The photo of the aircraft carrier shows one of the 9 nuclear-powered US Nimitz Class ships (the tenth called *George H.W. Bush* enters service in 2009). Each carries a crew of more 6,000 and over 70 aircraft.

See http://www.naval-technology.com/projects/nimitz/

For information about the photograph of the Kalashnikov AK-47 rifle, see **Background information** box below.

On the right-hand page, there's a picture of a smiling and rather avuncular-looking older man. These are all arresting images and the students will study them with interest. If you ask who they think the man is, they will of course quickly read the heading to the newspaper article and find out that this is Mikhail Kalashnikov, the inventor of the AK47 submachine gun. The headline I SLEEP SOUNDLY is a quote from him. *Soundly* means *well* in this context. Kalashnikov guns have their own website: http://kalashnikov.guns.ru/

At first sight, *The BIG question* seems rather simplistic. The answer would appear to be NO. But we hope that the target age audience for this book will have a certain amount of hope in the idea that things can change. Secondly, the information in this Unit may inform students about things they don't know.

The shocking facts in the **FACT** box about guns (*small arms* are hand-held weapons) and land mines (bombs buried in the ground so that they explode when people tread on them) will undoubtedly be new to most students. You can start the lesson by asking them if they knew or could imagine these facts, and what they think could or should be done about it. We hope that it is an essential desire of young people to put right the violent mistakes of previous generations, and that this will be proved (or not!) in the ensuing discussions.

See pages 42-45 SB, 22-23 WB

2 PREVIEW

Words

A This is an activity to make sure that the students know the words for the weapons which will be mentioned throughout this Unit. The words are either illustrated, easily demonstrated or possibly even cognates in your language. Unfortunately, English is the language of the international arms business.

2 PREVIEW Words A **Answers**

A People in the army, air force and navy use all the weapons, but mainly these weapons are associated with these branches of the armed forces:
The army – rifles, tanks and machine guns.
The air force – planes, helicopters and missiles.
The navy – aircraft carriers, other ships and helicopters.

B These are wide-ranging questions about weaponry and war, which some students may know very little about. However, it is possible that some students may have a fascination for war and guns (there are certainly enough successful video games, and films about war to suggest this). These students may find themselves better able to comment on these questions than others.

It is not a problem if discussions like this are dominated by one or two students, who have a more sophisticated prior knowledge of a particular subject than the rest of the class. In other Units of the book, there will be opportunities for other students to exhibit their knowledge of subjects that they know more about.

2 PREVIEW Words B **Possible answers**

B **1** Small arms like the AK-47 are used by national armies and also by guerrilla forces that operate against them. They are widely used in small-scale wars all over the world.
2 Land mines were used by many national armies in conflicts during the 20th century; now they are more commonly used by guerrilla forces. Unfortunately, the main victims worldwide are innocent civilians.
3 There are civilian victims because they are often caught in the cross-fire between national forces and guerrilla forces; also many civilians are killed and injured by bombs and other weapons which are intended for military or official targets.
4 Students can talk here about other weapons they have heard or read about.

Language

The language focus in this Unit is words and expressions which connect ideas and sentences. These are what we call *cohesive devices* or *discourse markers*. Some of these such as *however* and *consequently* are extremely useful in spoken English. Others like *furthermore* and *meanwhile* are more useful in written English. The important point about all of them is that they add a new level of sophistication to spoken and written work, and students should be encouraged to use them in examinations.

Key words / expressions

- furthermore = used when you want to add an extra fact or argument.

He went to live in Iceland. **Furthermore**, he met his wife there.

- however = another way of saying *but*.

He was unhappy at school. **However**, he loved the holidays.

- consequently = indicates the result of something.

Cathy did well in her exams. **Consequently**, she got a place at a top university.

- on the other hand = indicates an opposite argument.

The train was very expensive. **On the other hand**, it was much quicker than going by bus.

- meanwhile = at the same time

John cooked dinner. **Meanwhile**, Jane welcomed the guests.

- even so = used before a piece of information, if that information is a surprise (given what we have already heard or read).

He has no qualifications at all. **Even so**, he is now a millionaire with his own company.

Students should read the examples in the list, all of which are taken from the **READING** text. Encourage them to try to say the same idea in different words to make the concept of the words clear to themselves. If you want students to do more structure practice work before they proceed, they can at this point do the structure exercises in the **Language** section of the **Workbook** for Unit 9.

2 PREVIEW Language A / B / C / D

Answers

A furthermore
B however, on the other hand
C consequently
D meanwhile

Ideas

There are three quite extraordinary sentences in the **Ideas** section. The first is about the inventor of a weapon of war being *proud of* his invention. The second is the comparison between designing a weapon and childbirth. The third suggests that the designer of a weapon should take no responsibility for its use. The three subsequent questions ask students to consider these opinions.

3 READING CD 2 (Red) track 10, Page SB 43

The reading text is an article by Nick Paton Walsh from the British daily newspaper *The Guardian,* about Mikhail Kalashnikov, the inventor of the AK-47 submachine gun, the most successful small weapon in the history of war. The article contains an interview with Kalashnikov himself. Students may want to discuss the difference in meaning between *terrorists* and *revolutionary fighters.* Are they the same people, called a different name by their supporters and their enemies?

Key words / expressions

• award • combat • conflict • creation
• decade • invent • motherland
• outweigh • peasant • protect • proud of
• responsibility • revolutionary (adj) • rival
• submachine gun • terrorists • victims
• warfare • weapon
• arms = weapons in general, as in the arms industry, which makes weapons.
• small arms = personal weapons carried by soldiers.
• primary = most important (*secondary* is next in the list of importance).
• genie out of the bottle = once the genie (a spirit) has been released it is impossible to recapture it, with unexpected consequences.

The story of Aladdin, see **Background information** below.
• I sleep soundly = I sleep very well.
Soundly is a rarely used adverb and *sleep soundly* is one of the very few collocations that it appears in.

Background information / Internet references

The expression *genie out of a bottle* may be new to students, but they may have heard of the story of Aladdin and his magic lamp from the story of *The Arabian Nights*. When Aladdin rubs the lamp, a spirit or genie appears and offers him three wishes. This is marvellous for Aladdin to begin with, but the problems come later when the genie refuses to go back in the lamp. The story has become more famous in the West because it became a Disney film. The original is a much darker and more frightening piece. You can read the whole story at this website:
www.pagebypagebooks.com/Unknown/Aladdin_and_the_Wonderful_Lamp/

It is not clear how the lamp of the original Aladdin story became a bottle in the modern expression which is so common. For example, *Genie in a Bottle* is the name of the first single release by American singer Christine Aguilera.

Mikhail Kalashnikov's first job was as a technical clerk in the Turkistan-Siberian railway department but in 1938, he was called up for the Red Army. Despite the fact that he had no technical training, it was quite clear from the beginning that he was a genius with machines, and he invented several military devices, including a device to make pistol-firing through the small slits in tanks more effective. In 1941, he was transferred to Leningrad and became a tank commander. However, he was seriously wounded in battle and spent a long time in hospital. It was here that he came up with his idea for a new kind of submachine gun.

One of the most lasting symbols of his

influence on world events is the fact that various national flags, including the flag of Mozambique, have the AK-47 as a symbol. The revolutionaries who took power in those countries changed the flag, and they saw the AK-47 as the symbol of their victory, and also as the means to defend the revolution in future.

The full interview with Mikhail Kalashnikov is published at:
www.guardian.co.uk/g2/story/0,3604,1059879,00.html

The Kalashnikov AK-47 assault rifle has its own website. Mikahil Kalashnikov has also launched his own brand of vodka.
www.kalashnikov.guns.ru/models/ka50.html

According to Unicef, since 1975 land mines have exploded under more than 1 million people and are currently thought to be killing 800 people a month. There seems little prospect of any end to the carnage. In 64 countries around the world, there are an estimated 110 million land mines still lodged in the ground.
www.unicef.org/sowc96/9ldmines.htm

3A The pre-reading activity requires students to tell each other anything they know about Kalashnikov and his famous invention. You can if you wish give them the extra information in the **Background information** box above.

3B This is a scanning exercise, which uses the numbers and dates in the text. Students can locate the numbers quite easily and then read the surrounding words to get the context.

3 READING B **Answers**

1919: the year that Kalashnikov was born.
1947: the year that the Russian army started using the AK-47 (that year it won a competition for the design of a new submachine gun).
100 million: the number of AK-47s that have been manufactured.
300,000: the number of combat deaths every year in the 1990s (many of them caused by the AK-47).
40-plus: the number of wars in the 1990s.

3C Students now look at the expressions in bold in the text and explain the phrases in their own words. If you like, you can ask the students to work on this in groups, or it can even begin as a writing activity.

3 READING C **Suggested answers**

the world's most successful killing machine: the gun which has caused most deaths
300,000 annual combat deaths: the number of people killed every year in war
wars and conflicts of the 1990s: the word *conflicts* is usually given to fights where war has not actually been declared – for example, in the struggle between a government and an organisation of guerrillas or freedom fighters.
primary weapon: the weapon that people would choose first
a genie out of a bottle: (see the notes above) here it is used to mean *an uncontrollable force*
terrorists also want simple and reliable arms: Kalashnikov draws a parallel between government forces and others who have used his guns.

3D Finally, there are three more expressions from the text, with an *either / or* question about each one.

3 READING D **Answers**

1 I sleep soundly: he sleeps well
2 The Soviet government gave many of them away: the guns were free
3 The positive outweighs the negative: there are more good things than bad things

4 TALK ABOUT IT

Now that the students have dissected the text for meaning and language content, they can discuss the information and ideas contained in it. There are four questions for discussion and students are directed to **Language Bank 17**, where they will find cohesive words and expressions.

Note that these words are quite sophisticated discourse markers and they are not so easy to drop into a conversation. However (a good example!), when you listen to what your students say, you may hear a sentence where a cohesive device may have been useful. Our recommendation is not to stop the class, but to make a note and suggest it at the end of the discussion. Note also that the same discourse markers will be required to complete the writing task on the next page.

Picture notes

The two pictures reflect two aspects of worldwide peace movements. The left-hand photograph actually shows Rachel Corrie demonstrating in front of an Israeli-armoured bulldozer. You may not wish to point out to your students that this is a photograph of the actual scene that ended in her death. The right-hand picture shows the February 2003 peace demonstration passing the Roman Coliseum, where gladiators fought to the death 2000 years ago. The word on the multi-coloured flags is *pace*, Italian for *peace*. But the war started anyway in March 2003. You may want to read the **Background information** notes below to help you lead a discussion with the class, and also to find out more about two of the people who are mentioned in the listening text.

5 LISTEN IN CD 1 (Blue) track 9, Page 44 SB

The **Audio text** is in the **Workbook** (pages 67-68). It is an extract from a radio programme called *Peace News.* There are three items of news; the first concerns incidents involving two peace activists in Gaza, Rachel Corrie who was American and Tom Hurndall from Britain. Both Rachel and Tom were killed in separate incidents in Gaza. There is more about their stories in the **Background information** box below. The second news item is about Israeli air force pilots refusing to attack civilian targets in Palestine. The third is about the anti-war demonstrations that took place in the spring of 2003, just before the outbreak of hostilities in Iraq.

Background information / Internet references

The Gaza Strip is a narrow coastal strip of land in the Middle East, which is under the jurisdiction of the Palestinian authority. It is one of the most densely populated territories on Earth, with about 1.4 million residents in an area of 360 square kilometres. Parts of it were occupied by Israelis, but they were forced to withdraw from it by their government in 2005.

Rachel Corrie was a 23-year-old American peace activist who was crushed to death by a bulldozer as she tried to prevent the Israeli army from destroying Palestinian homes in the Gaza Strip in March 2003. Rachel's story has been made into a stage play. Young British photographer, Tom Hurndall, died as a result of being shot by an Israeli soldier in April 2003 in the town of Rafah, also in the Gaza Strip. He was trying to lead a child to safety.
http://www.rachelcorrie.org/
www.mynameisrachelcorrie.co.uk/
www.tomhurndall.co.uk

In early 2003 there were mass demonstrations in many cities of the world against the invasion of Iraq by American troops, with help from Britain and a few other countries, known by the American government as the 'Coalition of the Willing'. Italy was among the countries that took part. There was an anti-war demonstration in Rome on February 15th 2003 in which approximately a million people took part.
http://www.commondreams.org/headlines03/0215-10.htm

The Story of the 27 Israeli Defence Force pilots who refused to take part in attacks on the Palestinian Territories hit the news in September 2003. In light of the discussion and suggestions below about what is illegal and what is immoral, it is interesting to note that the pilots refused operations in the West Bank and Gaza because they considered them 'immoral and illegal'. At the same time, the deputy chief of the Israeli air force accused the pilots themselves of 'immoral' action.
http://news.bbc.co.uk/2/hi/middle_east/3140032.stm

Key words

- award • combat • conflict • creation
- decade • invent
- (anti-war) demonstration
- bulldozer • civilian target • conclude
- illegal • immoral • incident
- knock down • peace activist
- solution • tragic • volunteer

Note that we have identified *conflict* as a key word here, even though it appeared in the list of key words in the reading text earlier in the Unit. We do this because we are aware that teachers often skip items, or do them in an order, which may be different to that of the book.

You may want to start by asking students about the difference between *immoral* and *illegal.* However, we really **don't recommend** approaches like this:

- 'So ... what does *illegal* mean? And what does *immoral* mean?'

Or...

- 'Can anyone tell me the difference between *illegal* and *immoral*?'

Instead, we would recommend something like this: Write the two words *illegal* and *immoral* on the board, allow students to use their dictionaries if they need to, and then, in groups, get them to give an example of an illegal and / or an immoral act.

5A The pre-listening activity offers students the opportunity to say what they know about the Gaza Strip. Some of your students may have heard of the Gaza Strip but be unclear about where it actually is. In our experience, some students think that the Gaza Strip is part of the West Bank, the area east of the State of Israel that is under the jurisdiction of the Palestinian authority. There is information about the Gaza Strip in the **Background information** box above.

5B 1 The second pre-listening activity is designed to familiarise the students with some of the key words and expressions in the listening text. Here is a reminder of what we suggest in the Introduction about ways of doing this.

The list of words and expressions here is more or less the same as the list in the **Key words** box (above). Decide which of them the class probably already knows. Let's take the first word *volunteer.* Remember that we think that the approach of asking the question: *What does the word volunteer mean?* isn't actually a very good way to activate a word, whether it's being presented or revised.

Instead, we suggest giving examples involving the word under discussion, where an answer of *yes* or *no* from the students will indicate that they understand the meaning. Something like this:

Teacher: Let's talk about the word *volunteer.* Is a teacher a volunteer?
Students: No.
Teacher: OK. Imagine someone who works in a shelter for sick animals at the weekend. Is she a volunteer?
Students: Yes.
Teacher: Imagine you want to work for a bank when you leave school. *Volunteer*?
Students: No.

Then the conversation can move on to what volunteers actually do. Vocabulary gets activated more successfully if the teacher and the students engage in a dialogue, where the word gets repeated in different contexts.

5B 2 The final pre-listening activity offers students the chance to predict what the listening text will be about. They have the evidence of the title of the programme, *Peace News,* the photographs from the Gaza strip and Rome and the key vocabulary. Invite students to say what they think they will hear. Congratulate them whether they are right in their predictions or not.

5C Students now listen to the programme and then discuss if they were right in their predictions.

5D Finally, there are four questions for the class to answer. To answer them, students need to combine factual information from the radio programme and their own opinions.

5 LISTEN IN D — **Suggested answers**

1 Rachel Corrie was run over by a bulldozer because she was trying to prevent Palestinian homes from being destroyed.
2 Tom Hurndall was trying to take children to a safe place.
3 Students should give their own opinions.
4 The London demonstration was the biggest ever seen in Britain.

6 CONTROVERSY See Role cards Page 61-62 WB

Read the notes about this section in the Introduction. This is a formal debate. In a formal debate, four speakers speak. Two defend a motion and two oppose it. The first speaker proposes the motion (speaks in favour of it) and he / she is followed by the first opposing speaker. The third person to speak is the second speech in favour of the motion, and the last person to speak gives the second opposing speech. There are role cards for each of the speakers.

There is a basic problem with the staging of a debate: if only four people are going to speak, when do they prepare it and what do the others do while they're preparing? There are various possible answers to this question.

1 The whole class can prepare in groups of four, and then the teacher chooses one group to actually do it.
2 The teacher invites the whole class to read the role cards and then asks for volunteers for each role. They then work on what they are going to say during free periods.
3 The teacher arranges who is going to speak, then gives the four students time to work on what they are going to say while the rest of the class does something else, **Workbook** exercises, for example. If they do this, they will have to go to another room where they can talk.

A debate can be fun to watch, and the non-speakers can think of questions to ask the speakers. The class should be required to listen respectfully to the speakers and make notes of anything they want to question them about. All four speakers should finish before the rest of the class ask questions, or give their opinions. Questions can be directed at an individual speaker, a team or the whole panel of four speakers. Encourage students to make it clear who they are directing their questions at. Give them strategies for how to put their questions. For example:

- *I would like to ask Pedro / the last speaker to explain what he meant when he said …*
- *I would like to ask all the speakers what they think about …*

7 PORTFOLIO WRITING

The writing task is to write an article for a magazine. There are notes about writing an article on page 34 (Unit 7), but in this case, we want students to use the target language of the Unit to express their opinions. The instructions here are quite different, so we have included a different model below.

<u>Writing model</u> – **article for a peace magazine**

Interesting headline: Millions on the march

Interesting introduction: I spent last Saturday in Rome, a great city to spend some free time. There are amazing places to visit, great food and maybe the chance to see a fantastic soccer match. But I had more important things on my mind.

Opinions and reason: We went to Rome to be part of the biggest anti-war demonstration the country has ever seen. More than a million people took to the streets in protest at the military intentions of the United States and her allies, including Italy. We did it because we felt strongly that it was wrong to go to war against Iraq.

Support your opinion: The US government thinks that Iraq has weapons of mass destruction. Maybe they do, but in our opinion, the problem can be solved in other ways.

Arguments for the other side: On the other hand, it could be said that Iraq had a dangerous leader who had to be removed. However, if you start removing heads of state because you don't like them, where will it all end?

Conclusion: It was great to be part of such a wonderful march. There was a great sense of purpose. Consequently, we felt that we had had a great weekend and achieved something important.

<u>Picture notes / Internet reference</u>

The picture on this page is a very evocative image of a United Nations soldier and a child in Africa. Before you do anything else, ask students what they think is going on. Why is the soldier comforting the child? Do soldiers usually comfort children? Why is the soldier wearing a blue helmet? There is more information about UN peace missions on this website:
http://www.un.org/Depts/dpko/dpko/index.asp

8 *PEACE STUDIES in English* Page 45 SB

<u>Key words / expressions</u>

• civilians • conflict zone • contributors
• failure • genocide • (military) operation
• peacekeepers • peacekeeping • sky-blue

Background information / Internet references

The United Nations is an international organisation of nations which was founded in 1945 by 51 states. It was hoped that by uniting nations, it would be possible to prevent conflict between them. It now has more than 190 member states. UN headquarters are in New York.

The Nobel Peace Prize is one of five Nobel prizes, the gift of Swedish industrialist Alfred Nobel. According to Nobel's request, the prize is awarded to 'the person who does the most or the best work for fraternity between the nations.' The Peace Prize is awarded annually in Oslo, Norway. The other Nobel prizes, for physics, chemistry, medicine and literature, are awarded in Stockholm.

The Cold War was the name given to the struggle between the United States and the former USSR – the Union of Soviet Socialist Republics, also known as the Soviet Union. The Cold War lasted from the late 1940s, after the end of the Second World War, until the early 1990s, when the Soviet Union split up into independent nation states. The struggle was widely called the Cold War because it did not involve direct armed conflict between the contestants. Even so, the years of the Cold War were the time of the largest build-up of conventional and nuclear weapons on both sides.

The Bosnian War was one of many conflicts that took place between the various states of former Yugoslavia in the 1990s. The population of Bosnia-Herzegovina, like the other Yugoslavian states, was a mixture of many different peoples. The Bosnia-Herzegovina declaration of sovereignty in October 1991 and independence referendum in February 1992 led to conflict between all the ethnic groups, Bosnians, Bosnian Serbs and other groups. The worst of many terrible events in the conflict was the massacre of Bosnians by Serbs at Srebrenica in 1995.

Another conflict that is mentioned in the text is the conflict in **Rwanda** in 1995, where an estimated 800,000 Tutsis and some moderate Hutus were killed by extremist Hutu militia forces.

www.hrw.org/reports/1999/rwanda/Geno1-3-04.htm#P95_39230

Peace Studies is now established as a university course of study in many places. In the UK probably best known for this is the University of Bradford. See: http://www.bradford.ac.uk/acad/peace/

The main text of this cross-curricular section is a reading passage about the work of the United Nations peace-keeping forces.

8A1 Students are asked to share what they know about four aspects of the information which occurs in the reading text. The following is information for you to help them.

8A2 Before reading, students are asked to predict which countries provide UN peacekeeping forces. Students who follow politics will probably guess that the Scandinavian countries or perhaps Canada provide troops and support.

8A3 Students now scan the text to find the names of the countries which actually do provide troops. They will probably be surprised to discover that the main contributors during the 21st century have been the Asian nations of Pakistan, Bangladesh and India and also the West African nation, Ghana.

8B Students read the text and look for specific information.

8 *PEACE STUDIES in English* A / B Answers

A 2 / 3 the main contributors to the UN peace-keeping force during the 21st century have been the Asian nations of Pakistan, Bangladesh and India and also the West African nation, Ghana.

B 1 The first UN peacekeeping mission was in the Middle East at the time of the 1948 Arab-Israeli conflict.

2 Peacekeeping operations were the idea of Canadian Foreign Minister Lester Pearson.

3 The UN failed in Rwanda and Bosnia.

8C Finally, students are invited to comment on two statements relating to the UN and international conflict. You may want to put the students in small groups to discuss the two statements, who can then tell the rest of the class what they thought.

9 INTERACTIVE TASK

Read the notes about this section in the Introduction. The interactive task, as usual, requires students to work in groups of four, who work in two pairs. First of all, the two pairs make notes of their thoughts about two given questions. Pair A start the discussion, and the aim of the activity is for Pair B to try to take control of the situation, leading to an exchange of views. It is important for each pair to remember that when they try to take control of the conversation, they must do it respectfully and politely.

10 *Your answer:*

As always, the Unit finishes with a re-assessment of *The BIG question*. As we often do, we suggest three supplementary questions, and suggested ways of answering them. We recommend that you read out the questions one by one, let the students read the example opinions, and then offer their own.

Workbook answers — Pages 22-23 WB

1 Language: cohesive words

1A *Alternative answers are possible*

1 however, moreover **2** on the other hand
3 also **4** however
5 moreover, nevertheless **6** however

1B **1** Consequently **2** In the same way
3 For example **4** As a result
5 In addition **6** However / also

2 Use of English

2A *Alternative answers are possible*

1 I'm not interested in stories about war.
2 The soldiers don't intend to leave.
3 The peacekeepers managed to stop the fighting.
4 They've been attacking the city since nine a.m.

2B **1** (i) go to war **2** (b) demonstration
3 (c) marched **4** (d) singing
5 (g) demonstrators **6** (j) no **7** (a) them
8 (h) march **9** (e) who **10** (f) until

3 Portfolio writing

Students' own answers

4 Connections

4A **1** (b) fired **2**(a) joined **3** (a) made
4 (a) shot **5** (b) go to **6** (a) them

4B *Alternative answers are possible*

1 terrorists, civilians **2** terrorists
3 sailors **4** officers
5 prisoners **6** officers, soldiers

4C *Students' own answers*

1 War is terrible. A war is going on in Africa.
2 There was a civil war between different tribes in Rwanda. There was a war between Britain and Germany in the 1940s.
3 There was an important battle at Waterloo during the Napoleonic Wars.
4 The two countries decided to make peace. Peace is something we all dream about.

4D **1** (a) **2** (b) **3** (a) **4** (a)

What's new?

Subject:	Society and living standards
Function:	Expressing wishes and hopes
Grammar:	Verb patterns after *wish* and *hope*

Before you open the book ...
Write the title of the Unit on the board: *I must have one of those!* Ask the class what they think the Unit is about and elicit answers, teaching vocabulary as it arises, (*eg It's about the consumer society*). Tell students that the topic is *Society and living standards* (= the way in which people live, *eg* how comfortable their houses are or how much money they have to spend).

1 *The BIG question:* HOW MUCH IS ENOUGH?

FACT: There are over 9.5 million US dollar millionaires in the world. Meanwhile over 2.8 billion people live on less than two dollars a day.

Picture notes

Picture **1** shows African women sharing out beans from sacks. This is food aid – basic supplies donated to people in famine areas, in this case in East Africa, where crops have failed because of wars and drought.

Picture **2** shows young boys queuing to fill buckets of water at a public water tap. Obviously there is no clean water supply to their homes. Over a billion people in the world have to drink polluted water every day.

Picture **3** shows an open sports car with two people in it.

Picture **4** shows a motor-yacht. It is often called a powerboat. The object of these two pictures is to show that even if, to some people, cars and boats are a necessity, these are plainly luxury items, playthings for people who have enough money and time to enjoy a form of consumption that is not available to many communities that do not have the basics such as food and water.

Write *The BIG question* on the board. Ask: *How many in the class think they have enough?* You may need to clarify that *enough* means enough money, enough of the things they want. Count the show of hands. Ask those who put up their hands why they feel they have enough. Elicit answers. Ask: *How many in the class don't think they have enough and want more?* Again, count the show of hands. Ask members of the second group why they don't feel they have enough. Elicit answers.

Read out the **FACT**. Check students understand the difference between *a million* and *a billion* (= a thousand million). Ask students: *Does this* (the **FACT**) *surprise you?* Elicit reactions (*eg Yes, I didn't think there were so many rich people*). Elicit / teach the word *wealthy* as a synonym for *rich*. NB: The statistics change each year. See www.us.capgemini.com.

2 PREVIEW

Words

A Check students understand the words *luxury* (= something expensive that you enjoy but do not really need) and *necessity* (= some-thing that you must have or must do). Ask students for their answers and see if agreement can be reached on which items are luxuries and which are necessities.

B Question **1** refers to picture **1**. Elicit the fact that the African women in the picture are buying beans (you can see the words PINTO BEANS on the side of the sacks.) You may need to teach the word *beans*. Elicit the fact that beans are an important food in developing countries, and that the women in the picture probably live on very little money.

Elicit answers to question **2**. Students' answers may be very different, depending on which country they come from. An important point is that for students, who are well-known for having very little money, certain foods may be luxuries that are not regarded as luxuries by older people with good jobs. In question **3**, Students will probably know that it is Africa that has the most problems with drinking water, due to the droughts (= a long period of time when there is little or no rain) that regularly occur there.

C Put students into pairs to discuss these questions. Question **2**: The car in the photo is quite luxurious. It is a convertible. Elicit answers: *eg These days a car is a necessity, you can't get around otherwise. / A yacht is definitely a luxury. / You have to be wealthy to own a yacht.*

D Question **1**: Make sure that students understand that *mp3 player* and *iPod* refer to the same thing (= a little machine that you carry with you that has headphones and can store a great deal of music). Check that students understand the phrase *hi-fi* (= a piece of electronic equipment that is used for playing music). The word *stereo* refers to more or less the same thing. Elicit answers from the class: *eg I put my mobile phone first / I put the dishwasher last*, and ask students for their reasons, *eg I use my mobile to text my friends. That's very important to me.* Students can remain in pairs to discuss questions **2** and **3**. The answer to question **3** depends a great deal on the country. In New York, $2 will buy you very little but might buy three days' food in some African countries.

2 PREVIEW Words B **Answers**

B 1 Photo **1** shows sacks of beans (pinto beans). The people buying it are African women. The beans are probably sold in a local market. Beans are a staple food, eaten by people in developing countries.
2 Open answer: Some examples of luxury food for westerners: caviar, lobster, crab, truffles.
3 People have problems getting drinking water (picture **3** shows this situation) in countries where there is drought, *eg* in parts of tropical Africa.

Language

This section introduces verb patterns after *hope* and *wish*. See the **Workbook** for more explanation of these structures.

Verb patterns after *hope*

The second sentence is an example of the most common structure following *hope*:
I hope (that) one of them offers me a place. Hope can be followed by either the present simple or the future simple, but it always refers to the future. Ask students to make sentences about their hopes, *eg I hope I do well in my exams.*

The first sentence – *He is hoping to start a business* – gives an example of the structure *hope* + *to* + verb. It is rather more formal than the second sentence and often has the meaning *I hope that I can / am able to* (*He is hoping that he can start a business).* Ask students to make sentences beginning *I hope to …*

Verb patterns after *wish*

The last sentence – *I wish we hadn't moved* – refers to a past situation and is dealt with more fully in Unit 16. The structure *wish* + past simple, *eg I wish I had a TV in my room* refers to an ongoing present situation that you would like to change but do not think will change. (*I haven't got a TV, but I'd like to have one.*). Hence the situation is 'unlikely' (Question **B**). Here are some more examples:

- I wish my boyfriend rang me more often. *(He doesn't ring me.)*
- I wish I had more money. *(I haven't got much money.)*
- I wish my flat was bigger *(It's small.)*
- I wish it wasn't raining. *(It is raining.)*

Ask students to make their own sentences about present situations that they wish were different.

The structure *wish* + *would* + *verb* refers to a present or future situation where there is an element of choice.

- I wish he would ring. *(He could ring if he wanted.)*
- I wish they would explain. *(They can explain if they want to.)*

It is important to note that while *wish* + past simple always refers to an ongoing situation, or something that happens regularly, *eg I wish my boss paid me more*, *wish* + *would* often refers to a future situation that happens only once, *eg I wish they would leave.* With this latter example, you cannot say, *I wish they left,* as it would imply their leaving is an ongoing situation and not a single event. However, *I wish my boss would pay me more,* is perfectly correct.

Because of the element of choice in *wish + would,* we cannot say *I wish + I + would, eg I wish I would stop smoking.* (If I want to stop smoking, why don't I? Because I have no choice – I can't stop.) Instead we must say, *I wish I could stop smoking.* To give another example, we do not say, *I wish my son would read (because he is having difficulty reading).* Instead we would say, *I wish my son could read.*

To conclude, it is clear from the above notes that *wish + would* is a complex structure. Do not expect students to grasp all its complexities immediately. Instead, make sure that students understand that:

1 We MUST use *wish + would* to refer to something in the future that happens only once.
2 We cannot use the structure when there is no choice involved.

Write these sentences on the board and ask students to make sentences from them using *wish + would:*

1 Our guests are staying too long. (I wish they'd leave.)
2 You could help me if you wanted. (I wish you'd help me.)
3 My husband spends too much money. (I wish he'd spend less money.)
4 You should get another job. (I wish you'd get another job.)
5 My employers don't believe me. (I wish they would believe me.)

Finally, ask students to say for which sentences from the above could one also use the structure *wish + past simple.* The answers: *I wish he spent less money / I wish they believed me,* since both could also suggest an ongoing situation.

2 PREVIEW Language A / B / C / D / E / F
Answers

A The first and second sentences.
B The last two sentences.
C Sentences three and four.
D The final sentence.
E The first three sentences.
F The third sentence.

Ideas

Students will probably have very different reactions to the sentences, and it should be interesting to elicit their reactions. Do the students think that money can buy happiness? These sentences are taken from the text on the opposite page. Ask students to predict what they think it will be about (the pictures on the opposite page will provide some clues.) Elicit answers and teach any vocabulary that arises, but don't tell students if they are correct, as they will find out in the next session.

3 READING CD 2 (Red) track 11, Page SB 47

Key words / expressions
- banker • lawyer • gadget • coast
- financial advisor • former • feed • duck
- to adjust • to apply to • to go crazy
- Wales • Welsh
- to downshift = to choose to live in a less expensive and simpler way
- view = the things that you can see from a particular place
- panoramic view = when you can see a long way in all directions
- to go crazy = to go mad

This article describes the choice of two high-earning Londoners who give up their stressful jobs and expensive lifestyle, and move with their four children to a village on the coast of Wales (see **Background information** notes below) in order to live a simpler and less stressful life.

3A Tell students that they should be able to work out the meaning of *downshifting* by reading the text. Remind them that they should not try and understand every word at this point. Elicit answers and explain the meanings if necessary.

3B / C / D Activities **B-D** demand a more detailed reading of the text. For activity **B**, ask students to close their books and try and answer without looking at the text.

Picture notes / Background information

The portrait of the family group is by an artist called Luke Martineau. See http://www.lukemartineau.com/gallery/index.htm

Wales: The UK (United Kingdom) is composed of four parts, England, Northern Ireland, Scotland and Wales. Wales is in the west of the UK. It consists mainly of moorland and mountains and has an economy that is mostly agricultural, with an industrial area in the south, around the capital, Cardiff. There used to be many coal mines in South Wales, but they have been closed over the last 30 years. See http://www.welshcoalmines.co.uk/.

Since 1997, Wales has been largely self-governing, with its own National Assembly. See: http://www.bbc.co.uk/wales/storyofwelsh/content/devolutionandthelanguage.shtml

The national language of Wales is Welsh. It is an optional subject in Welsh schools and is spoken by some people as a first language and in addition to English in north Wales. There is a Welsh language TV station. See http://www.s4c.co.uk/

3 READING A / B / C / D **Answers**

A 1 Not really. Downshifting means to live in a less expensive and simpler way.
2 The two younger children, Paul and Daphne, are happy with the change. The two older children, Melissa and Joel, aren't very happy.
B 1 Because they were always stressed and spent very little time with each other or the children.
2 Rupert was a banker, Emma was a successful lawyer. They earned over £150,000 a year. The children were all at expensive private schools. The family took luxury holidays and owned a lot of expensive gadgets.
3 Their work life is very different and much less stressed. Rupert is hoping to start a business as a financial advisor. Emma looks after the house and works part-time in her daughter's school. The family now live in the countryside, with beautiful views from their house. They have less money and can't afford to give their children iPods.
C 1 Their new house is as big as their house in London.
2 In the garden you can see the nearby hills.
3 Paul is unhappy because he misses London and doesn't like the boys and girls in the village.
D **1** Daphne **2** Melissa **3** Joel

4 TALK ABOUT IT

Questions **1** and **2** give students the opportunity to use *I wish…*

Encourage them to complete the following sentences:

1 In the next year I hope to have ....
2 In the next five years I hope to have ....
3 In the next ten years I hope to have ....

Question **3** should lead to an interesting discussion. To help things along, ask this question: *Why do we need time?* Example answers: *I need time to relax / I need to time to see my friends / I need time to read and watch TV / I need time to think.*

Optional activity: Ask the class if they think that Rupert and Emma Woods made the right decision when they moved to Wales. Students' answers will reveal a lot about their attitudes to money, time and also relationships.

5 LISTEN IN CD 1 (Blue) track 10, Page 48 SB

Key words / expressions

- to recycle • to throw away
- tons of waste • truck • plastic (bottle)
- (computer) component • cell phone
- well-organised • to register • association
- to set up • to control • income
- massive • smell • foul • to risk
- injury • disease • medical waste
- syringe • chemicals
- economy = the system by which a country's money and goods are produced and used
- global economy = the idea that the world has a single economy
- garbage (AE) / rubbish (BE) dump = a place where we throw away our rubbish
- tons of waste = a ton is a Unit for measuring weight and is equal to 1016 kilograms. We use the expression *tons of* (something) to say that there is a great deal of something
- scavenger = someone who searches through things that other people have thrown away to

see if there is anything that he / she wants
- city authority = the organizations that control a city
- toxic fumes = poisonous gases
- rotting meat = meat that is old and no longer safe to eat

Note that a number of the more difficult vocabulary items are explained in activity **B.** The **Audio text** is in the **Workbook** (page 68). The listening passage describes the *garbage economy* that exists in countries such as Brazil and South Africa. The phrase *garbage economy* refers to whole sections of society who make a living by recycling other people's garbage. The passage describes how these people visit vast garbage dumps and go through them looking for items that can be recycled, such as computer components, plastic bottles, white paper.

The passage describes two groups of scavengers. The first group are from Brasilia (the capital of Brazil), where more than 3,000 people live off what the city throws away. The second group is a family from Soweto, which is 15 kilometres from the centre of Johannesburg, the financial capital of South Africa.

5A Write the phrase *the garbage economy* on the board and check students understand the meaning of the words *garbage* and *economy* when used separately. Then ask students to look at the photograph and elicit the fact that it is a picture of a *garbage / rubbish dump* – you will probably need to teach this phrase. Now ask the class to work out the meaning of *garbage economy* by looking at the photo. They will probably be able to work out that people make a living by finding things in the dump that they can recycle or sell. Explain that people who do this are known as *scavengers* (See *to scavenge* above). Explain that students will listen to a report about the garbage economy.

5B These vocabulary items are key words and phrases in the listening passage. Students should be able to do this exercise quite easily. If they have dictionaries, allow them to use them.

5C This activity is useful preparation for the listening passage, as it makes students think about the subject matter and how the vocabulary items are likely to fit in. Elicit answers but don't tell students if they are correct.

5D The passage is not easy, and the class will find it helpful if you divide the questions into two parts. Questions **1-3** are fairly general, so these questions can comprise Part **1**. Ask the class to listen and answer questions **1-3** only. They may need to hear the passage two or even three times in order to answer the questions. You may need to point out that the answers to question **3** are in the listening passage: Brasilia is *the nation's capital,* and Johannesburg is *the financial capital of South Africa* (but not the capital, which is Cape Town, although we are not told this in the listening passage). Students then read questions **4-9**. They listen and then answer the questions.

5E Students will probably need to listen again in order to pick up the similarities and differences between the two reports.

Similarities

Both reports describe the location of the dump, what people collect and how much money they can expect to make.

Differences

The Brazil report is a general report, whereas the South African report describes the life of a woman who lives as a scavenger. The Brazil report explains that the scavenging is well-organized. Scavengers in South Africa do not sound so well-organised. The South African report emphasizes the dangers of scavenging.

5 LISTEN IN B / C **Answers**

B **1** (b) **2** (d) **3** (e) **4** (a) **5** (h) **6** (c) **7** (f) **8** (g)

C **1** Brazil and South Africa

2 In Brazil, the dump is less than 20 kilometres from the centre of the nation's capital, Brasilia. In South Africa the dump is 15 kilometres from the centre of Johannesburg, the financial capital of South Africa.

3 Brasilia is 'the nation's capital, but Johannesburg is 'the financial capital', not the real capital (which is Cape Town).

4 More than 3,000 people.
5 Plastic bottles, computer components, other electronic items, clothes, shoes, watches, cell phones, white paper, clear plastic.
6 In Brasilia, they are well-organised. People have to register with an association if they want to work at the dump.
7 In Brasilia, people make from less than $20 a week up to $60 a week. In Soweto, Mapule Mohokare and her son usually make about $25 a week.
8 They're hoping to find things they can sell, like working watches and cell phones. They're also hoping to make more money than usual.
9 Because dumps have large amounts of medical waste, *eg* used syringes, there are also toxic fumes from rotting meat and chemicals.

6 CONTROVERSY

See Role cards Page 62 WB

Read the notes about this section in the Introduction. There is a role card for Group A and a role card for Group B. This means that students will be debating in groups of 8, with four students in group A and four students in group B.

Put students into their groups and hand out the role cards for each group. Explain that students will not necessarily be arguing according to their real opinion.Write the subject on the board: *Poverty is the most important problem in the world.* Check students understand the word *poverty* (= when people are extremely poor). In their groups students should discuss the arguments they will put forward to support their point of view. When they have done this, if you feel they need the help, elicit students' arguments and put them up on the board under two headings:
Poverty is the most important problem in the world / Poverty is not the most important problem in the world. Teach new vocabulary where needed. Here are some arguments both for and against:

Poverty is the most important problem in the world...

- It is wrong to ignore the suffering of millions of people.
- It is wrong that millions of people do not have enough food, water and money to live.
- It is possible to get rid of world poverty, if all the rich countries decide to do so.
- We could easily become poor ourselves. How will we feel then?
- Millions of people in developing countries are poor. Globalisation (see **Background information** notes below) only benefits rich countries. This situation needs to change.
- It would benefit the world economy if there were no poverty.

Poverty is NOT the most important problem in the world...

- There are other more important problems, for example, global warming, and the threat of terrorism from Islamic extremists.
- Poverty in a country is often caused by corrupt governments. If you give these governments money, they will just put it away in secret bank accounts.
- The most important task for governments is to maintain the world economy and make sure that it does well.

When the students are in their groups debating the subject, walk round and listen, making notes of mistakes, which you can then correct afterwards or in a later session.

Background information

Globalisation: People around the globe are more connected to each other than ever before. Information and money flow more quickly than ever. Goods and services produced in one part of the world are increasingly available in all parts of the world. International travel is more frequent. Multi-national companies like Toyota, Nike and McDonalds, act on a global scale with manufacturing bases in several countries.

Anti-globalisation: This term is commonly used to describe the attitude of those who protest against global trade agreements since they believe that these agreements often have negative consequences for the poor and for the environment.

7 PORTFOLIO WRITING

Go through the list of items in the activity, eliciting from students how much each thing is likely to cost. This should provoke discussion and also introduce some useful language for the writing task itself. Students then write the email, either in class or for homework.

Writing model

Hi (Juan)
Yes, I'm afraid that you will find that things are much more expensive over here. Here is a list of what some basic things are likely to cost in London.

If you share a flat with three or four people, you will probably pay between £400 and £500 a month, depending on the area. You'd be lucky to find somewhere at £300 a month.

With regard to entertainment, cinema tickets cost about £6, and a pint of beer costs about £3. To get into a club, you can pay anything between £6 and £15. If you go to street markets you can find cheap clothes, for example, you can find a pair of jeans for about £5. Charity shops are great for finding cheap second-hand clothes (even fashionable things) and also some of the supermarkets sell very cheap clothes. As for a cup of coffee in a café, it depends on the area again. It can cost anything from 60p to £4. The best place to buy cheap food is from street markets. There are a couple of supermarkets where the food is low-priced. Expect to spend about £35 a week.

See you when you get here.

Jane

8 *SOCIAL STUDIES in English* Page 49 SB

Key words / expressions
- essential • to increase • quarter
- population • washing machine • campaign
- proper • CD player • access
- to lack = to not have something or not have enough of something
- to go /do without = to manage, even though you do not have something you need
- to afford = to have enough money to pay for something
- to lift (children) out of poverty = to give (children) a better life, out of poverty
- to miss out on = to not have the chance to do something important or that you would enjoy
- after-school activity = things that children do after school, *eg* ballet, music lessons, riding, sports, martial arts classes
- satellite television = television programmes that are sent to your television by satellite

Write the title of the page on the board – *Social Studies in English.* Check students understand the word *social* (= relating to human society and the way it is organised). Ask the class what kind of thing you study in *Social Studies* and elicit answers, *eg poverty and the reasons for it, crime and the reasons for it, types of housing and its effect on people, different ethnic groups and their relations to each other.* Write the title of the text on the board – *Child poverty in Britain* – and, as preparation, ask students what they think the text might say. Elicit answers and use the opportunity to teach relevant vocabulary.

8A Students read the text and answer the questions. They should be able to work out the answers to question **2** from the context of the sentences.

8B Point to the graph at the bottom of the page and elicit / teach the word *graph.* Check students understand the vocabulary items listed there. Ask students to explain what the graph shows – the percentage of people who think the items are necessary and the percentage who can't afford the items. If students have not used the phrase *can't afford* before, take the opportunity to teach it and explain that it is a very common phrase, *eg I can't afford it / I can't afford to buy a car.*

Students list the items in the graph in the order of importance in their own lives. Ask students to read out their lists, and elicit reactions, *eg I think it's far more important to have a holiday abroad each year than to have satellite television.*

Optional activity: Ask students to look closely at the graph and say what surprises / doesn't surprise them, for example, *It surprises me that for many people a car is necessary. If you live in a big city, you don't need a car. / I absolutely agree that two meals a day and fresh fruit and vegetables are high on the list of necessary items.*

8 *SOCIAL STUDIES in English* **Answers**
A 1 Items that more than 50% of people believe they should be able to afford, for example, washing machines and televisions.
2 Yes, more or less.

9 CONVERSATION

Read the notes about this section in the Introduction. This activity allows students to choose which activity they want to do, **A**, **B** or **C**. However, if you feel the class need practice in describing pictures, ask them to do activity **A**.

9A Prepare for the activity by putting students into pairs. Ask them to choose other pictures in the book and use language from **Language Bank 12** to ask and answer questions about the pictures. Now ask students to choose a photo from this Unit that they would like to use as a basis for discussion. Explain that Student A should ask questions and Student B should respond. They should begin by describing the picture and then go on to discuss the topic that the picture suggests. The vocabulary for most of the pictures has been taught in previous sessions. However, you could briefly elicit / teach useful vocabulary for the picture on this page:
- The boys are playing on a pile of rubble.
- One of the boys is holding a cricket bat.
- Perhaps they're playing in a derelict house.
- The boys obviously live in a poor area.

9B Students will have acquired quite a lot of the vocabulary needed for these topics. However, if you feel students need help to discuss the topics before they go into pairs, then hold a preliminary discussion and use the opportunity to teach vocabulary and correct grammar mistakes. In answer to the question in **B**, encourage students to use the conditional form *would, eg I think they'd laugh or feel angry.* Write a second question on the board for students to discuss:
- For people who live on less than $2 a day, what are the real necessities of life?

9C Here are some answers to the question: *What do you think causes poverty?*
1 Lack of education / A poor (= bad) education: If you don't have a good education, you can't get a good job.
2 Corrupt governments: governments that use their country's money for private enrichment, not for the people.
3 Overpopulation: If there are too many people, then unemployment can be a problem.
4 Globalisation (See **Background information** notes above) can benefit rich countries more than poor countries.

10 *Your answer:*

Here is a suggestion for a different approach to ***Your answer:***

Students get into pairs, and in turn are given one minute to answer the first question. Students find a new partner and again, in turn, are given one minute to answer the second question. Finally, students find a third partner and repeat the process with the third question. Most students should be able to do this by simply turning in their seats.

Workbook answers — Pages 24-25 WB

1 Language: verb patterns after *wish* and *hope*

1A 1 I hope to become very rich. / I hope that I'll / I become very rich.
2 I hope that it won't be / isn't cold today.
3 Anna hopes to have her own flat one day. / Anna hopes that she owns / will own her own flat one day.
4 I hope to own a yacht one day. / I hope that I'll / I own a yacht one day.
5 We hope that she succeeds / she'll succeed.

1B 1 I wish I didn't have to share with my brother.
2 I wish we didn't live in such a selfish society.
3 I wish my father could afford a new car.
4 I wish my girlfriend wasn't so extravagant.

5 He wishes he didn't have to work so hard.

1C **1** I wish rich countries would do more to help more countries.
2 I wish the government would put more money into education.
3 I wish my parents would give me more money.
4 I wish I could find a better job.

1D **1** ✓ **2** I wish I knew more wealthy people.
3 ✓ **4** I wish Jenny had more time to relax.

2 Use of English

2A **1** She couldn't afford to buy food for her children.
2 Unless they work quickly, the trucks arrive and bury the garbage.
3 The city authority has set up an association so that they can control the numbers of workers.
4 He spent ten hours every day working in his office.

2B **(1)** as **(2)** called **(3)** by **(4)** where **(5)** were **(6)** raised **(7)** such **(8)** held **(9)** Instead **(10)** state / condition / plight

3 Portfolio writing

Students' own answers

4 Connections

4A **1** extravagant **2** mean **3** penniless **4** wealthy **5** generous

4B • *poverty / the poor: poverty* is a noun meaning *when people are extremely poor. The poor* refers to people who are poor (similarly, we say *the rich, the sick*).
• *cost of living / standard of living: The cost of living* refers to the amount of money that people need to pay for basic things. *Standard of living* refers to the type of life a person or society has according to the amount of money they have.
• *economics / economy: Economics* is the study of the way in which money, goods and services are produced and used. *The economy* is the system by which a country's trade, industry and money are organised.
• *developed / developing*: (when referring to countries) A *developed* country has a lot of industries. A *developing* country is poor and does not have many industries.

4C **1** the cost of living **2** economy **3** Developed **4** the poor

What's new?

Subject: Habits and obsessions
Function: Evaluating options
Grammar: *though, even though, although, in spite of, despite*

Before you open the book ...

The word *globesity* may be new to the students. It is a recently-coined word which combines the words *global* and *obesity*. 'Obese' in medical terms means being 20% or more above your ideal weight, 'overweight' means being anything up to 20% above your ideal weight. Being overweight is unhealthy, being obese is dangerous.

The topic of the Unit is the global epidemic of obesity. This may be a sensitive issue for some of your students, and therefore we suggest that you think about the consequences of working on this material if there are any overweight students in the class.

Even though it may be a sensitive issue, we felt that it was one that should be faced. Statistics suggest that, unless things change radically in the next few years, obesity may become a bigger threat to life than illnesses such as AIDS, malaria or cancer.

The facts speak for themselves. In the United States as an example, more than half of American adults are overweight, approximately one third are obese. See the **Background information** below to see what an effect this has on national health care.

Before you open the book, you may want to turn the following set of statistics into a gap-fill prediction quiz. Just photocopy this section. The answers are below.

QUIZ – Weight of the world

1 The World Health Organisation (WHO) estimates that the number of obese adults worldwide jumped from (a) .... million to (b) .... million between 1995 and 2000.

2 WHO also estimates that more than (a) .... million children around the world under the age of five are overweight.

3 Adult obesity rates average (a) .... in the United States, 24% in Mexico, and (b) .... in Great Britain. The rate is still a mere 11.3% in France, but that figure has risen from (c) .... since 2000.

4 In Greece, home of the 'healthy Mediterranean diet', more than (a) .... of adults 'are above their ideal size,' according to *The New York Times*.

5 About (a) .... of European adults will be obese by 2030, partly because of an emerging epidemic of obesity among children and adolescents.

6 Approximately (a) .... of Australian children and adolescents are currently overweight or obese.

7 In China, obesity is highest among wealthier city-dwellers, where one in every ten children is considered (a) ....

8 In Chile, (a) .... of children are overweight or obese.

9 Only (a) .... of 11-year-old English boys and 37% of girls exercise for two hours a week or more.

10 In a National Survey of Primary and Middle Schools in Japan between 1970 and 1997, obesity in 9 year-old children increased by (a) ....%.

1 *The BIG question:* ARE PEOPLE GETTING BIGGER?

FACT: More than a quarter of the people in the world (1.2 billion) are overweight. Of these, 300 million are obese.

Weight of the world		**Answers**
1 (a) 200 (b) 300	**2** (a) 17.5 million	
3 (a) 30% (b) 22%	**4** (a) 70%	
5 (a) half	**6** (a) 20%	**7** (a) obese
8 (a) 30%	**9** (a) 45%	**10** (a) 300%

If you did the background test suggested above, then the question is easily answered and the FACT will come as no surprise. Look at the photos. Ask students if they can give reasons for this epidemic. Questions **2A** and **2B** are based on the photos.

2 PREVIEW

Words

A This exercise makes sure that students know the exact meaning of *overweight* (heavier than you want to be for comfort) and *obese* (heavier than you should be for good health).

B This is a discussion about the people in the photos and their lifestyles. How do people get to look like this? Is it a medical condition or their lifestyle?

C This activity is a series of agree / disagree statements. As we often do in this book, we offer examples of opinions and ideas that the students can study before offering their own. They may not agree with any of the opinions that we suggest, but we feel that it is useful for them to see these models in order to help them express themselves on this topic. Allow the students some thinking time, and then let them compare their answers with others.

Language

The language point of this Unit looks at the meaning and use of the words *although, even though, though, in spite of* and *despite.* These are the kinds of words that can increase the sophistication of the students' speaking and writing, and it is important for them to learn to use them correctly. The structure words need to be presented before students read the examples in the **Language** section. So, how can we present them?

though, although, even though:

Technical stuff first – *though, although, even though* are conjunctions. *Though* is probably the easiest to present, as you can easily substitute it for *but.* It is more common in spoken than in written English. It can come in a different position – at the end of the phrase rather than the beginning – especially in spoken English. As you can see from these examples, in written English, it can mean turning one sentence into two.

- She's doing her best to lose weight, **but** she finds it very hard.
- She's doing her best to lose weight. She finds it very hard, **though**.

Once you have taught the meaning and use of *though,* you can use the same example to demonstrate the use of *although.*

- **Although** she's doing her best to lose weight, she finds it very hard.

This sounds more formal and is really useful in written English. Note that in spoken English, *although* at the beginning of a phrase like this is often reduced to *though.*

- **Though** she's doing her best to lose weight, she finds it very hard.

You can explain this as sheer laziness on the part of native speakers!

Even though really means the same as *although.* You can make a distinction by saying that it is more emphatic and indicates that you are surprised.

- **Even though** he's only 14, he weighs more than 100 kilos!!

In spite of, despite

In spite of and despite are prepositions, not conjunctions, and despite (!) some people trying to suggest otherwise, they mean exactly the same thing. Like the words above, they indicate that something is surprising or unexpected. But the first difference is that these words will, like all prepositions, be followed by a noun or a gerund. As before, your explanatory examples can contain the word *but.*

- He has tried everything to lose weight, **but** he hasn't been successful.
- **Despite** trying everything to lose weight, he hasn't been successful.

Both *despite* and (more commonly) *in spite of* are often followed by *the fact that …* and a phrase.

- In spite of **the fact that** he has tried everything to lose weight, he hasn't been successful.

When you are sure that the students understand the use and meaning of these expressions, ask them to read the examples in the **Language** section, which are as usual taken from the reading text on the following page, and then discuss the questions with other students.

2 PREVIEW Language A / B / C / D / E
Suggested answers

A Yes, the words in bold mean more or less the same thing.
B *Although* and *in spite of* are the most formal.
C Students should say the sentences to each other and decide which sounds the most emphatic.
D *But Dallas also has plenty of junk food, including 105 doughnut shops.*
E There are various ways to re-write these sentences. These are the best balanced versions:
- *Houston's sports facilities are excellent. However, people don't do enough exercise and sport.*
- *Houston folk can't do anything about the poor air quality. However, they could turn off the TV and get out to the parks.*

If you want students to do more structure practice work before they proceed, they can at this point do the structure exercises in the **Workbook** section. The target structure of this Unit doesn't have a direct correlation with a language function. The functional focus, *evaluating options,* uses different examples, which students will need to know in order to do section **4 TALK ABOUT IT**. You can find the words and expressions they need in **Language Bank 20**.

Ideas

Here are three more sentences from the reading text, for the students to think about as ideas, rather than simply for their language content. Then there are three questions for them to discuss with their partner or in small groups. Below is a **Background information** box to help you offer some extra ideas for the students to think about.

A How could people's weight have an effect on healthcare services?

B Fit US cities don't have to deal with sultry summers and arctic winters.

Background information

The health, economic and social consequences of obesity are substantial. Obesity is associated with numerous health complications which range from non-fatal debilitating conditions such as osteoarthritis, to life threatening chronic diseases such as coronary heart disease, diabetes, and certain types of cancer. The psychological consequences of obesity can range from low self-esteem to clinical depression. Recent estimates suggest that up to eight per cent of the total health care costs in Western countries are being spent on obesity-related problems.

Although the fittest US cities are in the West (San Francisco, Denver, Colorado Springs), according to the US Centers for Disease Control and Prevention, the five states which have the lowest rates of obesity in the country are Colorado, Massachusetts, Vermont, Rhode Island and Connecticut. All except Colorado are in New England, in the North east of the country. The five states with the highest rates of obesity are Mississippi, Louisiana, Texas, Alabama and Tennessee – all in the South east of the country. So, is obesity simply a geographical factor? What other factors are involved?

Factor 1: Climate

The five most obese states are too hot in the summers and sometimes too cold in the winter to go outside and exercise. Quite simply, it's easier to get out and be active if it's nice outside. If you live in an area that has a temperate year-round climate, you can go for a walk, run, bike ride or any other outdoor activity anytime you want. However, this can't be the whole truth – New England winters can be very hard!

Factor 2: Urban v Rural

People who live in urban areas rely on their own two feet for transportation as much as they can, often simply to avoid the city traffic. They probably use some public transport and are used to walking or cycling several blocks to the grocery store or bus stop, and they may not even own a car. Those in rural areas, on the other hand, may live miles from the nearest store and typically have no access to public transportation. If they are going to get anywhere, they need to drive to get there. Over time, the extra activity that city dwellers gain on a daily basis gives them an edge to avoid obesity.

Factor 3: Attitudes towards obesity

Opinion surveys suggest that people in certain areas of the USA don't think being overweight is important (either themselves or other people). In the south, local attitudes suggest being overweight is not something to worry about. This is not true in the north-east.

3 READING CD 2 (Red) track 12, Page 51 SB

Key words / expressions
• climate •humid • junk food
• natural resources • statistics • sultry
• pick on = victimise, single out

The two pictures on this page show very different people, a muscular man and an overweight boy. However, the muscular man is photographed in studio conditions and lighting and make-up accentuate his physique. So, is the photo real? And is this what the overweight boy in the other photo should aspire to look like? The reading text is an authentic magazine article, which was written as a reaction to a newspaper article which found that Houston, Texas had once again been named the fattest city in the USA.

It's worth noting the use of the phrasal verb *pick on,* which we normally use in the expressions like: *Stop picking on me / pick on someone your own size.* It is interesting to see it in this context – the editor of *Men's Fitness* magazine says: *We don't plan to pick on any particular city.* There is a question about this expression in activity **B**.

3A The pre-reading activity asks students to predict the content of the reading text. This should be clear by now!

3B This is another pre-reading activity, to establish the meaning of certain sentences.

3C Give students time to read the article in silence (or read the Introduction for other suggestions about how to deal with reading texts). Then decide if you want them to write the answers to the questions, discuss them in small groups or discuss them in full class.

3 READING B / C **Answers**
B 1 (a) **2** (a) **3** (b)
C Suggested answers
1 Houston residents are quite defensive about the statistics. Other cities are just as bad, they claim.
2 Residents of people at the top of the chart watch too much TV, eat too much and don't take enough exercise.
3 Fit city people exercise more and watch less TV.

4 TALK ABOUT IT

Students have a chance to recommend ways for fat city dwellers to get fit. To help them with this, they are directed to **Language Bank 20**, where they will find useful strategies for evaluating options. However, remember that the activity can still be a success even if the students don't manage to use many of the functional items. Try to encourage them to come up with fitness ideas that have NOT been mentioned already in the article, such as going to the gymnasium. Here are some other suggestions for ways to keep fit that you can give if the class can't think of any:

1 You could join a club and go mountaineering, or sailing.
2 Why not play a team sport, like soccer or rugby?
3 Get a dog and take it for a walk twice a day.

5 LISTEN IN CD 1 (Blue) track 11, Page 52 SB

The picture on this page may puzzle the students. It's of a rather uncertain-looking woman who is sitting opposite a man whose face we can't see. They appear to be in a bar, and the caption says: *Elaine buys a drink for Craig.*

Ask the students these questions:

1 Who are the people, what is their relationship and where are they?
2 What has this photo got to do with the Unit topic of globesity?

The second question may be harder to answer. Encourage the students to be as imaginative and inventive as possible with this, and don't discourage them by telling them that they are nowhere near the right answer! Remember that the process of trying to work out a puzzling situation like this is valuable language practice, even if they don't arrive at the right answer.

The **Audio text** is in the **Workbook** (pages 68-69). It is an audio diary spoken by Elaine, a woman who is rather worried by her weight. She seems to be in a state of anxiety and excitement because there is an attractive new man in her office. Her audio diary relates the progress of her friendship with him – and whether her weight has anything to do with it! She starts out by imagining that he won't find her attractive because she needs to go on a diet and ends by discovering that it makes no difference – he likes her anyway!

Key words / expressions

- ask (someone) out • bar of chocolate
- breakfast cereal • enormous • to fit
- to go on a diet • gorgeous • guy
- he will be mine • obsessed with
- oh dear! • to put on (weight) • salad
- skinny • things that make life worth living
- well done me! • who cares?

5A The pre-listening task lists all the food items that on the page (and mentioned in Elaine's diary). Students have to say which of them are fattening. There may be some disagreement about the answers here! Spaghetti, for example, is not fattening by itself, but it is often served with a sauce that could be fattening. It is also possible to make a pizza which isn't fattening. Students should be encouraged to bring their prior knowledge of such things into the discussion.

5 LISTEN IN A **Answers**
pizza (?) biscuits chocolate bars cream spaghetti (?) ice cream

5B The second pre-listening task highlights some of the expressions that appear in the text, plus some others that are related thematically. The key expressions that they need to know are *go on a diet, put on weight* and *feel faint with hunger* (to be so hungry that you almost lose consciousness). Read all the questions out first and make sure everyone knows what they mean. Then put the class in pairs or small groups to ask and answer them.

5C Students now listen and answer the comprehension questions.

5 LISTEN IN C **Suggested answers**
1 Because there's a new man in her office.
2 He's gorgeous!
3 Her diet is unlikely to be successful.
4 She decides to abandon her diet.
5 *Students' own answers*

5D For the second listening, students have to tick the diagram to indicate the days when specific things happen.

5 LISTEN IN D **Answers**
1 Elaine eats too much on Monday.
2 Elaine eats chocolate on Monday (chocolate cake), Tuesday, Wednesday, Thursday (chocolate biscuit), Saturday (possibly).
3 Elaine finds she has put on a kilo on Thursday.
4 Elaine decides she must lose four kilos on Friday.

5E Although this listening activity is quite light-hearted, the fact is that people like Elaine who eat and then starve themselves are not doing themselves any good. The final activity offers students the chance to discuss the situation more seriously. The instructions suggest that the students discuss three questions in small groups. Instead, you may want to do this as a whole class activity.

6 CONTROVERSY See Role cards Page 63 WB

Read the notes about this section in the Introduction. Groups of three work on this role play activity. There are two role cards. One of the characters is a student, the others are his / her parents. The student is dieting and exercising to make sure he / she doesn't get fat. The parents are worried about his / her behaviour.

This role play definitely needs a time-limit. We suggest that you give each group of three just five minutes to think about things they want to say, and then ask for a volunteer trio to act the scene out in front of the class. Stop the acting out when you feel they are running out of ideas and ask if there is another trio who would like to take over.

The thing to avoid in a role play like this is silence! If one of the groups runs out of ideas after just two or three minutes, then thank them and move on to another. Keep it brisk and congratulate everyone on their involvement, however long or short it may be.

Even if you decided that the Unit as a whole was not a problem for the class, you may feel that this particular activity may not be suitable. We fully understand if you feel that you want to skip it, especially if you have students in the class who suffer from eating disorders.

7 PORTFOLIO WRITING

The writing task is to produce an advertising brochure for a new fitness club. This is one of the most challenging writing tasks in the whole book, although it is the kind of thing that students might encounter in an examination.

The key requirements for the 'copy' (technical term for the words that are used in the writing of an advertisement) are outlined on the student's book page. The key to writing successful advertising copy is making it leap off the page. Certain words are very successful – words like *new, now, free, try, soon,* especially when followed by an exclamation mark.

As you will see from the model below, the position of the words and the size of the font are also important. If you give this activity as homework, you can ask the class to find suitable images from the internet to make it more interesting. NB At the time of going to press the URL (website address) below was not in use. However, new web addresses are constantly being registered and it is very possible that this and other similar internet addresses will be in use at the time that teachers and students are doing this activity.

Writing model

NEW IN TOWN!
THE
***FAT-OR-FIT* CLUB**

JOIN NOW AND GET THE FIRST MONTH
FREE!
Call 9232 – 9943 or visit
www.fat-or-fitness.com
***FAT OR FIT* – IT'S YOUR CHOICE!**

8 *HEALTH EDUCATION in English* Page 53 SB

Key words / expressions
- burn off (calories)
- calories
- equation
- hunger
- malnutrition

The text is a map of the world, annotated with information about the global problem of obesity clearly indicated regionally.

8A As always with the cross-curricular activities, it is good if there is someone in the class who can offer some information because of their specialised knowledge of a particular subject. In this case, it is nutrition. How many students know what calories are? Why are they important? And what are the results of malnutrition? What happens to someone, especially a child, when they don't get enough to eat, and don't eat the right things?

8B Comprehension questions.

8 *HEALTH EDUCATION in English* B

Answers

1 Obesity is a worldwide phenomenon.
2 When you store more (or less) food energy than your body needs.
3 *Students' own answers*

9 YOUR TOPIC

Read the notes about this section in the Introduction. This activity requires students to conduct a class survey and then explain the results of the survey to a partner.

9A Technically, an activity like this can be a bit chaotic, with people milling around the room. If you have a large class, you may want to restrict the movement of people by having students only interview people on their side of the room. It is also a problem to have everyone asking and answering the same questions. But if it works well, it is really worth it!

9B Students now have to present their findings to a partner, who asks questions. The questioner is directed to **Language Bank 5**, which offers them strategies for asking for clarification. If you wish, you can do this as a pair activity, followed by whole class discussion, as follows: Ask the students to work in pairs while they are collating information. One student mingles around collecting information and the other stays at his / her desk collating it. This makes it easier for people to do the interviewing; otherwise everyone is moving around at the same time!

10 *Your answer:*

And so we come back to *The BIG question*. As always, we sub-divide the main question into three more questions, which ask students to talk about the situation in their own countries.

Workbook answers — Pages 26-27 WB

1 Language: *although, though, even though, in spite of, despite*

1A *Alternatives are possible*

1 Although I was very tired after work, I still went swimming.
2 He works in a bakery. He never eats cakes, though.
3 Even though he exercises, he doesn't lose much weight.
4 Although there are some excellent gyms near me, I don't use them.
5 Even though he was hungry, he (still) ate very little food.

1B *Alternatives are possible*

1 Despite having a large meal, I was still hungry.
2 In spite of the fact that he was overweight, he was still very attractive.
3 Despite the cold weather, everyone had ice cream.
4 In spite of losing six kilos, I'm still not happy with my weight.
5 My boyfriend eats a lot of sweets in spite of my advice not to do so.

1C *Alternatives are possible*

1 In spite of the fact that I was very tired after work, I still went swimming.
2 Despite working in a bakery, he never eats cakes.
3 In spite of the fact that he exercises, he doesn't lose much weight.
4 Despite the fact that there are some excellent gyms near me, I don't use them.
5 Despite being hungry, he (still) ate very little food.

1D *Students' own answers*

2 Use of English

2A *Alternatives are possible*

1 If we don't start worrying about our weight, we will have a serious problem.
2 People's attitudes to keeping fit are affected by the weather.
3 Houston is fat, but every other city is fat too.
4 Most of us are using up fewer calories than we are taking in.

2B **1** a **2** c **3** b **4** c **5** b **6** a **7** a **8** b **9** c **10** a

3 Portfolio writing
Students' own answers

4 Connections

4A Less than ideal weight: skinny, thin
Ideal weight: shapely, slim, slender, well-built
More than ideal weight: fat, obese, chubby

4B starving, ravenous

4C Positive words: shapely, slender, starving, ravenous
Negative words: skinny, thin, obese, chubby, greedy, gluttonous
starving and *ravenous* – it's OK to be hungry
greedy and *gluttonous* – it's not OK to want to eat all the time!

What's new?

Subject: Design
Function: Eliciting further information
Grammar: Present perfect passive, future simple passive

Before you open the book ...
This Unit focuses on design, with a particular emphasis on imaginative and ambitious architectural and engineering projects such as the building of a 1.6 kilometre-high building in Japan in Tokyo Bay. These projects are only at the discussion stage. Whether they can actually be built in the near future remains unsure! Much of the reason for erecting extremely tall buildings is because the populations of cities are growing so fast. Hence ***The BIG question*** for this Unit: *Where will we all live?*

Introduce the Unit by writing its title, *Cities of the future,* on the board. Ask students to choose the answer they think is correct:

1 *What percentage of the world's population live in cities? a) 1/10 b) 1/4 c) 1/3 d) 1/2 e) 2/3*
2 *By 2030, how many people will live in cities? a) 2 billion b) 3 billion c) 4 billion d) 5 billion*

Elicit answers and ask students to write their answers down. Ask the class to open their books at page 54 and find the answers to the questions (the **FACT** gives the answers: *Already half of the world's population lives in cities. By 2030, five billion people will live in cities).* Elicit students' responses to the fact. Tell students that this Unit will look at imaginative architectural and engineering projects designed for cities. Check students understand the terms used (*imaginative / project* etc).

1 *The BIG question:* WHERE WILL WE ALL LIVE?

Picture notes / Internet references
The upper left-hand picture shows a sports stadium, the Allianz Arena in Munich, Germany, designed by Swiss architects Herzog & de Meuron. The stadium can accommodate almost 70,000 spectators. For more information go to this website:
http://www.allianz-arena.de/en/index.php
The upper right-hand picture shows the Ginger and Fred building in Prague. The office building was built in 1997 by American architect Frank Gehry together with Czech architect Vlado Miluni. It was given the nickname of Ginger and Fred because of its vague resemblance to a pair of dancing partners (See **Background information** notes below). It is also known as the Dancing House. For more information go to this website:
http://www.arcspace.com/gehry_new/
The bottom picture shows the Sydney Opera House designed by Danish architect Joern Utzon. Internationally famous, it is situated in Sydney, New South Wales, Australia and is located in Sydney Harbour. With its shells that resemble sailboats it is a major tourist sight. For more information go to this website:
http://www.utzon.dk/

Read out ***The BIG question***: *Where will we all live?* Point to the skyscraper in the photo on the opposite page and say: *This building is 1.6 kilometres high. Why do you think architects would put up such a tall building?* Elicit answers (*because if you build upwards you can house more people*). Ask: *Would you like to live in such a tall building?* Briefly elicit answers and tell students there will be time for longer discussion later in the Unit.

2 PREVIEW

Words

Background information
Fred Astaire was a famous Hollywood dancer, singer and actor. In the 1930s he teamed up with film star and dancer Ginger Rogers, and they made a succession of highly successful musicals, including Top Hat (1935) and Swing Time (1936).

Put students into pairs for these tasks, as questions **B** and **C** in particular are discussion questions.

A **1** Ask the class to look at the photos. Check they understand the rubrics. You may need to explain the word *arena* (= a large area surrounded by seats, used for sports or entertainment). Do students know which countries the buildings are in? (Alliance Arena – Munich, Germany / Ginger and Fred building – Prague, Czech Republic / Sydney Opera House – Sydney, Australia). Check students understand the vocabulary in choices **a) – f)**. Elicit answers and correct if necessary.

B Give students about 2-3 minutes to discuss the questions.

1 Help students by eliciting the fact / explaining that *Ginger and Fred* were two Hollywood dancing partners called Ginger Rogers and Fred Astaire who made some very famous musicals in the 1950s. Knowing this information, students should be able to answer this question (See **Answers** below), though they may have difficulty explaining – *The building looks like two people dancing.*

2 Be positive about students' suggestions – and use the opportunity to teach any new vocabulary that arises. The answers in the **Answers** section below are suggestions only – there are no correct answers.

C **1** Check students understand the vocabulary. You will probably need to teach the word *criterion* (plural *criteria*) (= standards that you use to judge something or make a decision about something). Allow about 2-3 minutes for discussion, then elicit answers. Most students should have the sense to put *safety* (choice **f**) as the most important criterion!

2 Explain that to some extent the criteria depend on the purpose of the building, for example, the Allianz Arena is a sports stadium. Ask students to decide which criteria are the most important according to the function of the building, for example, the Opera House is built to stage musical performances. Inform the class that the Ginger and Fred building is an office building.

Suggested answers:

The Allianz Arena: Criteria **(a)**, **(d)**, **(e)** and **(f)** are very important when designing a sports stadium.

The Ginger and Fred building: Again, choice **(c)** is very relevant: Ask: *Is the building beautiful?*

The Sydney Opera House: All the criteria **(a)** – **(f)** are probably relevant for an Opera House apart from **(b)**. Ask: *Has anyone actually seen it or been in it? What did you think of it?*

3 Elicit brief answers to this question, as students have limited information with which to answer it. Simply ask: *Do you like the buildings? Which building do you like best?*

2 PREVIEW Words A / B **Answers**

A Alliance Arena (d); The Ginger and Fred building (b); the Sydney Opera House (e)

B 1 The phrase *Ginger and Fred* refers to Ginger Rogers and Fred Astaire, two Hollywood movie star dancing partners of the 1930s. The part of the building that leans in can imaginatively be described as looking like a woman dancer – Ginger Rogers – leaning against her dancing partner, Fred Astaire.

2 Suggested answers: Allianz Arena – the tablet, the pill, the scarlet lozenge; the life-raft Sydney Opera House – the arches, the sailing boats…

Language

Check students understand the sentences, teaching new vocabulary where necessary. As the class have covered the present simple and past simple passives in Unit 6, they should have no difficulty in recognising the passive (question **A**).

When the class have completed the questions, ask them to say which tenses are used in the sentences (*have been shown* – present perfect; *may be built* – passive with *may*; *will be built / will be linked* – future simple (*will*).

Elicit from the class / explain, using the board, how these passives are formed.

will / may + *be* + past participle
have been + past participle

To provide practice in the future simple passive, do the following:

Draw a picture of tall, interesting-looking skyscraper on the board. Write these sentences on the board:

Frank Gehry will design this building.
They will start it in 2010,
They will finish it in 2015.
They will paint it silver and black.
People will live in it by 2016.

Ask the class to put the sentences into first the future simple passive, then the passive with *may*, and finally then the present perfect passive.

Note: The passive with modals is covered more fully in Unit 14.

2 PREVIEW Language A / B / C Answers
A They are all forms of the passive voice.
B Because the word *someone* (the subject of the active sentence) gives us very little information – we don't need it,
C The final sentence. This sentence rephrased in the active voice – *A series of hollow tubes will link the skyscrapers* – gives the same information equally well.

Ideas

Check students understand the sentences, teaching new vocabulary where necessary. You will need to explain the phrase *spider robots* (*robot* = a machine that can do work by itself, often work that humans do). A spider robot is a robot that looks like a spider. Put the class into pairs or small groups to discuss the questions.

A All these projects are unusual, for example, a building 1.6 kilometres high has never yet been built.

B / C / D Give the class about four minutes to discuss the questions, then elicit answers, making sure that students use the second conditional *would*, as they are discussing imaginary situations.

3 READING CD2 (Red) track 13, Page 55 SB

Key words / expressions
• extreme • engineering • development
• design • project • to construct • available
• space • dramatic • accommodation
• to go ahead • floor (storey) • resident
• pyramid • ambitious • to solve • series
• storey • structure • skyscraper • to link
• hollow • tube • spider • robot • volcanic
• eruption • earthquake
• seismic = relating to earthquakes
• to withstand = to be not damaged by heat, pressure, a force etc

The first of the two articles describes a project to build a 1.6 kilometre-high building in the sea, in Tokyo Bay, Japan. The second article describes an 'even more ambitious project' to build a 1,000 metre tall pyramid that would house three quarters of a million people.

Introduce the texts by writing the phrase *Extreme Engineering* on the board (see the reference to *Extreme Engineering* in the brief introduction to the articles). Ask students: What *does 'extremely' mean, for example, 'extremely tired'?* (Answer: *very*). Ask: *So what do you think Extreme Engineering means?* Elicit or give the answer (Engineering that is very imaginative and new). Tell the class that these two articles are about two very difficult and interesting building projects.

3A Point out that *house* is used as a verb here – *to house* (= to accommodate).

3B / C You may want to give students some more detailed comprehension questions. If so, write the following questions on the board for the class to answer:

Sky City
1 *Why are Japanese designers considering constructing such tall buildings?*
(Because there is less and less available building space.)
2 *Why is it possible that some residents would never leave Sky City?*
(Because accommodation, work and leisure facilities would all be in the same building.)
3 *What is the problem with Sky City?*
(No one knows for sure if it can be built.)

Pyramid City
1 *How big would each of the smaller pyramids be?*
(Each would be the size of the Great Pyramid of Giza in Egypt.)
2 *What will there be in-between the series of skyscrapers?*

(Parkland.)
3 *What is the 'ring of fire' and where is it?*
(It is an area of volcanic activity which stretches around the Pacific Ocean.)

3D Put the class into pairs to discuss these questions, allowing about 3-4 minutes. Elicit answers and encourage some discussion. Question **1**: Ask the class to guess what the word *futuristic* means (= appearing unusual and modern, as if it belongs in the future instead of the present). Encourage students to use the phrase: *It makes me feel (excited)*. Ask students to try and explain the reasons for their feelings. Question **2**: Ask students to write down the first word that comes into their head when they see the word *overcrowding* (=too many people). Write down students' answers on the board. Question **3**: Invite a student to the board to draw a picture of a *spider robot*.

3 READING A / B / C — **Answers**

A
1 Pyramid City, which would house three quarters of a million people.
2 Sky City would be taller, at 1.6 kilometres.
3 Both

B
1 Where will Sky City be built?
2 How high will Sky City be, if it is built?
3 How many people would Sky City house?
4 Will it just house people?

C
1 False. It will be twelve times higher.
2 True
3 True
4 True

4 TALK ABOUT IT

Put the class into pairs or small groups to discuss these statements. Ask students to say which statements they agree, or disagree with and why.

Optional activity: To provide more practice in the passive structures for this Unit, give the class these questions to discuss:

1 *What types of buildings have been built in the last 50 years to house large numbers of people? Have they been successful? What problems have they created?*
2 *What kind of buildings do you think will / may be built in the future?*

Use the first question to teach housing vocabulary: *skyscrapers / high-rise buildings / (housing) estates.* Elicit synonyms for the verb *to build*, such as *to construct / to put up / to erect.*

In answer to question **1**, students will probably reply that high-rise housing estates have been very unsuccessful, since they are usually very ugly and lonely, with no green spaces for children to play. They seem to have encouraged crime.

5 LISTEN IN — CD1 (Blue) track 12, Page 56 SB

Key words / expressions
- rail tunnel • to fix • to float • normal
- wheel • rail(s) • submarine • iceberg
- to operate = work
- rail tunnel = railway tunnel
- pre-constructed = built beforehand
- magnetically levitated = lifted by magnets
- transatlantic = across the Atlantic Ocean
- track(s) = railway tracks

NB: The vocabulary items in activities **A** and **B** are not included in the list above.

Picture notes / Internet references
The first picture on this page is of the Maglev train in Shanghai. For more information go to this website:
http://www.slate.com/id/2115114/
The second picture is of The Tunnel, also known as Transatlantic Tunnel, a 1935 British film directed by Maurice Elvey. For more information go to this website:
http://www.imdb.com/title/tt0027131/
The pictures on page 57 are of Walter Gropius and the Bauhaus building that he designed. For more information go to this website:
http://www.bauhaus.de/english/

The **Audio text** is in the **Workbook** (page 69). Introduce the listening passage by asking the class to look at the photos. Ask:

1 *What words would you use to describe the Maglev train?* (Futuristic, very modern, very fast.)
2 *How do you think a Maglev train is different from a normal train?*
3 *What is a transatlantic tunnel?* (A tunnel that goes

right across the Atlantic Ocean.)
4 *Do you think it would be possible to build a transatlantic tunnel?*

Elicit answers and explain that the class will hear a discussion about a possible railway under the Atlantic Ocean.

5A / B If students have dictionaries, ask them to use them to look up the vocabulary items focused on. If not, give the class some minutes to complete the task – they will have difficulty finding all the correct definitions – then go through the definitions, providing correct answers where necessary.

5C The class will probably need to listen to the passage up to three times in order to answer the questions. You may need to explain that *Maglev* is short for *magnetically levitated.*

5 LISTEN IN A / B / C **Answers**

A **1** (c) **2** (a) **3** (b) **4** (e) **5** (f) **6** (d)

B **1** (c) **2** (a) **3** (d) **4** (b)

C **1** Magnetically levitated trains don't have wheels and don't travel on rails. They travel in a vacuum between two magnets.
2 There are magnetically levitated trains (Maglev trains) in Shanghai (China).
3 The top speed could be 6,000 kilometres per hour.
4 They are very noisy.
5 The power of the ocean could cause the tunnel to bend or crack, damaging the train. A passing submarine or a drifting iceberg could hit the tunnel.

6 CONTROVERSY See Role cards Page 63 WB

Read the notes about this section in the Introduction. This activity provides an opportunity for the class to debate the advantages and disadvantages of the transatlantic tunnel described in the listening passage. Divide the class into groups of six or nine, with two or three students in each team A, B and C. Read out the rubric, which summarises the role play. Check that the class understand the word *waste* (= when something such as money or time is not used well). Check also that students understand their role cards and any new vocabulary. If you feel the class needs the help, before the role play, go through each role card eliciting arguments and suggestions for other options.

7 PORTFOLIO WRITING

Ask the class if they know the computer game Sim City, in which players design their ideal city. Some students will certainly know it. Ask students to imagine that they are part of a group of world-famous architects who have been asked to design their ideal city. Explain that this city must be built in their own country.

Direct attention to the categories in the box. For the category *What my city needs*, elicit from students what other facilities will be needed, *eg shops, shopping malls, parks, sports facilities.* Take the opportunity to teach the names of types of building, *eg detached / semi-detached houses, blocks of flats / apartments, high-rise buildings / apartments.*

Tell students to decide whether they want to build a futuristic city or a more conventional one. They should also decide on the exact location of their city, *eg on the south-east coast of their country or inland near another major city.* The size of the city is also important.

Give the class this plan for their report:

Paragraph 1: Location, size, type of city (futuristic / conventional) – and a name for the city
Paragraphs 2 & 3: Facilities and where they will be placed, types of building and transport. Explain that the report should be written in the future tense as it will definitely be built! (This will provide opportunities to use the future passive.)
Paragraph 4: Short conclusion

If students have access to the internet, encourage them to find photos they can use to illustrate their report.

Background information
SimCity: SimCity is a popular computer game in which the player's task is to create the ideal urban environment. Players create everything from mountains to the various problems and disasters that can strike a city, *eg traffic jams, fires* etc.

Writing model

Our city will be built on the south-west coast, in a part of England called Cornwall. It will be located there because it will bring business and money to a part of England that badly needs it. The city will not be big – the countryside is beautiful and we do not want to spoil it. The city will be called Tremorgan (a Cornish name).

We do not want the city to be obviously futuristic. We feel that it is more important for it to fit in with the countryside around it. There will be attractive high-rise office buildings in the centre of the city because high-rise buildings can accommodate a lot of offices and people, but in the more residential areas the buildings will not be more than three or four storeys high. Experience has shown that people are not happy living in high-rise buildings.

The city will be designed with plenty of tree-lined streets, squares and parkland. There will be spaces at train and bus stations where scooters are provided for people to hire and ride, so that for short journeys cars are unnecessary – this will help to reduce the amount of traffic.

We expect Tremorgan to be very popular – it will be a beautiful place for people to live and work.

8 *DESIGN in English*

Page 57 SB

Key words / expressions

- to design • to influence • to force
- cosmopolitan • to emigrate • to found
- architect • aim • to combine • practical
- to train • craftsperson • function
- sculpture • to associate
- design (n.) = the way that something is planned or made / a pattern used to decorate something / a drawing that shows how something will be made
- cosmopolitan = showing the influence of many different countries and cultures
- movement = a group of people who have the same beliefs and work together to achieve a particular aim
- craft = a traditional skill in which you make something using your hands, *eg jewellery*
- functional = designed to be useful and simple with no unnecessary decoration

Write the word *design* on the board and say that this session is about design. Point to a chair and ask: *Do you think this chair has a good design?* Elicit answers, *eg No, it's uncomfortable and not very attractive.* Ask: *Can you tell me the name of a famous clothes designer?* (*eg* Georgio Armani, Christian Dior*).* Ask if anyone in the class is interested in design – there are certain to be some students who are interested.

8A **1** Check students understand the words *revolutionary* (= completely new and different). Students might describe the building as *boring / ugly / unattractive / modern / ordinary / a glass box.*

2 Check students understand the word *architecture* (= the style and design of buildings). Only allow about 3-4 minutes for discussion of this question, as the purpose of this activity is simply to introduce the topic of design. However, you may want to continue the discussion in greater depth once students have completed activity **B**.

Example answers: *Of course architecture and design are important arts. We live in buildings and need them to be both attractive and functional. Beautiful buildings like the Taj Mahal and Versailles are great works of art. Everyone likes things that are well-designed, such as chairs, sofas, kettles. Fashion is one of the biggest design industries in the world!*

8B You may want to ask a few more detailed comprehension questions. If so, write the following questions on the board:

1 *Who started the Bauhaus movement?* (Architect Walter Gropius)

2 *Was designing chairs and lamps considered important?* (Yes)

3 *Can you name a famous Bauhaus artist?* (Paul Klee, Wassily Kandinsky)

4 *Why do you think the Bauhaus building was so revolutionary at the time?* (Because it's a very functional, simple building without decoration. It also used glass and concrete materials, which was unusual.)

8 *DESIGN in English* B **Answers**

1. To combine art with practical subjects like economics and engineering.
2. It was very successful. It influenced art and

design throughout the 20th century.
3 Because the Nazis did not think it was German enough.
4 Because the Bauhaus School had been closed. Perhaps they were unable to find work.

9 INTERACTIVE TASK

Read the notes about this section in the Introduction. Put students into pairs. Emphasise that although Student A begins the conversation, it is Student B who takes control of the conversation by asking questions and giving opinions etc.

To prepare the students playing part A, elicit students' opinions on modern architecture and design. Elicit the names of well-known modern buildings in their city / country, or other countries and their opinions of them. If they have no real opinions on the subject, suggest that one student supports modern architecture while the other criticises it.

Optional activity: Ask students to bring in a picture of their favourite modern building and describe it to the class, then put the photos up on the classroom wall.

10 *Your answer:*

Use the activity as a way of revising the various parts of the Unit. Put students in pairs or small groups to discuss the questions, giving students a time limit of three minutes for each question. Walk round and listen to students, noting mistakes. Then have a class discussion on the question(s) that students find most interesting.

WORKBOOK answers Pages 28-29 WB

1 Language: present perfect passive, future simple passive

1A **1** The plans have been examined by many experts.
2 Good shopping facilities will be provided by Sky City.
3 The final designs have only been seen by a few people.
4 Overpopulation has been described as one of their biggest problems.
5 If the pyramid is ever built, an amazing city will be created.
6 In future, taller and taller buildings will be designed by architects.

1B **1** First prize has been awarded to the team by the aircraft company Boeing.
2 Has the competition been entered by many schools?
3 Their cities have all been designed using the SimCity software program.
4 What form of energy will be used by the city of Noor?
5 Cars will be driven floating along magnetic roads.
6 Drivers will be guided to their destinations by a central computer.
7 Traffic and pollution will be reduced by this system.
8 A real city like this will not be constructed in the near future.

2 Use of English

2A **1** They must make the building strong, in case it falls down in an earthquake.
2 Inside a series of hollow tubes there will be a high-speed transport system.
3 It will take another 100 years to build it.
4 Because Maglev trains do not travel on rails, there is no noise.
5 If a submarine hit the tunnel it could damage it.

2B **1** location **2** connected **3** influential
4 construction **5** solutions

3 Portfolio writing

Students' own answers

4 Connections

4A **1** (b) **2** (d) **3** (a) **4** (c)

4B **(a)** A door is rectangular.
(b) The Pyramids are triangular.
(c) A high-rise building is rectangular.
(d) A roundabout is circular.
(e) A three-storey house is rectangular.
(f) The Eiffel Tower us rectangular.
(g) An apartment is square.
(h) A dome is circular.

4C **1** (e) set up **2** (g) carries on **3** (b) going up
4 (f) torn / pulled down **5** (a) falling down
6 (d) turned into **7** (h) taken over **8** (c) put up

What's new?

Subject:	National customs
Function:	Reporting the conversation of others; paraphrasing
Grammar:	Reported speech

Before you open the book ...

ELT materials written in the UK tend to address matters such as hunting (if they deal with them at all) from the rather liberal-minded anti-hunting point of view. This attitude probably doesn't represent the general views of the wider world, so we have tried in this Unit to be more even-handed about the whole idea of shooting animals. We have tried to recognise that, as ***The BIG question*** suggests, hunting can be a deeply-rooted tradition in many parts of the non-urban world. And of course, a lot of animals are killed for food, not just for sport.

The structure focus is reported speech, something which students really have to use confidently if they intend to do any examinations in English, as it is almost certain that they will encounter a reported speech exercise. Having said that, the reality is that young native English speakers don't use reported speech much, certainly not in spoken English. And yet the very nature of gossipy light conversation is the reporting of what other people said. So how do young native English speakers report what people said without using reported speech? Usually in one of the following informal ways:

1 By simply using *say* or *said* followed by the words that were said:
- He says / said: 'What are you doing tonight?' so I say / said: 'Nothing. Why do you want to know?' And he says / said: 'I was just asking!'

2 By using the verb *go* (present tense or past):
- He goes / went: 'What are you doing tonight?' so I go / went: 'Nothing. Why do you want to know?' And he goes / went: 'I was just asking!'

3 Using *be + like* (more common in US English):
- He's / He was like: 'What are you doing tonight?' so I'm / I was like: 'Nothing. Why do you want to know?' And he's / he was like: 'I was just asking!'

4 A combination of *go* and *be + like*, or *go / went + like* (used by British teenagers):
- He goes / went like: 'What are you doing tonight?' so I go / went like: 'Nothing. Why do you want to know?' And he goes / went like: 'I was just asking!'

5 You can often hear a combination of all the above:
- He says: 'What are you doing tonight?' so I'm like: 'Nothing. Why do you want to know?' And he went: 'I was just asking!'

In an examination, students would be expected to put sentences like these into 'real' reported speech – like this:

1 What are you doing tonight?
- He asked her what she was doing that night. (*tonight* might be allowed)

2 Nothing. Why do you want to know?
- She replied that she was doing nothing and asked him why he wanted to know.

3 I was just asking!
- He replied that he was just asking.

Do your students already know the 'basics' of reported speech? Whether they do or not, why not use this introduction as a way of teaching or reminding them of how people speak in 'real life' and at the same time make them aware of examination requirements? You may chose to photocopy the examples and use them as a reading text before you start.

This is a fun activity, and will help students to realise that there are divisions between the world of 'real' English and the specialised forms that they have to learn for examinations. However, you should emphasise to them that the normal reported speech forms are good written English style, and should always be used in any writing task.

1 *The BIG question:* IS HUNTING A SPORT, A TRADITION OR CRUELTY?

FACT: Rich tourists take hunting trips to kill lions in Tanzania, elephants in Botswana and bears in Russia.

Picture notes / Internet reference

There are three photos on this first spread. The photo of the lion shows a 'canned' hunt, as it is known in South Africa. Hunters pay up to £20,000 to shoot a lion which has been caught in the wild (or sometimes bred specially) and then confined in an enclosure so that it can be shot more easily. For more information go to these websites:
http://www.enkosini.com/CannedHunting.htm
http://www.enkosini.com/1997.05.02%20-%20Hunting%20Fenced%20Lions%20For%20Fun.htm

The photo of the boat shows First Nation Inuit traditional hunters in the Canadian arctic, with seals in their boat. The photograph was taken by Robert Semeniuk. To see more of his work go to this website:
http://www.robertsemeniuk.com/

The photo on page 59 shows a man with a brown bear that he has killed. There is more information on bear hunts in the **Background information** box below.

The photos on page 58 are dealt with in question **2A**.

As we said earlier, the usual liberal urban attitude to hunting is not always shared by people who live in rural areas. Urban dwellers may also have reasons to support hunting, perhaps because they have family members who live in rural areas. In fact, students may already have their own quite strong opinions about this and you may find that they want to talk about it now.

However, the information in the **FACT** box may be more disturbing. There is evidence that hunting trips are still being organised to Africa, where hunters are given the chance to shoot endangered or protected species, such as lions and elephants. International animal protection organisations seem unable to do anything about this. Meanwhile, in Russia and other countries, where bears are not yet well protected by law, hunting trips continue to be organised.

2 PREVIEW

Words

A Students answer questions about the photos.

2 PREVIEW Words A **Answers**

1 The first picture is a lioness. The hunter appears to have killed it for sport. In South Africa there has been a scandal surrounding what is called 'Canned hunting', in which wild animals are kept in an enclosure, so they can be shot by paying 'hunters'. There are moves to make this practice illegal. In the second photo, Inuit people of northern Canada have been hunting for seals. This traditional form of hunting is allowed, as it is for food and skins, which are used for clothing. There is much controversy, however, about culling baby seals on the ice in Canada. For more information go to this website:
http://www.newbuilder.co.uk/reports/sealcull.asp

2 From this list, you can say that these animals are killed for sport: bears, deer, seals, foxes, elephants and ducks; in some places, bears, deer and ducks are also killed for food. Wolves and foxes are killed because they pose a threat, and in Britain, foxes used to be killed for sport. The practice is now illegal but it still continues in some places. In some regions of the USA, wolves are considered an endangered species and cannot be hunted.

B Students now consider why these animals are hunted. There are a series of options – *because they are dangerous / for sport* etc – and students may have some knowledge about this. Encourage those who have specialist knowledge to say what they know. Here is some **Background information** about brown bears that might be useful. Students can find out more about other species by Googling the name of the species + *endangered.*

Background information

The North American brown bear (or grizzly bear, as it is known) used to live across the whole of North America, from the Arctic Ocean to central Mexico. Now its numbers are restricted, and it mainly lives in mountainous areas of national parks.

Brown bears have no natural enemies in the wild, except humans. A single brown bear needs up to 1,300 square kilometres of space in which to forage and live. But expanding human settlements are taking away the bear's habitat and threatening their ability to survive.

The decline of the grizzly began with the arrival of European settlers in America. In less than a hundred years from that time, numbers dropped from 100,000 to 10,000. By 1975, human expansion had eliminated 99 per cent of the bear's natural habitat and the grizzly was an endangered animal. It is now against the law in the United States to hunt brown bears.

The most widespread of the bear species, the brown bear also lives in the plains and mountains of Asia and Europe, where they are also in danger. There are estimated to be about 100,000 brown bears in the Russian Federation, over 50 per cent of the bear population worldwide. There are less than 100 animals in Italy and Greece. In Lebanon and Pakistan, the brown bear is believed to be extinct.

You can find out more about other endangered species on the US National Wildlife Federation website: www.nwf.org/wildlife

C This is the chance for students to discuss hunting in their own country. Discussions like this are usually easier if you are teaching a multilingual class, with students from different countries. If students are all from the same place, get them to say what they know about hunting practices in other countries. Opinions may be divided, you may have some quite heated exchanges. We would encourage this! It is interesting for students if they are allowed and able to express their feelings about such a sensitive and controversial subject.

Language

The examples of the target structure are, as usual, taken from the reading text on the next page and illustrate various uses of the written forms of reported speech. Your class may already be familiar with the basic forms, but it would be useful to write these examples on the board and point out certain recurring features and rules. By using the examples from the book on the board, you can do all the inductive questions **A-C** at the same time.

- You told me it would be interesting and you were right!
  What was actually said? *'It will be interesting.'*
  – *will* becomes *would* in reported speech
- They said that all the guides spoke English.
  What was actually said? *'All the guides speak English.'*
  – *speak* becomes *spoke* in reported speech
- I told the guide that they should change the information in the brochure.
  What was actually said? *'They should change the information in the brochure.'*
  – in some cases, *should* doesn't change
- The guide told him to stop.
  What was actually said? *'Stop!'*
  – when it's an order, you use *tell* + infinitive
- The guide told Curly that he had put all our lives in danger.
  What was actually said? *'You put* (possibly *you have put*) *all our lives in danger.'*

– when you use *tell,* you have to say who it is was spoken to.

If you want students to do more structure practice work before they proceed, they can do the structure exercises in the **Workbook** section (page 30 WB) at this point.

Ideas

The sentences in this section are also from the reading text. Taken out of context, they really seem astonishing. At this point, the class may look across at page 59 and realise that the text is actually an advertisement for a hunting tour in Kamchatka.

3 READING CD 2 (Red) track 14, Page 59 SB

There are in fact two reading texts. Text **1** is the advertisement for the hunting tour holiday, and Text **2** is an email from someone who has been on the holiday, writing to a friend. It would seem from the first line of the email that the friend told the man about it and possibly had been on the tour himself.

<u>Key words / expressions: Texts 1 and 2</u>
Scenery words: • glaciers • hot springs
• volcanoes • untamed • spectacular
Words to do with guns / hunting:
• to shoot (an animal) • to fire (a gun)
• to wound = injure • to miss = not hit
• to stalk • powerful • to spot = see
Other words: • exotic • guarantee
• inspiring • lifetime • to roam
• brochure • exhausting • puzzled
• to miss out = not see or do something

<u>Background information</u>

There are several websites devoted to information about bear hunting in Russia (and elsewhere) – search by entering 'bear hunting' into Google. They all describe the country as paradise for hunters. Here is some typical text from a hunting trip website:

'Animals you can expect to see while hunting in one of the many lush forests of the former Soviet Union, are: wild boars, moose, red deer, wolves, brown bears, lynx, foxes, wild ducks and geese. You should keep in mind though that the species you can hunt differ according to seasons. The best season for game is September – December, while for fowl spring is better.

A very popular region for hunting in Russia is the Republic of Sakha in Yakutia which has the largest hunting grounds in Russia. There is an area of 308 million hectares where various forms of hunting are permitted. With the brown bear population being so large and stable you can be 100% sure of a trophy in this region.'

In fact, the brown bear population is not 'large and stable' and these hunting expeditions are contributing to the disappearance of the species in several parts of the Russian Federation.

3A Before reading the whole of the advertisement, students are asked to match the words in bold in the text with three definitions.

3B Students have to read the two texts quickly and decide what kind of writing they are. There are three possible sources. The first option is quite clearly not a real option. There is no way that either the advertisement or the email would find their way into an environmental magazine!

3C This activity requires students to explain three short extracts from Text **1**.

3 READING A / C **Answers**
A **1** hot springs **2** glacier **3** volcano
C **1** *Untamed* is a word that should really be used about animals, but it is often used in articles about wild landscapes, particularly in holiday advertising like this, to give the impression that you are far from civilisation.
2 *Up to 600 kilos* means that 600 kilos is the maximum weight of one of these brown bears.
3 *Spotted* means *seen.* When you *stalk* an animal, you follow it with a view to killing it.

D This is a reference activity – which means that we want students to understand what pronouns like *it* and incomplete phrases like *told him to stop* actually refer to. Students should find the example in the text and then work out the reference from the context.

3 READING D **Answers**
1 The hunt was interesting.
2 The trip was neither short nor comfortable.
3 Stop shooting at the bear.
4 Go on a bear hunt again.

4 TALK ABOUT IT

This is a role-play activity, and can be done by small groups. Two students in each group act as reporters and the rest play the parts of hunters. Basically, the reporters have to collect information from all the hunters and report it to the rest of the class.

Obviously we hope they will report what they find out using reported speech! But as we often say at this point, the success of the activity is not solely dependent on this.

However, if they do use reported speech, and make lots of mistakes, this is an opportunity for you to capitalise on these mistakes and make corrections – but not during the reporting. Using reported speech in the hothouse conditions of a classroom can be a problem. If a student called Daniel says: *'It's my dream to hunt bears.'* It might be reported like this: *'Daniel says that it's his dream to hunt bears.'* Or perhaps like this: *'Daniel said that it's his dream to hunt bears.'*

There is nothing wrong with either of these sentences. But once again, it's best to remind students of what they will need to do in an examination. Therefore, if someone says: *'It's my dream to hunt bears,'* the exam-acceptable way of reporting this is to say: *'Daniel said that it was his dream to hunt bears.'* The best way to learn reported speech for an examination is to keep doing more and more exercises!

5 LISTEN IN CD 1 (Blue) track 13, Page 60 SB

Picture notes

There are three rather unusual photographs on this page. They are all from Kamchatka, the peninsula in Eastern Russia which is the venue for the hunting tour in the reading text on the previous page. You can see the volcanoes in the background of the village picture. You can draw students' attention to the tourist bus. In many remote parts of the Russian Federation (and ex-Soviet countries) left over military vehicles have been turned into civilian public transport. Imagine how you decide who the winner is in the fish-cleaning competition shown in the right-hand picture!

The **Audio text** is on page 69-70 of the **Workbook**. The listening text is a lecture at the Geographical Society given by someone called Robert Philpotts. Mr Philpotts illustrates his lecture with the three pictures that are on this page.

Key words / expressions

Food words: • cucumber • food combinations
• boil • soak • red caviar • salami
• salmon • salmon roe • salted • barrel

Geographical words: • peninsula
• wilderness • population density
• gold • nickel • copper
• deposits (of minerals etc)
• to mine = exploit underground minerals etc

Other words: • illustrated lecture
• non-existent • target
• time-consuming task
• wrestling match

In terms of vocabulary, this is one of the more challenging listening texts in the book, and we really recommend that you pre-teach some of the words and expressions in the box above. There are a lot of words to do with food here. It would help if you could illustrate them before the class listens to the tape. Google Images is a very good source of photographs for this kind of thing. If you have the technology to show the images in class, you could find *salmon, salmon roe, red caviar, salami, cucumber,* and maybe even images for *salt* and *boil.* If not, you can try to draw them. Or even better, ask one of the students to draw them for you!

5A The pre-listening task tells students what they are going to hear – an illustrated lecture about life on the Kamchatka Peninsula – and asks them to predict which topics they expect to be covered. As revision, you could ask students to say what they remember about Kamchatka from the reading text on the previous page – without turning back to see! Congratulate any student who remembers that there are volcanoes, glaciers and hot springs. In fact, all the items which are listed are mentioned in the illustrated lecture.

5B Because the vocabulary in this listening text is so varied and unusual, we have made the activities very vocabulary-oriented. Exercise 5B is in the style of the Cambridge ESOL 2008+ Paper 4 Listening Part 2. Students complete the sentences with information heard in the recording focusing on detail, specific information, and stated opinion. Ask students to read the ten incomplete extracts before they listen. This will give them an idea of what specific information they have to listen for and show them a lot of the words that will be used. As they read the extracts, ask them to imagine what KIND of word or words are missing. For example, the first one reads: *Kamchatka has a population density of less than one….* What kind of word will complete this sentence? Could you complete the sentence with the word hunting, for example? No. The sentence describes a statistic, and probably needs a noun to complete it. They listen again and find the answers.

5 LISTEN IN B **Answers**

1 person
2 mine
3 comfortable
4 survive
5 autumn
6 task
7 water
8 sell
9 important
10 variety

5C In this second listening activity, students can imagine that they are asking questions at the lecture. Now that they have heard the lecture once already, ask them to work in pairs to try to complete as much of the information as possible before they listen again.

5 LISTEN IN C **Answers**

1 **Q:** What percentage of the population lives in Petropavlovsk-Kamchatsky?
A: About 90 per cent.
2 **Q:** What mineral deposits are there?
A: Gold, copper and nickel.
3 **Q:** How long must bear meat be soaked?
A: For 24-36 hours (in fresh water).
4 **Q:** What happens on Fish Day?
A: There are fish-cleaning competitions, wrestling matches and horse races.
5 **Q:** What do they have for breakfast?
A: Bread, pink salmon roe, tomatoes and cucumbers.

We would like to thank conservationist Emma Wilson for her advice on this set of listening activities. Emma is co-editor of a book called *The Russian Far East: forests, biodiversity hotspots and industrial developments,* published by Friends of the Earth Japan. Emma has worked extensively in Kamchatka and was able to verify the information about the region that we found from various sources.

6 CONTROVERSY See Role cards Page 64 WB

Read the notes about this section in the Introduction. This activity is a debate. You can remind yourself of our recommendations about how to conduct a debate by reading the **Controversy** notes for Unit 6 in this **Teacher's Guide**.

This is a debate about hunting. In this case, there are three role cards, each proposing a different opinion on the subject. We recommend that you divide the class into three groups, and each group discusses how to speak in favour of one of the three opinions. Then you ask for a volunteer from each group to speak. As an extra team exercise, you can suggest to each group that they make notes and ask difficult questions to the speakers from the other groups.

7 PORTFOLIO WRITING

The writing task is to describe an old national custom, a festival for example. Because the structure focus of this Unit is reported speech, we have suggested that the students should write as if reporting the words of an older person, who knows about the history and / or origins of the festival.

On the other hand, you may want to make this a homework activity, and ask the students to genuinely ask an older person to give them details. It will help if you choose a local festival and ask the whole class to write about the same thing. There are details in the **Student's Book** of the kind of information they should include in the text.

The writing model below refers to a festival in a city in Lancashire called Preston. Every 20 years, they have a special celebration called 'The Preston Guild'.

Writing model – a traditional festival

Name and time:
Preston Guild; every 20 years!

History:
In 1179, the city of Preston was given the right to hold a Merchant Guild, a kind of festival for merchants, every 20 years. There were breaks in the tradition, but since 1902, it has been held every 20 years (except in 1942 when there was a war). The next one will be in 2012.

Who told you:
My grandfather told me about the Guild. He was born in 1935 and he remembers that everyone was very unhappy because the Guild festival was cancelled in 1942. Of course, he didn't know what it was that had been cancelled! But he told me that the Guild celebration of 1952 was the best ever. He said there was a party in every street in Preston!

What happens:
There are concerts, exhibitions and street parties. At the exhibitions, you can see wonderful souvenirs from previous Guilds, for example, commemorative cups and saucers from 1902!!! There are also a series of processions through the streets of the city. Grandfather said that he had been in the procession in 1952, when he was 17 years old. He told me that he had met my grandmother there! My grandmother told me that this was nonsense, and that she had met my grandfather at school. I don't know who to believe!

8 *CONSTITUTIONAL LAW in English* Page 61 SB

Guns have been central to the topics of this Unit so far, so we chose Constitutional Law as the featured cross-curricular topic because we wanted students to think and talk about the wider use and availability of guns, and the fact that 'the right to bear arms' is a constitutional right in the USA.

Picture notes / Background information

The photo shows CCTV image of the terrible events of 20th April 1999 at Columbine High School in the State of Colorado, USA. The two teenage Columbine students, Eric Harris and Dylan Klebold, killed 12 fellow students and a teacher, and wounded 24 others. They then committed suicide. It was the worst school shooting in US history. The massacre led to more debate about US gun control laws and the availability of firearms. This was also the subject of the opening sequences of the film *Bowling for Columbine* by Michael Moore, the campaigning American comedian and journalist. See http://www.bowlingforcolumbine.com/media/clips/index.php

Key words / expressions

Archaic and legal words: • amendment
• blessings • constitution • infringe
• insure • ordain • to provide for
• tranquillity • welfare
• well-regulated militia
• posterity = people who come after us

Other words: • defence
• to defend (the rights of)
• justice • liberty • right (noun)
• domestic = not foreign

There are some archaic words in this reading text, which you only need to explain and then move on. There is no need to try to activate them.

• ordain – in this formal sense, it means *to order that something should be done*. Nowadays, the word is used when someone is made a priest.

• infringe – here it means *take away someone's right*.

Apart from these words, students need to be clear about what a constitution is (the basis of government and law) and what an amendment is (a change in a constitution). There is some more detailed **Background information** below which you might find useful.

<u>Background information</u>
The US Constitution is the official document that is the basis of government and law in the United States. It was written in 1787 and ratified in 1789. Many amendments have been added since then. The first ten amendments are referred to as the Bill of Rights. The Constitution grants certain specified rights, often called constitutional rights, to the American people. It also places limits on the powers and activities of US federal and state governments.

After the American War of Independence (1775-1783), the thirteen states that formed the original USA (becoming independent from Britain) needed to arrange a federal government.

At the time, the only federal law they had was based on something called 'The Articles of Confederation of the United Colonies of New England' which had been established more than a hundred years before, in 1643.

In May 1787, representatives from twelve of the original thirteen states met in Philadelphia to discuss changes to the Articles of Confederation. In fact, the meeting went much further than that and they decided to propose a completely rewritten Constitution. Despite opposition from some politicians, who thought that a constitution would take away some of the power of the individual states, the new constitution was completed in September 1787. The form of government it recommended came into existence on 4th March 1789.

The authors of the Constitution were aware that changes would be necessary from time to time if the Constitution was to endure and cope with the effects of the anticipated growth of the nation. They realised that it would be necessary to occasionally have amendments.

What makes the US Constitution different, and almost unique, is the fact that amendments are added to the existing body of the text, rather than being revisions of the main articles. There is no provision for removing obsolete or disputed provisions from the text. This is why discussions such as changing the second amendment, the right to bear arms, become so complicated.

8A The first activity asks students to read the texts and say what they have learnt about the US Constitution. They then discuss the amendment which offers Americans the right to bear arms.

8B The second task is to interpret the old-fashioned Second Amendment to the US Constitution in more modern terms. It is not completely clear what it means, but the third interpretation is the closest.

9 CONVERSATION

Read the notes about this section in the Introduction. Students work in pairs and discuss one of the many photos in this Unit. This is a common examination task. The best way to do it is to ask both students to choose a different photo, and make notes about how to describe it. When Student A has finished describing it, Student B should ask questions about it. Students shouldn't just concentrate the immediate content of the photo, but should look at the wider implications.

10 *<u>Your answer:</u>*

Finally, back to *<u>The BIG question</u>* as usual, with some secondary questions and some suggested responses. So far, we have suggested that this activity should be a whole class or group discussion activity. If you prefer, you could ask the students to write their answers for homework. You might like to add to the discussion a saying that has become popular in the US: 'The right to bear arms is as logical as the right to arm bears.'

Workbook answers — Pages 30-31 WB

1 Language: reported speech

1A 1 He said everyone would get an opportunity to shoot a bear.

2 George said that one tourist had taken only three days to find and shoot a bear.

3 She said we were allowed to kill two bears each.

See pages 58-61 SB, 30-31 WB

4 The guide said that unfortunately they couldn't promise a kill.
5 He said that he refused to go hunting and (added that) it was cruel.
6 The man said that he believed that the bears were leaving the area.
7 The hunter said that he had always hunted there and would continue to do so.
8 They said that when they had returned to the area the previous year, it had still been just as wild.

1B **1** I asked the tour operator how much the trip cost.
2 He asked me if I had ever shot an animal before.
3 I told Jim that I didn't believe in hunting.
4 He told me to wait.
5 I asked him what I had to do.

2 Use of English

2A **1** People hunt because of their need for food.
2 Kluchi is typical of Kamchatkan villages / Kluchi is a typical village of Kamchatka.
3 They depend on salted bear meat for their winter food.
4 It is boiled for five hours so that it is safe to eat.

2B **1**j **2**e **3**i **4**h **5**d **6**b
7g **8**a **9**f **10**c

3 Portfolio writing

Students' own answers

4 Connections

4A1 **(a)** customary **(b)** traditional
(c) national **(d)** cultural
(e) celebratory / celebrate
(f) tend to **(g)** greet
(h) gesture

4A2 **(a)** national **(b)** gestures
(c) tend to (d) cultural
(e) traditional **(f)** greeting
(g) customary **(h)** celebrate

4B **1** The Spanish **2** The French
3 The Turks **4** The Russians
5 The Greeks

As we explained in the Introduction to this **Teacher's Guide**, the three Extended Reading Units contain texts which are longer and more substantial than the main reading texts of the other Units. Extended Reading 2 is an authentic newspaper article about the problem of waste computers and other electrical equipment. The article is taken from the London newspaper *The Guardian.* First of all, here is a list of the key words and expressions in the article.

Key words / expressions

• according to • **alarmed** • arise • bother with • bulk dealer • **cannibalised** • **civic amenity site** • computer monitor • developing countries/world • **discard** • dispose of • economic • environmental agency • estimate (vb) • **grey area** • **guidance** • handle (vb) • **injustice** • lead • **leaded glass** • legislation • pose (a danger) • reclassify • saleable • ship (vb) • **sift through** • spare parts • totter • **toxic waste materials** • unpublished • workers' conditions • **working models**

This is clearly a more complex reading text than the others the students have encountered. You must decide if you want to (a) examine the material in open class, (b) ask students to work on it in pairs or groups or (c) do it for homework, using dictionaries and other aids to study.

The underlined words are activated in the **2 PREVIEW** section. The words **in bold** are activated in the **3 READING** section. Here is some information about some of the other words. The word *totter* is used to describe someone who looks through rubbish to find things they can sell – the photo which accompanies the article on page 63 shows totters at work. A *bulk dealer* is someone who deals in large amounts of items. Note also that the noun *lead* here refers to the soft grey metal which has caused serious pollution and health problems. In this situation the word *economic* means good value.

Background information

Friends of the Earth (FoE) is an international network of environmental organisations in 70 different countries. The national groups in each country are composed of local groups working in their own areas. The various FoE groups consider environmental issues in their social, political and human rights contexts. Their campaigns stretch beyond the traditional arena of the conservation movement and address issues of sustainable development.

1 *The BIG read*: DUMPED COMPUTERS SOLD ILLEGALLY by Paul Brown

Each of these Extended Reading Units starts with a pre-reading text, something short and related to the topic. In this case, it is a Cree proverb about how we over-use and exploit natural resources.

Background information

The Cree are the largest of the native tribes of North America, and at one time lived in an area from the Rocky Mountains in the west to the Atlantic Ocean in the east, in both the United States and Canada. Their numbers were decimated when they encountered and fought English and French settlers. They were skilled buffalo hunters and horsemen and they cared a lot about preserving their environment. The proverb comes from the time when their world was being destroyed by the invading forces of Europeans.

2 PREVIEW

If you prefer, the class can work on these extended reading texts in examination conditions, having to deal with any new words and information by trying to understand the context. However, we still offer some preliminary exploitation of the vocabulary and ideas here in the **Teacher's Guide**. You can discuss the new words and expressions with students before they read, but even if you work on the text in class, rather than for homework, it may be more helpful for them if they encounter the new material in context. The latter method is more useful for the class if they are about to take an exam where the reading texts are of this complexity.

2A The first activity deals with the quotation at the beginning of the page. Students are asked to discuss it.

2B **1** Students read the headline of the article and work out from the context what *dumped computers* means. The correct answer is (a).
2 A less dramatic way to say *dumped* would be *abandoned* or *used.*

2C Students are asked to find the underlined words in the text. They then answer questions about the meaning of these words, contrasting them with other possible meanings and uses of the same words.

2 PREVIEW C **Answers**

1 *pose* means something different here. *Pose a danger* means to present a danger.
2 No. *Handle* as a noun means the part of a door that you use to open it. *Handle* as a verb indicates that something passes through your hands or that you have to deal with (*eg handle a difficult situation; handle stolen goods*).
3 *estimate* vb / estImeIt; noun /estimət / The noun ends in a /ə/, which is a shorter sound.
4 No. Here *arise* means *occur; problems arise …* this is a good collocation to remember!
5 No. In this case *bother with* means *do something about;* a common usage: *don't bother with that; don't bother to do that – it's not important.*

2D In this activity, we give the definitions of three expressions from the text, and ask students to talk about them. We ask what they know about civic amenity sites and toxic waste, and particularly about why lead is a pollution problem.

Background information

lead pollution: In the past, lead (Pb) was widely used in piping, including pipes that carried domestic water supplies, and also for paints for walls and art and glass-making. Until recently, it was also added to car fuel because it allowed better combustion, making engines more fuel-efficient. However, lead released in the air through car exhausts was absorbed into the bloodstream when inhaled and caused major damage. Although leaded fuel is no longer sold in the developed world, some estimates say that lead pollution has damaged the intelligence of 10% of British children, and 17% in the USA. Today, lead pollution primarily comes from lead smelters, metal processing factories and incinerators. There are also problems when items consisting of lead, such as leaded glass, are dumped.

3 READING CD 2 (Red) track 15, Page 63

3A In this activity, students are asked to work out the meaning of certain words and phrased from the context. Start by telling them that it may be impossible to work out the exact meaning of some of them from the context. Here are the words and expressions in context, and some notes about what the context should tell the students:

1 '…totters – people who *sift through* rubbish for saleable objects...'
We can see that *sift through* must be a verb, and it's something that people do with rubbish to find things to sell. From this, students should be able to realise that it is the action we can see in the photo on page 63.

2 'The agency is *alarmed* that half a million televisions … are being … dumped …'
Alarmed is obviously an adjective, and the thing that is *alarming* the agency is the size of the problem. So, probably it means *worried.*

3 'The agency … is planning to publish *guidance* to the industry soon.'
Guidance is obviously a noun; it has no article before it and it ends in *-ance,* so it's probably an abstract noun; and it's something you can publish. These are good clues!

4 'Action must be taken now to prevent this environmental *injustice* continuing.'
This is an unusual use of *injustice,* and the collocation has been used by the speaker for effect. If students know the words *just* and *justice,* they should work out that the speaker

thinks that this is wrong for the environment.

5 'many are *cannibalised* for spare parts.'
Another unusual use of a word. *Cannibals* of course eat people, but *cannibalise* has come to mean taking parts from something to use again.

6 '*working models* ... intended to be sold on the second-hand market.'
Items which are still functioning. They should work if they are saleable second-hand.

7 'there is a *grey area* here about some of the exports.'
The component words of this collocation are both very simple. Hopefully, the notion of a *grey area* – a situation where the law (or anything else) is not clear – may be the same in the students' own language.

8 '...if something has been *discarded,* even if it can be used again ...'
Again, *discarded* is a verb, used passively. And we know that we are talking about things which have been dumped, thrown away.

3B Now, finally, a comprehension exercise, with the slight difference that we ask students NOT to quote from the text in their answers. (This is a good homework exercise.)

3 READING B **Answers**

1. Computers can be recycled by taking them to places organised by local authorities. In some of these places, people look through the machines for items that they can resell.
2. The work of the totters who try to resell computers became illegal because they can no longer export these items because of the danger of toxic waste.
3. The text suggests that it must be half a million, the same number as television sets.
4. If a computer is still working, it can be legally sold. If it has been dumped, it is considered to be toxic waste. But this is a grey area.
5. It is expensive to repair things in the UK, and the implication is that people buy new things rather than repair old ones.

4 TALK ABOUT IT

The discussion offers the class the chance to be imaginative about how to recycle domestic items. Think of the parts of machines that can be used – not just the whole item. For example, electric motors could be used to power other machines. Think of some amusing and unlikely ways to recycle. In remote parts of Australia, people put old microwave ovens or even fridges at their front gate to act as mail boxes!

5 PORTFOLIO WRITING

The first writing task is a summary of the article in 200 words, and the second is an article suggesting how other product can be recycled. You could, if you wish, ask students to do the first task in class and the second as homework.

5A / B Below are writing models for these tasks.

Writing models

Making a summary

Environmental agencies are worried about the number of computers and other pieces of electrical equipment which are being discarded and then recycled in developing countries. Part of the problem is that the European Union law has changed, and nowadays it is illegal to send discarded computers to other countries because of the risk of pollution. Friends of the Earth is concerned because workers in developing countries may work in conditions where they are in more danger from handling these goods.

The Industry Council for Electronic Equipment Recycling (ICER) defends sending machines to other countries on the grounds that it is legal to sell machines if they are in working order. But the legal position of this is not clear.

Another problem is that totters – the people who go through piles of discarded computers for reusable items – often sell the parts on to dealers that they know nothing about. They have no idea where the parts will end up.

Another consideration is that some of the

machines are in good condition, but have been discarded because it's cheaper to buy a new machine, rather than repair old ones. If this is the case, why not allow the machines to be used in developing countries?

Writing an article

How goods can be recycled

In the developed world, there is a growing problem of discarded items. From cars to plastic bottles, too many things are being thrown away. In some countries, there is a serious attempt to recycle the paper, cardboard, glass and plastic products which make up the majority of waste that is produced.

However, it is in the area of cars, computer and other electronic goods and 'white products' – refrigerators, washing machines etc – that there is a very big problem. Not only are these items very big and heavy, they also often cause pollution when they are broken up. Washing machines, for example, contain chemicals called CFCs which are released if the machine is broken up and which damage the ozone layer.

Clearly, the best thing for these goods is to recycle them. With cars, the best thing is for totters to take anything that can be re-used – the tyres, seats and certain mechanical items. After that, the car should be broken up into metal, wood, glass, plastic and other items and these items should be recycled too. Some of the items are not so easy to recycle, but the metal can be reused in other cars. And the rest must be disposed of carefully.

What's new?

Subject: Dreams and nightmares
Function: Expressing abstract ideas
Grammar: Passives with modals (*can be seen, should be read*)

Before you open the book ...
Write the titles of the following books on the board: *Harry Potter / The Lord of the Rings.* Ask: *What do you know about these books?* Most students will probably know something about one or two of the titles. Elicit the fact / explain that they are fantasy stories, and if necessary, teach the word *fantasy* (= an experience or situation that you imagine that is not real). For each title, ask how many in the class have seen the films and whether they enjoyed them. Explain that the title of the Unit is *Fantasy worlds* and that the Unit will explore the world of fantasy. (See **Background information** notes below for information on *Harry Potter* and *The Lord of the Rings.)*

1 *The BIG question:* WHY IS FANTASY SO POPULAR?

FACT: More than 300 million copies of the Harry Potter fantasy stories have been sold in 200 countries.

Write *The BIG question* and the **FACT** on the board. Tell the class they will have the opportunity to discuss *The BIG question* later. Elicit the meaning of the word *copy* (= a single book, or a single CD that is one of many that are all exactly the same). Ask: *Have the Harry Potter stories sold well here / in your country?*

2 PREVIEW

Words

A Explain that the word *fantasy* can have slightly different meanings, and that this activity helps to explain these meanings.

B Explain that the phrase *to have in common*, as in *What do they have in common? = What are the similarities between them? / in what way are they the same?* A *show* is a performance for the public, especially one that includes dancing or singing.

C This activity will elicit students' attitudes to fantasy films, books etc. When the class has completed the activity, elicit answers, and briefly elicit students' reasons for their answers, *eg I enjoy fantasy because it helps me relax / I don't have to think about real life / I can't stand fantasy, I think it's ridiculous.*

D Put students in pairs for this activity. Then elicit answers, teaching new vocabulary where necessary.

Background information / Internet references
Star Wars: The film *Star Wars* was first shown in 1977. Directed by American George Lucas, it was a huge hit, particularly among teenagers, as were the two sequels, *The Empire Strikes Back* and *The Return of the Jedi*. The films were notable for their epic quality and their extraordinary use of special effects.

Star Wars was in fact planned by Lucas as the fourth in a series of six films. The first film in the series, *The Phantom Menace*, was released in 1999, 22 years after the release of the original *Star Wars*. Two more films followed, *The Attack of the Clones* (2002) and *Revenge of the Sith*, the third film in the series, in 2005.

The six-part series, which takes place at a time when planets and galaxies are linked together in a republic, tells the story of the downfall of the republic and the rise of an evil empire. It traces the rise of Anakin Skywalker as a warrior with magic powers (a Jedi) and his gradual fall into evil. The final three films in the series trace the rise of Anakin Skywalker's son as a good Jedi and the defeat of the evil Empire. *Star Wars* starred the American Harrison Ford, who became a huge star as a result.

Harry Potter: Harry Potter is the name of a popular series of fantasy novels by British author J.K Rowling. There are seven books planned in the whole series. The novels caught the imagination of children (and adults) all over the world and have had record sales. They tell the story of a boy, Harry Potter, who discovers that he is a wizard. He goes to wizard school and finds that there is a whole magic world of wizards and witches that ordinary people know nothing about.

Harry discovers that an evil wizard called Lord Voldemort had tried to destroy him as a baby but had failed. Voldemort, who has lost his power, is trying to regain it, and in each novel Harry finds that he has to fight his terrifying opponent. Rowling's novels are humorous, imaginative and exciting. Each of the novels has been eagerly awaited, and they have been made into highly successful films.

Nutcracker: The music for the ballet was written by Pyotr Ilyich Tchaikovsky in 1892. This version was directed by British dancer and choreographer Matthew Bourne, and first performed in 2002. Bourne is known for his exciting, very modern choreography. He once directed a performance of *Swan Lake* (1995) where all the parts were danced by men!

For more information go to these websites:
www.starwars.com
www.jkrowling.com

2 PREVIEW Words A / B / D **Answers**

A **1** (b) **2** (c) **3** (a)

B **1** They all show fantasy stories. (The Nutcracker ballet is a fantasy).

D A **witch** is a woman with magic powers. She is sometimes old, but also sometimes young and beautiful. A **dragon** is an imaginary animal that breathes fire and has wings and a tail. A **fairy** is an imaginary magical creature like a very small person. A fairy usually has wings. A **prince** is the son of a king / queen, a **princess** is the daughter of a king/queen. A **vampire** is an imaginary dead person who bites people's necks and sucks their blood.

http://www.matthewbournesnutcracker.com/

Language

This activity focuses on passives with modals: *can / should / must / have to / may / might* + *be* + past participle. The class have already covered the main passive forms, so should not find this structure too difficult. NB: You will probably need to teach the word *predecessor* (= something or someone that comes before someone else, often in a job), used in the first example sentence.

A Elicit the answer, and, to briefly check students remember the basic passive forms, ask them to put these sentences into the passive:

1 Millions of people enjoy fantasy stories.
Fantasy stories are enjoyed by millions of people.

2 Everyone will buy this book.
This book will be bought by everyone.

3 They showed the film all over the country.
The film was shown all over the country.

B This question checks students understand that just because a past participle is used in the passive structure, it does not mean that the sentence refers to the past.

C Students will find it helpful if they can actually explain how the structure is formed: *can / must* etc + *be* + past participle. For further practice, ask students to put this famous nineteenth century English saying into the passive:
You should see children and not hear them.

2 PREVIEW Language A / B / C **Answers**

A The sentences are passive.

B They refer to the present (or future).

C They have the same structure: modal (*can / must / should*) + *be* + past participle.

(Children should be seen and not heard).

Ideas

Explain that the novel the sentences are taken from tells the story of a boy wizard called Ged. Tell students that the novel was written about 20 years before the Harry Potter books, which have a similar subject. Explain that in the extract that the class will read, Ged *casts a spell* and the result is very frightening. You will almost certainly need to teach the following vocabulary items before students can answer the questions about the sentences: *(to cast) a spell / enchantment / oval / breach / lump / shadow.*

2 PREVIEW A **Answers**

A Through the bright crack climbs a lump of black shadow and it leaps straight out at Ged's face.

Definitions are in the **Key words** box below.

3 READING CD 2 (Red) track 16, Page 65 SB

Key words / expressions

- arrogant • law • fabric • spell
- to work • to embrace • to split apart
- sorrowful • to glimmer • to widen
- to stagger • to scream • to struggle
- to flee (p.p.*fled*) • to cling • beast
- paw • to sob • bound still • to fade
- edge • fountain • to heal
- (to cast) a spell = to say words or perform actions that make magic things happens
- predecessor = something or someone that comes before someone else, often in a job
- spirit = the part of a person that many people believes continues to exist after death
- oval = with a shape like a long narrow circle
- enchantment = spell
- to gleam = to shine brightly
- breach = a crack or break in something
- lump = a small piece of something without a regular shape
- shadow = an area of darkness created when something blocks light
- to tear (p.p.*torn*) = to pull something so that it separates or gets a hole in it
- to rip / the rip = to tear something quickly / a hole produced by tearing
- (the spell) works = the spell is successful
- bound still = made unable to move (from the verb *to bind*, p.p. *bound*)

If students have completed the **Ideas** section, they will know a little about the text they are going to read. Explain that the reading passage consists of a book review which introduces an extract from a fantasy novel called *The Wizard of Earthsea*, the first in a trilogy called *The Earthsea Trilogy*. Explain that the novel tells the story of Ged, a boy wizard.

Teach key vocabulary before students read the text. Tell the class not to worry about the new words they encounter. They should simply aim to understand the key points and events of the story, and to answer the questions.

When you come to question **3** in activity **C**, Point out to students that the answer is suggested rather than stated. Vech is *bound still, unable to move* because a voice is speaking softly nearby. This is a healing voice – *Starlight began to shine again ..... The night was healed.* Vetch is unable to move probably because he was going to touch the black shadow. That would probably have killed him. The person speaking protected him from this.

Background information / Internet reference

A Wizard of Earthsea is the first book, published in 1968, in a trilogy called *The Earthsea Trilogy* by Ursula K. Le Guin. The other books are *The Tombs of Atuan* (1970) and *The Farthest Shore* (1972). The Earthsea stories take place on a group of islands in an ocean world and involve the Wizard Ged, also called Sparrowhawk, at different points in his life. Ged is a peasant boy, who goes to the School of Wizards on Roke Island. Trying to show off his magical powers, he calls forth a terrible shadow from the dead. The novel follows his attempts to escape the shadow, which relentlessly follows him. Finally, he turns and confronts it and in doing so, achieves great wisdom. Ursula Le Guin is regarded as an important American writer of both science fiction and fantasy. For more information go to this website:
http://members.aol.com/misuly/leguin.htm

3 READING A / B / C **Answers**

A **1** Vetch is a friend of Ged's. He puts out his hand to try to pull the lump of shadow away from Ged.

2 The rip closes up. (… slowly the torn edges of the world closed together.)

B **1** True.

2 False. Ged calls up a spirit from the dead, which is 'something that must never be done, as it is against all the laws of nature.'

C **1** It is described as 'a tall woman looking back over her shoulder. Her face was beautiful, and

sorrowful, and full of fear.'
2 Jasper bends down to the ground and hides his eyes from the terrible light.
3 Because someone is speaking and casting another spell to protect Vetch. Probably, if he touched the black shadow, it would kill him.

4 TALK ABOUT IT

4A Encourage students to speculate. Ask: *What do you think happens after this?* If you wish, tell students a little more about the story (see **Background information** notes above).

4B This activity provides an opportunity to practise the structure focused on in the Unit, passives with modals. Walk round and read students' paragraphs. Choose one or two and write them on the board. Praise them and ask the class to say what they like about them. Then ask students to say how the paragraphs could be improved, encouraging them to use the passive form.

5 LISTEN IN CD 1 (Blue) track 14, Page 66 SB

Key words / expressions
- to vote • horror movie
- (I) can't stand (horror movies) • violence
- to terrify • the point • thriller
- channel (7) • joke • chip • nightmare
- the suspense (is killing me) • evil • awful
- gross • effect • stuff • entertainment
- to be sick • relief • horrifying • dream
- the point = the most important fact, idea
- scary = frightening
- to be over = to be finished
- sequel = a book, film, play etc that continues the story of an earlier one
- totally (slang) = absolutely

The **Audio text** is in the **Workbook** (page 70). In the listening passage, three American teenagers (two boys, Tom and Dave, and a girl, Nancy), discuss and watch a horror movie. The girl does not like horror movies and would prefer to watch a thriller. She leaves the room for some of the time. The boys enjoy the film precisely because it is so 'gross'. In fact the film is so horrifying that at one point Tom thinks he's going to be sick. The conversation ends with the two boys agreeing to watch the sequel the following week. The conversation is very typical of the way teenagers talk, with quite a lot of slang, such as *That was really gross! / That was bad! / Cool, man / I think that must totally be seen.*

5A The listening passage refers to both horror movies and thrillers. If students can explain the difference between horror movies and thrillers by saying that a horror movie is very frightening, while a thriller is exciting, that is an adequate explanation. Students may have seen the films pictured. Ask them: *What did you think of (Mission Impossible)?* Take the opportunity to teach adjectives, *eg It was brilliant / amazing,* and expressions, such as *It had great special effects* (= the artificial images and sounds in a film that are created by technology).

5B Elicit examples of abstract nouns like *happiness / the past* to check that students understand the meaning of *abstract noun* (= a word that names a quality, idea or feeling),

5C For words **1**, **4** and **5**, elicit both active and passive forms of the adjectives: *terrifying / terrified, horrifying / horrified, exciting / excited.* Ask students to make sentences showing they understand the difference, *eg The story was horrifying / I was horrified (by the story).*

5D Cambridge ESOL FCE 2008+ style activity, completing sentences with information in the recording - details, information, and opinion.

5E Explain that the conversation is between two boys, Tom and Dave, and a girl, Nancy. Explain also that they use typical teenage expressions.

5 LISTEN IN A / B / C / D / E Answers

A 1 The photo on the left is from a horror film. The photo on the right is from a thriller.
2 A horror film is about strange and frightening things. A thriller is an exciting film about murder or a crime.

B 1 (a) (b) (c) (d) (e) **2** (e) (f)
3 (b) (c) (d) (f) (g)

C 2 violent 3 afraid / fearful 4 horrified / horrifying 5 excited / exciting
D 1 votes 2 violence 3 horror 4 nightmare 5 suspense 6 entertainment 7 dreams 8 sequel
E 1 Audio: *The idea of witches and vampires **terrifies** me.* Terrifies is stronger than frightens.
2 Audio: ***I'm going to get** some drinks.* Same meaning.
3 Audio: ***This** is entertainment at its **best**.* The word *worst* gives the opposite meaning.
4 Audio: ***What** a relief **that's over**.* Audio words imply the film has ended. Sentence in exercise implies it has not ended yet.
5 Audio: *You don't like horror movies **either**.* Addition of the word *either* insinuates that the speaker also doesn't like horror movies.

6 CONTROVERSY See Role cards Page 64 WB

Read the notes about this section in the Introduction. Put students into pairs and allow them to choose which part they want to play. Explain that the conversation must end with them watching either a fantasy or a horror movie. Walk round while students are performing the role play and choose two pairs of confident students to perform the role play for the class. Afterwards, ask the class to say what they liked about the role plays and to point out mistakes.

7 PORTFOLIO WRITING

To practise the language used in the model, ask the class to agree on a film that most of them have seen. Ask them to talk about and give their opinion of the film using the language in the boxes, *eg (name of film) is a comedy directed by (name of director). / The story takes place in (New York). / It's about ......*

Encourage students to briefly describe the plot and say what they liked / disliked about the film. You may need to explain that the phrase *I find / found it (boring / exciting / slow)* is a phrase used to give an opinion. Having practised the language, students will be able to write their review (of a film of their own choice) with more confidence.

Writing model

Harry Potter and the Goblet of Fire is the fourth film in the series of Harry Potter films. It is directed by the British director Mike Newell. Like the first three films it stars Daniel Radcliffe as Harry, Rupert Grint as Harry's friend, Ron, and Emily Watson as their friend, Hermione.

As in the previous films, the story takes place at Hogworts, the school for wizards and witches. In this film, Harry takes part in a competition for which the prize is a 'goblet of fire'. To win the goblet Harry must perform very difficult and dangerous magical tasks, for example, defeating a dragon. As in all the Potter films, it ends with a terrifying encounter with Voldemort, the evil wizard who is trying to win back his power.

The three previous Harry Potter films were all very enjoyable, but the *Goblet of Fire* is, in my opinion, the best of them all. The film is visually very exciting. Daniel, Ron and Hermione are older in this film and consequently more interesting. Their teenage romances are an amusing part of the story. Emily Watson and Rupert Grint, in particular, give wonderful performances. For all those who enjoyed the first three movies, this film must not be missed.

8 *LITERATURE in English* Page 67 SB

Key words / expressions

- chilling • monster • villa • lake
- poet • to speculate • power • ghost
- vision • journal • engine • to rush (away)
- spark • to fade • curtain • to wonder
- novel • to publish • fiction
- to involve • mystery
- chilling = very frightening
- to speculate = to consider or discuss why something has happened
- journal = diary
- to clank = if a heavy metal object clanks, it makes a short, loud sound
- to stir = to move slightly
- horror-stricken = horrified
- horrid = very unpleasant
- genre = a particular type of film, writing or art

- (the) fantastic = strange or imaginary (one of several meanings)
- (the) supernatural = things that seem to be caused by magic, and do not have a natural or scientific explanation

Ask the class what the word *literature* means to them. Elicit answers and agree on a definition, *eg stories, poems and plays with artistic value.* Ask students to give examples of *literature* in their own language.

8A The photo shows a poster of the film, *Frankenstein* (see **Background information** notes below).

8B Teach key vocabulary items before asking students to read the text and answer the questions. When answering question **3**, make sure that students realise that an explanation of the Gothic fiction genre is given in the text: *Gothic novels involved the fantastic and supernatural and were full of suspense and mystery.*

8C Mystery and horror are still popular. Practice vocabulary and language from the audio.

8D If students know the story of Frankenstein, this activity could lead to a very interesting discussion. If they don't know the story, you could briefly describe it to them (see **Background information** notes below). To stimulate discussion, ask: *What is Frankenstein about? What is Mary Shelley trying to say? How is this relevant today?* Below are some suggestions for answers:

- *Frankenstein* is about the power of science. In *Frankenstein*, a scientist invents a creature that he cannot control. Scientists have done this today, with, for example, the atomic bomb. Another modern example is global warming, which is caused by scientific progress and may destroy the planet.
- *Frankenstein* is also about the need that living creatures have for love. The monster turns against his creator because the scientist does not recognise that he has feelings – he may be ugly but he is still capable of love. Today it is recognised more and more that if we do not receive love as children we become psychologically damaged.

Background information

Frankenstein (the novel) tells the story of a young scientist called Frankenstein who succeeds in creating a creature that resembles a human being. The creature is monstrous, ugly, and with huge strength, and all those who see it are terrified. But the creature has human feelings and is lonely and unhappy. It needs love and companionship and cannot find this. When Frankenstein refuses to give the monster a wife, the monster turns against his creator and kills Frankenstein's brother, his friend and his bride, Elizabeth. Frankenstein pursues the monster to the Arctic to destroy it, but dies there. The monster disappears into the ice and darkness to end its life.

The 1931 film *Frankenstein,* starring Boris Karloff as the monster and directed by James Whale, became hugely famous and remains famous today. Because the film is entitled *Frankenstein*, it has caused many people to believe that Frankenstein is the name of the monster. This is incorrect. Frankenstein is the name of the scientist who created him. The monster has no name.

8 *LITERATURE in English* B — Answers

1 Mary Shelley was only 18 when she began writing *Frankenstein.*

2 She and her group of friends were discussing electricity. That night, Mary couldn't sleep, and had a vision of a monster, created by a student, using electricity. The vision terrified her, and she realised it would be a wonderful story. She started work on the story the next day.

3 Modern horror stories are full of suspense, like gothic novels. Similarly, horror stories often involve the fantastic – strange, imaginary events.

9 CONVERSATION

Read the notes about this section in the Introduction. Allow students to choose which activity they would like to do, **A** or **B**. For activity **B**, ask students to decide on the genre (type of film, *eg* comedy), the basic plot, the main characters and who will play the parts. Each pair could then make a presentation to the class.

10 *Your answer:*

This activity gives the class the chance to discuss *The BIG question* in depth and to express their own feelings about fantasy literature and films. For a variation on this activity, ask students to find someone who has the opposite view to them about fantasy and to have a two / three minute discussion with them.

Workbook answers Pages 34-35 WB

1 Language: passives with modals

1A **1** This book should be read by everyone.
2 This film shouldn't be missed.
3 Nothing could be seen except a shadow.
4 The ghost can only be seen at night.
5 The monster must be killed.
6 What happened may never be forgotten.

1B **1** Can the story be written quickly?
2 When should the witches be followed to their homes?
3 Could it be completed this week?
4 Was the film made in Japan?
5 Why can't your daemon be separated from you?

1C **1** I want the truth to be discovered.
2 The grave is going to be opened.
3 I want someone to be told about this.
4 I'm sorry. It had to be done, Peter.

2 Use of English

2A **1** With them was another poet, Lord Byron, who had already become famous.
2 The poet Shelley married a girl who was eighteen years old.
3 Gothic stories were about the fantastic and supernatural.
4 What terrified me will be terrifying to others.
5 The story is still popular today.

2B **(1)** on **(2)** of **(3)** of **(4)** saw **(5)** over **(6)** later **(7)** with **(8)** in **(9)** was **(10)** believes

3 Portfolio writing

Students' own answers

4 Connections

4B **1** clanking **2** crashed **3** groan **4** spluttered / whirring

What's new?

Subject:	The world of work
Function:	Expressing likes and dislikes
Grammar:	Verbs + *ing* or an infinitive

Before you open the book ...

The topic of this Unit is the world of work. The structure item is verbs which are followed by the *-ing* form (*I enjoy cooking)* and those which are followed by an infinitive (*I'm planning to go to France for my holiday).* The verbs which will feature in the structure practice are *plan, aim, hope, decide, enjoy, consider, delay* and *imagine.*

Some or all of these verbs should be known to the students already, and we recommend presenting the ones that aren't before you open the book. As we have said before, a well thought out presentation at this stage is much better than encountering the word later and asking *What does it mean?* to the class. Always remember that even a native speaker would have trouble answering the question: *What does 'consider' mean?*

Most of the verbs can be built into a question and answer session about work ambitions. Some students may not want to talk about this topic to the rest of the class. For their own reasons, they may want to keep their work and other ambitions to themselves. Therefore, in the following activity, we suggest that you ask students to write answers on a piece of paper, rather than give their opinions in open class.

Start by writing *Plans and ambitions* on the board, followed by some questions, which activate some of the verbs that will appear in this Unit.

1 What do you plan to do (after this course / when you leave college / school?)
2 Do you hope to travel?
3 Can you imagine living in a foreign country?
4 Would you consider working in a developing country?

Ask the class to write answers to one or more of these questions on a piece of paper. The whole activity can be done anonymously, if the students prefer. They don't have to write their name on the piece of paper. You then collect the pieces of paper and read out some of the answers. Write some of the examples on the board.

If you do all the above activities before you open the book, you may find that you will talk about things which are discussion items later on. You may find, for example, that when you get to the **Ideas** section, you have already asked students the three questions which you will find there.

1 *The BIG question:* WOULD YOU LIKE TO MAKE A MILLION?

FACT: The most-trusted professionals are nurses, pharmacists, vets, doctors and teachers. The best-paid professionals are soccer players, racing drivers and people who work in legal and financial services.

At first sight, it would seem that everyone is going to answer *The BIG question* in the same way, with a loud 'YES PLEASE!' However, the topic of this Unit goes a little further than that and we offer students the chance to discuss other aspects of work. The FACT box gives statistics which distinguish between professionals who are trusted and those who are well-paid.

Begin by asking the class to define the professions. Write *someone who* on the board and ask students to give a definition (but not the profession) so that another student can guess the profession. For example:

Student A: someone who looks after animals
Student B: a vet

It is clear that the people who are most trusted are the ones who work in what we sometimes refer to as the 'caring professions'. Once we have established that everyone knows what all the people in the **FACT** box do, ask this question: *When you start your career, would you prefer to make a lot of money, or to be in a profession that helps people?* You don't need to discuss this for too long. In fact, you can let the students vote their answer with a simple show of hands.

2 PREVIEW

Words

A The four professions illustrated are nurse, teacher, racing driver and someone who works in financial services (for example a bank, the stock exchange or insurance).

B There are now three questions which refer to the professions in the **FACT** box. You may have discussed this earlier. The questions themselves are quite contentious - *Which of the people in the FACT box help others?* There is an argument for saying, for example, that people who work in the financial services help the whole country, because they contribute so much to the wealth of the nation (especially Britain, with London being the biggest international financial services centre in the world). Because there is so much room for disagreement about these questions, it is best to have this conversation as a whole class activity, so that students can be made aware of the views of their classmates.

C This activity focuses on some of the words and expressions to do with work which will appear later in the Unit.

2 PREVIEW Words C **Answers**

1 A *part-time job* is one which only takes part of your day or week; a *full-time job* means you should be doing it five (or more) days a week.
2 *Entrepreneur* is an interesting word for which there are several definitions: someone who recognises opportunities and organises resources to take advantage of the opportunity; someone who takes the risk of organising and operating a new business venture; an *executive* is someone in a management or directorial role.
3 *An experience* is an individual event: *Going to China was a great experience.* The abstract noun *experience* refers to the knowledge and skills you have because you have spent time doing a particular job.
4 *Legal services* refers to jobs such as solicitors or barristers, who are given the general name of lawyers (see the **Background information** box below); *Financial services* refers to people who trade on the financial markets, and also to accountants who help individuals with financial matters.

D This is a set of True-False questions with a difference – they are open to dispute. Is it possible to be a student and have a full-time job? In some countries, such as the USA and the UK, where getting an education is expensive, more and more people are working full-time to finance their studies.

Background information

A note about the difference between the terminology of legal professions in different parts of the English-speaking world. In the US, a *lawyer* is someone who is authorised to practise law, conduct lawsuits or give legal advice. This same person can give you advice, and also represent you in court.

In the UK, when we talk about lawyers, we distinguish between *barristers* and *solicitors*. A barrister is a lawyer who speaks in a court of law; he or she only practises in a court room. A solicitor advises clients and provides legal advice outside the courtroom, sometimes but not necessarily in preparation for a court case. Solicitors do appear in some lower courts to represent their clients.

Many Commonwealth countries use the British legal system, but with local variations. In Canada, lawyers sometimes use the title *barrister* and *solicitor* even though there is no legal distinction between the advising and litigating roles. Canadian lawyers can litigate or give legal advice, like their American counterparts. In Australia, solicitors give legal advice and also appear in many courts. However, there are also specialist barristers who are instructed by clients and solicitors to take a case to court. *Attorney* is an alternative word for lawyer, barrister or solicitor, and is used mostly in the United States.

Language

The examples in the **Language** section are taken from the reading text on page 69. At first sight, the target language of the four sentences may not be clear, which is a good thing! If the structure focus is too clear from the sentences in this section, then the text on the next page will read more like a structure vehicle than a genuine piece of writing.

Students read the four examples, comment on their meaning and what context they appear to be from. They appear to be experiences and advice from someone who is an entrepreneur. He / she doesn't seem to like working for other people.

If you want students to do more structure practice work before they proceed, they can at this point do the structure exercises in the **Workbook** section.

2 PREVIEW Language **Answers**

A The verbs in list 1 are followed by *to;* the verbs in list 2 are followed by *-ing*

B Verbs like the ones in list 1: *agree, dare, expect, fail, manage, mean, offer, prepare, pretend, promise, refuse, wish*

C Verbs like the ones in list 2: *avoid, deny, fancy, feel like, finish, give up, keep on, mind, miss, put off, risk, spend time, suggest*

Ideas

Students are given three more sentences from the reading text, and this time, they are asked about their own experience and ambitions regarding work. The topics may already have been dealt with if you did all the earlier tasks in this guide.

3 READING CD 2 (Red) track 17 , Page 69 SB

The reading text is about a real American entrepreneur called Geoff Cook, who became famous for making a million dollars while he was still a student. We contacted him after reading about him and he was extremely helpful in providing information about the way he made his millions, and in giving advice to other would-be student entrepreneurs. We would like to thank Geoff Cook for his time and patience in reading and commenting on the material we wrote about him.

We have provided some information about two other famous entrepreneurs at the end of this section. You can use this information as extra reading material. Students can compare the routes taken by different successful entrepreneurs.

While there is absolutely no suggestion that this in any way involves Geoff Cook's company, it is interesting to note separately that universities everywhere are becoming more and more concerned about the issue of plagiarism. With almost universal student access to the internet, it is tempting for students to cut and paste texts from the internet into their essays, without attribution. This is in fact plagiarism (= using someone else's ideas as if they were your own). American universities now often use special software that compares the texts of student essays to the entire internet, and highlights places where the words may not belong to the students themselves. Your students may also like to discuss whether it is right to have help of any kind in writing essays for school or university. Some may think that it is easier to learn if you have guidance, help or if a group works together collaboratively; others may think that people only learn by their own individual efforts and mistakes.

<u>Key words / expressions</u>
• benefit (of youth) • document • edit
• entrepreneur • essay • fast-food options
• financially independent • focus on
• funding • hire • instant success • invest
• investors • publicity • turn down

The new lexis is not difficult; students can probably work out the meaning of *financially independent, fast-food options* and *instant success,* either from the words themselves or from the context.

3A Students should show that they understand specific ideas in the text by choosing one of the sentences (A to E) for each of the spaces (1 to 4). There is one extra sentence that is not used (B). This is an activity type used in the Cambridge ESOL FCE 2008+.

In the exam there are seven sentences removed from a longer text, with an extra unused sentence also shown.

3B This exercise can be done first, with 3A quickly after it. By putting a time limit of about five minutes on these activities the students can be encouraged to skim the text rapidly in order to get the general sense of it, before they look for more specific details in the next exercise **3C**.

3C True or false questions about the content of paragraph **2**. Both sentences are false. If the students aren't sure about the first one, they should read the first line of paragraph **3**, which talks about what he did *the next year.*

3 READING A / B / C **Answers**

A **1** A **2** E **3** D **4** C (B ×)

B Geoff Cook's business was CyberEdit. He provided computer editing services for students.

C **1** False T **2** False

3D Students have two questions to answer, and you must encourage them to answer in their own words, and not simply lift sentences from the text. A good way to ensure that they do this is to ask them to close their books before they answer you!

3E The last reading task asks students to read specifically to find words which mean the same as the three definitions.

3 READING D / E **Example answers**

D **1** Investors became interested in the company and Cook got a million dollars of funding.
2 A young entrepreneur is likely to receive more publicity.

E **1** benefit **2** consider **3** combining

Background information / Internet reference

Geoff Cook: Google him. www.cyberedit.com is now www.writinglabedge.com.

Bill Gates, the founder of Microsoft, is the richest person in the world. He is worth about 100 billion dollars. Not only that, but as recently as 2000, two of his co-workers were also in the top five richest people in the world. Paul Allen, the co-founder of the company, and Steve Ballmer, the president, came in at three and four in the rich list. So how did it all start?

Gates was born in 1955 and grew up in Seattle. He began programming computers at the age of 13. In 1973, he went to Harvard University, where he met Steve Ballmer. While at Harvard, Gates developed a version of the programming language BASIC for the first microcomputer - the MITS Altair.

In his junior year, Gates left Harvard to devote his energies to Microsoft, a company he had begun in 1975 with his childhood friend Paul Allen. They began developing software for personal computers. This was a high-risk strategy in the mid-70s, when established companies such as IBM had already decided that the world market for personal computers was limited. At the time, a personal computer cost about half the average annual salary in the USA.

Gates gives a lot of his wealth to charity. The Bill and Melinda Gates Foundation has committed more than $3.2 billion to organisations working in global health and more than $2 billion to improve learning opportunities, including the Gates Library Initiative to bring computers, Internet Access and training to public libraries in low-income communities in the United States and Canada.

Richard Branson is the fourth richest British business person, and founder of the Virgin brand, which ranges from airlines to mobile phones. He began as a entrepreneur when he was still at school, founding *Student Magazine*. He then set up a mail order business supplying vinyl records (before the days of CDs). Eventually, he opened the Virgin Record Store, built a recording studio and started a record label. His first release was an instrumental album called *Tubular Bells* by Mike Oldfield, a huge best-seller. In most cases, Branson eventually sells his businesses to other companies and moves on to other things. The record stores now belong to the multinational EMI, and the airline is mainly owned by Singapore Airlines. His newest venture, Virgin Galactic, will take tourists into space. Branson says he has ten secrets for success:

1. You've got to challenge the big ones.
2. Keep it casual.
3. Haggle: everything is negotiable.

4. Have fun working.
5. Do the right things for the brand.
6. Smile for the cameras!
7. Don't lead 'sheep'; herd 'cats'.
8. Move like a bullet.
9. Size does matter.
10. Be a common, regular person.

4 TALK ABOUT IT

Students discuss their own likes and dislikes about work. They can consult **Language Bank 24** for useful expressions. This is recommended as a pair work activity but can work equally well in groups or as a whole class activity.

5 LISTEN IN — CD 1 (Blue) track 15, Page 70 SB

Key words / expressions
- advertise for • attract
- developing parts of the world
- engineer • (civil) engineering
- feel very strongly about
- first-/second-class degree
- human resources • specialise in
- come top = be first (in a class)
- CV = Curriculum Vitae
- quality = skill

The **Audio text** is in the **Workbook** (page 71) and contains two contrasting interviews for a job. Two candidates are interviewed by the same interviewer. Activity **B** will activate the main expressions from this list. It is worth pointing out here that though we refer to *first-class degree* and *second-class* degree, the colloquial way of referring to university qualifications is *a First, a Two-one (2.1), a Two-two (2.2)* and *a Third;* for example: *he thinks he's special because he got a First at Oxford and I only got a 2.2 at Birmingham!*

5A The illustration in this section is the advertisement that the two candidates saw when they applied for the job. The first pre-listening task puts the students in the same position as the people being interviewed. Assuming that not all (or even any) of your students are really qualified to apply for a job as a project engineer building a hospital in India, they must think of this as a role play.

More importantly, they must remember that attitude is almost as important as qualifications in an interview for a job. Therefore, in answering the two questions here, it isn't enough to say: *I'm well qualified to do this job.* You need to sell yourself much more strongly than this. Students should learn expressions such as: *I'm absolutely the best candidate you will see for this job because …*

5B The second pre-listening task is designed to make students familiar with some of the key expressions that they will hear on the tape. There are four questions. Depending on the amount of time you have, you can do this as a whole class activity, allowing the more advanced students to teach the rest, or you can let the class discuss it in groups first.

5 LISTEN IN B — Answers

1 The *successful candidate* is the one that gets the job.
2 A *first-class degree* is the best degree you can get from a British university.
3 The *Human Resources Department* of a company is responsible for recruiting new staff, and making sure their existing staff are doing their jobs adequately and are receiving the required in-service training.
4 Although not everyone is happy with these expressions, *the developed world* usually refers to the mainly northern hemisphere countries (plus the English-speaking countries of the southern hemisphere) which enjoy a relatively high standard of living through a strong high-technology economy. Most countries with a high per capita gross domestic product (GDP) are considered developed countries; *developing countries* are poor or middle-income countries, based upon the average income per person. Most countries in Africa, Asia and Latin America are in the *developing world.*

5C Students now listen and answer *yes / no* questions. However, we should expect more from our students at this level than merely a *yes* or *no*. Therefore, the instruction additionally asks them to give more details.

5 LISTEN IN C **Answers**

1 No. He seems to have no interest in the job, because he fails to take advantage of the questions that the interviewer asks.
2 Yes. She talks about the places where the company is involved in engineering projects.
3 Yes. He's been on the company website and seems to know a lot about what they do.
4 No. She isn't impressed with his qualifications because he only got a second-class degree.

5D This is an unusual activity, and one which the students might have difficulty with. They have to listen and judge the attitude of each of the people they hear.

5 LISTEN IN D **Suggested answers**

1 The first interviewer is friendly and makes every attempt to get the candidate to talk more about himself. Her attitude is helpful and good for the kind of work she does.
2 The first candidate does not make a very good impression of himself! He has made no attempt to find out anything about the company, and hasn't prepared any questions. He has a very good degree in a difficult subject, which is in his favour, but he seems rather arrogant about this. He seems to think that having a first-class degree is an automatic ticket to a job!
3 The second interviewer is less friendly. She reacts in a rather cool manner to the things that the candidate says, and doesn't congratulate him on the work he has done to find out about the company.
4 The second candidate has a good attitude. He has made an effort to find out about the company from its website, and has a pleasant manner throughout the interview. He deals very well with the interviewer's rather negative attitude to his second-class degree.

6 CONTROVERSY See Role cards Page 65 WB

Read the notes about this section in the Introduction. The role play is an interview for a job and is designed for four people to do together. Before the group works on the interview itself, they have to write an advertisement for the job that they are going to interview or apply for. Students may need some help with this. As a whole class activity, you can ask the class to give you some ideas for different types of jobs, and then write them on the board. If they have trouble thinking of anything, start with ones that the students might find attractive – media (TV, films, magazines, newspapers, websites), airlines (pilots, stewards), sports (motor-racing engineers, fitness coaches), fashion (designers, models), diplomacy (diplomat, interpreter), law, medicine, business, accounting.

When the group has decided on a job, they share out the roles. There are four very distinct roles, two for interviewers, two for candidates. One interviewer is nice (friendly and helpful), the other is nasty. They should both interview both candidates. The candidates also have different styles – one is very enthusiastic, the other simply wants to draw attention to his / her qualifications. As usual, give the groups less time than they THINK they want. The best work in these role plays is often the language they use when they are performing – things that they didn't rehearse.

7 PORTFOLIO WRITING

The writing task is a formal letter of application. There is another example of a letter of application in Unit 8. Check the suggestions we made there as well as the suggestions here.

Writing model - formal application

109 Lark Hill Rise
Blackbird Common
Hay Heath BN5 TH8

The Human Resources Manager
Anglo-Iberian Air Limited
Gatwick Airport
West Sussex RH6 0NP

15th May 200X

Dear Sir / Madam,

I would like to apply for the position of temporary ground steward, which was advertised in *Airline Magazine* this week. I am very well-qualified for the job, as I speak three languages, Italian, English and Spanish, and I am very good with people. I am very interested in working in the aviation industry full-time eventually.

I have a university degree in Economics and am studying at the moment for an MA at the University of Sussex. I live quite close to Gatwick Airport, so a part-time position there would be very suitable.

I am a native speaker of Spanish and I have passed the Trinity College Grade 9 examination and also the Cambridge First Certificate in English.

I hope you will consider my application favourably, and I look forward to hearing from you shortly. My CV is attached.

Yours faithfully,

Ana Martinez

8 *BUSINESS in English* — Page 70 SB

The cross-curricular activity continues the theme of work by looking at the kind of work that people do. As often is the case in this section, we have varied the visual and text content. There is a graph of working habits in the UK, plus a question and answer section, where the students match the questions with the texts.

Key words / expressions
- to account for
- auto engineering
- average income
- to decline
- ethnic group
- growth
- manufacturing industry (jobs)
- service industry (jobs)
- to work for yourself
- to be self-employed

The key words here are *growth* and *decline, manufacturing jobs* and *service industry.* There is no reason why your students should know percentages of work in manufacturing and service industries. However, they may be a little surprised to see what the graph tells us. In the UK, there are far more jobs in service industries than in manufacturing and this trend is increasing. Some of the statistics here came as a surprise to the authors, particularly the fact that financial and business services now account for one in five jobs, as opposed to one in ten jobs less than 30 years ago. As more and more manufacturing jobs move to new economies like China, this trend is set to continue in most developed, western countries. Meanwhile, even some developing countries, in particular India, are expanding their service industries, such as computing and call centres, very rapidly. Obviously, one of the key factors in this is having a large educated population that speaks good English.

8A The first activity tries to help students conceptualise service industry jobs and manufacturing jobs. Auto-engineering and paper-making are clearly manufacturing jobs and tourism is a service industry. But what about fashion? There is some manufacturing, but it is mainly a service industry (the manufacturing is usually contracted out, especially to low wage countries).

8B Make two lists of more jobs in both sectors. Write *Manufacturing* and *Services* on the board. Ask students to shout out jobs quickly until you have 10 jobs in each list. Here are some to help you start: Manufacturing - clothes, computers, steel-making; Services - supermarkets, financial advice, medical research.

8C Students have to look at the graph and analyse the facts. There are probably students in your class who find it easier to read graphs than to read text. Do you know who they are? If you don't, now is the time to ask! And when you know who they are, ask them if they would like to interpret the facts as shown by the graph.

The facts are as follows: Since the 1970s in the UK, jobs in manufacturing have declined significantly for men, and a little for women. Meanwhile, jobs in the service sector have grown dramatically for women and substantially for men. In the 1970s, there were more or less equal numbers of these jobs for men and women.

For the second part of this activity, students are asked if they know about changes in the world of work in their country. They may not know any of the national statistics on this matter, but they may have personal or anecdotal evidence, a factory closure for example, or the opening of a hypermarket on the outskirts of the town or city.

8D Finally, students read the three short texts which add more information about the change in work patterns. Students then match the texts to the questions.

8 *BUSINESS in English* A / C / D

Answers

A **1** manufacturing **2** manufacturing
3 both **4** service
C **1**(a) True **2**(b) False
D **1** Have the types of jobs in Britain changed?
2 Are more women working than men?
3 Who is more likely to be self-employed?

9 YOUR TOPIC

Read the notes about this section in the Introduction. This is an examination-style pair work activity which requires Student A to prepare a four-minute talk and Student B to ask questions about it. As we pointed out in the Introduction, you have to think about what Student B is going to do while Student A is preparing the talk. Student Bs could spend the time thinking of and writing down general questions on the topic that Student As have chosen. If the Student As need some help with choosing a topic, here are some ideas:

1 What people do best in this country (what is it famous for?).
2 Multinational companies (either those that are based in your country, or foreign companies that operate in your country).
3 How work in your country is changing.
4 How work in your country should change in future.

Student Bs are directed to **Language Bank 5**, where they will find useful expressions for asking for clarification.

10 *Your answer:*

Finally, we come back to *The BIG question* and, as usual, we offer some subsidiary questions and provide some specimen answers for them. Once again, remind the students that we don't expect them to agree with any of the stated opinions, merely to note the useful strategies that they provide. For example, in the examples given, the expressions *My ambition is to …* and *I'd enjoy working as a…* will be useful to help them express their thoughts and opinions.

Workbook answers Pages 36-37 WB

1 Language: verbs + gerund or infinitive

1A **1** He denied stealing the money.
2 Everyone feels like leaving.
3 He suggested starting a company.
4 We've finished asking questions.
5 My sister is considering taking a part-time job.
6 I've given up smoking.
7 He'll carry on his studies at school.
8 We don't mind leaving the party now.

1B *Alternative answers are possible*
1 The manager attempted to lock his office door.
2 The salesman agreed to send the customer a brochure.
3 They are refusing to help us.
4 In our business, we aim to please our customers.
5 I'm hungry. I plan to go to the restaurant.

1C *Students' own answers*

2 Use of English

2A *Alternatives are possible*

1 While I was at university, I worked for an internet company.

2 It took me fifty hours a week to edit up to ten essays a night.

3 I was asked by *Wired* magazine to write an article about my life.

4 If young people want to start a company, I advise them to do it now!

2B **1**g **2**i **3**a **4**e **5**d **6**h
7j **8**c **9**b **10**f

3 Portfolio writing

Students' own answers

4 Connections

4A **1**f **2**g **3**b **4**c **5**a **6**h
7d **8**e

4B / C

1 A *salary* is paid monthly; a *wage* is usually paid by the hour.

2 ✓

3 *To take someone on* means to give them a job; *to promote someone* means to give them a higher position in the same company.

4 A *career* is work in a particular field, theoretically for life; a *job* is something you do.

5 An *employer* is the boss; an *employee* works for the boss.

6 ✓

7 ✓

8 *To be hired* is to be given a job; *to be laid off* means to lose that job.

What's new?

Subject: Crime and punishment
Function: Expressing regrets
Grammar: Third conditional; past use of *wish*

Before you open the book ...

The topic of this Unit is crime and punishment, and especially about why people are sent to prison, and how penal systems differ in different countries. The reading pages focus on attitudes to drug users and drug dealers in different countries.

Drug use is a topic that students may have some anecdotal or 'street' awareness of and / or it may be something they want to talk about. It is also likely that there are words and expressions that they need to learn to be able to talk about the subject. Nowhere in the Unit is there anything which suggests that drugs are safe or 'cool' and students are never asked to defend or condone the use of drugs.

There are two language points focused on in this Unit – the third conditional and the past use of *wish.* The functional focus – regrets – is linked to both of these structure items. You may want to focus on forms used with the verb *wish,* which can relate to the present or the past. Present wishes may refer to future time, but the wish refers to now.

Start by writing the word *I wish* on the board. Ask students if there is anything that they haven't got that they would like. Make a list on the board – *iPod, car, digital camera, Sony Playstation, girl friend* etc. Then ask them if there are any skills that they haven't got that they would like. Make a list on the board – *I can't sing, play a musical instrument, run, swim etc.* Give a marker sentence to show how *wish* is used to express these things:

- I wish I had an iPod.
- I wish I could swim.

There are further uses of *wish,* which can indicate your feelings about events or other people's actions. Give some examples at this point:

- I wish it would stop raining.
- I wish he wouldn't say things like that.

Wish is also used to express regrets in the past. It may not be so easy for students to talk about things they regret having done, but you can start with a simple one of your own – *I didn't work very hard in my maths class.* Again, try to make a list on the board, then give a marker example of how to use *wish* to express these ideas.

- I wish I'd (I had) worked harder in my maths class.

You can also teach the idiomatic use with *I bet ...*

- I bet he wishes he hadn't done that!!

For homework, ask students to write a list of regrets – their own and any others they know about or can imagine.

The third conditional in English is conceptually simple, but a little complex in format. It can be easily taught using a simple example. Two people talking about an event in the past.

A: Did you see Fred on the TV news last night?
B: No! I didn't know he was on the news!

Therefore B can say: If *I had known Fred was on the news, I would have watched it!*

Did he know? No. Did he watch the TV news? No. A series of examples like this will clearly demonstrate the form and meaning.

See pages 72-75 SB, 38-39 WB

1 *The BIG question:* IS PRISON THE BEST WAY TO STOP CRIME?

FACT: Between the late 1970s and the late 1990s, deaths from the use of heroin dropped by 40% in the Netherlands and tripled in the US.

The BIG question is about prison, the FACT is about death from heroin use. You may want to allow students to discuss *The BIG question* now. The obvious subsidiary question is: If we don't put criminals in prison, what do we do with them? Students might have their own opinions about this.

Picture notes

The pictures on page 72 all relate to drugs. There is a photo of someone with an ecstasy pill on her tongue, a photo of someone smoking marijuana, and a picture of Rachel Whitear, a British girl who died of a heroin overdose in 2000, aged only 21. After her death, her parents allowed this horrific police photograph to be used as part of a nationwide anti-drugs campaign.

None of the activities relate directly to the photos. If you like, you can ask students what they know about ecstasy, heroin and marijuana. Here are some background notes that may help you. You can if you wish turn this into a reading text.

Background information

Ecstasy is the common name for a synthetic drug called MDMA. Research in animals indicates that MDMA is neuro-toxic, which means it is harmful to nerve tissue; it is still not clear if this is also true in humans.

What we do know for sure is that chronic users of MDMA perform more poorly than non-users on certain types of cognitive or memory tasks. Some of these effects may be due to the use of other drugs in combination with MDMA, among other factors. Users of MDMA face many of the same risks as users of other stimulants such as cocaine and amphetamines. These include an increase in heart rate and blood pressure and other symptoms such as nausea, blurred vision, faintness, chills or sweating.

Psychological effects can include confusion, depression, sleep problems, drug craving and severe anxiety. These problems can occur sometimes days or weeks after taking the drug. You can find more information at this website:
www.nida.nih.gov/Infofacts/ecstasy.html

Marijuana is a dry, green / brown mix of flowers, stems, seeds, and leaves of the hemp plant cannabis sativa. It is usually smoked as a cigarette (joint) or in a pipe (bong). Its more concentrated resinous form is called hashish. Marijuana smoke has a pungent and distinctive odour. Street terms for marijuana include pot, herb, weed, grass and ganja. You can find more information at this website:
www.nida.nih.gov/Infofacts/marijuana.html

Heroin is an addictive drug, which is processed from morphine, a naturally occurring substance extracted from the seedpod of the Asian poppy plant. Heroin usually appears as a white or brown powder. Street names for heroin include smack, H, skag, and junk.

Heroin abuse is associated with serious health conditions, including fatal overdose and, particularly in users who inject the drug, infectious diseases, including HIV / AIDS and hepatitis. The short-term effects of heroin abuse appear soon after a single dose and disappear in a few hours. After an injection of heroin, the user reports feeling a surge of euphoria ('rush') accompanied by a warm flushing of the skin, a dry mouth, and heavy extremities. Following this initial euphoria, the user goes 'on the nod', an alternately wakeful and drowsy state. Mental functioning becomes clouded due to the depression of the central nervous system. You can find more information at this website:
www.nida.nih.gov/Infofacts/heroin.html

NB: The recommended websites are US government websites. The information there relates almost exclusively to use of these drugs in the USA.

2 PREVIEW

Words

A The first activity introduces the class to the expressions *hard drugs, soft drugs* and *social drugs.* It seems unlikely that these words will need to be taught at this level. It should be easy for them to match them with their meanings.

2 PREVIEW Words A **Answers**
1(b) **2**(c) **3**(a)

B Now we introduce a list of words that include some items which are classed as drugs and some which are not. Most of the words should be familiar to the students. The one new word may be *amphetamines.* Amphetamines are stimulants or 'uppers'. They are available on prescription, but are also made synthetically in illegal laboratories. The effects include stimulation of the central nervous system, a sense of well-being and high energy, a release of social inhibitions, and feelings of cleverness, competence and power. There are three questions to answer and we recommend that students work in groups to answer them.

2 PREVIEW Words B **Answers**
1 The simple answer is that they are ALL drugs; some of them are legal drugs (*caffeine, alcohol, tobacco)* and some are illegal in most countries.
2 Students discuss this and list the drugs according to their opinions.
3 The situation regarding these drugs is different in every country. The **Background information** box below indicates the legal response in the UK to using and dealing in these drugs.

<u>Background information</u>
Drug law in the UK: In the UK, **amphetamines** are prescription-only drugs under the Medicines Act, and are also controlled as Class B drugs under the 1971 Misuse of Drugs Act. Therefore it is possible for doctors to legally prescribe them to patients, but to be in possession of amphetamines without a prescription is an offence. It is also an offence to supply them or allow premises to be used to produce or supply them. Maximum penalties for possession are five years imprisonment, and 14 years for supplying.

It is illegal to grow, possess or supply **cannabis** to another person in the UK. It is also an offence to allow your house to be used for growing cannabis or smoking it. Cannabis is controlled under the Misuse of Drugs Act and is categorised as a Class C drug. The maximum penalty for supply, dealing and production and trafficking remains at 14 years imprisonment. The maximum penalty for possession has been reduced from 5 years to 2 years' imprisonment.
Cocaine and heroin are defined as a Class A drugs under the Misuse of Drugs Act 1971, and being caught in possession can lead to a maximum of seven years in prison and / or a fine. Being caught supplying cocaine or being in possession with intent to supply, means a maximum prison sentence of life.
Ecstasy is a Class A drug under the Misuse of Drugs Act 1971, which means that doctors cannot prescribe it, and it is illegal to be in possession of it, or supply it. Maximum penalties for possession are seven years imprisonment plus a fine, and the penalty for supplying, or possession with intent to supply, is a maximum sentence of life imprisonment.
Caffeine is a mild stimulant found in coffee and is legal. **Alcohol and tobacco** are sold legally in the UK to people over 18.

Language

The first part of the language section contains an example of both the uses of *wish* that we demonstrated in **Before you open the book...** above. There is an inductive question about them (**A**) and then another example, followed by two more questions (**B** / **C**). If you want students to do more structure practice work before they proceed, they can at this point do the structure exercises in the **Workbook**.

2 PREVIEW Language A / B / C
Suggested answers
A The first sentence refers to now, the second to the past.
B The third sentence refers to the past.
C It is clear from the use of the third conditional that the speaker doesn't think Mr Walters checked his facts.

Ideas

As usual, three more sentences are taken from the reading text on the following page, which are designed to give students an introduction to the content. It also introduced students to the idea of *soft* punishment, and the difference between *therapy* and *punishment.*

2 PREVIEW Ideas A / B / C

Suggested answers

A The meaning of *soft punishment* is very much dictated by your political beliefs. For some people, soft punishment is giving prisoners TV sets in their cells and allowing them to play soccer. However, a more likely attitude is that community service is a soft punishment option, compared to a term in prison.
B In the case of drug use, *therapy* refers to attempts to stop people using the drug; *punishment* would be a prison term or a fine.
C A *rehabilitation centre* is where someone would go to seek therapy, especially for drug addiction, also for alcoholism and some forms of behavioural problems.

3 READING CD 2 (Red) track 18, Page 73 SB

There are two very different authentic reading texts here, both of them news items. The first relates to a difference of opinion between the director of the US Office of National Drug Control Policy and a Dutch prosecutor about the attitude to soft drugs in the Netherlands. The second is taken from an English language newspaper in China, and deals with the trial and conviction of some drug dealers, leading to the death penalty.

Key words / expressions, Text 1
- blame • creation • concentrate on
- direct (vb) (criticism at) • effort
- end up • enormous • irrational
- justified • last resort • recreational drug
- soft drugs / hard drugs • tolerate
- concerned = worried • soft = lenient

Text 2
- gang • jail (AE); gaol (BE)
- methamphetamine • trial
- rehabilitation centre
- sentence (vb) (to death)
- court = where trials take place

It is worth pointing out the two uses of the word *soft* in the first text, referring to leniency and less dangerous drugs. In second text, there is a reference to the Guangzhou Public Security Bureau. This really means the police department. In China, policing, customs and immigration and all other similar activities are dealt with by the Department of Public Security. People who work there are trained at Public Security University.

Background information
Attitudes to drugs in various countries

In the United States, most non-violent first-time offenders guilty of drug possession get a mandatory minimum sentence of 5 years, 10 years if he / she has a large quantity of drugs. This prison time is doubled if he / she has been imprisoned for drug possession before. In 1996, 59.6% of prisoners were drug-related criminals. The US war on drugs has led to a prison-overcrowding problem. The USA has the highest prison population in the world, both in total numbers (almost 1.5 million) and as a proportion of the population. The UK has the highest prison population in the EU. See: http://www.homeoffice.gov.uk/rds/pdfs2/r188.pdf

In the Netherlands, cannabis and other soft drugs are fully de-criminalised in small quantities. Cannabis is still illegal, mostly to satisfy the country's agreements with the United Nations. Coffee shops that sell cannabis are tolerated across the country, and pay taxes like any other business for their drug sales. Like the rest of the European Union, the use and sale of hard drugs is theoretically illegal.

The Chinese government believes that most drugs come from other countries, so attempts are constantly made to stamp out transit drug trafficking, particularly in the south-west of the country, near the borders of Burma, Vietnam and Laos. The word 'trafficking' rather than 'dealing' is always used in official Chinese documents. There are 118 drugs on the government's control list, although some of these are legally available for medical purposes. During the 1990s, there were more than 800,000 drug-related cases in China, although not all of them came to trial. China's anti-drug law enforcement almost always involves the death penalty for drug trafficking.

3A This is a scanning activity to identify the people who are mentioned in both texts.

3 READING A **Answers**

1 John Walters is director of the US Office of National Drug Control Policy.
2 Martin Witteveen is a Dutch prosecutor for drug crimes.
3 Yu Zhuixiong is a Chinese drug trafficker.
4 Xie Fuxing is vice-director of Guangzhou City Public Security Bureau.

3B This activity is related specifically to Text **1**. It focuses on two sentences in the text, and asks a question about each.

3C This activity focuses on three words which are used in Text **2**, and asks students to think about the wider context that they are used in.

3D Now students read both texts more carefully and answer questions. We emphasise the need for them to answer in their own words, not simply to quote directly from the text.

3 READING B / C / D **Suggested answers**

B 1 No. A *resort* is definitely a place where people go for a holiday, but the expression *last resort* refers to what is done when all other possibilities have been tried.

2 No. Although *justified* and *justice* are related to the same root word *just* (meaning legal or fair), *justified* does not refer to the justice process. The meaning here is that the criticism is not fair.

C 1 (a) sentenced: the word (verb) is used to indicate the outcome of a trial when the defendant is found guilty – *sentenced to death, sentenced to life imprisonment.*

(b) convicted: this indicates that a defendant has been found guilty of a specific crime – *convicted of robbery;* not to be confused with *convinced.*

(c) trafficking: this means *illegal dealing,* with the added meaning that there has been some kind of movement of the items which are being sold; the word is not used so much in the West.

2 All three words are used in phrases connected with crime and justice.

3 No, not generally.

D 1 John Walters thinks that the Dutch are too soft on drug users and he claims that a lot of illegal drugs are made there.

2 The Chinese gang produced methamphetamine (ice) and sold it mainly in South Africa.

3 The provincial government of Guangdong is building rehabilitation centres.

4 TALK ABOUT IT

There are two sections to this activity. The first is a group discussion and the second is a role play. The discussion asks students to relate the official attitudes to drug use they have read about to the situation in their own countries, and to comment on the use of the death penalty.

The role play is a pair-work activity, where one student is a jailed drug trafficker, who is invited to reflect on his / her actions. Students are directed to **Language Bank 25**, where they will find expressions of regret, using *I wish.*

5 LISTEN IN CD 1 (Blue) track 16, Page 74 SB

The **Audio text** is in the **Workbook** (page 71). The listening text is a radio discussion about the Three-Strikes Law in California. Students will hear two people, Carl Brewer and a serving police officer called Kelly McGuire, giving their opinions about the law. Below is some **Background information.**

Picture notes / Background information

The picture on this page is a very evocative protest over the Three-Strikes Law. A man sits inside a cage, and over the cage is a provocative statement about the California law. If students didn't know anything about the law before they turned the page, we feel they are sure to want to know something now.

The Three-Strikes Law means that people who are convicted of three felonies (crimes and offences) may end up facing life in prison. Although it is usually associated with California, the first Three-Strikes Law was approved in 1993 by voters in the state of Washington (on the West Coast, not the capital city in the East, which is Washington DC - District of Columbia). California followed a year later. Voters in California approved Proposition 184 by an overwhelming majority of 72% in favour to 28% against.

The idea quickly spread to other states, but none of them adopted a law as tough and wide-ranging as California's. Some states required all three felony convictions to be for violent crimes before a life sentence could be imposed, whereas in California, convicted felons faced life imprisonment for ANY third conviction, as long as the first two felonies were deemed to be either 'violent' or 'serious,' or both. A life sentence in most US states usually means 25 years.

In 2000, 60% of voters in California voted for Proposition 36, which scaled back the Three-strikes Law by providing for drug treatment instead of life in prison for some of those convicted of possessing drugs. Felony is the US English word for a serious crime. Less serious crimes, known in British English as offences, are called misdemeanours in US English.

Finally, an explanation of why it is called the Three-Strikes Law. What are these 'strikes' that are referred to? It comes from baseball, where a batter has three attempts to hit the ball before he has to run or is out. Hence, 'three strikes and you're out'.

Key words / expressions
- anger / angry • approve of
- arguments for and against
- car tire (AE); tyre (BE)
- commit a crime
- criminal / minor offense (AE); offence (BE) • decrease
- kidnapping • national average
- non-violent offenders
- on parole • repeat offenders
- sharply divided (opinions)
- shoplifting • victims of crime
- violent crime

It is clear from the list of words in the box that the majority of lexical items are collocations to do with crime. Many of these words and expressions are dealt with in the pre-listening and listening tasks.

5A The pre-listening activity is simply to read three facts about the Three-Strikes Law. To be absolutely fair to the system (which has recently changed in California, although not in other states), the first two offences must be for violent crimes. Theoretically, the third crime does not have to be for a violent crime.

5B Students read five expressions from the listening text and then listen and decide which of two possible meanings is the more likely. We recommend, of course, that the class read all the possibilities and make a preliminary decision before they listen. As usual, we have used an activity of this type to give the students a chance to read some of the key expressions before they hear them.

5 LISTEN IN B				Answers
1b	2a	3b	4b	5a

5C This activity presents the students with four opinions from the text. This activity is not as easy as it looks. Carl Brewer probably holds the opinions that violent people should be given long prison sentences, and that the majority of Three-Strikes offenders are violent, but he does not actually say so. Students may infer his opinions, but strictly speaking they cannot give any answer at all to questions **2** and **3**.

5 LISTEN IN C				Answers
Carl Brewer	1✓	2 -	3 -	4✓
Kelly McGuire	1x	2✓	3✓	4✓

5D This is a class survey. There are various ways to carry out a class survey, some of which involve a lot of mingling and potential class disruption. The simplest way is a show of hands. You could turn it into a secret ballot by asking people to write what they think on a piece of paper. Whatever happens, the next activity offers them the chance to debate the idea.

6 CONTROVERSY See Role cards Page 65 WB

Read the notes about this section in the Introduction. This serious topic deserves a serious debate, so we have devised two sets of role cards, one for the team proposing the motion *We believe the Three-Strikes Law should be introduced in our country,* and one for the team opposing the motion.

Remind the students that in an examination situation, they may be asked to express opinions which are not their own.

7 PORTFOLIO WRITING

The writing task is to write a page from the diary of a released prisoner, and the recommendation is that students once again check the expressions in **Language Bank 25**, where they will find expressions of regret. If students choose not to use these expressions, this is not a reason to mark them down. This is a good homework activity.

Writing model

> It's my first day out of prison and I'm feeling a mixture of emotions; first, a sense of excitement that I'm out. Second, I feel a sense of panic. Everything seems to be happening so fast – cars are going past so quickly, people are talking so quickly. Thirdly, I feel disorientated. In prison, everything is organised for you. Outside, you have to do everything yourself. You have to buy food, and pay for it, and then cook it yourself. You can go anywhere you want, whenever you want – but this doesn't feel like a good thing if you haven't got any money.
>
> The most important thing is that I have to find a job, and I have to tell any possible employer that I have been in prison. I wish I didn't have to do that. I don't think it makes any difference to my ability to do a job. I stole some money, so I'm not going to apply for a job as an accountant. All I want is a job in a factory, or driving a van. I realise now how stupid I was to steal the money. I didn't need it, but the opportunity was there. I wish I hadn't done it.

8 *HUMAN RIGHTS in English* Page 75 SB

Picture notes / Internet reference

There are two arresting images on this page, which deserve attention before you work on the activities. The first is a painting by William T Ayton, who, with his wife Diana, came up with the idea for an exhibition of paintings to draw attention to the Universal Declaration of Human Rights. There are 30 paintings in all, one for each article in the Declaration. The caption under the painting invites students to discuss it.

You can find more information about the paintings on Ayton's own website:
www.ayton.net

The second image is a photograph of Eleanor Roosevelt with a copy of the Declaration of Human Rights. Eleanor Roosevelt, born 1884, was the wife of Franklin D Roosevelt, the 32nd president of the United States, from 1933-1945 (the last president who served three consecutive terms). After her husband's death in 1945, she became involved in civil rights in the USA, and human rights worldwide. She is credited with helping to write the Universal Declaration.

For more information about Eleanor Roosevelt and the Declaration of Human Rights go to this website:
http://www.udhr.org/history/Biographies/bioer.htm

The text is a short explanation of the Declaration, followed by a summary of the first five articles.

Key words / expressions
- adopt (a declaration) • atrocities
- cruel • degrading • entitled to
- in response to • inhuman • liberty
- security • status • torture
- race (n)=ethnic identity

8A The opening activity gives students the chance to say what they already know at this point. As we have said before, we hope at this point that someone whose main skills are in another subject area may step forward and say what they know. This of course may not happen without some prompting. An indication of genuine ignorance on the part of the teacher may help here! Or putting the class into groups to discuss it amongst themselves.

8B Students read the text and find words and expressions with the same meaning as expressions quoted here.

8 *HUMAN RIGHTS In English* B Answers
1 summary **2** liberty **3** torture

8C Now we give students the chance to actually interpret the information in the notes about the declaration. The questions are quite easy to answer in general terms, and we hope they can provide some specific details of where in the world people don't have the human rights that they deserve.

9 INTERACTIVE TASK

Read the notes about this section in the Introduction. This examination format pair activity allows students to discuss a central issue here, and at the same time practise the skill of taking turns in a conversation in a respectful way. Students are directed to **Language Bank 26** where they can find ways of showing respect in discussion and understanding other people's views.

10 *Your answer:*

As usual, we return to *The BIG question*. Here we sub-divide it into three more specific questions, and give examples of ways in which people can express their opinions about these new questions. This time, the sub-questions concentrate on drug-related crime, which was focused on in the first two pages of the Unit.

WORKBOOK answers — Pages 38-39 WB

1 Language: third conditional, past use of *wish*

1A *The answers can also be written without contractions (would not etc)*

1 If Mike had known the danger, he wouldn't have accepted the pills.
2 If you'd told me the truth, I wouldn't have been angry.
3 The police would have found the drugs if they'd had more help.
4 Would you have gone to the party if you'd known the guests?
5 What would you have done if you'd known he took heroin?

1B 1 If he hadn't become addicted to drugs, he wouldn't have needed therapy.
2 Rachel wouldn't have died if she hadn't taken a heroin overdose.
3 If marijuana hadn't been classed as a soft drug, there wouldn't have been less crime.
4 If he hadn't needed money for drugs, he wouldn't have started stealing.
5 If the government hadn't made drugs legal, many criminals wouldn't have lost money.

1C *Example answers; alternatives are possible*
1 I wish I hadn't decided to try hard drugs.
2 If only our son hadn't starting taking drugs at school.
3 I wish my friend hadn't refused to go to a drug rehabilitation centre.
4 I wish our daughter had talked to us about her problems.
5 If only we'd known she was in trouble.

1D 1 If only we hadn't made a mistake.
2 I wish I'd known it was so dangerous.
3 If only I hadn't been such a fool!
4 If only the police had listened to my side of the story.
5 I wish she'd asked someone for advice.

2 Use of English

2A *Example answers; alternatives are possible*
1 Despite the efforts of the police, the use of hard drugs has risen.
2 Most of the ecstasy in the USA comes from the Netherlands.
3 It is legal to use marijuana in the Netherlands.
4 The prisoner regretted stealing the money.

2B 1 more **2** been **3** However
4 leads **5** best **6** allowed / permitted
7 warning **8** despite **9** than **10** past

3 Portfolio writing

Students' own answers

4 Connections

4A 1 in prison **2** steal
3 fault **4** in a prison
5 in court **6** rob
7 blame **8** the court

4B 1 (a) ✓ (b) ✓ **2** (a) ✓ (b) ✓ **3** (b) ✓
4 (b) ✓ **5** (b) ✓ **6** (b) ✓ **7** (b) ✓

4C *Students' own answers*

What's new?

Subject:	Risk and adventure
Function:	Evaluating past actions / course of events
Grammar:	*should / could* + present perfect

Before you open the book …

The topic of this Unit is surviving dangerous situations. It also asks why some people seem to crave danger in their free time activities. The structure which is featured is *should have / could have,* which is linked to the target function area of evaluating past actions.

If your class is not familiar with the structure, you can start the lesson with the following presentation. Draw on the board, or better still, ask your students to draw on the board, people doing the following things.

1 someone walking in the rain without an umbrella	2 people missing a bus, tram or train	3 cars colliding with bicycle (or another car)

If you ask a student to do the drawing, whisper the instruction, so that the rest of the class don't know what he / she is supposed to be drawing. Ask students to describe what is happening, and then ask: *What did the people do wrong?* You can then elicit: *He forgot his umbrella; they were late arriving at the bus stop / train station; they didn't drive carefully.*

Then ask: *What advice would you give them?* Elicit: *He should take an umbrella* etc. But of course, it's too late for advice, so you have to tell people not what they *should do,* but what they *should have done.*

1 He should have taken his umbrella.

2 They should have got to the bus stop / train station earlier.

3 She should have driven more carefully.

Note also the use of *so* in negative 'past advice':

- They shouldn't have got to the bus stop SO late.
- They shouldn't have driven SO carelessly.

Remember that if you have internet access, you can usually find excellent graphics by searching Google images. You can use these personally, providing that you only use them in the classroom and don't photocopy them, or print out copies to distribute to students.

The inductive activities in the **Language** section are also a useful way to present the new language.

Could have (done) will also be introduced in the Unit. You can extend the presentation of the *should have* examples by asking for other possibilities.

- He should have taken an umbrella. Are there any other possible things he COULD have done? He could have taken a raincoat … or …

We use *could have* to indicate the possibility of alternative courses of action. By adding more examples, the concept becomes clearer.

See pages 76-79 SB, 40-41 WB

1 *The BIG question:* ARE YOU A SURVIVOR?

FACT: More than 1,400 people have climbed Mount Everest. More than 170 of them died, about one in eight.

Looking at *The BIG question* and the FACT together, students can imagine the dangers of climbing the world's tallest mountain. They can think about who in the class they would expect to do best if conditions were bad on such a climb.

Picture notes / Background information

There are three captioned photos on the first page, and there is no exercise to accompany them. All the photos show outdoor activities. Ask the students to write *mountaineering* and *hiking in the wilderness* on separate pieces of paper. Then ask them to write an adjective on each piece of paper to describe the activities. Collect the pieces and then read some or all of them out. Write some of the words on the board, especially if the words are opposites – *exciting – boring*. Without asking for the person who wrote the word to say anything if they don't want to, ask the class to justify saying that mountaineering and / or hiking are boring, dangerous, scary etc. You can ignore words which you don't want to use or which are mis-spelt.

Lynn Hill, who was born in 1961 in the USA, is one of the top sports climbers of the 1980s, famous for being the first person (male or female) to make a free ascent of the notoriously difficult Nose Rose on a mountain called El Capitan in Yosemite National Park, California. Free ascent means climbing with ropes but without bolts or pitons. She has won more than 30 international titles and is credited for making mountain climbing popular amongst women and short people (1.55 metres tall).

2 PREVIEW

Words

Some words from the reading text are highlighted and students have to find the meanings and activate the words.

2 PREVIEW Words A / B **Answers**

A 1 mountaineer / climber / hiker
2 canyon / boulder
3 to survive / rescue / search
B 1 (a) *survival* is the act of surviving; *survivor* is someone who survives.
(b) *rescue* is the act of saving someone who is in danger; *rescuer* is the person who does it.
2 The combinations that are normal usage are *take risks, set off* and *set out.* Both the *set* verbs mean *to start a journey.*

Language

In this section, the use of *should have (done)* is made clear through a series of inductive activities. *Could have* is also introduced.

2 PREVIEW Language **Answers**

A 1 He didn't do the things – this is why we use *should have.*
2 He did set off, but he was unprepared. This is why we use *shouldn't have.*
B 1 although the action took place in the past, it is not the intention of the speaker to point this out.
2 It's really too late to recommend another action!
3 This is correct.
C 1 This could be the meaning of the sentence, where *could have* has the same meaning as *might have.* With the sentence taken out of context, students have every right to think that the sentence describes something that might have happened.
2 This is the meaning of the sentence in context – the speaker is recommending one of a series of things that someone could have done.
3 This is not a possible meaning for either of the sentences.

If you want students to do more structure practice work before they proceed, they can at this point do the structure exercises in the **Workbook** section.

Ideas

Now the students read another three extracts from the reading text, and discuss the ideas that they contain.

2 PREVIEW Ideas — Answers

A No. *Expected* means that he predicted the length of the trip based on his previous experience.

B Students can discuss what the most important rule of climbing might be – wearing the right clothes? carrying food and water? taking a mobile phone? telling people where you're going? They will find out in the reading text.

READING — CD 2 (Red) track 19, page 77 SB

Picture notes / Background information

The picture on this page is of **Aron Ralston**, the subject of the reading text. The photo is one that he took of himself off his arm trapped by a boulder in a remote canyon.

One of the reasons that we have notes about the photos and artwork is that we know from experience and research that this is what students look at first. We also know that they then try to synthesise the information that the photo gives them with some other evidence on the page about the context – either a caption or some nearby text. This is how newspapers, especially the more sensational ones, engage their readers, drawing them towards reading the main content.

In this case, you can ask students to look at the picture and look for other easy-to-see information. They can then tell you if they know anything already about this true story.

Aron Ralston was hiking in a remote canyon in Utah, USA when his arm became trapped under a boulder, a huge rock. He had to cut off his own arm to survive. The details of the story are included in the text. Ralston took the photograph himself later when he returned to the exact place where he had to cut off his own arm.

The first two paragraphs of the text tell you what happened to Ralston. The rest is an interview with a search and rescue veteran called Rex Tanner, who says what he thinks about Ralston's actions. His advice is given in the kind of language that the students practised in the **Language** section. Many of the new words in the text were glossed in the **Words** activity on the previous page.

Key words / expressions

- to amputate • boulder • break a rule
- canyon • cell phone • elbow
- to figure out • frame of mind
- to get (yourself) into trouble
- to hike • to keep your head
- to manage to • narrow • pocket knife
- to run out • search and rescue
- search party • to trap • stable (adj)
- veteran • wilderness
- to set out = start a journey

3A Students read the first two paragraphs and then explain in their own words what happened. It is best if they close their books when they do this.

3B This activity focuses on some key expressions in the text. Students decide which of the two suggested meanings is more likely.

3 READING B — Suggested answers

1 A stable frame of mind is definitely a good thing for an airline pilot, maybe not essential for an artist.

2 *To keep your head* means to be calm.

3 *The wilderness experience* refers to the feeling of adventure.

Students now read the article carefully. Most of the new vocabulary items are clear from the context.

3C These are *yes / no* questions, where the students must give evidence from the text to support their answer. Once again, it would be useful if they closed their books when they are answering to prevent them from simply quoting phrases and sentences from the text.

3 READING C — Suggested answers

1 No. Rex Tanner thinks that he did well not to panic.

2 No. The fact is he lists a number of different possibilities – *he could have asked someone to do the hike with him.*

3 No. He is clearly not pleased that the media

chose not to write about how Ralston got himself into trouble. They merely concentrated on his dramatic decision to free himself by amputating his arm.

4 TALK ABOUT IT

There are two separate activities here, a pair activity and a group activity.

4A In the pair activity Student A pretends to be Rex Tanner giving his thoughts about what Aron Ralston should and could have done. This student works with his / her book closed. Student B asks questions, with the book open.

4B This is a group or whole class activity, a discussion about the reasons why people do adventurous things. Students are invited to talk about any other survival stories they have heard.

5 LISTEN IN

CD 1 (Blue) track 17, Page 78 SB

Picture notes

The illustration on this page is a map of Central Edinburgh and a photograph of a hill called Arthur's Seat. Ask students if they can find the hill on the map. They can see from the map how close to the centre the hill is.

Key words / expressions
- annoyed (with myself)
- to behave (like a baby) • boots
- boulder • carry • to complain
- fit / unfit (adj) • to gasp for breath
- helicopter • to hover • to hurt
- to persuade • pullover • shelter
- shorts • trainers • to turn cold
- to pass out = faint
- to slip = lose your footing

The **Audio text** is in the **Workbook** (page 76-77). The listening text is an interview with three students who had to be rescued from Arthur's Seat, the majestic hill which can be seen from many parts of Central Edinburgh. The three who climbed the hill were not experienced climbers and were completely unprepared for the drama which befell them.

5A The pre-listening task is a list of words and expressions which are taken from the text and which form a short-hand narrative of what happened. Students read the notes and try to make sense of the story.

5B Exercise 5B is in the style of the Cambridge ESOL 2008+ Paper 4 Listening Part 2. Students complete the sentences with information heard in the recording focusing on detail, specific information, and stated opinion. Ask students to read the ten incomplete extracts before they listen. This will give them an idea of what specific information they have to listen for.

5 LISTEN IN B **Answers**
1 warned **2** experienced **3** fit **4** surprised
5 complained **6** persuaded **7** sheltered
8 shivering **9** annoyed **10** hovered

5C Students now discuss what the three people did and what they should have done. They also surmise what would have happened if Michael had gone down the mountain earlier (he was the only one with a mobile phone).

6 CONTROVERSY

See Role cards Page 66 WB

Read the notes about this section in the Introduction. This role play involves three people, a sailor who has to be rescued by a lifeboat, a lifeboat captain and a journalist. Put the class into groups of three, direct them to the role cards and give them a limited amount of time to complete the task. Remember – when students are working in groups, particularly on a role play, thcy will only work hard to get things ready if they are told that their time is very limited. A good rule is that you should give them enough time for you to spend a minimum of one minute checking with each group. So, if there are five groups, tell them they only have five minutes! They may complain (and you can actually give them more than five minutes) but we believe that this leads to greater productivity.

With these activities, group practice should lead to performance. Depending on your relationship with your class, you can ask for volunteers to act out the interview, or you can choose one of the groups. Don't let the performance last too long, and don't force them to continue when they clearly have nothing more to say.

7 PORTFOLIO WRITING

The writing task is a narrative. The stages of the narrative are clearly laid out on the page. Encourage students to use all the narrative devices they know – time expressions, adverb forms etc. And emphasise the importance of not starting every sentence with *I* or *we*!

Writing model

Title: The Car Journey
Set the scene: My friends and I decided to drive into the mountains for a day of skiing. We left the city at about 4am. It was still dark.
Explain your plan: Our plan was to drive to a small town at the foot of the mountains, drink some hot coffee there, and then continue up the mountain, so we would reach the ski station by first light.
What you did: We drove to the small town, had the coffee and then set off to drive the remaining 100 kilometres to the ski station. It was still dark when we left. About a kilometre outside the town, when the road began to climb up the mountain, the driver took a corner too fast and the car hit the barrier and fell down the side of the mountain! Fortunately, we all survived the accident, but Frank, the driver of the car, was trapped and in great pain. And we were in a ravine and could not be seen from the road.

At first, we just felt lucky to be alive, but then we realised we were in a difficult situation. Not only could we not be seen from the road, but we were too far down the side of the mountain to be heard if we tried to shout. And the mountain was too steep to climb back up. To make matters worse, the only person who had brought a mobile phone couldn't find it! Somehow, it had disappeared into the snow.

There was only one thing we could do. Two people stayed with the car and two started climbing down the mountain. There was no road there, but we hoped we would find someone who could help. We were lucky. We walked for about a kilometre and found a small chalet. We were able to call the emergency services and Frank was freed from the car and taken to hospital.
Conclusion: We should all have taken our mobile phones and Frank should have driven more carefully.

8 *PHYSICAL GEOGRAPHY in English* Page 79 SB

Picture notes / Background information

There is a photo of the Andean fishing people who live and fish on Lake Titicaca. There is also a diagram which shows the height of the lake and the amount that the temperature falls with altitude. The geographical term for this is the 'Lapse rate'. Before doing any reading, encourage someone who is good at science to interpret the information.

There is information in the reading text about both Lake Titicaca and the people who live near it. Lake Titicaca is on the border of Peru and Bolivia.

Peru is a republic on the west coast of South America, which borders Ecuador, Colombia, Brazil, Bolivia and Chile. The country is rich in cultural anthropology and was the centre of the Inca Empire in pre-Columbian (pre-Spanish) times. Peru was colonised by Spain and declared independence in 1821. Almost half of all Peruvians are Amerindians. The population is nearly 28 million and the capital is Lima. Peru has two official languages, Spanish and the Amerindian language Quechua.

Bolivia is situated to the south-east of Peru, and is landlocked. It was a Spanish colony and became independent in 1825. Bolivia is one of the least developed countries in South America. Almost two-thirds of its people live in poverty. More than 60 per cent of the inhabitants are either Quechua or Aymara-speaking. The population is nearly nine million and the capital, La Paz, is the highest capital in the world. Bolivia hit the headlines in December 2005, when Evo Morales was elected president. Morales is not only the first person of Amerindian descent who has ever been elected president of a South American country; he is also a socialist.

The cross-curricular subject is geography. We link it to the Unit topic by describing the living conditions of people who live in a very inhospitable region, high in the Andes Mountains of Bolivia.

Altitude sickness: We take oxygen into our lungs and the oxygen must enter the blood-stream. This is a straightforward process until you find yourself at high altitude. At the summit of Mont Blanc (4807m), the highest mountain in Western Europe, the pressure of oxygen is about half of that at sea level and on the summit of Mount Everest (8850m), it is one third of sea level pressure. At these altitudes, each breath you take carries less oxygen to your lungs, and less oxygen therefore enters your bloodstream. For climbers and trekkers at such altitudes, the lack of oxygen may cause illness that is potentially life-threatening. Reports from Nepal have revealed that the mortality of trekkers is about 14 per 100,000, with 25% of these attributed to altitude illness.

Key words / expressions
- altitude sickness • haemoglobin
- light-headed • oxygen
- rapid heartbeat • sea level • severe
- sunburn • ultra-violet rays

One word which you may not know the exact meaning of (although one of your students may!) is *haemoglobin. Haemoglobin* is a complex protein-iron compound in the blood that carries oxygen to the cells from the lungs and carbon dioxide away from the cells to the lungs. More simply, it can be described as the part of the red blood cells that carries oxygen.

8A The first exercise requires students to read the information and use it to answer questions, the first of which they have to do some calculations for.

8 *PHYSICAL GEOGRAPHY in English* A Suggested answers

1 This question is answered by reading the caption under the cross-section illustration of the position of Lake Titicaca in the Andes, which tells you that the temperature drops by 1° Celcius for every 150 metres of altitude. Therefore, at an altitude of 1,500 metres, the temperature will drop by 10° Celcius. If the temperature at sea level is 10° Celcius, the temperature at 1,500 metres will be 0° Celcius.
2 Altitude sickness is something that affects people who are not used to heights – they can get short of breath and have a rapid heartbeat.
3 Haemoglobin carries oxygen through the blood.
4 Ultra-violet rays cause sunburn.

9 INTERACTIVE TASK

Read the notes about this section in the Introduction. As always with the interactive task, students work in pairs. Student A starts a conversation with a sentence based on the topic of the Unit. The sentence doesn't have to contain an example of the structure under review. Three example sentences are given. Student B has to 'take control' of the conversation, but in a respectful way.

The way this pair work activity works is explained in the Introduction to this **Teachers' Guide**, but the success of it depends on your students working at the task with a sense of purpose. It isn't enough to tell them that they may encounter a test like this in an examination. It is just as important for them to realise that it will give them practice of the kind of give-and-take conversation that is a reality in social (as opposed to more formal) encounters.

10 *Your answer:*

As always, we end the Unit coming back to the original question. The statements and answers given are only there for guidance.

WORKBOOK answers — Pages 40-41 WB

1 Language: *should, could* + present perfect

1A 1 He could have taken a cell phone with him (but he didn't).
2 I could have written an article for the newspaper.
3 I could have joined the expedition.
4 I could have gone scuba-diving.

1B 1 He should have worn more warm clothing.
2 They shouldn't have gone up the mountain without a torch.
3 You should have told me you were going.
4 They should have booked the trip on the internet.
5 They shouldn't have set off without a map.

1C 1c 2d 3a 4b

2 Use of English

2A *Example answers; alternatives are possible*
1 It was impossible for him to move.

2 What made Aron Ralston set out on this adventure?
3 Having enough water was important.
4 What advice would you give?
5 To be able to start a fire is important.

2B **1**f **2**g **3**h **4**i **5**d
6e **7**j **8**a **9**c **10**b

3 *Students' own answers*

3 Portfolio writing

Students' own answers

4 Connections

4A Least fearful:

(b) concerned (e) worried
(f) jumpy (i) tense

Most fearful:

(a) anxious (c) frightened to death
(d) terrified (g) panicky
(h) scared stiff

4B **1**f **2**e **3**d
4c **5**a **6**b

What's new?

Subject:	The supernatural
Function:	Hypothesising
Grammar:	*must / might / could / can't* + present perfect

Before you open the book ...

The function of this Unit is *hypothesising.* A *hypothesis* is a suggested explanation that has not yet been shown to be correct. The grammar structure for this Unit – *must / might / could / can't* + present perfect – hypothesises about the past.

Begin the session by teaching the word *hypothesis.* Give these examples:

Example 1 – *A group of scientists believe that healthy food will improve schoolchildren's work. That is their 'hypothesis'. They give the schoolchildren healthy food for three months and their schoolwork improves.* Ask: *Is the scientists' hypothesis correct?* (Yes, it is, the hypothesis has been proved.)

Example 2 – Ask students: *What do you think of this hypothesis: Fat people are not as happy as thin people? Do you think it is true?* Elicit answers. Then tell students that in fact the opposite is true. It's been shown that fat people are happier than slim people. The hypothesis 'fat people are not as happy as thin people' is not correct.

Note: It may help to write each hypothesis on the board, with the label *hypothesis.*

Move on to the grammar points for this Unit, and explain to students that we hypothesise when we speak, talking about explanations that may or may not be correct. Ask: What kind of language do you think we use when we hypothesise? Since students have covered the structures *might / may* + *must / can't be* they should be able to answer this. Give this example:

A person is passing a friend's house and decides to visit him. He rings the bell but there is no answer. The friend has a garden. Ask: *What does the person think?* Elicit answers, for example, *My friend might be asleep / He might be in the garden.*

Then say: *The person sees that his friend's car is not there. What does he think?* Elicit answers, for example, *He must be out.* Explain that all these thoughts can be described as ways of hypothesising, but that *must* is a stronger hypothesis than *might*, which is more about possibility.

Write the sentence *He must be out* on the board. Ask students if they can put it into the past. They may or may not be able to. If not, give them the sentence yourself: *He must have gone out.* Elicit the fact that the present perfect is used. Give this example for students to make sentences from:

A man goes to a fish restaurant and eats a large dish of seafood. The next day he is very sick.

Ask: *What does the man think?* Elicit answers: *eg The seafood must / might / could have been bad.* Go on to say: *The man rings the restaurant to complain. The manager says: The seafood was very fresh.* Elicit the sentence: *The seafood can't have been bad.*

1 *The BIG question:* ARE WE ALONE IN SPACE?

FACT: A survey revealed that five million Americans believe they have seen UFOs.

Write ***The BIG question*** on the board and check that students understand the word *space* (= the whole of the universe outside the Earth's atmosphere).

Ask: *How many people think we are alone in space?* Count the show of hands and write the figure down. Tell the class that you will ask the same question at the end of the Unit and see if students have changed their minds. Read out the **FACT**. You will probably have to teach the word *UFO* (= Unidentified Flying Object). Explain that it is something in the sky that people see and can't identify – it's not an aeroplane, for example. It may come from outer space.

Picture notes /Background information

The pictures on this page show:

(a) something that looks like a UFO (Unidentified Flying Object). We would also use the phrase *flying saucer* to describe it. There are lots of sites on the internet with pictures of what are supposed to be UFOs. Here are a few:
http://www.alien-ufos.com/img/ufos/popocatepeti/pop.jpg
http://www.alien-ufos.com/img/ufos/belgium.jpg
http://www.alien-ufos.com/img/ufos/ca6.jpg
http://www.alien-ufos.com/img/ufos/neenah_wisconsin_2.jpg
http://www.alien-ufos.com/img/cropcirclephotographs/german.jpg

(b) This shows the planet Saturn. We know it is Saturn because of the rings around it.

(c) This shows a galaxy. The internet is also a wonderful resource for real scientific information about space, stars and the universe. Here are a few sites which students may find interesting.
http://www.seti.org/site/pp.asp?c=ktJ2J9MMIsE&b=178899
http://www.firstscience.com/site/articles/rees2.asp
http://planetquest1.jpl.nasa.gov/TPFDarwinConf/proceedings/open/Beichman.pdf
http://www.vt-2004.org/Background/Infol2/EIS-G5.html
http://grin.hq.nasa.gov/BROWSE/HSTI_1.html

2 PREVIEW

Words

A The reading text on the opposite page explores the idea of aliens (= a creature from another planet) visiting the Earth. This activity introduces vocabulary connected with the topic. Go through each of the alternatives, teaching new vocabulary: *illusion* (= an appearance that is different from the way things really are). Use a drawing on the board to teach the word *alien*. Elicit answers to the question, *eg It must be a UFO. / It might be a visual illusion.*

B The class will encounter this vocabulary group on pages 82 and 83 of this Unit. Again, go through the alternatives, teaching new vocabulary: *Comet* = a very bright object in the sky, like a star with a tail.

C This activity checks students have learnt the vocabulary items in **B**.

2 PREVIEW Words B / C — Answers

B Photo (b) shows Saturn, a planet.
Photo (c) shows a galaxy.

C a comet, a planet, the Sun, the solar system, a galaxy, the universe

Language

The class should find it fairly easy to answer the questions, since you have already been through the grammar of this section. Check that students understand the vocabulary in the sentences and that they understand the word *deduction* (= something you feel quite sure of from the information that you have). Explain that *spaceman* is another word for *alien*.

D Explain that this question refers to the structures (*could / might / can't / must have*) rather than the context of the sentences.

2 PREVIEW Language A / B / C / D / E — Answers

A All the sentences.
B The first two sentences.
C The last two sentences.
D In the first two sentences, *could have* and *might have* have more or less the same meaning.
E The final sentence.

Ideas

Go through the sentences teaching new vocabulary: *disc* = a flat, circular object or shape. Elicit answers to the questions. Question **B** provides practice in the structure for this Unit. Encourage students to have fun with question **C**. You could invite students to the board to draw 'an alien', and then ask the rest of the class to describe the drawings.

3 READING CD 2 (Red) track 20, Page 81 SB

Key words / expressions

- shining • disc • aircraft
- UFO (Unidentified Flying Object) • alien
- spacecraft • injured • to conclude
- dummy • human • balloon • research
- to invent • publicity • suggestible • tribe
- knowledge • spaceman • mythology
- companion • visible • telescope
- rational • missionary • anthropologist
- astronomy • to combine
- dummy = a figure or model of a person
- balloon = a large bag filled with gas or hot air that can be used for travelling through the air
- suggestible = if you are suggestible, you believe things very easily, even if there is not much evidence for them
- companion = someone or something that stays with you (the meaning in this context)
- missionary = someone who is sent on a mission, especially one sent to do religious or charitable work in a territory or foreign country
- anthropologist = a social scientist who studies the origin, behaviour, and cultural development of humans
- rational = based on real facts or scientific knowledge

Note: Many of the key vocabulary items in the passage have been introduced in the first page of the Unit.

The reading passage discusses the possibility of aliens visiting the Earth. It gives two examples of well-known UFO stories, and also describes an African tribe called the Dogon who have knowledge of the star Sirius that they say was given to them by spacemen. The article seems to conclude that there is a rational explanation for all these mysteries.

Introduce the passage by asking students to look at the title and the pictures. Ask, *What do you think the passage is about?* Elicit answers, such as, *It's about aliens or alien bodies.* Encourage speculation about the picture on the right, for example, *Does it show a photo of an alien?* Ask students to describe the picture on the left, *eg It shows a star, Sirius A. Behind it you can see its smaller companion star, Sirius B.* Teach the word *companion* (= someone or something that stays with you). This will help students to understand the information in the passage about the Dogon tribe and their knowledge of the Sirius stars.

3A Students read the text and match paragraphs 1-6 with the paragraph headings (a)-(f) given in the first question. Tell students not to worry about understanding every word. They are only asked to understand the general meaning. Elicit suggestions for the heading for the final paragraph, eg *Possible explanations.*

3B / C These sections test students' comprehension in more detail.

3D Tell students that they should not try to understand every word, but to concentrate on answering the questions. Check students understand that the mystery about the Dogon tribe is that they knew that the star, Sirius A, had a companion, Sirius B, even though the companion (Sirius B) is not visible in the sky. Dogon mythology says that visitors from the star Sirius gave them this information.

Background information

The Roswell Incident (event): On July 18, 1947, the US Army Air Force reported the recovery of a 'flying disk'. Within hours, higher authorities officially stated that it was the remains of a weather balloon. Thirty years later a Roswell intelligence officer stated that a flying saucer (UFO) had indeed crashed. In 1997 the US Air force investigated all the stories that had built up around the incident, including stories of alien bodies. They concluded that these stories were caused by faulty memory on the part of witnesses. The incident is still much disputed by UFO researchers.

The Dogon: The Dogon are an African tribe who live near Timbuktu in Mali. They are said to have known in the 19 century that Sirius had a companion star, long before its discovery through the use of powerful telescopes. They also apparently knew that the planet Saturn had rings and that Jupiter had four moons (in fact Jupiter has many more moons but this has only been discovered relatively recently). Careful research reveals that visiting researchers may have actually imparted this astronomical information to the Dogon people, but this is disputed by UFO researchers who prefer to believe that the Dogons were indeed visited by aliens from Sirius.

Explanation for UFO sightings: Recent research suggests that there is a scientific explanation for UFO sightings. Scientists now believe that 'plasmas' of gas are created by charges of electricity. Air flows then sculpt the plasmas into aerodynamic shapes which appear to fly at extraordinary speeds through the sky – and may appear to be UFOs!

3 READING A / B / C / D **Answers**

A **1** (d) **2** (b) **3** (e) **4** (c) **5** (a) **6** (f)
(g) Suggested title for the missing paragraph
7 Possible explanations

B **1** True **2** Maybe **3** False

C **1** …the bodies at Roswell were aliens.
2 …they wanted publicity.
3 …imagine experiences.

D **1** The Dogon believe that they have knowledge given to them from spacemen from the star Sirius. This says that the star Sirius has a dark companion (which is not visible in the night sky). This belief is hundreds of years old.
2 Because Sirius does have a dark companion, another star called Sirius B, but this fact was not discovered until 1922.
3 French missionaries and anthropologists.

4 TALK ABOUT IT

For a variation on this activity, put the class into groups, and tell the groups that they should choose one question to discuss. Allow five minutes for discussion and then choose a representative from each group to summarise the group's discussion.

5 LISTEN IN CD 1 (Blue) track18, Page 82 SB

Key words / expressions

- studio • astronomer • organisation
- extra-terrestrial life • radio signal • vast
- billion • to orbit • to search • distance
- to exist • evidence • form • gravity
- microbe • simple • ice
- The Big Bang • explosion • God
- studio = rooms were a TV show, radio show or interview is recorded
- extra-terrestrial life = life in or from a place that is not the Earth
- radio wave / signal = electromagnetic radiation of a certain wavelength
- to orbit = to travel in space around a larger object, eg the Moon orbits the Earth
- form = the way something exists, eg life has many forms
- gravity = the force that makes objects fall to the ground
- microbe = an extremely small living thing that you cannot see
- The Big Bang = the explosion of energy and matter that started the universe (see **Background information** notes below)

The **Audio text** is in the **Workbook** (page 72). The listening passage consists of an interview with an astronomer called Simon Hanworth for an organisation called SETIL (Search for Extra-Terrestrial Intelligence and Life). As its name suggests, since 1959 the organisation has been looking for intelligent life in space by searching for radio signals from outer space. Simon thinks there may be intelligent life in outer space but says that they have not yet received any radio signals that might show this. He also talks about the Big Bang, the explosion that scientists believe may have begun the universe about 12 billion years ago.

Explain that the class will listen to an interview with an astronomer. To teach the words *astronomy / astronomer* use the picture on the opposite page. Also use the picture to teach the words *Mars* and *(the) Earth*. (Take the opportunity to point out that we say both *Earth* and *the Earth*.) Explain that the astronomer belongs to an organisation called *SETIL* (Search for Extra-Terrestrial Intelligence and Life). Explain the meaning of *extra-terrestrial*.

5A This activity prepares the class for the listening passage by introducing some of the ideas and vocabulary that they will hear. Go through the sentences checking comprehension and teaching new vocabulary.

Sentence 4: Check students understand that a

radio telescope can receive *radio signals*, ie signals of a certain electromagnetic wavelength. Ask: *What would it mean if radio telescopes received signals from outer space?* Elicit answers: *eg It would mean that something in outer space was sending the radio signals* (in other words, some kind of intelligent life form!).

The Big Bang: Teach the word *bang* (a sudden loud noise, *eg The door closed with a bang.*) Explain that the Big Bang is a scientific theory about the way the universe started. There will surely be some students in the class who know a little about this, so allow them to explain (see **Background information** notes below).

Some students in the class may react strongly to the final sentence: *The Big Bang was created by God*. Tell students that they will be able to discuss this later. All that is asked of them now is an opinion – True / False / Maybe.

5B In this activity, students listen to the passage and check the sentences in activity **A.**

5C If you think students are able to answer a few more detailed questions, write the following sentences and phrases from the listening passage on the board. Ask students to try and complete the sentences. Then play the tape and ask students to check if their answers are correct. **Note:** If you do this activity, make sure that you have taught the necessary vocabulary at the start of the session.

1 Our Sun is just one star among ....
2 Because the .... in space are so great ...
3 If there is ...., what might it be like?
4 For example, on a planet where .... is very strong, all life forms could be the size of ....
5 For example, we think there is .... on Mars.

Answers: 1 billions **2** distances **3** life **4** gravity / microbes **5** ice

5D Write the word *God* on the board and ask students if they have other words for God (eg Divine Being, Higher Intelligence). Ask the class if they would like to have a discussion about the existence of God / a Higher Intelligence – they may not want to. If so, respect their wishes and move on to the next activity.

If the class wish to discuss the topic, ask: *Who believes that there is a God or Higher Intelligence?* Count the show of hands, and divide these people up into groups of three. Then divide the remaining individuals (those who don't believe or aren't sure) into groups of three. Groups then each find three arguments to support their beliefs.

A spokesperson for each group presents their arguments to the class. The arguments for and against are written on the board. Ask the class to agree on the best arguments. At the end take another vote on the topic – has anyone changed their mind?

Background information / Internet reference

The Big Bang: This is the current scientific theory about how the universe began. According to the theory, the universe was created somewhere between 10 and 20 billion years ago from a cosmic explosion that threw matter in all directions. The Big Bang was initially suggested because it explains why distant galaxies are travelling away from us at great speeds. Although the Big Bang Theory is widely accepted, it probably will never be proved.

For more information on the Big Bang, go to this website:
http://liftoff.msfc.nasa.gov/academy/universe/b_bang.html

5 LISTEN IN B / C **Answers**

B	**1** True	**2** Maybe	**3** Maybe
	4 False	**5** Maybe	**6** Maybe

C **1** Simon believes there may be intelligent life in space.
2 No, he says there is no real evidence for this.
3 He says that scientists don't know.

6 CONTROVERSY

See Role cards, Page 66 WB

Read the notes about this section in the Introduction. The role play is based on the Roswell incident, which was described in the reading passage on page 81. Ask the class to say what they remember from the reading passage about the Roswell incident. The class may find it helpful if you photocopy the

Background information above about the incident and give them the notes to read.

If you think students need the help, prepare them more fully for the role play by asking them to give arguments for and against the Roswell Incident. Write the arguments up in note form on the board.

7 PORTFOLIO WRITING

To help students with the kind of language used for a story, photocopy the **Writing model** below and erase the following words:

• believed • however • for • eyes • that
• remote • from • surrounded • sound
• spinning • As • came • light • When
• lying • which • spacecraft

Photocopy the resulting gap passage and give it to the class to complete. If you think the class needs help with the actual creation of a story, put students in groups to plan a 'UFO' story. Ask each group to tell their story and teach new vocabulary as it arises.

Writing model

I am not a very imaginative or suggestible person and have never believed in UFOs or things like that. However, I do now believe that aliens – creatures from outer space – exist, and that they have visited the Earth. I have changed my mind for a very good reason – I have seen a UFO and aliens with my own eyes!

The event that changed my opinions – and my life – happened in August of last year. At the time, my sister and I were staying in a cottage in a very remote part of Wales. The cottage was about two kilometres away from the nearest village. One afternoon, I went for a long walk by myself in the woods that surrounded the cottage. I heard a strange sound above me and looked up. I saw a huge silver disc spinning about 100 metres above the trees. I couldn't believe my eyes! As I stood looking at the disc a ray of green light suddenly came from the disc. I was immediately covered in the green light.

After that I remember nothing at all. When I woke up two hours later, I was lying on the ground. On my face and arms (which were bare) there was a red rash. The spacecraft was gone.

8 *ASTRONOMY in English* Page 83 SB

Key words / expressions

• astronomy • astronomer • speed of light
• cosmos • light year • spaceship
• the Milky Way • trillion
• statistical probability • civilisation
• to base / basis (n.) • element • carbon
• nitrogen • to depend • silicon
• the Milky Way = our galaxy, that contains the Earth, the Sun etc.
• trillion = a thousand thousand million
• carbon = a chemical element that exists in all living things and in coal and diamonds
• nitrogen = a gas with no colour or smell that exists in large quantities in the air

In activity **A**, students are asked to check the meaning of the following words and phrases in bold in the text:

speed of light = the speed at which light travels (299,792,458 metres per second)
cosmos = universe
light year = the distance light can travel in a year
statistical probability = how probable something is according to statistics (if here are ten million billion trillion planets, it is statistically likely that somewhere on these planets there is life). **Statistics** are sets of numbers that represent facts or measurements, *eg Statistics show that one-fifth of students do not complete their courses.*
extraterrestrial life = life in or from a place that is not the Earth.
element = a substance that consists of only one type of atom, *eg hydrogen.*
silicon = a chemical element used especially for making computer chips.

Ask the class to look at the picture of the solar system. Go through the names of the planets. Ask: *Are these names very different from the names in (your own language)?* Continue by asking some questions: *Is anyone in the class interested in astronomy? / Does anyone have a telescope? / Do you enjoy looking at the night sky, with all the stars? / Can you name any of the stars? / Can you name the planets in order without looking at the book?*

8A When students have read the text, ask them to

explain the meaning of the vocabulary items in bold (see explanations above), the task for question **1**. They should be able to explain most of the words and phrases. Students should then re-read the text a second time before answering questions **2-4**.

8 *ASRONOMY in English* A **Answers**

A **2** Travelling at the speed of light, it would take seven hours to get from Earth to Pluto. To reach our nearest neighbour in the cosmos would take at least 25,000 years. The Milky Way is one of about 140 billion other galaxies. There could be as many as ten billion trillion planets.

3 Because there could be as many as ten billion trillion planets, it is a statistical probability that there are millions of other life forms and civilisations in the universe.

4 It might not be based on the carbon, hydrogen, oxygen and nitrogen on which we depend. Some scientists think it could be based on the element silicon.

9 YOUR TOPIC

Read the notes about this section in the Introduction. Encourage students to think widely when choosing a topic to talk about, *eg* they might wish to talk about astronomy, Mars, the solar system, the Roswell incident, the supernatural, the existence of God. Since they have to talk for 5 minutes, one alternative is to allow the class to prepare their talk as homework for the next session.

Since this is the final **Your Topic** in the book, do not offer support to the class in preparing their talk since it will be interesting to see how they manage on their own. When the time comes for students to give their talk, put the class into pairs. Student A (the person giving the talk) should tell Student B (the person listening) the topic title. Student B can then write down a few questions that he / she would like to ask. Explain that part of Student B's role is to ask for clarification, if there is something he / she does not understand (direct students to **Language Bank 5**) or would like more information about.

While students are giving their talks, walk round and listen, noting mistakes. After students have given their talk, invite their partners to say what they liked about the talk and say how the talk could be improved. Finally, invite one or two students (the brave ones!) to give their talks to the class.

10 *Your answer:*

As a variation on the activity, and as preparation for the discussion, ask the class, for homework, to do some research about the possibility of alien life. This research could either be some pieces of scientific information or a strange UFO story, for example. Ask students to come to the session with their story / information and begin the activity by asking two or three students to talk about what they have learnt. Explain that the intention of the homework was to make students think more deeply about the questions in this activity.

Now ask the class to say whether or not they believe that we are alone in space (***The BIG question***). Remind them that you asked ***The BIG question*** at the start of the Unit. Write down the number of students who replied *yes / no* in answer to the question then. Ask the same question again and count the show of hands. Has it changed? Ask: *Why hasn't / has it changed?* and elicit answers. Go through the three questions A, B, C and encourage students to use information from the Unit and from their own research in the discussion.

Workbook answers **Pages 42-43 WB**

1 Language: *must, might, could, can't* + present perfect

1A **1** The aliens can't / couldn't have abducted people from Earth.
2 There must have been life on other planets, before ours on Earth.
3 You can't / couldn't have seen a UFO.
4 The Dogon people can't have known about Sirius B from French scientists.
5 The Dogon people must have learnt all this by watching the sky.

1B *Suggested answers*
1 must have
2 must have / can't / couldn't have

3 must have / must have
4 must have
5 can't / couldn't have

1C **1** (a) **2** (b) **3** (d) **4** (c)

2 Use of English

2A **1** According to Dogon mythology, Sirius has a dark companion.
2 It's true that Sirius has a dark companion.
3 But you can only see these things with a telescope.
4 But it was not until 1862 that this was discovered.
5 It is not possible that spacemen have visited the Earth.

2B **1** permission **2** glowing **3** metallic
4 illuminated **5** flashing
6 approaching **7** hysterical

3 Portfolio writing

Students' own answers

4 Connections

4A **1** (a) dream (b) imagine
2 (a) discover (b) invent
3 (a) Star (b) planet
4 (a) claim (b) exclaim
5 (a) spacecraft (b) aircraft

4B **1** dreamt **2** lonely **3** alone
4 invent **5** star **6** planets
7 claim / an aircraft **8** imagine
9 spacecraft / exclaimed **10** explain

The Extended Reading Units contain longer and more substantial texts. This one is an extract from the autobiography of Beryl Markham, who was the first person to fly solo and non-stop from east to west across the Atlantic. She achieved this remarkable feat at the age of 34 in 1936. The extract deals with the end of her flight, when she crashed in Nova Scotia, Canada, about a thousand kilometres short of her target, New York.

First of all, here are the key words and expressions that appear in the text. The words and expressions which are in **bold** are activated in the **2 PREVIEW** section. The underlined words are in expressions which are dealt with in the **3 READING** section. Below is some information about some of the words. As you can see from the list, Beryl Markham is fond of words beginning with the letter *s*! This literary device is known as alliteration.

Key words / expressions

• airlock • **altitude** • blood • **bog** • boulder • breed (vb) • **confidence** • crippled
• **cut** (vb) • earthward • failure • firm (adj) • following wind • forced landing • **hut**
• **land** • lifeless • limp • motionless • muck • **mud** • non-stop • on (my) course
• propeller • seep into • shatter • shipwreck • short-lived • **shudder** • snatch • splutter
• stumble • submerge • **swamp** • (petrol) tank • trudge • visibility

Background information

Charles Lindbergh was the first person to fly solo and non-stop across the Atlantic, a feat which he achieved in 1927. He flew from Roosevelt Airfield in Long Island, New York in a single-engine plane called the Spirit of St Louis. He landed near Paris 33 hours later.

1 *The BIG read:* WEST WITH THE NIGHT by Beryl Markham

The opening box contains biographical information about Beryl Markham and students can of course see a picture of her on the next page. Ask them to imagine what kind of woman she was. Do you think it would have been normal for a woman to do something like this in the 1930s? What were women's lives like in the 1930s? Exercise **2 PREVIEW** has more questions about this text.

Background information

Abingdon: A town in Oxfordshire, England, where Beryl Markham started her journey.

Nova Scotia: One of the eastern provinces of Canada, which are collectively known as the Maritime Provinces; if you look at the position of Nova Scotia on the map, and realise that Beryl Markham was heading for New York, you will realise that, in those days, transatlantic flights followed a route which kept as close to land as possible. Cape Breton is part of the north-east part of Nova Scotia.

Sydney: No, this isn't a mistake! Sydney, Nova Scotia is less famous than its namesake in Australia. It has a population of 26,000, making it the second largest city on the Province. It is known as the Steel City and is a major industrial centre.

Floyd Bennett Field: An airport in New York. Opened in 1931 and located at the south-eastern end of Brooklyn, it was New York City's first municipal airport. It was named after the aviator who flew across the North Pole in 1926. With its long concrete runways, it was an ideal airport for record-breaking flights in the 1930s.

2 PREVIEW

If you prefer, the class can work on these extended reading texts in examination conditions, having to deal with any new words and information by trying to understand the context. However, we still offer some preliminary exploitation of the vocabulary and ideas here in the **Teacher's Guide**. You can discuss the new words and expressions with students before they read, but even if you work on the text in class, rather than for homework, it may be more helpful for them if they encounter the new material 'cold', having to work things out for themselves. The latter method is more useful for the class if they are about to take an exam where the reading texts are of this complexity.

2A This pre-reading activity highlights some of the plane vocabulary.

2 PREVIEW A		**Answers**
1T	2F	3T

2B This activity directs students back to the information about Beryl Markham at the top of the page.

2 PREVIEW B **Suggested answers**
1 Beryl Markham was unusual because (a) she was a pilot when there were probably very few women pilots (b) because she trained racehorses when she was still a teenager (c) because she embarked on a solo flight that most people, men or women, would have been too frightened to do.
2 She landed in Nova Scotia, Canada.

2C Students now read the text quickly and match the words in bold with given definitions. These are not as easy as it seems, as *swamp, mud* and *bog* are quite similar words. Beryl Markham is very good at using words that convey a certain atmosphere, but she's not particularly interested in using the correct word for the terrain!

2 PREVIEW C		**Answers**	
1 altitude	**2** mud	**3** hut	**4** land
5 swamp	**6** bog	**7** shudder	**8** failure
9 cuts	**10** confidence		

3 READING CD 2 (Red) track 21 Page 85 SB

This is a more complex reading text than the others the students have encountered. You should decide if you want to (a) examine the material in open class, (b) ask students to work on it in pairs or groups or (c) do it for homework, using dictionaries and other aids to study. Here is an indication of what you can ascertain about their meaning from the context and the style of this autobiographical extract.

1 'Success breeds confidence.'
Note the sentence that opens the text. *Breed* in this sense means *leads to* or *creates.*

2 'the realisation of failure seeped into my heart.'
To seep into is clearly a verb and means *to enter slowly;* the context doesn't really tell you how fast it entered, but the word *seep* suggests a slow movement, like water slowly flowing into the earth. The author uses strong, atmospheric words to give vivid descriptions of her adventure.

3 'hearing it (glass) shatter'
Clearly *shatter* is something that glass does, when there's an accident. This is an onomatopoeic word – one that sounds like the noise it describes.

4 'my engine began to shudder before I saw the land'
Shudder is a verb which describes something that the engine does, which tells us that the engine isn't working properly, so it probably isn't good! It is also onomatopoeic.

5 'I snatch my map and stare at it,'
Tell students that *to snatch* means to pick up quickly; quite clearly she is in danger but also a little angry.

6 'it (the engine) died, it spluttered, it started again.'
Splutter is a wonderful word (more onomatopoeia), describing the noise of an engine that isn't working properly, starting and stopping irregularly.

7 'I stumble out of the plane and sink to my knees.'
Stumble is obviously a verb of movement; that movement is affected by the fact that she's getting out of a crashed plane and she has injured her head.

8 'my wheels touch and I feel them submerge'
She's landing on wet earth; the prefix *sub-* may tell the students that it is something about going under, sinking into the ground.

The reading text is divided into two parts (two different columns of text). Activities **A** and **B** relate to part **1**, and activity **C** relates to part **2.**

3A Students read the first part and answer some True / False questions.

3 READING A **Answers**

1 This is true, although it involves careful reading of the first paragraph, especially the sentence which begins *If I had been wiser ...*
2 True
3 True – it says that the land is under her when she snatches the map.
4 False – she has to *stumble out*, which indicates that she had to make a movement; *fall out* would suggest that this happened accidentally and without her own volition.

3B In this section, questions are asked about four specific phrases from the text.

3 READING B **Possible answers**

1 This is a big question, and students may have their own ideas. A possible explanation of the confidence of the gods is that they are all-seeing and all-knowing.
2 As we mentioned above, *seep into* suggests that the feeling came slowly.
3 Planes make forced landings when something goes wrong; sometimes planes are forced to land by the military forces of another country, for example because they have strayed into that country's air space.
4 The plane was *crippled* (another of the author's strong descriptions) because of a blockage in the fuel system.

3C The final reading activity is a multiple choice exercise based on part **2** of the text.

3 READING C **Answers**

1b **2**a **3**b **4**a

4 TALK ABOUT IT

There are three talking points for the students to discuss relating to Beryl Markham. Here are some thoughts to help you with the discussion.

4A Beryl Markham seemed to be devastated by failure at the time that it happened, and later wished that she had been successful in her goal of reaching New York. But she admits that time moved on and it became less important.

Students may have some similar experiences that they'd like to talk about, when they thought something very good or bad was going to happen; it didn't and at the time this seemed important; but later the importance faded.

4B She was undoubtedly an optimist, and she equates optimism with innocence, so that when she has to make a forced landing, she wishes she hadn't been so innocent.

4C Students will of course have their own opinions about whether she was brave or mad, but it would seem to be necessary to be both to undertake a trip like this.

5 PORTFOLIO WRITING

The task is to write a newspaper report about Markham's flight and the obvious question is – do you write it in a contemporary style, in other words, in the style of the 1930s, or in a modern style? If this book was being used on a Creative Writing course, then there would be a reason to suggest trying a contemporary style. But in most cases, it quite hard enough to imitate modern newspaper style in English.

Remind the students that they must have a headline on their article. Tell them that in headlines, it is normal for the verbs to be in the present tense and that definite and indefinite articles are usually omitted. If they are using contemporary style, they should write a place and date at the beginning of the piece – this would have been normal in the 1930s.

Writing model

A newspaper article

British woman flies solo across Atlantic

New York, April 1st 1936

Beryl Markham, a 34-year-old British pilot and racehorse trainer, yesterday became the first person to fly solo and non-stop across the Atlantic from east to west in her plane *The Gull*. She completed this amazing trip in less than 24 hours.

Ms Markham took off from an airfield near Abingdon in Oxfordshire, England and was aiming to reach New York. The actual crossing of the Atlantic went without problem, but things started to go wrong as she approached the coast of Nova Scotia, Canada. She had engine problems and unfortunately had to make a forced landing near the city of Sydney, Nova Scotia. Thankfully, she wasn't badly hurt in the crash, although her plane was badly damaged.

She was found walking around near the accident scene by a local fisherman, who raised the alarm. After being treated at a local hospital, Ms Markham flew in another plane to Floyd Bennett Airfield in New York. She said she was very disappointed not to have reached New York in her own plane, but 'life goes on'.

Supplementary Grammar

These Photocopiable Resources include 15 Units of Supplementary Grammar explanation and practice. These follow the grammar syllabus of the Cambridge ESOL First Certificate (FCE). They are in addition to the Language page of each Unit of the Workbook. The FCE Exam is set at the Council of Europe's Common European Framework of Reference (CEF) Level B2. At the back of this Teacher's Guide there are lists of 'Can-do' statements, for self-assessment by students (pages 251-255). They do not pretend to be comprehensive. A full list is available from the Council of Europe website http://www.coe.int/t/dg4/linguistic/CADRE_EN.asp.

FCE Exam Practice

The authors have chosen to practise particularly the Use of English (Paper 3), Speaking (Paper 5) and Writing (Paper 2) sections of the FCE examination in these photocopiable pages. The Listening and Reading components are extensively covered in the Student's Book.

Quick Smart Tests

Each of the 19 **Quick Smart Tests** is marked out of 30 points. This makes it easy for students to check their own progress by seeing how they perform in tests as they work through the book. The marking scheme for the individual sections, Vocabulary or Language for example, varies, but the overall total for each Test is the same. The authors have a slight preference for self-assessment, and encouraging students to compete against themselves, rather than against each other for the highest mark in the class.

Contents list of Photocopiable Resources

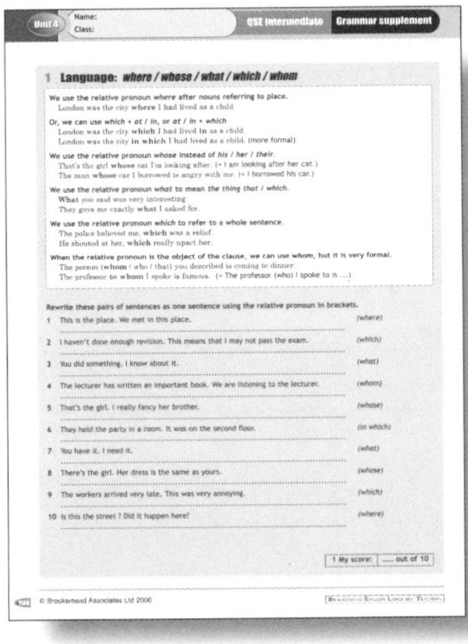
Unit 4 Name: Class: QSE Intermediate Grammar supplement

1 Language: where / whose / what / which / whom

Supplementary Grammar (pages 190-204)

These pages can be used in addition to the **Language** pages which are in every Unit of the **Workbook.** Together they provide 33 separate grammar exercises that can be done in class or for homework. **Answers** to the exercises are on pages 244-245. Teachers should note that the grammar element of each Unit begins with exercise **2 Preview Language** on the opening page of the **Student's Book.** This is an inductive grammar activity with a cross-reference to the Workbook page where the grammar point is explained and practiced.
There is no Supplementary Grammar for Units 0, 3, 9, 16.

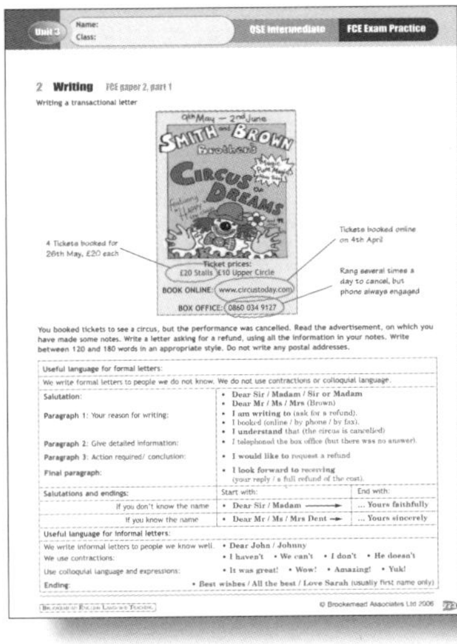
Unit 3 Name: Class: QSE Intermediate FCE Exam Practice

2 Writing FCE paper 2, part 1

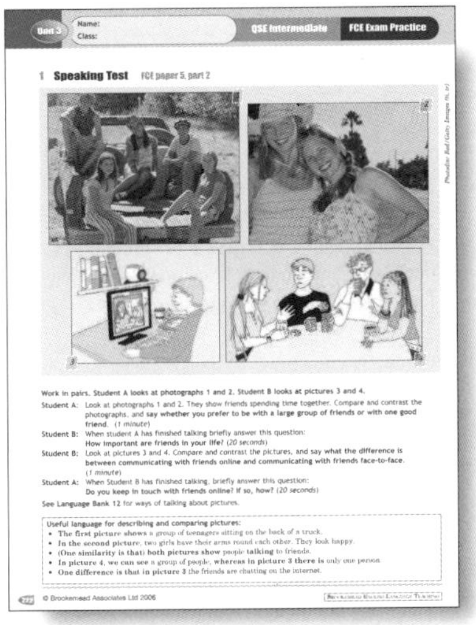
Unit 3 Name: Class: QSE Intermediate FCE Exam Practice

1 Speaking Test FCE paper 5, part 2

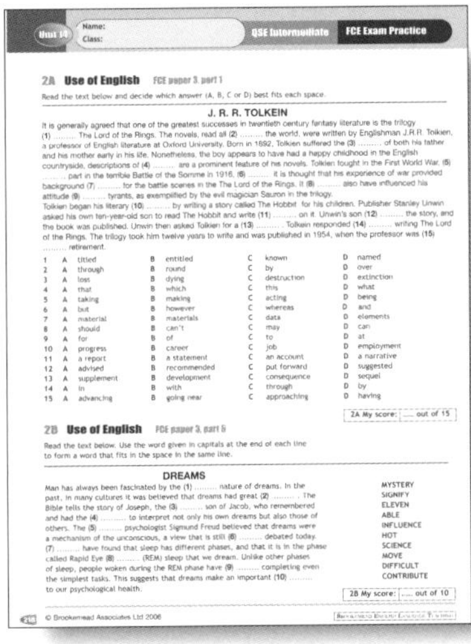
Unit 14 Name: Class: QSE Intermediate FCE Exam Practice

2A Use of English FCE paper 3, part 1

J. R. R. TOLKEIN

2B Use of English FCE paper 3, part 5

DREAMS

FCE Exam Practice (pages 205-225)

These pages are in the formats of three of the Cambridge ESOL FCE Exam papers.
There are 15 **Paper 3 Use of English** pages in the various different styles of the exam. In addition to these there are Use of English style exercises in every Unit of the **Workbook.** The **Photocopiable Resources** feature **Paper 5 Speaking Test** activities with pictures to act as discussion starters. There are also **Paper 2 Writing** activities, which give writing models and suggestions as well as typical questions. **Answers** are on pages 246-247.

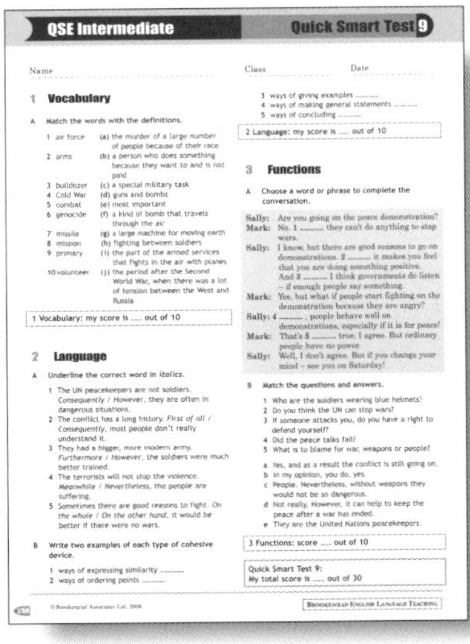
QSE Intermediate Quick Smart Test 9

1 Vocabulary

2 Language

3 Functions

Quick Smart Tests (pages 226-243, 267)

For every Unit of the book there is a **Quick Smart Test.** This checks what students have learned in the Unit under three headings: **Vocabulary, Language** (grammar) and **Functions.** These are the headings given in the **What's new?** section at the beginning of each Unit in the **Student's Book,** providing students and teachers alike with clear aims and a means of testing if they have achieved them. **Answers** to the exercises are on pages 248-250. The **Quick Smart Test** for Unit 0 is on page 267 with answers on page 266.

1 Language: *so / such / too / enough*

We use *so* to express emphasis:		
so + adjective:	• I'm **so tired**!	= I'm very tired.
so + adjective + (*that*) + verb:	• He was **so tired** (**that**) he fell asleep in front of the TV.	= He was very tired. As a result, he fell asleep.
We also use *such* in order to express emphasis:		
such + (adjective) + noun	• It's **such a pity**! • It's **such a lovely day**! • They're **such nice people**! • They're **such nice people** (**that**) they won't be angry. • It was **such beautiful weather** (**that**) **we** stayed out all day.	
• It's **too difficult** (**for me**) **to** do that.	= It's very difficult. I can't do it.	
Look at these ways of using *enough*:		
enough + noun:	• Are there **enough** books?	
enough + noun + *to*:	• Are there **enough people to** start the class?	
Adjective + *enough* + *to*:	• Is it **cold enough** (for us) **to** turn on the heating?	

Rewrite these sentences as one sentence, using the word in brackets.

1 The film was very sad. Everyone cried. (*so*)
....

2 I can't understand him. He speaks too fast. (*too*)
....

3 How much money have we got? Can we pay for the tickets? (*enough*)
....

4 It was a very good meal. We ate far too much. (*such*)
....

5 The teacher was very stupid. He believed the children. (*enough*)
....

6 The trousers were very cheap. I bought six pairs. (*such*)
....

7 How much food is there? Can we feed everyone?. (*enough*)
....

8 The film was very bad. Most people walked out. (*so*)
....

9 He can't walk far. He's old. (*too*)
....

10 My boss was kind. He paid for the meal. (*enough*)
....

1 My score:	...... out of 10

1 Language: word formation – prefixes and suffixes

A prefix is added to the beginning of a word to change its meaning.

Here are some examples of prefixes added to nouns:	
mis (= bad or wrong)	• **mis**understanding • **mis**spelling • **mis**use
non- (= not, usually with a hyphen)	• **non**-smoker • **non**-fiction • **non**-payment
in (= without)	• **in**accurate • **in**ability • **in**decision
mis (= to do something badly or wrongly)	• **mis**understand • **mis**spell
Common prefixes added to verbs include the following:	
re (= to do again)	• **re**write • **re**do • **re**make
dis (= to not do something)	• **dis**agree • **dis**approve • **dis**obey
Prefixes added to adjectives include those that give a negative meaning to the adjective:	
im (used before *b*, *m*, *p*)	• **im**possible • **im**mature • **im**balance
in	• **in**active • **in**elegant
il (used before *l*)	• **il**legal • **il**literate
un	• **un**recognised • **un**comfortable • **un**attractive
A suffix is added to the end of a word to change its meaning. Here are some examples of common suffixes added to words in order to make adjectives:	
able (= able to be)	• drink**able** • wash**able**
less (= without)	• hope**less** • pain**less**
en (= made of something)	• wood**en** • gold**en**
ish (= approximately)	• twenty**ish** • green**ish**

Put the word in brackets into the correct form.

1 They have no children. They are .... *(child)*
2 I can't accept this situation. It's .... *(accept)*
3 I think we should discuss this project again. Let's .... it. *(think)*
4 It was not sensitive of them to do that. It was very .... *(sensitive)*
5 It was not practical to go to London. It was .... *(practical)*
6 The money they make is for charity. It's a .... organisation. *(profit)*
7 She was a little bit too early for dinner. She was .... for dinner. *(early)*
8 He wasted his time at university. He .... his time at university. *(spend)*
9 She was not satisfied with the restaurant service. She was .... *(satisfied)*
10 He doesn't enjoy being with people. He's .... *(sociable)*
11 I was .... , but luckily I caught the bus. *(late)*
12 He kept warm in the snow. He wore a .... sweater. *(wool)*
13 I couldn't ever take a bribe. It would be .... *(think)*
14 .... the video. I want to see that shot again. *(wind)*
15 He has very bad handwriting. It is completely .... *(legible)*

1 My score:	...... out of 15

1 Language: *where / whose / what / which / whom*

We use the relative pronoun *where* after nouns referring to place.
London was the city **where** I had lived as a child.

Or, we can use *which + at / in*, or *at / in + which*
London was the city **which** I had lived **in** as a child.
London was the city **in which** I had lived as a child. (more formal)

We use the relative pronoun *whose* instead of *his / her / their*.
That's the girl **whose** cat I'm looking after. (= I am looking after her cat.)
The man **whose** car I borrowed is angry with me. (= I borrowed his car.)

We use the relative pronoun *what* to mean *the thing that / which*.
What you said was very interesting.
They gave me exactly **what** I asked for.

We use the relative pronoun *which* to refer to a whole sentence.
The police believed me, **which** was a relief.
He shouted at her, **which** really upset her.

When the relative pronoun is the object of the clause, we can use *whom*, but it is very formal.
The person (**whom** / who / that) you described is coming to dinner.
The professor **to whom** I spoke is famous. (= The professor (who) I spoke to is ...)

Rewrite these pairs of sentences as one sentence using the relative pronoun in brackets.

1 This is the place. We met in this place. *(where)*
....
2 I haven't done enough revision. This means that I may not pass the exam. *(which)*
....
3 You did something. I know about it. *(what)*
....
4 The lecturer has written an important book. We are listening to the lecturer. *(whom)*
....
5 That's the girl. I really fancy her brother. *(whose)*
....
6 They held the party in a room. It was on the second floor. *(in which)*
....
7 You have it. I need it. *(what)*
....
8 There's the girl. Her dress is the same as yours. *(whose)*
....
9 The workers arrived very late. This was very annoying. *(which)*
....
10 Is this the street ? Did it happen here? *(where)*
....

1 My score:	...... out of 10

1 Language: defining / non-defining relative clauses

A defining relative clause tells you *which* person or thing it is referring to.
- She's the woman **who / that** helped me.
- That's the book (**which / that**) everyone is talking about.

Defining relative clauses do not have commas.

In non-defining relative clauses, we already know which person or thing the speaker is talking about. The relative clause simply gives more information about the person or thing.
- We went to Prague, **which** was very beautiful.

With non-defining clauses, we use *who / whom* (not *that*) for people.
- This is my father, **who / whom** you've already met, I think.

We use *which* (not *that*) for things.

This car, **which** won the 1965 Grand Prix, will be put in the Motor Museum.

You cannot omit the relative pronoun in non-defining clauses.
Commas MUST be used in non-defining clauses, as shown in the examples above.

Rewrite these two sentences as one sentence, inserting commas where necessary.

1 We had lunch in a village. My friend knew the village well.
....

2 People never remember my birthday. It's on 25th December.
....

3 The children welcomed the teacher. She smiled warmly at them.
....

4 The man has left the room. He was the one that asked the question.
....

5 Marie Heather had a fantastic voice. I had never heard of her.
....

6 Where's the dog? It bit the child.
....

7 The Ferrari team is famous. It won the Formula 1 trophy this year.
....

8 'Have you met James? He lives in the same street as you.'
....

9 The things are on the table. You bought them.
....

10 'Officer, it was that man. He damaged my car.'
....

1 My score:	...... out of 10

1 Language: countable nouns / uncountable nouns; plurals

These nouns are usually uncountable:
• news • luggage • baggage • information • weather • accommodation • advice • furniture
• traffic • work • behaviour • luck • travel • permission • progress • damage

To make some of these nouns countable, we use the expression *a piece of*:
• **a piece of** news / **a piece of** luggage / **a piece of** information / **a piece of** advice / **a piece of** furniture

Many abstract nouns can be both countable and uncountable.	
When they are uncountable they have a general meaning.	**When they are countable, they have a particular meaning.**
• There's **room** in the car for one more. (room = space in the car) • What a large **room** this is! (room = a particular room in a house)	• Do you have much **experience** as a teacher? (= practice in teaching) • My visit to America was a wonderful **experience**. (experience = the things that happened to me).
Words for materials (wood, paper, glass) are uncountable. →	**But when we refer to something made of a material, the noun is countable.**
• We need some more **paper**. • **Glass** is transparent.	• Did you buy a **paper** this morning? (= a newspaper) • I'd like a **glass** of water.

Some nouns only have a plural form. But we can say a pair of *trousers* / a pair of *scissors*.
• trousers • jeans • scissors • glasses / spectacles • the English / French / Spanish

Some of these sentences have mistakes. Tick (✓) the sentences that are correct. If a sentence is incorrect, rewrite the sentence correctly.

1 Happiness is something all human beings want. ....
2 It was pity that we couldn't help him. ....
3 The scissors are over there. ....
4 The news are wonderful! ....
5 That's an interesting information. ....
6 Where are my luggage? ....
7 When they told her, she felt nothing but joy. ....
8 We need to buy some new furnitures for the sitting room. ....
9 My uncle has a flock of sheeps on his farm. ....
10 Have you got a time to help me? ....

1 My score:	...... out of 10

1 Language: the future tense / the future perfect tense

We use the future perfect tense (*will have* + past participle) to say that something will have been done by a certain time in the future.

- Let's talk about things at the weekend, when **I'll have seen** the doctor.
  (= I'll have seen him anytime between now and the weekend, eg, on Thursday, or Friday).

We often use *by* (*by 4 o'clock*, *by Friday*), or *by then* / *by the time* (*that*) to signify the latest time by which something will have happened.

- The builders **will have finished** the house **by** Friday (and maybe before then).
- **By the time** you arrive here tomorrow, I **will have** gone.

To talk about plans and intentions, we use the *going to* future.

- I'm **going to** talk to him tomorrow. (= I've already decided to talk to him).

To talk about something you have decided to do at the moment of speaking, we use *I'll* + verb.

- Jane hasn't heard the news. **I'll tell** her.

To talk about personal arrangements, we often use the present continuous future.

- The Smiths **are leaving** on Friday.
- **I'm seeing** her next week.

When we make predictions, we use *will* or *going to*. We use *going to* when there is outside evidence for a future situation.

- Don't worry, **you'll pass** the exam.
- Look at those clouds, it's **going to** rain!

We can use the future simple (*will* / *won't* + verb) when talking about future facts (not a personal arrangement or prediction).

- The train **will leave** at 10.40 pm.
- The Prime Minister **will visit** the hospital.

We can use the present simple tense to talk about events which are part of a timetable.

- **We fly** to Spain on Friday and then **leave** for Italy on Sunday.

Complete the sentences with the correct future form, using the verb(s) in brackets.

1 By next weekend the ship .... (*arrive*) at its destination.
2 You're too tired to cook. I .... (*cook*) tonight.
3 You've worked all night. You .... (*be*) very tired tomorrow.
4 We .... (*have*) dinner with our neighbours on Saturday.
5 The meeting ...... (*take place*) tomorrow at nine.
6 By the time the boys .... (*get*) there, everyone ...... (*leave*).
7 The term .... (*start*) on 8th September.
8 The party .... (*end*) by the time we .... (*get*) there.
9 If you .... (*not do*) some revision, you .... (*not pass*) the exam.
10 I .... (*go*) skiing in Switzerland this year.

1 My score:	...... out of 10

1 Language: *I prefer / I'd rather*

When we talk about preferences in general we use *prefer*, or *prefer + (do)ing*, or *prefer + (do)ing to…*
- **I prefer** dogs **to** cats.
- **I prefer** swim**ming** to run**ning**.

We can also use *prefer + to (do) rather than (to) (do).*
- **I prefer to** write letters **rather than (to)** use email.
- **I prefer to** cook **rather than (to)** eat out.

To talk about a particular preference we can use *would prefer (not) + to (do).*
- **Would you prefer** tea or coffee? → **I'd prefer** coffee.
- Would you like to go out tonight? → **I'd prefer not to** go out.
  → **I'd prefer to** stay in.

When talking about particular preferences, we can also use *I'd rather (not) (do).*
- Shall we go by car? → **I'd rather not** go by car.
  → **I'd rather** walk.

When comparing particular preferences, we can use *I'd rather (do) than (do).*
- **I'd rather** walk **than** drive.

When we want somebody to do something, we can say *I'd rather (you) (did).*
- Do you want to do it? → No, **I'd rather you did** it.

Although we use the past (*did*), we are referring to the present or to the future.

Rewrite the sentences using the words in brackets.

1 I like pop music more than jazz. (*prefer*)
....
2 Can you tell him about it please? (*rather*)
....
3 I don't want to do my homework now. (*prefer*)
....
4 I like spending time with one friend more than with a group. (*prefer*)
....
5 I don't want to go to the theatre. I'd like to see a movie. (*rather*)
....
6 I don't want to go by car. I'd like to walk. (*prefer*)
....
7 I like England, but Italy is my favourite place for a holiday. (*prefer*)
....
8 Mozart was a great composer, but I like Beethoven's music better. (*prefer*)
....
9 I don't feel like going to the movies tonight. (*rather*)
....
10 I would prefer to go by car because it's more comfortable. (*rather*)
....

1 My score:	...... out of 10

1 Language: *to / so as to / in order to / so that*

There are various ways to talk about purpose. Very often, we use *to*. There is no negative form of this. • I did it **to** help you. • We sat down **to** eat.	
More formally, we use *so as (not) to*. • I've started working longer hours **so as to** earn more money.	***In order (not) to* is even more formal.** • He wrote a letter **in order to** explain why he missed the meeting.
We can also use *so that* + *can / could / will / wouldn't*. **We MUST use this structure when the subjects of the two clauses are different.** • My sister went to China **so that** she **could** learn Chinese. **or** • My sister went to China **to** / **so as to** learn Chinese. • I'm speaking slowly **so that** she **will** understand. • I spoke slowly **so that** she **would** understand.	
Less formally, we use *so* without *that*.	• I will arrive early **so** I can get a good seat.

Complete Complete the sentences using *to / so as (not) to / in order to / so that*.

1 The students paid the top price .... they would get good seats.

2 He had to stay up late .... complete his homework on time.

3 I've written everything down .... you'll know what to do.

4 Turn the music down .... disturb the neighbours.

5 You need to fill in the form .... enter the competition.

6 You must sign the contract .... make it legally valid.

7 We walked slowly .... the children could keep up with us.

8 I'll say it very slowly .... help him understand.

9 I got up very early .... miss the train.

10 We went by car .... grandmother wouldn't have to walk very far.

1 My score:	...... out of 10

1 Language: ability and possibility - *can / could / to be able to*

Can **and** ***to be able to*** **are both ways of talking about ability and possibility.**
- I **can** drive (= I *am able to* drive.)
- I **can't** do it (= I'*m not able to* do it.)
- I **can** see you tomorrow (= I *will be able to* see you tomorrow.)

We can also use the negative form ***to be unable to.***
- They are **unable** to help.

Can / cannot **is more usual than** ***to be able to.***
Can **has only two forms:** ***can*** **(present tense) and** ***could / could not*** **(past tense).**
- You **can** see the doctor now.
- The doctor **could not** see you yesterday. He had to answer an emergency call.
- This morning, I **have been able** to talk to the doctor. (there is no equivalent form of *can*)

When we talk about general ability in the past we use ***could. Was / were able to*** **is also possible.**
- He **could** swim (= He had the ability to swim.)

BUT, when we talk about ability in a particular situation we use ***was able to,*** **not** ***could.***
- Luckily he **was able to** swim, so he survived when the boat sank.
- Because he spoke English he **was able to** help her. (= He managed to help her.)

The negative ***couldn't*** **is also possible.**
- He **couldn't** swim, so he drowned.

Other ways of talking about ability:
- He **managed to** open the door.
- Do you **know how to** do this?

1A Rewrite the sentences using the words in brackets.

1 They've managed to find it.
.... (able)

2 We can't go until next week.
.... (unable)

3 The child couldn't explain.
.... (know)

4 How were you able to persuade them?
.... (manage)

5 The army was not able to stop the invasion.
.... (couldn't)

1B Complete the sentences with ***could*** **or** ***was / were able to.***

1 They didn't want to do it but I .... persuade them.
2 When I was younger I .... run for miles.
3 The men were badly wounded but the surgeons .... save them.
4 .... complete the Marathon last year?
5 My son .... walk at the age of ten months.

1 My score:	...... out of 10

1 Language: participle clauses

We use *-ing* clauses to say what somebody / something is doing or was doing at a particular time.	
• Who's the man **who is talking** to your sister?	• Who's the man **talking** to your sister?
• The light that **is flashing** on and off is an alarm.	• The light **flashing** on and off is an alarm.
We can also use *-ing* clauses to talk about something that happens all the time.	
• The motorway **that passes** the town has . a lot of traffic.	• The motorway **passing** the town has a lot of traffic.
• The carpet **that hangs** on the wall is from Iran.	• The carpet **hanging** on the wall is from Iran.
We use *-ed* clauses to do the same thing with the passive.	
• The car **was parked** badly. The police took it away.	• The car **parked** badly was taken away by the police.
• The man **who was caught** by the police is a murderer.	• The man **caught** by the police is a murderer.
• It's an animal **that is** only **found** in tropical countries.	• It's an animal **found** only in tropical countries.

Rewrite the sentences as one sentence using participle clauses.

1 It's a new book. It was written by three famous journalists.
....

2 Did you see an object? The object was moving very fast across the sky.
....

3 The map shows the route. The map is on the table.
....

4 The present was perfect. It was bought for me by my parents.
....

5 Do you know that woman? She is standing in the corner.
....

6 Children are taught by these methods. The children often do better.
....

7 The man is sitting opposite me. He keeps smiling at me.
....

8 The picture is painted by your sister. It is absolutely awful!
....

9 It's a herb. It's used only in certain parts of the country.
....

10 The stars shine in the sky. They have been there for billions of years.
....

1 My score:	...... out of 10

1 Language: reporting verbs

When quoting direct speech, many different verbs are used. Here are some of the most common ones: exclaim cry laugh whisper scream shout murmur grunt

Verbs used for quoting direct speech: • 'That was wrong of you,' he **exclaimed.** → • 'I'm sorry,' the girl **whispered.** →	**The same verbs in reported speech:** • He **exclaimed (that)** it was wrong of her. • The girl **whispered (that)** she was sorry.
Other reporting verbs follow the rules of reported speech. We say: ***explain / complain / deny / admit / agree / promise / warn / demand / suggest / recommend + (that) +*** **verb.**	
• 'It's very dangerous,' he said. →	• He **warned** us **(that)** it **was** very dangerous.
• 'Why don't you buy the car, John?' I said. →	• I **suggested (that)** John **bought** the car.
Some reporting verbs are followed by to + verb. These verbs include: ***offer / promise / agree / refuse.***	
• 'I'll lend you the money,' my father offered. →	• My father offered to lend me the money.
Other reporting verbs are followed by *someone + to*. These verbs include: ***invited / persuade / advise.***	
• 'You should discuss it,' said the doctor. →	• The doctor advised us to discuss it.
The verb *suggest* can be followed by *should* OR the subjunctive form, which is the same as the present simple. • 'Ring the company,' my friend said. →	• My friend suggested (that) we **should ring** the company. • My friend suggested (that) we **ring** the company.
Note these structures: *accuse someone of + (do)ing / apologise for + (do)ing.*	
• 'I know you stole the money, Simon!' she cried. →	• She accused Simon of stealing the money.

Rewrite the sentences as reported speech using verbs from the box. complain accuse grunt apologise deny advise admit invite suggest exclaim

1 'Come and stay the weekend,' Matthew said to me.
....

2 The customer said, 'The food isn't hot.'
....

3 'Alright, it's true, I borrowed the car,' said the boy.
....

4 The man said, 'I'm so sorry I behaved badly.'
....

5 'I didn't break the window,' the child said.
....

6 My neighbour said, 'Lock up your house,'
....

7 The teacher said, 'John, you're lying.'
....

8 'You could buy it,' my father said to me.
....

9 'I hate school!' exclaimed the girl.
....

10 'All right, I'll do it,' he grunted.
....

1 My score:	...... out of 10

1 Language: the gerund and the infinitive

The gerund (verb + *-ing*) can be used as a noun, eg as the subject of a sentence. • **Swimming** is very enjoyable. • **Watching** television is entertaining.	
However, when a noun has a similar meaning to a gerund, we usually use the noun. • **Work** has to be done. NOT Working has to be done.	
The infinitive can also be used as the subject of a sentence, but it is very formal and no longer used much. We more often use *it* + adjective + *to*.	
• **To go** to bed early is healthy. →	• **It's** healthy **to** go to bed early.
• **To eat** in restaurants is expensive. →	• **It's** expensive **to** eat in restaurants.
Look at these different forms of the infinitive:	Examples of their use:
• **to (do)** =ordinary infinitive →	• I'm so glad **to see** you.
• **not to (do)** = negative infinitive →	• I'm glad **not to study** today.
• **to be (do)ing** = progressive infinitive →	• It's great **to be talking** to you.
• **to have (done)** = perfect infinitive →	• I'm happy **to have finished** my exams.
• **(not) to be (done)** = passive infinitive →	• I'd like **to be included** in the plans.
• **to have been (done)** = perfect passive infinitive →	• She ought not **to have been told**.
Certain adjectives can be followed by *of* + the infinitive: nice kind polite rude silly good generous stupid • It's **nice of** you **to visit** the old lady. • It was **rude of** him **to say** you can't come with us.	
But we say: kind / polite / generous / good / generous / rude / nice to someone: • He is very **nice to the old lady**. • He was very **rude to you**. • Please be **kind to them**.	

Rewrite the sentences as shown using either the gerund or an infinitive form. Sometimes both are possible.

1 It was wrong of him to do that.
He ought ....

2 I think the gate has been mended.
The gate seems ....

3 It can be risky to invest in the stock market.
.... can be risky.

4 I stupidly forgot my passport.
It was ....

5 It can be dangerous to ski off-piste, but many people love it.
.... dangerous but many people love it.

6 Is taking vitamin pills sometimes a good idea?
Is it a good idea .... ?

7 Someone should clean the kitchen.
The kitchen needs ....

8 To meet you again is wonderful.
It's ....

9 I'm delighted I'm working here.
I'm delighted ....

10 I can't see it anywhere.
It's ....

1 My score:	...... out of 10

1 Language: verbs followed by gerund or infinitive

Some verbs can be followed by the gerund (verb + *ing*) or the infinitive, but with a change of meaning in each case. These verbs include: *to remember / to regret / to go on / to try / to stop / to mean.*

- **I remember phoning** him. (= I telephoned him and I remember that I did this.)
- You must **remember to phone** him. (= This is something you must do.)
- I **regret to say** / **tell you** / **inform you** that I am leaving. (= I am sorry, but I must tell you that…)
- I **regret** not **telling** the truth. (= I did not tell the truth and now I am sorry I did this.)
- The students **went on talking** when the teacher came in. (= The students continued talking when the teacher came in).
- The class discussed unemployment and then **went on to discuss** the economy. (= First the class discussed unemployment and then it did something else.)
- I wanted to stop smoking so I **tried to smoke** less each day. (= It was difficult to do this.)
- I wanted to stop smoking so I **tried visiting** a hypnotist. (= I used the method of hypnotism).
- I've **stopped looking** in shop windows. (= I don't look in shop windows any more.)
- Sarah was walking home but **stopped to look** in a shop window. (= She stopped in order to look …)
- I didn't **mean to upset** him. (= I didn't intend to upset him).
- I don't want to tell him if it **means upsetting** him. (= if the result is that he will be upset.)

Put the verbs in brackets in either the gerund or the infinitive form.

1 I stopped (*talk*) .... because I could see no one was listening.
2 John stood up angrily and left the dinner table but everyone went on (*eat*) ....
3 Before you leave on holiday, remember (*give*) .... our neighbour the house key.
4 Did you mean (*tell*) .... him the answer?
5 The boy tried (*climb*) .... the wall but it was too high.
6 Do you remember (*meet*) .... the Watson family last year?
7 It was a mistake and I regret (*do*) .... it.
8 I don't remember (*see*) .... him at the party.
9 If we decide to go, it will mean (*leave*) .... very early.
10 The company did badly at first but went on (*do*) .... very well.

1 My score:	...... out of 10

1 Language: *It is said that . . . / He is said to . . .*

We use the phrase:
They say / believe / think (that) + verb to talk about general opinion.

- **They say (that) the Prime Minister has lost his party's support.**
- **They think (that)** the climate is getting warmer.

To say the same thing more formally, we use the phrase:
It is said / thought / believed / known / feared / whispered (that) + verb.

- **It is said (that)** the actor has left his wife and family.
- **It is thought (that)** the Antarctic glaciers are melting.

The infinitive is used in the following very formal structure to talk about general opinion. Notice that the infinitive form corresponds to the tense in the first sentence.

For example: the past tense... →	...the perfect infinitive
• The terrorists **have left** the country. →	• The terrorists **are said to have left** the country.
For example: future tenses... →	...progressive infinitive
• The Prime Minister **will retire** soon. →	• The Prime Minister **is known to be retiring** soon.
Here are some more examples:	
• The singer **remains** silent before a performance. →	• The singer **is said to remain** silent before a performance.
• The workers **have not been told.** →	• The workers **are not thought to have been told.**

Rewrite the sentences using the phrases in brackets.

1 The council will build a new road round the town. *(They say)*
....

2 He does not always tell the truth. *(It is known)*
....

3 The economy is deteriorating. *(It is feared)*
....

4 The actor will star in a film about Hitler. *(is believed to)*
....

5 The bears have left the region. *(are thought to)*
....

6 The author's new book has been completed. *(is said to)*
....

7 The climber has been lost in the snow storm *(It is thought)*
....

8 The new group plays very popular music. *(is known to)*
....

9 It is very dangerous to go hiking alone on this mountain. *(They say)*
....

10 The scientist is working on a new invention. *(is known to)*
....

2B My score:	...... out of 10

1 Language: *to have / get something done / its time we . . .*

We use the structure: to *have something (done)* to talk about an arrangement in which somebody else does something for us.

- I **had the car repaired**. (= Someone repaired the car for me.)
- I'm going to **have my hair cut**. (= Someone will cut my hair.)

We can also use the structure to talk about an experience that happens to us.

- I **had my watch stolen** last week. (= Someone stole my watch last week.)

We can use the same structure but with the word *get: to get something (done)*. It is slightly more informal.

- We must **get** the carpet **cleaned**.
- I must **get** my hair **cut**.

We use the structure: *It's time we (left)* to say that it is the right time for something to happen. Although we use the past tense, we are talking about the present or the future.

- **It's time someone told** her the truth.
- **It's time you left** home, young man!

We can also say: *It's time for someone to (do) something*.

- **It's time for her to give** him the real story.
- **It's time for us to leave** the party.

Rewrite the sentences using either the structure *to have / get something (done)* or the structure *It's time...*

1 I think we should ask someone to redecorate the house.
....

2 He ought to return to work.
....

3 Why hasn't she got up yet?
....

4 Someone stole our car last month.
....

5 We need to install a new kitchen.
....

6 I love it when someone manicures my nails.
....

7 We should tell him what really happened to his father.
....

8 The computer was upgraded for me.
....

9 I injured my leg playing football last week.
....

10 My hair's too long, I must get it cut.
....

1 My score:	...... out of 10

2A Use of English FCE paper 3, part 2

Read the text below and think of the word which best fits each gap. Use only one word in each gap. There is an example at the beginning. Write your answers IN CAPITAL LETTERS.

Example: 0 | I | N

OBEDIENCE TO AUTHORITY

(0) .... a famous psychological experiment, psychologists asked volunteers to give electric shocks to subjects if they did not **(1)** .... a task correctly. The psychologists encouraged the volunteers to give the subjects bigger and **(2)** .... shocks each time they got the task wrong. On **(3)** .... the shocks the subjects cried out and often asked the volunteers to stop. **(4)** .... the end of the experiment the shocks were so strong that some of the volunteers seemed to become unconscious. However, the volunteers **(5)** .... unaware that they were the true subjects of the experiment. The aim of the experiment was to discover **(6)** .... people behaved when a person in authority asked them to punish someone. **(7)** .... surprised the psychologists was the discovery that many of the volunteers went on **(8)** .... their 'subjects' despite the **(9)** .... that the latter begged them to stop. The volunteers felt that they should obey the psychologists; they felt **(10)** .... afraid of them to refuse to punish the subjects. The experiment explained **(11)** .... ordinary soldiers in Nazi Germany, for example, had followed the often cruel orders of superior officers. It seems that many people have such a powerful need to do what those in authority tell them that they pay no **(12)** .... to the suffering of others.

2A My score:	...... out of 12

2B Use of English FCE paper 3, part 3

Read the text below. Use the word given in capitals at the end of some of the lines to form a word that fits in the gap in the same line. There is an example at the beginning (0). Write your answers IN CAPITAL LETTERS.

Example: 0 | S | U | C | C | E | S | S | F | U | L

SUCCESSFUL MARRIAGES?

The factors that help couples make their marriages **(0)** .... are now the subject	**SUCCESS**
of urgent research. Is marriage more **(1)** .... for some people than others?	**SUIT**
Recent work reveals that happily married couples are more willing to compromise than people	
who have divorced. They have less **(2)** .... in accepting that their partner	**DIFFICULT**
has faults and do not expect their **(3)** .... to be perfect. Researchers have	**RELATION**
also made the **(4)** .... that people really do change as they get older.	**DISCOVER**
(5) .... when a person says to their partner, 'You're not the person I married,'	**SURPRISE**
it is likely to be the truth. But some people have a greater **(6)** .... to accept	**ABLE**
their partners' changes than others. Again, **(7)** .... tell us that people with	**PSYCHOLOGY**
happy marriages tend to be a lot more **(8)** .... than those who have made	**TOLERATE**
the difficult **(9)** .... to divorce. The evidence does seem to suggest that	**DECIDE**
divorcees are more **(10)** .... than those who stay married.	**DEMAND**

2B My score:	...... out of 10

2A Use of English FCE paper 3, part 1

Read the text below and decide which answer (A, B, C or D) best fits each gap. There is an example at the beginning (0).

Example: 0 A the west B the western C west D western

0	A	B	C	D
	▬	▭	▭	▭

URBANISATION

During the last two centuries, all over the world, but particularly in (0) ...., huge numbers of people have moved from the country to the city – a (1) .... called 'urbanisation'. The loss of much of its population has had a huge (2) .... on the countryside. Industrialisation has created (3) .... greater changes. Agriculture, although it (4) .... has great importance, is not as important as it once was. (5) .... general, the effect of these changes on the countryside has not been (6) .... Public services in rural (7) .... are poor. Hospitals and schools are not usually as good as those in the cities. Farmers, in particular, often have an extremely difficult time. The big supermarkets buy (8) .... from all over the world, and try to pay as little as they can. As a result, farmers often have to accept (9) .... low prices for their crops. All over the world, farmers are finding that the farm that has been in their family for so many years no longer (10) .... a profit. Another problem is (11) .... people from the city who buy second houses in the countryside. This often pushes up (12) .... prices so high that country people cannot afford to buy houses in their own village.

1	A process	B move	C way	D description
2	A result	B affect	C change	D effect
3	A far	B even	C further	D much
4	A yet	B no more	C still	D just
5	A on	B in	C at	D by
6	A beneficial	B nice	C bad	D optimistic
7	A parts	B areas	C countryside	D fields
8	A harvest	B vegetable	C agriculture	D produce
9	A silly	B ridiculously	C strangely	D sadly
10	A provides	B buys	C earns	D makes
11	A middle	B middling	C well-off	D comfortable
12	A neighbour	B local	C building	D street

2A My score:	...... out of 12

2B Use of English FCE paper 3, part 4

Complete the second sentence so that it has a similar meaning to the first sentence, using the word given. Do not change the word given. You must use between two and five words, including the word given. **See example (0) on p.208.**

Example: 0 | N | O | T | | O | L | D | | E | N | O | U | G | H |

1 'It is still light,' she said.
YET
'It .... ,' she said.

2 I've lived in the country for ten years now and I love it.
1995
I've lived in the country .... and I love it.

3 The fact is, the weather was so awful that we stayed in all week.
SUCH
The fact is .... that we stayed in all week.

4 I like this town a lot because it's quiet and pretty.
FOND
I .... because it's quiet and pretty.

5 The family doesn't live here any more, thank goodness.
LONGER
The family .... , thank goodness.

6 My father stopped smoking years ago.
GAVE
My father .... years ago.

7 What was the cause of the argument, do you know?
REASON
What was .... the argument, do you know?

8 The tall, good-looking man started the discussion.
WHO
The man .... started the discussion.

2B My score:	...... out of 8

2A Use of English FCE paper 3, part 1

Read the text below and decide which answer (A, B, C or D) best fits each gap. There is an example at the beginning (0).

Example: 0 **A** common **B** true **C** well-known **D** popular

0	A	B	C	D
	☐	☐	■	☐

CHIMPANZEES

It is a **(0)** .... fact that chimpanzees, members of the primate (1) ...., are man's closest living relatives, so similar in fact that they **(2)** .... as much as 96% of their genes with us. **(3)** ...., chimpanzees resemble human beings more closely in their genetic make-up than even gorillas, their larger cousins. It is unsurprising, therefore, that the more we learn about these **(4)** .... animals, the more we discover that both their emotions and intelligence are far more complex than we had ever suspected.

Those who work with chimpanzees confirm that as well **(5)** .... having feelings such as happiness and sadness, they also feel emotions such as despair and **(6)** .... embarrassment. One researcher **(7)** .... how a mature chimpanzee, on falling off a branch, looked **(8)** .... in what was obviously embarrassment to see if another chimp had seen it fall. Chimpanzees are even capable of showing empathy for another species, for example, by feeding a turtle.

(9) .... intelligence, chimpanzees in captivity have shown that they are capable of reasoning and abstract thought. They use more tools than any other species **(10)** .... from humans and have the **(11)** .... abilities of a three-year old child. They have been taught ASL (American Sign Language) and are capable of learning more than 300 signs. However, one thing is sure – chimpanzees will never acquire **(12)** ....!

	A	B	C	D
1	kind	species	variety	classification
2	match	share	combine	meet
3	truly	however	truthfully	indeed
4	lively	alive	enthusiastic	excited
5	as	of	with	in
6	even	actually	equally	moreover
7	commented	declared	told	explained
8	behind	ahead	around	out
9	Regarding	About	With	For
10	apart	except	exception	besides
11	number	numerical	counting	numerous
12	communication	speaking	talk	speech

2A My score:	...... out of 10

2B Use of English FCE paper 3, part 3

Read the text below. Use the word given in capitals at the end of some of the lines to form a word that fits in the gap in the same line. There is an example at the beginning (0). Write your answers IN CAPITAL LETTERS.

Example: 0 T R O P I C A L

OUR RAINFORESTS

It is a well-known fact that the **(0)** .... rainforests of the world are of great importance to all **TROPIC**
(1) .... creatures. A few thousand years ago they covered 14% of the world's surface. **LIVE**
They now cover less than 5%, but because of their **(2)** .... weather conditions, **FAVOUR**
(3) .... two-thirds of the planet's species live in them. Furthermore, it is estimated that **FULL**
hundreds of millions of new species are still **(4)** .... Rainforests take in carbon dioxide, a **DISCOVER**
(5) .... gas, and clean the atmosphere. They give out oxygen, which we need in order to **POISON**
(6) .... They are also home to 50 million indigenous forest people. Tragically, because of **BREATH**
their **(7)** .... timber, the rainforests are being destroyed at a frightening rate. An area **VALUE**
more than twice the size of Florida **(8)** .... every year. If, as seems likely, the present **APPEAR**
rate of **(9)** .... continues, by 2025, only half our rainforests will be in **DESTROY**
(10) ...., and by 2060 there will be no rainforests left. **EXIST**

2B My score:	...... out of 10

2A Use of English FCE paper 3, part 2

Read the text below and think of the word which best fits each gap. Use only one word in each gap. There is an example at the beginning. Write your answers IN CAPITAL LETTERS.

Example: 0 C O N T R O L

SLAVERY – A WORLDWIDE INJUSTICE

Slavery is a terrible condition in which one person, the slave, is under the (**0**) .... of an owner who (**1**) .... them to work unpaid. When we think of slavery, most people think of the USA, (**2**) .... imported millions of Africans to pick cotton in the American South. (**3**) .... , slavery seems to have existed in almost every culture throughout history. In ancient Mediterranean societies, prisoners of war were often taken (**4**) .... slaves. Alternatively, people (**5**) .... became slaves as a punishment for crime, or because they owed money. In Europe during the medieval period, there were markets in many cities (**6**) .... people used to buy and sell slaves. Cities such (**7**) .... Marseilles, Dublin and Prague all held slave markets. (**8**) .... many other cultures, the Arab world also traded in slaves. During the eighteenth century, North African ships (**9**) .... raid countries as far north as Britain and Scandinavia. Slavery was common in African societies, where tribes used to capture slaves from other nearby groups. (**10**) .... Britain was a major slave-trading country, it was the first (**11**) .... officially abolish slavery by law in 1833. More and more countries followed (**12**) .... example and in 1926, the League of Nations banned slavery.

2A My score:	...... out of 12

2B Use of English FCE paper 3, part 4

Complete the second sentence so that it has a similar meaning to the first sentence, using the word given. Do not change the word given. You must use between two and five words, including the word given.

Example:
0 My brother is too young to drive a car.
NOT
My brother is .... to drive a car.

Example: 0 N O T O L D E N O U G H

1 The police haven't found the robbers yet, which is terrible.
STILL
The police .... , which is terrible.

2 I can't remember anything about the story.
FORGOTTEN
I .... about the story.

3 The only person who didn't enjoy the film was my brother.
EXCEPT
Everyone .... the film.

4 We like each other a lot.
GET
We .... well.

5 I'm afraid that I didn't understand anything he said.
WHAT
I'm afraid that .... he said.

6 It's ages since I last saw him.
FOR
I .... ages.

7 It was a relief that they brought the money.
WHICH
They brought .... a relief.

8 In my opinion, you should buy it.
YOU
If ...., I'd buy it.

2B My score:	...... out of 8

2A Use of English FCE paper 3, part 1

Read the text below and decide which answer (A, B, C or D) best fits each gap. There is an example at the beginning (0).

Example: 0 **A** thing **B** accident **C** circumstance **D** event

0	A	B	C	D
	☐	☐	☐	■

AN UNSEEN THREAT

For many Americans, the most important **(0)** .... of the 21st century so far has been 9/11 – the attack against the World Trade Centre on 11th September, 2001. Almost 3,000 people were killed, the largest number of American civilian deaths at one time that has ever been **(1)** .... Many westerners think that since that moment, **(2)** .... has changed considerably. They have become **(3)** .... for the first time of the anti-western **(4)** .... of people in many parts of the world. For months after 9/11, New Yorkers lived in fear of **(5)** .... attack. Then came the terrorist bombing in Madrid, **(6)** .... on a crowded commuter train, on 11th March 2004. Then, on 7th July 2005, came the suicide bombing of buses and an Underground train in London. Fifty-two people died and over 700 people were badly **(7)** .... Since then, the police and **(8)** ....-terrorist forces have been on high alert. In Britain, young Muslim men are regularly stopped by police and **(9)** ...., often for no reason. This inevitably **(10)** .... anger in Muslim communities. For many months after the attacks, commuters felt real fear when they travelled on **(11)** .... There was a feeling that westerners face a threat to their **(12)** .... of life.

	A	B	C	D
1	noted	recorded	observed	done
2	life	condition	living	survival
3	aware	knowledgeable	wise	sensitive
4	actions	business	methods	feelings
5	second	other	another	next
6	committed by	carried out	made in	performed on
7	murdered	injured	attacked	killed
8	against	destroy	fighting	anti
9	examined	looked at	searched	explored
10	occurs	causes	bring	see
11	public transport	Underground	railway	transport
12	style	habit	way	method

2A My score:	...... out of 12

2B Use of English FCE paper 3, part 3

Read the text below. Use the word given in capitals at the end of some of the lines to form a word that fits in the gap **in the same line.** There is an example at the beginning (0). Write your answers IN CAPITAL LETTERS.

Example: 0 R E P E A T E D L Y

SPEED KILLS

Speed kills. Drivers are told this **(0)** .... If you have an accident on the highway driving at **REPEAT**
120kph, you are far more likely to be seriously hurt, or to hurt other people, than if you are driving
at 30kph. **(1)** ...., there are now speed limits on almost all roads and in recent years, road **CONSEQUENCE**
humps and speed cameras have been used to keep **(2)** .... speeds down further. However, **DRIVE**
both methods are extremely **(3)** .... Drivers dislike road humps because they fear that **POPULAR**
they will damage their cars. There is also a lot of **(4)** .... about how effective cameras **ARGUE**
actually are at preventing accidents. Roadside speed cameras are **(5)** .... useful tools for **DOUBT**
catching **(6)** .... drivers, who then have to pay fines. Some drivers think that the **SPEED**
government is more **(7)** .... in the revenue from fines than promoting road safety. It is also **INTEREST**
claimed that cameras can actually cause accidents because people slow down too suddenly when
they see them. However, both the **(8)** .... organisations and the police now view **MOTOR**
road humps and speed cameras **(9)** .... as an effective method for the **FAVOUR**
(10) .... of accidents. The likelihood is that both types of speed controls are here to stay. **PREVENT**

2B My score:	...... out of 10

2A Use of English FCE paper 3, part 1

Read the text below and decide which answer (A, B, C or D) best fits each gap. There is an example at the beginning (0).

Example: 0 A climate B global C weather D atmosphere

0	A (marked)	B	C	D

GLOBAL WARMING

It is strange to think that less than a decade ago scientists could not agree whether **(0)** .... change was occurring. Today there is universal agreement that it is taking place and happening far faster than most experts could have **(1)** .... We see it clearly in the great **(2)** .... in hurricanes, floods and fires **(3)** .... the world, while studies show that ice sheets in the polar region are melting at a **(4)** .... rate, releasing methane gas into the atmosphere, one of the most dangerous of the global-warming gases. Finally, the world is realizing the **(5)** .... of the situation, which gives hope that if urgent action is **(6)** ...., the worst consequences may be avoided. For some years now individuals have been **(7)** .... to take responsibility by, for example, recycling rubbish and reducing heating **(8)** .... Many, however, are suffering from 'green fatigue', a **(9)** .... that it is all too late and nothing can be done. It is therefore important to realize that each and every person **(10)** .... to global warming. In the UK about 40% of energy emissions are the result of decisions taken directly by individuals. The biggest source of emissions are **(11)** .... to be energy use in the home (the main use is heating), driving and air travel. If each person concentrates on reducing these a great difference can be **(12)** ....

	A	B	C	D
1	told	prophesied	predicted	understood
2	progress	movement	raise	increase
3	throughout	through	around	over
4	frightening	quick	speedy	serious
5	fear	seriousness	disaster	terror
6	done	performed	made	taken
7	persuaded	urged	recommended	desired
8	requirements	needs	necessities	uses
9	thought	doubt	guess	belief
10	leads	contributes	causes	gives
11	likely	probably	certainly	mainly
12	made	done	caused	created

2A My score:	...... out of 12

2B Use of English FCE paper 3, part 3

Read the text below. Use the word given in capitals at the end of some of the lines to form a word that fits in the gap in the same line. There is an example at the beginning (0). Write your answers IN CAPITAL LETTERS.

Example: 0 S U R V I V A L

NUCLEAR ENERGY OR WIND FARMS?

With global warming now a real threat to mankind's **(0)** ...., governments everywhere **SURVIVE**
are **(1)** .... debating which forms of energy they should make a priority for green **URGENT**
(2) .... Many experts see nuclear energy as the best option. Its great advantages are that **INVEST**
it does not produce carbon dioxide (CO_2), and that nuclear power plants can **(3)** .... produce large **RELY**
amounts of electricity, **(4)** .... of the weather or the season. However, it also has big disadvantages. **REGARD**
Firstly, nuclear waste is extremely dangerous and lasts for thousands of years. Secondly, there is
always the risk of an **(5)** .... explosion, a new Chernobyl, or the even more frightening **ACCIDENT**
possibilities of a natural disaster or terrorist attack on a nuclear **(6)** .... Many experts think **INSTALL**
that wind and **(7)** .... energy are far better. Wind farms provide the cheapest and cleanest **SUN**
form of **(8)** .... energy that there is. However, many people, particularly those who live in **RENEW**
the country near wind farms, are against them, saying that they pollute the landscape **(9)** .... **VISUAL**
and are a danger to birds. Some experts also argue that **(10)** .... energy sources cannot **ALTERNATE**
supply all the electricity we need 24 hours a day, 365 days a year.

2B My score:	...... out of 10

2A Use of English FCE paper 3, part 2

Read the text below and think of the word which best fits each gap. Use only one word in each gap. There is an example at the beginning. Write your answers IN CAPITAL LETTERS.

Example: 0 M O R E

STUDYING ABROAD

All over the world, more and **(0)** .... students are choosing to study abroad. Chinese students are opting to **(1)** .... time at colleges in the USA while American students are going to study in China. Young people are making the **(2)** .... to study abroad for many reasons. With regard **(3)** .... future employment, it is obviously a great advantage to have a detailed **(4)** .... of another country and its language. Also, there is the excitement of **(5)** .... to know the country and its people. Neil Wilson, a language student from the USA at a university in Beijing says, 'I definitely prefer studying here **(6)** .... studying in the States. It's much more interesting.' Another reason why students study abroad **(7)** .... because they believe that they will get a better standard of education. However, there are disadvantages to spending three or four years **(8)** .... a young age in a foreign country. Homesickness is the most obvious problem. Italian student Carla Fontini says, 'If my parents **(9)** ...., I would go back home tomorrow and never come back.' There is also the question **(10)** .... cost. **(11)** .... for your child to study abroad can be hugely expensive, since you not **(12)** .... have to pay the university fees, but also the cost of accommodation and living expenses.

2A My score:	...... out of 12

2B Use of English FCE paper 3, part 4

Complete the second sentence so that it has a similar meaning to the first sentence, using the word given. Do not change the word given. You must use between two and five words, including the word given.

Example:

0 My brother is too young to drive a car.
NOT
My brother is .... to drive a car.

Example: 0 N O T O L D E N O U G H

1 You don't need to explain.
NECESSARY
It's .... explain.

2 Why did they build the shopping mall so far away from the centre of town?
WAS
Why .... so far away from centre of town?

3 It took him a long time to recover from his illness.
GET
It took him a long time .... his illness.

4 You've put the wrong answer again.
MISTAKE
You've .... again.

5 The children left for school at eight-thirty, as usual.
SET
The children .... at eight-thirty, as usual.

6 I borrowed a car belonging to that man.
WHOSE
He's .... I borrowed.

7 I haven't been in the office for a month.
SINCE
It's .... in the office.

8 Stephen walks to the station in ten minutes.
TAKES
Stephen .... walk to the station.

2B My score:	...... out of 8

2A Use of English FCE paper 3, part 1

Read the text below and decide which answer (A, B, C or D) best fits each gap. There is an example at the beginning (0).

Example: 0 A chain B connection C join D tie

0	A	B	C	D
	☐	■	☐	☐

WHAT MAKES YOU HAPPY?

Is there a strong **(0)** .... between the amount of money you have and how happy you are? Many people would say 'yes'. Certainly many people **(1)** .... as if this was true, working long hours and sacrificing their family life in order to earn a high income. However, **(2)** .... in more than 65 countries appears to show that money cannot buy happiness. The studies show that happiness levels have **(3)** .... almost the same in most industrialised countries over the last 60 years, although incomes have risen **(4)** .... The exception is Denmark, where people have become more satisfied with life **(5)** .... the last three decades. The study reveals that the world's happiest people live on the island of Malta, although the Maltese themselves **(6)** .... this hard to believe! Denmark, Switzerland and Colombia come close behind in the happiness league. The USA is **(7)** .... at number 16 and the UK at number 21. **(8)** ...., the least happy people in the world are the Ukrainians. It seems that the things that make people happy are different in different countries. For example, in the US people hope to **(9)** .... personal success, whereas in Japan, people work hard to fulfil the **(10)** .... of their families and society. Religion appears to play a part in making people happy, since religion stresses the **(11)** .... of being happy with what you have got. It is perhaps **(12)** .... that Malta is 97% Catholic.

	A	B	C	D
1	A perform	B pretend	C act	D do
2	A examination	B research	C investigation	D survey
3	A rested	B remained	C lasted	D persisted
4	A a great deal	B not much	C very largely	D extremely
5	A through	B by	C with	D over
6	A find	B say	C tell	D talk
7	A graded	B arranged	C ordered	D placed
8	A clearly	B apparently	C obviously	D evidently
9	A complete	B carry out	C achieve	D reach
10	A expects	B exits	C expectations	D apparitions
11	A weight	B importance	C position	D worth
12	A suggestive	B peculiar	C significant	D thoughtful

2A My score: ...... out of 12

2B Use of English FCE paper 3, part 3

Read the text below. Use the word given in capitals at the end of some of the lines to form a word that fits in the gap in the same line. There is an example at the beginning (0). Write your answers IN CAPITAL LETTERS.

Example: 0 B I G G E S T

CHANGES IN CHINA

China, with about 1.3 billion people, has the **(0)** .... human population of any nation in the world. **BIG**
It has vast **(1)** .... resources and is the largest oil-producing country in the Far East. In the **NATURE**
last decade, China has also emerged as one of the most **(2)** .... forces in the entire **POWER**
(3) .... economy. It is predicted that by 2050 it will have overtaken America to be the world's **GLOBE**
leading **(4)** .... power. In spite of the recession, Chinese industry is booming, and major **ECONOMY**
(5) .... cities such as Shanghai are constantly changing as newer and taller skyscrapers are built **COAST**
at an **(6)** .... speed. Huge numbers of people are migrating from the Chinese countryside to the **ASTONISH**
cities, where there is a **(7)** .... and growing middle class with tastes and buying power resembling **WELL**
similar groups of people everywhere in the developed world. Nowadays, Chinese **(8)** .... are just **COMMUTE**
as likely to travel by car as by bike. Shenzhen and other cities have official policies to cut down on the
number of motorcycles. However, there are still approximately 200 million people living in **(9)** .... **POOR**
in inland China. Many cannot afford medical **(10)** ...., or even to send their children to school. **TREAT**

2B My score: ...... out of 10

2A Use of English FCE paper 3, part 2

Read the text below and think of the word which best fits each gap. Use only one word in each gap. There is an example at the beginning. Write your answers IN CAPITAL LETTERS.

Example: 0 A S

EATING DISORDERS

The women acknowledged **(0)** .... the world's most beautiful women are, almost without exception, thin, sometimes too thin, and their fame in movies and the media puts enormous pressure **(1)** .... young women and girls to emulate them in the belief that to be attractive you must be thin. **(2)** ...., eating disorders have become increasingly common and mothers are right to watch their daughters, and also their sons, for signs that they are developing a problem **(3)** .... food. There are two main types of eating disorder. In anorexia, an **(4)** .... serious illness, sufferers have a distorted body image, believing themselves to be a lot bigger than they really are. Victims can almost stop eating **(5)** ...., and sometimes die of starvation. Bulimia, on the other hand, is an illness in **(6)** .... sufferers deliberately make **(7)** .... vomit after overeating, thus controlling their weight. The most famous victim of bulimia was probably Princess Diana, ex-wife of Prince Charles, heir to the British throne. **(8)** .... she first came to the attention of the public, Prince Charles' young fiancée was described **(9)** .... 'nicely rounded'. A famous photo of Diana's legs **(10)** .... revealed them to be quite plump. Diana was horrified and in response developed a serious case of bulimia. As the princess became increasingly thinner, the world responded **(11)** .... admiration and delight. It took several years before Diana found **(12)** .... courage to admit she had the condition and got treatment for it.

2A My score:	...... out of 12

2B Use of English FCE paper 3, part 3

Read the text below. Use the word given in capitals at the end of some of the lines to form a word that fits in the gap **in the same line.** There is an example at the beginning (0). Write your answers IN CAPITAL LETTERS.

Example: 0 C E L E B R A T E D

SCHOOL LUNCHES

One of the most **(0)** .... chefs on British television is a young man called **CELEBRATE**
Jamie Oliver, who is famous for his **(1)** .... approach to cooking and his popular **RELAX**
(2) .... books and TV programmes. Some years ago, Oliver decided to make a television **COOK**
series about the meals served to children in British schools. He first spent
time finding out exactly what kind of food was being provided at lunchtime every day.
He soon made the **(3)** .... that many of the meals consisted of unhealthy, **DISCOVER**
(4) .... food such as chips and hamburgers, none of which had much **FAT**
(5) .... value, and that children were given hardly any vegetables and fruit. **NUTRITION**
For a month Oliver worked with the cooks at a London school, producing food that
provided real **(6)** .... for over 200 children, while keeping within the limited school **NOURISH**
budget. He gave them vegetables, fish, fruit, yoghurt and freshly-made salads. However,
he quickly learnt that many of the children and even some of the parents had a strong
(7) .... for the old menus and disliked the fresh food. The TV programme began an **PREFER**
important **(8)** .... debate about the quality of food, resulting in many changes **NATION**
in school meals. However, to the nation's **(9)** ...., some parents could not see **ASTONISH**
the value in this to their children's **(10)** .... and a few were even filmed handing **DEVELOP**
their children chips and pies through the school gates. There is still some way to go,
it seems, before the British acquire a taste for good food!

2B My score:	...... out of 10

2A Use of English FCE paper 3, part 2

Read the text below and think of the word which best fits each gap. Use only one word in each gap. There is an example at the beginning. Write your answers IN CAPITAL LETTERS.

Example: 0 | A | S

MODERN AND POST-MODERN ARCHITECTURE

The design movement known **(0)** .... Modern Architecture began around 1900. The work of architects such as Frank Lloyd Wright and Charles Rennie Mackintosh was a reaction **(1)** .... the excessive use of ornamentation which characterized nineteenth century building designs. Modern Architecture was simple, without ornament, **(2)** .... new building materials such as steel, glass and concrete. In the 1920s, the designs of Mies van der Rohe and Walter Gropius became famous, but it wasn't **(3)** .... the 1950s and 60s that many skyscrapers were built in the Modern style, of **(4)** .... one of the best-known examples was the United Nations building in New York. Many people disliked Modern Architecture, claiming that it did not regard people as **(5)** .... beings. The architect Le Corbusier famously regarded Modern buildings as being 'machines **(6)** .... living in'. However, he went **(7)** .... to say, 'People are not machines and do not want to live in machines.' After the 1950s, architects reacted to Modern Architecture by **(8)** .... a new movement called Post-modernism which **(9)** .... back some ornamentation. In Post-modern Architecture, different, often conflicting styles are used, **(10)** .... angles and surfaces that are often unusual. The Piazza d'Italia, in New Orleans, designed by Charles W. Moore, is a good example of this style. Modern and Post-modern Architecture are very different. **(11)** .... Modernist architects see Post-modern Architecture as vulgar, Post-modern architects feel that Modernists have no soul. **(12)** .... with all forms of art, there is probably some truth in both views.

2A My score:	...... out of 12

2B Use of English FCE paper 3, part 4

Complete the second sentence so that it has a similar meaning to the first sentence, using the word given. Do not change the word given. You must use between two and five words, including the word given.

Example:

0 My brother is too young to drive a car.
NOT
My brother is .... to drive a car.

Example: 0 | N O T | O L D | E N O U G H

1 I think it will be interesting and fun to meet them.
FORWARD
I'm .... them.

2 She said that the children could not go outside.
LET
She .... go outside.

3 We've planned our departure.
ARRANGEMENTS
We've .... our departure.

4 I did not find it easy to explain what had happened.
DIFFICULTY
I .... what had happened.

5 Gina always wears fashionable clothes.
SOMEONE
Gina .... always looks fashionable.

6 The maths problem was so difficult that no one could find the solution.
TOO
The maths problem was .... to find a solution.

7 If you don't follow the boss's orders, he'll be very angry.
CARRY
If you don't ...., he'll be very angry.

8 'This is the best meal I've ever eaten,' John said.
NEVER
'I've ....,' John said.

2B My score:	...... out of 8

2A Use of English FCE paper 3, part 1

Read the text below and decide which answer (A, B, C or D) best fits each gap. There is an example at the beginning (0).

Example: 0 A going B travelling C also D together

0	A	B	C	D
	▭	▭	▭	■

FOX HUNTING

In Britain, foxhunting is a sport in which hunters on horses, **(0)** .... with dogs, chase and kill a fox. Foxhunters describe foxes as predators, killing **(1)** .... and other small animals, while farmers have always viewed foxes as dangerous **(2)** .... that need to be exterminated. The sport has a long history, starting in the sixteenth century, when farmers, either on **(3)** ...... or on horseback, hunted foxes with dogs as a way of **(4)** .... their numbers. By the end of the seventeenth century, organised **(5)** .... of hunters were hunting stags, hares and foxes with dogs, and hunting was regarded as a healthy sport. During the nineteenth century foxhunting became a **(6)** .... of the **(7)** .... classes since the cost of running foxhunts amounted to about £50,000 a year in today's money. The **(8)** .... of red coats, tight trousers and riding boots became very fashionable and foxhunting became an enjoyable way of taking **(9)** .... in an exciting sport and socializing at the same time. The sport's **(10)** .... continued during the twentieth century. However, in the final decades of the twentieth century many people became increasingly concerned about the sport, **(11)** .... foxhunters of cruelty. Foxhunters denied this, claiming that foxes suffered little physical pain when hunted and that hunting them was a more humane way of killing them than poisoning them. In 2004 a law was **(12)** .... making it illegal to hunt with dogs, although shooting foxes was still allowed.

	A	B	C	D
1	chickens	leopards	alligators	cattle
2	pests	troubles	worries	threats
3	cars	foot	legs	feet
4	murdering	stopping	controlling	killing
5	packs	numbers	gangs	crowds
6	pleasure	habit	game	pastime
7	top	low	upper	important
8	dress	clothes	uniform	costume
9	fun	part	time	enjoyment
10	popularity	fashion	practice	tradition
11	accusing	charging	blaming	criticising
12	made	passed	done	created

2A My score: ...... out of 12

2B Use of English FCE paper 3, part 4

Complete the second sentence so that it has a similar meaning to the first sentence, using the word given. Do not change the word given. You must use between two and five words, including the word given.

Example:
0 My brother is too young to drive a car.
NOT
My brother is .... to drive a car.

Example: 0 | N O T | O L D | E N O U G H

1 I like eating at home more than eating in restaurants.
PREFER
I .... eating in restaurants.

2 Someone cuts my hair about once every two weeks.
HAVE
I .... about once every two weeks.

3 The customer said he was sorry he had been rude to the shopkeeper.
APOLOGIZE
The customer .... rude to the shopkeeper.

4 It took my sister a long time to recover from her illness.
GET
It took my sister a long time to .... her illness.

5 It's so late it's not worth going to the party.
POINT
It's so late .... going to the party.

6 I've been told we must complete everything by Friday.
BE
I've been told .... by Friday.

7 They told us it would be a good idea to buy it.
ADVISE
They .... buy it.

8 I don't like flying and my brother doesn't either.
NEITHER
I don't like flying and .... my brother.

2B My score: ...... out of 8

2A Use of English FCE paper 3, part 1

Read the text below and decide which answer (A, B, C or D) best fits each gap. There is an example at the beginning (0).

Example: 0 A fantasy B dream C fantastic D fiction

0	A	B	C	D
	■	□	□	□

J. R. R. TOLKIEN

It is generally agreed that one of the greatest successes in twentieth century **(0)** .... literature is the trilogy **(1)** .... 'The Lord of the Rings'. The three novels, read all over the world, were written by Englishman J.R.R. Tolkien, a professor of English literature at Oxford University. Born in 1892, Tolkien suffered from the **(2)** .... of both his father and his mother early in his life. Nonetheless, the boy appears to have had a happy childhood in the English **(3)** ...., descriptions of which are a prominent **(4)** .... of his books. Tolkien was a soldier in the First World War, taking part in the **(5)** .... Battle of the Somme in 1916, and it is thought that his experience of war provided background material for the battle **(6)** .... in 'The Lord of the Rings'. It may also have influenced his **(7)** .... towards tyrants, as exemplified by the evil magician Sauron in the trilogy. Tolkien began his literary **(8)** .... by writing a story called 'The Hobbit' for his own children. Publisher Stanley Unwin asked his ten-year-old son to read 'The Hobbit' and write **(9)** .... on it. Unwin's son **(10)** .... the story highly and the book was published. Unwin then asked Tolkien for a **(11)** .... Tolkien responded by writing 'The Lord of the Rings'. The trilogy took him twelve years to write and was first published in 1954, when the professor was **(12)** .... retirement.

1	A named	B titled	C entitled	D known
2	A loss	B dying	C destruction	D extinction
3	A country	B countryside	C landscape	D territory
4	A theme	B ingredient	C quality	D feature
5	A deadly	B harmful	C deathly	D bitter
6	A parts	B scenes	C sections	D events
7	A view	B opinion	C attitude	D position
8	A progress	B career	C advance	D profession
9	A a report	B a statement	C an account	D a narrative
10	A advised	B recommended	C put forward	D suggested
11	A supplement	B development	C consequence	D sequel
12	A advancing	B going near	C approaching	D having

2A My score: ...... out of 12

2B Use of English FCE paper 3, part 3

Read the text below. Use the word given in capitals at the end of some of the lines to form a word that fits in the gap in the same line. There is an example at the beginning (0). Write your answers IN CAPITAL LETTERS.

Example: 0 M Y S T E R I O U S

DREAMS

People have always been fascinated by the (0) .... nature of dreams. In the past, **MYSTERY**
in many cultures it was believed that dreams had great (1) .... The Old Testament **SIGNIFY**
of the Bible tells the story of Joseph, who remembered and had the ability to interpret not
only his own dreams but also those of others. The (2) .... psychologist Sigmund Freud **INFLUENCE**
believed that dreams were a **(3)** .... of the unconscious mind and in 1899 he published **MECHANIC**
a **(4)** .... book called 'The Interpretation of Dreams'. He thought that **LONG**
(5) .... dreams could give us an insight into emotions that we may have buried. Today, while **REMEMBER**
many people **(6)** .... place much importance on their dreams, the question of whether dreams **INSTINCT**
actually have meaning is **(7)** .... debated by brain scientists. They have found that sleep has **HOT**
different phases, and that it is in the phase called Rapid Eye **(8)** .... (REM) sleep that we dream. **MOVE**
Unlike other phases of sleep, people woken during the REM phase have difficulty completing even
the simplest tasks. This suggests that dreams make an important contribution to our **(9)** .... **PSYCHOLOGY**
health, even though REM sleep only makes up about 20% of the total sleep time. People can go
through the REM stage of sleep five or six times **(10)** .... **NIGHT**

2B My score: ...... out of 10

2A Use of English FCE paper 3, part 2

Read the text below and think of the word which best fits each gap. Use only one word in each gap. There is an example at the beginning. Write your answers IN CAPITAL LETTERS.

Example: 0 | F | E | W

JOB INTERVIEWS

(0) ...... people like going for a job interview, which can be very daunting, **(1)** .... for experienced interviewees, and it is advisable to be as **(2)** .... prepared for the interview as possible. Before going for the interview, you should find out everything you can about the organization you hope to join. **(3)** .... possible, find out who will be interviewing you and their position in the company. **(4)** .... done this, think carefully about questions that may be asked. You answers **(5)** .... be carefully worded and it is important to prepare questions to ask your interviewers. To do well at the interview you will not **(6)** .... need to convince interviewers you have the necessary qualifications for the job and the right motivation, you will also need to convince them that you are capable of **(7)** .... as part of a team. One of the best ways to prepare for an interview is to role-play it with a friend. Do this **(8)** .... giving your friend the list of questions you have prepared and ask them to **(9)** .... constructive comments on your replies and the way in **(10)** .... you present yourself. One common mistake of interviewees is to talk too much. Replies should be brief and to the point. With **(11)** .... to the interview itself, it is important to dress appropriately and arrive **(12)** .... time. Good luck!

2A My score: ...... out of 12

2B Use of English FCE paper 3, part 4

Complete the second sentence so that it has a similar meaning to the first sentence, using the word given. Do not change the word given. You must use between two and five words, including the word given.

Example:

0 My brother is too young to drive a car.
NOT
My brother is .... to drive a car.

Example: 0 | N O T | O L D | E N O U G H

1 'Have you completed the project yet, Liz?' asked her boss.
SHE
Liz's boss asked her .... the project yet.

2 The students threw away all their old exam papers.
RID
The students .... all their old exam papers.

3 It's true that it's getting more and more difficult to find a job.
FINDING
It's true that .... more and more difficult.

4 I'll only phone her if you tell me to.
UNLESS
I .... you tell me to.

5 We told the manager we were not satisfied with the food.
COMPLAINED
We .... the food.

6 The boy was sorry that he had stolen the money.
REGRETTED
The boy .... the money.

7 His friends told him that it wasn't a good idea to mention the subject.
WARNED
His friends .... mention the subject.

8 I'll try as hard as I can to improve my grades.
BEST
I'll .... to improve my grades.

2B My score: ...... out of 8

2A Use of English FCE paper 3, part 2

Read the text below and think of the word which best fits each gap. Use only one word in each gap. There is an example at the beginning. Write your answers IN CAPITAL LETTERS.

Example: 0 A B O U T

EXTREME SPORTS

A friend of mine went bungee jumping in Kenya two years ago and came back really enthusiastic **(0)** .... extreme sports. The next year he went as far as New Zealand in **(1)** .... to go sky diving. This summer he went white-water rafting in America and returned with, if possible, **(2)** .... greater enthusiasm. 'I nearly came **(3)** .... the raft a couple of times,' he said delightedly. I couldn't understand his enthusiasm for **(4)** .... a dangerous sport – people occasionally drown when white-water rafting. But he explained **(5)** .... makes a sport like that so exciting is the fact that it is actually dangerous. My friend is one of the growing band of enthusiasts **(6)** .... part in extreme sports such as bungee jumping and skydiving that feature a much higher degree of risk than normal sports. There is a theory that extreme sports are becoming more popular **(7)** .... to the fact that people get bored in societies **(8)** .... everything is made as safe as possible. Whenever anything appears remotely dangerous, we pass a law that will make it **(9)** .... so. **(10)** ...., for example - and very sensibly - motor cyclists are required to wear helmets, and drivers and car passengers must wear seat belts. But it seems to be the case that some people have a need to **(11)** .... risks, hence the desire to seek out extreme sports. One thing is **(12)** ...., I won't be joining them!

2A My score:	...... out of 12

2B Use of English FCE paper 3, part 3

Read the text below. Use the word given in capitals at the end of some of the lines to form a word that fits in the gap in the same line. There is an example at the beginning (0). Write your answers IN CAPITAL LETTERS.

Example: 0 A D M I R A T I O N

BORN WITH TALENT AND LUCK

We all feel enormous **(0)** ...., for those who achieve greatness, whether it is in a sporting, **ADMIRE**
(1) ...., business or artistic area of achievement. We tend to believe that these **SCIENCE**
(2) .... people are born with natural talent and that success is easier for them as **FORTUNE**
a result of a **(3)** .... advantage of some kind. But the truth is that often their **GENE**
(4) .... are also the result of incredibly hard work in their chosen field. While it **ACHIEVE**
is **(5)** .... true that high-achievers need both talent and hard work, recently an idea **CERTAIN**
has been put forward by American sociologist Malcolm Gladwell that as well being
(6) .... and hardworking, people also need the right opportunities in order to be **TALENT**
successful. A **(7)** .... example is the fact that 40% of top ice hockey players are **CONVINCE**
born in the months of January, February and March. Children born after January
1st are **(8)** .... accepted into youth hockey leagues, which begin in the **RARE**
autumn each year. **(9)** ...., children born in the first three months of the year, **CONSEQUENCE**
being bigger and stronger, are more likely to get places. They then receive
further **(10)** .... training which will puts them well ahead of those born later in **INTENSE**
the year. But what if they had been born in December? Would they have had time to
grow and develop into first class players, whatever their natural ability?

2B My score:	...... out of 10

2A Use of English FCE paper 3, part 1

Read the text below and decide which answer (A, B, C or D) best fits each gap. There is an example at the beginning (0).

Example: 0 A being B continuation C survival D existence

0	A	B	C	D
	▭	▭	▭	■

DO GHOSTS EXIST?

In previous times a belief in the **(0)** .... of ghosts was quite **(1)** .... but in the twenty-first century, as science finds more and more explanations for what was **(2)** .... described as 'supernatural', fewer people tend to believe in them. However, **(3)** ...., newspapers report stories of ghosts being seen in **(4)** .... buildings and while there is doubtless a good explanation for these **(5)** ...., it is always interesting to ask yourself what the scientific explanation could be. A good example is a story that received **(6)** .... in all the British national newspapers in January 2009. The city of Derby's new hospital had been built on the **(7)** .... of a much older hospital and the papers reported that hospital **(8)** .... were claiming that a strange figure in a black cloak was stalking the corridors and wards. It seemed that **(9)** .... several weeks the ghostly apparition had been seen dozens of times, moving between rooms and through walls, especially in departments near the morgue. Workers were so terrified that hospital managers were forced to **(10)** .... the claims seriously. A theory was put **(11)** .... that the figure was the ghost of a Roman soldier who had been killed in the **(12)** .... of the original hospital.

1	A frequent	B common	C known	D ordinary
2	A previously	B before	C earlier	D then
3	A to some extent	B unusually	C irregularly	D from time to time
4	A national	B public	C architectural	D social
5	A views	B sights	C sightings	D spectacles
6	A news	B interest	C coverage	D public
7	A place	B position	C location	D site
8	A members	B colleagues	C staff	D people
9	A during	B over	C through	D for
10	A accept	B take	C think	D believe
11	A forward	B up	C in	D on
12	A district	B vicinity	C region	D area

2A My score:	...... out of 12

2B Use of English FCE paper 3, part 4

Complete the second sentence so that it has a similar meaning to the first sentence, using the word given. Do not change the word given. You must use between two and five words, including the word given.

Example:
0 My brother is too young to drive a car.
NOT
My brother is .... to drive a car.

Example: 0 | N | O | T | | O | L | D | | E | N | O | U | G | H

1 It looks as if the workers have left the building.
SEEM
The workers .... the building.

2 They claimed that he had planted the bomb.
ACCUSED
They .... the bomb.

3 Jack, I'd prefer it if you told him the news.
RATHER
Jack, ... the news.

4 The children are tired, they should go to bed.
TIME
It's .... to bed.

5 I can't tolerate her criticisms any more.
PUT
I can't .... her criticisms any more.

6 Alfonso wouldn't let anyone else pay for the meal.
INSISTED
Alfonso .... the meal.

7 I wonder if they realized what was happening.
AWARE
I wonder if .... what was happening.

8 I'd like you to explain why you did it.
WISH
I .... explain why you did it.

2B My score:	...... out of 8

Name:
Class:

1 Speaking Test FCE paper 5, part 2

1

2

3

4

Work in pairs. Student A looks at photographs 1 and 2. Student B looks at pictures 3 and 4.

Student A: Look at photographs 1 and 2. They show friends spending time together. Compare and contrast the photographs, and **say whether you prefer to be with a large group of friends or with one good friend.** (*1 minute*)

Student B: When student A has finished talking briefly answer this question:
How important are friends in your life? (*20 seconds*)

Student B: Look at pictures 3 and 4. Compare and contrast the pictures, and say **what the difference is between communicating with friends online and communicating with friends face-to-face.** (*1 minute*)

Student A: When Student B has finished talking, briefly answer this question:
Do you keep in touch with friends online? If so, how? (*20 seconds*)

See Language Bank 12 for ways of talking about pictures.

Useful language for describing and comparing pictures:
- **The first picture shows** a group of teenagers sitting on the back of a truck.
- **In the second picture**, two girls have their arms round each other. They look happy.
- **(One similarity is that) both pictures show** people **talking** to friends.
- **In picture 4**, **we can see** a group of people, **whereas in picture 3 there is** only one person.
- **One difference is that in picture 3** the friends are chatting on the internet.

2 Writing FCE paper 2, part 1

Writing a transactional letter

4 Tickets booked for 26th May, £20 each

Tickets booked online on 4th April

Rang several times a day to cancel, but phone always engaged

You booked tickets to see a circus, but the performance was cancelled. Read the advertisement, on which you have made some notes. Write a letter asking for a refund, using all the information in your notes. Write between 120 and 180 words in an appropriate style. Do not write any postal addresses.

Useful language for formal letters:		
We write formal letters to people we do not know. We do not use contractions or colloquial language.		
Salutation:	• **Dear Sir / Madam / Sir or Madam** • **Dear Mr / Ms / Mrs** (Brown)	
Paragraph 1: Your reason for writing:	• **I am writing to** (ask for a refund). • I booked (online / by phone / by fax). • **I understand** that (the circus is cancelled).	
Paragraph 2: Give detailed information:	• I telephoned the box office (but there was no answer).	
Paragraph 3: Action required/ conclusion:	• **I would like to** request a refund.	
Final paragraph:	• **I look forward to** receiving (your reply / a full refund of the cost).	
Salutations and endings:	Start with:	End with:
If you don't know the name	• **Dear Sir / Madam** →	**... Yours faithfully**
If you know the name	• **Dear Mr / Ms / Mrs Dent** →	**... Yours sincerely**
Useful language for informal letters:		
We write informal letters to people we know well.	• **Dear John / Johnny**	
We use contractions:	• **I haven't** • **We can't** • **I don't** • **He doesn't**	
Use colloquial language and expressions:	• **It was great!** • **Wow!** • **Amazing!** • **Yuk!**	
Ending:	• **Best wishes / All the best / Love, Sarah** (usually first name only)	

1A Speaking Test FCE paper 5, part 2

Work in pairs.

Student A: Explain that you want to ask Student B some questions about him or herself. Ask Student B each of these three questions.

- Where are you from?
- Do you live in (the local town)?
- What do you like about living in (student's home town)?

Listen to B's replies.

Student B: Ask Student A the same three questions above. Listen to A's replies.

Student A: Now choose one question from each of the headings below to ask your partner.

Student B: Answer A's questions. *(1½ minutes)*

Student B: From each of the headings below, ask the other question that Student A did not ask you.

Student A: Answer B's questions. *(1½ minutes)*

Family life
- Can you tell me something about your family, or your friends?
- Do you miss your family and friends when you're away from home?

Daily life
- Do you have a daily routine? What usually happens?
- What do you normally do at the weekend?

Future plans
- What are your plans for your next holidays?
- What are your plans with regard to work and career?

Leisure
- How do you spend your free time?
- Do you have a hobby or sport that you really enjoy?

House and home
- Do you live in a house or an apartment? What's it like?
- Can you tell me something about your neighbourhood?

Language learning
- How do you think you will use English in the future?
- Do you speak any other languages?

1B Speaking Test FCE paper 5, part 3

Work in pairs. Look at the pictures. Imagine that you are in your last year at a school or college where students can join a cadet force - army, navy or air force. First, talk to each other about what kind of training activities students would do as cadets in each of the three different armed forces. Then decide which armed force you will join as cadets. You must both join the same one. *(3 minutes)*

See Language Bank 12 for ways of talking about pictures.

Useful language:
- **This picture shows** army cadets train**ing**.
- **Army cadets would probably do** lots of exercises to get fit.
- **I should imagine that** navy cadets **would** learn to sail.
- **Do you think** air force cadets **might** learn to fly?
- **I dislike** flying, **so I wouldn't** join the air force cadets.
- **I think** the navy cadet force **would / might** be the most fun.
- **I'd prefer to** join the army cadets.

2 Writing FCE paper 2, part 2

Writing a discursive composition

You have recently had a class discussion about violence. Now your teacher has asked you to write a composition, giving your opinions on the following statement:

- There should not be so much violence on television.

Plan your composition as follows:

Paragraph 1: Introduction State the topic and make one or two general statements about it. • **There is a lot of discussion about** whether there is too much violence on television today. • **It is certainly true that** there is a lot of violence on television these days.
Paragraphs 2 and 3: Give your opinion, with two to four arguments in support of it. Try to give one or two examples. • **In my opinion**, the violence which we see on television is very harmful, **for several reasons. Firstly, ... Secondly, ... Lastly, ...** • **For example,** police detective series show very high levels of violence. War films show shooting and...
Use cohesive devices: see Language Bank 17. • **Moreover,** violent scenes on TV are not good for young children. • **As a result,** there is more crime than ever before.
Final Paragraph: Conclusion Present your final opinion. • **To conclude, my opinion is that** there is **indeed** too much violence on TV.

1 Speaking Test FCE paper 5, part 4

Work in groups of three. The task is to take part in a three-way discussion.
(4 minutes)

Student A: Play the part of the examiner. Ask some or all of the following questions. Give each student time to fully answer the questions and take part in the discussion yourself.

- Were your parents strict when you were a child?
- Did they believe that discipline was important?
- Do you think children should be punished?
- Do you think that your generation are well-brought-up?
- Do you think that manners are important?
- If you have children, how will you bring them up?

Students B and C:

Answer the examiner's questions. Try and give full answers.
Interact with the other participants, asking for their opinions and agreeing or disagreeing. Give reasons for your opinions.

Change roles. Students B and C take turns at playing the part of the examiner.

See these Language Banks for useful interview language:

Language Bank 2:	Ways of asking for and giving opinions
Language Bank 5:	Ways of asking for clarification
Language Bank 9:	Ways of agreeing and disagreeing
Language Bank 7/11:	Hesitation fillers
Language Bank 19:	Ways of checking that you understood what someone said
Language Bank 21:	Ways of asking for and eliciting further information
Language Bank 26:	Ways of showing respect for other people's views

2 Writing FCE paper 2, part 2

Writing a non-transactional letter

You are in your final year at school. Your class teacher has asked you to write a letter to a social worker inviting him/her to come to our school to give a talk on drugs. In the letter, you should give relevant details such as how many students will attend the lecture and how long the talk should last.

Write your letter. Do not write any postal addresses. This should be a formal letter.
Plan your composition as follows:

Begin:	• Dear Mr (Smith)
Paragraph 1: Explain who you are: Explain why you are writing:	• I am a student in my final year at (name of school). • We feel it would be helpful for students to hear an expert talk about the dangers of drug abuse.
Paragraph 2: Give practical information:	• The week beginning March 12th would be suitable. • I suggest that the talk should last about an hour. • About 100 students will attend. • We will provide refreshments after the talk.
Paragraphs 3/4: Give some background information: Suggest suitable topics for discussion:	• We know that some of the younger students have started experimenting with drugs. • The connection between cannabis and mental illness
Conclusion:	• We think that your experience will help to give students a better understanding of the problems of drugs.
Polite farewell:	• We do hope that you will be able to come. • I look forward to hearing from you.

Name ______ Class ______ . Date ______

1 Vocabulary

A Choose the correct word or phrase to fill the gaps.

1 Have you ever .... an advertisement on a dating website?
(a) posted (b) sent (c) described

2 A lot of young people .... the internet hoping to meet people online.
(a) follow (b) surf (c) look at

3 The word is .... that online dating is fun.
(a) looking around (b) getting around
(c) getting up

4 .... research, 25% of high school students regularly visit dating websites.
(a) Because of (b) About (c) According to

5 The internet dating market is .... to grow in the next four years.
(a) liking (b) probably (c) likely to

B Match the words with the definitions.

1 psychologist (a) a person who is used in a test
2 subject (b) a person who studies the human mind
3 trial (c) to behave in the same way as other people in a group
4 majority (d) a test
5 conform (e) most of the people or things in a group

1 Vocabulary: my score is ...... out of 10

2 Language

A Complete the advice using *should* or *shouldn't*.

Keep your identity secret. You **1** .... put your personal details on a website. Your first meeting **2** .... be in a public place. Don't go to someone's house alone. You **3** .... meet in a coffee shop or a shopping centre. If you are already going out with someone, you **4** .... tell the new person before you meet. And finally, you **5** .... always be honest – don't tell lies about yourself!

B Match the sentences.

1 You shouldn't eat so much chocolate. (a) You're going to be late.
2 I hate my new hairstyle! (b) I've got an exam tomorrow.
3 I want to go out later. (c) You'll get spots.
4 Why don't you hurry up and get ready? (d) You shouldn't have cut it.
5 I ought not to stay up late. (e) You'd better do your homework now.

2 Language: my score is ...... out of 10

3 Functions

A Choose a suitable word or phrase from Language Bank 1 to fill the gaps.

Lisa: I've just changed schools and I don't know anyone. **1** .... to make new friends?
Alex: Well, you **2** .... joining some school clubs and activities. Or **3** .... taking up a new sport?
Lisa: I suppose so but I'm not very fit – I don't really like sports. I prefer sitting at my computer and surfing the Internet.
Alex: OK, then **4** .... post an ad on the school website? **5** .... for some new friends online. I know a great site for meeting people and chatting.
Lisa: Oh great – what's the address?

B Answer the questions.

1 Do you think people Internet dating is safe?
2 Would you like to meet a boyfriend or girlfriend online?
3 Do you think parents approve of their children using websites to make friends?
4 Where should you meet someone on a first date?
5 Do you think internet dating will increase in the future?

3 Functions: my score is ...... out of 10

Quick Smart Test 1:
My total score is ...... out of 30

Name ______________________ Class ______________ Date ______________

1 Vocabulary

A Underline the correct answer in *italics*.

1 I couldn't sleep because people in the street were being so *noisy / hectic*.
2 My friends *emigrated / immigrated* from India twenty years ago.
3 Population is always very high in *rural / urban* areas because so many people live close together.
4 I would prefer to live in the *environment / suburbs* of a city rather than the city centre.
5 There was a carnival and the streets were very *crowded / exotic*.

B Choose a word from the box to fill the gaps.

peaceful	transport	high-rise building
refugee	agricultural	

1 If a region has many farms, we describe it as an .... region.
2 A very tall building is known as a ....
3 If someone has to leave their country because of a war, they are a ....
4 A place that is very quiet can be described as ....
5 Buses, trains and cars are all forms of ....

1 Vocabulary: my score is ...... out of 10

2 Language

Complete the gaps with a suitable word or phrase.

The centre of a city is always **1** .... busier than the suburbs. There are **2** .... more cars, and during the rush hour the city centre is **3** .... busier than it is at other times. In the evenings the streets are not **4** .... full, but even then, the traffic can be bad. During the month of August, when people go on holiday, the congestion is **5** .... better - but not much! Of course, when you are young, living in the city is a lot **6** .... exciting than living in the boring suburbs, where life moves much more **7** .... To a teenager eager to leave for the city lights, a suburb can be the most boring place **8** .... the world. To his parents, however, the suburbs are far more attractive **9** .... the city centre. They are **10** .... happy to return to the suburbs each evening as their teenage children are to leave them.

2 Language: my score is ...... out of 10

3 Functions

A Choose a suitable word or phrase from Language Bank 5 to fill the gaps.

Nick: More and more people are moving from the country to the city.
Ben: Sorry. **1** .... again ?
Nick: Yes. More and more people are moving to the city. There are lots of push factors.
Ben: Could you **2** .... by 'push factors'?
Nick: Yes, things that make people want to leave the countryside.
Ben: Sorry, **3** would .... ?
Nick: Things that make people want to leave the countryside.
Ben: That's interesting. Can **4** .... that?
Nick: Yes, it's things such as high unemployment, lack of services.
Ben: I didn't **5** .... word.
Nick: Services.
Ben: Ah yes, there aren't enough trains or buses in the countryside, I know.

B Complete the gaps using a different word each time.

Karen: I've just come back from a holiday in California. We spent a week in San Francisco. It's **1** .... more beautiful than Los Angeles.
Jane: Oh, you can't compare the two. LA is **2** .... larger and dirtier.
Karen: And not **3** .... interesting.
Jane: I think San Francisco is one of the loveliest cities **4** .... the US.
Karen: I agree. And people are a lot **5** .... I'd love to live there.

3 Functions: my score is ...... out of 10

Quick Smart Test 2:
My total score is ...... out of 30

Name ______________________ Class ______________ Date ______________

1 Vocabulary

Match the words with the definitions.

1 stalker	(a) newspapers, television and radio
2 celebrity	(b) luxuries that rich people can afford to buy
3 disguise	(c) having a special ability in something
4 keep up appearances	(d) when people know who you are and what you do
5 trappings	(e) not be successful or not last as long as you might like
6 media	(f) a person who is famous for some reason
7 talented	(g) when someone gets a lot of attention from the public and in the media
8 not work out	(h) someone who takes too much interest in a celebrity and follows them everywhere
9 public recognition	(i) pretend that everything in life is wonderful
10 limelight	(j) something you wear so that people will not recognise you

1 Vocabulary: my score is ...... out of 10

2 Language

A **Match the sentences with the meanings.**

1 If you're famous, you may have people asking for your autograph.
2 I might be famous in ten years time.
3 A lot of the stories about celebrities in the media may be untrue.
4 The public will lose interest in her if she doesn't make any more films.
5 Celebrities may or may not be very interesting as people.

(a) a situation that will definitely happen
(b) a situation that could happen in the future
(c) something that is possibly true
(d) a situation that can happen at any time
(e) something that you are not sure about

B **Complete the gaps with a suitable word or phrase.**

1 You .... that fame will last.
2 Famous people .... like all the attention they get and want to be left alone.
3 Although celebrities .... pretend not to like having their photo taken all the time, I think they're secretly happy about it.
4 Sam is a very talented child. He .... grow up to be a famous musician one day.
5 It's .... that man in the restaurant was Michael Jackson in disguise!

2 Language: my score is ...... out of 10

3 Functions

Complete the gaps with a suitable word or phrase.

Karen: Do you want to have a look at my *Hello* magazine? There are some great pictures of all our favourite **1** ....
Jane: Yes, I'd love to. Let's see the photos of Nicole Kidman.
Karen: She looks happy! But don't you think she **2** .... be getting a bit too thin?
Jane: Oh, **3** .... about that. It **4** .... just be the camera.
Karen: Well, **5** .... she has to go on a diet all the time because Hollywood wants actresses to be really thin.
Jane: You know what? I think they like all the attention. Having their **6** .... trying to get their **7** .... all the time and all the photographers waiting around!
Karen: Oh, **8** .... about that!
Jane: I think celebrities worry that people **9** .... lose interest in them.
Karen: Well, that may or **10** .... be true – but I still like looking at the magazine photos!

3 Functions: my score is ...... out of 10

Quick Smart Test 3:
My total score is ...... out of 30

Name ____________________ Class ____________ Date ____________

1 Vocabulary

A Complete the gaps with the correct word.

joy	survival	mammal	grief	feeling

1 An emotion is the same as a ....
2 Sadness is the opposite of ....
3 Dolphins and whales are both ....
4 The .... of many animals is endangered.
5 When someone dies we feel ....

B Match the words with the definitions.

1 gorilla
2 threaten
3 pleasure
4 extinction
5 hunter

(a) a situation in which a type of animal or plant stops existing
(b) a large strong African wild animal that is similar to a monkey but much larger
(c) someone who catches wild animals
(d) a feeling of happiness or enjoyment
(e) to be likely to harm or destroy something

1 Vocabulary: score is ...... out of 10

2 Language

A Rewrite the sentences using relative pronouns.

1 The dolphin has died. You saw the dolphin.
....
2 I met a man. He worked at a zoo.
....
3 I am reading a book. The book is about ecology.
....
4 These are plants. They grow well in sunny environments.
....
5 She's the woman. She wrote a book about chimpanzees.
....

B Put *a* or *the* where necessary, or leave a blank (-).

1 Some monkeys were lying on .... ground.
2 Are you afraid of............ dogs?
3 Whales are .... largest of all mammals.
4 This is .... very young animal.
5 This is .... book they were discussing on television.

2 Language: my score is ...... out of 10

3 Functions

Choose a suitable word or phrase from Language Banks 8 and 9 to fill the gaps.

A: What are **1** .... vivisection?
B: I think it's terrible.
A: I don't **2** .... it, but I sometimes I think it's necessary.
B: I can see **3** .... saying, but I **4** .... agree. I love animals. It **5** .... so sad when I read about cruelty to them.
A: I feel **6** .... way, but sometimes we need to test medicines on animals first.
B: I think **7** .... wrong. I'm sure it's not necessary.
A: Scientists say it is. How **8** .... cancer, for example?
B: It's a terrible disease.
A: Well, would you like to be given a drug for cancer that perhaps wasn't safe? We have to test on animals first.
B: Oh **9** .... That's not true!
A: I can see we'll never agree on this.
B: That's **10** .... right.

3 Functions: my score is ...... out of 10

Quick Smart Test 4:
My total score is ...... out of 30

Name ______________________ Class ______________ Date ______________

1 Vocabulary

A Match the words with the definitions.

1 imagination (a) something you can remember
2 reminder (b) to remember a fact or experience from the past
3 memories (c) the ability to form pictures and ideas in your mind
4 recollection (d) something that helps you remember
5 recall (e) things you remember from the past

B Choose a word from A to fill the gaps.

1 You need a lot of .... to write stories for children.
2 I love this song, it's a good .... of last summer.
3 Annie Burton had happy .... of her childhood on the plantation.
4 She cannot .... anything about the accident at all.
5 Do you have any .... of when you were a baby?

1 Vocabulary: score ...... out of 10

2 Language

Choose a word or phrase from the box to fill the gaps.

ate	had	used to x 2	would x 3
had eaten	was	didn't use to	

The young children **1** .... to wander from plantation to plantation and **2** .... care about what was happening in the world outside.
The slaves that were not married **3** .... serve the food. They **4** .... send the older children with food to the workers in the fields. Before they got to the fields, they **5** .... nearly all the food. The workers **6** .... complain if there wasn't enough food and the children **7** .... be whipped. The children **8** .... no supper and only a little food in the morning. Sometimes there **9** .... bread in their bowls and sometimes dogs and ducks **10** .... from the bowl as well.

2 Language: score ...... out of 10

3 Functions

A Underline the correct word in *italics*.

Nick: Did you see the programme about the slave trade?
Ben: No. I missed it. Was it interesting?
Nick: **1** *Well / You know*, yes, it was really good.
Ben: Did it describe how the Africans went to work as slaves in the USA?
Nick: **2** I *mean / Actually*, most of the Africans were taken to the Caribbean islands and South America.
Ben: Oh, really? How long did it take to cross the Atlantic?
Nick: **3** *Let me think / What can I say*? It was between one and two months. But they were chained together on the ships and many people died.
Ben: It's hard to believe that really **4** *went / happened*. I can't even **5** *imagine / believe* what it was like.
Nick: No, I don't think anyone can.

B Answer the questions about your own life.

1 What television programmes did you use to watch when you were a child?
2 What was your favourite programme last year?
3 Do you remember your first friend at primary school?
4 Are there any foods that you didn't use to like when you were a child, but that you like now?
5 Have you got a pet or did you use to have a pet?

3 Functions: score ...... out of 10

Quick Smart Test 5:
My total score is ...... out of 30

Name ______ Class ______ Date ______

1 Vocabulary

A Complete the gaps with one word.

Speed cameras and surveillance cameras are examples of new **1** t ………… . They **2** m ………… people as they drive or walk about in the streets. Many people dislike the use of surveillance cameras because they reduce our **3** p ………… . On the other hand, they **4** r ………… us and make us feel more **5** s ………… .

B Choose the correct word or phrase to fill the gaps.

1. This machine doesn't ……….. . It's broken.
   (a) go **(b)** march **(c)** work
2. Can you ………… the man in the photograph?
   (a) identify **(b)** know **(c)** notice
3. ………… is the science that studies heat, light and other forms of energy.
   (a) physics **(b)** chemistry **(c)** biology
4. Who ………… the computer?
   (a) discovered **(b)** made **(c)** invented
5. The boy fell into the water and almost ………… .
   (a) drowned **(b)** sank **(c)** floated

1 Vocabulary: my score is …… out of 10

2 Language

Rewrite the sentences using the passive.

1. They pulled LeRoy out of the water. ………… .
2. A security officer identified the thief. ………… .
3. Today, surveillance cameras monitor people in the street. ………… .
4. Most people dislike the idea of RFID tags. ………… .
5. They transmitted the images all around the world. ………… .
6. Who recognised him? ………… .
7. They place RFID tags in all kinds of items, don't they? ………… .
8. Where did they put the computer? ………… .
9. The police didn't catch the shoplifters. ………… .
10. Why do cameras photograph drivers? …………

2 Language: my score is …… out of 10

3 Functions

Complete the gaps with a suitable word or phrase.

Sara: There are some great photographs in the photo competition.
Jill: Tell me about them.
Sara: Well, the best photo, in my opinion, is a **1** ………… a small child. She's **2** ………… on a street corner all alone. She looks **3** ………… she's crying. There are people **4** ………… by her and no-one has noticed her.
Jill: That sounds rather sad.
Sara: Well, there are two more photos. The photo next to it **5** ………… a man coming down the same street who **6** ………… very worried. Terrified, in fact.
Jill: And what does the third photo **7** ………… ? I think I can guess. Is it a photo **8** ………… the man and the girl?
Sara: Yes. The man's **9** ………… the little girl in his arms. **10** People ………… as they watch them. It's very sweet.

3 Functions: my score is …… out of 10

Quick Smart Test 6:
My total score is …… out of 30

Name ____________________ Class __________ Date __________

1 Vocabulary

A Choose the correct word or phrase to fill the gaps.

1 When cars burn petrol, they produce ...., which causes pollution.
(a) hydrogen (b) carbon dioxide
(c) gasoline
2 Carbon, hydrogen and oxygen are all........... .
(a) elements (b) fossil fuels
(c) fractions
3 Sun, wind and water are all sources of........... .
(a) greenhouse gases (b) renewable energy
(c) acid rain
4 If oil production goes down there might be an oil ....
(a) crop (b) problem
(c) crisis
5 Coal, oil and natural gas are examples of ....
(a) global warming (b) hydrocarbons
(c) fossil fuels

B Choose a word to fill the gaps.

In the future I'm going to build my own **1** .... This is a modern house which uses **2** .... technology and produces electricity from **3** .... on the roof. **4** .... runs down a pipe into a **5** .... in the garden and this saves a lot of water.

1 Vocabulary: score ...... out of 10

2 Language

A Match the two parts of the sentences.

1 When oil production goes down,
2 When half the planet's oil is used up,
3 If we make enough solar panels,
4 If we run out of oil,
5 When cars burn petrol,

(a) we will reach peak oil.
(b) we will have to stop driving cars.
(c) they produce greenhouse gases.
(d) the price will go up.
(e) we can make limitless quantities of electricity.

B Choose a word from the box to fill the gaps.

unless	in case	when	if x2

1 .... crude oil is heated, it divides into different gases and liquids.
2 .... we start saving energy, we will face major problems in the future.
3 We need to save rainwater, ... there is a water shortage.
4 .... you burn PVC, it produces dioxins.
5 There will be an economic crisis, ... the price of oil increases dramatically.

2 Language: score ...... out of 10

3 Functions

A Choose a suitable word or phrase from Language Banks 13 and 14 to fill the gaps.

William: What do you think governments will do about the oil situation?
Alex: **1** It's .... , but I **2** .... they will start looking for alternative sources of energy.
William: Well, **3** .... , we'll find alternatives before it is too late.
Alex: Yes, because if we don't, **4** .... there will be oil wars.
William: Or **5** .... the world will become more peaceful.
Alex: I hope you're right!

B Write answers to the questions.

Q Do you think there is an oil crisis at the moment?
1 No, but there .... if ....
Q What will happen if the oil runs out?
2 We will not ....
Q What do we need to do to stop an energy crisis?
3 We need to ....
Q What alternative sources of energy are there?
4 ....
Q If we all use less oil, what will happen to the environment?
5 Perhaps ....

3 Functions: score ...... out of 10

Quick Smart Test 7:
My total score is ...... out of 30

Name Class Date

1 Vocabulary

A Underline the correct answer in *italics*.

1 He worked hard and succeeded in *passing / failing* all his exams.
2 I have a *degree / test* from Oxford University.
3 My daughter would like to do *research / study* in psychology.
4 Do you have the right *qualifications / paper* for this job?
5 Before an exam it's important to *revisit / revise*.

B Match the words with the definitions.

1 academic	**(a)** to try to persuade someone to do something that you believe would be good
2 grade	**(b)** doing something for the number of hours that people normally work in a week
3 full-time	**(c)** relating to education, especially in a college or university
4 encourage	**(d)** a letter or number given by a teacher that shows how good a student's work is
5 stress	**(e)** a strong feeling of worry that stops you from relaxing

1 Vocabulary: my score is ...... out of 10

2 Language

A Rewrite the sentences using the second conditional.

1 I'd like to buy a car but I don't have the money.
....
2 You don't do enough work. That's why you don't do well in exams.
....
3 I think you should find a counsellor. They could help you with your problems.
....
4 The teacher isn't very good, so the students aren't very interested in the subject.
....
5 I'm not going to take the course because I haven't got the time.
....

B Write complete questions using the second conditional.

1 What / you / study / you / have the opportunity?
....
2 What / you / buy / someone / give you $100,000?
....
3 Who / you / interview / you / can / interview anyone in the world? ....
4 Which country / you / live in / you / can / live anywhere in the world? ....
5 You / build / a swimming pool / you / have the money? ....

2 Language: my score ...... out of 10

3 Functions

Put the verbs in brackets into the correct form.

Anna: What are you doing tomorrow?
Carol: I'm staying in and revising all day.
Anna: **1** You (not / need) .... revise all day! The exams aren't till next week. If you **2** (work) .... in the afternoon, you can go out in the evening, surely?
Carol: No, I've got a lot of work to do.
Anna: You **3** (be) .... fine in the exams. You **4** (do) .... well, your grades are fine.
Carol: They're not good enough.
Anna: **5** (not / say) .... that, that's rubbish. If I **6** (have) .... your grades, I **7** (be) .... really pleased. Anyway, you **8** (need) .... go out and enjoy yourself. Listen, if you **9** (come) .... to the cinema with me, I **10** (pay) ....
Carol: No, I've got to revise – otherwise I'll fail, I know I will!

3 Functions: my score is ...... out of 10

Quick Smart Test 8:
My total score is ...... out of 30

Name ______________ Class ______________ Date ______________

1 Vocabulary

A Match the words with the definitions.

1 air force
2 arms
3 bulldozer
4 Cold War
5 combat
6 genocide
7 missile
8 mission
9 primary
10 volunteer

(a) the murder of a large number of people because of their race
(b) a person who does something because they want to and is not paid
(c) a special military task
(d) guns and bombs
(e) most important
(f) a kind of bomb that travels through the air
(g) a large machine for moving earth
(h) fighting between soldiers
(i) the part of the armed services that fights in the air with planes
(j) the period after the Second World War, when there was a lot of tension between the West and Russia

1 Vocabulary: my score is ...... out of 10

2 Language

A Underline the correct word in *italics*.

1 The UN peacekeepers are not soldiers. *Consequently / However*, they are often in dangerous situations.
2 The conflict has a long history. *First of all / Consequently*, most people don't really understand it.
3 They had a bigger, more modern army. *Furthermore / However*, the soldiers were much better trained.
4 The terrorists will not stop the violence. *Meanwhile / Nevertheless*, the people are suffering.
5 Sometimes there are good reasons to fight. *On the whole / On the other hand*, it would be better if there were no wars.

B Write two examples of each type of cohesive device.

1 ways of expressing similarity ....
2 ways of ordering points ....
3 ways of giving examples ....
4 ways of making general statements ....
5 ways of concluding ....

2 Language: my score is ...... out of 10

3 Functions

A Choose a suitable cohesive device to fill the gaps.

Sally: Are you going on the peace demonstration?
Mark: No. **1** .... they can't do anything to stop wars.
Sally: I know, but there are good reasons to go on demonstrations. **2** .... it makes you feel that you are doing something positive. And **3** .... I think governments do listen – if enough people say something.
Mark: Yes, but what if people start fighting on the demonstration because they are angry?
Sally: **4** .... , people behave well on demonstrations, especially if it is for peace!
Mark: That's **5** .... true, I agree. But ordinary people have no power.
Sally: Well, I don't agree. But if you change your mind – see you on Saturday!

B Match the questions and answers.

1 Who are the soldiers wearing blue helmets?
2 Do you think the UN can stop wars?
3 If someone attacks you, do you have a right to defend yourself?
4 Did the peace talks fail?
5 What is to blame for war, weapons or people?

a Yes, and as a result the conflict is still going on.
b In my opinion, you do, yes.
c People. Nevertheless, without weapons they would not be so dangerous.
d Not really, However, it can help to keep the peace after a war has ended.
e They are the United Nations peacekeepers.

3 Functions: score ...... out of 10

Quick Smart Test 9:
My total score is ...... out of 30

Name ____________ Class ____________ Date ____________

1 Vocabulary

A Choose the correct word or phrase to fill the gaps.

1 Supermarkets try to please ………… .
(a) their clients **(b)** the consumer
(c) their patients
2 Wealthy people are not always ………… with their money.
(a) generous **(b)** kind **(c)** warm
3 The country is getting richer – the ………… has improved.
(a) economy **(b)** economics
(c) cost of living
4 Far too many people ………. the necessities of life.
(a) miss **(b)** don't own
(c) lack
5 A yacht is a ………. most of us will never have.
(a) luxury **(b)** speciality **(c)** necessity

B Match the words with the definitions.

1 can / can't afford
2 poverty
3 garbage
4 dishwasher
5 social

(a) something that you throw away
(b) a machine that washes dishes and cutlery
(c) a situation when you do not have enough money for your basic needs
(d) relating to society and to people's lives in general
(e) have enough money to pay for something

1 Vocabulary: my score is …… out of 10

2 Language

A Rewrite the sentences using *I wish*.

1 I haven't got an iPod.
I wish …………
2 I'd like them to stop.
I wish …………
3 I want him to go.
I wish …………
4 I'd like to live there.
I wish …………
5 I can't play the guitar.
I wish …………

B Write sentences using the words below. Begin *I hope* …………

1 have children: …………
2 pass your exams: …………
3 sunny tomorrow : …………
4 catch the train: …………
5 not rain: …………

2 Language: my score is …… out of 10

3 Functions

Complete the gaps with one or two words.

Linda: I wish we **1** (have) ………… a bigger flat. This place is tiny.
Mark: I wish you **2** (not / talk) ………… like that. I like it here.
Linda: It's nice, but it's too small. I wish **3** (there be) ………… a garden.
Mark: Well, I've got that job interview tomorrow. The salary's really good. If I get the job, we can move to a bigger place.
Linda: That would be wonderful. I hope you **4** (get) ………… it.
Mark: Yes, I really hope they **5** (like) ………… me.
Linda: How are you travelling there?
Mark: By train. I hope they **6** (not / cancel) ………… the trains. I wish we **7** (have) ………… a car.
Linda: Well, we just don't have enough money.
Mark: Oh, we never have enough money, that's our problem. Anyway, I'm going to bed.
Linda: I hope you **8** (sleep) ………… well.
Mark: Yes, I wish I **9** (not / feel) ………… so nervous.
Linda: And I wish you **10** (not / worry) ………… so much! You'll be fine!

3 Functions: my score is …… out of 10

Quick Smart Test 10:
My total score is …… out of 30

Name ______________________ Class ______________ Date ______________

1 Vocabulary

A Match the words with the meanings.

1 calories
2 malnutrition
3 imbalance
4 in a row
5 starving

(a) one after the other
(b) very, very hungry, dying because of a lack of food
(c) units for measuring how much energy you get from food
(d) a lack of balance
(e) an illness caused by not eating enough food

B Underline the correct word in *italics*.

1 My jeans are too small! think I'd better *go on a diet / put on weight*.
2 Millions of people in the world are hungry and millions are *gluttonous / obese*.
3 Helen is quite *obsessed / greedy*. Today she ate three doughnuts!
4 Why do they *pick on / put on* Americans? A lot of Europeans are overweight as well.
5 It's not attractive to be fat but it's not good to be too *skinny / slim* either.

1 Vocabulary: score ...... out of 10

2 Language

A Match the two parts of the sentence.

1 Matthew's one of those people who never puts on weight,
2 In spite of all the fitness clubs in Houston,
3 Although I've been on a diet for three months,
4 Despite being really hungry,
5 I try not to eat chips,

(a) I've only lost one kilo.
(b) many people who live there are overweight.
(c) even though he eats anything he likes.
(d) though I really love them.
(e) I couldn't eat the food on the plane as it was disgusting!

B Rewrite the sentences using the word in brackets.

1 Nicky never seems to eat very much but she still seems to be overweight. (although) ....
2 In spite of being very slim already, she worries about her weight. (even though) ....
3 I went to the fitness club after work, even though I didn't feel like it. (despite) ....
4 Freya works in a pizza restaurant but she never eats anything there. (though) ....
5 In spite of there being plenty of sports facilities in the city, people still prefer watching TV. (in spite of the fact that) ....

2 Language: score ...... out of 10

3 Functions

Complete the gaps with a suitable word.

If you want to lose weight, the best **1** .... is to go on a diet. You should have regular meals and not eat too many calories. You should be careful to avoid fattening food like chocolate, biscuits and cake **2** .... that **3** .... be difficult for some people. Remember to **4** .... enough **5** .... as well. You **6** .... join a fitness club or gym, but don't forget to go at least twice a week. My **7** .... is to take up a sport which helps you to burn energy and there are plenty of **8** .... .You **9** .... try swimming, weights or jogging – whichever activity you **10** .... The most important thing is to do a sport you enjoy, so that you don't give it up!

3 Functions: score ...... out of 10

Quick Smart Test 11:
My total score is ...... out of 30

Name ____________ Class ____________ Date ____________

1 Vocabulary

A Choose the correct form of the words in the box to fill the gaps.

crack	section	circle	design	location

That building, with its **1** .... windows, is beautifully **2** .... and it's in a wonderful **3** .... But it's only two years old and already there are big problems. The concrete has started **4** .... And there are **5** .... that need replacing.

B Choose the correct word or phrase to fill the gaps.

1 The earthquake .... the building but didn't destroy it.
(a) crashed (b) damaged (c) broke
2 He was the last .... to leave the building.
(a) citizen (b) inhabitant (c) resident
3 Artists are often .... by other artists.
(a) influenced (b) changed (c) persuaded
4 We need cheap .... for a family with two children.
(a) spaces (b) accommodation (c) room
5 Do objects of art need to have a .... ?
(a) task (b) function (c) role

1 Vocabulary: my score is ...... out of 10

2 Language

A Rewrite the sentences using the passive.

1 They have designed the skyscrapers to withstand earthquakes. ....
2 Engineers haven't yet tested the strength of the tunnel. ....
3 The country's top architects have discussed the plans. ....
4 Have they found homes for all the refugees? ....
5 Why haven't they completed the project? ....

B Rewrite the sentences using the passive.

1 They won't include leisure facilities in the building. ....
2 Hollow tubes will link the skyscrapers. ....
3 The vertical city will house more than 35,000 people. ....
4 Where will they build it? ....
5 Waves and wind will provide power. ....

2 Language: my score is ...... out of 10

3 Functions

A Write questions using the words given.

1 The tunnel will be made safe.
How .... ?
2 The first Maglev train was built some years ago.
When .... ?
3 Maglev trains don't use rails.
Why .... ?
4 The skyscraper will be pulled down.
Which .... ?
5 The anchors have been placed.
Where .... ?

B Complete the sentences with a phrase asking for further information.

1 **A:** The Bauhaus School was considered too cosmopolitan.
B: Can you .... mean by 'cosmopolitan'?
2 **A:** Some of the Bauhaus artists are very famous.
B: Can you .... example .... Bauhaus artist?
3 **A:** The artists developed a new sense of functional design.
B: I'm not sure .... by 'functional design'.
4 **A:** Laszlo Maholy-Nagy started a new Bauhaus in Chicago in 1937.
B: Tell me ....
5 **A:** Of course, many of the things they designed were very unattractive.
B: Do you .... that .... don't like them?

3 Functions: my score is ...... out of 10

Quick Smart Test 12:
My total score is ...... out of 30

Name

Class Date

1 Vocabulary

A Underline the odd one out.

1 bear	elephant	wolf	duck
2 bullring	hot springs	glacier	volcano
3 hunt	infringe	stalk	shoot
4 caviar	fish	bread	salmon roe
5 custom	celebration	festival	trophy

B Choose an alternative for the word or phrase underlined.

1 The right to carry guns is established in the US Bill of Rights.
2 This is a very beautiful untamed part of the country.
3 After the bears wake up, they start to wander around the forest.
4 Many people condemn hunting and think it is cruel.
5 We need to make sure there are enough fish in the sea for people in the future.

1 Vocabulary: score ...... out of 10

2 Language

A Rewrite the sentences in reported speech.

1 "I would never go hunting, I think it's cruel," said John. ....
2 "The best time to see the bears is early in the morning," the guide told us............
3 "Why do people want to hunt wild animals?" she asked. ....
4 "Do you want to come on the trip with us?" asked Tom. ....
5 "I want to go to Alaska and see the hot springs," said Ella. ....

B Rewrite the sentences in direct speech.

1 The guide told us the weather was perfect. ....
2 She said that seals were hunted for their fur. ....
3 Chris said he wanted to go back to the mountains. ....
4 The hunters asked if we wanted to go with them on the trip. ....
5 I asked why she agreed with a sport that was so cruel. ....

C Rewrite the questions in reported speech.

1 'Why do so many Americans carry guns?' the child asked. ....
2 'Has the salmon fishing season started?' the tourist wanted to know. ....
3 'Did you catch any fish, Mike?' Jacky asked. ....
4 The man said, 'Where will the hunt take place?' ....
5 'When are you going to the festival?' I asked my sister. ....
6 The reporter asked, 'Can anyone explain the shootings?' ....

2 Language: score ...... out of 10

3 Functions

A Choose a phrase from Language Bank 22 to fill the gaps.

1 **A:** Hunting isn't just a sporting pastime, you know.
B: .... villagers don't just hunt for pleasure.
2 **A:** Kamchatka has a very low population density.
B: ...., not many people live there.
3 **A:** The hunter put all our lives in danger.
B: .... he behaved recklessly.
4 **A:** Tourism is almost non-existent.
B: .... very few tourists visit the area.

B Write answers to the questions.

Q Do you agree with hunting?
1 ....
Q What about hunting for sport?
2 ....
Q Would you go fishing?
3 ....
Q What national customs in your country do you like?
4 ....
Q Are there any traditions you don't like?
5 ....

3 Functions: score ...... out of 10

Quick Smart Test 13:
My total score is ...... out of 30

Name Class Date

1 Vocabulary

A Choose the correct word or phrase to fill the gaps.

1 The sick man lay on his bed ....
(a) clanging (b) groaning (c) splashing
2 The horror film was really ....
(a) terrifying (b) fearful (c) horrified
3 It's not a very .... story.
(a) realistic (b) real (c) living
4 Do you believe in .... ?
(a) the unreal (b) the supernatural
(c) ghostly things
5 The lion .... and came out from the trees.
(a) whispered (b) growled
(c) spluttered

B Match the words with the definitions.

1 thriller
2 nightmare
3 fantasy
4 witch
5 imaginative

(a) good at thinking of interesting ideas
(b) a woman who is believed to have magic powers
(c) an experience or situation that you imagine but is not real
(d) an exciting film or book about murder or a crime
(e) a very frightening dream

1 Vocabulary: my score is ...... out of 10

2 Language

A Rewrite the sentences using the passive.

1 It's a film that you must see.
....
2 People used to think that we should kill witches.
....
3 Can we do it immediately?
....
4 The writers may change the ending.
....
5 In some countries they can't show the film.
....

B Rewrite the sentences using the passive.

1 A big film company is going to make the book into a movie. ....
2 Why do they have to change the ending?
....
3 The director has to explain the roles to the actors. ....
4 The writer didn't want the story to frighten people. ....
5 They are not going to show the film at the local cinema. ....

2 Language: my score is ...... out of 10

3 Functions

A Match the two parts of the sentences.

1 Fear
2 Terror
3 Excitement
4 Entertainment
5 Suspense

(a) is provided by films and books.
(b) is a feeling that you want to run away.
(c) is what you feel when you are waiting for something to happen.
(d) is what you feel when something good is going to happen.
(e) is a stronger feeling than fear.

B Rewrite the sentences using the words given.

1 I felt excited.
I had ....
2 For me, horror films are amusing.
I find ....
3 Films are often very violent.
There is ....
4 The audience was very amused by the film.
The audience found ....
5 I won't forget how terrifying the journey was.
I won't forget the ....

3 Functions: my score is ...... out of 10

Quick Smart Test 14:
My total score is ...... out of 30

Name ______ Class ______ Date ______

1 Vocabulary

A Match the words with the definitions.

1 to be hired	(a) to refuse
2 to be fired	(b) to get a job
3 to be laid off	(c) to give someone a more important job
4 to promote	(d) to lose your job
5 to turn down	(e) to lose your job because there is not enough work

B Choose the correct form of the words in the box to fill the gaps.

entrepreneur	publicity	graduate
candidate	apply for	

1 Josh .... last summer and now he's working in America.
2 I've .... for several jobs that were advertised in the paper.
3 Andrew was definitely the best .... for the job because he had the most experience.
4 Good .... is very important for a new business.
5 He was a young .... who made his first million when he was only 16.

1 Vocabulary: my score is ...... out of 10

2 Language

A Rewrite the sentences using the words given.

1 I think I might go to Italy to work for a few months. I'm considering ....
2 My parents said they will buy me a car when I finish university. My parents promised ....
3 We have no more exams to take – today was the last one! We've finished ....
4 He doesn't have enough money to have a holiday this year. He can't afford ....
5 You shouldn't wait until next week to go to the doctor – go now. Don't put off ....

B Complete the sentences using the correct form of the verbs in brackets.

1 They .... (offer / pay) for my training while I am working.
2 Tim .... (suggest / go) into business together, but I'm not so sure.
3 Will you .... (continue / study) English when you leave school?
4 I have to .... (avoid / eat) any food that contains eggs.
5 She .... (refuse / give) me extra time to finish my homework.

2 Language: my score is ...... out of 10

3 Functions

A Choose a suitable word or phrase from Language Bank 24 to fill the gaps.

What sports do I like? Well, that's easy. I **1** .... swimming, that's my favourite sport. And I'm **2** .... tennis but I'm not very **3** .... on football. I **4** .... other sports like basketball but I **5** .... watching them on TV. I prefer to play them myself.

B Match the questions and answers.

1 Was there any subject you really disliked at school?
2 And tell me – what kind of work do you really enjoy?
3 Has work changed for women in your country?
4 What kind of organisation would you like to work for?
5 Do you think money is the most important thing about a job?

(a) Well, not really. It's important to do something you're good at and that you enjoy.
(b) I couldn't stand Maths although I was quite good at it.
(c) I think I'd like to work for a small company rather than a big one.
(d) I really enjoy working outside in the fresh air - I don't like offices.
(e) Yes I think it has. A lot more women work full-time now.

3 Functions: score ...... out of 10

Quick Smart Test 15:
My total score is ...... out of 30

Name ____________ Class ____________ Date ____________

1 Vocabulary

A Choose the correct form of the words in the box to fill the gaps.

commit	sentence	send	carry out	take

1 When was the murder .... ?
2 Why do you feel the need to .... drugs?
3 The men .... the robbery late at night.
4 If you do that, you'll be .... to prison.
5 He was .... to fifteen years in prison.

B Choose the correct word to fill the gaps.

1 The .... was attacked by three teenagers.
(a) offender (b) victim (c) criminal
2 .... is a drug which is illegal all over the world.
(a) cocaine (b) tobacco (c) caffeine
3 Do you think people who use heroin should be .... ?
(a) sentenced (b) punished (c) offended
4 It is the .... that decides how long a person will stay in prison.
(a) police (b) court (c) crime
5 The use of hard drugs is ....
(a) incorrect (b) unsocial (c) illegal

1 Vocabulary: my score is ...... out of 10

2 Language

A Put the verbs in brackets into the third conditional.

1 If I (know) .... , I (warn) .... you.
2 What (happen) .... if the police (catch) .... him?
3 If they (wake up) .... , they (see) .... the thief.
4 If his behaviour (be) .... better, they (release) .... him by now.
5 He (not / buy) the heroin .... if he (known) .... the police were watching him.

B Rewrite the sentences using *I wish*.

1 I didn't know what they were doing.
I wish ....
2 Why didn't they tell me about it?
If only ....
3 They introduced the Three-Strikes Law.
If only ....
4 Unfortunately, it happened.
I wish ....
5 They didn't put him in prison after the first attack.
If only ....

2 Language: score ...... out of 10

3 Functions

A Choose suitable words or phrases from Language Bank 26 to fill the gaps.

Ben: What do you think of the Three-Strikes Law?
Susie: I think it's a very good idea.
Ben: I **1** .... with you. I think it's terrible. People who haven't done anything very wrong spend many years in prison.
Susie: I respect **2** .... but sometimes we have to be tough.
Ben: I can see **3** .... , but in many cases I think the law is too tough.
Susie: I'm **4** .... view. Criminals need to be frightened of spending a long time in prison.
Ben: I think **5** .... point, but the thing is, there's less violent crime in states that don't have the Three-Strikes Law.
Susie: **6** That's an interesting .... but I still don't agree with you.
Ben: How about the argument that offenders who stay in prison cost the state about 1.5 million dollars?
Susie: **7** I understand what .... We need to reduce the cost.
Ben: That isn't what I meant. Surely what we need to do is stop people from re-offending.
Susie: That's **8** .... too. The Three-Strikes Law does exactly that!
Ben: I have to **9** .... argument, but the problem is, the Three-Strikes Law is very cruel.
Susie: I don't think we'll ever see this in the same way.
Ben: **10** I fully .... !

3 Functions: my score is ...... out of 10

Quick Smart Test 16:
My total score is ...... out of 30

Name ______________________ Class ____________ Date ____________

1 Vocabulary

A Match the words with the definitions.

1 mountaineer
2 hiker
3 boulder
4 climber
5 hike

(a) a person who goes up rocky mountains using ropes
(b) a very large rock
(c) a long walk in the country
(d) a person who climbs mountains
(e) a person who goes for long walks in the country

B Choose a phrase from the box to fill the gaps.

keep / lose your head	presence / frame of mind
against all the odds	

1 Simpson survived the climbing accident ....
2 If you get into difficulty, ... and call the emergency services.
3 Thanks to their .... , they were able to escape the dangerous situation.
4 She always has a very positive .... , whatever the situation.
5 You must not .... Just try and stay calm and not panic.

1 Vocabulary: my score is ...... out of 10

2 Language

A Match the sentences with the meanings.

1 You shouldn't have gone without telling anyone.
2 You could have had a terrible accident.
3 You should always take a mobile phone with you.
4 You should have asked your friend to go climbing with you.
5 You could have gone when the weather was better.

(a) I recommend that you do this.
(b) What you did was wrong.
(c) You had the possibility to make a different choice.
(d) This was possible but it didn't happen.
(e) You didn't do this, but it was a good idea.

B Complete the advice using *should / shouldn't have*, or *could / couldn't have*.

1 I .... gone to the party because I was ill that day.
2 Emily .... given her parents her new phone number.
3 You .... got so angry about such a small thing.
4 I .... gone on holiday with my friends, if I had had enough money.
5 I'm completely exhausted. I really .... walked any further today!

2 Language: my score is ...... out of 10

3 Functions

A Complete the gaps with a suitable word or phrase from Language Bank 27.

1 What do you think you .... done to stop Mark leaving?
2 I don't think it .... been possible to save his arm when he had the accident.
3 It .... for you to go for a hike without taking any water.
4 I don't think there was much they could do. Do you think they........... done anything about it?
5 You .... had to wait so long at the airport.

B Rewrite the sentences using the words in brackets.

1 It was stupid of him not to take a mobile phone. (should) ....
2 Why didn't you listen to me? You wouldn't have broken your leg. (if) ....
3 I decided not to go on the trip, although I had the opportunity to do so. (could) ....
4 It was very unwise of him to take those risks. (should) ....
5 How stupid it was to climb so high without oxygen! (idea) ....

3 Functions: score ...... out of 10

Quick Smart Test 17:
My total score is ...... out of 30

Name Class Date

1 Vocabulary

A Complete the sentences with a suitable word.

1 Mars is the third.............. in the solar system.
2 What is the .... that there is life in outer space?
3 Aeroplanes and helicopters are both types of ....
4 A .... has millions of stars in it.
5 Do people .... UFO experiences in order to attract attention?

B Match the words with the definitions.

1 tribe
2 probability
3 astronomy
4 universe
5 alien

(a) a creature that comes from another world
(b) how likely it is that something will happen
(c) a group of people with the same language and customs, who usually live together in the same area
(d) all the stars and planets and all of space
(e) the scientific study of the stars and planets

1 Vocabulary: score is ...... out of 10

2 Language

A Rewrite the sentences using *must have* or *can't / couldn't have*.

1 I feel certain they imagined the whole thing.
....
2 I don't think you understood me.
....
3 I don't believe he told the truth.
....
4 The Dogon used telescopes, I'm sure.
....
5 It seems clear that the alien bodies were dummies.
....

B Complete the gaps using the verbs in brackets and *might / could / couldn't have*.

1 It (not / be) .... a spaceship that I saw.
2 Anthropologists (tell) .... the Dogons about Sirius B.
3 The stories (not / invent) ....
4 The pilot (see) .... a military aircraft.
5 Many people believe that our planet (visit) .... by aliens.

2 Language: my score is ...... out of 10

3 Functions

Complete the gaps using the verbs in brackets and *must / might / could / couldn't / can't have*.

Mike: What do you think it was that we saw last night?
Tessa: Well, I think it **1** (be) .... a UFO.
Mike: You're crazy. It **2** (be) .... There's no such thing as UFOs!
It **3** (be) .... something else, for example a military aircraft. Or we **4** (imagine) .... the whole thing.
Tessa: Don't be stupid. How **5** (imagine) .... the whole thing? We both saw it.
Mike: That's true. Well, it was sunset and the clouds were amazing colours. They **6** (create) .... a visual illusion.
Tessa: It's possible, but I don't think so. It looked just like the UFOs you see in pictures.
I really believe that aliens **7** (visit) ....us at some time in the past.
Mike: If you believe that, you'll believe anything! I think it was that wine we had.
We **8** (be) .... drunk.
Tessa: We **9** (be) .... drunk. We only drank one glass of wine each. It **10** (be) .... a UFO!

3 Functions: my score is ...... out of 10

Quick Smart Test 18: My total score is ...... out of 30

UNIT 1

1 Language

1 The film was so sad that everyone cried.
2 He speaks too fast for me to understand him.
3 Have we got enough money to pay for the tickets?
4 It was such a good meal that we ate far too much.
5 The teacher was stupid enough to believe the children.
6 They were such cheap trousers that I bought six pairs.
7 Is there enough food to feed everyone?
8 The film was so bad that most people walked out.
9 He's too old to walk far.
10 My boss was kind enough to pay for the meal.

UNIT 2

1 Language

1 childless	2 unacceptable	3 rethink
4 insensitive	5 impractical	6 non-profit
7 earlyish	8 misspent	9 dissatisfied
10 unsociable	11 lateish	12 woollen
13 unthinkable	14 Rewind	15 illegible

UNIT 4

1 Language

1 This is the place where we met.
2 I haven't done enough revision, which means I may not pass the exam.
3 I know about what you did.
4 The lecturer to whom we are listening has written an important book.
5 That's the girl whose brother I really fancy.
6 The room in which they held the party was on the second floor.
7 You have what I need.
8 There's the girl whose dress is the same as yours.
9 The workers arrived very late, which was very annoying.
10 Is this the street where it happened?

UNIT 5

1 Language

1 We had lunch in a village which my friend knew well.
2 People never remember my birthday, which is on 25th December.
3 The children welcomed the teacher, who smiled warmly at them.
4 The man who asked the question has left the room.
5 Marie Heather, whom I had never heard of, had a fantastic voice.
6 Where's the dog that bit the child?
7 The Ferrari team, which won the Formula 1 trophy this year, is famous.
8 'Have you met James, who lives in the same street as you?'
9 The things that you bought are on the table.
10 'Officer, it was that man who damaged my car.'

UNIT 6

1 Language

1 ✓
2 It was a pity that we couldn't help him.
3 ✓
4 The news is wonderful!
5 That's interesting information.
6 Where is my luggage?
7 ✓
8 We need to buy some new furniture for the sitting room.
9 My uncle has a flock of sheep on his farm.
10 Have you got time to help me?

UNIT 7

1 Language

1 will have arrived	2 'll
3 're going to be	4 are having
5 will take place	6 get there/will have left
7 starts	8 will have ended/get
9 don't do/won't pass	10 'm going

UNIT 8

1 Language

1 I prefer pop music to jazz.
2 I'd rather you told him about it.
3 I'd prefer not to do my homework now.
4 I prefer spending time with one friend rather than a group.
5 I'd rather see a movie than go to the theatre.
6 I'd prefer to walk rather than go by car.
7 I prefer Italy to England for a holiday.
8 I prefer Beethoven to Mozart.
9 I'd rather not go to the movies tonight.
10 I'd rather go by car because it's more comfortable.

UNIT 10

1 Language

1 so that	2 to/so as to/in order to
3 so that	4 so as not to
5 to/so as to/in order to	6 to/so as to/in order to
7 so that	8 to/so as to/in order to
9 so as not to	10 so that

UNIT 11

1 Language

1A

1 They have been able to find it.
2 We are unable to go until next week.
3 The child didn't know how to explain.
4 How did you manage to persuade them?
5 The army couldn't stop the invasion.

1B

1 was able to
2 could/was able to
3 were able to
4 Were you able to
5 could/was able to

UNIT 12

1 Language

1 It's a new book written by three famous journalists.
2 Did you see an object moving very fast across the sky?
3 The map showing the route is on the table.
4 The present bought for me by my parents was perfect.
5 Do you know that woman standing in the corner?
6 Children taught by these methods often do better.
7 The man sitting opposite me keeps smiling at me.
8 The picture painted by your sister is absolutely awful!
9 It's a herb used only in certain parts of the country.
10 The stars shining in the sky have been there for billions of years.

UNIT 13

1 Language

1 Matthew invited me to stay the weekend.
2 The customer complained that the food wasn't hot.
3 The boy admitted that he had borrowed the car.
4 The man apologised for behaving badly.
5 The child denied breaking the window.
6 My neighbour advised me to lock up my house.
7 The teacher accused John of lying.
8 My father suggested that I buy it/should buy it/bought it.
9 The girl exclaimed that she hated school.
10 He grunted that he would do it.

UNIT 14

1 Language

1 He ought not to have done that.
2 The gate seems to have been mended.
3 Investing/to invest in the stock market can be risky.
4 It was stupid of me to forget my passport.
5 Skiing/To ski off-piste can be dangerous, but many people love it.
6 Is it a good idea to take vitamin pills?
7 The kitchen needs to be cleaned.
8 It's wonderful to meet you again.
9 I'm delighted to be working here.
10 It's nowhere to be seen.

UNIT 15

1 Language

1 talking 2 eating 3 to give 4 to tell
5 to climb 6 meeting 7 doing 8 seeing
9 leaving 10 to do

UNIT 17

1 Language

1 They say that the council will build a new road round the town.
2 It is known that he does not always tell the truth.
3 It is feared that the economy is deteriorating.
4 The actor is believed to be starring in a film about Hitler.
5 The bears are thought to have left the region.
6 The author's new book is said to have been completed.
7 It is thought that the climber has been lost in the snow storm.
8 The new group is known to play very popular music.
9 They say that it is very dangerous to go hiking alone on this mountain.
10 The scientist is known to be working on a new invention.

UNIT 18

1 Language

1 I think we should have/get the house redecorated.
2 It's time he returned to work.
3 It's time she got up.
4 We had our car stolen last month.
5 It's time we installed a new kitchen.
6 I love having my nails manicured.
7 It's time we told him what really happened to his father.
8 I had/got my computer upgraded.
9 I got my leg injured playing football last week.
10 It's time I had/got my hair cut.

UNIT 1

Ex 2A page 205

(1) perform	(2) bigger	(3) receiving
(4) By / At	(5) were	(6) how
(7) What	(8) shocking	(9) fact
(10) too	(11) why	(12) attention

Ex 2B page 205

(1) SUITABLE	(2) DIFFICULTY
(3) RELATIONSHIPS	(4) DISCOVERY
(5) SURPRISINGLY	(6) ABILITY
(7) PSYCHOLOGISTS	(8) TOLERANT
(9) DECISION	(10) DEMANDING

UNIT 2

Ex 2A page 206

(1) A process	(2) D effect	(3) B even
(4) C still	(5) B In	(6) A beneficial
(7) B areas	(8) D produce	(9) B ridiculously
(10) D makes	(11) C well-off	(12) B local

Ex 2B page 206

1 'It's not yet dark,' she said.
2 I've lived in the country since 1995 and I love it.
3 The fact is it was such awful weather that we stayed in all week.
4 I am fond of this town because it's quiet and pretty.
5 The family no longer lives here, thank goodness.
6 My father gave up smoking years ago.
7 What was the reason for the argument, do you know?
8 The man who was tall and good-looking started the discussion.

UNIT 4

Ex 2A page 207

(1) B species	(2) B share	(3) D indeed
(4) A lively	(5) A as	(6) A even
(7) D explained	(8) C around	(9) A Regarding
(10) A apart	(11) B numerical	(12) D speech

Ex 2B page 207

(1) LIVING	(2) FAVOURABLE
(3) FULLY	(4) UNDISCOVERED
(5) POISONOUS	(6) BREATHE
(7) VALUABLE	(8) DISAPPEARS
(9) DESTRUCTION	(10) EXISTENCE

UNIT 5

Ex 2A page 208

(1) made	(2) which	(3) However
(4) as	(5) often	(6) where
(7) as	(8) like	(9) would
(10) Although	(11) to	(12) Britain's

Ex 2B page 208

1 The police still haven't found the robbers, which is terrible.
2 I've forgotten everything about the story.
3 Everyone except my brother enjoyed the film.
4 We get on very well.
5 I'm afraid that I didn't understand what he said
6 I haven't seen him for ages.
7 They brought the money, which was a relief
8 If I were you, I'd buy it.

UNIT 6

Ex 2A page 209

(1) B recorded	(2) A life	(3) A aware
(4) D feelings	(5) C another	(6) B carried out
(7) B injured	(8) D anti	(9) C searched
(10) B causes	(11) A public transport	(12) C way

Ex 2B page 209

(1) CONSEQUENTLY	(2) DRIVERS'	(3) UNPOPULAR
(4) ARGUMENT	(5) DOUBTLESS	(6) SPEEDING
(7) INTERESTED	(8) MOTORING	(9) FAVOURABLY
(10) PREVENTION		

UNIT 7

Ex 2A page 210

(1) A predicted	(2) D increase
(3) A throughout	(4) A frightening
(5) B seriousness	(6) D taken
(7) B urged	(8) D requirements
(9) D belief	(10) B contributes
(11) A likely	(12) A made

Ex 2B page 210

(1) URGENTLY	(2) INVESTMENT	(3) RELIABLY
(4) REGARDLESS	(5) ACCIDENTAL	(6) INSTALLATION
(7) SOLAR	(8) RENEWABLE	(9) VISUALLY
(10) ALTERNATIVE		

UNIT 8

Ex 2A page 211

(1) spend	(2) decision	(3) to
(4) knowledge	(5) getting	(6) to
(7) is	(8) at	(9) agreed
(10) of	(11) paying	(12) only

Ex 2B page 211

1 It's not necessary to explain.
2 Why was the shopping centre built so far away from the centre of town?
3 It took him a long time to get over his illness.
4 You've made a mistake again.
5 The children set off for school at eight-thirty as usual.
6 He's the man whose car I borrowed.
7 It's a month since I was in the office.
8 Stephen takes ten minutes to walk to the station.

UNIT 10

Ex 2A page 212

(1) C act	(2) B research	(3) B remained
(4) A a great deal	(5) D over	(6) A find
(7) D placed	(8) B apparently	(9) C achieve
(10) C expectations	(11) B importance	(12) C significant

Ex 2B page 212

(1) NATURAL	(2) POWERFUL	(3) GLOBAL
(4) ECONOMIC	(5) COASTAL	(6) ASTONISHING
(7) WELL-OFF	(8) COMMUTERS	
(9) POVERTY	(10) TREATMENT	

UNIT 11

Ex 2A page 213

(1) on (2) Consequently (3) with
(4) extremely (5) completely / altogether
(6) which (7) themselves (8) when
(9) as (10) then (11) with
(12) the

Ex 2B page 213

(1) RELAXED (2) COOKERY
(3) DISCOVERY (4) FATTENING
(5) NUTRITIOUS (6) NOURISHMENT
(7) PREFERENCE (8) NATIONAL
(9) ASTONISHMENT (10) DEVELOPMENT

UNIT 12

Ex 2A page 214

(1) against (2) using (3) until
(4) which (5) human (6) for
(7) on (8) developing / starting
(9) brought (10) with (11) While
(12) As

Ex 2B page 214

1 I'm looking forward to meeting them.
2 She did not let the children go outside.
3 We've made the arrangements for our departure.
4 I had difficulty (in) explaining what happened.
5 Gina is someone who always looks fashionable.
6 The maths problem was too difficult for anyone to find a solution.
7 If you don't carry out the boss' orders, he'll be very angry.
8 'I've never had a better meal,' John said.

UNIT 13

Ex 2A page 215

(1) A chickens (2) A pests (3) B foot
(4) C controlling (5) A packs (6) D pastime
(7) C upper (8) D costume (9) B part
(10) D popularity (11) A accusing (12) B passed

Ex 2B page 215

1 I prefer eating at home to eating in restaurants.
2 I have my hair cut about once every two weeks.
3 The customer apologized for being rude to the shopkeeper.
4 It took my sister a long time to get over her illness.
5 It's so late it's pointless going to the play.
6 I've been told everything must be completed by Friday.
7 They advised me to buy it.
8 I don't like flying and neither does my brother.

UNIT 14

Ex 2A Page 216

(1) C entitled (2) A loss (3) B countryside
(4) D feature (5) A deadly (6) B scenes
(7) C attitude (8) B career (9) A a report
(10) B recommended (11) D sequel (12) C approaching

Ex 2B page 215

(1) SIGNIFICANCE (2) INFLUENTIAL
(3) MECHANICAL (4) LENGTHY
(5) REMEMBERED (6) INSTINCTIVE
(7) HOTLY (8) MOVEMENT
(9) PSYCHOLOGICAL (10) NIGHTLY

UNIT 15

Ex 2A page 217

(1) even (2) well (3) If
(4) Having (5) should (6) only
(7) working (8) by (9) make
(10) which (11) regard (12) on

Ex 2B Page 217

1 Liz's boss asked her if she had completed the project yet.
2 The students got rid of all their old exam papers.
3 It's true that getting a job is more and more difficult.
4 I won't phone her unless you tell me to.
5 We complained to the manager about the food.
6 The boy regretted stealing the money.
7 His friends warned him not to mention the subject.
8 I'll do my best to improve my grades.

UNIT 17

Ex 2A page 218

(1) order (2) even (3) off
(4) such (5) what (6) taking
(7) due (8) where (9) less
(10) So (11) take (12) certain

Ex 2B page 218

(1) SCIENTIFIC (2) FORTUNATE (3) GENETIC
(4) ACHIEVEMENTS (5) CERTAINLY (6) TALENTED
(7) CONVINCING (8) RARELY
(9) CONSEQUENTLY (10) INTENSIVE

UNIT 18

Ex 2A page 219

(1) B common (2) A previously
(3) D from time to time (4) B public
(5) C sightings (6) D coverage
(7) D site (8) C staff
(9) B over (10) B take
(11) A forward (12) B vicinity

Ex 2B page 219

1 The workers seem to have left the building.
2 They accused him of planting the bomb.
3 Jack, I'd rather you told him the news.
4 It's time the children went to bed.
5 I can't put up with her criticisms any more.
6 Alfonso insisted on paying for the meal.
7 I wonder if they were aware of what was happening.
8 I wish you would explain why you did it.

For UNIT 0 QS Test answers, see page 266.

UNIT 1

1 A (a) 2 (b) 3 (b) 4 (c) 5 (c)
B 1 (b) 2 (a) 3 (d) 4 (e) 5 (c)
2 A 1 shouldn't 2 should 3 should 4 should 5 should
B 1 (c) 2 (d) 3 (e) 4 (a) 5 (b)
3 1 What should I do 2 could try 3 how about 4 why don't you 5 Look

UNIT 2

1 A 1 noisy 2 emigrated 3 urban 4 suburbs 5 crowded
B 1 agricultural 2 high-rise building 3 refugee 4 peaceful 5 transport
2 1 much 2 a lot 3 much 4 as 5 a little 6 more 7 slowly 8 in 9 than 10 as
3 A 1 Could you say that 2 explain what you mean 3 you mind repeating that
4 you say more about 5 quite get that
B 1 much 2 a lot 3 as 4 in 5 friendlier

UNIT 3

1 1 (h) 2 (f) 3 (j) 4 (i) 5 (b) 6 (a) 7 (c) 8 (e) 9 (d) 10 (g)
2 A 1(d) 2 (b) 3 (c) 4 (a) 5 (e)
B1 can't be certain 2 may not 3 may 4 might 5 possible
3 1 celebrities 2 may/might 3 I'm not sure 4 may/might 5 it's possible 6 fans 7 autograph 8 you can't be sure/certain 9 may/might 10 may not

UNIT 4

1 A 1 feeling 2 joy 3 mammals 4 survival 5 grief
B 1 (b) 2 (e) 3 (d) 4 (a) 5 (c)
2 A 1 The dolphin that/which you saw at the zoo has died. 2 The man who I met worked at the zoo. 3 The book that/which I'm reading is about ecology. 4 These are plants that/which grow well in sunny environments. 5 She's the woman who wrote a book about chimpanzees.
B 1 the 2 - 3 the 4 a 5 the
3 1 your feelings about 2 agree 3 what you're 4 don't 5 makes me 6 the same way 7 you're 8 do you feel about 9 come on 10 absolutely

UNIT 5

1 A 1 (c) 2 (d) 3 (e) 4 (a) 5 (b)
B 1 imagination, 2 reminder 3 memories 4 recall 5 recollection
2 1 used to 2 didn't use to 3 used to 4 would 5 had eaten 6 would 7 would 8 had 9 was 10 ate
3 A 1 Well 2 Actually 3 Let me think 4 happened 5 imagine
B Students' own answers

UNIT 6

1 A 1 technology 2 monitor 3 privacy 4 reassure 5 secure
B 1 (c) 2 (a) 3 (a) 4 (c) 5 (a)
2 1 LeRoy was pulled out of the water.
2 The thief was identified by a security guard.
3 Today, people are monitored in the street by surveillance cameras. 4 The idea of RFID tags is disliked by most people. 6 Who was he recognised by? 7 RFID tags are placed in all kinds of items, aren't they? 8 Where was the computer put?
9 The shoplifters weren't caught (by the police).
10 Why are drivers photographed by cameras?
3 1 picture of 2 standing 3 as if 4 walking 5 shows 6 looks 7 show 8 of 9 holding 10 are smiling

UNIT 7

1 A 1 (b) 2 (a) 3 (b) 4 (c) 5 (c)
B 1 eco-house 2 alternative 3 solar panels 4 Rainwater 5 tank
2 A 1 (d) 2 (a) 3 (e) 4 (b) 5 (c)
B 1 when 2 unless 3 in case 4 if 5 if
3 A 1 difficult to say 2 think 3 hopefully 4 it's possible that 5 perhaps
B Students' own answers

UNIT 8

1 A 1 passing 2 degree 3 research 4 qualifications 5 revise
B 1 (c) 2 (d) 3 (b) 4 (a) 5 (e)
2 A 1 If I had the money, I'd buy a car.
2 If you did enough work, you'd do well in exams.
3 If you found a counsellor, they could help you with your problems. 4 If the teacher was better, the students would be more interested in the subject.
5 If I had more time, I would take the course.
B 1 What would you study if you had the opportunity? 2 What would you buy if someone gave you $100,000? 3 Who would you interview if you could interview anyone in the world?
4 Which country would you live in if you could life anywhere in the world? 5 Would you build a swimming pool if you had the money?
3 1 don't need 2 work 3 will be 4 will do 5 Don't say 6 had 7 would be 8 need to 9 come 10 'll pay

UNIT 9

1 1 (i) 2 (d) 3 (g) 4 (j) 5 (h) 6 (a) 7 (f) 8 (c) 9 (e) 10 (b)
2 A 1 However 2 Consequently 3 Furthermore 4 Meanwhile 5 On the other hand
B 1 Similarly, in the same way 2 first of all, firstly, secondly, lastly 3 for instance, for example 4 on the whole, generally, in general 5 finally, in conclusion, to conclude
3 A 1 In my opinion 2 Firstly 3 Secondly 4 On the whole 5 generally
B 1 (e) 2 (d) 3 (b) 4 (a) 5 (c)

UNIT 10

1 A 1 (b) 2 (a) 3 (a) 4 (c) 5 (a)

B 1 (e) 2 (c) 3 (a) 4 (b) 5 (d)
2 A 1 I wish I had an iPod. 2 I wish they'd stop. 3 I wish he would go. 4 I wish I hadn't done that. 5 I wish I could play the guitar.
B 1 I hope I have children. 2 I hope you pass your exams. 3 I hope it'll be sunny tomorrow. 4 I hope we catch the train. 5 I hope it won't rain.
3 A 1 had 2 wouldn't talk 3 there was 4 get 5 like 6 don't cancel 7 hadn't sold 8 sleep well 9 wasn't feeling 10 wouldn't worry

UNIT 11

1 A 1 (c) 2 (e) 3 (d) 4 (a) 5 (b)
B 1 go on a diet 2 obese 3 greedy 4 pick on 5 skinny
2 A 1 (c) 2 (b) 3 (a) 4 (e) 5 (d)
B 1 Although Nicky never seems to eat very much, she still seems to be overweight. 2 Even though she is very slim already, she (still) worries about her weight. 3 Despite not feeling like it, I went to the fitness club after work. 4 Freya works in a pizza restaurant, though she never eats anything there. 5 In spite of the fact that there are plenty of sports facilities in the city, people still prefer watching TV.
3 1 option 2 although 3 might 4 take 5 exercise 6 could 7 advice/suggestion 8 possibilities 9 could 10 prefer

UNIT 12

1 A 1 circular 2 designed 3 location 4 cracking 5 sections
B 1 (b) 2 (c) 3 (a) 4 (b) 5 (b)
2 A 1 Skyscrapers have been designed to withstand earthquakes. 2 The strength of the tunnel has not yet been tested. 3 The plans have been discussed by the country's top architects. 4 Have homes been found for all the refugees? 5 Why hasn't the project been completed?
B 1 Leisure facilities won't be included in the building. 2 The skyscrapers will be linked by hollow tubes. 3 More than 35,000 people will be housed in the vertical city. 4 Where will it be built? 5 Power will be provided by waves and wind.
3 A 1 How will the tunnel be made safe? 2 When was the first Maglev train built? 3 Why don't Maglev trains use rails? 4 Which skyscraper will be pulled down? 5 Where have the anchors been placed?
B 1 explain what you 2 give me an example of a 3 what you mean 4 more 5 mean that you

UNIT 13

1 A 1 duck 2 bullring 3 infringe 4 bread 5 trophy
B 1 bear arms 2 wild 3 roam around 4 say hunting is morally wrong 5 posterity
2 A 1 John said he would never go hunting because he thinks it's cruel. 2 The guide told us the best time to go hunting was early in the morning. 3 She asked why people wanted to hunt wild animals. 4 Tom asked if I/we wanted to come on the trip with them. 5 Ella said she wanted to go to Alaska and see the hot springs.
B 1 'The weather is perfect,' the guide told us. 2 'Seals are hunted for their fur,' she said. 3 'I want to go back to the mountains,' said Chris. 4 'Do you want to come with us on the trip?' the hunters asked. 5 'Why do you agree with a sport that is so cruel,' I asked.
C 1 The child asked why so many Americans carried guns. 2 The tourist wanted to know if the salmon fishing season had started. 3 Jacky asked Mike if he had caught any fish. 4 The man asked where the hunt would take place. 5 I asked my sister when she was going to the festival. 6 The reporter asked if anyone could explain the shootings.
3 A 1 You mean 2 So you're saying that 3 So you feel that 4 So what you're saying is

UNIT 14

1 A 1 (b) 2 (a) 3 (a) 4 (b) 5 (b)
B 1 (d) 2 (e) 3 (c) 4 (b) 5 (a)
2 A 1 It's a film that must be seen. 2 People used to think that witches should be killed. 3 Can it be done immediately? 4 The ending may be changed. 5 In some countries the film can't be shown.
B 1 The book is going to be made into a film by a big film company. 2 Why does the ending have to be changed? 3 The roles have to be explained to the actors. 4 The writer didn't want the people to be frightened by the story. 5 The film is not going to be shown at the local cinema.
3 A 1 (b) 2 (e) 3 (d) 4 (a) 5 (c)
B 1 I had a feeling of excitement. 2 I find horror films amusing. 3 There is often a lot of violence in films. 4 The audience found the film very amusing. 5 I won't forget the terror of the journey.

UNIT 15

1 A 1 (b) 2 (d) 3 (e) 4 (c) 5 (a)
B 1 graduated 2 applied for 3 candidate 4 publicity 5 entrepeneur
2 A 1 going.. 2 to buy .. 3 our last exam .. 4 to have .. 5 going ..
B 1 offered to pay 2 suggested going 3 continue to study 4 avoid eating 5 refused to give
3 A 1 love 2 crazy about 3 keen on 4 don't mind 5 mind
B 1 (b) 2 (d) 3 (e) 4 (c) 5 (a)

UNIT 16

1 A 1 committed 2 take 3 carried out 4 sent 5 sentenced
B 1 (b) 2 (a) 3 (b) 4 (b) 5 (c)

2 A **1** had known / would have warned **2** would have happened / had caught **3** had woken up / would have seen **4** had been / would have released **5** would not have bought / had known
B **1** I had known what they were doing. **2** they had told me about it. **3** they hadn't introduced the Three-strikes Law. **4** it hadn't happened. **5** they had put him in prison after the first attack.
3 **1** I don't / can't agree **2** your opinion about this **3** where you're coming from **4** afraid it isn't my view **5** you have a very good point **6** way of looking at it **7** you are trying to say **8** an interesting way of looking at it **9** admit that's a very strong **10** agree with you/with what you're saying

UNIT 17

1 A **1** (d) **2** (e) **3** (b) **4** (a) **5** (c)
B **1** against all the odds **2** keep your head **3** presence of mind **4** frame of mind **5** lose your head.
2 A **1** (b) **2** (d) **3** (a) **4** (e) **5** (c)
B **1** couldn't have **2** should have **3** shouldn't have **4** could have **5** couldn't have
3 A **1** should have **2** would have **4** could have **5** shouldn't have
B **1** He should have taken a mobile phone. **2** If you had listened to me you wouldn't have broken your leg. **3** I could have gone on the trip, but I didn't. **4** He shouldn't have taken those risks. **5** It wasn't a good idea to climb so high without oxygen.

UNIT 18

1 A **1** planet **2** evidence **3** aircraft **4** galaxy **5** invent
B **1** (c) **2** (b) **3** (e) **4** (d) **5** (a)
2 A **1** They must have imagined the whole thing. **2** You can't have understood me. **3** He can't have told the truth. **4** The Dogon must have used telescopes. **5** The alien bodies must have been dummies.
B **1** couldn't have been **2** might/could have told **3** couldn't have been invented **4** might/could have seen **5** might/could have been visited
3 **1** might have been **2** can't have been **3** must have been **4** might have imagined **5** could we have imagined **6** might have created **7** could have visited **8** must have been **9** couldn't have been **10** must have been

Progress check 1 Answer key
Page 18-19 WB

1 Reading
1=G, 2=C, 3=A, 4=D, 5=E, 6=F, 7=B, H=✗ (not used)

2 Language and vocabulary
A **1** *may*, **2** *will*, **3** *will*, **4** *won't*, **5** *may*
B **1** *were painted*, **2** *are made*, **3** *are designed*, **4** *was won*, **5** *was invented*
C **1** album, **2** grief, **3** horrified, **4** remind, **5** attractive
D **1** (a), **2** (b), **3** (a), **4** (b), **5** (b)
E **1** (b), **2** (c), **3** (a), **4** (a), **5** (b)

Progress check 2 Answer key
Page 32-33 WB

1 Reading
1=C, 2=A, 3=B, 4=C, 5=A, 6=B, 7=D, 8=A
9=C, 10=C, 11=A, 12=D, 13=B, 14=B, 15=D

2 Use of English
A **1** (b), **2** (a), **3** (c), **4** (d), **5** (a)
B **1** *If I were you, I wouldn't drink so much coffee.*
2 *If I were you, I would buy that car.*
3 *If I were you, I wouldn't ask her to marry me.*
4 *If I were her, I wouldn't argue with the policeman.*
5 *If I were him, I would take Spanish lessons.*
C **1** *Sky City will never be built.*
2 *I was told to lose weight (by my doctor).*
3 *The trip has been postponed until next week (by the guide).*
4 *The garbage will be taken away on Friday (by the men).*
5 *Several children have been injured badly.*
D **1** *Even though he was 39 years old, they accepted him in the army.*
2 *Despite losing his passport, he still enjoyed his holiday.*
3 *In spite of his reluctance to fly, he is still going to make the journey.*
4 *I can take you there, though you'll have to pay extra.*
5 *Although there may be delays, most planes are leaving on time.*
E 1 (a), 2 (c), 3 (b), 4 (a), 5 (b)

Progress check 3 Answer key
Page 44-45 WB

1 Reading
1=C, 2=B, 3=A, 4=A, 5=D, 6=B

2 Language and vocabulary
A **1** (d), **2** (a), **3** (d), **4** (b), **5** (c), **6** (b), **7** (b), **8** (b), **9** (c), **10** (a), **11** (b), **12** (a), **13** (c), **14** (c), **15** (c)
B **1** *to study*, **2** *meeting*, **3** *going*, **4** *to send*, **5** *to see*
C **1** *he can't have*, **2** *should have*, **3** *could you have*, **4** *had told*, **5** *had known / would have acted*
D **1** (b), **2** (c), **3** (d), **4** (a), **5** (b)

Name ______________________ Class ______________ Date ______________

LISTENING

I can:	Very well	OK	Not very well
... understand standard spoken language, live or broadcast, on both familiar and unfamiliar topics normally encountered in personal, social or academic life			
... understand in detail what is said to me in standard spoken language even when there is some background noise			
... understand the main ideas of complex speech delivered in standard language, including technical discussions in my field of specialisation			
... follow extended speech and complex lines of argument provided the topic is reasonably familiar, and the direction of the talk is signposted by explicit markers			
... understand announcements and messages spoken in standard language at normal speed			
... understand most radio programmes and other recorded material delivered in standard language and identify the speaker's mood, tone etc.			
... understand most TV news and current affairs programmes, and the majority of films in standard dialect			
... listen and understand in other ways, such as...			

I find that it is useful to practise my listening skills by:

- ☐ listening to music with English words
- ☐ listening to English language radio
- ☐ watching music television
- ☐ watching other English language TV
- ☐ watching films in English in the original version
- ☐ watching films in English with subtitles
- ☐ talking to English or American native speakers
- ☐ talking to people from other countries using English as a common language

Name ____________________ Class ____________ Date ____________

READING

I can:	Very well	OK	Not very well
... understand a variety of texts with a large degree of independence, reading at different speeds and in different ways according to the type of text, and using appropriate reference sources selectively			
... quickly identify the content and relevance of news items, articles and reports on a wide range of professional topics			
... understand articles and reports concerned with contemporary problems in which the writers adopt particular viewpoints			
... understand specialised articles outside my field, provided I can use a dictionary to check meanings			
... read correspondence related to my fields of interest and easily understand the essential meaning			
... make use of a broad active reading vocabulary, though I may experience some difficulty with less common words and phrases			
... read in English in other ways such as...			

I find that it is useful to practise my reading skills by:

- ☐ reading magazines in English
- ☐ reading books in English
- ☐ reading English language websites online
- ☐ reading letters, emails and texts from friends in English
- ☐ reading signs, notices and advertising in English
- ☐ reading for homework
- ☐ reading for pleasure in English
- ☐ having extra English lessons

Name ______________________ Class ______________ Date ______________

SPEAKING

I can:	Very well	OK	Not very well
... use the language fluently, accurately and effectively on a wide range of general, academic or leisure topics, marking clearly the relationships between ideas			
... engage in extended conversation on most general topics, even in a noisy environment			
... give clear, detailed descriptions and presentations on a wide range of subjects related to my field of interest			
... communicate spontaneously with good grammatical control without much sign of having to restrict what I want to say, adopting a level of formality appropriate to the circumstances			
... interact with a degree of fluency and spontaneity that makes regular interaction with native speakers quite possible			
... take an active part in discussion in familiar contexts, accounting for and sustaining my views			
... express my ideas and opinions with precision			
... speculate about causes, consequences and hypothetical situations			
convey degrees of emotion and highlight the personal significance of events and experiences			
... speak English in other ways, for example...			

I find that it is useful to practise my speaking skills by:

- ☐ talking to my teachers and fellow students
- ☐ talking to English native speakers
- ☐ talking to people from other countries using English as a common language
- ☐ talking to friends on the phone
- ☐ having extra English conversation lessons

Name ____________________ Class ____________ Date ____________

WRITING

I can:	Very well	OK	Not very well
... produce clear, detailed text on a wide range of subjects related to my interests and evaluate information and arguments from a number of sources			
... explain a viewpoint on a topical issue giving the advantages and disadvantages of various options			
... write an essay or report which develops an argument, giving reasons for or against a particular point of view			
... write personal letters or emails conveying degrees of emotion, highlighting the personal significance of events and experiences and commenting on the correspondent's news and views			
... write an essay or report which develops an argument systematically with appropriate highlighting of significant points and relevant supporting detail			
... evaluate different ideas or solutions to a problem			
... write clear, detailed descriptions of real or imaginary events, marking the relationship between ideas in clear connected text and following established conventions of the genre concerned			
... write English in other ways, for example...			

I find that it is useful to practise my writing skills by:

- ☐ writing emails in English
- ☐ writing texts in English on my mobile phone
- ☐ writing letters in English to a penfriend
- ☐ writing my blog or diary in English
- ☐ writing stories in English
- ☐ having extra English lessons

Name ______________________ Class ____________ Date ____________

IN FUTURE

English will be:	Very useful for me	Fairly useful for me	Not useful at all
... for future study, work and my career			
... for going on holiday in English-speaking countries			
... for travelling to any part of the world where my own language is not widely spoken			
... for making new friends in the 'global village'			
... for understanding other cultures			
... for helping to make the world a better place			
... for reading news and literature in English			
... for technical and scientific purposes			
... for other reasons such as....			

Introduction

Following the guidelines of the Trinity College, London Examinations 2010 and the Cambridge ESOL FCE Examinations 2008+, this new Unit 0 (Zero) has been added to *QSE Intermediate B1-B2*.

- Unit 0 (Zero) covers the new subject areas, grammar and functions of Trinity Grade 7 GESE. Unit 0 is also useful as a bridge between *QSE Pre-Intermediate* and *Intermediate* at B1 level.
- The Revised edition of the *QSE* course includes changes to various exercise types in the Cambridge ESOL Examinations.
- **Unit 0 Audio** (Listening passages and recorded Reading texts) can both be found on the Revised *QSE Intermediate CD 1* (Blue - ISBN 978-1-905248-24-7).
- **Unit 0 Grammar** and **Use of English** exercises are included in the *QSE Intermediate* Workbook.
- **Unit 0 Answer keys** and relevant changes to the **Teacher's Notes** are in this Teacher's Guide and also provided online at www.brookemead-elt.co.uk.
- This Revised edition of the *QSE Intermediate* Student's Book contains **Reading** activities with gapped text and **Listening** activities in line with the FCE 2008+ changes.
- **Writing** tasks include the Portfolio Writing types for Trinity ISE, while those in the Workbook provide practice for the FCE Writing (Paper 2).
- **Speaking** activities remain central to the skills practice in QSE Intermediate and follow mainly the format of the GESE, with 'long turns' conversations and discussion topics suitable for both GESE and FCE throughout the course.
- The *QSE Intermediate* Workbook contains FCE-type exercises (key word transformations and open cloze texts).

What's new?

Subject:	National and local produce and products
Function:	Advantages and disadvantages
Grammar:	*should*; present simple passive; *because of, due to*

Preliminary notes

This unit was added to the second edition of QSE in order to cover the new Subject area, Functions, Grammar and Communicative skills for Grade 7 of the GESE. The unit is also useful as a bridge between QSE Pre-Intermediate and this book.

As a result of the above, these Teacher's Notes don't have some of the lengthier explanations about teaching the unit that you will find in Units 1 and 2. If you are an inexperienced teacher, you will find further guidance in the Introduction.

Should and the present simple passive are also covered in Unit 1 (*should / ought to / could / you'd better*) and Unit 6 (Present and Past simple passives), so you have the option of not doing much work on them here. However, extra language practice is always useful, and since the passive voice is one of the most difficult grammar points for many nationalities, this unit provides a good opportunity to work on it before practising it once again in Unit 6.

Before you open the book …

The main topics of this unit are shops and their products, our habits, particularly our shopping habits, how we dispose of rubbish, and the effect of all these on the environment. The title of the unit, *Think global, act local*, was a slogan for the very influential British environmental organisation, *Friends of the Earth*, when it was first founded in 1969. The slogan is a catchy phrase that is often used to spur people on to take local actions that will help the environment, and as we all know, the environment – *ie* the natural world (land, air, animals, plants, sea) that is affected by human activity – is in need of a great deal of help!

Write the title of the unit on the board and check students understand the words *global, local*. Put students in pairs and ask them to explain:

- the meaning of the title in one or two sentences.
- what the unit will be about.

Elicit answers and write the best sentences on the board, which should be something like this: *Think about the whole world but take small local actions to help it.*

1 *The BIG question:* ARE YOU A GOOD SHOPPER?

FACT: Over the past decade, Britain has lost nearly 30,000 independent food and drink shops - more than 40% of the total.

Read out *The BIG question* and ask students what they think it means. Elicit the fact that it could mean 'good' in the sense of *good at shopping, ie* someone who doesn't waste money, or 'good' in the sense that their shopping habits help the environment. You may want to teach the adjective *ethical* here, *eg Are you an ethical shopper*? Ask for answers to the question using both meanings. Tell them they'll return to the question at the end of the unit with more information.

Ask students: *What's your reaction to the FACT?* Ask them if they know why so many food and drink shops have closed. Don't give any answers yet and say there will be more discussion about this later.

2 PREVIEW

Words

A Put students into pairs to do the activities and check they understand the vocabulary. A *hypermarket* sells a much wider range of goods than a supermarket and is often out of town. A *farmer's market* is a street market that sells local produce. Note that a farmer's market is different from a market, which sells all kinds of things, not just food, *eg* clothes, kitchen equipment, jewellery. *A mountain bike* can ride over rough ground and up hills.

B *Manufactured products* and *agricultural produce* are phrases that are often used. A *product* is something that is grown or made in large quantities and is for sale, whereas, *produce* is what a farmer grows, *eg* fruit and vegetables. Point out that *produce* is uncountable.

C If time allows, ask students for other examples in each category.

2 PREVIEW Words A / B / C **Answers**

A **1** a, b, c, d, e **2** b, c, d **3** b, c, d **4** c, d
B **1** a, b, e **2** c, d
C **1** i **2** c **3** e **4** g **5** b **6** a **7** h **8** d **9** f

Language

The work on the present simple passive is most probably revision for students. Check students understand that it is the beginning of a sentence that we pay most attention to and that the second passive sentence therefore places more emphasis on *global brands*. Elicit the fact / explain that we use the passive when the subject of the active sentence is less important.

If students have difficulty with question **C,** ask them to look at the first two sentences, and ask: *What tense is the first sentence in?* Analyse the second sentence:

Object of Active verb	+ *to be* in present simple	+ past participle	+ *by*	+ Subject of active sentence
Global brands	are	worn	by	everyone.

Elicit more passive sentences by writing these sentences on the board without including the final word (*eg milk*). Elicit the final words from the students.

1 Cows make … (milk).
2 Humans eat … (meat / vegetables / fruit).
3 Chickens produce … (eggs).
4 Farmers grow … (crops).
5 They grow rice in … (China / India).
6 They drink a lot of wine in (France / Italy).

Elicit / point out the fact that when the subject is impersonal and not important, *eg They*, there's no need to add *by*: *Rice is grown in China (by people).*

Put students into pairs to make the sentences passive.

Students will have a lot of opportunity to practise the present simple passive in this unit.

Due to and *owing to* both mean *because of*. Point out the following:

- Both phrases are followed by a noun or a pronoun.
- *Because of* is a lot more common and less formal.
- We can use both phrases in the second half of a sentence, *eg I never have much time because of the children and my job.*
- When *due to* and *because of* begin a sentence, we often use a comma.
- These phrases can also follow the verb *to be*: *The delay was because of / due to the rain.*

For further practice, put students in pairs to complete these sentences:

1 The plane didn't leave on time, … (due to the weather / the snow / the storm / the rain)
2 … , I was unable to finish the work. (Because of my headache / the interruption / the noise)
3 I had to give up / leave my job … (because of illness / my age / an accident)
4 … , I didn't get to work on time. (Due to the traffic / the delay)
5 …., the planet is getting warmer. (Because of pollution/ carbon dioxide / industrialisation)
6 She got the job … (due to her personality / qualifications / previous experience)

At this level students should know that *should* is used for advice, so this is a brief revision. Students will practise giving advice in **4 Talk about it**.

Point out that in everyday conversation it's very common to use the imperative when giving advice, as in the example. (*…try the weekly farmer's market.*)

To practice the use of *should*, meaning *the right thing to do*, write these sentences on the board: *You should do things to help the environment. It's wrong not to do this.*

Ask if the sentence with *should* is giving advice and elicit the answer / explain that it's more about saying that it's the right thing to do / our duty.

If you feel students need practice, give them a situation where one's parents are old and ill and ask students what the right thing to do is. Example answers: *You should look after / help / visit /shop / care for them.*

If you want students to do more structure practice work before they proceed, they can do the structure exercises in the **Workbook Language** section (page 2 WB) at this point.

2 PREVIEW Language A / B / C / D / E
Answers

A Yes
B 'Everyone', 'Global brands'
C All our food is produced by local farmers.
D Sentences 3 & 4
E Yes

Ideas

These sentences pick out three aspects of supermarkets highlighted in **3 Reading** and prepare them for the passage.

B For sentence 2, point out / elicit from students that the phrase used for the distance flown by air is *air miles*. Student will almost certainly know that air travel is a great cause of pollution, so elicit / teach the phrase: *Air travel creates pollution*. Food often travels long distance because we want exotic food from other, often hotter, countries.

C Elicit answers but don't encourage students to say too much as there'll be a lot more discussion about this subject in **4 Talk about it**.

2 PREVIEW Ideas A / B / C **Answers**

A Hypermarket
B Yes, they are true.
C *Students' own answers.*

3 READING CD 1 (Blue) track 19, page 5 SB

<u>Background information</u>

There has been a lot of controversy in the West about supermarkets. It is of course generally recognised that supermarkets offer huge advantages for shoppers (See notes below in **4 Talk about it**) but environmentalists in particular protest about the following:

- the long distances supermarket food is flown.
- the fact that supermarkets often force local shops out of business.
- the fact that supermarkets bring traffic to a town.

<u>Key words / expressions</u>

Text 1: • take-away food = food that you buy from a shop that is cooked and ready to eat, *eg* pizzas. It is often delivered to your home.
• iPod = a small portable music player with headphones that can store large amounts of music, especially from the Internet.
• PlayStation = a computer on which you can only play video games
• DVD = A silver disc with a film or TV programme recorded on it.
• online globalisation = the idea that the world has become a single economy and that multi-national companies have offices in many countries.

Text 2: chef • regional • mango
• global warming = the fact that the planet is getting warmer due to gases (carbon dioxide in particular) produced by industrialisation.

Text 3: • global brands = products made by multi-national companies
• second-hand = not new • designer • save money • individual looks = individual styles

Text 4: import • souvenir • region • pottery textile • leather goods
• goods = objects made for sale
• ceramics = objects made from clay and baked at a very high temperature
• mug • vase

These four texts focus on four very different people and where they shop and why. *Globalisation* and *global warming* are two important phrases in this text that need to be checked and focused on. Check understanding of *air miles* by asking why air miles increase global warming (planes produce huge amounts of carbon dioxide).

For *globalisation*, ask students where their computers were probably made (perhaps China) and why products made in third world countries and sold here are often very cheap. (Because workers are paid very low wages in developing countries.)

3 READING A / B / C / D **Answers**

A **1** a **2** c **3** c **4** b **5** c
B **1** leather goods
2 shop online
3 a designer
4 I'm not bothered!
5 regional produce
C **1** are sold
2 second-hand clothes
3 global warming
4 are produced
D **1** Text 1: 'The advantage is that it sells everything and it's cheap.'
Text 2: 'Supermarket food often travels long distances and is very bad for the environment.'
Text 3: 'The advantage is that we save money and help the environment.'
Text 4: 'It's a disadvantage that some of the local shops have closed since the supermarket arrived a few years ago.'
Text 5: 'The disadvantage is the cost – they're more expensive than the supermarket.'

2 Because it supports the local shops, because supermarket food travels long distances, and it helps the environment, and in the markets the clothes are cheaper and the food is delicious.
3 Others prefer to go to the supermarkets because it saves time and to the hypermarkets because they sell everything and it's cheap.

4 TALK ABOUT IT

Read the notes about this section in the Introduction. Activities **A** and **C** involve talking about the advantages and disadvantages of local shops, so they are listed below:

<u>Advantages and disadvantages of supermarkets</u>
Advantages: They're cheap. / They have long opening hours. / They provide employment. / You can do a weekly shop there and buy everything you need so they save time. / They offer a very wide range of products.
Disadvantages: Local shops close because of them, *eg* butchers, greengrocers. / The food is often flown long distances, which is bad for the environment.

<u>Advantages and disadvantages of local shops and markets</u>
Advantages: They're a meeting place for local people and make people feel they belong to a neighbourhood. / A neighbourhood feels empty without local shops. /They may sell products / produce that are produced locally. / They're convenient. They're often much nearer than supermarkets so if you want one or two things it's easy to go there. / Organic food is likely to be better in local shops and markets.
Disadvantages: They're often more expensive than supermarkets. / If you only shop locally, it takes time and you have to carry heavy bags.

A Ask: *What are the (dis)advantages of supermarkets / hypermarkets / local shops?* Elicit answers practising the language in **Language Bank 0.** You will find the accompanying exercise in the **Workbook Language Bank** section. (Page 46, LB 0)

Ask students how and where they buy things other than the three places mentioned. Students will almost certainly mention these places:

Shopping online / online shopping (compound noun): Advantages: Things are cheaper online, you can shop from home / in the comfort of your home. Disadvantages: People are afraid to shop online because of internet fraud.
Second-hand clothes shops: Advantages: Clothes are cheap and if you look carefully you can find real bargains, *ie* good, fashionable clothes. Disadvantages: Clothes can look rather old / worn and may not be at all fashionable!
Charity shops: Shops owned by charity organisations. People bring second-hand clothes, books and other goods to the charity shop, and these things are given away to the people whom the charity supports. Charity shops also sell second-hand clothes, books etc very cheaply. Advantages and disadvantages: Same as second-hand clothes.
eBay: eBay is an online auction and shopping website where people can buy and sell goods worldwide. Besides its original American website, it has websites in 30 countries, including Japan, South Korea and India. Students may well be very enthusiastic about eBay, as it's a great source of bargains.

The word *bargain* will keep coming up here, so teach it:

bargain (noun): *It's a bargain* (*ie* very cheap) / *You can get (real) bargains on eBay.*
bargain (verb): *In the Middle East they expect you to bargain* (discuss the price to get a better deal).

B This activity provides an opportunity to practise *should* and the imperative for giving advice.
C See **Background information** above for more about this. Finish by asking students if they feel angry about supermarkets.

Optional activity

Do a role-play in a situation where a very successful hypermarket wants to buy a site on the edge of a small town which already has one supermarket. Put students in groups of four to six and give them these roles. Make sure the roles are evenly balanced for and against.

- A **greengrocer** who fears he will have to close if the hypermarket arrives.
- A **working mother** with three small children. She likes the idea of a hypermarket because it gives more choice and goods will be cheap. She would like to use local shops more but doesn't have time.
- An **elderly man** who can still drive. He would welcome a hypermarket as he could do most of his shopping there.
- A **male student** who is very pro-environment and anti-supermarkets because of air miles flown by supermarket goods and the fact that local shops often close because of them.
- A **single mother** with two children. She hopes the hypermarket will come because goods will be cheap. She says she can't afford to use local shops much.
- A **woman in her fifties** whose children have left home. She likes the idea of a hypermarket but fears that the local shops will go as a result. She thinks this would be a disaster for the town.

Tell students they have 12 minutes to present their arguments and decide whether or not the supermarket should be allowed to buy the site.

5 LISTEN IN CD 1 (Blue) track 20, page 6 SB

Background information / Internet reference

The **Audio text** is in the **Workbook** (page 67).

The listening passage evolved from the work of an English couple, Neil and Ruth Thompson. For over ten years they have travelled in Africa, Asia and the Americas collecting artefacts made from recycled material. They have called their collection of more than 1000 contemporary recycled artefacts *kNOwtrash*. The artefacts are made from recycled rubber, paper, metal, glass plastic and textiles. These materials have been made into highly attractive goods as diverse as handbags, lamps, toy aeroplanes and jewellery. They're mostly made by poor people in small industries where they are paid to gather used material for recycling, *eg* rubber and cans. They are then taught how to make the artefacts and get paid for their work. These small industries are therefore helpful both for the workers and the environment.

See the Thompsons' website, www.knowtrash.com for more information and for photos of the artefacts. It's fascinating!

The title *kNOwtrash* for the Thompson's collection is a pun, *ie* it has two meanings. It means: *Know that all trash can be recycled* and NO trash, *ie* everything can be recycled so there's no need for trash.

Pictured on the page is *the Eden Project*, an environmental theme park in south-west England (Cornwall). The Thompsons have held several exhibitions of kNOwtrash there. The Eden project is one of the UK's top tourist attractions. It is a 'global garden' with over a million plants representing 5000 different species from the world's different climate zones. Its greenhouses, which are massive and bubble-shaped (see Picture 1), are called Biomes. There are two indoor Biomes for plants which cannot grow in the temperate English climate. The project's aim is to teach people how biodiversity and looking after the environment (environmental sustainability) can go together. For example, all the plants' water is recycled and the heating system uses solar energy. For more information see www.edenproject.com.

Key words / expressions

- exhibition • recycled / natural materials • drinks can • flag • trash • wood
- nature = the physical world, including the land, sea, and all living things
- waste • energy • throw away • precious • car tyre
- developing countries = poor countries that don't have many industries
- plastic (bag) • rubbish

A Ask students to look at the picture as this is a good opportunity to tell them something about the Eden Project. Then ask students to name the objects in the pictures. (Picture 3 is a chicken.) Teach the phrase *recycled material* and encourage students to express their astonishment on learning that these objects are made from them. Don't tell students what the objects are made out of yet, as they will learn some of the answers from the Listening passage.

B Encourage students to work out what the title *kNOwtrash* means. Explain that the British say rubbish and the Americans say *trash*. Both words are uncountable.

D When students have completed the activity, ask them what the handbag, the hat and the shoes / sandals are made out of. (The handbag is made out of drinks cans, the hat is made out of newspaper, and the shoes / sandals are made out of car tyres.) Students will probably need to hear that section of the listening passage again in order to answer. Tell them that the cup is made out of glass bottles.

E This activity practises the present simple passive. Answers may differ widely, depending on which country and region students are from. Answers could include: *They don't recycle much in my neighbourhood. / In my neighbourhood paper and cans are recycled but not plastic bottles. / Ordinary rubbish is collected every week. / Cans and paper are collected once a fortnight. / We take recycled stuff down to the recycling centre once a week. / We put our rubbish in different containers / bins and take it down to the recycling centre / dump once a week.*

Use this activity to highlight the distinction between the active and the passive. Students should say, *eg I / We recycle most things*, *ie* use the active voice because the subject is important but, *eg Cans are recycled / rubbish is collected once a week* because it's clear from the sentence who recycles (the local council) and who collects the rubbish (the garbage disposers / dustmen) so it's not necessary to say it.

Encourage students to be honest about whether they recycle and if so, how much, *eg I know I should recycle more but I don't do it very much. / I recycle as much as I can. / I'm a bit lazy about it. / I don't always have time to go down to the recycling centre.*

Optional activities

- Photocopy the **Background information** and give it to students as a short reading comprehension. Teach the word *artefact* with the meaning of *man-made object*. Ask students what new information they have learnt from the passage.
- Students write an interview with the Thompsons. (See **Background information**.) They can research this task by going to the website mentioned.

5 LISTEN IN A / B / C / D — **Answers**

A **1** d **2** c **3** f **4** b **5** a **6** e

B (a) 4 (b) 2 (c) 1 (d) 3

C **1** drinks cans
2 trash, know
3 everything
4 energy
5 use
6 precious
7 toy aeroplane, sun hat, shoes
8 developing countries
9 recycle
10 money

D **1** The toy aeroplane is made out of drinks cans.
2 In nature nothing is wasted.
3 In the West, products are used for a short time.
4 A lot of rubbish is thrown away.

6 CONTROVERSY

Read the notes about this section in the Introduction. Ask students if they or their families grow or have grown their own vegetables / fruit. Teach these phrases: *(We) grow our own vegetables. / These are home-grown vegetables.* Encourage those who have done so to talk about how the food compares with *supermarket* or *market vegetables* and how much work it involves. Teach the compound adjective *home-grown* (*vegetables*). Explain that we often use the word veg in conversation, *eg Grow your own veg.*

If possible, put students into pairs in which one student has at some time lived in a family that has grown their own vegetables.

7 PORTFOLIO WRITING

This writing task provides an opportunity to practise the present simple passive. Put students into pairs to plan the review. They may want to hear the passage again and you could suggest that they take notes. All the language students need is in the listening passage, but if you look at the **Writing model** below you will see that it's very natural to use the passive with a relative clause in this task:

There are handbags and toy planes which are made out of drink cans and hats which are made out of newspaper.

Write the sentences on the board. Ask students to complete these sentences:

1 There's a cup .... (which is made out of glass bottles.)
2 There are shoes .... (which are made out of car tyres.)
3 There's a chicken .... (which is made out of plastic bags.)

Write this sentence on the board:

It shows objects which are made in developed countries .... Brazil.

Elicit phrases that fill the gap, *eg for example / such as*. Point out that *for example* should have commas *(... developed counties, for example, Brazil.)*

If students are familiar with the reduced relative clause, *eg There are hats made out of newspaper*, then encourage them to use this structure.

Writing model

Most people know about the Eden project, the environmental theme park. At present they have a wonderful exhibition called k**NO**wtrash, and yes, this exhibition is all about rubbish! It shows objects which are made in developed countries such as Brazil, and they're all made out of recycled materials.

The exhibition is divided into four parts. The first part shows natural things such as wood. The lesson here is that everything in nature is recycled - nothing is wasted. The second part shows things that come out of the ground, for example, oil. We manufacture products from these things but only use them for short time, then throw them away. But we shouldn't do this, we should recycle them instead.

Part 3 of the exhibition shows the recycled products. They're wonderful! There are handbags and toy planes which are made out of drinks cans and hats which are made out of newspaper. A lot of these products are very attractive and I wanted to buy at least half of the things there. The final part of the exhibition gives useful advice about recycling.

k**NO**wtrash is a fantastic exhibition and I learnt a lot from it. If you can, you should visit it, it's definitely worth it.

8 *ECONOMICS in English*

Background information

You'll see that the topic of the reading passage is the BRIC economies. BRIC is an acronym for **B**razil, **R**ussia, **I**ndia and **C**hina. These countries are the fastest growing developing economies in the world and were named the BRIC(s) economies in 2001 by the American bank, Goldman Sachs. It was this bank that made the prediction in the text that these economies are growing so fast that by 2050, they could be the most powerful economies. The fact is that these four countries have over 40% of the world's population and more than 25% of the world's land. For more information go to this website: www.rediff.com/money/2003/oct/16guest1.htm

Key words / Expressions

- Economics = The study of how money is managed and how goods and services are used.)
- economy = (1) a country's industry, business and trade and the money they produce. (2) a country considered as an economic system.
- rapid • predict • population • unfortunately • growth • pollution

A Find out if anyone is interested in or is studying Economics. Elicit from students / explain that countries with a lot of industry are known as *industrialised / developed countries*. Check students understand the two different meanings of *economy*.

B One way to deal with the text is to give students two or three minutes to read it and then put them in pairs to answer the questions without looking at the book.

C Elicit from students that the words in the box are all examples of a country's *products*. Explain that when talking about a country, the word *products* includes the idea of *agricultural produce* as well. Tell students that instead of *trees* we often say *timber* (uncountable noun).

Optional activity

A discussion on why the BRIC economies are growing so fast. Answers include:

> The BRIC economies are countries with huge mineral and agricultural resources. They also have huge populations, another very important resource. These are great advantages.
>
> Now that China and Russia have accepted capitalism, they are trading with the West. This brings in money which they can invest, *eg* in building factories, housing.
>
> With such huge populations, labour is very cheap. Goods are therefore made very cheaply and are exported at cheap prices. This creates a huge advantage.

8 *ECONOMICS in English* A / B **Answers**

A **1**, **2** *Students' own answers*

B **1** Brazil, Russia, India and China
2 China
3 USA, Japan, Germany, Britain, France and Italy

C **1** Films (e) are made in India.
2 Computers (c) are manufactured in China.
3 Gas (f) is produced in Russia.
4 Oil (b) is found in Russia.
5 Beef cattle (d) are raised in Brazil.
6 Trees (a) are cut down in Brazil.
7 Textiles (h) are exported from China/India.
8 Pollution (g) is created in China/India.

9 YOUR TOPIC

Read the notes about this section in the Introduction. How you deal with this task depends on whether your class is multilingual or monolingual.

If the class is multilingual, put students into pairs, and if possible, according to nationality.

If the class is monolingual, put them into pairs. Encourage students to use their dictionaries for this activity.

Explain that students will talk about their country's economy and its products.

A Ask each pair (or individual if no one else has the same nationality) to choose one of the categories listed and make their list. How students choose will probably depend on where they're from. Students from cities will probably choose national products while students from smaller towns or the countryside may opt for regional or local products.

B If the class is monolingual, divide the board into three columns, *national*, *regional* and *local* and elicit answers. Use the opportunity to expand students' vocabulary in this area and encourage them to say where products are manufactured, grown etc.

If the class is multilingual, divide the board into nationalities, then further subdivide the board.

C Keep students in pairs. If they are not used to making this kind of presentation, shorten the task to one minute.

Give students a general outline. Choose a confident pair and get them to go through the outline. Help them by asking questions and teach vocabulary as it arises:

- Explain what the talk is about, *eg We're going to talk about the Dordogne region in France and its products.*
- Make some general statements, *eg The Dordogne is one of the most beautiful parts of France with very old villages and towns. It's also a very agricultural region.*
- Talk about the products: *The Dordogne produces wonderful wine. / Of course, the Dordogne's most important product is probably tourism.*

- Try and give some interesting information and make comments: *We think the best Dordogne wine is .... / If you haven't had any wine from the Dordogne, you should try it.*
- End by making one or two general statements: *So you can see that it's a very productive region and contributes a lot to the country's economy.*

Students can then prepare their presentation. Students then give their presentation to another pair. Walk round and listen, noting mistakes.

Finally, choose some pairs to make their presentation to the class. Again, make notes of their mistakes.

Alternative approach: Having gone through Activities **A** and **B** in class, ask students to do some research for homework, either through books or the Internet. They can then come to the next lesson with more information and do Part **C**.

Ask students to write up their talk for homework.

10 *Your answer:*

Read the notes about this section in the Introduction. Having worked through the unit, students should have a lot to say about all the questions.

A Encourage students to use *should, eg A good shopper should ...*

C This question gives students the opportunity to talk about recycling and what they do with their rubbish, so elicit this kind of information from students. The examples given extend the area of discussion by mentioning other ways in which one can help the environment. You may want to do more work on this subject. Point out the use of *recycled* (adj.).

Here are some more ideas: *I use low-energy light bulbs. / I travel by bike. / I try not to use the car. / I turn off the lights. / I switch off at night. / I keep my energy bills low.*

You may want to do **A** and **B** and then work with the whole class eliciting answers to the question in **C** in order to teach them vocabulary. You can then put students into pairs or small groups to discuss their answers.

Workbook answers — Pages 2-3 WB

1 Language: *should* / present simple passive / *due to, because of*

A **1** You should get fish from that shop.
2 Should I buy this handbag?
3 That factory should not create so much pollution.
4 Do you think I should leave before the market closes?
5 I think you should take that to the recycling centre.

B **1** Second-hand clothes are sold here.
2 Souvenirs are bought by tourists.
3 Cheap computers are made by Chinese companies.
4 Dairy produce is eaten by many people.
5 The exhibition is described in the article.

C *Due to* and *because of* are both correct in all sentences.
1 ...*because of* (d) the price.
2 *Due to* (c) the weather...
3 ...*due to* (a) its huge population.
4 ...*because of* (b) you.

2 Use of English

A **1** I went to the farm shop to buy some cheese.
2 Did you like the exhibition?
3 It's a fact / The fact is that China's economy is growing very fast.
4 It's an advantage that they use recycled materials.
5 I don't mind supermarkets.

B **1** since
2 century
3 most
4 supply
5 are
6 produced
7 world
8 of
9 due
10 national

3 Writing

A, B *Students' own answers*

4 Connections

A agriculture – farming
business – company
products – goods
manufacturing - industry

B 1 Manufacturing / Industry
2 business / company
3 industry / agriculture
4 goods / products
5 company / business
6 products / goods
7 agriculture / industry
8 agriculture / farming

C *Students' own answers*

QUICK SMART TEST ANSWER KEY UNIT 0

See page 267 for Quick Smart Test Unit 0.

1 A 1 economy
2 crop
3 rubbish
4 products
5 goods
B 1 mineral
2 exports
3 wheat
4 agricultural
5 Plastic

2 A 1 due to / because of
2 flown
3 due to / because of
4 is
5 should
B 1 How many people know a global-warming gas is emitted by rice fields?
2 The oil is found in a remote part of the country and piped to nearby countries.
3 Where are these beautiful vases sold?
4 The rubbish is collected by our local council and recycled.
5 Vegetables aren't usually grown by people who live in flats.

3 A

Sarah: What are the advantages of living in the country? You've lived there for almost a year now.

Simon: There are a lot of advantages, there really are.

Sarah: I suppose one advantages is (that) it's very peaceful.

Simon: Yes, it's lovely. And another / a big advantage is (that) it's so much better for the children.

Sarah: It must be.

Simon: But of course, it's a disadvantage (that) there's no big supermarket near us.

B

1 **A:** Name two advantages of learning English.
B: One advantage is / It's an advantage (that) it gives you more job opportunities.
Another advantage is (that) it's very helpful when you travel.

2 **A:** What are the disadvantages of (using) local shops?
B: They're usually more expensive.

3 **A:** It must be great living next to a supermarket!
B: Yes, there are / it has advantages. But the disadvantage is (that) I can't sleep at night!

Name ______________________ Class ____________ Date ____________

1 Vocabulary

A Choose the correct form of the words in the box to fill the gaps.

goods	economy	rubbish	crop	product

1 The .... has not grown as fast as the government predicted.
2 Wheat is not a .... that grows well in tropical climates.
3 It's important to recycle as much of your .... as you can.
4 One of the company's most important .... is handbags.
5 The factory failed to deliver the .... on time.

B Underline the correct answer in *italics*.

1 Coal is a *mineral / textile* that produces carbon dioxide when it burns.
2 Brazil is a country that *exports / manufactures* a lot of timber.
3 In the West, bread is usually made from *beef / wheat*.
4 It's an *agricultural / industrial* region and grows a lot of olives.
5 *Plastic / leather* goods are not good for the environment.

1 Vocabulary: my score is......out of 10

2 Language

A Complete the gaps with a suitable word or phrase.

One reason why supermarkets are not good for the environment is **(1)** .... the long distances that goods are often **(2)** .... This is a problem **(3)** .... the fact that aeroplanes emit a lot of carbon dioxide, one of the worst global warming gases. If a product **(4)** .... grown or produced locally, some people feel we **(5)** .... therefore make efforts to buy it.

B Rewrite the sentences in the present simple passive. Use *by* only when necessary.

1 How many people know that rice fields emit a global-warming gas?
....?
2 They find the oil in a remote part of the country and pipe it to nearby countries.
....?
3 Where do they sell these beautiful vases?
....?
4 Our local council collects the rubbish and recycles it.
....?
5 People who live in flats don't usually grow vegetables.
....?

2 Grammar: my score is..... out of 10

3 Functions

A Complete the sentences using phrases with the words *advantage* or *disadvantage*.

Sarah: What are .... living in the country? You've lived there for almost a year now.
Simon: .... , there really are.
Sarah: I suppose .... it's very peaceful.
Simon: Yes, it's lovely. And .... it's so much better for the children.
Sarah: It must be.
Simon: But of course, it's .... there's no big supermarket near us.

B Complete the sentences using phrases with the words *advantage* or *disadvantage*.

1 A: Name two advantages of learning English.
B: .... it gives you more job opportunities.
.... it's very helpful when you travel.
2 A: .... local shops?
B: They're usually more expensive.
3 A: It must be great living next to a supermarket!
B: Yes, ... But .... I can't sleep at night!

3 Functions: my score is...... out of 10

Quick Smart Test 0:
My total score is ...... out of 30

Language bank exercises **Example answers** **See pages 46-56 WB**

Language bank 0

1 A: I grow all my own vegetables. Of course, the disadvantage is (that) you have to work quite hard.
B: So what's the advantage?
2 A: There are several advantages. For example, they taste much better than supermarket vegetables. Another advantage is (that) they haven't travelled very far.
B: I am sure that's true. But I just buy all the produce I need from the local farmer's market.
3 A: That's great, Well done.
B: Of course, the disadvantage is the cost.
4 A: True.
B: But the advantage is (that) it's better for the environment.

Language bank 1

1 A: I need a boyfriend! But it's so difficult to meet new people.
B: Do you think I should look online? A lot of people do that now.
2 A: That's a great idea.
B: But you should be / you'd better be careful.
3 A: How do you mean?
B: Well, for example, you should keep your identity a secret at first. And you shouldn't arrange to meet immediately.
4 A: That sounds like good advice. And if I like someone, where do you think we should meet?
B: I think you ought to meet in a public place. For example, you could meet in a coffee bar. Or how about meeting outside, in a park?
A: Yes, maybe I'll do that - if I meet someone for the first time.

Language bank 2

1 A: What do you think about online dating?
B: I think it's OK.
2 A: In my opinion, it sounds dangerous. You don't know who you're talking to.
B: I think people should be careful when they meet someone.

Language bank 3

1 A: Can you suggest some good places to meet someone? Um / Er, somewhere I can find a girlfriend / boyfriend! You see, I haven't had a relationship for ages!
B: Well, you know, how about joining a club? Or an evening class?
2 A: Well, maybe I'll join a sports club. You know, I think I might enjoy that. I mean, you meet people there, don't you?

Language bank 4

1 In my opinion, New York is a lot more exciting than San Francisco.
2 I like small towns because they're far friendlier than big cities.
3 One of the problems with cities is that houses are twice as expensive.
4 One of the best things about cities is that there are many more things to do and see.
5 Compared with city life, life in the country is much quieter and more peaceful and there is much less traffic.

Language bank 5

1 A: Refugees leave their country for many reasons.
B: Sorry, would you mind explaining that, please?
2 A: Well, for example, they might leave because their government puts people of their race or religion in prison.
B: What do you mean by the word 'race'?
3 A: I mean 'nationality'.
B: Sorry, I didn't quite get that. Could you explain that word, please?
4 A: I mean people from a particular country. But it could be the same for an ethnic group, or a minority who have a different religion or culture.
B: Oh, I see. That's interesting. Can you say more about that?
5 A: Yes. Some people leave because they are political refugees and some people are economic refugees.
B: What does 'refugee' mean? What do you mean by 'economic refugee'?
C: They're people who leave their country to look for a better job and life abroad.

Language bank 6

1 A: What are you doing tomorrow evening?
B: I'm not sure. I may go to a film.
2 A: Which one?
B: Well, I might go to that film about the famous rock band drummer. But I might have to work. At the moment, I can't be certain (about that).

3 A: It's possible I'll be free tomorrow evening. If you're not working, I'll come with you.
B: Great!

Language bank 7

1 A: Do you think it's fun to be famous?
B: Yes, but I think it has lots of disadvantages.
2 A: For example?
B: Um... How can I put it? Let me think. Well, if you're very famous, the media watch you all the time.
3 A: A famous person might like that.
B: Yes, but, what's the best way of putting it? In that situation, you have no privacy. No one likes that.
4 A: True, but if you're very famous, you're probably very rich. That's nice!
B: I agree, but, well, how can I explain? I think it can very difficult to be real if you're famous. You have an image and people want you to be that image.

Language bank 8

1 How does sunny weather make you feel? It makes me feel great. I love it.
2 When was the last time you felt really happy? I felt really happy when I was on holiday.
3 How do you feel about animals? I dislike them. They make me feel terrible.
4 What are your feelings about your family? I love them. I feel very happy (when I'm with them).

Language bank 9

1 I think *Dark Star* is the best band in the charts. I totally agree with you / I couldn't agree more.
2 Fame and celebrity always change people. Oh come on! That's not true. I think you're (completely) wrong.
3 The media only show us the news they want us to see. I can see your point of view, but I have a different one.
4 Zoos help protect animals. I don't agree with you at all / I couldn't agree less.
5 Vivisection is necessary. I can see your point of view. You're right.
6 Most people treat animals badly. I think you're wrong.
7 Some animals are almost as intelligent as humans. I feel the same way / That's absolutely right.

Language bank 10

1 Where did the children used to play? (fields) The children used to play in the fields.
2 When would the older children take food to the workers? (At about 11:30) The older children would take food to the workers at about 11:30.
3 What did the children usually have for breakfast? (a piece of bread) The children usually / often had a piece of bread for breakfast.
4 What did they eat from? (wooden bowls) They used to eat from wooden bowls.

Language bank 11

Slavery has always existed.
1 Well, actually, for example, we know that there were slaves in ancient times.
2 You know (that) slaves were often ...
3 ... what's the word? prisoners of war. Or they could be the children of slaves. But it was sometimes possible for a slave to, ...
4 ... what can I say, win his freedom.

Language bank 12

1 Can you describe this picture? It shows / It's a picture of people walking in the street.
2 What else does the picture show? It looks as if that person is stealing a car.
3 What's happening here? There is someone watching the man stealing the car.
4 Can you say more about the picture? Yes. The man looks very suspicious and anxious.

Language bank 13

1 Perhaps people will start driving hydrogen-powered cars.
2 If oil becomes very expensive, it's possible (that) we will be prepared for the situation.
3 Peak Oil may happen sooner than we expect.
4 If the oil runs out, we'll need to use other energy resources.
5 We need to prepare now, in case Peak Oil happens soon.

Language bank 14

1 Things may change a lot in the next ten years.
2 We don't know exactly when, but some day soon / sooner or later the oil is going to run out.
3 By / In 2020, oil supplies may be very low.
4 Sometime soon we're going to reach Peak Oil.
5 What will life be like in 20 years' time?

Language bank 15

1 A: This science course is so difficult. I've decided to give up.
B: Don't give up so easily. If you didn't do it, you'd feel bad.
2 A: I'm doing so badly.
B: Rubbish! It's easier than you think, and if you do your revision, you'll pass.
3 A: No, I think I'm going to stop.
B: Don't do that. Everything will be fine.

Language bank 16

1 People feel very differently about exams. For instance / For example, my brother finds them really easy.
2 You can do a lot to help stress. To give you an example, taking exercise is very relaxing.
3 An activity such as running can make you feel much better.

Language bank 17

1 We should punish deserters. What's more, if many soldiers are deserting, the government should ask why.
2 I believe that we should love our country. As a result, we should always be ready to fight for it.
3 I don't believe in this war. However, I'm fighting in it.
4 Michael Peel is a deserter from the war. In addition, his friend Paul Harber has been hiding from the army for many months.
5 The air force is bombing towns. Consequently, many civilians have been killed.
6 I don't believe we can prevent countries from selling weapons. Firstly, how would we do this? Secondly, countries need weapons to protect themselves.

Language bank 18

1 I haven't got a car. I wish I had one.
2 I'm sorry I didn't believe them. I wish I had believed them.
3 They're talking so loudly. I wish they would talk more quietly.
4 My father may change his job. He hopes to change his job.
5 My friends may come to the party. I hope they'll come to the party.

Language bank 19

1 A: Child poverty in Britain has decreased.
B: Sorry / Excuse me, what did you say?
2 A: I said that child poverty in Britain has decreased.
B: Can you say that again?
3 A: Sure, I said that child poverty in Britain is less than it was.
B: I'm sorry, I didn't hear what you said. Could you say that more slowly, please?
4 A: Yes. There are fewer poor children now because the government has spent more money on them.
B: Did you say that the government has spent more money on poor children?
A: That's right. A government spending programme has helped a lot of families.

Language bank 20

1 A: What could people in our city do to get fit?
B: Lots of things. For example, one possibility is to do more sports, like football.
2 A: I don't think that's very helpful. You have to be very fit to do that.
B: All right, they could go swimming.
3 A: I think that's a good suggestion. Most people love swimming. But some people can't swim, of course.
B: Another possibility is to go for a half-hour walk every day. It's very good for you and anyone can do it.
4 A: I think the best option is to play football. I like football and I'm quite fit.

Language bank 21

1 A: I think we're going to build taller and taller buildings.
B: That's interesting. Why do you think that?
2 A: Because populations are exploding.
B: Can you explain what you mean by that?
3 A: I mean that populations are getting a lot bigger all the time
B: Can you give me an example?
4 A: Yes, China and India are very good examples.

Language bank 22

1 A: I really care about my privacy.
B: So you feel that privacy is something you really care about?

2 A: Speed cameras mean that people drive more slowly.
B: So you're saying that speed cameras do mean that people drive more slowly?
3 A: I don't think RFID tags are a good idea.
B: You mean they're a bad idea?
4 A: RFID tags are sometimes placed on airline luggage.
B: So what you're saying is, it's a good idea to use RFID tags on airline baggage?

Language bank 23

suspense / horror excitement / fear
violence fantasy

1 I did not enjoy the feeling of suspense in the film. I like romance more.
2 This book is about liberty and happiness, not about love.
3 The novel is about the friendship between three women living in New York.
4 Humour is the best kind of entertainment on TV.
5 The main character in the film showed honesty, courage and patience.

Language bank 24

1 A: What aspects of work do you like?
B: Well, I like working with people.
2 A: Anything else?
B: Yes, I love being independent.
3 A: That's good. You start work very early, don't you?
B: Yes. Actually, I hate working late. I like to get up early.
4 A: Me too. Do you have to work late sometimes?
B: Yes, but that's OK. I don't mind working late sometimes.

Language bank 25

I got angry and argued with my girlfriend. Now she has left me.
1 I wish I hadn't got angry with her.
2 If only I had known she would leave me, I wouldn't have argued with her!
They suggested I catch the 9 o'clock train to get to the interview on time. I overslept and missed the train so that I arrived very late. I didn't get the job.
3 If only they had told me to catch the 8 o'clock train, I wouldn't have been late.
4 I wish I hadn't overslept. If I hadn't been late, I would have got the job.

Language bank 26

1 A: In my opinion, prison doesn't stop people from re-offending.
B: I think you have a very good point, but I don't agree with you.
2 A: There are other good alternatives to prison.
B: That's an interesting way of looking at it, and I fully agree with you.
3 A: But sometimes I think it's necessary to send someone to prison.
B: I respect your opinion about this, but I don't agree with you because...
4 A: Particularly when they've committed a very violent crime.
B: I have to admit that's a very strong argument and it's my view too.

Language bank 27

1 Tracy went out hiking without a coat or umbrella. She got very bad flu.
She shouldn't have gone hiking without a coat. If she'd taken a coat, she wouldn't have got flu.
2 Martin set out on a long car journey when he had had very little sleep. He had an accident.
Martin was wrong to set out when he'd had very little sleep. If he'd had some sleep, he wouldn't have had an accident.

Language bank 28

1 A: Has Ursula arrived yet?
B: No, I went to the station but she wasn't on the train. She must have missed it.
2 A: She can't have missed it. She rang me to say she was on the train.
B: That's strange.
3 A: She might have got off at an earlier station.
B: Why would she want to do that?
4 A: She might have thought it was the right station.
B: Oh dear!